NINTH EDITION

THE HUMAN SPECIES

An Introduction
to Biological Anthropology

JOHN H. RELETHFORD

State University of New York
College at Oneonta

McGraw Hill

Connect
Learn
Succeed™

THE HUMAN SPECIES: AN INTRODUCTION TO BIOLOGICAL ANTHROPOLOGY, NINTH EDITION

Published by McGraw-Hill, a business unit of The McGraw-Hill Companies, Inc., 1221 Avenue of the Americas, New York, NY 10020. Copyright © 2013 by The McGraw-Hill Companies, Inc. All rights reserved. Printed in the United States of America. Previous editions © 2010, 2008 and 2005. No part of this publication may be reproduced or distributed in any form or by any means, or stored in a database or retrieval system, without the prior written consent of The McGraw-Hill Companies, Inc., including, but not limited to, in any network or other electronic storage or transmission, or broadcast for distance learning.

Some ancillaries, including electronic and print components, may not be available to customers outside the United States.

This book is printed on acid-free paper.

1 2 3 4 5 6 7 8 9 0 RJE/RJE 1 0 9 8 7 6 5 4 3 2

ISBN: 978-0-07-803498-5
MHID: 0-07-803498-1

Vice President & Editor-in-Chief: *Michael Ryan*
Vice President of Specialized Publishing: *Janice M. Roerig-Blong*
Publisher: *William Glass*
Senior Sponsoring Editor: *Debra B. Hash*
Marketing Coordinator: *Angela R. FitzPatrick*
Project Manager: *Jolynn Kilburg*
Design Coordinator: *Margarite Reynolds*
Cover Designer: *Studio Montage, St. Louis, Missouri*
Cover Image: *Ryan McVay/Getty Images*
Buyer: *Susan K. Culbertson*
Media Project Manager: *Sridevi Palani*
Compositor: *MPS Limited*
Typeface: *10.5/12.5 Legacy Serif Book*
Printer: *R. R. Donnelley*

All credits appearing on page or at the end of the book are considered to be an extension of the copyright page.

Library of Congress Cataloging-in-Publication Data
Relethford, John.
 The human species : an introduction to biological anthropology / John Relethford.—9th ed.
  p. cm
 ISBN 978-0-07-803498-5 (pbk.)
 1. Physical anthropology. I. Title.
GN60.R39 2012
599.9—dc23

2012004922

BRIEF CONTENTS

CONTENTS

PREFACE

This text is an introduction to the field of biological anthropology (also known as physical anthropology), the science concerned with human biological evolution and variation. The text addresses the major questions that concern biological anthropologists: What are humans? How are we similar to and different from other animals? Where are our origins? How did we evolve? Are we still evolving? How are we different from one another? What does the future hold for the human species?

ORGANIZATION

This book is divided into four parts. Part I, "Evolutionary Background," provides the basic background in genetics and evolutionary theory used throughout the remainder of the text. Chapter 1 introduces the science of biological anthropology, the nature of science, and the history of evolutionary thought. Chapter 2 reviews molecular and Mendelian genetics as applied to humans, providing genetic background for later chapters. Chapter 3 focuses on evolutionary forces, the mechanisms that produce evolutionary change within and between populations. Chapter 4 looks at evolution over longer periods of time, focusing on the origin of new species, and includes discussion on how species are classified.

Part II, "Our Place in Nature," examines the biology and behavior of the primates, the group of mammals to which humans belong. The focus of this section is on two basic questions: What are humans? How are we related to other living creatures? Chapter 5 looks at the basic biology and behavior of mammals in general and primates in particular, and reviews the different types of living primates. Chapter 6 examines the diversity in primate behavior and ecology, and includes a number of brief case studies of different primate species. Chapter 7 looks specifically at the human species and includes a comparison of human traits with those of apes.

Part III deals with questions of "Our Origins." Chapter 8 begins with a discussion of the methods of analyzing the fossil record and concludes with a brief history of life on earth prior to the appearance of the first primates. Chapter 9 examines the fossil and genetic evidence for primate evolution from the appearance of the primate-like mammals through the split of ape and human lines by 6 to 7 million years ago. Chapter 10 deals with the beginning of human evolution, focusing on the fossil evidence for the first hominins and the evolution of bipedalism. Chapter 11 examines the origin and biological and cultural origins of the genus *Homo,* including *Homo habilis* and *Homo erectus.* Chapter 12 looks at the fossil and archaeological records of "archaic humans"—*Homo heidelbergensis* and the Neandertals. Chapter 13 reviews the fossil, archaeological, and genetic evidence for the origin of modern humans and includes a discussion of current controversies.

Part IV, "Our Diversity," examines human biological variation in our species today from an evolutionary perspective. Chapter 14 focuses on the analysis of human variation and contrasts racial and evolutionary approaches to human diversity. Chapter 15 reviews a number of case studies of recent human microevolution, including studies of population history and natural selection in human populations. Chapter 16 continues examining human variation from the broad perspective of human adaptation, both biological and cultural. Chapter 17 concludes the text by examining recent human evolution (over the past 12,000 years), focusing on the biological impact of agriculture and civilization, with particular emphasis on changing patterns of disease, mortality, fertility, and population growth. Two appendices provide additional detail on cell biology and skeletal biology.

The organization of this text reflects my own teaching preference in terms of topics and sequence. Not all instructors will use the same sequence of chapters; some may prefer a different arrangement of topics. I have attempted to write chapters in such a way as to accommodate such changes whenever possible. For example, although I prefer to discuss human evolution before human variation, others prefer the reverse, and the chapters have been written so that this alternative organizational structure can be used.

FEATURES

Throughout the text, I have attempted to provide new material relevant to the field and fresh treatments of traditional material. Key features include the following:

- All areas of contemporary biological anthropology are covered. In addition to traditional coverage of areas such as genetics, evolutionary theory, primate behavior, and the fossil record, the text includes material on genetics and population history, human growth, epidemiology, and demography.

- The relationship between biology and culture is a major focus. The biocultural framework is introduced in the first chapter and integrated throughout the text.

- Behavior is discussed in an evolutionary context. The evolutionary nature of primate and human behavior is emphasized in a number of chapters, including those on primate biology and behavior (Chapters 5–7) and the fossil record of human evolution (Chapters 10–13).

- Emphasis is on the human species in its context within the primate order. Discussions of mammals and nonhuman primates continually refer to their potential relevance for understanding the human species. In fact, Chapter 7 is devoted entirely to treating our species from a comparative perspective.

- Hypothesis testing is emphasized. From the first chapter, in which students are introduced to the scientific method, I emphasize how various hypotheses are tested. Rather than provide a dogmatic approach with all the "right" answers, the text examines evidence in the context of hypothesis testing. With this emphasis, readers can see how new data can lead to changes in basic models and can better understand the "big picture" of biological anthropology.

NEW TO THIS EDITION

The text has been revised in light of new findings in the field and comments from users of the eighth edition and reviewers. Two chapters have been revised extensively and sections of others have been rewritten to provide additional clarity. In addition to updating material throughout the text, specific changes to this addition include:

- Extensive revision of the chapter on the first hominins (Chapter 10) in order to make the material more accessible to students. The material on the origin of bipedalism has been moved to the beginning of the chapter so that students have contextual background when reading about the fossil evidence. As the number of early hominin species has increased in recent years, this chapter often is a challenge to students. Consequently, the review of the fossil record has been simplified and clarified to provide a clearer presentation of the general trends in early human evolution. The robust forms have now been referred to the genus *Paranthropus* but this material is written in such a way that instructors who prefer alternative classifications will not have any difficulty.

- The chapter on the study of human variation (Chapter 14) has been rewritten to focus on the contrast between racial and evolutionary approaches to human variation. Because of the continued confusion in both the public and in science over the meaning of race as applied

to human variation, this chapter now begins with a discussion of the
biological race concept, including a brief history of race and racial
classification. Problems with a strict application of the race concept to
humans are then discussed, followed by an evolutionary perspective on
global genetic variation.

- The strepsirhine/haplorhine classification of primate suborders is now
  used.

- New information is covered throughout the text, including new
  findings on hunting in chimpanzees, *Ardipithecus, Australopithecus sediba,*
  new dates for *Homo erectus* in Southeast Asia, the Neandertal genome,
  the Denisovans, and the genetics of human skin color, among other
  topics.

- Thirty-two information boxes have been added throughout the text.
  These boxes serve as supplements to the main text, much in the same
  way that tables and figures provide additional information. The information boxes are short summaries that either expand upon material in
  the main text or provide information on additional topics of interest.
  In both cases, these boxes provide information that is useful without
  breaking up the flow of the main text. The topics included in these
  boxes include epigenetics, punctuated equilibrium, brain size and intelligence, genetic estimates of divergence time, the Piltdown hoax, possible
  tool use in *Australopithecus,* the "Hobbit," monogenism and polygenism
  in the history of race, the Lemba, ongoing natural selection, and possible
  changes in future life expectancy, among others. These boxes replace the
  "Special Topics" boxes used in previous editions.

- An appendix has been added on skeletal biology, particularly as
  applied to forensic anthropology and bioarchaeology. This appendix
  expands upon a number of topics in skeletal biology from throughout
  the text, including identification of sex, estimation of age, estimation
  of height, identification of ancestry, and analysis of disease and
  trauma.

STUDY AIDS

To make the text more accessible and interesting, I have included frequent
examples and illustrations of basic ideas to help orient students. I have kept
the technical jargon to a minimum, yet every introductory text contains
a number of specialized terms that students must learn. At first mention
in the text, these terms appear in **boldface** type, and accompanying short
definitions appear in the text margins. A glossary is provided at the end
of the book. Each chapter ends with a summary and a list of supplemental
readings. A list of references appears at the end of the book, providing the
complete reference for studies cited in the text.

Visit our Online Learning Center Web site at **www.mhhe.com/relethford9e**
for student and instructor resources.

ANCILLARIES

For Students
Student resources include self-quizzes, Internet links as well as other chapter study aids.

For Instructors
The password-protected instructor portion of the Web site includes the Instructor's Manual, a comprehensive computerized test bank, PowerPoint lecture slides, and a variety of additional instructor resources.

ACKNOWLEDGMENTS

My thanks go to the dedicated and hardworking people at McGraw-Hill, both those whom I have dealt with personally and those behind the scenes. I give special thanks to my sponsoring editor, Debra Hash, for encouragement and support. My heartfelt thanks also go to Nicole Bridge, developmental editor, for her valuable suggestions and incredible patience in answering the same questions repeatedly. Special thanks also go to Karyn Morrison, permissions editor; Susan Norton, manuscript editor; Margarite Reynolds, design coordinator; Jennifer Blankenship, photo researcher; and Jolynn Kilburg, project manager.

I also thank my colleagues who served as reviewers: David Andrew Merriwether, Binghamton University; Beth Shook, California State University, Chico; Christopher Stojanowski, Arizona State University; Eric J. Bartelink, California State University, Chico; Diana C. Crader, University of Southern Maine; Darryl de Ruiter, Texas A&M University; and Arthur Durband, Texas Tech University. Having been a reviewer myself, I appreciate the extensive time and effort these individuals have taken. I also thank my colleague Tracy Betsinger, SUNY College at Oneonta, for her advice on the skeletal biology appendix.

Last, but not least, I dedicate this as always to my family. To my wonderful sons, David, Benjamin, and Zane—thanks for your support and love, and for all those questions over the years that really made me think (the ones I couldn't answer as well as those I could). Finally, to my wife, Hollie, love of my life and my best friend—thanks for the love, friendship, and support. I couldn't have done this without you.

Anthropology and Biological Anthropology

One of the often-agonizing decisions a college student must make is to pick a major. Like you, I also went through this decision-making process, which was made even more difficult by the fact that I was interested in many different subjects. At one time or another, I contemplated (even if for only a day) a major in psychology, biology, philosophy, sociology, geography, and mathematics, among others. Part of my problem (apart from not being prepared for many of these majors) was that I could not even narrow my choice down to a general area, such as natural science, social science, or the humanities. Through a series of accidents, I stumbled across anthropology several times before eventually realizing that it was the choice for me, as it encompassed aspects of many different fields, including both natural and social sciences.

As practiced in North America, anthropology has an unusual character and history that defies the typical categorization of an academic discipline as being natural science *or* social science *or* in the humanities. Anthropology has connections with all of these different approaches, making it (for me, at least) a perfect liberal arts discipline. However, the sheer breadth of anthropology also makes it difficult to explain to someone exactly what it is and exactly what an anthropologist does.

What is anthropology? To many people, it is the study of the exotic extremes of human nature. To others, it is the study of ancient ruins and lost civilizations (Figure 1). The study of anthropology seems strange to many, and the practitioners of this field, the anthropologists, seem even stranger. The stereotype of an anthropologist is a pith-helmeted, pipe-smoking eccentric, tracking chimpanzees through the forest, digging up the bones of million-year-old ancestors, interviewing lost tribes about their sexual customs, and recording the words of the last speakers of a language.

A popular image presented in the media of an anthropologist is Indiana Jones, the intrepid archaeologist of *Raiders of the Lost Ark* and other movies. Here is a man who is versed in the customs and languages of many societies past and present, feels at home anywhere in the world, and makes a living teaching, finding lost treasures, rescuing beautiful women in distress, and fighting Nazis. Of course, Indiana Jones is a fictional character and more a

FIGURE 1

Stone statues from Easter Island in the eastern Pacific Ocean. These statues are an example of the archaeological record studied by anthropologists.

treasure hunter than a scientific archaeologist. However, some real-life anthropologists are almost as well known: Jane Goodall, the late Margaret Mead, and the late Louis Leakey. These anthropologists have studied chimpanzees, Samoan culture, and the fossils of human ancestors. Their research conjures up images of anthropology every bit as varied as the imaginary adventures of Indiana Jones. Anthropologists do study all these things and more. The sheer diversity of topics investigated by anthropologists seems almost to defy any sort of logic. The methods of data collection and analysis are almost as diverse. What pulls these different subjects together? In one obvious sense, they all share an interest in the same subject—human beings. In fact, the traditional textbook definition of anthropology is the "study of humans." Though this definition is easy to remember, it is not terribly useful. After all, scientists in other fields, such as researchers in anatomy and biochemistry, also study humans. And there are many fields within the social sciences whose sole interest is humans. History, geography, political science, economics, sociology, and psychology are all devoted to the study of human beings, and no one would argue that these fields are merely branches of anthropology.

WHAT IS ANTHROPOLOGY?

What, then, is a suitable definition of anthropology? **Anthropology** could be described as the science of human cultural and biological variation and evolution. The first part of this definition includes both human culture and biology. Although there are more complex definitions, for the moment we will consider **culture** to be shared learned behavior. Culture includes social and economic systems, marriage customs, religion, philosophy, and all other behaviors that are acquired through the process of learning rather than through instinct. The joint emphasis on culture and biology is an important feature of anthropology, and one that sets it apart from many other fields. A biochemist may be interested in specific aspects of human biology and may consider the study of human cultural behaviors to be less important. To a sociologist, cultural behaviors and not human biology are the focus of attention. Anthropology, however, is characterized by a concern that both culture and biology are vital in understanding the human condition.

anthropology The science that investigates human biological and cultural variation and evolution.

culture Behavior that is shared, learned, and socially transmitted.

The Biocultural Approach

To the anthropologist, humans must be understood in terms of shared learned behavior as well as biology. We rely extensively on learned behaviors in virtually all aspects of our lives. Even the expression of our sex drive must be understood in light of human cultural systems. Although the actual basis of our sex drive is biological, the ways in which we express it are shaped by behaviors we have learned. The very inventiveness of humans, with our vast technology, is testimony to the powerful effect of learning. However, we are not purely cultural creatures. We are also biological organisms. We need to eat and breathe, and we are affected by our external environment. In addition, our biology sets certain limits on our potential behaviors. For example, all human cultures have some type of social structure that provides for the care of children until they are old enough to fend for themselves. This is not simply kindness to children; our biological position as mammals requires such attentiveness to children for survival. In contrast to some animal species, whose infants need little or no care, human infants are physically incapable of taking care of themselves.

Anthropology is concerned not only with culture and biology but also with their interaction. Just as humans are not solely cultural or solely biological, neither are we simply the sum of these two. Humans are biocultural organisms, which means that our culture and biology influence each other. The **biocultural approach** to studying human beings is a main theme of this book, and you will examine many examples of biocultural interaction. For now, however, consider one—population growth (which will be covered in detail in Chapter 17). The growth of a population depends, in part, on how many people are born relative to how many die. If more people are born than die in a given period, then the population will grow. Obviously, population growth is in part caused by biological factors affecting the birth and death rates. A variety of cultural factors, such as economic

biocultural approach Studying humans in terms of the interaction between biology and culture in evolutionary adaptation.

system and marriage patterns, also affect population growth. Many factors, including technological changes and ideological outlooks, affect the birth rate. Developments in medicine and medical care change the death rate. The entire process of population growth, and its biological and cultural implications, is considerably more complicated than described here. The basic point, however, should be clear: By studying the process of population growth, we can see how cultural factors affect biological factors, and vice versa. The biocultural perspective of anthropology points to one of the unique strengths of anthropology as a science: It is **holistic,** meaning that it takes into consideration all aspects of human existence. Population growth again provides an example. Where the sociologist may be concerned with effects of population growth on social structure, and the psychologist with effects of population growth on psychological stress, the anthropologist is interested potentially in *all* aspects of population growth.

holistic Integrating all aspects of existence in understanding human variation and evolution.

Variation

variation The differences that exist among individuals or populations.

comparative approach Comparing human populations to determine common and unique behaviors or biological traits.

A key characteristic of anthropology is its concern with **variation.** In a general sense, variation refers to differences among individuals or populations. The anthropologist is interested in differences and similarities among human groups in terms of both biology and culture. Anthropologists use the **comparative approach** to attempt to generalize about those aspects of human behavior and biology that are similar in all populations and those that are unique to specific environments and cultures. How do groups of people differ from one another? Why do they differ? These are questions about variation, and they apply equally to cultural and biological traits (Figure 2).

FIGURE 2

Biological variation in a group of children. Anthropologists study the differences and similarities among human populations over time.

Evolution

Evolution is change in living organisms over time. Anthropologists are interested in the origin and evolution of both human culture and biology. For example, anthropologists may be interested in the origin of marriage systems. When, how, and why did certain marriage systems evolve? For that matter, when did the custom of marriage first originate, and why? In terms of human biology, questions about evolution concern where, when, and why human ancestors first walked on two legs, or the evolution of our larger brains.

evolution Change in populations of organisms from one generation to the next.

Adaptation

In addition to the concepts of variation and evolution, the anthropologist is interested in the process of **adaptation.** At the broadest level, adaptations are advantageous changes. Any aspect of biology or behavior that confers some advantage on an individual or population can be considered an adaptation. Cultural adaptations include technological devices such as clothing, shelter, and methods of food production. Adaptations can also be biological. Some biological adaptations are physiological in nature and involve metabolic changes. For example, when you are too hot, you sweat. Sweating is a short-term physiological response that removes excess heat through the process of evaporation. Biological adaptations can also be genetic in nature. Here, changes in genes over many generations produce variation in biological traits. The darker skin color of many humans native to regions near the equator is one example of a long-term genetic adaptation. The darker skin provides protection from the harmful effects of ultraviolet radiation (see Chapter 15 for more information on skin color and variation).

adaptation The process of successful interaction between a population and an environment.

THE SUBFIELDS OF ANTHROPOLOGY

In a general sense, anthropology is concerned with determining what humans are, how they evolved, and how they differ from one another. Where other disciplines focus on specific issues of humanity, anthropology is unique in dealing simultaneously with questions of origins, evolution, variation, and adaptation.

Even though anthropology has a wide scope and appears to encompass anything and everything pertaining to humans, the study of anthropology in North America is often characterized by four separate subfields, each with a specific focus. These four subfields are cultural anthropology, archaeology, linguistic anthropology, and biological anthropology.

Cultural Anthropology

Cultural anthropology deals primarily with variations in the cultures of populations in the present or recent past. Its subjects include social, political,

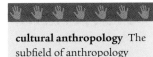

cultural anthropology The subfield of anthropology that focuses on variations in cultural behaviors among human populations.

economic, and ideological aspects of human cultures. Cultural anthropologists look at all aspects of behavior within a society. Even when they are interested in a specific aspect of a culture, such as marriage systems, they look at how these behaviors relate to all other aspects of culture. Marriage systems, for example, may have an effect on the system of inheritance and may be closely related to religious views. Comparison of cultures is used to determine common and unique features among different cultures. Information from cultural anthropology will be presented later in the book to aid in the interpretation of the relationship between human culture and biology.

Archaeology

Archaeology is the study of cultural behaviors in the historic and prehistoric past. The archaeologist deals with such remains of past societies as tools, shelters, and remains of animals eaten. These remains, termed artifacts, are used to reconstruct past behavior. To help fill in the gaps, the archaeologist makes use of the findings of cultural anthropologists who have studied similar societies. Archaeological findings are critical in understanding the behavior of early humans and their evolution. Some of these findings for the earliest humans are presented later in this text.

Linguistic Anthropology

Linguistic anthropology is the study of language. Spoken language is a behavior that appears to be uniquely human. This subfield of anthropology deals with the analysis of languages, usually in nonliterate societies, and with general trends in the evolution of languages. A major question raised by linguistic anthropology concerns the extent to which language shapes culture. Is language necessary for the transmission of culture? Does a language provide information about the beliefs and practices of a human culture? Biological anthropology must consider many of the findings of linguistic anthropology in the analysis of human variation and evolution. When comparing humans and apes, we must ask whether language is a unique human characteristic. If it is, then what biological and behavioral differences exist between apes and humans that lead to the fact that one species has language and the other lacks it? Linguistics is also important in considering human evolution. When did language begin, and why?

Biological Anthropology

The subject of this book is the subfield of **biological anthropology,** which is concerned with the biological evolution and variation of the human species, past and present. Biological anthropology is often referred to by another name—physical anthropology. The course you are currently enrolled in might be known by either name; the two names refer to the same field. Early in the twentieth century, the field was known as physical anthropology, reflecting

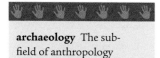

archaeology The subfield of anthropology that focuses on cultural variations in prehistoric (and some historic) populations by analyzing the culture's remains.

linguistic anthropology The subfield of anthropology that focuses on the nature of human language, the relationship of language to culture, and the languages of nonliterate peoples.

biological anthropology The subfield of anthropology that focuses on the biological evolution of humans and human ancestors, the relationship of humans to other organisms, and patterns of biological variation within and among human populations. Also referred to as physical anthropology.

its then-primary interest in the physical variation of past and present humans and our primate relatives. Much of the research in the field focused on descriptive studies of physical variations, with little theoretical background. Starting in the 1950s, physical anthropologists became more familiar with the rapidly growing fields of genetics and evolutionary science. As a result, the field of physical anthropology became more concerned with biological processes, particularly genetics. After a while, many in the field began using the term "biological anthropology" to emphasize the new focus on biological processes. In most circles today, the two terms are used more or less interchangeably.

It is useful to consider the field of biological anthropology in terms of three very basic questions that are addressed in Parts II, III, and IV of this text. First, what is our place in nature? That is, how are we related to other living creatures? How are we unique? The second major question concerns our past. What are our origins? Where did we come from? What does the history of our species look like? How were our earlier ancestors similar to us, and how different from us? The third question concerns our diversity. How are humans around the world like, or unlike, each other? What causes the patterns of human variation that we see? What is the pattern of recent evolution of our species, and how do we continue to evolve?

There are several traditionally defined areas within biological anthropology, such as primate studies, human evolution, and human variation. Primates are the group of mammals to which we belong, and studies of the anatomy, ecology, and behavior of the nonhuman primates provide us with a comparative perspective from which to view our own evolutionary history. In this way, we learn something about what it is to be human. Primate studies are covered in Chapters 5–7 in this text. The study of human evolution necessarily involves analysis of the fossil and archaeological remains of our ancestors in order to determine where, when, how, and why they evolved. The fossil record for primate and human evolution is covered in Chapters 8–13. The study of human variation deals with how and why humans differ from each other in their biological makeup, including studies of ancestry and population history, recent and ongoing human evolution, and ways in which changes in human culture have affected our biology. The study of human variation and recent evolution is covered in Chapters 14–17.

Applied research is an expanding focus in biological anthropology. Forensic anthropologists apply their knowledge of human skeletal variation to the identification of human skeletal remains. These remains (including the teeth) are used to classify individuals by sex, age, stature, and, where possible, likely ancestry. Information about the cause of death and existing pathologies is recorded, and these clues, combined in some cases with identification of DNA from skeletal remains, provide information that is used in legal cases, for identification of missing persons, in analysis of mass gravesites, and for other forensic applications (Steadman 2009). Some aspects of forensic anthropology (and a related field known as bioarchaeology) are mentioned throughout this text and covered in more detail in a separate appendix at the end of the book.

Having read this introduction, you realize that the major focus of biological anthropology is evolution. In order to make sure we are all on the same page regarding evolutionary theory, including relevant aspects of human genetics, the first part of this text (Chapters 1–4) reviews what we need to know about evolution in general.

EVOLUTIONARY BACKGROUND

How does life change over time? A variety of evidence, ranging from the fossil record to anatomic and genetic comparisons of living organisms, shows us that all life has a common origin and that the diversity in living creatures (including humans) is the result of biological evolution. The science of biological anthropology is one of a number of fields that deal with evolution: in this case, the evolution of humans and their close relatives. How does evolution occur? The first section of this book looks at the evolutionary process. Chapter 1 provides background on the nature of evolutionary science and its historical development. Chapter 2 reviews some basic concepts of human genetics that are necessary for understanding evolution. Chapter 3 builds on this background to focus on the details of the evolutionary process. Chapter 4 extends these ideas to evolution over long periods of time, including the origin and classification of new species.

Charles Darwin (1809–1882) was the author of *On the Origin of Species*, a monumental work that collected evidence for the evolution of life and presented a hypothesis of evolutionary change, natural selection, that has stood the test of time and remains a central component of modern evolutionary thought.

Science and Evolution

Do you believe that humans evolved?

More specifically, how would you respond to the statement "Human beings, as we know them, developed from earlier species of animals"? This question has been asked as part of a national survey given since 1985, and people are asked if they consider this statement true or false, or are not sure. The most recent survey shows that about 40 percent of Americans agree with the statement, about 40 percent disagree with the statement, and about 20 percent are not sure (Miller et al. 2006). Would you have expected to find that the majority (60 percent) of Americans either rejected or were not sure about the facts of human evolution?

You might argue that this is not really a matter of facts. After all, we have all probably heard a frequent assertion that "evolution is only a theory, not a fact." If this is true, should we not err on the side of caution and take human evolution (or evolution in general) as simply a theory that remains to be tested, and not assume that it is a solid and given fact? And if evolution is not a fact, but "only" a theory, then should we in all fairness be open to alternative explanations? If so, then should not science classes present these different explanations? Would not the best approach be to provide students with all sides of an argument and let them make their own choice?

The above chain of reasoning (or variants on it) is common today, and has often been the stated motivation behind a number of legal attempts to mandate the teaching of alternatives to evolutionary theory in the public schools. One of the more recent and famous examples took place in Dover, Pennsylvania, when the local school board passed a resolution in 2004 that stated "Students will be made aware of gaps/problems in Darwin's theory and of other theories of evolution including, but not limited to, intelligent design." (*Kitzmiller et al. v. Dover Area School District*, p. 1). The model of intelligent design will be described in more detail later in this chapter, but in short, it refers to the idea that the Darwinian theory of evolution cannot explain adequately the complex structure of biological organisms, which in turn implies that life was designed, which in turn implies an intelligent designer (God?). Those who oppose the teaching of intelligent design argue that the subject matter is not science, but rather religion. As such, it should not be taught in a public school science class. Proponents of intelligent

CHAPTER OUTLINE

- Characteristics of Science

- The Development of Evolutionary Theory

- Science and Religion

design argue back that intelligent design *is* a science, and therefore should be considered as a valid alternative to evolutionary theory. Supporters of intelligent design also argue that in order to be fair, all different views and opinions should be taught, and we should let the students make up their own minds.

At this point, you probably realize that these discussions often go beyond the content matter in a high school class and cross over into religious and philosophical realms, which makes the issue much less abstract and (for most) quite personal (especially when we consider *human* evolution as compared with the evolution of butterflies or squid). Before deciding where you stand on the Dover school board resolution, it is important to take some time to consider some very basic questions. What exactly is a science, and do evolutionary theory and intelligent design qualify as science? When we talk about "theory," exactly what do we mean, and are we all using the term in the same way? How does science work, and does "fairness" enter into it? These and other questions need to be addressed more fully before considering examples such as the Dover school board resolution.

As noted in the Introduction, biological anthropology is an evolutionary science focused on human biological origins, evolution, and variation. In order to understand the findings of biological anthropology, we need to understand more clearly the nature of science in general, and the nature of evolutionary science in particular. The remainder of this chapter examines the characteristics of science and the historical development of evolutionary science, ending with a broader consideration of the issues raised by the Dover case, specifically the supposed conflict between science and religion.

CHARACTERISTICS OF SCIENCE

Before we consider how evolution works, it is important to understand exactly what a science is and what the relationship between facts, hypotheses, and theories is.

Facts

As noted earlier, sometimes we hear evolution referred to as a fact and sometimes as a theory. Which is it, theory or fact? The truth of the matter is that someone who makes either of these statements does not understand what a theory or a fact is. Evolution is *both* fact and theory. A fact is simply a verifiable truth. It is a scientific fact that the earth is round. It is a fact that when you drop something, it falls to the ground (assuming you are in the presence of a gravitational field and are not dropping something that floats or flies away!). Evolution is a fact. Living organisms have changed in the past, and they continue to change today. There are forms of life today that did not exist millions of years ago. There are also forms of life that existed in the past but are not around today, such as our ancestors (Figure 1.1). Certain organisms have shown definite changes in their biological makeup. Horses, for example,

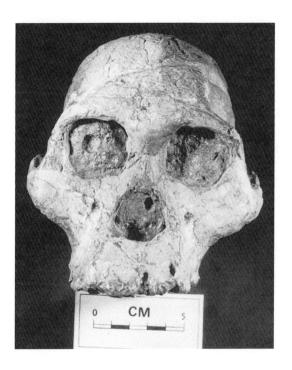

FIGURE 1.1

A skull of *Australopithecus africanus*, a human ancestor that lived 2.5 million to 3.3 million years ago. Paleoanthropologists use the fossil record to learn about our evolution.

used to have four toes, then three, and today only one. Human beings have larger brains and smaller teeth today than they did a million years ago. Some changes are even apparent over shorter intervals of time. For example, human teeth are on average smaller today than they were only 10,000 years ago. All of these statements and many others are verifiable truths. They are facts.

Hypotheses

What is a hypothesis? A **hypothesis** is simply an explanation of observed facts. For example, consider gravity. Gravity is a fact. It is observable. Many hypotheses could be generated to explain gravity. You could hypothesize that gravity is caused by a giant living in the core of our planet drawing in air, thus causing a pull on all objects on the earth's surface. Bizarre as it sounds, this is a scientific hypothesis because it can be tested. It is, however, easily shown to be incorrect (air movement can be measured, and it does not flow in the postulated direction).

To be scientific, a hypothesis must be testable. The potential must exist for a hypothesis to be rejected. Just as the presence of the hypothetical giant in the earth can be tested (it doesn't exist!), predictions about gravitational strength can also be tested. Not all hypotheses can be tested, however, and for this reason, they are not scientific hypotheses. That doesn't necessarily mean that they are true or false, but only that they cannot be tested. For example, you might come up with a hypothesis that all the fossils we have ever found were put in the ground by God to confuse us. This is not a scientific hypothesis because we have no objective way of testing it.

hypothesis An explanation of observed facts.

Many evolutionary hypotheses, however, are testable. For example, specific predictions about the fossil record can be made based on our knowledge of evolution. One such prediction is that humans evolved after the first appearance of mammals. The potential exists for this statement to be rejected; all we need is evidence that humans existed before the first mammals. Because we have found no such evidence, we cannot reject the hypothesis. We can, however, imagine a situation in which the hypothesis could be rejected. If we cannot imagine such a situation, then the hypothesis cannot be tested. Suppose someone tells you that all the people on the earth were created five minutes ago, complete with memories! Any evidence you muster against this idea could be explained away. Therefore, this hypothesis is not scientific because there is no possible way to reject it.

Theories

theory A set of hypotheses that have been tested repeatedly and that have not been rejected. This term is sometimes used in a different sense in social science literature.

What is the difference between a theory and a hypothesis? In some disciplines, the two terms are sometimes used to mean the same thing. In the natural and physical sciences, however, theory means something different from hypothesis. A **theory** is a set of hypotheses that have been tested repeatedly and that have not been rejected. Evolution falls into this category.

There seems to be continuing confusion about the difference between "fact" and "theory" in our culture, giving rise, for example, to arguments about whether evolution is a fact *or* a theory. Such arguments show unfamiliarity with the definitions of "fact," "hypothesis," and "theory." Too often, there is a tendency to view a theory as a mere speculation as opposed to the more accurate definition as a set of confirmed hypotheses. The argument about whether evolution is a fact *or* a theory incorrectly suggests that evolution may or may not exist. One only has to use the same debate over atoms and atomic theory to see the problem with such reasoning. When you hear about atomic theory, does that suggest to you that atoms may or may not exist? Of course not. Atoms are real (facts), and atomic theory refers to a set of confirmed hypotheses used to explain these facts. As such, atoms refer to *both* a fact *and* a theory.

Likewise, evolution is *both* a fact *and* a theory. As noted below, we have evidence that evolution has occurred in the past and continues to occur today. Various hypotheses have been suggested in the past to explain *why* and *how* evolution has occurred. Over time, the hypothesis of natural selection, developed by Charles Darwin and explained below, has stood the test of time as a major component (along with other mechanisms discussed in later chapters) of modern evolutionary theory.

THE DEVELOPMENT OF EVOLUTIONARY THEORY

As with all general theories, modern evolutionary theory is not static. Scientific research is a dynamic process, with new evidence being used to support, clarify, and, most importantly, reject previous ideas. There will always be continual refinements in specific aspects of the theory and its applications. Because science is a dynamic process, evolutionary theory did not come about overnight. Charles Darwin (1809–1882) is most often credited as the "father of evolutionary thought" (Figure 1.2). It is true that Darwin provided a powerful idea that forms the center of modern evolutionary thought. However, he did not work in an intellectual vacuum; rather, he built on the ideas of earlier scholars. Darwin's model was not the first evolutionary theory; it forms, instead, the basis of the one that has stood the test of time.

Pre-Darwinian Thought

To understand Darwin's contribution and evolution in general, it is necessary to take a look at earlier ideas. For many centuries, the concept of change, biological or otherwise, was unusual in Western thought. Much of ancient Greek philosophy, for example, posited a static, unchanging view of the world. In later Western thought, the universe, earth, and all living creatures were regarded as having been created by God in their present form, showing little if any change over many generations. The tendency to view the universe through the lens of biblical interpretation gave way to the rise of science and the scientific method during the European Renaissance and the later period of Enlightenment (Age of Reason). In astronomy, for example, the view of an earth-centered universe declined due to the influence of Copernicus and Galileo. Eventually, the idea of a static world gave way to an appreciation for the evolution of living creatures, although this took time. Before the eighteenth century, biology was a descriptive science, with much attention given to the description and classification of organisms. In the mid to late 1600s, the minister John Ray (1627–1705) argued for a scientific system of comparisons among organisms and was the first to define and use the terms *genus* and *species*. Ray's initial work was later developed more fully by the Swedish naturalist Carolus Linnaeus (1707–1778), who compiled a massive formal classification of all living things (Figure 1.3).

FIGURE 1.2

Charles Darwin developed the idea of natural selection as a way of explaining how organisms evolve over time by adapting to their environment. Organisms that are more likely to survive and reproduce pass their genetic material on to future generations.

FIGURE 1.3

Carolus Linnaeus, the Swedish naturalist who compiled one of the first formal taxonomies of all living organisms.

taxonomy The science of describing and classifying organisms.

species A group of populations whose members can interbreed naturally and produce fertile offspring.

genus Groups of species with similar adaptations.

Taxonomy is the science of describing and classifying organisms. Linnaeus's taxonomic research produced a classification of all known living creatures into meaningful groups. For example, humans, dogs, cats, and many other animals are mammals, characterized primarily by the presence of mammary glands to feed offspring. Linnaeus used a variety of traits to place all then-known creatures into various categories. Such a classification helps clarify relationships between different organisms. For example, bats are classified as mammals because they possess mammary glands—and not as birds simply because they have wings.

Following Ray, Linnaeus also gave organisms a name reflecting their genus and species. A **species** is a group of populations whose members can interbreed and produce fertile offspring. A **genus** is a group of similar species, often sharing certain common forms of adaptation. Modern humans, for example, are known by the name *Homo sapiens*. The first word is the genus, and the second the species (more detail on genus and species is given in Chapter 4).

The reason for the relationships among organisms, however, was not often addressed by early natural historians. The living world was felt to be the product of God's work, and the task of the natural historian was description and classification. This static view of the world began to change in the eighteenth and nineteenth centuries. One important reason for this change was that excavations began to produce many fossils that did not fit neatly into the classification system. For example, imagine that you found the remains of a modern horse. This would pose no problem in interpretation; the bones are those of a dead horse, perhaps belonging to a farmer several years ago. Now suppose you found what at first glance appeared to be a horse but was somewhat smaller and had three toes instead of the single hoof of a modern horse. If you found more and more of these three-toed horses, you would ask what creature the toes belonged to. Because horses do not have three toes today, your only conclusion would be that there once existed horses with three toes and that they do not exist anymore. This conclusion, though hardly startling now, was a thunderbolt to those who believed the world had been created as it currently was, today, with no change.

Apart from fossil remains of creatures that were somewhat similar to modern-day forms, excavations also uncovered fossil remnants of truly unusual creatures, such as the dinosaurs. This fossil record led scientists to chip away at the view that the world was as it always had been, and the concept of change began to be incorporated into explanations of the origin of life. Not all scholars, however, came up with the same hypotheses.

One French anatomist, Georges Cuvier (1769–1832), analyzed many of the fossil remains found in quarries. He showed that many of these belonged to animals that no longer existed; that is, they had become extinct. Cuvier used a hypothesis called catastrophism to explain these extinctions. The hypothesis posited a series of catastrophes in the planet's past during which many living creatures were destroyed. Following these catastrophes, organisms from unaffected areas moved in. The changes over time observed in the fossil record could therefore be explained as a continual process of catastrophes followed by repopulation from other regions (Mayr 1982). A problem with Cuvier's hypothesis is that it does not explain where organisms from other regions came from. Some interpreted his idea of catastrophism as a sequence of creations and extinctions.

The work of the French scientist Jean-Baptiste Lamarck (1744–1829) more explicitly attempted an explanation of evolution. He believed that the environment would affect the future shape and organization of animals (Mayr 1982). His specific mechanism stressed the use and disuse of body parts. For example, a jungle cat that developed stronger legs through constant running and jumping would pass these changes on to its offspring. This type of change does not actually happen; if you work out every day, you will not pass on your larger muscles to your children. Although we now know that Lamarck's ideas are not genetically correct, it is important to note that he was quite astute in noticing the relationship between organisms, their environment, and evolution.

Uniformitarianism and Geologic Time

Central to an explanation of biological evolution is the nature of the passage of time and the age of the earth. In earlier times, it was generally thought that the earth was young, with age estimates based on biblical interpretations. Perhaps the most well-known estimate of earth's antiquity is that of Archbishop James Ussher (1581–1656). Based on his analysis of biblical writings and events, Ussher concluded that the earth was less than 6,000 years old, and he assigned a precise date of 4004 B.C. as the year God created the universe (his most precise estimate was that creation took place the night before Sunday, October 23, 4004 B.C.!).

Geological research, however, was moving in a different direction with the growing realization that the earth was considerably older than several thousand years. Scottish geologist James Hutton (1726–1797) developed the idea of **uniformitarianism,** which means that the geologic processes we observe in the world today, such as erosion or continental drift, operated in the same way in the past. This important principle means that we can study the world around us in the present and use what we see to make inferences about the past. The principle of uniformitarianism was adopted and extended by another Scottish geologist, Charles Lyell (1797–1875), who provided considerable geologic evidence for a slowly changing earth. Critical to the development of evolutionary thought was the observation that because the earth was shaped slowly over time, it would have therefore taken a considerable amount of time to form the many geologic features present in the world today. Thus, geological research was showing that the earth was *much* older than several thousand years. Indeed, according to current estimates, based on a variety of physical and chemical methods (see Chapter 8), the earth is 4.6 *billion* years old—over 750,000 times as old as estimated by Ussher! The work of Lyell also suggested that small biological processes could add up over time to produce considerable evolutionary change. In fact, Lyell's work greatly influenced the key figure in the history of evolutionary thought—Charles Darwin.

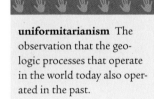

uniformitarianism The observation that the geologic processes that operate in the world today also operated in the past.

Charles Darwin and Natural Selection

With this background in mind, let us look at Darwin and his accomplishments. Charles Darwin had been interested in biology and geology since he was a small child. Born to well-to-do parents, Darwin attended college and had planned to enter the ministry, although he was not as enthusiastic about this career as he was about his studies of natural history. Because of his scientific and social connections, Darwin was able to accompany the scientific survey ship *Beagle* as an unpaid naturalist. The *Beagle* conducted a five-year journey around the world collecting plant and animal specimens in South America and the Galapagos Islands (in the Pacific Ocean near Ecuador), among other places (Figure 1.4).

During these travels, Darwin came to several basic conclusions about variation in living organisms. First, he found a tremendous amount of observable variation in most living species. Instead of looking at the world in terms of fixed, rigid categories (as did mainstream biology in his time), Darwin saw that individuals within species varied considerably from place to place. With careful attention, you can see the world in much the same way that Darwin did. You will see, for example, that people around you vary to an incredible degree. Some are tall, some short; some are dark, some light. Facial features, musculature, hair color, and many other characteristics come in many different forms, even in a single classroom. Remember, too, that what you see are only those visible characteristics. With the right type of equipment, you

FIGURE 1.4

The voyage of the HMS *Beagle*. Darwin's observations of variation in the different regions he visited aboard the HMS *Beagle* shaped his theory of natural selection.

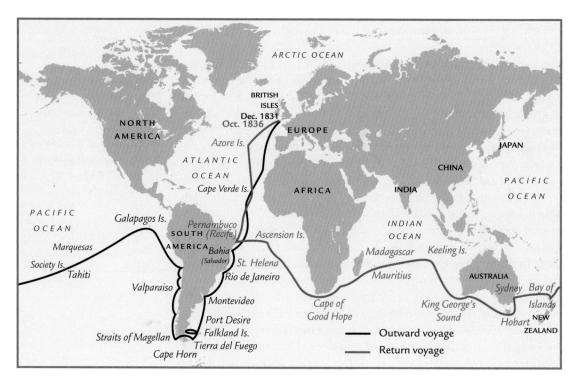

could look at genetic and biochemical variation within your classroom and find even more evidence of tremendous diversity.

Darwin also noted that the variations he saw made sense in terms of the environment (Figures 1.5 and 1.6). Creatures in cold climates often have fur for protection. Birds in areas where insects live deep inside tree trunks or branches have long beaks to enable them to extract these insects and eat them. In other words, organisms appear well adapted to specific environments. Darwin believed that the environment acted to change organisms over time. But how?

To help answer this question, Darwin turned to the writings of the economist Thomas Malthus (1766–1834), who had noted that more individuals are born in most species than can possibly survive. In other words, many organisms die before reaching maturity and reproducing. If it were not for this mortality, populations would grow too large for their environments to support them. Malthus is best known for extrapolating the principle of population growth into human terms; his lesson is that unless we control our growth, there will soon be too many of us to feed.

To Darwin, the ideas of Malthus provided the needed information to solve the problem of adaptation and evolution. Not all individuals in a species survive and reproduce. Some failure to reproduce may be random, but

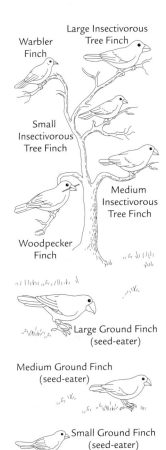

FIGURE 1.5

The sizes, beak shapes, and diets of this sample of Darwin's finches show differences in adaptation among closely related species. (From E. Peter Volpe, *Understanding Evolution*, 5th ed. © 1985 Wm. C. Brown Communications, Inc., Dubuque, Iowa. All rights reserved. Reprinted by permission of The McGraw-Hill Companies.)

FIGURE 1.6

The long-necked subspecies of the Galapagos tortoise, a form that has adapted to living in a dry climate. The long neck allows greater access to higher vegetation that grows in this climate.

some is related to specific characteristics of an individual. If there are two birds, one with a short beak and one with a long beak, in an environment that requires reaching inside trees to feed, it stands to reason that the bird with the longer beak is more likely to feed itself, survive, and reproduce. In certain environments, some individuals possess traits that enhance their probability of survival and reproduction. If these traits are due, in part or whole, to inherited characteristics, then they will be passed on to the next generation.

In some ways, Darwin's idea was not new. Animal and plant breeders had applied this principle for centuries. Controlled breeding and artificial selection had resulted in many traits in domesticated plants and animals, such as livestock size and milk production in cows. The same principle is used in producing pedigreed dogs and many forms of tropical fish. The difference is that Darwin saw that nature (the environment) could select those individuals that survived and reproduced. Hence, he called his concept **natural selection.** Given the influence of Lyell's thoughts on uniformitarianism, as well as the great antiquity of the earth, Darwin further argued that small changes due to natural selection could add up over long periods to produce the diversity of species we see in the world today.

natural selection A mechanism for evolutionary change favoring the survival and reproduction of some organisms over others because of their biological characteristics.

Although the theory of evolution by natural selection is most often associated with Charles Darwin, another English natural historian, Alfred Russel Wallace (1823–1913), came up with essentially the same idea. In fact, Darwin and Wallace communicated their ideas to each other and first presented the theory of natural selection in a joint paper in 1858. Many scholars feel that Wallace's independent work impelled Darwin finally to put forward the ideas he had developed years earlier but had not published. To ensure timely publication, Darwin condensed his many years of work into a book titled *On the Origin of Species by Means of Natural Selection,* published in 1859.

An Example of Natural Selection

One example of how natural selection works involves populations of the peppered moth in England over the past few centuries (Figure 1.7). These moths come in two distinct colors, dark and light. Early observations found that most of these moths were light-colored, thus allowing them to camouflage themselves on tree trunks covered by light-colored lichen. By blending in, they had a better chance of avoiding the birds that tried to eat them. Roughly 1 percent of the moths, however, were dark-colored and thus at an obvious disadvantage. In the century following the beginning of the Industrial Revolution in England, naturalists noted that the frequency of dark-colored moths increased to almost 90 percent (Grant 1985). The explanation for this change was the massive pollution in the surrounding countryside brought about by industrialization. The pollution killed the lichen, exposing the dark trees. The light moths were at a disadvantage, whereas the dark moths, now better camouflaged, were better off. Proportionately, more dark moths survived and passed their dark color to the next generation. In evolutionary terminology, the dark moths were *selected for* and the light moths

FIGURE 1.7

Adaptation in the peppered moth. The dark-colored moth is more visible on light-colored tree trunks and therefore at greater risk of being seen and eaten by a bird (*left*). The light-colored moth is at greater risk of being eaten on dark-colored tree trunks (*right*).

were *selected against*. After antipollution laws were passed and the environment began to recover, the situation was reversed: Once again, light moths survived better and were selected for, whereas dark moths were selected against (Cook et al. 1999).

To illustrate one of the ways that natural selection can be detected, consider the relationship between moth color and survival revealed in a recapture experiment. In such a procedure, moths of different colors are marked and then released into the environment in known proportions of light and dark. Later, moths are recaptured, the relative proportions of light and dark compared, and the ratio of observed to expected used as a measure of survival rate. For example, in one study of a polluted area in Birmingham, England, 158 moths were recaptured, of which 18 were light-colored and 140 were dark-colored. Given the initial proportions, the expected numbers (given a total of 158 recaptured moths) were 36 light-colored moths and 122 dark-colored moths. In other words, fewer light-colored moths and more dark-colored moths survived than was to be expected if there were no survival value in color. In another recapture experiment, conducted in an unpolluted area, the findings were the opposite—more light-colored moths and fewer dark-colored moths survived than expected. This observation also makes sense, as the survival rate of light-colored moths is expected to be higher in an area without industrial pollution (Ridley 2004).

The peppered moth example shows us more than just the workings of natural selection. It also illustrates several important principles of evolution. First, we cannot always state with absolute certainty which traits are "good" and which are "bad." It depends on the specific environment. When the trees were light in color, the light-colored moths were at an advantage, but when the situation changed, the dark-colored moths gained the advantage. Second, evolution does not proceed unopposed in one direction. In certain situations, biological traits can change in a different direction. In the case of the moths, evolution produced a change from light to dark to light again. Third, evolution does not occur in a vacuum. It is affected by changes in the environment and in other species. In this example, changes in the cultural evolution of humans led to a change in the environment, which further affected the evolution of the moths. Finally, the moth study shows us the critical importance of variation to the evolutionary process. If the original population of moths had not possessed the dark-colored variation, they might have been wiped out after the trees turned darker in color. Variation must exist for natural selection to operate effectively.

The peppered moth example also provides a good example of the application of the scientific method. Although the relationship between changing frequency of moth color and bird predation has long been considered a "classic" example of natural selection, there have also been criticisms of the underlying methods of the studies. The point here is that criticism of methods and interpretations is an important part of science; results must be repeatable. In the case of the peppered moth studies, there have been sufficient analyses employing different methods to confirm early observations of differential survival (Cook 2000; Ridley 2004). It is also important to note that such criticism and reanalysis revealed that the geographic distribution of moth colors is a bit more complicated than once thought; apparently, migration, in addition to bird predation, has affected the evolution of the peppered moth (Ridley 2004).

Modern Evolutionary Thought

Darwin provided part of the answer to the question of how evolution worked, but he did not have all the answers. Many early critics of Darwin's work focused on certain questions that Darwin could not answer. One important question concerns the origins of variation: Given that natural selection operates on *existing* variation, where do those variations come from? Why, at the outset, were some moths light and others dark? Natural selection can act only on preexisting variation; it cannot create new variations. Another question is, How are traits inherited? The theory of natural selection states that certain traits are selected for and passed on to future generations. How are these traits passed on? Darwin knew that traits were inherited, but he did not know the mechanism. Still another question is, How do new forms and structures come into being?

Darwin is to be remembered and praised for his work in providing the critical base from which evolutionary science developed. He did not, however, have all the answers; no scientist does. Even today, people tend to equate evolutionary science with Darwin, to the exclusion of all work since that time. Some critics of evolutionary theory point to a single aspect of Darwin's work, show it to be in error, and then claim that all of evolutionary thought is suspect. In reality, a scientific theory will continue to change as new evidence is gathered and as further tests are constructed.

Modern evolutionary theory relies not only on the work of Darwin and Wallace but also on developments in genetics, zoology, embryology, physiology, and mathematics, to name but a few fields. The basic concept of natural selection as stated by Darwin has been tested and found to be valid. Refinements have been added, and some aspects of the original idea have been changed. We now have answers to many of Darwin's questions.

Biological evolution consists of changes in the genetic composition of populations. As shown in Chapter 3, the relative frequencies of genes change over time because of four mechanisms, or evolutionary forces. Natural selection is one of these mechanisms. Those individuals with genetic characteristics that improve their survival or reproduction pass their genetic material on to the next generation. In the peppered moth example, the dark moths were more likely to survive in an environment where pollution made the trees darker in color. Thus, the relative frequency of genes for dark moth color increased over time (at least until the environment changed again).

Evolutionary change from one generation to the next, or over many generations, is the product of the joint effect of the four evolutionary forces. Our discussion here simplifies a complex idea, but it does suggest that evolution is more than simply natural selection. Modern evolutionary theory encompasses all four evolutionary forces and will be discussed in greater detail in the next three chapters.

Evidence for Evolution

Because this book is concerned with human variation and evolution, you will be provided with numerous examples of how evolution works in human populations, past and present. It is important to understand from the start that biological evolution is a documented fact and that the modern theory of evolution has stood up under many scientific tests.

The fossil record provides abundant evidence of evolution (see Figures 1.8–1.10 for some examples). The story the fossils tell is one of change: Creatures existed in the past that are no longer with us. Sequential changes are found in many fossils showing the change of certain features over time, as in the case of the horse. Apart from demonstrating that evolution did occur, the fossil record also provides tests of the predictions made from evolutionary

FIGURE 1.8

A pair of trilobites, an extinct arthropod, found in Morocco and dating to the Cambrian Period (542–488 million years ago) of the Paleozoic Era.

FIGURE 1.9

Dinosaur (Tyrannosaurus rex) teeth from South Dakota. Tyrannosaurus rex lived during the Upper Cretaceous Period (67–65.5 million years ago) of the Mesozoic Era.

FIGURE 1.10

Fossil fish (genus Knightia) from the Green River Formation in Wyoming dating to the Eocene Epoch (56–34 million years ago) of the Paleogene Period in the Cenozoic Era. Knightia is the state fossil of Wyoming.

theory. For example, the theory predicts that single-celled organisms evolved before multicelled organisms. The fossil record supports this prediction—multicelled organisms found in layers of the earth appeared millions of years after the first single-celled organisms. Note that the possibility always remains that the opposite could be found. If multicelled organisms were indeed found to have evolved before single-celled organisms, then the theory of evolution would be rejected. A good scientific theory always allows for the possibility of rejection. The fact that we have not found such a case in countless examinations of the fossil record strengthens the case for evolutionary theory. Remember, in science, you do not prove a theory; rather, you fail to reject it.

The fossil record also provides numerous examples of transitional forms, such as fossils of early whales with reduced hind limbs (Gingerich et al. 1990). Whales are aquatic mammals that have lost their hind limbs and pelvic bones since their evolutionary separation from other mammals more than 50 million years ago. The discovery of fossil whales with small hind limbs provides an example of shared characteristics that can be explained only through evolution. This discovery also provides an excellent example of a transitional form linking both early and modern forms. Another example of a transitional form is the species known as *Tiktaalik roseae*, which is a link between early fish and the first vertebrates with limbs (Daeschler et al. 2006). Another example is *Seymouria*, a transitional form linking amphibians and reptiles (Figure 1.11). Such fossils are exactly what are predicted by evolutionary theory.

FIGURE 1.11

Fossil of the species *Seymouria baylorensis,* which lived in Texas 280 million years ago and represents forms that are transitional between amphibians and reptiles.

The fossil record is not the only evidence that evolution has occurred. Comparison of living organisms provides further confirmation. For example, the African apes are the closest living relatives of humans. We see this in a number of characteristics. African apes and humans share the same type of dental pattern, have a similar shoulder structure, and have DNA (the genetic code) that is over 98 percent identical. Even though any one of these traits, or others, could be explained as coincidental, why do so many independent traits show the same pattern? One possibility, of course, is that they were designed that way by an ultimate creator. The problem with this idea is that it cannot be tested. It is a matter of faith and not of science. Another problem is that we must then ask ourselves why a creator would use the same basic pattern for so many traits in different creatures. Evolution, on the other hand, offers an explanation: Apes and humans share many characteristics because they evolved from a common ancestor.

Another example of shared characteristics is the python, a large snake. Like many vertebrates, the python has a pelvis, the skeletal structure that connects the lower legs to the upper body (Futuyma 1983). From a structural standpoint, of what possible use is a pelvis to a creature that has no legs? If the python was created, what purpose could there have been to give it a pelvis? We can, of course, argue that no one can understand the motivations of a creator, but that is hardly a scientific explanation. Evolutionary reasoning provides an answer: The python has retained the pelvis from an earlier ancestor that did have legs. In fact, fossil discoveries dating back 95 million years provide evidence of early snakes that actually had limbs (Tchernov et al. 2000).

SCIENCE AND RELIGION

The subject of evolution has always been controversial, and the implications of evolution have sometimes frightened people. For example, the fact that humans and apes evolved from a common ancestor has always upset some people who feel that their humanity is somehow degraded by having ancestors supposedly less worthy than themselves. Another conflict lies in the implications evolution has for religious views. In the United States, even

FIGURE 1.12

The Scopes trial. William Jennings Bryan (*right*) represented the state of Tennessee, and Clarence Darrow (*left*) represented John Scopes, who was on trial for violating the law that prohibited teaching evolution in public schools.

into the late 1960s, a number of laws prohibited teaching evolution in public schools.

Numerous legal battles have been fought over these anti-evolution laws. Perhaps the most famous was the "Scopes Monkey Trial" in 1925. John Scopes, a high school teacher in Dayton, Tennessee, was arrested for violating the state law prohibiting the teaching of evolution. The town and trial quickly became the center of national attention, primarily because of the two celebrities in the case—William Jennings Bryan, a former U.S. secretary of state, who represented the state of Tennessee, and Clarence Darrow, one of the most famous American trial lawyers ever, who represented Scopes. The battle between these two eloquent speakers captured the attention of the nation (Figure 1.12). In the end, Scopes was found guilty of violating the law and fined $100. The fine was later suspended on a legal technicality. The story of this trial, which has been dramatized in play and movie versions as *Inherit the Wind,* is a powerful portrayal of those who feel strongly about academic freedom and freedom of speech fighting against ignorance and oppression. In reality, the original arrest of Scopes was planned by several local people to gain publicity for the town (Larson 1997).

Creation Science

In retrospect, the Scopes trial may seem amusing. We laugh at early attempts to control subject matter in classrooms and often feel that we have moved beyond such battles. Nothing could be further from the truth, however. For many people, evolution represents a threat to their beliefs in the sudden creation of all life by a creator. Attempts to legislate the teaching of the biblical view of creation in science classes, however, violate the First Amendment of the Constitution as an establishment of religion. To circumvent this problem, opponents of evolution devised the strategy of calling their teachings "creation science"—supposedly, the scientific study of special creation. The word *God* does not always appear in definitions of creation science, but the word *creator* often does.

In March 1981, the Arkansas state legislature passed a law (Act 590) requiring that creation science be taught in public schools for equal amounts of time as evolution. The American Civil Liberties Union challenged this law, and it was overturned in a federal district court in 1982. A similar law passed in Louisiana in 1981 was later overturned. The Louisiana case was later appealed and brought to the U.S. Supreme Court, which upheld the ruling of the lower court in 1987. Among other legal problems they raise, both the Arkansas and Louisiana laws have been found to be unconstitutional under the First Amendment.

What is "creation science"? Why shouldn't it be taught in science classes? Shouldn't science be open to new ideas? These questions all center on the issue of whether creation science actually is a science. As typically applied, creation science is not a science; at best, it is a grab bag of ideas spruced up with scientific jargon.

One of the original definitions is found in Act 590 of the Arkansas law, which defines creation science as

> the scientific evidence for creation and inferences from these scientific evidences. Creation-science includes the scientific evidences and related inferences that indicate: (1) Sudden creation of the universe, energy, and life from nothing; (2) The insufficiency of mutation and natural selection in bringing about development of all living kinds from a single organism; (3) Changes only within fixed limits of originally created kinds of plants and animals; (4) Separate ancestry for man and apes; (5) Explanation of the earth's geology by catastrophism, including the occurrence of a worldwide flood; and (6) A relatively recent inception of the earth and living kinds. (quoted in Montagu 1984:376–377)

None of these statements is supported by scientific evidence, and creationist writers generally use very little actual evidence to support their views. The main "scientific" work of the creationists consists of attempting to find fault with evolutionary theory. The reasoning is that if evolution can be rejected, then "special creation" must be true. This strategy actually uses an important feature of scientific research by attempting to reject a given hypothesis. The problem is that none of the creationists' attacks on evolution has been supported by scientific evidence. Certainly, some predictions of evolutionary theory have been proven incorrect, but that is to be expected because science is a dynamic process. The basic findings of evolution, however, have been supported time and time again.

On an emotional level, the doctrines of creation science attract many people. Given the concept of free speech, why shouldn't creation science be given equal time? The problem with this plea is that it assumes that both ideas have equal merit. Consider that some people still believe the earth is flat. They are certainly entitled to their opinion, but it would be absurd to mandate "equal time" in geography and geology classes for this idea. Also, the concept of equal time is not really that fair-minded after all. The specific story many creationists refer to is the biblical story of Genesis. Many other cultures have their own creation stories. Shouldn't they receive equal time as well? In one sense, they should, though the proper forum for such discussions is probably a course in comparative religion, not a science class.

Perhaps the biggest problem advocates of creation science have introduced is that they appear to place religion and science at odds with each other. Religion and science both represent ways of looking at the world, and though they work on different levels, they are not contradictory. You can believe in God and still accept the fact of evolution and evolutionary theory. Only if you take the story of Genesis as a literal, historical account does a conflict exist. Most major religions in the world accept the findings of evolution. Many people, including some scientists, look to the evolutionary process as evidence of God's work, an idea known as **theistic evolution.** As such, many religions support the teaching of evolution in science education rather than creation science. As further evidence that there is no necessary conflict between religion and evolution, Pope John Paul II stated in his October 22, 1996, message to the Pontifical Academy of Sciences that "knowledge has led to the recognition of the theory of evolution as more than a hypothesis" (Gould 1999:81).

theistic evolution The belief that God operates through the natural process of evolution.

Intelligent Design

In recent years, another approach to creationism has become popular in the United States. Known as **intelligent design creationism,** this approach centers on the idea that the biological world was created by an intelligent entity, although "God" is not generally specified directly as the creator, thus trying to divorce intelligent design from objections regarding the establishment of religion under the First Amendment.

The basic concept of intelligent design is that certain characteristics of biological organisms are too complex to be explained through natural processes such as natural selection, and therefore *must* have been created. This idea actually dates back to the "watchmaker analogy" of the eighteenth-century theologian William Paley, who argued that a complex mechanical object such as a watch, with its intricate mechanisms, could not have arisen naturally, and so its existence automatically implies the existence of a watchmaker (Dawkins 1987).

This basic idea has been extended by proponents of intelligent design to the concept of "irreducible complexity," whereby if any part of a system were removed, the entire system would fail (Scott 2004). A classic example of the concept of irreducible complexity is a mousetrap, a simple mechanical device consisting of only several parts. If any of these parts were removed, the mousetrap would fail to operate. Thus, a mousetrap is "irreducibly complex." Extending this concept to biological organisms suggests that biochemical

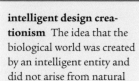

intelligent design creationism The idea that the biological world was created by an intelligent entity and did not arise from natural processes.

structures that are irreducibly complex could not have arisen piece by piece through natural selection, and that such complex structures or phenomena, such as the animal eye or the mechanism of blood clotting, must therefore have been "designed."

One major problem with the argument of irreducible complexity is that complex biological structures *can* arise through natural selection operating on intermediate forms, often for separate purposes, to produce what appears to us today as irreducibly complex (Dawkins 1987; Pennock 1999; Scott 2004). In addition, the function of different structures can change over time, giving an end result that is quite different from an original function. An example of this is the evolution of the jaw joint in the first mammals. As parts of the jaw joint became superfluous, they were then available to evolve through natural selection to serve a different need. In this case, the bones that had made up part of an ancestral reptilian jaw joint but were no longer necessary for the function of chewing served a new purpose—sound reception—and evolved into the inner ear of mammals (Strickberger 2000).

There is also a logical problem with the idea of irreducible complexity. The basic premise is that if we cannot explain something through natural processes, then it must constitute evidence of design. This has been termed the "argument from ignorance" (Scott 2004), whereby an intelligent designer is the explanation for anything that we do not know. If science does not at present have a natural explanation, does that necessarily imply a creator? A simpler explanation is that we lack sufficient evidence for a natural explanation. As such, intelligent design creationism uses the same either-or dichotomy as biblical creation science. Anything that is not explained by evolutionary theory at present must therefore constitute proof of a creation, even though science never claims to have all the answers at any given point in time.

From a scientific perspective, there are no testable hypotheses regarding the specific actions of a creator, or any way to check on the proposed hypothesis. In short, intelligent design creationism is not science. It is important to note that science deals with testable hypotheses about natural processes. Supernatural actions or entities do not fall within the realm of science. Science does not *require* a creator or creation, but it does not rule them out; creationism, on the other hand, requires both.

Science and Society

Despite scientific, legal, and theological objections, creationism has not gone away. Various surveys have shown a sizable number of people wanting the teaching of intelligent design as an alternative to evolutionary theory in the public schools. In some cases, debate over the attempt to present intelligent design as a valid science in the public schools has spilled over into the legal system, as is the case with the Dover school board resolution introduced at the beginning of this chapter. Following the school board's decision, the parents of 11 students filed a civil suit that culminated in a federal district court ordering the school to remove references to intelligent design from the biology curriculum.

In his ruling, Judge John Jones stated that intelligent design (ID), with its focus on supernatural explanation, was *not* a science (Mervis 2006). Another key point in his decision was the recognition that the strategy of ID, whereby criticism of evolutionary theory equates to proof of a designer, is invalid. The language of the decision states this clearly and unequivocally:

> ID proponents primarily argue for design through negative arguments against evolution, as illustrated by Professor Behe's argument that "irreducibly complex" systems cannot be produced through Darwinian, or any natural, mechanisms . . . However, we believe that arguments against evolution are not arguments for design. Expert testimony revealed that just because scientists cannot explain today how biological systems evolved does not mean that they cannot, and will not, be able to explain them tomorrow. (*Kitzmiller et al. v. Dover Area School District,* pp. 71–72)

The Dover case is no doubt not the last battle, but it is illustrative of the basic problem of educating the public as to what science is and is not.

Perhaps one of the more noticeable casualties of the debate over teaching evolution has been the erosion in science education. Due to continued and often very vocal opposition to the teaching of evolution, educational standards have sometimes been altered to appease anti-evolution forces or to avoid confrontation.

The arguments about creationism and evolution also play a role in individuals' views on ethics, morality, and social philosophy. Many creationists fear that science has eroded our faith in God and led to a decline in morals and values. They imply that science (and evolution in particular) makes statements about human morality. It does not. Science has nothing to say about right and wrong; that is the function of social ethics, philosophy, and religion. Religion and science are important to many people. To put them at odds with each other does both a disservice. It is no surprise that many ministers, priests, and rabbis have joined in the fight against creationism.

Summary

As a science, biological anthropology has certain requirements and characteristics. Hypotheses must be testable and verifiable. The main theoretical base of biological anthropology is the theory of evolution. A major feature of evolutionary theory is Darwin's idea of natural selection. In any environment in which resources are necessarily limited, some organisms are more likely to survive and reproduce than others because of their biological characteristics. Those who survive pass these traits on to the next generation.

A current controversy involves the efforts of people who advocate that creationism be taught in public schools. Examination of this field shows that it is not a science at all. Apart from these debates, it should be noted that today there is little conflict between religion and science in the United States. Each perspective addresses different questions in different ways.

Supplemental Readings

Futuyma DJ. 2009. *Evolution*, 2d ed. Sunderland, Mass: Sinauer Associates. A comprehensive textbook on evolution, including material on the history of evolutionary thought, evolutionary theory, and the fossil record and other evidence for evolution.

Humes E. 2007. *Monkey Girl: Evolution, Education, Religion, and the Battle for America's Soul.* New York: HarperCollins. An excellent account of the Dover trial over the teaching of intelligent design, including much history on the conflict between some scientific and religious views.

Larson, E. J. 1997. *Summer for the Gods: The Scopes Trial and America's Continuing Debate over Science and Religion.* Cambridge, Mass.: Harvard University Press. Winner of the Pulitzer Prize for History, an excellent book that provides a comprehensive description and analysis of the Scopes trial and creationism in the United States.

Scott, E. C. 2009. *Evolution vs. Creationism: An Introduction,* 2d ed. Berkeley: University of California Press. An excellent and comprehensive review of the evolution–creationism debate, including excerpts from scientific and creationist writings.

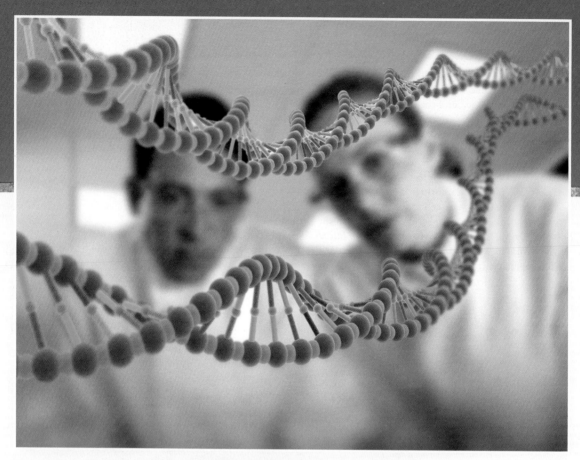

Two scientists examining a model of DNA. The study of human genetics includes the bio-chemical makeup of DNA and the transmission of genes from one generation to the next.

Human Genetics

"It's all in your genes."

The above is a statement that is sometimes used in connection with some new development of genetics, usually some aspect of behavior. I suspect that most of us realize that this statement is simplistic and inaccurate. As will be clear throughout this text, our biology is a reflection of both genetics and environment, often interacting in complex ways. Quite simply, it is *not* all in our genes. Still, new research in human genetics is so widespread today that scarcely a week goes by without hearing about the genetic *influence* on some aspect of our being. We are used to seeing genetics discussed (sometimes accurately, sometimes not) in relation to heart disease, obesity, sexual orientation, cancer, addiction, ancestry, and many other aspects of health and behavior.

Much of our interest in genetics is concerned with the here and now—our health, for example. Yet genetics is also part of our evolution, as we inherit genetic material from the previous generation (our parents) and pass some of it on to the next generation (our children). Although genetics is definitely important in understanding one's current biology, it is also important to view genetics as a long-term dynamic process that unites all life—past, present, and future. The purpose of this chapter is to review some basics of human genetics, but not as an end in and of itself, but as background for understanding genetic *change* over time—evolution.

The emphasis throughout this chapter is on viewing genetics as *information* that is passed along from one generation to the next to the next over time, rather than a focus on the biochemical nature and cellular biology of genetics. Although these topics are needed and are covered here, at the broadest level, we are interested in the general question of what happens over time if this information changes. This chapter connects genetics, particularly inheritance, to evolution, and the next chapter follows up by looking specifically at the forces of evolution.

Genetics can be studied at a number of different levels, ranging from the cell to the species. We can look at genetics from the level of the cell, the individual, or the group. At the level of the cell, the field of **molecular genetics** is concerned with what genes are and how they act to produce biological structures. Much of molecular genetics focuses on the structure and function of the DNA and RNA molecules (discussed later). Even at this level, we can look

molecular genetics The branch of genetics concerned with the structure and function of genes and DNA sequences at the molecular level.

at genetics as information, as the process of cellular replication can be viewed as the transmission of genetic material from one cell to the next (for example, we all start off as a single cell—a fertilized egg—and as our cells replicate the genetic information is passed on from cell to cell).

Much of our attention focuses on genetic information at an individual level in terms of what we inherit (and what we pass on to our children). To what extent are we a reflection of our parents? How are traits inherited? What will our children inherit? The branch of genetics concerned with inheritance is called **Mendelian genetics,** named after Gregor Mendel, who in the nineteenth century first worked out many of the principles of inheritance.

Genetics can also be studied in groups, such as populations within a species. Here we are interested in describing the patterns of genetic variation within and among different populations, and their relationship with biological evolution. Why do certain genes change in frequency over time (for example, recall the peppered moth example from Chapter 1)? Why are some human populations different from one another in some traits, such as blood types or skin color? All of these questions (and more) are part of the field of **population genetics,** which deals with the patterns of genetic transmission in populations over time, and which forms the mathematical basis of evolutionary theory. The primary concern of population genetics is on genetic changes within populations from one generation to the next, which is often termed **microevolution.** Understanding these relatively short-term changes allows us to make projections about **macroevolution,** the long-term pattern of evolution over thousands and millions of years, as well as the origin of new species. The current chapter focuses on molecular and Mendelian genetics and provides the needed background for the study of population genetics and microevolution in Chapter 3, which in turn leads to a discussion of macroevolution in Chapter 4. The discussion in the current chapter includes a brief review of high school biology; for those wanting additional review, Appendix 1 at the end of the book provides more detail on selected aspects of cell biology.

Mendelian genetics The branch of genetics concerned with patterns and processes of inheritance, named after Gregor Mendel, the first scientist to work out these principles.

population genetics The branch of genetics concerned with the changes in the frequency of genes and DNA sequences in populations over time.

microevolution Short-term evolutionary change.

macroevolution Long-term evolutionary change.

MOLECULAR GENETICS

DNA: The Genetic Code

The study of genetics at the molecular level concerns the amazing properties of a molecule known as deoxyribonucleic acid, or **DNA** for short. The DNA molecule provides the genetic code for biological structures and the means to translate this code. It is perhaps best to think of DNA as a set of instructions for determining the makeup of biological organisms. Quite simply, DNA provides information for building, operating, and repairing organisms. In this context, the process of genetic inheritance is seen as the transmission of this information, or the passing on of the instructions needed for biological structures. Evolution can be viewed in this context as the transfer of information from one generation to the next, along with the possibility that this information will change.

DNA The molecule that provides the genetic code for biological structures and the means to translate this code.

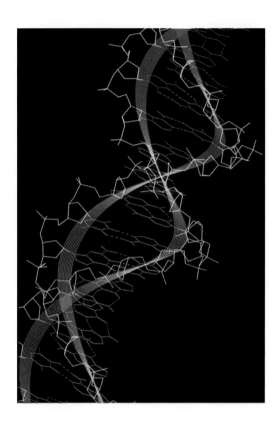

An understanding of both the structure and function of DNA is necessary to understand the processes of genetic inheritance and evolution. The exact biochemistry of DNA is beyond the scope of this text, but its basic nature can be discussed in the context of information transfer.

The Structure of DNA   In many organisms (including humans), most of the DNA is contained in the nucleus of cells. However, a small amount of DNA (16,569 base pairs) also exists in the mitochondria, the parts of the cell that produce energy. (See the cell biology review in Appendix 1 if needed.) Physically, the DNA molecule resembles a ladder that has been twisted into the shape of a helix (Figure 2.1). In biochemical terms, the rungs of the ladder are of major importance. These rungs are made up of chemical units called **bases.** There are four possible types of bases, identified by the first letter of their longer chemical names: A (adenine), T (thymine), G (guanine), and C (cytosine). These bases form the "alphabet" used in specifying and carrying out genetic instructions.

All biological structures, from nerve cells to blood cells to bone cells, are made up predominantly of proteins. Proteins in turn are made up of amino acids, whose chemical properties allow them to bond together to form proteins. Each amino acid is coded for by three of the four chemical bases just discussed. For example, the base sequence CGA provides the code for the amino acid alanine, and the base sequence TTT provides the code for the amino acid lysine. There are 64 (4^3) possible codes that can be specified, using some combination of three bases. This might not seem like a lot, but in fact there are

base Chemical units (adenine, thymine, guanine, cytosine) that make up part of the DNA molecule and specify genetic instructions.

TABLE 2.1   DNA Base Sequences for Amino Acids

First Base	Second Base			
	A	T	C	G
A	AAA Phenylalanine	ATA Tyrosine	ACA Cysteine	AGA Serine
	AAT Leucine	ATT Stop	ACT Stop	AGT Serine
	AAC Leucine	ATC Stop	ACC Tryptophan	AGC Serine
	AAG Phenylalanine	ATG Tyrosine	ACG Cysteine	AGG Serine
T	TAA Isoleucine	TTA Asparagine	TCA Serine	TGA Threonine
	TAT Isoleucine	TTT Lysine	TCT Arginine	TGT Threonine
	TAC Methionine	TTC Lysine	TCC Arginine	TGC Threonine
	TAG Isoleucine	TTG Asparagine	TCG Serine	TGG Threonine
C	CAA Valine	CTA Aspartic acid	CCA Glycine	CGA Alanine
	CAT Valine	CTT Glutamic acid	CCT Glycine	CGT Alanine
	CAC Valine	CTC Glutamic acid	CCC Glycine	CGC Alanine
	CAG Valine	CTG Aspartic acid	CCG Glycine	CGG Alanine
G	GAA Leucine	GTA Histidine	GCA Arginine	GGA Proline
	GAT Leucine	GTT Glutamine	GCT Arginine	GGT Proline
	GAC Leucine	GTC Glutamine	GCC Arginine	GGC Proline
	GAG Leucine	GTG Histidine	GCG Arginine	GGG Proline

Rows refer to the first of the three bases, and columns refer to the second of the three bases. These base sequences are for the DNA molecule. The 64 different combinations code for 20 amino acids and one termination sequence ("Stop"). To convert to messenger RNA, substitute U for A, A for T, G for C, and C for G. To convert to transfer RNA, substitute U for A.

only 20 amino acids that need to be specified by the genetic code. The three-base code provides more than enough possibilities to code for these amino acids. In fact, some amino acids have several different codes; alanine, for example, can be specified by the base sequences CGA, CGT, CGC, and CGG. Some of the base sequences, such as ATT, act to form "punctuation" for the genetic instructions; that is, they provide the code to start or stop "messages." Table 2.1 lists the different DNA sequences.

The ability of four different bases, taken three at a time, to specify all the information needed for the synthesis of proteins is astounding. It boggles the mind that the diverse structure of complex protein molecules can be specified with only a four-letter "alphabet." As an analogy, consider how computers work. All computer operations, from word processing to complex mathematical simulations, ultimately are translated into a set of instructions that use only a simple binary code—1s and 0s! These two instructions make up a larger set of codes that provide information on computer operations. These operations are combined to generate computer languages that can be used to write a variety of programs.

The ability of the DNA molecule to use the different amino acid codes derives from a simple property of the chemical bases. The base A bonds with the base T, and the base G bonds with the base C. This chemical property enables the DNA molecule to carry out a number of functions, including making copies of itself and directing the synthesis of proteins.

Functions of DNA   The DNA molecule can make copies of itself. Remember that the DNA molecule is made up of two strands that form the long arms of the ladder. Each rung of the ladder consists of two bases. If one part of the rung contains the base A, then the other part of the rung will contain the base T because A and T bond together.

To understand how DNA can make copies of itself, consider the following sequence of bases on one strand of the DNA molecule—GGTCTC. Because A and T bond together and G and C bond together, the corresponding sequence of bases on the other strand of the DNA molecule is CCAGAG. The DNA molecule can separate into two distinct strands. Once separate, each strand attracts free-floating bases. The strand GGTCTC attracts the bases CCAGAG, and the strand CCAGAG attracts the bases GGTCTC. When the new bases have attached themselves to the original strands, the result is two identical DNA molecules. This process is diagrammed in Figure 2.2. Keep in

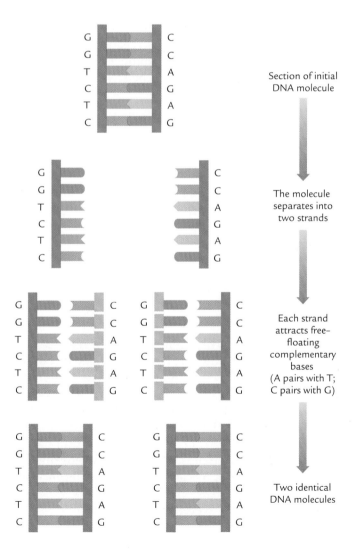

FIGURE 2.2

Replication of the DNA molecule.

mind that this description is somewhat oversimplified—in reality, the process is biochemically much more complex.

The ability of the DNA molecule to control protein synthesis also involves the attraction of complementary bases, but with the help of another molecule—ribonucleic acid, or **RNA** for short. In simple terms, RNA serves as the messenger and decoder for the information in the DNA molecule. One major difference between DNA and RNA is that in RNA the base A attracts a base called U (uracil) instead of T.

Consider the DNA base sequence GGT. In protein synthesis, the DNA molecule separates into two strands, and one strand (containing CCA) becomes inactive. The active strand, GGT, attracts free-floating bases to form a strand of **messenger RNA.** Because A bonds with T and G bonds with C, this strand consists of the sequence CCA. The strand then travels to the site of protein synthesis. Once there, the strand of messenger RNA transfers its information via **transfer RNA,** which is a free-floating molecule. The sequence of messenger RNA containing the sequence CCA attracts a transfer RNA molecule with a complementary sequence—GGU. The result is that the amino acid proline (specified by the RNA sequence GGU or the DNA sequence GGT) is included in the chain of amino acids making up a particular protein. To summarize, one strand of the DNA molecule produces the complementary strand of messenger RNA, which attracts a complementary strand of transfer RNA, which carries the specified amino acid. This process is illustrated for the DNA sequence GGT in Figure 2.3.

This simplified discussion shows the basic nature of the structure and functions of the DNA molecule. More advanced discussion can be found in most genetics textbooks. It is interesting to note that the conventional view of the relationship between DNA, RNA, and proteins has increasingly been shown to be more complex than once thought (Pearson 2006). For our purposes, however, the broad view will suffice. If we consider DNA as a "code," we can then look at the processes of transmission and change of information without actually having to consider the exact biochemical mechanisms.

Chromosomes and Genes

As noted above, most of the DNA is contained in the nucleus—and hence is known as **nuclear DNA.** The nuclear DNA sequences are bound together by proteins in long strands, called **chromosomes,** that are found within the nucleus of each cell. With the exception of those in the sex cells (egg and sperm), chromosomes occur in pairs. Most body cells contain both members of these pairs. Different species have different numbers of chromosomes. For example, humans have 23 pairs, chimpanzees have 24, fruit flies have 4, and certain plant species have thousands. There is no relationship between the number of chromosome pairs a species has and its intelligence or biological complexity.

With certain exceptions, each cell in the human body contains a complete set of chromosomes and DNA. Nerve cells contain the same DNA as

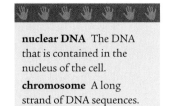

RNA The molecule that functions to carry out the instructions for protein synthesis specified by the DNA molecule.

messenger RNA The form of RNA that transports the genetic instructions from the DNA molecule to the site of protein synthesis.

transfer RNA A free-floating molecule that is attracted to a strand of messenger RNA, resulting in the synthesis of a protein chain.

nuclear DNA The DNA that is contained in the nucleus of the cell.

chromosome A long strand of DNA sequences.

1. Section of the initial DNA molecule.

2. The DNA molecule temporarily separates, and one strand becomes active. Free-floating complementary bases (with U replacing T) are attracted to form messenger RNA.

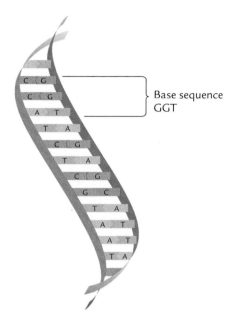

Base sequence GGT

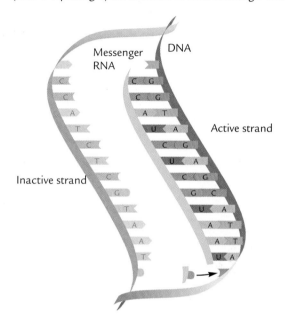

Messenger RNA

DNA

Active strand

Inactive strand

3. Messenger RNA travels to the ribosomes, the site of protein synthesis. As ribosomes move along messenger RNA, transfer RNA picks up amino acids and lines up according to the base complements. Each transfer RNA molecule transfers its amino acid to the next active transfer RNA as it leaves, resulting in a chain of amino acids.

4. This chain of amino acids forms a protein.

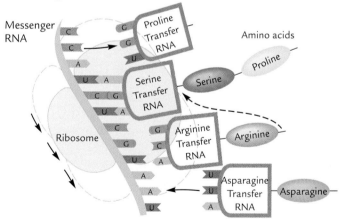

Messenger RNA

Proline Transfer RNA

Amino acids

Proline

Serine Transfer RNA

Serine

Arginine Transfer RNA

Arginine

Ribosome

Asparagine Transfer RNA

Asparagine

Proline

Serine

Arginine

Asparagine

FIGURE 2.3

Protein synthesis.

bone cells, for example, and vice versa. Some type of regulation takes place within different cells to ensure that only certain genes are expressed in the right places, but the exact nature of this regulation is not known completely at present.

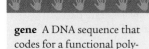

gene A DNA sequence that codes for a functional polypeptide or RNA product.

hemoglobin The molecule in blood cells that transports oxygen.

exon A section of DNA that codes for the amino acids that make up proteins. It is contrasted with an intron.

intron A section of DNA that does not code for the amino acids that make up proteins. It is contrasted with an exon.

regulatory gene A gene that acts as a genetic switch to turn protein-coding genes on or off.

homeobox genes A group of regulatory genes that encode a sequence of 60 amino acids regulating embryonic development.

Genes   The term *gene* can have a number of different meanings depending on the context. One use of the term **gene** refers to a DNA sequence that includes the code for a functional polypeptide (a compound containing many amino acids) or RNA product (Strachan and Read 1996)—that is, a section of DNA that has an identifiable function, such as the gene that determines a particular blood group. One example, referred to in later chapters, is the **hemoglobin** molecule in your blood (which transports oxygen), which is made up of four protein chains. For each chain, a section of DNA (the gene) contains the genetic code for the proteins in that chain.

Not all DNA contains genes; much of our DNA is made up of noncoding sequences of DNA whose purpose (if any) is not known. Even within genes, not all of the DNA sequence results in a polypeptide product. The DNA sequence of a gene can contain both sections that code for amino acids that make up proteins—called **exons**—and sections that do not code for amino acids that make up proteins—called **introns.** The formation of mature RNA involves the removal of the noncoding sections and the splicing together of the coding sections (Figure 2.4).

Although some genes code for proteins, another class of genes, known as **regulatory genes,** act as switches that turn protein-coding genes on or off, thereby affecting how these genes are expressed. The same coding gene can be used for a number of different traits. An example of this is a dark pigment found in fruit flies. Different species of fruit flies have different patterns of pigmentation, with some having dark spots on their abdomens and some having dark spots on their wings. The different types of pigmentation are all affected by the same gene, but the expression of this gene is turned on or off in different body parts in different species (Carroll et al. 2008). Differences in regulatory genes have great evolutionary significance and help explain how large physical differences can exist between species that have very similar genes.

A group of regulatory genes known as **homeobox genes** encodes a sequence of 60 amino acids that regulate embryonic development.

FIGURE 2.4

Diagram of messenger RNA (mRNA) showing regions of coding (exons) and noncoding (introns). The introns are removed from the pre-mRNA, and the exons then splice together to form the mature mRNA.

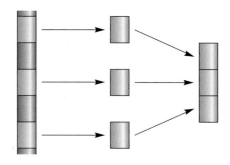

Pre-mRNA consists of exons (green) and introns (red).

Introns are removed.

Exons are spliced together to form mature mRNA.

BOX 2.1

Epigenetics

As an organism develops from a single fertilized egg, the cells duplicate. One cell becomes two, which then become four, and so on, doubling each cycle of cell replication. The genetic code of the organism is transmitted from cell to cell. Along the way, cells differentiate, forming different types of tissues and organs. Although each cell contains all of an organism's genes, only some genes are expressed in different types of cells, such as bone, skin, nerve, and so on. What controls this process of differentiation? The field of *epigenetics* is concerned with the general process of gene expression and looks at how some genes are turned on or off in different contexts. The word "epigenetics" literally means "above genetics" and deals with non-genetic influences on gene expression.

DNA is wrapped around proteins and the activation and inactivation of different genes is controlled by various chemical "tags." These tags make up the *epigenome,* which literally translates as "above the genome." Both the genome (the actual DNA code) and the epigenome are needed for gene expression; the influence of the epigenome is that different genes are active in different types of cells. Although DNA sequences remain the same, the epigenetic tags (sometimes called "marks") can change because of environmental factors. Understanding how and why certain genes are activated can provide valuable insight (and possible cures) for some diseases. Epigenetics might provide insight into why identical twins sometimes diverge from each other in terms of disease susceptibility as they age (Bird 2007).

There is some epigenetic inheritance. Epigenetic tags can persist over a number of cell divisions, and these tags can even be passed on from one generation to the next. Normally, epigenetic tags in sperm and egg are erased following fertilization so that the cells can develop into different types during the organism's development. It turns out, however, that some of these tags can be passed on for several generations. This is not evolution, however, because the underlying DNA sequences are not changed. It will be interesting to see how future epigenetic research might enhance our understanding of genotypic and phenotypic variation.

Specifically, they subdivide a developing embryo into different regions from head to tail that then form limbs and other structures (De Robertis et al. 1990). Thus, the same genes are found in different species, but their expression is modified by regulatory genes to produce physical differences in body shape. Expression and regulation of genes is affected by mechanisms apart from the actual DNA sequence, processes studied by the field of epigenetics (see Box 2.1).

Mitosis and Meiosis   The DNA molecule provides for the transmission of genetic information. Production of proteins and regulation are only two aspects of information transfer. Because organisms start life as a single cell that subsequently multiplies, it is essential that the genetic information within the initial cell be transferred to all future cells. The ability of DNA to replicate itself is involved in the process of cell replication, known as **mitosis** (Figure 2.5). When a cell divides, each chromosome duplicates and then splits. Each chromosome has replicated itself so that when the cell finishes dividing, the result is two cells with the full set of chromosomes.

The process is different when information is passed on from one generation to the next. The genetic code is passed on from parents to offspring through the sex cells—the sperm in males and the egg in females. The sex cells, however, contain not the full set of chromosomes but only one chromosome from each pair (i.e., only one-half of the set). Whereas your other body cells have a total of 46 chromosomes (2 each for 23 pairs), your sex cells

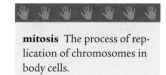

mitosis The process of replication of chromosomes in body cells.

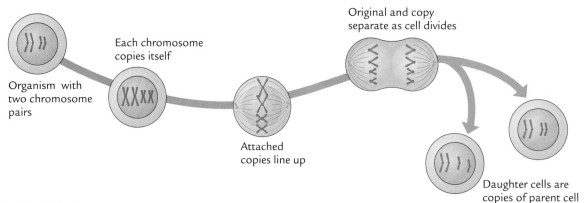

Organism with two chromosome pairs

Each chromosome copies itself

Attached copies line up

Original and copy separate as cell divides

Daughter cells are copies of parent cell

FIGURE 2.5

The process of mitosis is the formation of body cells. Each chromosome copies itself, the attached copies line up in the cell, and the original and copy split when the cell divides. The result is two identical cells. (From *Human Antiquity: An Introduction to Physical Anthropology and Archaeology*, 4th ed., by Kenneth Feder and Michael Park, Fig. 4.4. Copyright © 2001 by Mayfield Publishing Company. Reprinted by permission of The McGraw-Hill Companies.)

contain only 23 chromosomes (1 from each pair). When you have a child, you contribute 23 chromosomes and your mate contributes 23 chromosomes. Your child then has the normal complement of 46 chromosomes in 23 pairs.

Sex cells are created through the process of **meiosis** (Figure 2.6). In this process, chromosomes replicate themselves, and then the cell divides and then divides again without replicating. For sperm cells, four sex cells are produced from the initial set of 23 pairs of chromosomes. The process is similar in egg cells, except that only one of the four cells is functional.

The process of meiosis is extremely important in understanding genetic inheritance. Because only one of each pair of chromosomes is found in a functional sex cell, this means that a person contributes half of his or her genes to his or her offspring. The other half of their offspring's genes comes from the other parent. Usually, each human child has a full set of 23 chromosome

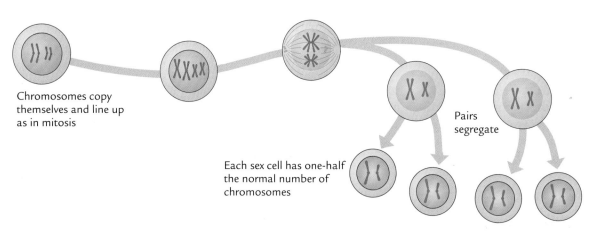

Chromosomes copy themselves and line up as in mitosis

Each sex cell has one-half the normal number of chromosomes

Pairs segregate

FIGURE 2.6

The process of meiosis is the formation of sex cells. Meiosis begins in the same way as mitosis: Each chromosome makes a copy of itself. The pairs of chromosomes then segregate, forming four sex cells, each with one chromosome rather than a pair of chromosomes. (Adapted from *Human Antiquity: An Introduction to Physical Anthropology and Archaeology*, 4th ed., by Kenneth Feder and Michael Park, Fig. 4.4. Copyright © 2001 by Mayfield Publishing Company. Reprinted by permission of The McGraw-Hill Companies.)

BOX 2.2

The Human Genome Project

It is increasingly common to read in the newspapers about DNA sequencing. A number of living humans, as well as other organisms, have had their entire genome sequenced. We now take for granted accomplishments in genetic technology that until recently had been considered an incredible task. Keep in mind the immense length of the human genome—over 3 billion base pairs. Here is one way to appreciate the total length of the human genome: If you were to read the sequence aloud (A, T, T, etc.) at the rate of one letter per second, it would take you 95 years to read the entire sequence (assuming no breaks for food or sleep)! Despite the immensity of the genome, by the end of the twentieth century, new technologies had enable researchers to sequence the complete genomes for a number of organisms, including humans.

The Human Genome Project (HGP) began in 1990 as an international effort devoted to sequencing the entire human genome. The "complete" sequence was finished in April 2003 according to the goals of the project (Collins et al. 2003), although gaps are still being filled in. It will take many researchers a long time to learn about the specific relationship of genes to biological structures and function. The analysis of such large amounts of data is daunting, but some preliminary findings are quite interesting. For one thing, it turns out that only a small fraction of

our genome (less than 1.5 percent) actually codes for proteins. Although much of the rest of the DNA sequences may have no current function (and is sometimes referred to as "junk DNA"), some of this non-coding DNA might actually be involved in gene regulation, acting as switches (Carroll et al. 2008). Perhaps the most interesting finding is that there are only about 20,500 actual genes in the human genome (National Human Genome Research Institute web page, http://www.genome.gov/12011238, retrieved June 10, 2011). This number seems surprisingly low given the biological complexity of human beings. It appears that the action of regulatory genes allows various protein-coding genes to be used in different ways throughout the body.

For biological anthropologists, one of the most significant uses of human genome data is the comparison of the human genome with the genomes of our closest living relatives, the apes. Such comparisons are allowing us to construct accurate "family trees" from genetic data and to identify which DNA sequences have changed during the course of human evolution. If we know which DNA sequences we have in common with apes and which are different, we will be able to identify the genetic basis of what makes us unique. Some preliminary findings are discussed in Chapter 7.

---

pairs, one of each pair from each parent (Figure 2.7). The total of all DNA sequences of an organism is known as its **genome.** In humans, the genome is approximately 3 billion base pairs in length (see Box 2.2 for more information on the human genome).

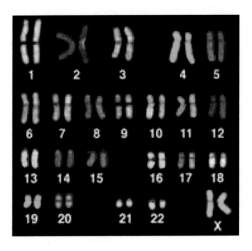

FIGURE 2.7

All 23 pairs of chromosomes typically found in a human being. This set of chromosomes came from a woman—note that the 23rd pair has two X chromosomes (see page 49).

meiosis The creation of sex cells by replication of chromosomes followed by cell division.

genome The total DNA sequence of an organism.

MENDELIAN GENETICS

Many of the facts about genetic inheritance were discovered over a century before the structure of DNA was known. Although people knew where babies came from and noted the close resemblance of parents and children, the mechanisms of inheritance were unknown until the nineteenth century. An Austrian priest, Gregor Mendel (1822–1884), carried out an extensive series of experiments in plant breeding. His carefully tabulated results provided the basis of what we know about the mechanisms of genetic inheritance.

Before Mendel's research, it was commonly assumed that inheritance involved the blending together of genetic information in the egg and sperm. The genetic material was thought to mix together in the same way that different color paints mix together. Mendel's experiments showed a different pattern of inheritance—that the genetic information is inherited in discrete units (genes). These genes do not blend together in an offspring.

In one experiment, Mendel crossed pea plants whose seeds were yellow with pea plants whose seeds were green (Figure 2.8). Under the idea of blending, we might expect all offspring to have mustard-colored seeds—a mixture of the yellow and green. In reality, Mendel found that all the offspring plants had yellow seeds. This discovery suggested that somehow one trait (yellow seed color) dominated in its effects.

When Mendel crossed the plants in this new generation, he found that some of their offspring had yellow seeds and some had green seeds. Somehow the genetic information for green seeds had been hidden for a generation and

FIGURE 2.8

The seven phenotypic characteristics investigated by Gregor Mendel in his experiments on breeding in pea plants. Each of the seven traits has two distinct phenotypes.

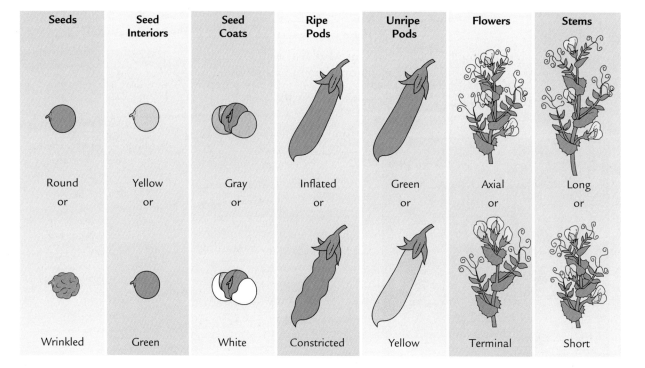

Seeds	Seed Interiors	Seed Coats	Ripe Pods	Unripe Pods	Flowers	Stems
Round or Wrinkled	Yellow or Green	Gray or White	Inflated or Constricted	Green or Yellow	Axial or Terminal	Long or Short

then reappeared. Mendel counted how many there were of each color. The ratio of plants with yellow seeds to those with green seeds was very close to 3:1. This finding suggested to Mendel that a regular process occurred during inheritance that could be explained in terms of simple mathematical principles. With these and other results, Mendel formulated several principles of inheritance. Though Mendel's work remained virtually unknown during his lifetime, his work was rediscovered in 1900. In recognition of his accomplishments, the science of genetic inheritance is called *Mendelian genetics.*

Genotypes and Phenotypes

The specific position of a gene or DNA sequence on a chromosome is called a **locus** (plural *loci*). The alternative forms of a gene or DNA sequence at a locus are called **alleles.** As an example, consider the fact that some human adults are lactose intolerant, which means they cannot easily digest milk or milk products, leading to a variety of health issues such as cramps, diarrhea, and flatulence. As infants, humans produce the enzyme lactase, which allows them to digest lactose, which is milk sugar (humans, as mammals, are nourished by breast milk as infants—see Chapter 5). Once mammals are weaned, production of the lactase enzyme ceases and they become lactose intolerant. Yet some humans can continue to digest milk as adults because of genetic variation in this gene. In humans, the gene that controls lactase activity (the lactase activity locus) is located on chromosome 2. There are two major forms (alleles) of this gene. One allele codes for lactase persistence (the enzyme continues to be produced) and the other allele codes for lactase restriction (the enzyme stops being produced).

As another example, consider the different loci that control your blood type, which refers to the type of molecules that are present on the surface of your red blood cells. One of these blood groups, known as the MN system, determines whether you have M molecules, N molecules, or both on the surface of your red blood cells. The MN system has two forms, or alleles—*M* and *N*. Another blood group system, the ABO system, has three alleles—*A, B,* and *O.* Even though three different forms of this gene are found in the human species, each individual has only two genes at the ABO locus. Some genetic loci have only one allele, some have two, and some have three or more.

Mendel's Law of Segregation   The genetic basis of any trait is determined by an allele from each parent. At any given locus, there are two alleles, one on each member of the chromosome pair. One allele comes from the mother, and one allele comes from the father. Within body cells, alleles occur in pairs, and when sex cells are formed, only one of each pair is passed on, according to **Mendel's Law of Segregation.**

The two alleles at a locus in an individual specify the **genotype,** the genetic endowment of an individual. The two alleles might be the same form or might be different. If the alleles from both parents are the same, the genotype is **homozygous.** If the alleles from the parents are different, the genotype is **heterozygous.**

locus The specific location of a gene or DNA sequence on a chromosome.

allele The alternative form of a gene or DNA sequence that occurs at a given locus. Some loci have only one allele, some have two, and some have many alternative forms. Alleles occur in pairs, one on each chromosome.

Mendel's Law of Segregation States that sex cells contain one of each pair of alleles.

genotype The genetic endowment of an individual from the two alleles present at a given locus.

homozygous When both alleles at a given locus are identical.

heterozygous When the two alleles at a given locus are different.

phenotype The observable appearance of a given genotype in the organism.

dominant allele An allele that masks the effect of the other allele (which is recessive) in a heterozygous genotype.

recessive allele An allele whose effect is masked by the other allele (which is dominant) in a heterozygous genotype.

The actual observable trait is known as the **phenotype.** The relationship between genotype and phenotype is affected by the relationship between the two alleles present at any locus. If the genotype is homozygous, both alleles contain the same genetic information. But what happens in heterozygotes, where the two alleles are different?

Dominant and Recessive Alleles   In a heterozygote, an allele is **dominant** when it masks the effect of the other allele at a given locus. The opposite of a dominant allele is a **recessive** allele, whose effect may be masked. A simple example helps make these concepts clearer. One genetic trait in human beings is the ability to taste certain substances, including a chemical known as PTC. The ability to taste PTC appears to be controlled by a single locus and is also affected to some extent by environmental factors such as diet. There are two alleles for the PTC-tasting trait: the allele T, which is also called the "taster" allele, and the allele t, which is also called the "nontaster" allele. Given these two alleles, three combinations of alleles can be present in an individual. A person could have the T allele from both parents, which would give the genotype TT. A person could have a t allele from both parents, giving the genotype tt. Both TT and tt are homozygous genotypes because both alleles are the same. The third possible genotype occurs when the allele from one parent is T and the allele from the other parent is t. This gives the heterozygous genotype of Tt. It does not matter which parent provided the T allele and which provided the t allele; the genotype is the same in both cases.

What phenotype is associated with each genotype? The phenotype is affected both by the relationship of the two alleles and by the environment. For the moment, let us ignore possible environmental effects. Consider the T allele as providing instructions for tasting and the t allele as providing instructions for nontasting. If the genotype is TT, then both alleles code for tasting, and the phenotype is obviously "taster." Likewise, if the genotype is tt, then both alleles code for nontasting, and the phenotype is "nontaster." What of the heterozygote Tt? One allele codes for tasting and one codes for nontasting. Does this mean that both will be expressed and that a person will have the tasting ability, but not to as great a degree as a person with genotype TT? Or does it mean that only one of the alleles is expressed? If so, which one?

There is no way you can answer this question using only the data provided so far. You must know if either the T or t allele is dominant, and this can be determined only through experimentation. For this trait, it turns out that the T allele is dominant and the t allele is recessive. When both alleles are present in a genotype, the T allele masks the effect of the t allele. Therefore, a person with the genotype Tt has the "taster" phenotype (Table 2.2). The relationship between genotype and phenotype does not take into consideration known environmental effects on PTC tasting. Under certain types of diet, some "tasters" will show less ability to taste weaker concentrations of PTC.

The action of dominant and recessive alleles explains why Mendel's second-generation pea plants all had yellow seeds. The allele for yellow seed color is dominant, and the allele for green seed color is recessive.

Dominance and recessiveness refer only to the effect an allele has in producing a phenotype. These terms say nothing about the frequency or value of an allele. Dominant alleles can be common or rare, harmful or helpful.

TABLE 2.2	Genotypes and Phenotypes for PTC Tasting
Genotype	*Phenotype*
TT	Taster
Tt	Taster
Tt	Nontaster

Because *T* is dominant, the genotypes *TT* and *Tt* both produce the taster phenotype. This example is somewhat oversimplified because in reality the phenotype can also be affected by diet.

Codominant Alleles   Some alleles are **codominant,** meaning that when two different alleles are present in a genotype, both are expressed. That is, neither allele is dominant or recessive. One example of a codominant genetic system in humans is the MN blood group, mentioned previously. There are two alleles—*M,* which codes for the production of M molecules, and *N,* which codes for the production of N molecules. Therefore, there are three possible genotypes: *MM, MN,* and *NN.*

The phenotypes for the homozygous genotypes are easy to determine. Individuals with the genotype *MM* will have two alleles coding for the production of M molecules and will have the M molecule phenotype. Likewise, individuals with the genotype *NN* will have two *N* alleles and will have the N molecule phenotype. But what of the heterozygote genotype *MN?* Again, there is no way to answer this question without knowing the pattern of dominance. Experimentation has shown that the *M* and *N* alleles are codominant. When both are present (genotype *MN*), both are expressed. Therefore, an individual with genotype *MN* will produce both M and N molecules. Their phenotype is MN, indicating the presence of both molecules (Table 2.3).

In complex genetic systems with more than two alleles, some alleles may be dominant and some may be codominant. A good example of dominance and codominance in the same system is the ABO blood group. The alleles, genotypes, and phenotypes of this system are described in Table 2.4.

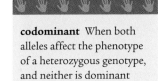

codominant When both alleles affect the phenotype of a heterozygous genotype, and neither is dominant over the other.

TABLE 2.3	Genotypes and Phenotypes of the MN Blood Group System
Genotype	*Phenotype*
MM	M molecules
MN	M and N molecules
NN	N molecules

The *M* and *N* alleles are codominant, so they are both expressed in the heterozygote.

TABLE 2.4	Genotypes and Phenotypes of the ABO System

The ABO system has three alleles (*A, B, O*) that code for the type of molecule on the surface of the red blood cells (A, B, and O molecules). The *A* and *B* alleles are codominant, and the *O* allele is recessive to both *A* and *B.*

Genotype	*Phenotype*
AA	A
AO	A
BB	B
BO	B
AB	AB
OO	O

Predicting Offspring Distributions

When parents each contribute a sex cell, they are passing on to their offspring only one allele at each locus. The possible genotypes and phenotypes of the offspring reflect a 50 percent chance of transmittal for any given allele of a parent. This simple statement of probability allows prediction of the likely distribution of genotypes and phenotypes among the offspring.

Figure 2.9 illustrates this method using the MN blood group system for two hypothetical parents, each with the genotype *MN*. Each parent has a 50 percent chance of passing on an *M* allele and a 50 percent chance of passing on an *N* allele. Given these probabilities, we expect one out of four offspring (25 percent) to have genotype *MM,* and therefore phenotype M. In two out of four cases (50 percent), we expect the offspring to have genotype *MN,* and therefore phenotype MN. Finally, in one out of four cases (25 percent), we expect the offspring to have genotype *NN,* and therefore phenotype N. Of course, different parental genotypes will give a different set of offspring probabilities.

Remember that these distributions give the expected probabilities. The exact distributions will not always occur because each offspring is an independent event. If the hypothetical couple first has a child with the genotype *MN,* this will not influence the genotype of their next child. The distributions give the proportions expected for a very large number of offspring.

To help understand the difference between expected and actual distribution, consider coin flipping. If you flip a coin, you expect to get heads 50 percent of the time and tails 50 percent of the time. If you flip 10 coins one after another, you expect to get five heads and five tails. You may, however, get four heads and six tails, or six heads and four tails, and so on.

Analysis of possible offspring shows that recessive alleles can produce an interesting effect: It is possible for children to have a different phenotype from either parent. For example, consider two parents, both with the genotype *Tt* for the PTC-tasting locus. Both parents have the "taster" phenotype. What genotypes and phenotypes will their children be likely to have? The expected genotype distribution is 25 percent *TT,* 50 percent *Tt,* and 25 percent *tt* (Figure 2.10).

FIGURE 2.9

Inheritance of MN blood group genotypes for two parents, both with the *MN* genotype.

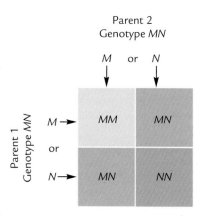

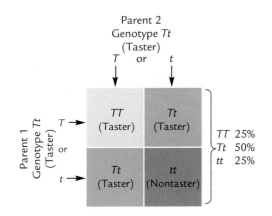

Parent 2
Genotype *Tt*
(Taster)
T   or   *t*

Parent 1
Genotype *Tt*
(Taster)

	TT (Taster)	*Tt* (Taster)
T		
t	*Tt* (Taster)	*tt* (Nontaster)

TT 25%
Tt 50%
tt 25%

FIGURE 2.10

Inheritance of PTC-tasting genotypes and phenotypes for two parents, both with the *Tt* genotype. Phenotypes are shown in parentheses.

Given this distribution of genotypes, what is the probable distribution of phenotypes? Genotypes *TT* and *Tt* are both "tasters," and therefore, 75 percent of the children are expected to also be "tasters." Twenty-five percent of the children, however, are expected to have the genotype *tt*, and therefore will have the "nontaster" phenotype. These children would have a different phenotype from either parent. An additional example, also using the PTC-tasting locus, is shown in Figure 2.11, which looks at the genotype and phenotype offspring distributions in the case where one parent has the *Tt* genotype and the other has the *tt* genotype.

A recessive trait, then, can remain hidden in one generation. This fact has strong implications for genetic disease. For example, the disease cystic fibrosis occurs when a person is homozygous for a recessive allele. Therefore, two parents who have the heterozygous genotype do not manifest the disease, but they have a 25 percent chance of giving birth to a child who has the recessive homozygous condition, and therefore the disease.

Chromosomes and Inheritance

Alleles occur in pairs. Mendel showed that when alleles are passed on from parents to offspring, only one of each pair is contributed by each parent. The

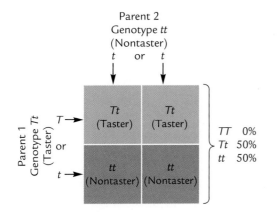

Parent 2
Genotype *tt*
(Nontaster)
t   or   *t*

Parent 1
Genotype *Tt*
(Taster)

	Tt (Taster)	*Tt* (Taster)
T		
t	*tt* (Nontaster)	*tt* (Nontaster)

TT 0%
Tt 50%
tt 50%

FIGURE 2.11

Inheritance of PTC-tasting genotypes and phenotypes for two parents, one with the *Tt* genotype and one with the *tt* genotype. Phenotypes are shown in parentheses.

specific chromosome at any pair that is passed on is random. There is a 50 percent chance of either chromosome being passed on each time a sex cell is created.

Mendel's Law of Independent Assortment   Mendel's experiments revealed another aspect of probability in inheritance and the creation of sex cells. **Mendel's Law of Independent Assortment** states that the segregation of any pair of chromosomes does not influence the segregation of any other pair of chromosomes. In other words, chromosomes from separate pairs are inherited independently.

For example, imagine an organism with three chromosome pairs, which we will label 1, 2, and 3. To keep the members of each pair straight in our minds, we will also label each chromosome of each pair as A or B. This hypothetical organism has six chromosomes: 1A, 1B, 2A, 2B, 3A, and 3B. During the creation of a sex cell, the 1A chromosome has a 50 percent chance of occurring, and so does the 1B chromosome. This same logic applies to chromosome pairs 2 and 3. According to Mendel's Law of Independent Assortment, the segregation of one pair of chromosomes does not affect the segregation of any other pair of chromosomes. It is just as likely to have a sex cell containing chromosomes 1A, 2A, and 3A as it is to have a sex cell containing chromosomes 1A, 2A, and 3B. There are eight possible and equally likely outcomes for the sex cells: 1A-2A-3A, 1A-2A-3B, 1A-2B-3A, 1A-2B-3B, 1B-2A-3A, 1B-2A-3B, 1B-2B-3A, and 1B-2B-3B (Figure 2.12). Given that any individual could have any one of the eight possible sex cells from *both* parents, the total number of combinations of offspring in this hypothetical organism is $8 \times 8 = 64$.

Independent assortment provides a powerful mechanism for shuffling different combinations of chromosomes, and thus introduces great potential for

Mendel's Law of Independent Assortment
States that the segregation of any pair of chromosomes does not affect the probability of segregation for other pairs of chromosomes.

FIGURE 2.12

Schematic diagram illustrating Mendel's Law of Independent Assortment. This hypothetical organism has three pairs of chromosomes (1, 2, and 3), each of which has two chromosomes, indicated by the letters A and B. For example, the chromosomes for chromosome pair 1 are 1A and 1B. During meiosis, only one of each pair is passed on to a sex cell, that is, 1A or 1B, 2A or 2B, and 3A or 3B. The probability of a particular chromosome being passed on from any pair is independent of the other pairs, so there are eight possible combinations.

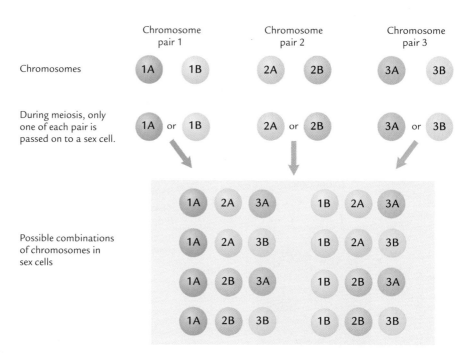

genetic diversity. In humans, who have 23 chromosome pairs, the numbers are even more impressive. From any given individual, there are $2^{23} = 8,388,608$ possible combinations of chromosomes in sex cells. This means that two parents could produce a maximum of 70,368,744,177,664 genetically unique offspring!

Linkage A major implication of Mendel's Law of Independent Assortment is that genes are inherited independently. This is true only to the extent that genes are on different chromosomes. Remember, it is the pairs of chromosomes that separate during meiosis, not each individual pair of alleles. When alleles are on the same chromosome, they are inherited together, in a process called **linkage.** Linked alleles are not inherited independently because they are, by definition, on the same chromosome.

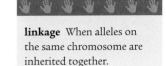

linkage When alleles on the same chromosome are inherited together.

Recombination When loci are linked, they will tend to be inherited as a unit. As an example, imagine that two loci, each with two alleles (A and a for the first locus and B and b for the second), are located on the same chromosome. Further, imagine that one of the chromosomes contains the A allele for the first locus and the B allele for the second one, and that the other chromosome contains the alleles a and b (Figure 2.13). Under linkage, we expect the two loci to be inherited as a unit. That is, your possible sex cells could have A and B or

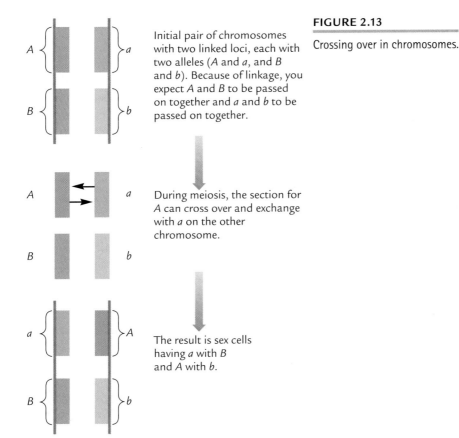

Initial pair of chromosomes with two linked loci, each with two alleles (A and a, and B and b). Because of linkage, you expect A and B to be passed on together and a and b to be passed on together.

During meiosis, the section for A can cross over and exchange with a on the other chromosome.

The result is sex cells having a with B and A with b.

FIGURE 2.13

Crossing over in chromosomes.

a and *b*. Any offspring inheriting the *A* allele would also inherit the *B* allele, and any offspring inheriting the *a* allele would also inherit the *b* allele.

This does not always happen. During meiosis, chromosome pairs sometimes exchange pieces, a process known as **crossing over.** For example, the segment of DNA containing the *a* allele could switch with the segment of DNA containing the *A* allele on the other chromosome. Therefore, you could have a sex cell with *a* and *B* or a sex cell with *A* and *b* (see Figure 2.13). The result of crossing over is known as **recombination,** the production of new combinations of genes and DNA sequences. (Recombination describes the result, and crossing over describes the process.)

Recombination does not change the genetic material. The alleles are still the same, but they can occur in different combinations. Recombination provides yet another mechanism for increasing genetic variation by providing new combinations of alleles.

Sex Chromosomes and Sex Determination

One of the 23 pairs of human chromosomes is called the *sex chromosome pair* because these chromosomes contain the genetic information relating to an individual's sex. There are two forms of sex chromosomes, X and Y. Females have two X chromosomes (XX), and males have one X and one Y chromosome (XY).

The Y chromosome is much smaller than the X chromosome. Therefore, almost all genes found on X are not found on Y. This means that males possess only one allele for certain traits because their Y chromosome lacks the corresponding section of DNA. Therefore, males will manifest a trait for which they have only one allele, whereas females require the same allele from both parents to show the trait. An example of this sex difference is hemophilia, a genetic disorder that interferes with the normal process of blood clotting. The allele for hemophilia is recessive and is found on the segment of the X chromosome that has no corresponding portion on the Y chromosome. For females to be hemophiliac, they must inherit two copies of this allele, one from each parent. This is unlikely because the hemophilia allele is rare. Males, however, need to inherit only one copy of the X chromosome from the mother. As a result, hemophilia is more common in males than females.

Inheritance from One Parent

Thus far, patterns of human inheritance have been described in terms of two parents—a mother and a father. Although most of our DNA is inherited from both parents, there are two important exceptions to this general rule. The first concerns **mitochondrial DNA,** the small amount of DNA that exists in the mitochondria of the cell. Unlike the DNA in the nucleus, mitochondrial DNA is inherited *only* through the mother. This happens because in conception the female sex cell (egg) contains mitochondria, whereas the male sex cell (sperm) does not. Your mitochondrial DNA came only from your mother, who inherited it from her mother, who inherited it from her mother, and so on. If you are female and have children, you will pass on your mitochondrial DNA to your children, whereas if you are male, you cannot.

Another form of single-parent inheritance is through the Y chromosome in males. Males (XY) inherit the Y chromosome from their fathers and their

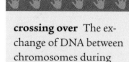

crossing over The exchange of DNA between chromosomes during meiosis.

recombination The production of new combinations of DNA sequences caused by exchanges of DNA during meiosis.

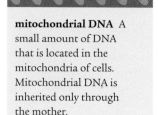

mitochondrial DNA A small amount of DNA that is located in the mitochondria of cells. Mitochondrial DNA is inherited only through the mother.

X chromosome from their mothers. Because most of the Y chromosome does not recombine with the X chromosome, this means that almost all of the Y chromosome is passed on intact from father to son, with no genetic contribution from the mother.

The Genetics of Complex Traits

The discussion of genetics thus far has focused on simple discrete genetic traits. Traits such as the MN blood group are genetically "simple" because they result from the action of a single locus with a clear-cut mode of inheritance. These traits are also discrete, meaning that they produce a finite number of phenotypes. For example, you have the M or the N or the MN phenotype for the MN blood group system; you cannot have an intermediate phenotype. Your MN phenotype is also produced entirely from genetic factors. It is not influenced by the environment. Except for a complete blood transfusion, your MN blood group phenotype is the same all of your life.

These simple discrete traits are very useful for demonstrating the basic principles of Mendelian inheritance. It is not wise, however, to think of all biological traits as resulting from a single locus, exhibiting a finite number of phenotypes, or not being affected by the environment. Many of the characteristics of interest in human evolution, such as skin color, body size, brain size, and intelligence, do not fall into this simple category. Such traits have a complex mode of inheritance in that one or more genes may contribute to the phenotype, and they may be affected by the environment. The combined action of genetics and environment produces traits with a continuous distribution. An example is human height. People do not come in 3 different heights (short, medium, and tall), nor 5, nor 20. Height can take on an infinite number of phenotypes. People can be 1,700 mm tall, 1,701 mm tall, and any value in between, such as 1,700.3 mm or 1,700.65 mm.

Complex traits tend to produce more individuals with average values than extreme values. It is not uncommon to find human males between 1,676 and 1,981 mm (5.5 and 6.5 feet) tall. It is much rarer to find someone taller than 2,134 mm (7 feet). A typical distribution of a complex trait, human height, is shown in Figure 2.14.

Polygenic Traits and Pleiotropy Many complex traits are **polygenic,** the result of two or more loci. When several loci act to control a trait, many different genotypes and phenotypes can result. A number of physical characteristics, such as human skin color and height, may be polygenic. A single allele can also have multiple effects on an organism. When an allele has effects on multiple traits, this is referred to as **pleiotropy.** For example, in humans, the sickle cell allele affects the structure of the blood's hemoglobin and also leads to changes in overall body growth and health.

The concepts of polygenic traits and pleiotropy are important in considering the interrelated nature of biological systems. Analysis of simple discrete traits on a gene-by-gene basis is useful in understanding genetics, but

polygenic A complex genetic trait affected by two or more loci.

pleiotropy A single allele that has multiple effects on an organism.

FIGURE 2.14

The distribution of a normally distributed continuous trait. This figure is based on the actual distribution of height (mm) of 1,986 Irish women (author's unpublished data). The height of the curve represents the proportion of women with any given height. Most individuals have a value close to the average for the population (the highest point on the curve, which corresponds to a height of 1,589 mm). The solid line is the fit of the normal distribution.

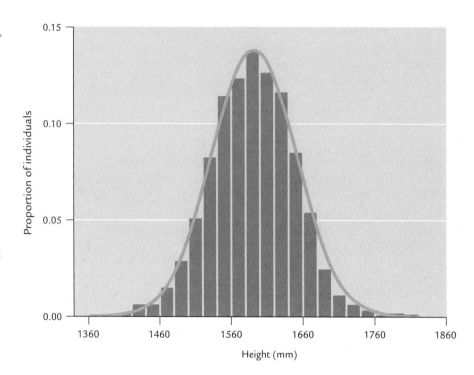

it should not lead you to think that any organism is simply a collection of single, independent loci.

Figure 2.15 shows several different models of genetic interaction. Figure 2.15a represents the nature of some simple genetic traits, whereby each cause has a single effect. Figure 2.15b represents a polygenic trait, whereby many loci contribute to a single effect. Pleiotropic effects are shown in Figure 2.15c, whereby a single allele has multiple effects. Figure 2.15d is the most

FIGURE 2.15

The relationship between a gene and a biological effect: (a) single gene, single effect; (b) polygenic trait; (c) pleiotropy; (d) polygenic trait and pleiotropy.

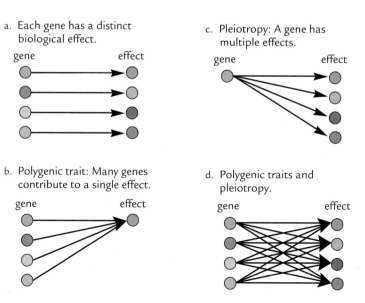

a. Each gene has a distinct biological effect.

b. Polygenic trait: Many genes contribute to a single effect.

c. Pleiotropy: A gene has multiple effects.

d. Polygenic traits and pleiotropy.

realistic model for many complex traits; each allele has multiple effects, and each effect has multiple causes. In this case, the trait is caused by polygenic and pleiotropic effects. To complicate matters, consider variations of this model in which not all alleles have the same effect, some alleles are dominant and some are not, and environmental factors act to obscure what we actually observe. It is no wonder that the study of the genetics of complex traits is extremely difficult, requiring sophisticated mathematical methods.

Nature versus Nurture How much are complex traits, particularly behavioral traits such as intelligence or sexual orientation, the result of genes ("nature") versus the physical and cultural environment ("nurture")? The "nature–nurture" debate has a long history. At the beginning of the twentieth century, the prevalent view was that nature was the more important determinant of many behaviors, particularly intelligence. This emphasis shifted to nurture from the 1930s to the 1960s, when environmental factors were seen as being the most, if not the only, important factor. Much of the debate over nature *versus* nurture is nonsense, however. Any attempt to relegate human behaviors to either genetics *or* environment is fruitless. Genes and environment both have a significant effect on human behaviors. The proper question is not which is more important but rather how they interact. Evidence of *some* genetic influence has been found for a variety of human behaviors, including intelligence test scores, autism, reading and language disabilities, eating disorders, schizophrenia, and sexual orientation. These studies do not support a view that behavior is *caused* by genes, but rather suggest that genes can *influence* behavior. In a review of genetic studies of human behavior, Plomin et al. (1994) note that these analyses have consistently shown that there is at least as much environmental variation related to phenotypic variation as to genetic variation. In other words, *both* genetic and environmental variation has been related to behavioral variation. Genetic analysis can be used to determine the relative proportion of total variation due to genetic variation in a population (Box 2.3).

MUTATIONS

As shown earlier, the process of genetic inheritance produces genetic variation in offspring. The independent assortment of chromosomes during meiosis and the action of crossing over both act to create new genetic combinations. They do not act to create any new genetic material, however. To explain past evolution, we need a mechanism for introducing new alleles and variation. The origin of new genetic variation was a problem for Darwin, but we now know that new alleles are brought about through the process of mutation.

The Evolutionary Significance of Mutations

A **mutation** is a change in the genetic code. Mutations are the ultimate source of all genetic variation. Mutations are caused by a number of environmental

mutation A mechanism for evolutionary change resulting from a random change in the genetic code; the ultimate source of all genetic variation.

BOX 2.3

Heritability

When we discuss the relative influence of genes ("nature") and environment ("nurture") on a complex trait such as height or test scores, we often hear mention of the trait's heritability. Even without defining the word "heritability," we assume rightly that it has something to do with what we inherit (genes). It is often the case that a specific number is attached, such as a claim that trait X shows 80 percent heritability. What exactly does this 80 percent figure mean, and what does it *not* mean?

Heritability is the percentage of total phenotypic variation of a trait that is due to genetic variation. In order to understand fully what this number means, consider first what we mean by phenotypic variation. Imagine, for example, that you have measured height on a group of adult women in a village in the countryside. As with most complex traits, you will see a certain amount of variation in height—some women will be taller, and some will be shorter—and most often the pattern of variation you see will be the bell-shaped curve you saw in Figure 2.14. The difference between the women is the phenotypic variation.

Some of the total variation that we see in this sample will be due to genetic variation; some of the women might be related, but others have different genetic background and could have different genes that affect height. Some of the variation is also due to environmental variation, where different women have different diets, health, and other factors affecting height. Mathematically, we can express the total variation that we see in the sample as the sum of the amount of variation due to genes and the amount of variation due to environment:

Total variation = Genetic variation + Environmental variation

Heritability is simply the proportion of total variation that is due to genetic variation, or

$$\text{Heritability} = \frac{\text{Genetic variation}}{\text{Total variation}}$$

$$= \frac{\text{Genetic variation}}{\text{Genetic variation} + \text{Environmental variation}}$$

A number of methods exist for determining the expected amount of genetic variation in a population when we know how people are related to each other (for example, a specific amount of genetic variation is expected when comparing siblings or comparing parents and offspring).

Two thought experiments help illustrate what heritability means. Imagine that everyone in the population had the exact same alleles for all of the genes affecting height. Because all of the alleles are the same, there would be no genetic difference between anyone, and the genetic variation would be zero, which means that the heritability would also be zero, even though some genes affect height! On the other hand, imagine that everyone in a population varied genetically but had the exact same environment—the same upbringing, the same diet, the same exercise, and so forth. If the environmental differences were zero, then there would be no environmental variation (= 0), and heritability would be equal to 1. This figure would not mean that the environment had no effect, but instead that the environment affected everyone the same. In actual situations where there is *both* genetic *and* environmental variation, the level of heritability can change from one case to the next. Heritability could be different in different populations, and it can even change within the same population over time (if, for example, environmental differences are reduced in a population over time, heritability will by definition increase). Thus, heritability is a statistic that only has meaning in reference to a population, and even here, it is a number that can change as the relative amounts of genetic and environmental variation change over time.

Finally, because heritability is a property of a population, it has no direct relevance to an individual's phenotype. For example, suppose you live in a population where the heritability of height is 0.9 and you are 67 inches tall (5 foot, 7 inches). Would you infer that the proportion of your height due to genetics is 0.9 times 67 inches = 60.3 inches and the remainder is due to the environment? If so, you would be making a major mistake, as heritability refers to variation within a group and does not refer to an individual person. To do so would be ludicrous mathematically and genetically.

heritability The proportion of total variation of a trait due to genetic variation.

factors, such as background radiation, which includes radiation from the earth's crust and from cosmic rays. Such background radiation is all around us, in the air we breathe and the food we eat.

Mutations can take place in any cell of the body. To have evolutionary importance, however, the mutation must occur in a sex cell. A mutation in a skin cell on the end of your finger has no evolutionary significance because it will not be passed on to your offspring.

Mutations are random. That is, there is no way of predicting when a specific mutation will take place or what, if any, phenotypic effect it will have. All we can do is estimate the probability of a mutation occurring at a given locus over a given time. The randomness of mutations also means that mutations do not appear when they might be needed. Many mosquitoes have adapted to insecticides because a mutation was present in the population that acted to confer some resistance to the insecticide. If that mutation had not been present, the mosquitoes would have died. The mosquitoes' need for a certain genetic variant had no effect on whether the mutation appeared.

Mutations can have different effects depending on the specific type of mutation and the environment. The conventional view of mutations has long been that they are mostly harmful. A classic analogy is the comparison of the genetic code with the engine of an automobile. If an engine part is changed at random, the most likely result is that the car will not operate, or at least not as well as it did before the change.

Some mutations, however, are advantageous. They lead to change that improves the survival and reproduction rates of organisms. In recent decades, we have also discovered that some mutations are neutral; that is, the genetic change has no detectable effect on survival or reproduction. There is continued controversy among geneticists about the relative frequency of neutral mutations. Some claim that many mutations are neutral in their effect. Others note the difficulties in detecting the effects of many mutations.

Whether a mutation is neutral, advantageous, or disadvantageous depends in large part on the environment. Genetic variants that are harmful in certain environments might actually be helpful in other environments.

Types of Mutations

We now recognize that mutations can occur in a variety of ways. Mutations can involve changes in a single DNA base, in larger sections of DNA, and in entire chromosomes. One example is the substitution of one DNA base for another, such as the widely studied **sickle cell allele.** The red blood cells produced in individuals with two copies of this allele (one from each parent) are misshapen and do not transport oxygen efficiently. The result is a severe form of anemia (sickle cell anemia) that leads to sickness and death. The specific cause of this allele is a mutation in the sixth amino acid (out of 146 amino acids) of the beta chain of hemoglobin. The DNA for the normal beta hemoglobin allele contains instructions for the amino acid, glutamic acid, at this position (CTC). The sickle cell mutation occurs when the base T is changed to an A, which specifies the amino acid valine (CAC). This small change affects the entire structure of the red blood cells and, in turn, the well-being of the individual.

Substitution of one base for another is only one type of mutation. Mutations can also involve the addition or deletion of a base or of large sections of DNA. In these cases, the genetic message is changed. Also, sections of DNA

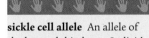

sickle cell allele An allele of the hemoglobin locus. Individuals homozygous for this allele have sickle cell anemia.

FIGURE 2.16

Facial appearance of a child with Down syndrome. Down syndrome is often caused by the duplication of one chromosome in the 21st chromosome pair.

can be duplicated or moved from one place to another, and sections of DNA can be added or lost when crossing over is not equal.

The genetic information contained in the chromosomes can also be altered by the deletion or duplication of part or all of the chromosome. For example, an entire chromosome from a pair can be lost (**monosomy** = one chromosome) or can occur in duplicate, giving three chromosomes (**trisomy**). One result of the latter is Down syndrome, a condition characterized by certain cranial features (Figure 2.16), poor physical growth, and mental retardation (usually mild). Down syndrome is caused by the duplication of one of the 21st chromosome pair. Affected individuals have a total of 47 chromosomes, one more than the normal 46. Down syndrome can also be caused by mutations of the 21st chromosome. In some individuals, the change involves the exchange of parts of the 21st chromosome with other chromosomes.

Several chromosomal mutations involve the sex chromosomes. One, known as Turner syndrome, occurs when an individual has only one X chromosome instead of two. These individuals thus have only 45 chromosomes and develop as females. Those with Turner syndrome are generally short, have undeveloped ovaries, and are sterile. Another condition, known as Klinefelter syndrome, occurs in males with an extra X chromosome. Instead of the normal XY combination, these males have an XXY combination for a total of 47 chromosomes. They are characterized by small testes and reduced fertility.

Rates of Mutations

Specific mutations are relatively rare events. In humans, an average rate for mutation for a single nucleotide site per person per generation is about 2.3×10^{-8} (Jobling et al. 2004). Some sections of DNA have higher mutation rates, such as mitochondrial DNA and repeated DNA sequences (discussed

monosomy A condition in which one chromosome rather than a pair is present in body cells.

trisomy A condition in which three chromosomes rather than a pair occur in body cells.

in Chapter 14). Regardless of the specific mutation rates for a given gene or DNA sequence, one thing is clear—mutation rates are generally low. Given these low probabilities, it might be tempting to regard mutation as being so rare that it has no special evolutionary significance. The problem with this reasoning is that the estimated rates refer to a *single* DNA base. Human chromosomes have many loci. The probability that a specific locus will show a mutation rate in any individual is low, but the probability of *any* locus in an entire population is much higher. This is particularly true in humans today; the large current size of the human species generates more potential for new mutations (Hawks et al. 2007).

Summary

The DNA molecule specifies the genetic code or set of instructions needed to produce biological structures. DNA acts along with a related molecule, RNA, to translate these instructions into proteins. The DNA is contained along structures within the cell called chromosomes. Chromosomes come in pairs. A segment of DNA that codes for a certain product is called a gene. The different forms of genes present at a locus are called alleles. The DNA molecule has the ability to make copies of itself, allowing transmission of genetic information from cell to cell and from generation to generation.

Meiosis is the process of sex cell formation that results in one of each chromosome pair being transmitted from parent to offspring. An individual receives half of his or her alleles from each parent. The two alleles together specify the genetic constitution of an individual—the genotype. The physical manifestation of the genotype is known as the phenotype. The relationship between genotype and phenotype depends on whether an allele is dominant, recessive, or codominant. In complex physical traits, the phenotype is the result of the combined effect of genetics and environment.

The ultimate source of all genetic variation is mutation—a random change in the genetic code. Some mutations are neutral in effect; others are helpful or harmful. The effect of any mutation often depends on the specific environmental conditions. Mutations for any given allele are relatively rare events, but given the large number of loci in many organisms, it is highly probable that each individual has at least one mutant allele.

Supplemental Readings

Baker, C. (2004) *Behavioral Genetics: An Introduction to How Genes and Environments Interact Through Development to Shape Differences in Mood, Personality, and Intelligence*. Washington, D.C.: American Association for the Advancement of Science. Available at: http://www .aaas.org/spp/bgenes/publications.shtml. An exceptionally clear overview of behavior genetics.

Genetic Science Learning Center, University of Utah. A comprehensive multimedia Web page with discussions of all aspects of genetics: http://learn.genetics.utah.edu/

Variation among dogs. Similarity and differences within species and between species is the focus of evolutionary investigation. Changes over time reflect the action of the four evolutionary forces: mutation, natural selection, genetic drift, and gene flow.

The Forces of Evolution

CHAPTER

3

Change is all around us. In the physical environment, we can see erosion, rivers changing course, climates changing, and (given precise equipment) the movement of the continents. We can also observe biological change either by observing organisms from generation to generation, or by detecting past change through anatomic and genetic analysis. For example, biologists Peter and Rosemary Grant have observed physical changes in finch populations in the Galapagos Islands for decades, noting for example how the size and shape of beaks change in response to changes in the environment (Weiner 1994). As another example, consider that some human populations have high frequencies of the lactase persistence allele described in Chapter 2, which allows individuals to digest milk and milk products throughout their lifetime. Genetic analysis shows us that those populations with higher frequencies of this allele are those that rely on dairy farming (which makes sense), and that this allele arose as a mutation only within the last 9,000 years (Tishkoff and Gonder 2007). As a final example, consider that random genetic differences between Italian villages are greater in the more isolated mountain regions than in the more densely populated hills and valleys (Cavalli-Sforza et al. 2004).

These examples are only a handful of countless examples accumulated since the time of Darwin that demonstrate evolution in action. Regardless of the species studied (finch or human) or the type of measure (physical measures or DNA), all of these studies share a common question—what causes evolutionary change? In the first half of the twentieth century, scientists merged Darwin's ideas with the rediscovered principles of Mendelian genetics and developed a theory that provides the explanation for evolutionary changes from one generation to the next. You have seen some parts of this evolutionary theory in the past two chapters; Darwin provided the basis for understanding how natural selection worked on existing variation but had no explanation for the ultimate origin of variation. The rise of genetics provided that answer—mutation. Both mutation and natural selection are evolutionary forces, but are not the only ones. This chapter reviews all of the evolutionary forces that act to cause changes in the frequency of alleles over time. Whereas Chapter 2 looked at molecular and Mendelian genetics, this chapter focuses on population genetics. The focus here will be on relatively short-term changes, typically over several dozen generations. However, the principle of uniformitarianism (Chapter 1) means that we can extend these short-term changes (microevolution) to much longer periods of time by considering how they add up over time. Chapter 4 will examine evolution over these longer time periods, including the origin of new species (macroevolution).

POPULATION GENETICS

Microevolution takes into account changes in the frequency of alleles from one generation to the next. The focus is generally not on the specific genotypes or phenotypes of individuals but rather on the total pattern of an entire biological population. We are interested in defining the relative frequencies of different alleles, genotypes, and phenotypes for the entire population being studied. We then seek to determine if any change in these frequencies has occurred over time. If changes have occurred, we try to explain them.

What Is a Population?

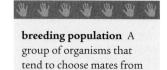

breeding population A group of organisms that tend to choose mates from within the group

The term **breeding population** is used frequently in evolutionary theory. In an abstract sense, a breeding population is a group of organisms that tend to choose mates from within the group. This definition is a bit tricky, however, because it is not clear what proportion of mating within a group defines a breeding population.

For example, suppose you travel to a village in a remote mountain region. You find that 99 percent of the people in the villages are married to others who were born in the same village. In this case, the village would appear to fit our ideal definition. But what if only 80 percent of the people chose their mates from within the village? What if the number were 50 percent? At what point do you stop referring to the population as a "breeding population"? There is no quick and ready answer to this question.

On a practical level, human populations are initially most often defined on the basis of geographic and political boundaries. A small, isolated island, for example, easily fits the requirements of a defined population. In most cases, the local geographic unit (such as town or village) is used. Because many human populations have distinct geographic boundaries, this solution often provides the best approach. We must take care, however, to ensure that a local geographic unit, such as a town, is not composed of distinct subpopulations, such as groups belonging to different religious sects. A rural Irish village fits this criterion because most of its residents belong to the same religion, social class, and occupational group. New York City, on the other hand, clearly contains a number of subpopulations defined in terms of ethnicity, religion, social class, and other factors. In this case, subpopulations defined on the basis of these factors would serve as our units of analysis.

In many cases, the definition of a population depends on the specific research question asked. For example, if the goal of a study is to look at spatial patterns of biological variation, populations defined on the basis of geography are most suitable. If, however, the goal of a study is to look at genetic variation among ethnic groups, then ethnicity should be used to define the populations.

Another potential problem in defining populations is determining the difference between the total census population and the breeding population. Microevolutionary theory specifically concerns those individuals who contribute to the next generation. The *total* population refers to everybody, whether or not they are likely to breed. The *breeding* population is smaller than the total population because of a number of factors. First, some individuals in the total population will be too young or too old to mate. Second, cultural factors and geographic distribution may act to limit an individual's choice of mate, and as a consequence, some individuals will not breed. If, for example, you live in an isolated area, there may not be enough individuals of the opposite sex from which to choose a mate. Such factors must be taken into consideration in defining a breeding population.

Once a population has been defined, the next step in microevolutionary analysis is to determine the frequencies of genotypes and alleles within the population.

Genotype Frequencies and Allele Frequencies

The genotype frequency is a measure of the relative proportions of different genotypes within a population. Likewise, an allele frequency is simply a measure of the relative proportion of alleles within a population. Genotype frequencies are obtained by dividing the number of individuals with each genotype by the total number of individuals. For example, consider a hypothetical population of 200 people for the MN blood group system in which there are 98 people with genotype *MM,* 84 people with genotype *MN,* and 18 people with genotype *NN.* The genotype frequencies are therefore:

Frequency of *MM* = 98/200 = 0.49

Frequency of *MN* = 84/200 = 0.42

Frequency of *NN* = 18/200 = 0.09

Note that the total frequency of all genotypes adds up to 1 (0.49 + 0.42 + 0.09 = 1). These frequencies are *proportions.* If you find it easier to think about the frequencies in terms of *percentages,* then simply multiply the proportions by 100. Thus, we see that 0.49 × 100 = 49 percent of the population with genotype *MM.* Likewise, 42 percent have genotype *MN,* and 9 percent have genotype *NN.*

Allele frequencies are computed by counting the number of each allele and dividing that number by the total number of alleles. In the example here, the total number of alleles is 400 because there are 200 people, each with 2 alleles. To find out the number of *M* alleles for each genotype, count up the number of alleles for each genotype, and multiply that number by the number of people with that genotype. Finally, add up the number for all genotypes. In the example, 98 people have the *MM* genotype, and therefore 98 people have

> ## TABLE 3.1   Example of Allele Frequency Computation
>
> Imagine you have just collected information on *MN* genotypes for 250 humans in a given population. Your data are:
>
> Number of *MM* genotype = 40
> Number of *MN* genotype = 120
> Number of *NN* genotype = 90
>
> The allele frequencies are computed as follows:
>
> | Genotype | Number of People | Total Number of Alleles | Number of M Alleles | Number of N Alleles |
> |----------|------------------|-------------------------|---------------------|---------------------|
> | *MM* | 40 | 80 | 80 | 0 |
> | *MN* | 120 | 240 | 120 | 120 |
> | *NN* | 90 | 180 | 0 | 180 |
> | Total | 250 | 500 | 200 | 300 |
>
> The relative frequency of the *M* allele is computed as the number of *M* alleles divided by the total number of alleles: 200/500 = 0.4.
>
> The relative frequency of the *N* allele is computed as the number of *N* alleles divided by the total number of alleles: 300/500 = 0.6.
>
> As a check, note that the relative frequencies of the alleles must add up to 1.0 (0.4 + 0.6 = 1.0).

two *M* alleles. The total number of *M* alleles for people with the *MM* genotype is $98 \times 2 = 196$. For the *MN* genotype, 84 people have one *M* allele, giving a total of $84 \times 1 = 84$ *M* alleles. For the *NN* genotype, 18 people have no *M* alleles, for a total of $18 \times 0 = 0$ *M* alleles. Adding the number of *M* alleles for all genotypes gives a total of $196 + 84 + 0 = 280$ *M* alleles. The frequency of the *M* allele is therefore $280/400 = 0.7$. The frequency of the *N* allele can be computed in the same way, giving an allele frequency of 0.3. Note that the frequencies of all alleles must add up to 1. Another example of allele frequency computation is given in Table 3.1.

The method of counting alleles to determine allele frequencies can be used only when the number of individuals with each genotype can be determined. If one of the alleles is dominant, this will not be possible, and we must use another method.

Hardy-Weinberg Equilibrium

Now that we have computed the allele frequencies for the MN blood group for our hypothetical population, we turn to another question: What are the *expected* genotype frequencies in the next generation? If the population reproduces, what proportion of children in the next generation will have genotype *MM*? What proportion will have *MN*, or *NN*?

As shown in Chapter 2, we can easily answer this question for any specific pair of parents. For example, if a man with genotype *MN* mates with a woman with genotype *MN*, we expect that 25 percent of the offspring will have genotype *MM*, 50 percent will have genotype *MN*, and 25 percent will have genotype *NN* (see Figure 2.9). Extending this computation to the entire population means that we would need to consider *all* possible pairings (e.g., *MM* and *MN*, *MM* and *NN*, and so forth) and the number of each pairing (e.g., how many men with *MN* mate with women with *MN*, and so forth).

Although this might seem to be an overly complex question to answer, two scientists, G. H. Hardy and W. Weinberg, independently arrived at a simple and elegant solution in 1908, known today as **Hardy-Weinberg equilibrium.** This is a mathematical statement that relates the allele frequencies in a population to the expected genotype frequencies in the next generation. It is best explained using a simple model of a single locus with two alleles, such as the MN blood group above. First, we need to know the allele frequencies, which were derived above as 0.7 for the frequency of the *M* allele and 0.3 for the frequency of the *N* allele. By convention, we use the symbols p and q to refer to the allele frequencies, and in this case, p is shorthand for "the frequency of the *M* allele" and q is shorthand for "the frequency of the *N* allele." Using these symbols, we say that $p = 0.7$ and $q = 0.3$.

The Hardy-Weinberg equilibrium model states that, given allele frequencies p and q, the expected genotype frequencies in the next generation are:

Frequency of the *MM* genotype $= p^2$

Frequency of the *MN* genotype $= 2pq$

Frequency of the *NN* genotype $= q^2$

For our hypothetical example (where $p = 0.7$ and $q = 0.3$), we can now predict the genotype frequencies in the next generation using these formulae:

Frequency of the *MM* genotype $= p^2 = (0.7)^2 = 0.49$

Frequency of the *MN* genotype $= 2pq = 2 \times 0.7 \times 0.3 = 0.42$

Frequency of the *NN* genotype $= q^2 = (0.3)^2 = 0.09$

Thus, we expect that in the next generation, 49 percent of the offspring will have genotype *MM*, 42 percent will have genotype *MN*, and 9 percent will have genotype *NN*.

As another example, suppose we have a locus with two alleles, *A* and *a*, where the frequency of the *A* allele is 0.9 and the frequency of the *a* allele is 0.1. How many offspring would we expect to see in the next generation with the homozygous genotype *aa*? We can easily answer this question by using Hardy-Weinberg. If p is the frequency of the *A* allele ($p = 0.9$) and q is the frequency of the *a* allele ($q = 0.1$), then the expected proportion of the population having the *aa* genotype is $q^2 = (0.1)^2 = 0.01$. As a real life example, consider the fact that there is an allele for something called the *CCR5* gene that has a frequency of about 0.1 in some European populations (see Chapter 15). If you have two copies of this allele, you resistant to the HIV virus that causes AIDS. Given an allele frequency of 0.1, we see from Hardy-Weinberg that about one percent of the population $[(0.1)^2 = 0.01]$ will have the HIV-resistant genotype.

Hardy and Weinberg also showed that *given certain conditions* genotype and allele frequencies would stay the same from one generation to the next.

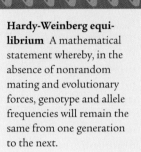

Hardy-Weinberg equilibrium A mathematical statement whereby, in the absence of nonrandom mating and evolutionary forces, genotype and allele frequencies will remain the same from one generation to the next.

That is, the genetic composition of the population would be at equilibrium. Of course, these conditions cannot apply to all populations, or else there would be no evolution! The role of Hardy-Weinberg equilibrium in population genetics is a baseline with which to compare the real world, which helps us determine *why* populations do change (Box 3.1). During the early twentieth century, population geneticists discovered that change in genotype frequencies could result from the effects of evolutionary forces and/or nonrandom mating. **Evolutionary forces** are those mechanisms that can actually lead to a change in allele frequency over time. There are four evolutionary forces: mutation, natural selection, genetic drift, and gene flow (each is described in detail in the following section). These four forces are the only mechanisms that can cause the frequency of an allele to change over time. For example, if you study a population with an allele frequency of 0.5 and return a generation later to find an allele frequency of 0.4, then you have observed evolution. This change could be due to mutation, natural selection, genetic drift, and/or gene flow. Given the large amount of change in a single generation, it is unlikely that mutation would be responsible because mutation usually causes much lower amounts of change in a single generation. In that case, you could conclude that the observed change was due to natural selection, genetic drift, and/or gene flow. You would need to examine more information, such as migration rates, population size, and environmental variation, to determine which factors were responsible for the change.

When allele frequencies change, so do genotype frequencies, but genotype frequencies can change without altering the underlying allele frequencies. This happens when there is significant **nonrandom mating,** which refers to the patterns of mate choice within a population and its genetic effects. One form of nonrandom mating is **inbreeding,** which occurs when there is mating between biologically related individuals (Figure 3.1). Inbreeding increases

evolutionary forces Four mechanisms that can cause changes in allele frequencies from one generation to the next: mutation, natural selection, genetic drift, and gene flow.

nonrandom mating Patterns of mate choice that influence the distributions of genotype and phenotype frequencies.

inbreeding Mating between biologically related individuals.

FIGURE 3.1

A white tiger. Inbreeding had been used in the past to produce larger numbers of white tigers. The pale color of the white tiger is due to a recessive allele.

BOX 3.1

Hardy-Weinberg Equilibrium—What Does It Predict?

As presented in the text, Hardy-Weinberg equilibrium provides us with a way to figure out genotype frequencies in the next generation. But this equilibrium has a broader meaning that was mentioned only briefly. *Given certain assumptions*, both genotype and allele frequencies will remain the same from one generation to the next to the next. For example, imagine a population with a locus with two alleles, *A* and *a*, where the frequency of the *A* allele is 0.8 and the frequency of the *a* allele is 0.2. If this population is at Hardy-Weinberg equilibrium, this means that the frequency of the *A* allele will stay at 0.8 in the next generation, and stay at 0.8 in the generation after that, and so on into the future. Furthermore, Hardy-Weinberg equilibrium states that the genotype frequencies will stay the same over time.

Many students find Hardy-Weinberg equilibrium perplexing because it is used to explain evolution, yet the model predicts no evolution—everything stays the same! After all, if we define evolution as a change in allele frequencies over time, and if Hardy-Weinberg equilibrium predicts *no* change, then what relevance does it have? The key to understanding the importance of Hardy-Weinberg equilibrium is to recall and examine that critical phrase made in the third sentence of this box: "*Given certain assumptions.*" When Hardy and Weinberg showed that there was no inherent tendency of allele frequencies to change over time, they used a simple model that had a number of assumptions. Simply put, the model makes a prediction—no change in allele frequency over time. In the real world, however, we have countless examples of evolutionary change in many species. When observed reality does not match the predictions of the model, this means that one or more of the assumptions of the model is incorrect. By framing the process of evolutionary change in terms of the equilibrium model, population geneticists were able to discover exactly what *does* cause evolutionary changes.

What are the assumptions of the mathematically simple Hardy-Weinberg equilibrium? Here is a list:

1. Random mating (this means someone does not mate with a close biological relative or choose a mate based on their genotype).
2. There is no mutation.
3. The population is very large so that there are no random changes in allele frequency because of small population size (actually the assumption is for infinite population size, but this translates practically into an assumption of a very large population).
4. There is no natural selection, and every genotype has the same probability of survival and reproduction.
5. The population is closed, so no changes in allele frequency are possible due to migration from outside the group.

When the first assumption is not true, there can be a change in genotype frequency. When any of the other four assumptions are not true, then allele and genotype frequencies can change. Each of the other four assumptions corresponds to a particular evolutionary force—mutation, natural selection, genetic drift, and gene flow. See Relethford (2012a) for more details on Hardy-Weinberg equilibrium.

---

the proportion of individuals who are homozygous but does not change the allele frequency. In other words, under inbreeding, more individuals will be homozygous and fewer will be heterozygous.

THE EVOLUTIONARY FORCES

This section discusses the four evolutionary forces in detail. Although they are described here one at a time, keep in mind that in the real world all four operate at the same time.

Mutation

Mutation introduces new alleles into a population. Therefore, the frequency of different alleles will change over time. Consider a genetic locus with a single allele, *A,* for a population of 100 people (and therefore 200 alleles, because each person has 2 alleles). Everyone in the population will have genotype *AA,* and the frequency of the *A* allele is 1.0 (100 percent). Now, assume that one of the *A* alleles being passed on to the next generation changes into a new form, *a.* Assuming the population stays the same size (to make the mathematics a bit easier), there will be 199 *A* alleles and 1 *a* allele in the next generation. The frequency of *A* will have changed from 1.0 to 0.995 (199/200), and the frequency of *a* will have changed from 0.0 to 0.005 (1/200).

If there is no further evolutionary change, the allele frequencies will remain the same in future generations. If this mutation continues to recur, the frequency of the *a* allele will slowly increase, assuming no other evolutionary forces are operating. For typical mutation rates, such a process would take a very long time.

Although mutations are vital to evolution because they provide new variations, mutation rates are low and do not lead, by themselves, to major changes in allele frequency. The other evolutionary forces increase or decrease the frequencies of mutant alleles. If you visited a population over two generations and noted that the frequency of a given allele had changed from 0.30 to 0.40, it would be extremely unlikely that this magnitude of change was due solely to mutation. The other evolutionary forces would be responsible for such large changes.

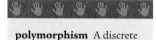

polymorphism A discrete genetic trait in which there are at least two alleles at a locus having frequencies greater than 0.01.

Many discrete genetic traits are **polymorphisms** (many forms). A genetic polymorphism is a locus with two or more alleles having frequencies too large to be a result of mutation alone. The usual, somewhat arbitrary, cutoff point for these allele frequencies is 0.01. If an allele has a frequency greater than 0.01, we can safely assume that this relatively high frequency is caused by factors other than mutation. For example, a locus with allele frequencies of *A* = 1.0 and *a* = 0.0 would not be polymorphic because only one allele (*A*) is present in the population. Likewise, a locus with frequencies of *A* = 0.999 and *a* = 0.001 would not be a genetic polymorphism because only one allele has a frequency greater than 0.01. If the allele frequencies were *A* = 0.2 and *a* = 0.8, this would be evidence of genetic polymorphism. Both alleles have frequencies greater than 0.01. Such frequencies are explained by natural selection, genetic drift, and/or gene flow.

Natural Selection

As discussed in Chapter 1, natural selection filters genetic variation. Individuals with certain biological characteristics that allow them to survive to reproduce pass on the alleles for such characteristics to the next generation. Natural selection does not create new genetic variation (only mutation can do that), but it can change the relative frequencies of different alleles.

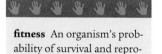

fitness An organism's probability of survival and reproduction.

The analysis of natural selection focuses on **fitness,** the probability of survival and reproduction of an organism. For any locus, fitness is measured as the relative genetic contribution of a genotype to the next generation. Imagine a locus with two alleles, *A* and *a,* and the genotypes *AA, Aa,* and *aa.* If all individuals with genotypes *AA* and *Aa* survive and reproduce but only half of those with genotype *aa* do so, then the fitness of genotype *aa* is half that of genotypes *AA* and *Aa*. Fitness refers to the proportion of individuals with a given genotype who survive and reproduce.

Examples of How Natural Selection Works It is easy to see how natural selection works using a simple mathematical simulation. For the purposes of illustration, let us imagine a case where there is a gene with two different alleles, which we call *A* and *a*. This means that there will be three different genotypes: *AA, Aa,* and *aa*. Our simulation starts with 200 people before selection takes place, of which 128 have genotype *AA,* 64 have genotype *Aa,* and 8 have genotype *aa*. Using the methods described earlier (see Table 3.1), we can add up the number of *A* and *a* alleles, giving a total of 2(128) + 64 = 320 *A* alleles and 64 + 2(8) = 80 *a* alleles, for a total of 400 alleles. This means that the frequency of the *a* allele is 80/400 = 0.2.

The assumption of no selection means that each genotype has the same chance of surviving and reproducing. In other words, the genotypes all have the same fitness. If this were the case, then the allele frequencies would stay the same, generation after generation. What happens, however, if this is not the case, and the different genotypes have different fitness? For purposes of illustration, consider a hypothetical example with the following fitness values: *AA* = 100 percent, *Aa* = 100 percent, and *aa* = 50 percent. These numbers correspond to a case of selection against a recessive homozygote, where the *A* allele is dominant over the *a* allele. Thus, individuals with the dominant phenotype (*AA* and *Aa*) all survive, whereas individuals with the recessive homozygote (*aa*) have only a 50 percent chance of survival. Under this situation, what do you expect to happen to the frequency of the *a* allele over time? Intuitively, the fact that fitness is lower for individuals with the *aa* genotype means that there is selection against the *a* allele, and it will decrease in frequency over time.

Table 3.2 shows how this works in a single generation. Using the above hypothetical fitness values, we see that all individuals with the *AA* genotype survive (= 128) and all individuals with the *Aa* genotype survive (= 64) because a fitness of 100 percent was assigned for both of these genotypes. The assigned fitness of *aa* is 50 percent, meaning that only 50 percent of the individuals with the *aa* genotype survive, leaving 0.5(8) = 4. Thus, selection has removed 4 of the 8 individuals with the *aa* genotype. This causes a reduction in the frequency of the *a* allele. After selection, the allele frequency (computed using the method in Table 3.1) is 0.184. Evolution has occurred due to natural selection!

The simulation of natural selection can be extended to future generations, as shown in Figure 3.2. Over time, the frequency of the *a* allele is reduced and will ultimately approach zero. Note that the actual amount of selection slows down over time. As the frequency of *a* slowly declines, an increasingly lower percentage of the population will be recessive homozygotes; consequently, fewer will be eliminated every generation.

Selection against an allele will lead to a reduction in the allele frequency over time. In this case, selection occurred because the fitness of the recessive

TABLE 3.2   Example of Natural Selection

This example uses an initial population size before selection of 200 individuals. The locus has two alleles, *A* and *a*. Initially, there are 128 individuals with genotype *AA,* 64 individuals with genotype *Aa,* and 8 individuals with genotype *aa.* The allele frequencies before selection are 0.8 for *A* and 0.2 for *a* (using the method from Table 3.1). The fitness values have been chosen to illustrate selection against the recessive homozygote (*aa*).

	Genotype			
	AA	Aa	aa	*Total*
Number of Individuals before Selection	128	64	8	200
Fitness (Percentage that Survive)	100%	100%	50%	
Number of Individuals after Selection	128	64	4	196

There are 196 individuals after selection (4 individuals did not survive). Using the method of allele frequency computation shown in Table 3.1 and the text, the allele frequencies after selection are 320/392 = 0.816 for the *A* allele and 0.184 for the *a* allele.

homozygote was lower than that of other genotypes. This is the case for a number of genetic diseases, where having two copies of a recessive allele leads to a genetic disease that reduces fitness. An example in the human species is Tay-Sachs disease, an affliction caused by a metabolic disorder that results in blindness, mental retardation, and destruction of the nervous

FIGURE 3.2

Change over time in the frequency of an allele (*a*) that has been selected against. The fitness values are *AA* = 100 percent, *Aa* = 100 percent, and *aa* = 50 percent. The initial frequency of the *a* allele is 0.2.

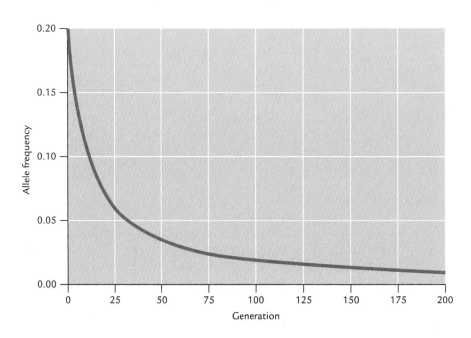

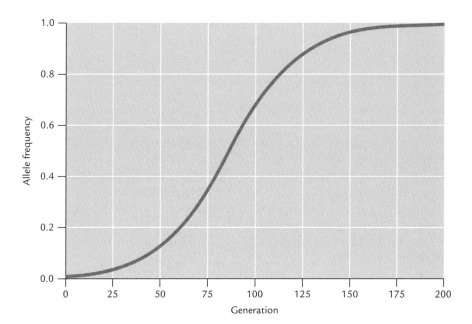

FIGURE 3.3

Change over time in the frequency of an allele (*A*) that has been selected for. The fitness values are *AA* = 100 percent, *Aa* = 95 percent, and *aa* = 90 percent. The initial frequency of the *A* allele is 0.01

system. Children with Tay-Sachs disease generally die within the first few years of life. The disease is caused by a recessive allele and occurs in those individuals who are homozygous. Heterozygotes carry the allele but do not show any major biological impairment. In terms of natural selection, the fitness of individuals with Tay-Sachs disease is zero.

Selection can also act to increase the frequency of an allele that results in an increase in fitness. Figure 3.3 shows an example of how this can occur. Here, the simulation starts with allele frequencies of *A* = 0.01 and *a* = 0.99. The fitness values in this case are *AA* = 100 percent, *Aa* = 95 percent, and *aa* = 90 percent. This represents a case where the *A* allele is selected for, as fitness is higher in individuals with a single *A* allele (*Aa*) and higher still in those with two *A* alleles (*AA*). Because fitness is higher in those individuals with one or more *A* alleles, the frequency of the *A* allele will increase over time. Figure 3.3 shows the results for this hypothetical example. Note that over 200 generations, the frequency of *A* increases to almost 100 percent. This example also reinforces the concept introduced earlier that natural selection can act over relatively short periods to produce very significant change. A number of examples of rapid natural selection in recent human evolution are discussed in Chapter 15.

Selection for the Heterozygote The examples discussed thus far deal with natural selection acting to either increase or decrease the frequency of an allele. If an allele is selected for, it will increase in frequency over time, and if an allele is selected against, it will decrease in frequency over time. We can also consider what happens to mutant alleles. If the mutant form increases fitness, it will increase in frequency. If the mutant form decreases fitness, it will be eliminated. With time, we might therefore expect selection to result in an allele frequency of either 0 or 1, depending on whether the allele is selected against or selected for, over time.

These models might lead us to expect patterns of genetic variation whereby most populations have allele frequencies close to either 0 or 1, and few populations have intermediate values. In reality, studies of human genetic variation have found that for some loci the allele frequencies produced by natural selection are intermediate. Is there a way that natural selection can produce such values? A classic example of an intermediate allele frequency in human populations is the sickle cell allele, discussed briefly in Chapter 2. Because people homozygous for this allele have sickle cell anemia and are likely to die early in life, this appears to be a classic situation of selection against a homozygote. If this were the case, we might expect most human populations to have frequencies of the sickle cell allele close to 0, and, in fact, many do. A number of populations in parts of Africa, India, and the Mediterranean, however, show higher frequencies. In some African groups, the frequency of the sickle cell allele is greater than 20 percent (Roychoudhury and Nei 1988). How can a harmful allele exist at such a high frequency?

The answer is a form of selection known as selection for the heterozygote (and therefore against the homozygotes). Consider fitness values of $AA =$ 70 percent, $Aa = 100$ percent, and $aa = 20$ percent. Here, only 70 percent of those with genotype AA and 20 percent of those with genotype aa survive for every 100 individuals with genotype Aa (the heterozygote). Selection is for the heterozygote and against the homozygotes. Figure 3.4 shows how this works. In this example, the initial frequency of the a allele is set at 0.01. Note that the frequency of the allele increases rapidly at first, but stops increasing after a certain point and levels off at a frequency of about 0.27.

This is the expected pattern when there is selection for the heterozygote. A balance is reached between selection for and against the A and a alleles. The exact value of this balancing point will depend on the fitness values of the homozygous genotypes. Selection for the heterozygote is also called

FIGURE 3.4

Changes over time in the frequency of an allele (a) when there is selection for the heterozygote (Aa). The fitness values of the genotypes are $AA = 70$ percent, $Aa = 100$ percent, and $aa = 20$ percent. The initial frequency of the a allele is 0.01.

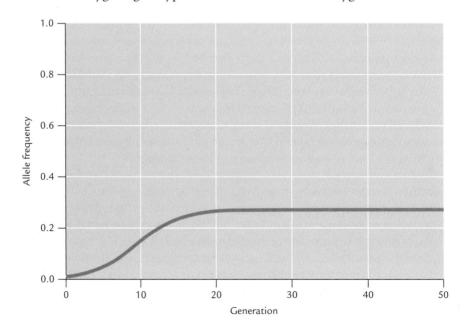

balancing selection. Given this model, the distribution of sickle cell allele frequencies in humans makes sense. In many environments, there is selection against the sickle cell homozygote, and the frequency is low. In environments in which malaria is common, the heterozygotes have an advantage because they are less susceptible to malaria. People homozygous for the sickle cell allele are likely to suffer from sickle cell anemia. People homozygous for the normal allele are more likely to suffer from malaria. Thus, there is selection against both homozygotes (although more selection against those with sickle cell anemia) and selection for the heterozygote. A balance of allele frequencies is predicted and has been found in many human populations. A more complete discussion of the sickle cell example is given in Chapter 15.

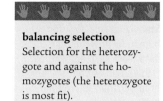

balancing selection
Selection for the heterozygote and against the homozygotes (the heterozygote is most fit).

Selection and Complex Traits   The previous examples used simple genetic traits to illustrate basic principles of natural selection. Selection also affects complex traits, however, such as those discussed in Chapter 2. For complex traits, we focus on measures of the average value and on variation around this average. Because complex traits are continuous, we look at the effects of selection on the average value of a trait and on the lower and higher extremes.

There are several forms of selection on complex traits. **Stabilizing selection** refers to selection against both extremes of a trait's range in values. Individuals with extreme high or low values of a trait are less likely to survive and reproduce, and those with values closer to the average are more likely to survive and reproduce. The effect of stabilizing selection is to maintain the population at the same average value over time. Extreme values are selected against in each generation, but the average value in the population does not change.

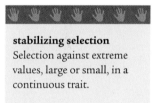

stabilizing selection
Selection against extreme values, large or small, in a continuous trait.

Human birth weight is a good example of stabilizing selection. The weight of a newborn child is the result of a number of environmental factors, such as mother's age, weight, and history of smoking, among many others. There is also a genetic component to birth weight. Newborns who are very small (less than 2.5 kg) are less likely to survive than are newborns who are heavier. Very small babies are more prone to disease and have weaker systems, making their survival more difficult. Newborns who are too large are also likely to be selected against, because a very large child may cause complications during childbirth and both mother and child may die. Thus, there is selection against both extremes, small and large.

Stabilizing selection for birth weight has been documented for a number of human populations. These studies show a definite relationship between birth weight and mortality. The results of one study based on 13,730 newborns (Karn and Penrose 1951) are shown in Figure 3.5. Mortality rates are highest for those newborns with low and high birth weights.

Another type of selection for complex traits is known as **directional selection,** selection against one extreme and/or for the other extreme. In other words, a direct relationship exists between survival and reproduction on the one hand and the value of a trait on the other. The result is a change over time in one direction. The average value for a trait moves in one direction or the other. Perhaps the most dramatic example of directional selection in human evolution has been the threefold increase in brain size over the past

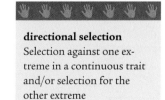

directional selection
Selection against one extreme in a continuous trait and/or selection for the other extreme

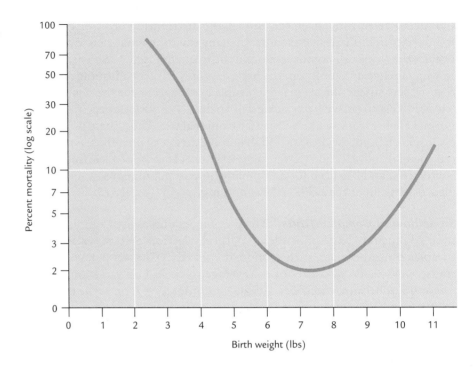

4 several million years. Another example is the lighter skin that evolved in prehistoric humans as they moved north out of Africa (see Chapter 15).

Genetic Drift

genetic drift A mechanism for evolutionary change resulting from the random fluctuations of gene frequencies from one generation to the next.

Genetic drift is the random change in allele frequency from one generation to the next. These random changes are the result of the nature of probability. Think for a moment about flipping a coin. What is the probability of its landing with the head facing up? It is 50 percent. The coin has two possible values, heads and tails, and when you flip it, you will get one or the other. Suppose you flip a coin 10 times. How many heads and how many tails can you expect to get? Because the probability of getting a head or a tail is 50 percent, you expect to get five heads and five tails. Try this experiment several times. Do you always get five tails and five heads? No. Sometimes you get five heads and five tails, but sometimes you get different numbers. You may get six heads and four tails, or three heads and seven tails, or, much less likely, all heads.

The probability for different numbers of heads from flipping a coin 10 times is shown in Figure 3.6. The probability of getting all heads is rather low—a little less than 0.1 percent of the time (about 1 in 1,000 times). Note, however, that the probability of getting four heads and six tails (or six heads and four tails) is much higher—almost 21 percent of the time. Also note that you can expect exactly five heads and five tails about 25 percent of the time. This means that there is roughly a 75 percent chance of *not* getting exactly five heads and five tails.

The probability of 50 percent heads and 50 percent tails is the expected distribution. If you flip 10 coins enough times, you will find that the number

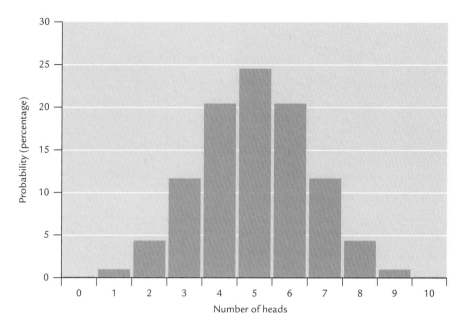

FIGURE 3.6

The probability (in percentages) of flipping a coin 10 times and getting different numbers of heads.

of heads and tails grows closer to a 50:50 ratio. Often, we hear about the "law of averages." The idea here is that if you flip a coin and get heads several times in a row, then you are very likely to get a tail the next time. This is wrong, and applying this "law" is an easy way to lose money if you gamble. *Each* flip of the coin is an independent event. Whatever happened the time before cannot affect the next flip. *Each* time you flip the coin, you have a 50 percent chance of getting a head and a 50 percent chance of getting a tail.

What does all this have to do with genetics? The reproductive process in this way is like a coin toss. During the process of sex cell replication (meiosis), only one allele out of two at a given locus is used. The probability of either allele being passed on is 50 percent, just like a coin toss. Imagine a locus with two alleles, *A* and *a*. Now imagine a man and a woman, each with genotype *Aa,* who have a child. The man can pass on either an *A* allele or an *a* allele. Likewise, the woman can pass on either an *A* allele or an *a* allele. As we saw in the previous chapter, the probable distribution of genotypes among the children is 25 percent *AA,* 50 percent *Aa,* and 25 percent *aa.* If the couple has four children, you would expect one with *AA,* two with *Aa,* and one with *aa.* Thanks to random chance, however, the couple may get a different distribution of genotypes.

When genetic drift occurs in populations, the same principle applies. Allele frequencies can change because of random chance. Sometimes the allele frequency will increase, and sometimes it will decrease. The direction of allele frequency change caused by genetic drift is random. The only time drift will not produce a change in allele frequency is when only one allele is present at a given locus.

Genetic drift occurs in each generation. Such a process is too complicated to simulate using coins, but computers or random number tables can be used to model the effects of drift over time (see Cavalli-Sforza and Bodmer 1971:389). Figure 3.7 shows the results of three computer simulations of

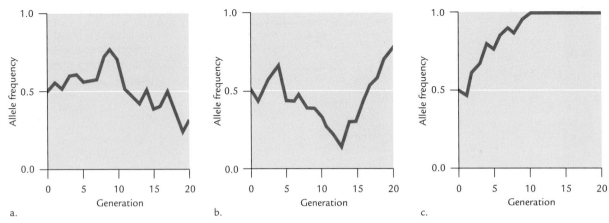

FIGURE 3.7

Three computer simulations of 20 generations of genetic drift for populations of 10 individuals. Each simulation started with an initial allele frequency of 0.5.

drift. In each case, the initial allele frequency was 0.5, and the population size was equal to 10 individuals (20 alleles) in each generation. The simulation was allowed to continue in each case for 20 generations. The graphs show the changes in allele frequency over time. Note that each of the three simulations shows a different pattern. This is to be expected because genetic drift is a random process. Each simulation is an independent event.

In each of these three graphs, the allele frequency fluctuates up and down. In Figure 3.7a, the allele frequency after 20 generations is 0.3. In Figure 3.7b, the allele frequency after 20 generations is 0.75. In Figure 3.7c, the allele frequency is equal to 1.0 after 10 generations, and it does not change any further. Given enough time, and assuming no other evolutionary forces affecting allele frequencies, genetic drift will ultimately lead to an allele's becoming fixed at a value of 0.0 or 1.0. Thus, genetic drift leads to the reduction of variation within a population, given enough time.

Population Size and Genetic Drift   The effect of genetic drift depends on the size of the breeding population. The larger the population size, the less change will occur from one generation to the next. Thinking back to the coin toss analogy will show you that this makes sense. If you flip a coin 10 times and get three heads and seven tails, it is not that unusual. If you flip a coin 1 million times, however, you will be much less likely to get the same proportions—300,000 heads and 700,000 tails. This is because of a basic principle of probability: the greater the number of events, the fewer deviations from the expected frequencies (50 percent heads and 50 percent tails).

The effect of population size on genetic drift is shown in Figure 3.8. These graphs show the results of 1,000 simulations of genetic drift for four different values of breeding population size: $N = 10, 50, 100, 1,000$. In each computer run, the initial allele frequency was set to 0.5, and the simulation was allowed to continue for 20 generations. The four graphs show the distribution of allele frequency values after 20 generations of genetic drift. Figure 3.8a shows this distribution for a population size of $N = 10$. Note that the majority of the 1,000 simulations resulted in final allele frequencies of less than 0.1 or greater than 0.9. In small populations, genetic drift more often results in a quick loss of one allele or another. Figure 3.8b shows the distribution of final

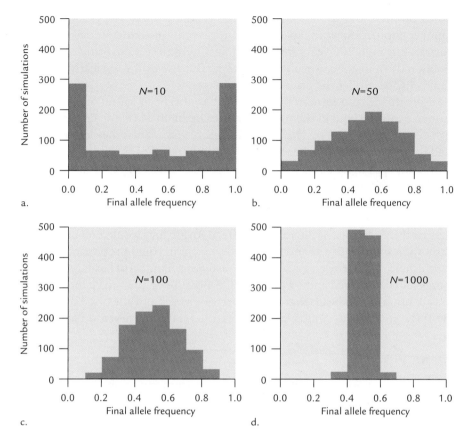

FIGURE 3.8

Allele frequency distributions for 1,000 computer simulations of 20 generations of genetic drift. The distributions show the number of times a given allele frequency was reached after 20 generations of drift. In all cases, the initial allele frequency was 0.5. Each graph represents a different value of population size: (a) = 10, (b) = 50, (c) = 100, (d) = 1,000.

allele frequencies for a population size of $N = 50$. Here there are fewer extreme values and more values falling between 0.3 and 0.7. Figures 3.8c and 3.8d show the distributions for population sizes of $N = 100$ and $N = 1,000$. As these graphs show, the larger the population size, the fewer deviations in allele frequency caused by genetic drift. The main point here is that genetic drift has the greatest evolutionary effect in relatively small breeding populations.

Examples of Genetic Drift Genetic drift in human populations is shown in a case study of a group known as the Dunkers, a religious sect that emigrated from Germany to the United States in the early 1700s. Approximately 50 families composed the initial group. Glass (1953) studied the genetic characteristics of the descendants of the original founding group living in Pennsylvania. These populations have never been greater than several hundred people and thus provide a unique opportunity to study genetic drift in a small human group. Glass found that the Dunker population differed in a number of genetic traits from both the modern German and U.S. populations. Further, the allele frequencies of Germany and the United States were almost identical, suggesting that other factors such as natural selection were unlikely. For example, the allele frequencies for the MN blood group were roughly $M = 0.55$ and $N = 0.45$ for both the U.S. and German samples. In the Dunker population, however, the allele frequencies were $M = 0.655$ and $N = 0.345$.

Based on these and additional data, Glass concluded that the genetics of the Dunker population was shaped to a large extent by genetic drift over two centuries. Although 200 years may seem like a long time to you and me, it is a fraction of an instant in evolutionary time. Genetic drift can clearly produce rapid changes under the proper circumstances.

Genetic drift in human populations has also been found on Tristan da Cunha, a small island in the south Atlantic Ocean. In 1816, the English established a small garrison on the island (Roberts 1968). When they left, one man and his wife remained, to be joined later by a handful of other settlers. Given such a small number of original settlers, what do you suppose is the probability that the families represented all the genetic variation present in the population they came from? The probability would be very low. Genetic drift is often caused when a small number of founders form a new population; this type of genetic drift is known as the **founder effect.** An analogy would be a barrel containing thousands of red and blue beads, mixed in equal proportions. If you reached into the barrel and randomly pulled out a handful of beads, you might not get 50 percent red and 50 percent blue. Because of random chance, founders are not likely to be an exact genetic representation of the original population. The smaller the number of founders, the greater the deviation will be.

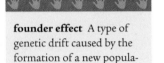

founder effect A type of genetic drift caused by the formation of a new population by a small number of individuals.

Gene Flow

gene flow A mechanism for evolutionary change resulting from the movement of genes from one population to another.

The fourth evolutionary force is **gene flow,** the movement of alleles from one population to another. The term *migration* is often used to mean the same thing as gene flow, although this is not completely accurate. Migration refers to the more or less permanent movement of individuals from one place to another. Why the confusion? After all, excepting artificial insemination, your alleles do not move unless you do. You can migrate, though, without passing on any alleles. You can also be involved in gene flow without actually making a permanent move to a new place. In many texts on microevolution, the terms *gene flow* and *migration* are used interchangeably. Keep in mind, however, that there are certain distinctions in the real world.

Genetic Effects of Gene Flow   Gene flow involves the movement of alleles between at least two populations. When gene flow occurs, the two populations mix genetically and tend to become more similar. Under most conditions, the more the two populations mix, the more similar they will become genetically (assuming that the two environments are not different enough to produce different effects of natural selection).

Consider a genetic locus with two alleles, *A* and *a*. Assume two populations, 1 and 2. Now assume that all the alleles in population 1 are *A* and all the alleles in population 2 are *a*. The allele frequencies of these two imaginary populations are:

Population 1	*Population 2*
Frequency of *A* = 1.0	Frequency of *A* = 0.0
Frequency of *a* = 0.0	Frequency of *a* = 1.0

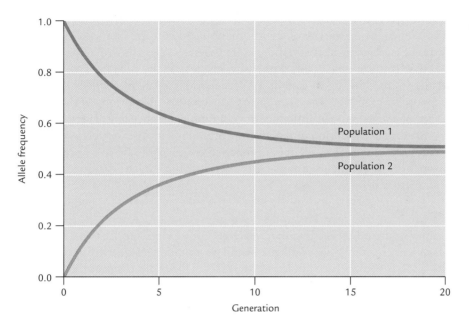

FIGURE 3.9

Effects of gene flow over time. Population 1 started with an allele frequency of 1.0, and population 2 started with an allele frequency of 0.0. The two populations exchanged 10 percent of their genes in each generation. Over time, the continued gene flow acts to make the two populations more similar genetically.

Now imagine a situation in which 10 percent of the people in population 1 move to population 2, and vice versa. This movement constitutes gene flow. What effect will the gene flow have? After gene flow has taken place, population 1 is made up of 90 percent *A* alleles and 10 percent *a* alleles. Population 2 is made up of 10 percent *A* alleles and 90 percent *a* alleles. The allele frequencies of the two populations, though still different, have become more similar as a consequence of gene flow. If the same rate of gene flow (10 percent) continues generation after generation, the two populations will become more and more similar genetically. After 20 generations of gene flow, the two populations will be almost identical. The accumulated effects of gene flow over time for this hypothetical example are shown in Figure 3.9.

Apart from making populations more similar, gene flow can also introduce new variation within a population. In the example, a new allele (*a*) was introduced into population 1 as the result of gene flow. A new mutation arising in one population can be spread throughout the rest of a species by gene flow.

Compared to many other organisms, humans are relatively mobile creatures. Human populations show a great deal of variation in degree of migration. Even today, many humans live and work within a small area and choose mates from nearby. Some people are more mobile than others with the extent of their mobility depending on a number of factors, such as available technology, occupation, and income.

In spite of local and regional differences, humans today all belong to the same species. Even though genetic variation exists among populations, they are in fact characterized more by their similarity. A critical factor in the cohesiveness of the human species, gene flow acts to reduce differences among groups.

What Affects Gene Flow?   The amount of gene flow between human populations depends on a variety of environmental and cultural factors. Geographic distance is a major determinant of migration and gene flow. The farther two populations are apart geographically, the less likely they are to exchange mates. Even in the highly mobile modern world, you are more likely to choose a spouse from nearby than from across the country. Exceptions to the rule do occur, of course, but the influence of geographic distance is still very strong.

Studies of migration and gene flow often look at distance between birthplaces or premarital residences of married couples. If, say, you were born in New York City and your spouse was born in Chicago, the distance between your birthplaces would be 810 miles. If both you and your spouse came from the same neighborhood in the same city, your marital distance would be close to zero. The relationship between migration and geographic distance is similar in most human populations (Relethford 1992). Most marriages take place within a few miles, and the number of marriages quickly decreases as the distance between populations increases. This indicates that the majority of genes flowing into human populations come from a local area, and a small proportion from farther distances.

An example of the relationship between the frequency of marriages and geographic distance is shown in Figure 3.10. This graph presents the results of a historical study of migration into the town of Leominster, Massachusetts, using marriage records for 1800–1849. A total of 1,066 marriages took place in the population over the 50-year period. Of these, over half (58.2 percent) were between a bride and groom who lived within 5 miles of each other. An additional 15.4 percent of the marriages took place between couples who lived between 5 and 10 miles of each other before marriage. Note that the percentage of marriages decreases quickly with distance. Also note that over 4 percent of the couples came from locales over 50 miles apart. This type of long-range migration acts to keep populations from diverging too much from the rest of the species.

Geographic distance is a major determinant of human migration and gene flow, but it is not the only one. Ethnic differences also act to limit them. Most large cities have distinct neighborhoods that correspond to different ethnic communities. A large proportion of marriages takes place within these groups because of the common human preference for marrying within one's own social and cultural group. Likewise, religious differences act as barriers to gene flow because many, though not all, people prefer to marry within the same religion. Social class and educational differences can also limit gene flow.

Interaction of the Evolutionary Forces

It is convenient to discuss each of the four evolutionary forces separately, but in reality, they act together to produce allele frequency change. Mutation acts to introduce new genetic variants; natural selection, genetic drift, and gene flow act to change the frequency of the mutant allele. Sometimes the evolutionary forces act together, and sometimes they act in opposition. Their exact interaction depends on a variety of factors, such as the biochemical and

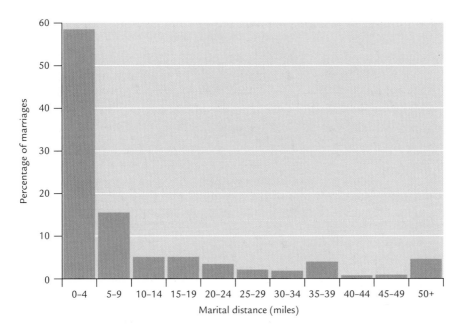

FIGURE 3.10

Percentage of marriages taking place at various marital distances (the distance between the premarital residences of bride and groom) for the town of Leominster, Massachusetts, 1800–1849. (*Source:* author's unpublished data.)

physical effects of different alleles, the presence or absence of dominance, population size and distribution, and the environment, to name but a few. Many biological anthropologists attempt to unravel some of these factors in human population studies.

In general, we look at how natural selection, genetic drift, and gene flow act to increase or decrease genetic variation within and between groups. An increase in variation within a population means that individuals within the population will be more genetically different from one another. A decrease in variation within a population means the reverse: Individuals will become more similar to one another genetically. An increase in variation among populations means that two or more populations will become more different from one another genetically, and a decrease in variation within populations means the reverse.

Genetic drift tends to remove alleles from a population and therefore acts to reduce variation within a population. On the other hand, because genetic drift is a random event and occurs independently in different populations, the pattern of genetic drift tends to be different on average in different populations. On average, then, genetic drift acts to increase variation between populations. Gene flow acts to introduce new alleles into a population and can have the effect of increasing variation within a population. Gene flow also acts to reduce variation between populations in most cases.

Natural selection can either increase or decrease variation within a population, depending on the specific type of selection and the initial allele frequencies. Selection against recessive homozygotes, for example, will lead to the gradual decrease of one allele and consequently reduce variation. Selection for an advantageous mutation, however, will result in an increase in the frequency of the mutant allele and act to increase variation within the population. Selection can also either increase or decrease variation between populations, depending on environmental variation. If two populations have

TABLE 3.3   Summary of the Effects of Natural Selection, Genetic Drift, and Gene Flow on Variation within and among Populations

Evolutionary Force	Variation within Populations	Variation between Populations
Natural selection	Increase or decrease	Increase or decrease
Genetic drift	Decrease	Increase
Gene flow	Increase	Decrease

A decrease in variation within a population makes individuals more similar to one another, whereas an increase in variation within a population makes individuals less similar to one another. A decrease in variation among populations makes the populations more similar to one another, whereas an increase in variation among populations makes the populations less similar to one another. Note that natural selection can either increase or decrease variation; the exact effect depends on the type of selection and on differences in environment.

similar environments, then natural selection will take place in the same way in both groups and so will act to reduce genetic differences between them. On the other hand, if the two populations are in different enough environments that natural selection operates in different ways, then variation between the populations may be increased. Table 3.3 summarizes the effects of different evolutionary forces on variation within and among populations.

Different evolutionary forces can produce the same or opposite effects. Different forces can also act in opposition to one another. Genetic drift and gene flow, for example, have opposite effects on variation within and between populations. If both of these forces operate at the same time, they can counteract each other.

Several examples will help illustrate the ways in which different evolutionary forces can interact. Consider the forces of mutation and genetic drift. How might these two forces interact? Mutation acts to change allele frequency by the introduction of a new allele, whereas genetic drift causes random fluctuations in allele frequency from one generation to the next. If both operate at the same time, drift may act to increase or decrease the frequency of the new mutation. Most of the time, the random nature of genetic drift will result in the quick loss of a new mutant allele, because, by chance, it may not be passed on to the next generation. In some cases, however, drift will rapidly increase the frequency of a mutant allele, again by chance.

Many other possibilities for interaction also exist. For example, natural selection reduces the frequency of a harmful recessive mutant allele. Gene flow tends to counter the effects of genetic drift on variation among populations. Genetic drift can increase the frequency of a harmful allele even if it is being selected against.

Studies of actual populations must take these interactions into account and try to control for them in analysis. There are some basic rules for interpreting genetic variation. If populations are large, then drift is unlikely to have much of an effect. Gene flow can be measured to some extent by looking at migration rates to determine how powerful an effect it would have. Natural selection can be investigated by looking at patterns of fertility and mortality among different classes of genotypes.

Imagine that you have visited a population over two generations, and you note that the frequency of a certain allele has changed from 0.4 to 0.5. Further, assume that the population has been totally isolated during the last generation and that the size of the breeding population has stayed at roughly 50 people. What could have caused the allele frequency change? Because mutation occurs at much lower rates, it could not be responsible. Given that the population was totally isolated, gene flow could not be responsible. Drift may have caused the change in allele frequency, for the size of the breeding population is rather low. Natural selection could also have produced the change. You would have to know more about the specific alleles and genotypes involved, environmental factors, and patterns of mortality and fertility to determine whether selection had an effect. Even given this rather limited information, you can rule out mutation and gene flow and proceed to develop tests to determine the relative influence of drift and selection.

The study of any natural population is much more complex. With laboratory animals, you can control for a variety of factors to help your analysis. In dealing with human populations, however, you must rely on observations as they occur in nature.

Summary

The study of microevolution looks at changes in the frequencies of alleles from one generation to the next. Such analyses allow detailed examination of the factors that can alter allele frequencies in the short term and also provide us with inferences about long-term patterns of evolution. Changes in allele frequencies stem from four evolutionary forces: mutation, natural selection, genetic drift, and gene flow.

Mutation is the ultimate source of all genetic variation, but it occurs at low enough rates that additional factors are needed to explain polymorphic frequencies (whereby two or more alleles have frequencies greater than 0.01). The other three evolutionary forces are responsible for increasing or decreasing the frequency of a mutant allele. Natural selection changes allele frequencies through the process of differential survival and reproduction of individuals having certain genotypes. Genetic drift, the random change in allele frequencies from one generation to the next, has the greatest effect in small populations. Gene flow, the movement of alleles between populations, acts to reduce genetic differences between different groups.

Supplemental Readings

Hartl, D. L., and A. G. Clark. 2006. *Principles of Population Genetics,* 4th ed. Sunderland, Mass.: Sinauer. A comprehensive and advanced treatment of population genetics.
Relethford, J. H. 2012. *Human Population Genetics.* Hoboken, NJ: Wiley-Blackwell. An introduction to population genetics that includes case studies from human populations.

Skeleton of *Tyrannosaurus,* a dinosaur that lived over 65 million years ago. The study of long-term evolution, or macroevolution, focuses on the origin and evolution of new species (and their extinction).

The Evolution and Classification of Species

Little things add up over time.
     When we stop to take a close look at the world, we see many examples of change accumulating over time, sometimes slowly, and sometimes rapidly. For example, we can see the steady process of erosion altering the landscape, or a flood washing away a riverbank. As the years pass, even small changes in the physical world can add up to produce major change, something that early geologists such as Hutton and Lyell (Chapter 1) realized when developing the concept of uniformitarianism. Likewise, the evolutionary forces described in the last chapter act generation after generation and can produce dramatic evolutionary change even within relatively short intervals of time (on a geologic scale)—macroevolution.

     When so-called creation scientists dispute evolution, they generally mean macroevolution. Few doubt the existence of short-term, microevolutionary changes; we can see such changes in our daily lives, from changing patterns of disease to the kinds of alterations brought about by animal and plant breeding. The long-term pattern of evolution, including the origin and evolution of species, is generally more difficult to grasp. Creationism argues that we cannot directly observe changes over millions of years and therefore cannot conduct scientific tests. It is true that we cannot undertake laboratory tests lasting for millions of years, but we can still make scientific predictions. Many sciences, including geology and astronomy, are historical in nature. That is, we rely on some record—geologic strata or stellar configurations, for example—to note what has happened. We can establish the facts of change. The same is true of macroevolution. The fossil record provides us with information about *what* has happened. We must then utilize other information available to us to determine *why* such change occurred. Geology makes use of the fact that geologic processes occur in a regular manner and so occurred in the same way in ancient times; that is, available information about current geologic processes helps explain patterns of change in the past. In much the same way, evolutionary science takes what we know about microevolution and extends it to explain the long-term pattern of macroevolution.

     This chapter deals with three related aspects of the central focus of macroevolution—the origin and evolution of species. In addition to outlining the nature of species and the process by which species change over time (including the birth and death of species), we examine several common misconceptions about how macroevolution works and discuss the relationship between macroevolutionary change and the classification of living organisms.

THE BIRTH AND DEATH OF SPECIES

The origin of new species has been observed in historical times and in the present. Some new species have been brought about by human intervention and controlled breeding; examples include many species of tropical fish. New species have also arisen naturally in the recent past, such as certain types of fruit flies. In addition, we have information on populations in the process of forming new species, such as certain groups of snails. We also have seen (and contributed to) many examples of extinction—the death of a species.

How do new species come into being? Why do some species die out? Even though the title of his book is *On the Origin of Species,* ironically, Charles Darwin did not focus much on this question. Instead, he sought to explain the basic nature of evolutionary change, believing that extension of these principles could explain the formation of new species.

What Is a Species?

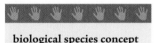

biological species concept
A definition of species that focuses on reproductive capabilities, whereby organisms from different populations are considered to be in the same species if they naturally interbreed and produce fertile offspring.

The term *species* is used in a number of different ways in evolutionary biology (Ereshefsky 1992). One common use is the **biological species concept,** which defines species in terms of reproductive capability. If organisms from two populations are capable of breeding naturally and can produce fertile offspring, then they are classified in the same species. Note that this definition has several parts. First, organisms from different populations must be capable of interbreeding. Second, these matings must occur in nature. Organisms that breed together in zoos, such as lions and tigers, are still considered separate species because they do not breed together *in nature.* In understanding evolutionary history, we are interested in breeding that takes place naturally. Third, the offspring must be *fertile,* that is, capable of producing further offspring.

Perhaps the best-known example of an application of the biological species concept is the mule. Mules are farm animals produced as the offspring of a horse bred with a donkey. The horse and donkey interbreed naturally, which satisfies the first and second parts of the species definition. However, the offspring (mules) are sterile and cannot produce further offspring. The only way to get a mule is to mate a horse and a donkey. Because the offspring are not fertile, the horse and the donkey are considered separate species (Figure 4.1). All human populations around the world belong to the same species (*Homo sapiens*) because members can interbreed and produce fertile offspring.

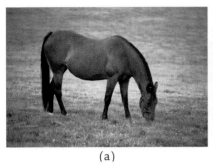
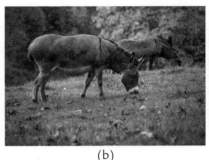
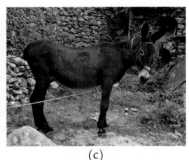

(a)   (b)   (c)

FIGURE 4.1

Illustration of different species using the biological species concept. The horse (a) and donkey (b) are considered separate species because even though they can interbreed their offspring, mules (c), are sterile.

The biological species concept assumes that two organisms either belong or do not belong to the same species. It does not allow for any kind of intermediate state. Why should this be a problem? Consider two modern species that had a common ancestor at some point in the past. We usually draw an evolutionary "tree," showing the point at which a new "branch," or species, came into being (known as a **phylogenetic tree**). If some populations of species A evolved into species B, at what point did those populations stop being species A and start being species B? The species concept suggests that this change was instantaneous, because a creature belongs to either one species or the other. Any system of classification tends to ignore variation within groups. In the real world, however, evolution and variation work to break down rigid systems of classification. Organisms become difficult to classify when they are constantly changing.

Species Change

As outlined above, the biological species concept is useful in comparing two or more populations in the world today. How does the concept of species work when we consider changes in populations over time? There are two different ways of looking at species over time. First, a single species can change over time such that enough differences accumulate that we would choose to give it a different species name. According to this mode of evolutionary change, a single species exists at any given point in time, but evolves over time. This mode of species change is known as **anagenesis,** or straight-line evolution. It is illustrated as a straight line, as shown in Figure 4.2, where form A evolves into form B and then into form C. Although this mode of evolutionary change is fairly straightforward, complications arise when naming species. Should form A be called a different species from form B? The problem is that the traditional biological species concept doesn't really apply. Form A and form B are, by necessity, isolated from each other reproductively because they lived at different times. There is no way they could interbreed any more than you could mate with a human who lived 2 million years ago (we'll leave out science fiction and time machines here).

Many researchers modify the species concept to deal with this situation. Different physical forms along a single lineage (an evolutionary line such as

Species C

Species B

Species A

Time

FIGURE 4.2

Anagenesis, the linear evolution of a species over time. Species A changes over time into species B and then further changes into species C.

phylogenetic tree A diagram showing the evolutionary relationships between species.

anagenesis The transformation of a single species over time.

chronospecies Labels given to different points in the evolutionary lineage of a single species over time. As a species changes over time, the different stages are labeled as chronospecies in recognition of the biological changes that have taken place.

cladogenesis The formation of one or more new species from another over time.

that shown in Figure 4.2) are given different species names out of convenience and as a label to represent the types of physical change shown over time. Such forms are referred to as **chronospecies** and are used as labels for different stages of biological change over time, even though only one species exists at any point in time. As such, the different physical forms illustrated in Figure 4.2 would be labeled as chronospecies A, chronospecies B, and chronospecies C. The important point here is that there is only *one* species at any point in time. As an analogy, consider the different labels given to humans as they grow: "infant," "child," "teenager," and "adult." These labels indicate the different stages of a person's life, but they all refer to the same individual. In evolution, chronospecies are different stages in the evolution of a single evolutionary lineage.

Anagenesis is not the only mode of species change. If you think about it, anagenesis is not completely sufficient as an explanation of macroevolution. Where do new species come from? The other mode of species change is **cladogenesis,** or branching evolution. Cladogenesis involves the formation of new species (speciation) whereby one or more new species branch off from an original species. In Figure 4.3, a portion of species A first branches off to produce species B (living at the same time), then a portion of species B branches off to produce species C. This example starts with one species and ends up with three. The factors responsible for speciation will be discussed later in this chapter.

The problem of species naming is complicated by the fact that evolutionary relationships among fossil forms are not always clear. Some of these problems will be addressed later. For now, keep in mind that species names often mean different things to different people. The naming of species might adhere to an evolutionary model or might serve only as convenient labels of physical variation.

FIGURE 4.3

Cladogenesis, the origin of new species. Species A splits and forms a new species B, which later splits to form species C. The process begins with a single species (A) and ends with three species (A, B, C).

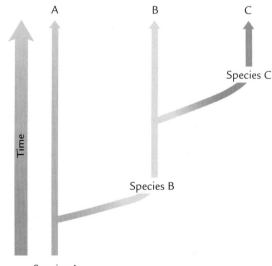

Speciation

The fossil record shows many examples of new species arising through clado-genesis. How does this come about? You know that genetic differences between populations come about as a result of evolutionary forces. For a population to become a new species, these genetic differences must be great enough to prevent successful interbreeding with the original parent species. For this to occur, the population must become reproductively isolated from the original parent species.

Reproductive Isolation   **Reproductive isolation** is genetic change that can lead to an inability to produce fertile offspring. How does this happen? Evolutionary forces can produce such a situation. The first step in **speciation**—the formation of a new species from a parent species—is the elimination or reduction of gene flow between populations. Because gene flow acts to reduce differences between populations, its continued action tends to keep all populations in the same species. Gene flow does not need to be eliminated altogether, but it must be reduced sufficiently to allow other evolutionary forces to make the populations genetically different. Populations must become genetically isolated from one another for speciation to occur.

The most common form of isolation in animal species is geographic isolation. When two populations are separated by a physical barrier, such as a river or mountain range, or by great distances, gene flow is cut off between the populations. As long as the populations remain isolated, genetic changes occurring in one group will not spread to other groups. As we saw in Chapter 3, geographic distance limits gene flow even in our own highly mobile species. The effects of geographic distance in causing reproductive isolation are even more dramatic in other species.

Geographic separation is the most common means of producing reproductive isolation among animal populations, but other mechanisms may also cause isolation. Some of these can operate within a single region. Populations may be isolated by behavioral differences such as feeding habits. Some groups may eat during the day, and others at dusk. Because the groups are not in frequent contact with one another, there is opportunity for isolation to develop.

Genetic Divergence   Isolation is the first step in the speciation process. By itself, this isolation does not guarantee speciation. Reduction of gene flow merely provides the *opportunity* for speciation. Other evolutionary forces must then act upon this isolation to produce a situation in which the isolated groups have changed sufficiently to make fertile interbreeding no longer possible. Isolation, however, does not always lead to speciation.

How can evolutionary forces lead to speciation? Mutation might act to increase variation among populations because it occurs independently in the genetic composition of separate groups. Without gene flow to spread them, individual mutations will accumulate in each group, making isolated

reproductive isolation
The genetic isolation of populations that may render them incapable of producing fertile offspring.

speciation The origin of a new species.

FIGURE 4.4

A simplified view of the process of speciation where two populations become increasingly different genetically over time once gene flow has been eliminated or reduced.

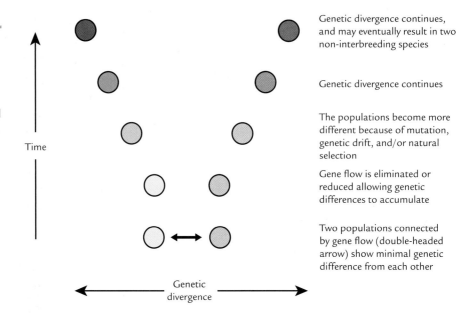

Genetic divergence continues, and may eventually result in two non-interbreeding species

Genetic divergence continues

The populations become more different because of mutation, genetic drift, and/or natural selection

Gene flow is eliminated or reduced allowing genetic differences to accumulate

Two populations connected by gene flow (double-headed arrow) show minimal genetic difference from each other

Time

Genetic divergence

populations genetically divergent. Genetic drift also contributes to differences in allele frequencies among small populations. In addition, if the two populations are in separate environments, then natural selection will lead to genetic differences. Once gene flow has been eliminated, the other evolutionary forces will act to make the populations genetically divergent. When this process continues to the point at which the two populations can no longer interbreed and produce fertile offspring, they have become separate species (Figure 4.4).

It may be tempting to consider speciation as a slow and gradual process, but the fossil record shows us that there are times when evolutionary change is slow, and times when it is fast (in geologic terms). Different models have been proposed for dealing with the tempo of macroevolution (see Box 4.1).

Adaptive Radiation

The process of speciation minimally results in two species: the original parent species and the new offspring species. Under certain circumstances, many new species can come into being in a short period of time. This rapid diversification of species is associated with changing environmental conditions. When new environments open up or when new adaptations to a specific environment develop, many new species can form—a process known as **adaptive radiation.**

An example of adaptive radiation is the Darwin finches mentioned in Chapter 1. All of the finch species that Charles Darwin observed descended from a single original finch species. The availability of new environmental niches led to the rapid speciation of finches in the Galapagos Islands.

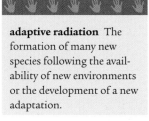

adaptive radiation The formation of many new species following the availability of new environments or the development of a new adaptation.

BOX 4.1

Punctuated Equilibrium

How fast do new species form? How fast does macroevolution take place? These questions continue to be debated. Charles Darwin saw much of evolution and speciation as a relatively slow and gradual process that could take thousands or millions of years. To Darwin, natural selection acted on populations slowly, ultimately producing new species. The view that macroevolution is a slow and gradual process is called **gradualism.** According to this view, small changes in each generation over time result in major biological changes, and speciation is a slow, lengthy process in which new species form from large portions of an original species.

An alternative hypothesis has been suggested known as **punctuated equilibrium** (Eldredge and Gould 1972; Gould and Eldredge 1977). This hypothesis suggests that the pattern of macroevolution consists of long periods when little evolutionary change occurs (stasis, or equilibrium), broken up by short periods of rapid evolutionary change. According to Eldredge and Gould, the tempo of macroevolution is not gradual; rather, it is static at times and rapid at other times. Eldredge and Gould also view speciation as a rapid event occurring within small, isolated populations on the periphery of a species range. Mutations can spread quickly in small populations because of inbreeding and genetic drift. If such genetic changes are adaptive, and if the newly formed species gains access to the parental species' range, it may then spread throughout an area, replacing the original parent species. According to this model, most biological change occurs during speciation. Once a species has been established, it changes little throughout time. Eldredge and Gould argue that stabilizing selection and other factors act to keep a species the same over time. This view contrasts with the gradual model, which sees biological change occurring at a slow rate, ultimately leading to new species. Punctuated equilibrium makes a prediction about how the fossil record should look. Given stasis, we should see long periods when little evolutionary change takes place. Many examples of stasis have been found in the fossil record (Futuyma 2009).

Although the claim of stasis has been widely accepted, there are also examples of gradual change (Futuyma 2009) so that punctuated equilibrium is not universal. In addition, other parts of the model of punctuated equilibrium have been critiqued. Perhaps the most contentious claim made originally by Eldredge and Gould was that most major changes in physical morphology took place during speciation. In their original view, speciation was the trigger for morphological change. Later, they realized this was not the case (e.g., Gould 2002). In fact, we now recognize that the pattern of periods of stasis punctuated by rapid shifts in morphology can occur *within* species, a phenomenon known as "punctuated gradualism" (Futuyma 2009).

The main lesson to keep in mind with this discussion of gradual versus rapid change is that we are using such terms relative to *geologic* time, where a period of several thousand years is often but a brief moment in a span of dates that we might be looking at in the fossil record. A shift in morphology over time, such as an increase in tooth size, can be relatively slow when looked at from generation to generation but appear very rapid when looked at in intervals of thousands of years in the fossil record.

Another example is the adaptive radiation of major mammalian groups that took place between 45 and 65 million years ago (Figure 4.5).

Extinctions and Mass Extinctions

In considering macroevolutionary trends, we must not forget the most common pattern of all—extinction (Figure 4.6). It is estimated that more than 99 percent of all species that ever existed have become extinct (Futuyma 1986). In historical times, humans have witnessed (and helped cause) the extinction of a number of organisms.

What causes extinction? When a species is no longer adapted to a changed environment, it may die. The exact causes of a species' death vary from situation to situation. Rapid ecological change may render an environment hostile to a species. For example, temperatures may change and a species may not

gradualism A model of macroevolutionary change whereby changes occur at a slow, steady rate over time.

punctuated equilibrium A model of macroevolutionary change in which long periods of little evolutionary change (stasis) are followed by relatively short periods of rapid evolutionary change.

(a)

(b)

(c)

(d)

(e)

FIGURE 4.5

Examples of mammalian diversity. The origin of modern groups of mammals all took place in a relatively short period of time (about 45 to 65 million years ago), representing an example of adaptive radiation. (a) Bat, (b) Whale, (c) Squirrel, (d) Zebra, (e) Baboon.

be able to adapt. Food resources may be affected by environmental changes, which will then cause problems for a species requiring these resources. Other species may become better adapted to an environment, resulting in competition and, ultimately, the death of a species.

FIGURE 4.6

Artist's reconstruction of a wooly mammoth, a species that became extinct about 10,000 years ago.

FIGURE 4.7

Artist's reconstruction of an asteroid hitting the earth, the likely cause of a mass extinction event that took place 65.5 million years ago.

Extinction seems, in fact, to be the ultimate fate of all species. Natural selection is a remarkable mechanism for providing species with the ability to adapt to change, but it does not always work. When the environment changes too rapidly or when the appropriate genetic variations do not exist, a species can become extinct.

The fossil record shows that extinction has occurred throughout the history of the planet. Recent analysis has also revealed that on some occasions a large number of species became extinct at the same time—a **mass extinction.** The fossil record documents five mass extinctions in the history of our planet (and some suggesting that we are currently in a period of extinction that might be the sixth). One of the best-known examples occurred 65 million years ago when an asteroid hit the planet, altering the environment and causing the extinction of an estimated 76 percent of all then-living species, including dinosaurs (Figure 4.7). The most severe mass extinction took place 251 million years ago and resulted in the extinction of 96 percent of species (Barnosky et al. 2011). Mass extinctions can be caused by a relatively rapid change in the environment, compounded by the close interrelationship of many species. If, for example, something were to happen to destroy much of the plankton in the oceans, then the oxygen content of our planet would drop, affecting even organisms not living in the oceans. Such a change would probably lead to a mass extinction.

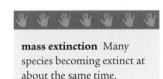

mass extinction Many species becoming extinct at about the same time.

MISCONCEPTIONS ABOUT EVOLUTION

Evolution is a frequently misunderstood subject. Many of our basic ideas regarding evolution are misconceptions that have become part of the general culture. The often-used phrase "survival of the fittest" conjures up images that are sometimes at odds with the actual findings of evolutionary science. Such misconceptions may continue even after initial exposure to evolutionary theory.

The Nature of Selection

Many people have a basic understanding of the general principles of natural selection. The problem lies in their misinterpretation of the nature of selection.

Misconception: Bigger Is Better   A common misconception is that natural selection will *always* lead to larger structures. According to this idea, the bigger the brain and the bigger the body, the better. At first, this idea seems reasonable. After all, larger individuals may be more likely to survive because they can compete more successfully for food and mates, and pass their genes on to the next generation. Natural selection is expected to lead to an increase in the size of the body, brain, and other structures. However, this isn't always true. There are numerous examples of species in which *smaller* body size or structures were more adaptive. Keep in mind that in evolution nothing is free. A larger body may be more adaptive because of sheer size, but a larger body also has greater energy needs. Any advantage gained by a larger body may be offset by the disadvantage of needing more food. What we have to focus on is a *balance* between the adaptive and nonadaptive aspects of any biological characteristic. By walking upright, humans have their hands free, which is rather advantageous. However, we pay the price with varicose veins, back pain, fallen arches, and other nonadaptive consequences of walking on two legs. Again, we need to focus on the relative costs and benefits of any evolutionary change. Of course, this balance will vary in different environments.

Misconception: Newer Is Better   When we buy new products, such as televisions and cars, we tend to prefer the newer, up-to-date models (Figure 4.8). The idea of "newer is better" can certainly apply to much technology, but we must be careful not to extend this analogy to the natural world. If we do so, we might assume that traits more recent in origin are superior because they are newer. Humans walk on two legs, a trait that appeared close to 6 million years ago. We also have five digits (fingers and toes) that date back many hundreds of millions of years. Is upright walking better because it is newer? Of course not. Both features are essential to our toolmaking way of life. The age of a structure has no bearing on its usefulness.

Misconception: Natural Selection Always Works   The idea that natural selection will always provide an opportunity for some members of a species to survive is not accurate. Occasionally, I hear statements such as "we will evolve to tolerate air pollution." Such statements are absurdities. Natural selection operates only on variations that are present. If no genetic variation occurs to aid in breathing polluted air, natural selection will not help us. Even in cases in which genetic variation is present, the environment may change

FIGURE 4.8

A couple looking to buy a new car. There is a tendency to view "newer" as "better." Although this might be true for technology, it is not the case for evolution, where the antiquity of a trait or adaptation is not important; only its effect on overall fitness.

orthogenesis A discredited idea that evolution will continue in a given direction because of some vaguely defined "force."

too quickly for us to respond through natural selection. All we have to do is examine the fossil record to see how inaccurate this misconception is—that 99 percent of all past species are extinct shows us that natural selection obviously doesn't always work!

Misconception: There Is an Inevitable Direction in Evolution An idea popular in the nineteenth century was **orthogenesis,** the notion that evolution would continue in a given direction because of a vaguely defined nonphysical "force" (Mayr 1982). As an alternative to the theory of natural selection, orthogenesis suggested that evolutionary change would continue in the same direction until either a perfect structure was attained or a species became extinct. Apart from the problem of metaphysical "forces," orthogenesis has long been rejected on the basis of analysis of the fossil record and the triumph of natural selection as an explanatory mechanism for evolutionary change. Some of its basic notions, however, are still perpetuated. A common belief is that humans will evolve larger and larger brains, as a continuation of earlier trends (Figure 4.9). The view of orthogenesis is tied in with notions of "progress" and with the misconception that bigger is necessarily better. There are many examples from the fossil record of non-linear change and many examples of reversals in sizes of structures. In the case of human evolution, brains actually stopped getting larger 50,000 years ago. In fact, the average brain size of humans since that time has decreased slightly as a consequence of a general decrease in skeletal size and ruggedness (Henneberg 1988).

Is it possible for a trend to continue in a given direction under the right circumstances? Of course, but change comes through the action of natural

FIGURE 4.9

Illustration of the idea of orthogenesis, which predicts continued change in a given direction. One popular but incorrect notion is that humans in the future will have progressively larger brains.

selection, not through some mysterious internal force. Continuation of any trend depends on the environment, present genetic variation, and basic biological limits. (A 50-foot spider can't exist because it wouldn't be able to absorb enough oxygen for its volume.) Such change also depends on the relative costs and benefits of change. Suppose an increase in human brain size was combined somehow with an increase in pelvic size (assuming genetic variation was present for both features). A larger pelvis would make walking difficult or even impossible. Evolution works on the entire organism, not one trait at a time. Any change can have both positive and negative effects, but it is the net balance that is critical to the operation of natural selection.

Structure, Function, and Evolution

A number of misconceptions about evolution focus on the relationship between biological structures and their adaptive (or nonadaptive) functions.

Misconception: Natural Selection Always Produces Perfect Structures
There is a tendency to view nature as the product of perfect natural engineering. Granted, there are many wondrous phenomena in the natural world, but a closer examination shows that biological structures are often far from perfect. Consider human beings. Is the human body perfect? Hardly. Just to note one aspect, consider your skeleton when you stand upright. What is holding in your internal organs? Skin and muscles. Your rib cage provides little support for lower internal organs because it reflects ancestry from a four-legged form. When humans stood up (adaptive), the rib cage offered less support (Figure 4.10). The result? A variety of complaints and complications, such as hernias. The human skeleton is not perfect but rather is the result of natural selection operating on the variation that was present.

Misconception: All Structures Are Adaptive   Natural selection is such a powerful model that it is tempting to apply it to all biological structures.

FIGURE 4.10

The rib cage in (a) a dog, which is a quadruped, and (b) a human, who is a biped. In quadrupeds, the rib cage provides more support for the internal organs, support that humans have lost to some extent after evolving upright walking.

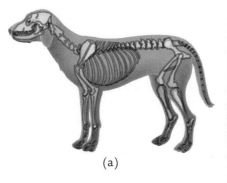

(a)

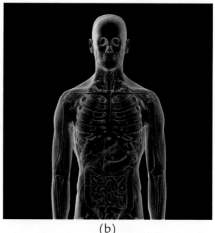

(b)

Indeed, many anthropologists and biologists have done so. They examined a structure and explained its function in terms of natural selection. But are all structures adaptive? Many structures are simply a by-product of other biological changes and have no adaptive value of their own (Gould and Lewontin 1979). Other structures, such as the human appendix, may have served a function in the past but appear to have no present function.

An example involves an old question: Why do human men have nipples? Earlier explanations suggesting that in ancient times men could assist women in breast-feeding are ludicrous. The true explanation is simple. Both males and females develop from the same basic body plan during the embryonic stage of prenatal life. Under the influence of sex hormones, various structures develop in different ways (just as the same structure develops into a penis in men and a clitoris in women). The basic body plan for nipples is present in both sexes; for women, these structures develop into breasts capable of lactation. In men, nipples serve no functional purpose. Thus, male nipples are a by-product of the fact that males and females share a similar developmental path and are not the result of some adaptive value (Gould 1991).

Misconception: Current Structures Always Reflect Initial Adaptations   The idea here is that any given structure, with an associated function, originally evolved specifically for that function (see Figure 4.11). Human beings, for example, walk on two legs; this allows us to hold tools and other objects we constructed with the aid of our enlarged brain. Although it is tempting to say that both upright walking and a larger brain evolved at the same time because of the adaptive value of having both structures, this is not what happened. Upright walking evolved millions of years before the use of stone tools and the expansion of the brain (see Chapter 10).

As another example, consider your fingers. You have five of these digits on each hand, which enables you to perform a variety of manipulative tasks.

FIGURE 4.11

A flightless cormorant, a species that lives in the Galapagos Islands and that has lost the use of its wings for flight. The reduced wings are instead used to help steer when swimming under water.

We use our hands to manipulate both natural and human-made objects. Manipulative digits are essential to our nature as tool-using creatures. We might therefore suggest that our grasping hands *first* evolved to meet this need, but this is not the case. Grasping hands *first* developed in our early primate ancestors to meet the needs of living in trees (see Chapter 9). Even though we don't live in trees, we have retained this trait and use it *for a different purpose*. Natural selection operates on the variation that is present. Structures are frequently modified for different uses.

CLASSIFICATION OF SPECIES

In Chapter 1, you read about Linnaeus's system of classification for all living creatures. Instead of simply making a list of all known organisms, Linnaeus developed a scheme by which creatures could be grouped according to certain shared characteristics. Even though we now make use of Linnaeus's scheme to describe patterns of evolution, Linnaeus himself did not have this objective in mind. Rather, he sought to understand the nature of God's design in living organisms.

We use systems of classification every day, often without being aware that we do so. We all have the tendency to label objects and people according to certain characteristics. We often use terms such as "liberal" and "conservative" to describe people's political views and terms such as "white" and "black" to describe people's skin color. Movies are classified into different groups by a rating, such as G, PG, PG-13, and R.

If you think about it, a great deal of your daily life revolves around your use and understanding of different systems of classification. In biology, we are interested in a system of classification that shows relationships between different groups of organisms. This may sound simple but can actually be rather difficult. For example, consider the following list of organisms: goldfish, bat, shark, canary, lizard, horse, and whale (Figure 4.12). How would you classify these creatures? One way might be to put certain animals together according to size: the goldfish, bat, canary, and lizard in a "small" category; the shark and horse in a "medium" category; and the whale in a "large" category. Another method would be to put the animals in groups according to where they live: the goldfish, shark, and whale in the water; the bat and canary in the air; and the lizard and horse on the land. Still another method would be to put the shark in a separate category from all the others because the shark's skeleton is made of cartilage, not bone.

The problem with this example is that none of these three ways of classification agrees with the other two. There is no consistency. Biologists actually classify these animals into the following groups: fish (goldfish and shark), reptiles (lizard), birds (canary), and mammals (bat, horse, whale). These groups reflect certain common characteristics, such as mammary glands for the mammals. What makes this system of classification any better than those based on size or habitat or skeletal form? For our purposes, we require classifications that reflect evolutionary patterns. As you will see,

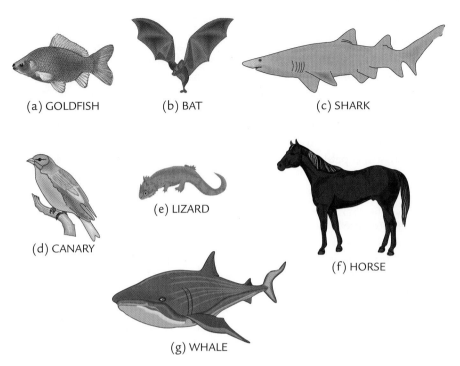

(a) GOLDFISH   (b) BAT   (c) SHARK

(d) CANARY   (e) LIZARD

(f) HORSE

(g) WHALE

FIGURE 4.12

How would you classify the following animals: (a) goldfish, (b) bat, (c) shark, (d) canary, (e) lizard, (f) horse, (g) whale?

organisms can have similar traits because they inherited these traits from a common ancestor. Thus, the presence of mammary glands in the bat, horse, and whale represents a trait that has been inherited from a common ancestral species.

Classifications are useful in trying to understand evolutionary relationships. In order to reflect the evolutionary process, the classifications must reflect evolutionary changes. The groups of mammals, birds, reptiles, and fish are based on characteristics that reflect evolutionary relationships. The bat and the whale are placed in the same group because they have a more recent common ancestor than either does with the lizard, as reflected by certain shared characteristics such as mammary glands. Biological classification should reflect evolutionary processes, but only careful analysis of both living and extinct life forms allows us to discover what characteristics reflect evolutionary relationships.

Taxonomic Categories

The Linnaean system is a hierarchical classification. That is, each category contains a number of subcategories, which contain further subcategories, and so on. Biological classification uses a number of categories. The more commonly used categories are kingdom, phylum (plural *phyla*), class, order, family, genus (plural *genera*), and species. In addition, we often add prefixes to distinguish further breakdowns within a particular category, such as subphylum or infraorder. The scientific name given to an organism consists of the genus and species names in Latin or Latinized form. The scientific name for the common house mouse, for example, is *Mus musculus.* Modern human beings are known as *Homo sapiens,* translated roughly as "wise humans."

Any given genus may contain a number of different species. The genus *Homo,* for example, contains modern humans—**Homo sapiens**—as well as extinct human species (*Homo erectus,* among others). These species are placed in the same genus because of certain common characteristics, such as large brain size. Another level of classification that is sometimes used is **subspecies,** which are groups within a species that are physically distinct from one another but still capable of interbreeding. Subspecies labels are indicated by a third name attached to that of the genus and species. For example, the subspecies *Papio cynocephalus cynocephalus* is one of three subspecies of the yellow baboon, a monkey.

The categories of classification are often vaguely defined. Genus, for example, refers to a group of species that share similar environments, patterns of adaptation, and physical structures. An example is the horse and the zebra, different species that are placed in the genus *Equus* (there are several species of zebra). These species are four-legged, hoofed grazers. The basis for assigning a given species to one genus or another is often unclear. This uncertainty is even more problematic when fossil remains are assigned to different categories. The only category with a precise meaning is the species, and even that has certain problems in application.

Methods of Classification

Classification involves making statements regarding the similarity of traits between species. The process can be somewhat confusing because biological similarity can arise for different reasons.

Homology and Homoplasy   Two species may have the same trait for two different reasons. They may have inherited this trait from a common ancestor, or they may have evolved the same trait independently.

Homology refers to similarity due to descent from a common ancestor. Humans and apes, for example, share certain features of their shoulder anatomy that enables them to hang by their arms. In this case, the similarity is because both humans and apes inherited this anatomy from a common ancestor. Homology is often revealed by comparing the actual structure of different species. For example, Figure 4.13 shows the forelimb anatomy of three different animals—a human, a whale, and a bird. In each case, the basic anatomical structure is similar; all three have a limb made up of a single upper limb bone (humerus) and two lower limb bones (radius and ulna). Further, note that the "hand" of each has five digits made up of carpal and metacarpal bones. These three animals use their limbs for different purposes, but the basic structure is the same; they are the same bones, but they differ in size, shape, and function. The reason for this similarity is descent from a common ancestor (an ancient vertebrate).

Homoplasy refers to similarity due to the independent evolution of the same trait(s) in both species. Birds and flies, for example, are both capable

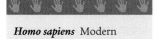

Homo sapiens Modern humans.

subspecies Groupings within a species that are quite physically distinct from one another but capable of fertile interbreeding. When used, subspecies are often listed as a third name in a taxonomic classification, such as *Homo sapiens sapiens,* the subspecies to which all living humans belong.

homology Similarity due to descent from a common ancestor.

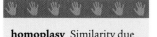

homoplasy Similarity due to independent evolution.

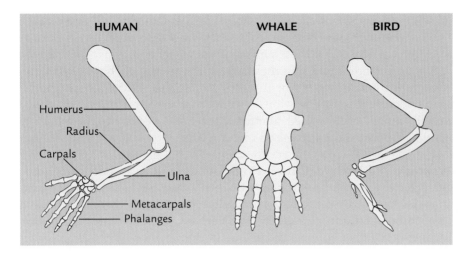

FIGURE 4.13

An example of homology: the forelimbs of a human, whale, and bird. Note that the same bones are found in all three vertebrates. Even though the limbs are used differently by all three organisms, the bones show a structural correspondence, reflecting common ancestry. (Adapted with permission from T. Dobzhansky, F. J. Ayala, G. L. Stebbins, and U. W. Valentine, *Evolution*, 1977, page 264. Copyright © 1977 by W. H. Freeman and Company.)

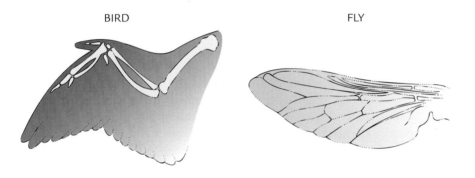

FIGURE 4.14

The wings of a bird and a fly. Even though both structures provide the same function (flight), they are structurally different, reflecting independent evolutionary origin. (Adapted with permission from T. Dobzhansky, F. J. Ayala, G. L. Stebbins, and U. W. Valentine, *Evolution,* 1977, page 264. Copyright © 1977 by W. H. Freeman and Company.)

of flight, but this similarity is due to independent evolution of an anatomy capable of flight and not to descent from a common ancestor. This becomes apparent when we consider their anatomy (Figure 4.14); both creatures can fly, but their anatomy is quite different and reflects independent origins.

There are two different types of homoplasy. **Parallel evolution** is the independent evolution of similar traits in closely related species, such as the increase in dental size among a number of early human ancestors (see Chapter 10). **Convergent evolution** is the independent evolution of similar traits in more distantly related species, such as the evolution of flight in both birds and flies.

If we want our classification system to reflect evolutionary relationships, we need to focus on traits that exhibit homology. We would not want to include traits that reflect homoplasy, because those reflect independent evolutionary origins. For this reason, we classify birds and flies into different taxonomic categories—their similarity does not tell us anything about evolutionary relationships.

As an example, consider three of the organisms mentioned earlier in this chapter—horse, shark, and whale. Which two are more similar to each other than to the third? Looking at overall similarity (including body shape,

parallel evolution
Independent evolution of traits in closely related species.

convergent evolution
Independent evolution of similar traits in rather distinct evolutionary lines.

presence of fins rather than limbs, and habitat), you might conclude that the shark and the whale are more similar to each other than either is to the horse. The problem here is that these similarities all reflect homoplasy—specifically, the independent evolution in the shark and the whale of characteristics related to living in the water. Focusing on homologous structures, such as the limb structure described previously, we see that the horse and the whale are actually more closely related, and for that reason, we classify them both as mammals, whereas the shark is classified as a fish.

Primitive and Derived Traits   Homologous biological traits can also be characterized as primitive or derived. When a trait has been inherited from an earlier form, we refer to that trait as **primitive.** Traits that have changed from an ancestral state are referred to as **derived.** As an example, consider the number of digits in humans and horses. Both humans and horses are mammals. From fossil evidence, we know that the first mammals had five digits on each hand and foot (as did other early land vertebrates). Humans have retained this condition, and we refer to the five digits of the human hand and foot as primitive traits. The horse's single digit (a toe), however, is a derived trait relative to the first mammals.

The concept of primitive and derived traits is relative. What is considered primitive at one level of comparison might be considered derived at another level. For example, neither modern apes nor modern humans have a tail. If apes are compared to humans, the absence of a tail is a primitive characteristic—they share this absence because they inherited this characteristic from a common ancestor. Monkeys, however, do have tails. If modern monkeys are compared to modern apes, the lack of a tail in the modern apes is a derived condition—it has changed since the common ancestor of monkeys and apes. The relative nature of primitive and derived traits must always be kept in mind.

To make any comparison, we must have information on modern and fossil forms so that we can determine whether a trait is primitive or derived. We cannot assume that any given organism will be primitive or derived for a given trait without knowing something about the ancestral condition. In other words, we cannot equate the terms *primitive* and *derived* with biased notions of "higher" or "lower" forms. In the past, there was a tendency to regard all traits of modern humans as derived relative to the apes. For some traits, such as increased brain size and upright walking, this holds true. For other traits, such as certain features of the teeth, the opposite is true.

When we compare the distribution of derived traits between two or more species, we are also interested in whether these traits are *shared* or *unique*. For example, in comparing humans and apes, the absence of a tail is a *shared derived* trait, as both apes and humans lack a tail. On the other hand, upright walking in humans is a *unique derived* trait because it is not found in any other primates. Different methods of taxonomic classification consider the use of primitive traits, shared derived traits, and unique derived traits in different ways.

primitive trait A trait that has not changed from an ancestral state.

derived trait A trait that has changed from an ancestral state.

Approaches to Classification

The problem of biological classification may be approached in many different ways, but there are two major schools of classification: evolutionary systematics and cladistics. Although they both rely on the analysis of homologous traits, they differ in how they treat primitive and derived homologous traits.

Evolutionary Systematics   The traditional method of classification is based on **evolutionary systematics,** a school of thought that considers *all* homologous traits, whether primitive or derived, when classifying organisms into taxonomic groups. Species that share the largest number of homologous traits are placed into the same group even if all of these traits do not reflect an ancestor–descendant relationship. As a result, species that do not necessarily share a common ancestor may be placed in the same taxonomic group. Consider, for example, crocodiles, lizards, and birds. The evolutionary systematics approach would place crocodiles and lizards in the same taxonomic class—Reptilia (reptiles)—and birds in a different class—Aves—because crocodiles and lizards share more homologous traits. Although this classification fits traditional views on overall similarity, it does not show the actual evolutionary relationship between these organisms. When derived traits are considered, birds and crocodiles are found to be more closely related to each other than either is to lizards (Harvey and Pagel 1991).

evolutionary systematics A school of thought that stresses the overall similarity of all (primitive and derived) homologous traits in classification.

Cladistics   An alternative approach is **cladistics,** which looks only at shared derived homologous traits and classifies organisms based solely on their evolutionary relationship. A cladist would place birds and crocodiles in the same taxonomic group, and lizards in another. The guiding principle of cladistics is that *only* shared derived traits should be used to construct classifications; primitive traits and unique derived traits are not considered. The fact that humans, apes, and monkeys all have five digits would not be used to judge their relationship to each other because comparative data and the fossil record show us that having five digits is a *primitive* trait. Because all of these organisms share the same trait, that trait cannot help us determine which two groups are more closely related to each other than the third group.

cladistics A school of thought that stresses evolutionary relationships between organisms based on shared derived traits.

The large brain of humans would not be used to separate humans from monkeys or apes because the large brain is a *unique* derived trait. As such, it cannot tell us whether we are more closely related to the apes or the monkeys. Cladistics uses only homologous traits that are shared and derived. For example, both humans and apes share certain features of their shoulder anatomy (see Chapter 5) that are not shared with monkeys or other primates. Humans and apes have these traits in common because they inherited them from a common ancestor that had changed from an ancestral state.

How do we tell if a given trait is primitive or derived? A commonly used method is to compare the groups of interest with an **outgroup,** a group that is more distantly related to the species being classified. For example, consider the presence or absence of a tail in three different but related groups—humans, apes, and monkeys. Humans and apes do not have tails, but monkeys

outgroup A group used for comparison in cladistic analyses to determine whether the ancestral state of a trait is primitive or derived

BOX 4.2

Primitive and Derived Traits in Apes and Humans

Throughout this book, you will see the statement that apes and humans are more closely related to each other than either is to monkeys. Does this make sense given what you know about monkeys, apes, and humans? We will go into more detail about apes and monkeys in future chapters, but for the moment, you can simply consider what you might have seen on television, a book, or the zoo. It would be common for most people to note the similarity of monkeys and apes and the difference of humans. After all, both apes and monkeys are hairy, walk on all fours, have a smaller brain than we have, and have large canine teeth. Humans on the other hand are relatively hairless, walk on two legs, have a big brain, and have smaller canine teeth. If we were to consider only these traits, we would conclude that because apes and monkeys *look* more like each other, they are more closely related. As noted in the main text, an evolutionary classification would need to take into consideration whether the traits we are looking at are primitive, derived and unique, or derived and shared. Cladistics looks only at shared derived traits for classification. Some examples here might make this point more clearly by comparing monkeys, apes, and humans. Again, the details of these traits will be covered in more detail later in the book, but for the moment, we are going to rely on short descriptions.

Consider the following traits: four limbs and five digits on each limb. What do these traits tell us about the relationship of monkeys, apes, and humans? Nothing, because they are all *primitive* traits that are found in a variety of different creatures descended from the first vertebrates hundreds of millions of years ago. Monkeys, apes, and humans all inherited these traits from earlier ancestors, and because they are all the same, we cannot use these traits to distinguish between them.

Now, consider the following traits: large brains, walking on two legs, small canines, and hairless. These are all *derived* traits relative to early primate ancestors (see later chapters). However, they are also *unique derived* traits because they are found only in humans. This tells us what has changed specifically during the course of human evolution, but does not tell us whether an earlier stage of evolution was more like that of a monkey or that of an ape. In other words, we cannot tell from this list whether apes and monkeys are more closely related, whether monkeys and apes are more closely related, or whether apes and humans are more closely related.

Finally, consider the following traits: lack of a tail, shoulder blades on the back of the torso rather than on the side, and the structure of lower molar teeth. These are all *derived* traits compared to most primate species. The most important thing here is that although they are derived, they are not unique but are found in both apes and humans. That is, they are *shared derived* traits. These traits tell us that apes and humans shared a more recent common ancestor than did monkeys, and are therefore apes and humans are more closely related to each other than to monkeys.

The above example is a bit simplistic because we examined only a small number of traits for illustrative purposes. However, this simple example does show us how cladistics works—classifying species based on shared derived traits. Neither primitive nor unique derived traits are useful in this context. In a real life analysis, we would need to look at dozens or hundreds of traits and take into account the possibility of homoplasy among other complications.

do. According to the cladistic method, we would place humans and apes in the same group if the absence of a tail were a shared derived trait—that is, one that was present in the common ancestor of humans and apes but not in the common ancestor of humans, apes, and monkeys. How do we know whether the common ancestor of all three groups had a tail or not? An appropriate outgroup for this example might be more distantly related primates or other mammals. Because a tail is found in most of these mammals, we would conclude that the primitive state was the presence of a tail and that the absence of a tail in both humans and apes reflects their descent from a common ancestor not shared with monkeys (Figure 4.15). Some further examples of the distinction between primitive, unique derived, and shared derived traits are given in Box 4.2.

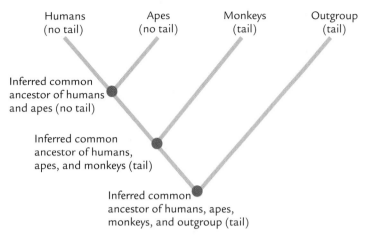

FIGURE 4.15

Illustration of the use of an outgroup in cladistic analysis. This diagram shows the relationship among humans, apes, and monkeys based on the presence or absence of a tail. Humans and apes lack a tail, which makes them different from monkeys. According to the principles of cladistics, lack of a tail can be considered a shared derived trait in humans and apes if the presence of a tail was indeed the primitive condition. Using an outgroup, such as other mammals, shows that the presence of a tail is very widespread apart from humans and apes, and it is the primitive condition. According to this model, monkeys have tails because they retained this primitive trait, whereas the inferred common ancestor of humans and apes lost the tail, a trait inherited in both from this common ancestor.

Summary

Macroevolution, the process of long-term evolution, can occur in two ways: anagenesis, the evolution of a species over time, or cladogenesis, the splitting off of one or more new species from the original parent species. In cladogenesis, new species form through the process of reproductive isolation followed by genetic divergence. Both steps are understood in terms of evolutionary forces. Reduction or elimination of gene flow provides for the beginning of reproductive isolation. Mutation, genetic drift, and selection can then act on this isolation to produce a new species. The relative importance of the evolutionary forces in speciation is still debated. When new environments open up, many new species may diversify as part of the process of an adaptive radiation.

The most common evolutionary pattern is extinction. Some scientists have argued that the evolutionary record is best understood as the process of new species forming from old, with many species becoming extinct. The evolutionary trends we observe in the fossil record may reflect the differential survival of species with certain adaptations.

There are many misconceptions regarding natural selection and evolution. Some of the more common of these are that bigger is better, that newer is better, that natural selection always works, and that there is an inevitable direction to natural selection. There are also misconceptions regarding the relationship of biological structures, their functions, and their evolutionary origin.

Species are classified according to similarity in traits that arose because of descent from a common ancestor (homology) and not according to similar traits that evolved independently (homoplasy). Homologous traits can be categorized as primitive (unchanged since the time of a common ancestor) or derived (having changed since the time of a common ancestor). Different approaches to classification place different weight on primitive or derived traits depending on whether the purpose of classification is to provide a measure of overall similarity or to reveal evolutionary relationships.

Supplemental Readings

Futuyma, D. J. 2009. *Evolution,* 2d ed. Sunderland, MA: Sinauer Associates. A comprehensive treatment of evolutionary theory and the fossil record.

OUR PLACE IN NATURE

What are humans? This question has been asked over and over again throughout human history by scientists, artists, philosophers, and others. Where do we fit into the animal world? In this section, we look at human beings in a comparative framework, considering our species as part of the total diversity of life. The emphasis in this section is on the primates, a group of mammals to which humans belong. Chapter 5 reviews the basic characteristics of mammals and primates and the diversity of living primates. Chapter 6 examines the relationship of primate behavior and ecology, including a number of case studies of primate behavior. Chapter 7 focuses on the human species, emphasizing the similarities to and differences from our closest living relatives, the African apes.

A chimpanzee sitting in a tree. Chimpanzees are one type of ape. The zoological order Primates includes lemurs, lorises, tarsiers, monkeys, apes, and humans, all sharing certain traits such as grasping hands and depth perception.

The Primates

Given that humans, like all living creatures, have evolved, we turn now to a very basic question: Who are our relatives? When Darwin demonstrated to the scientific community that all living creatures were related, this also meant that we humans have closer kinship with some creatures than with others. Even a casual glance at living animals gives us some basic clues. We are clearly more similar to dogs, cats, and apes than to birds, lizards, or sharks. When we look more closely, we can see a number of characteristics than we humans share with a variety of other animals classified as mammals. Looking even more closely, we see that we belong to a particular group of mammals known as the **primates.**

To understand what we are, we also have to know something about our basic mammalian and primate nature. How much of what we are today is a reflection of what we inherited from earlier primate ancestors and how much has changed in our specific evolutionary history since our line branched off from an earlier ancestor? To put this question in terms of the discussion from the last chapter, we want to know what about humans is primitive, what is shared and derived, and what is unique and derived. In order to make these comparisons, we need to look at the biology, behavior, and ecology of our closest living relatives, the primates. However, to understand primates in evolutionary perspective, we also need to look at our nature more broadly, by considering primates as a group relative to mammals. Because mammals in turn belong to a larger group known as vertebrates, it is first necessary to understand the basic characteristics of this larger taxonomic group. We begin, therefore, by discussing first vertebrates and then mammals, and then go on to discuss the special characteristics of primates.

As with all living creatures, human beings can be classified according to the different levels of Linnaean taxonomy—kingdom, phylum, class, and so on. A traditional taxonomic description of modern humans is given in Table 5.1. Kingdom is the most inclusive taxonomic category. All living organisms can be placed into one of five kingdoms: plants, animals, fungi, nucleated single-celled organisms, and bacteria. Major differences among these kingdoms are their source of food and their mobility. Whereas plants produce their own food through photosynthesis, animals must ingest food. Humans belong to the animal kingdom. Given that animals must ingest

primates The order of mammals that has a complex of characteristics related to an initial adaptation to life in the trees.

TABLE 5.1	Classification of Humans	
Taxonomic Category	*Taxonomic Name*	*Common Names*
Kingdom	Animalia	Animals
Phylum	Chordata	Chordates
Subphylum	Vertebrata	Vertebrates
Class	Mammalia	Mammals
Subclass	Eutheria	Placental mammals
Order	Primates	Primates
Suborder	Haplorrhini	Haplorhines
Infraorder	Simiiformes	Simians/Anthropoids
Parvorder	Catarrhini	Catarrhines/Old World anthropoids
Superfamily	Hominoidea	Hominoids
Family	Hominidae	Hominids
Subfamily	Homininae	Hominines
Tribe	Hominini	Hominins
Genus/Species	*Homo sapiens*	Modern humans

Chordata A vertebrate phylum consisting of organisms that possess a notochord at some period during their life.

notochord A flexible internal rod that runs along the back of an animal.

Vertebrata A subphylum of the phylum Chordata, defined by the presence of an internal, segmented spinal column and bilateral symmetry.

bilateral symmetry Symmetry in which the right and left sides of the body are approximately mirror images.

food, it is no surprise that most animals have well-developed nervous, sensory, and movement systems to enable them to acquire food.

Humans belong to the phylum **Chordata** (the chordates, animals with a spinal cord). Perhaps the most important characteristic of chordates is that they possess at some point in their life a **notochord,** a flexible internal rod that runs along the back of the animal. This rod acts to strengthen and support the body. In humans, it is present early in gestation and is later reabsorbed.

Humans belong to the subphylum **Vertebrata** (the vertebrates, animals with backbones). One characteristic of vertebrates is that they have **bilateral symmetry,** which means that the left and right sides of their bodies are approximately mirror images. Imagine a line running down a human being from the top of the head to a spot between the feet. This line divides the body into two mirror images. This pattern contrasts with other phyla of animals such as starfish.

Another characteristic of vertebrates is an internal spinal cord covered by a series of bones known as vertebrae. The nerve tissue is surrounded by these bones and has an enlarged area of nerve tissue at the front end of the cord—the brain.

The general biological structure of human beings can be found in many other vertebrates. Most vertebrates have the same basic skeletal pattern: a single upper bone and two lower bones in each limb, and five digits. Some vertebrates have changed considerably from this basic pattern. For example, a modern horse has one digit (a toe) on the end of each limb. Humans may seem to be rather specialized and sophisticated creatures, but they actually have retained much of the earliest basic vertebrate skeletal structure.

The subphylum of vertebrates also includes several classes of fish along with the amphibians, reptiles, birds, and mammals. Humans belong to the class of mammals, and much of our biology and behavior can be understood in terms of what it is to be a mammal.

CHARACTERISTICS OF MAMMALS

The first primitive mammals evolved from early reptiles over 200 million years ago. The distinctive features of modern mammals and modern reptiles are the result of that long period of separate evolution in the two classes. It is important to realize that the further back in time we look, the more difficult it is to tell one form from another. Keep in mind that the definition and characteristics of any modern form reflect continued evolution from an earlier ancestor.

Because mammals and reptiles are related through evolution, it is logical and useful to compare these two classes to determine the unique features of each. Modern mammals differ from modern reptiles in reproduction, temperature regulation, diet, skeletal structure, and behavior. As we look at each of these factors separately, do not forget that they are interrelated.

Reproduction

Mammals are often identified as animals that give birth to live offspring, whereas other vertebrates lay eggs. This is not completely accurate. Some fish, such as guppies, give birth to live infants. Also, some mammals, such as the platypus, lay eggs. Others, such as kangaroos, give birth to an extremely immature fetus that completes development inside a pouch in the mother. The most common mammal found today belongs to the subclass of placental mammals, characterized by the development of the fetus inside of the mother's body. Humans are placental mammals.

Placental Mammals   The **placenta** is an organ that develops inside the female during pregnancy. It functions as a link between the circulatory systems of the mother and the fetus, acting to transport food, oxygen, and antibodies, as well as to filter out waste products. The efficiency of the placenta means that the developing offspring of placental mammals have a much greater chance of survival than does a reptile developing in an egg or in a nonplacental mammal (both egg layers and marsupials, Figures 5.1 and 5.2). Development inside the mother provides warmth and protection along with proper nutrition. Although placental mammals appear at first glance to be superior to egg-laying reptiles, the presence of a placenta has a cost as well as a benefit. Pregnant mammals consume a great deal of energy, making ample food resources vital to successful birth. Also, the demand on energy sets a limit on the number of offspring any female mammal can have at one time.

A main feature of mammals is the female mammary glands, which provide food for the newborn infant. Important immunities are also provided in mother's milk. The ready availability of food increases the child's chance of survival. Although advantageous, nursing also has a price; energy is expended by the mother during this process, and only a limited number of offspring can be taken care of at one time.

placenta An organ that develops inside a pregnant placental mammal that provides the fetus with oxygen and food and helps filter our harmful substances.

FIGURE 5.1

The spiny anteater, an egg-laying mammal.

FIGURE 5.2

Mother kangaroo with baby in her pouch. Kangaroos are marsupial mammals.

prenatal The period of life from conception until birth.

postnatal The period of life from birth until death.

Parental Care The **prenatal** (before birth) and **postnatal** (after birth) patterns of parental care in mammals contrast with those of reptiles, which expend less energy during reproduction and care of offspring. Pregnancy and the raising of offspring take energy; the more offspring an organism has, the less care a parent can give each of them. Consequently, some animals have many offspring but provide little care to them, whereas other animals have few offspring and provide much more care to each.

Species vary in terms of the balance between number of offspring and degree of parental care. One extreme example is the oyster, which produces roughly half a billion eggs a year and provides no parental care. Fish can produce 8,000 eggs a year and provide a slight amount of parental care. Frogs can lay 200 eggs a year and provide slightly more parental care.

Compared to other animals, mammals have relatively few offspring but provide much more parental care. The development of the placenta and the mammary glands are biological features that maximize the amount of care given to an offspring. A female lion, for example, has only two offspring per year and provides a great deal of care to them. An extreme example among mammals is the orangutan, an ape that has roughly one offspring every eight years (Galdikas and Wood 1990).

From an evolutionary viewpoint, which strategy is better: having many offspring but providing little care, or having fewer offspring and providing greater care? Each strategy has its advantages and disadvantages. In general, those species that have many offspring tend to be at an advantage in rapidly changing environments, whereas those that provide greater care are at an advantage in more stable environments (Pianka 1983).

Temperature Regulation

Modern mammals are **homeotherms;** they are able to maintain a constant body temperature under most circumstances. Modern reptiles are cold-blooded and cannot keep their body temperature constant; they need to use the heat of the sun's rays to keep themselves warm and their metabolism active. Mammals maintain a constant body temperature in several ways. They are covered with fur or hair that insulates the body, preventing heat loss in cold weather and reducing overheating in hot weather. Temporary changes in the size of blood vessels also aid in temperature regulation. When blood vessels contract, blood flow is reduced, and less heat is lost from the mammal's extremities. When blood vessels dilate, blood flow is increased to the extremities, thus allowing greater heat loss.

Mammals also maintain a constant body temperature by ingesting large quantities of food and converting the food to energy in the form of heat. When you feel hot, your body is not losing the produced heat quickly enough. When you feel cold, you are losing heat too quickly. The ability to convert food energy to heat enables mammals to live comfortably in many environments where reptiles would slow down or even die.

Mammals are thus able to exploit a large number of environments. However, heat production and temperature regulation, though obviously useful adaptations in certain environments, are not without a price. To obtain energy, mammals need to consume far greater quantities of food than do reptiles. In environments where food resources are limited, mammals may be worse off than reptiles. Again, the evolutionary benefits of any trait must be looked at in terms of its costs.

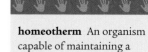

homeotherm An organism capable of maintaining a constant body temperature under most circumstances.

Teeth

The saying "You are what you eat" is not usually meant literally, but in fact, it embodies an important truth of ecology and evolution. The nutritional requirements of organisms dictate, in part, their environmental needs. Also, diet is reflected in the physical structure of organisms, particularly the teeth and jaws. Because mammals maintain a constant body temperature by converting food energy to heat, they require a considerable amount of food. The physical features of mammalian teeth reflect this need.

The teeth of modern reptiles are all the same, that is, **homodontic;** they all have sharp sides and are continually replaced throughout life (Figure 5.3). A major function of reptilian teeth is to hold and kill prey. The food is then most often eaten whole. Mammals, on the other hand, have different types of teeth; that is, they are **heterodontic.** Mammals usually have two sets of teeth during their lives: a set of deciduous ("baby") teeth and a set of permanent teeth. As a mammal grows and matures, the baby teeth fall out and are replaced with the adult teeth. In modern humans, this replacement normally starts around age 6 and takes 18–20 years of life to complete.

Types of Teeth   Most mammals have four types of teeth: **incisors, canines, premolars,** and **molars.** These teeth in a chimpanzee and a human are shown in Figure 5.4. The incisor teeth are chisel- or spatula-shaped and located in the front of the jaw. Both the human and the chimpanzee (and other higher primates) have a total of four incisors in each jaw. These teeth are used for cutting and slicing food. You use your incisors when you eat an apple or corn on the cob. Behind the incisors are the canine teeth, which are often long and sharp, resembling fangs or tusks. Apes and humans have two canine teeth in each jaw. In many mammals, the canine teeth are used as weapons or for killing prey. Although the canine teeth of most mammals are rather large and project beyond the level of the rest of the teeth, human canines are usually small and nonprojecting.

homodontic All teeth are the same.

heterodontic Having different types of teeth.

incisor The chisel-shaped front teeth, used for cutting, slicing, and gnawing food.

canine The teeth located in the front of the jaw behind the incisors, which are normally used by mammals for puncturing and defense.

premolar One of the types of back teeth, used for crushing and grinding food.

molar The teeth farthest back in the jaw, used for crushing and grinding food.

FIGURE 5.3

A crocodile with its mouth open, showing how the teeth of reptiles are all the same (homodontic).

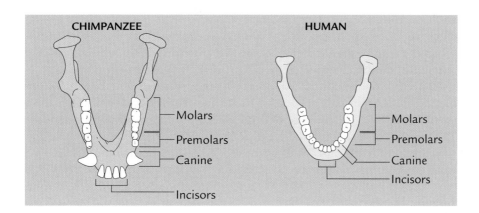

FIGURE 5.4

The lower jaws and teeth of a chimpanzee and a modern human.

The premolars and molars are also known collectively as the back teeth or cheek teeth. Both of these types of teeth are often large in surface area and are used for grinding and chewing food. When you chew food between your back teeth, you do not simply move your lower jaw up and down. Instead, your upper and lower back teeth grind together in a circular motion as your jaw moves up and down and sideways as well. The structures of the premolar and molar teeth are different, and in some mammals, these teeth have different functions as well.

Dental Formulae Mammals can be characterized by the number of each type of tooth they have. The usual method of counting teeth is to consider the number of each type of tooth in one-half of one jaw, upper or lower. Only one-half of the jaw is considered because both the right and left sides of the jaw contain the same number of teeth. These numbers are expressed using a **dental formula,** which lists the number of incisors, canines, premolars, and molars in one-half of a jaw. A dental formula looks like this: I-C-P-M. Here I = number of incisors, C = number of canines, P = number of premolars, and M = number of molars. For example, the typical dental formula of humans (as well as apes and some monkeys) is 2-1-2-3 (see Figure 5.4). This means that in one-half of either jaw there are two incisors, one canine, two premolars, and three molars. Each half of each jaw therefore contains 2 + 1 + 2 + 3 = 8 teeth. The typical number of teeth in humans is therefore 8 × 4 = 32 (two sides of each of two jaws). Some mammals have different numbers of teeth in the top and bottom jaws. In these cases, we use two dental formulae.

dental formula A shorthand method of describing the number of each type of tooth in one-half of the jaw in a mammal.

Diet and Teeth The basic description of the types of teeth is somewhat simplistic. Many mammals have evolved specialized uses of one or more of these tooth types. As noted earlier, human canines are rather different in form and function from those of many other mammals. The general description is useful, however, in showing the importance of differentiated teeth in mammals. By having different types of teeth capable of slicing, cutting, and grinding, mammals are able to eat a wide variety of foods in an efficient way. In addition, the ability to chew food rather than swallow it whole allows greater efficiency in eating. By chewing, mammals break down the food into smaller pieces that can be digested more easily and efficiently. Also, saliva released in the mouth during chewing begins the process of digestion.

The nature of mammalian diet and teeth relates to mammals' warm-bloodedness. Mammals need more food than reptiles, and their teeth allow them to utilize a wider range of food and to process it more productively. The benefits of differentiated teeth lie in these abilities. The cost is the fact that the teeth tend to wear out over time. When a mammal's adult teeth are worn down, it may not be able to eat or may develop serious dental problems, which could lead to death. As far as recent humans are concerned, we can circumvent these potential problems to a certain extent with dental technology, personal hygiene, and processed foods. Even so, dental problems continue to pose a serious threat to human health.

Skeletal Structure

Both mammals and reptiles share the basic skeletal structure of all vertebrates, but there are some differences, especially in movement. In reptiles, the four limbs come out from the side of the body for support and movement (Figure 5.5). In four-legged mammals, the limbs slope downward from the shoulders and hips. Having the limbs tucked in under the body allows more

FIGURE 5.5

The orientation of the limbs is different in reptiles and mammals. In reptiles, such as the iguana (*left*), the limbs are splayed out to the sides. In mammals, such as the lion (*right*), the limbs are under the body, providing better support and movement.

efficient and quicker movement, and the weight of the body is supported better. Humans differ from the pattern of many mammals in using only two limbs for movement. Even so, the configuration of the legs follows the basic pattern; the legs slope inward from the hips and are not splayed out to the sides.

Behavior

The brains of all vertebrates have similar structures but differ in size, relative proportions, and functions. All vertebrates have a hindbrain, a midbrain, and a forebrain. In most vertebrates, the hindbrain is associated with hearing, balance, reflexive behaviors, and control of the autonomic functions of the body, such as breathing. The midbrain is associated with vision, and the forebrain is associated with chemical sensing, such as smelling ability. Compared to fish, reptiles have a relatively larger midbrain and hindbrain because they rely more extensively on vision and hearing. The midbrain of a reptile is particularly enlarged because it functions to coordinate sensory information and body movements.

The brain of a mammal reveals several important shifts in structure and function. The mammalian brain has a greatly enlarged forebrain that is responsible for the processing of sensory information and for coordination. In particular, the forebrain contains the **cerebrum,** the outermost layer of brain cells, which is associated with learning, memory, and intelligence. The cerebrum becomes increasingly convoluted, which allows huge numbers of interconnections between brain cells. It accounts for the largest proportion of the mammalian brain.

The overall functions of a brain include basic body maintenance and the ability to process information and respond accordingly. Mammals rely more on learning and flexible responses than do reptiles. Behaviors are less instinctual and rigid. Previous experiences (learning) become more important in responding to stimuli. As a consequence, mammals are more capable of developing new responses to different situations and are capable of learning from past mistakes. New behaviors are more likely to develop and can be passed on to offspring through the process of learning. Humans have taken this process even further; our very existence depends on flexible behaviors that must be learned. Although our behavior is to a large extent cultural, our ability to transfer information through learning relies on a biological trait: the mammalian brain.

The behavioral flexibility of mammals ties in with their pattern of reproduction. In general, the more a species relies on parental care, the more intelligent it is, and the more it relies on learning rather than instinct. Extensive parental care requires increased intelligence and the ability to learn new behaviors in order to provide maximum care for infants. The increased emphasis on learning requires, in turn, an extended period of growth during which the information needed for adult life is absorbed. Furthermore, the extension of childhood requires more extensive child care so that offspring are protected during the time they are completing their growth and learning.

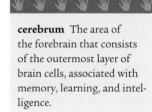

cerebrum The area of the forebrain that consists of the outermost layer of brain cells, associated with memory, learning, and intelligence.

PRIMATE CHARACTERISTICS

There are many different forms of mammals—they are as diverse as mice, whales, giraffes, cats, dogs, and apes. Patterns of biology and behavior vary considerably, although all mammals share to some extent the basic characteristics outlined in the previous section.

Recall that the mammalian class is broken down into a number of orders. Humans, as noted, are primates, as are the apes, such as the chimpanzee, bonobo, and gorilla, which are our closest living relatives. Monkeys are also primates. The basic characteristics of primates are discussed in this section.

No single characteristic identifies primates; rather, they share a set of features. Many of these features relate to living in trees. Though humans, as well as a few other modern primates, clearly do not live in trees, they still retain certain features inherited from ancestors who did.

An **arboreal** (tree-living) environment presents different challenges than a **terrestrial** (ground-living) environment. Living in the trees requires an orientation to a three-dimensional environment. Animals that live on the ground generally contend with only two dimensions: length and width. Arboreal animals must also deal with the third dimension, height. Perception of distance and depth is vital to a tree-living form, which moves quickly from one branch to the next and from one level of the forest to another. Agility is also important, as is the ability to anchor oneself in space (Figure 5.6).

Many forms of animals, such as squirrels and birds, have adapted to living in the trees. Primates, too, are capable of extensive rapid movement through the trees and are able to move to all areas of a tree, including small terminal branches. A squirrel can climb up and down the trunk of a tree and traverse larger branches, but primates are even better equipped to move out to feed on the smallest branches. The two major characteristics of primates

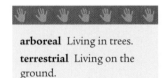

arboreal Living in trees.
terrestrial Living on the ground.

FIGURE 5.6

Baboons, a form of Old World monkeys, sitting in trees. The three-dimensional nature of arboreal life poses problems. Primates have evolved characteristics such as grasping hands and depth perception that allow use in arboreal environments.

that account for their success in the trees are the ability to use hands and feet to grasp branches (rather than digging in with claws) and the ability to perceive distance and depth.

Not all modern primates have kept the original adaptations of the first primates. For example, humans can still use their hands to grasp objects but cannot do so with their feet. We do not normally use our hands to grasp and hang onto branches. We have taken our inherited ability to grasp and put it to work in another arena: We hold tools, weapons, food, and children. The grasping hands of a human and a tree-living monkey are homologous—that is, they are similar structures because of common descent. The different functions of the hands of humans and tree-living monkeys reflect adaptive changes from the original primate ancestors. Even though humans do things differently, we are still primates and have the basic set of primate characteristics.

The Skeleton

First, let us consider some general characteristics in the primate skeletal structure.

Grasping Hands   A characteristic of the earliest known mammals (and reptiles) is five digits on each hand or foot. Certain mammals, such as the horse, have changed from this ancestral condition and have only a single toe on each limb. Other mammals, such as the primates, have kept the ancestral condition.

In the case of primates, the retention of the primitive characteristics of five digits on the hands and feet turned out to be an important adaptation. The hands and feet of primates are **prehensile,** that is, capable of being used to grasp objects. The ability to grasp involves the movement of the fingers to the palm, thus allowing the fingers to wrap around an object. In many primates, the toes can also wrap around an object. This grasping ability is a remarkable adaptation to living in the trees. Primates can grab onto branches to move about, to provide support while eating, and in general to allow for a high degree of flexibility in navigating their environment. More specialized structures, such as the horse's single hoof, would be useless in the trees because there would be no way to grasp branches.

Another feature of primate hands and feet is their expanded tactile pads (such as the ball of your thumb) and nails instead of claws. Nails serve to protect the sensitive skin at the ends of the fingers and the toes. The numerous nerve endings in the tips of fingers and toes of primates provide an enhanced sense of touch that is useful in manipulating objects (Figure 5.7).

As mentioned earlier, the characteristics possessed by primates are not the only possible solution to the challenge of living in the trees. Squirrels, for example, use their claws to dig into the bark of limbs and branches when they climb in the trees. The grasping ability of primate hands, however, provides much greater flexibility. They can reach food at the end of small branches by grasping surrounding branches for support, using a free arm to reach out

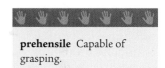

prehensile Capable of grasping.

FIGURE 5.7

Primates have grasping hands, which allow them to grab onto tree branches and other objects. As shown here, a human uses a grasping hand to use tools.

and grab the food, and then bringing it to the mouth. A small branch might not provide enough surface area for a squirrel to dig its claws into, but a primate can use its grasping hands and feet to hold onto it.

Variations on these themes occur even within primates. Humans differ from the general primate conditions. We have lost the ability to use our feet for grasping as a result of anatomical changes relating to our ability to walk on two legs.

Generalized Structure   Biological structures are often classified as specialized or generalized. **Specialized structures** are used in a highly specific way, whereas **generalized structures** can be used in a variety of ways. The hooves of a horse, for example, are a specialization that allows rapid running over land surfaces. The basic skeletal structure of primates is generalized because it allows movement flexibility in a wide variety of circumstances.

The arm and leg bones of primates follow the basic pattern of many vertebrates: Each limb consists of an upper bone and two lower bones (refer back to Figure 4.13). This structure allows limbs to bend at the elbows or knees. In climbing or jumping in a tree, you must have this flexibility, or you would not be able to move about (imagine trying to jump from one branch to another with arms and legs each made up of one long bone). That the lower part of the limb is made up of two bones provides even greater flexibility. Hold your arm out straight in front of you with your palm down. Now turn your hand so that the palm side is up. This is easy to do, but only because you have two lower arm bones. When turning the hand over, one lower arm bone crosses over the other. Imagine trying to climb in a tree without the ability to move your hand into different positions. This flexibility is obtained by the retention of a generalized skeletal structure.

specialized structure A biological structure adapted to a narrow range of conditions and used in very specific ways.

generalized structure A biological structure adapted to a wide range of conditions and used in very general ways.

Vision

The three-dimensional nature of arboreal life requires keen eyesight, particularly depth perception. This feature has evolved from the need to judge distances successfully. (Jumping through the air from branch to branch

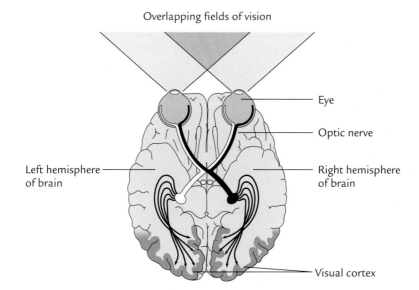

Overlapping fields of vision

Eye

Optic nerve

Left hemisphere
of brain

Right hemisphere
of brain

Visual cortex

FIGURE 5.8

Binocular stereoscopic vision
in primates. The fields of
vision for each eye overlap,
and the optic nerve from
each eye is connected to both
hemispheres of the brain. (From
*Human Antiquity: An Introduction
to Physical Anthropology and
Archaeology,* 4th ed., by Kenneth
Feder and Michael Park, Fig. 5.1.
Copyright © 2001 by Mayfield
Publishing Company. Reprinted by
permission of The McGraw-Hill
Companies.)

demands the ability to judge distances. After all, it is not very adaptive to fall short of your target and plunge to the ground!)

Depth perception involves **binocular stereoscopic vision.** *Binocular* refers to overlapping fields of vision. The eyes of many animals are located at the sides of the skull so that each eye receives a different image with no overlap. The eyes of primates are located in the front of the skull so that the fields of vision overlap more than most other mammals (Figure 5.8). Primates see objects in front of them with both eyes. The *stereoscopic* nature of primate vision refers to the way in which the brain processes visual signals. In non-stereoscopic animals, the information from one eye is received in only one hemisphere of the brain. In primates, the visual signals from both eyes are received in both hemispheres of the brain. The result is an image that has depth. Moving quickly and safely in three dimensions requires depth perception.

Many primates also have the ability to perceive colors. Color vision is extremely useful in detecting objects in moderate-contrast environments. In fact, color vision is found in other animals for this reason, including whales, fish, bumblebees, and certain birds. Color vision is also important in primate species that use color as a visual signal of various emotional states, such as anger or receptivity to sexual relations.

Primates are vision oriented. On average, their sense of smell is less keen. As a result, the areas of the face devoted to smelling are reduced in primates. Compared to other mammals, primates have short snouts.

The Brain and Behavior

Primates have expanded on the basic pattern of mammalian brains. Their brains are even larger relative to body size. Primate brains have larger visual areas and smaller areas for smelling, corresponding to their increased emphasis on vision over smell as the main sense. Also, primate brains are even

**binocular stereoscopic
vision** Overlapping fields of
vision, with both sides of the
brain receiving images from
both eyes, thereby providing
depth perception.

more complex than those of most other mammals. Primates have larger proportions of the brain associated with learning and intelligence. Areas of the brain associated with body control and coordination are also proportionately larger, as expected given the demands of arboreal life. Hand–eye coordination, for example, is crucial for moving about in trees.

The greater size and complexity of primate brains are reflected in their behaviors. Many primates rely extensively on learned behaviors. As a result, it is often difficult to assign specific behaviors to a given species of primate because the increased emphasis on learning allows a great deal of flexibility in behavior patterns.

The increased emphasis on learning means that primates spend a greater proportion of their lives growing up, both biologically and socially, than do other animals. The more an animal needs to learn, the longer the time needed for learning. An increase in the amount of time spent learning as an infant or child also means that greater amounts of attention and care are required from parents. Again, we see the intimate relationship among reproduction, care of offspring, learning, and intelligence.

PRIMATE DIVERSITY

In terms of both biology and behavior, primates are an extremely variable group of mammals. For example, some primates are small enough to sit in the palm of your hand, and others typically weigh several hundred pounds. Some primates live exclusively in the trees, some live exclusively on the ground, and some live both in the trees and on the ground. Primate societies range in size from a mother and her dependent offspring to groups numbering in the dozens. The remainder of this chapter explores some of the basic biological, behavioral, and evolutionary diversity of the living primates. This diversity is now in danger as environmental changes have led to a number of primate species becoming endangered (Box 5.1).

Primate Suborders

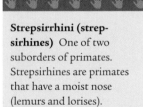

Strepsirrhini (strepsirhines) One of two suborders of primates. Strepsirhines are primates that have a moist nose (lemurs and lorises).

Haplorrhini (haplorhines) One of two suborders of primates. Haplorhines are primates without a moist nose (tarsiers, monkeys, apes, and humans).

Figure 5.9 shows a classification of the living primates. The two major subgroups of the primates are the suborder **Strepsirrhini** and the suborder **Haplorrhini.** These are the official scientific names for the two suborders, although we will use the more common terms *strepsirhines* and *haplorhines.* As shown in Figure 5.9, each of these suborders is broken down into smaller taxonomic units, such as infraorders, pavorders, and superfamilies.

A difference between strepsirhines and haplorhines has to do with the nose (the common root "rhine" translates as "nose" from Greek). The word "strepsirhine" literally translates as "turning nose," indicating the curly nostrils, and contrasts with the translation of "haplorhine" as "simple nosed" or "dry nosed." In typical use, the major difference between the noses is that strepsirhines have moist noses and haplorhines (which includes humans) have dry noses.

BOX 5.1

Endangered Primates and Conservation

Almost half of the primate species in the world today are threatened. Counting subspecies as well as species, a report issued in 2009 by Mittermeier and colleagues identified 634 distinct types of primates. Many, however, live a precarious existence. As of 2008, 32 percent of these taxa had been classified as "Endangered" or "Critically Endangered" by conservation experts, with an additional 15 percent classified as "Vulnerable" (Mittermeier et al. 2009).

What has caused this danger to living primates? One major factor is the destruction of native habitats. More than 90 percent of all primate species live in tropical rain forests, which are disappearing at an alarming rate as forest is cleared for human use (Wright 1992; Chapman and Peres 2001). Other primates, such as the mountain gorilla, have had their habitats reduced through farming to meet the demands for food of growing human populations (Mittermeier and Sterling 1992). Hunting by humans is another threat to primate survival (Strier 2011; Mittermeier et al. 2009). The demand for bushmeat (the meat of wild animals) has increased in parts of the world even when it is illegal. In addition to being a food resource, primates are hunted in many parts of the world for use as bait for other animals, for

sale of their body parts for ornaments, or because they are considered agricultural pests. Logging is another human activity that has endangered many primate species, as the loss of habitat contributes significantly to the endangered status of many primates (Chapman and Peres 2001).

What can be done? There is no single solution; a series of conservation efforts must be applied at the international level to have the greatest impact. Strier (2011) lists several general strategies, including developing economic incentives for conservation, raising public awareness of the potential problems, and increasing the role of nongovernmental organizations (NGOs) in providing an opportunity for interaction and information exchange among conservationists, primate researchers, and policy makers. Other approaches to primate conservation include developing protected parks and preserves, implementing less harmful agricultural practices, and breeding endangered primate species in captivity (Mittermeier and Sterling 1992; Wright 1992). Chapman and Peres (2001) emphasize the role that scientists can play in such conservation efforts. All of these efforts, and more, are needed if we are to save these remarkable relatives of ours.

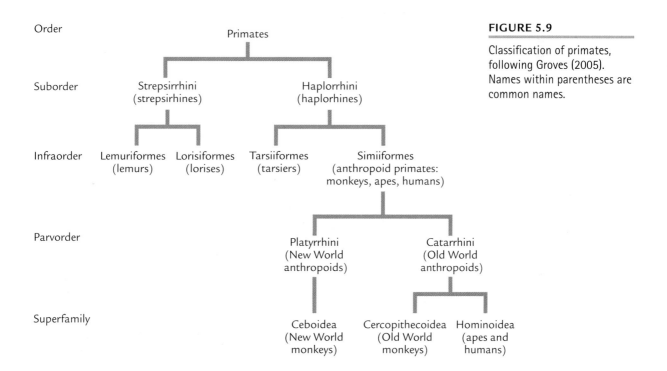

FIGURE 5.9

Classification of primates, following Groves (2005). Names within parentheses are common names.

Strepsirhines   The strepsirhines are the more primitive of the two primate suborders, having a number of traits more similar to early primate ancestors than the haplorhines. The moist nose, associated with an emphasis on smell, is one of these primitive traits, as are larger olfactory lobes in the brain. Strepsirhines rely more on a sense of smell than do haplorhines. Another primitive trait of strepsirhines is that they typically retain a claw on one digit instead of having only nails as do haplorhines. The strepsirhines tend to have lower brain to body ratios than the more intelligent haplorhines. Strepsirhines also tend to have more elongated snouts and have a **postorbital bar,** which is a bone that runs along the eye socket. By contrast, haplorhines have a fully enclosed eye socket. Many strepsirhines have incisor teeth that protrude from their jaws, forming a "tooth comb" used for grooming. Finally, many strepsirhine species are **nocturnal** (active at night), whereas most (but not all) haplorhines species are **diurnal** (active during the day).

There are two subgroups of strepsirhines—lorises and lemurs. The **lorises** are small, solitary, and nocturnal. A number of different loris species live in Asia and Africa (Figure 5.10). The more biologically diverse group of strepsirhines is the **lemurs,** which are found only on the island of Madagascar off the southeast coast of Africa (Figure 5.11). The lemurs show a wide range of biological and behavioral characteristics; some species are diurnal, and some live in much larger social groups. The diversity of the lemurs may reflect their isolation on Madagascar. Because the island has no competing monkey or ape species and not many other mammals either, the lemurs have expanded into a variety of ecological niches. Apart from these variations, the lemurs are definitely strepsirhines—having the moist nose, postorbital bar, and other defining characteristics of the suborder.

Haplorhines   As shown in Figure 5.9, there are two major groups (infraorders) of the dry-nosed haplorhines—the Tarsiiformes (tarsiers) and the Simiiformes (anthropoids). The **tarsiers** are small, relatively solitary, and nocturnal primates found in Indonesia. As shown in Figure 5.12, their nocturnal lifestyle is apparent from their enlarged eyes, the size of which serves to gather available light. Tarsiers eat only insects, spiders, and other invertebrate animals, as well as some vertebrates, an unusual dietary pattern among

postorbital bar The bony ring that separates the eye orbits from the back of the skull in strepsirhines.

nocturnal Active during the night.

diurnal Active during the day.

loris A nocturnal strepsirhine found today in Asia and Africa.

lemur A strepsirhine found today on the island of Madagascar.

tarsier A nocturnal haplorhine found today in Indonesia.

FIGURE 5.10

A slow loris, a nocturnal strepsirhine that lives in parts of South and Southeast Asia.

FIGURE 5.11

Ring-tailed lemurs from the island of Madagascar.

FIGURE 5.12

A tarsier, a nocturnal haplorhine from Southeast Asia. See Box 5.1 for discussion of debates over the classification of tarsiers.

nocturnal primates, which typically eat fruits and leaves. Although tarsiers have many similarities to lorises and lemurs, their dry nose (and other traits) link them with the haplorhines using cladistic principles. Until recently, many scientists tended to classify the tarsiers with the lorises and lemurs (see Box 5.2 for additional detail on alternative primate classifications).

The other subgroup of haplorhines is the anthropoids (the group humans belong to), the focus of most of our attention in this book. Although the technical name of this infraorder is the Simiiformes (simians), we typically use the name **anthropoid** to be consistent with earlier classifications (Box 5.2). The anthropoid primates consist of primates we typically assign to the general groups of monkeys, apes, and humans. The everyday use of

Anthropoids A group of haplorhine primates consisting of monkeys, apes, and humans.

BOX 5.2

Alternatives in Primate Classification

Taxonomic classifications are always evolving. As we discover more about genetic and anatomic similarities and differences between different species, we may want to revise our system of classification. Whether or not we should reclassify can depend on tradition as well as our preference for one philosophy of classification—cladistics versus evolutionary systematic (see Chapter 4). The classification used in this text is based on cladistics and divides the primates into two suborders, the strepsirhines and the haplorhines. The more traditional approach, still used in many books and journals, divides all primates into two suborders, the prosimians and the anthropoids. Here, the term "anthropoid" is elevated from the rank of infraorder (as in Figure 5.9) to suborder.

In this system, the prosimians consist of lemurs, lorises, and tarsiers, and the anthropoids consist of monkeys, apes, and humans. The difference between these two different classifications is how they classify the tarsiers. As summarized in the table below, under the strepsirhine/haplorhine system, the tarsiers are placed with monkeys, apes, and humans, whereas the tarsiers are placed along with lemurs and lorises using the more traditional division between prosimians and anthropoids.

The difference between these two systems boils down to deciding where to classify the tarsiers. Do they belong with the more primitive primates, the lemurs and lorises, or do they belong with the anthropoids (monkeys, apes, humans)? As is often the case with questions of classification, the answer depends on the underlying philosophy of classification. If we consider the adaptive niche of tarsiers, we see they have a lot in common with lemurs and lorises, and it has long been considered most appropriate to lump them into the same taxonomic category as these primitive primates—prosimians. On the other hand, tarsiers lack the wet nose of the lemurs and lorises and instead have the dry nose of the anthropoids, a shared derived trait. In addition, some genetic investigations have supported the greater kinship of tarsiers and anthropoids. Thus, if we want to emphasize evolutionary relationships rather than adaptive nature in classification, the strepsirhine/haplorhine division is more appropriate. None of this debate has great impact on our primary focus in this book, which is the evolutionary placement of humans within the order primates, but it does show some of the difficulties in taxonomic analyses.

Strepsirhines	Lemurs and lorises	Prosimians
Haplorhines	Tarsiers	
	Monkeys, apes, and humans	Anthropoids

---

these terms is sufficient for some descriptive purposes but does not fit the cladistic philosophy of classification based on evolutionary relationship. For one thing, some monkey species are actually more closely related to apes and humans than to other monkey species. Thus, we will use terms such as "monkey" and "ape" as descriptive, not classificatory, terms.

Anthropoids are often called the "higher" primates and tend to have larger bodies and larger and more complex brains, they rely more on vision than do other primates. There are two subgroups of anthropoids, defined in part by their native lands—the platyrrhines and the catarrhines. As you can see from the words, one of the physical differences between platyrrhines and catarrhines has to do with their noses. **Platyrrhines** have broad and flat noses with nostrils on the side of the nose, whereas **catarrhines** have narrower noses where the nostrils face down.

The two kinds of anthropoids are also distinguished by geography—platyrrhines are also known as New World anthropoids and catarrhines are known as Old World anthropoids. Here, the "New World" refers to the Americas, and the "Old World" refers to Afric, Asia, and Europe. The only type of New World anthropoids (past or present) are the New World monkeys.

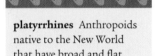

platyrrhines Anthropoids native to the New World that have broad and flat noses with nostrils on the side. This group consists of New World monkeys.

catarrhines Anthropoids native to the Old World that have narrow noses with downward-facing nostrils. This group consists of Old World monkeys, apes, and humans.

The Old World anthropoids include the Old World monkeys, the apes, and humans. Even if you live in the New World, you are not a New World anthropoid because the initial origin of the catarrhines was in the Old World. Any humans living in the New World are migrants, having moved here sometime in the past 20,000 years or so (see Chapter 15).

New World Monkeys

New World monkeys are found today in Central and South America. Like Old World monkeys, they typically walk on all fours (**quadrupedal**) and their arms and legs are generally of similar length so that their spines are parallel to the ground. Although they share many similarities with Old World monkeys, several important differences reflect separate lines of evolution over the past 30 million years or so. For example, New World monkeys have four more premolar teeth than do Old World monkeys. The dental formula for many New World monkeys is 2-1-3-3, compared to the 2-1-2-3 dental formula of all Old World monkeys. Other differences relate to the way in which the monkeys live; for example, some New World monkeys have prehensile tails. Because the tail of some New World monkeys is capable of grasping, it is highly useful in moving about and feeding in the trees (Figure 5.13). Typically, the

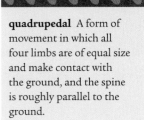

quadrupedal A form of movement in which all four limbs are of equal size and make contact with the ground, and the spine is roughly parallel to the ground.

FIGURE 5.13

A spider monkey, a New World monkey capable of using its tail as a "fifth limb."

monkey uses this "fifth limb" to anchor itself while feeding on the ends of small branches. Old World monkeys have tails, but not prehensile tails. Those New World monkeys with prehensile tails are thus more proficient in terms of acrobatic agility. This difference probably relates to the fact that all New World monkeys are arboreal, whereas some Old World monkeys are terrestrial. The prehensile tail of many New World monkeys is a derived trait that did not develop in the Old World monkeys.

Old World Monkeys

Old World monkeys are biochemically and physically more similar to humans than are New World monkeys. They inhabit a wide range of environments. Many species live in tropical rain forests, but other species have adapted to the savanna, or open grasslands. One species has even learned to survive in the snowy environment of the Japanese mountains (Figure 5.14).

The Old World monkeys, like the New World monkeys, are quadrupedal, running on the ground and on tree branches on all fours. Though Old World monkeys are agile in the trees, many species have adapted to spending more time on the ground in search of food (Figure 5.15). Most Old World species eat a mixed diet of fruits and leaves, although some show dental and digestive specializations for leaf eating. Some Old World species occasionally supplement their primarily vegetarian diet with insects or small animals that they hunt. Social structure is highly variable among Old World monkeys. Some species have social groups with only one adult male, whereas others have more than one adult male (variation in social structure is discussed in more detail in Chapter 6).

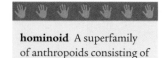

hominoid A superfamily of anthropoids consisting of apes and humans.

The Hominoids

The superfamily of **hominoids** consists of apes and humans. The similarity of apes and humans (hence their placement in the same group) has long been a source of fascination. One of our most memorable images of this relatedness comes from the classic 1933 movie *King Kong* (and subsequent remakes). The giant gorilla discovered on "Skull Island" is captured and brought to New York City for display as the eighth wonder of the world. Ignoring the fantastic nature of some of the plot elements (gorillas could not be that large and still walk), the film draws close comparisons between Kong's behavior and that of the humans in the film. Kong shows love, curiosity, and anger, among other emotions and behaviors. Kong is a mirror for the humans, and the humans are a mirror for Kong. We see ourselves in the beast and the beast in ourselves.

Hominoid Characteristics   Whether we choose to look at apes as humanlike or at humans as apelike, the fact remains that of all living creatures the apes are the most similar to humans in both biology and behavior. Unlike monkeys, hominoids do not have tails. Another hominoid characteristic is size: In general, most hominoid species are larger than monkeys. Hominoid brains as a rule are larger than monkey brains, both in terms of absolute size and in relation to body size. Their brains are more complex as well, which correlates

FIGURE 5.14

Japanese macaques, an Old World monkey, are the most northerly living nonhuman primates. They adapted to their climate with thick winter coats and lighter summer coats.

with the hominoid characteristics of greater intelligence and learning abilities. Hominoids also invest the most time and effort in raising their young.

Hominoids share with Old World monkeys the 2-1-2-3 dental formula (two incisors, one canine, two premolars, and three molars in each half of the upper and lower jaws). The structure of the molar teeth, however, is different in monkeys and hominoids. The most noticeable difference is that the lower molars of hominoids tend to have five **cusps** (raised areas) as compared to the four cusps in the lower molars of monkeys. The deeper grooves between these five cusps form the shape of the letter Y. As such, this characteristic shape is

cusp A raised area on the chewing surface of a tooth.

FIGURE 5.15

A mandrill, an Old World monkey. Mandrills are terrestrial monkeys that live in West Africa. Adult males are known for their vividly colored faces.

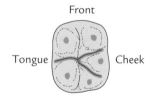

FIGURE 5.16

The Y-5 lower molar pattern of hominoids. Colored dots represent cusps. The heavier line resembles the letter Y on its side.

called the "Y-5" pattern (Figure 5.16). This difference helps us in identifying fossils because we can often tell whether a form is a monkey or a hominoid from the structure of the molars.

Perhaps one of the most important characteristics of hominoids is their upper body and shoulder anatomy. Hominoids can raise their arms above their heads with little trouble, whereas monkeys find this difficult. This ability of hominoids to raise their arms above their heads is based on three basic anatomical features. First, hominoids have a larger and stronger collarbone than monkeys. Second, the hominoid shoulder joint is very flexible and capable of a wide angle of movement. Third, hominoid shoulder blades are located more toward the back. By contrast, monkeys' shoulder blades are located more toward the sides of the chest (Figure 5.17). And whereas hominoid shoulder joints face outward, the shoulder joints of monkeys face downward.

Most hominoids have longer front limbs than back limbs. Modern humans are an exception to this rule, with longer legs than arms. This trait facilitates upright walking (discussed later). In apes, the longer front limbs represent an adaptation to hanging from tree limbs. In addition, hominoids generally have long fingers that help them hang suspended from branches. The wrist joint of hominoids contains a disc of cartilage (called a *meniscus*) between the lower arm bones and the wrist bones. This disc cuts down on contact between bones. As a result, the wrist joints of hominoids are more flexible than those of monkeys, allowing greater hanging ability.

Hominoid anatomy allows them a different type of movement from that of monkeys. Hominoids are adept at climbing and hanging from branches;

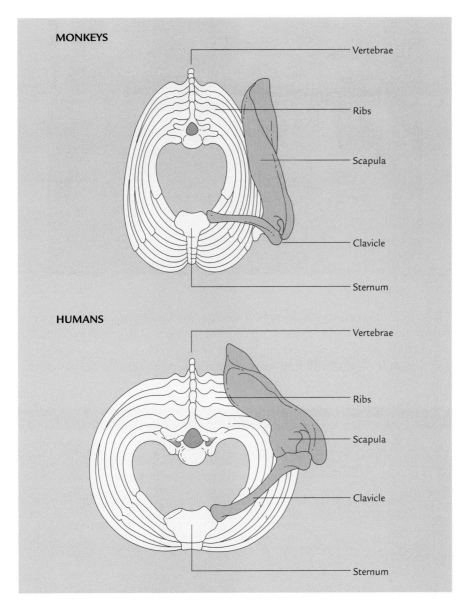

FIGURE 5.17

Top view of the shoulder complex of a monkey (*top*) and a human (*bottom*) drawn to the same scale top to bottom. In hominoids (apes and humans), the clavicle is larger and the scapula is located more toward the rear of the body.

they are **suspensory climbers.** As hominoids, humans have retained this ability, although we seldom use it in our daily lives. One exception is children playing on so-called monkey bars at playgrounds (which should more properly be called "hominoid bars"). The ability to suspend by the arms and then swing from one rung of the bars to the next is a basic hominoid trait (Figure 5.18).

Living hominoids all share this basic ability but vary quite a bit in terms of their normal patterns of movement. Some apes, for example, are proficient arm swingers, whereas others are expert climbers. Humans have evolved a very different pattern in which the arms are not used for movement; this allows us to carry things while walking on two legs. In spite of these differences in function, the close relationship between apes and humans is seen in their shared characteristics of the upper body and shoulder.

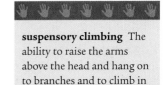

suspensory climbing The ability to raise the arms above the head and hang on to branches and to climb in this position.

FIGURE 5.18

Children playing on so-called monkey bars. Being able to hang by one's arms is a trait shared by apes and humans, but not as often in monkeys.

Classification and Evolutionary Relationships   Many different types of hominoids have lived over the past 20 million years. Today we have only the representatives of a few surviving species from this once diverse, widespread group (Table 5.2). Living hominoids are divided into three categories: the

TABLE 5.2   Species of Living Hominoids

	Genus	Species	Common Name(s)
Lesser apes	Hoolock	hoolock	Western hoolock gibbon
	Hoolock	leuconedys	Eastern hoolock gibbon
	Hylobates	agilis	Agile gibbon
	Hylobates	klossi	Mentawai/Kloss's gibbon
	Hylobates	lar	White-handed gibbon
	Hylobates	moloch	Javan silvery gibbon
	Hylobates	muelleri	Grey/Mueller's gibbon
	Hylobates	pileatus	Pileated/capped gibbon
	Nomascus	concolor	Black crested gibbon
	Nomascus	gabriellae	Yellow-cheeked crested gibbon
	Nomascus	hainanus	Hainan black crested gibbon
	Nomascus	leucogenys	White-cheeked crested gibbon
	Nomascus	nasutus	Cao-Vit black crested gibbon
	Symphalangus	syndactylus	Siamang
Great apes	Pongo	abelii	Sumatran orangutan
	Pongo	pygmaeus	Bornean orangutan
	Gorilla	beringei	Mountain/Grauer's gorilla
	Gorilla	gorilla	Western lowland/Cross River gorilla
	Pan	troglodytes	Chimpanzee
	Pan	paniscus	Bonobo
Humans	Homo	sapiens	Modern human

Source: Strier (2011).

(a) Gibbon

(b) Orangutan

(d) Chimpanzee

(c) Gorilla

(e) Bonobo

FIGURE 5.19

The living apes. The gibbon (a) and orangutan (b) are Asian apes, and the gorilla (c), chimpanzee (d), and bonobo (e) are African apes, and are our closest living relatives. Apes and humans are hominoids.

lesser apes, the great apes, and humans. The biology and behavior of the living apes are discussed at length in Chapter 6 and are only mentioned briefly here. The lesser apes are the gibbons of Asia (14 species), which are smaller than other apes, and are the least related to humans. The great apes, on the other hand, are larger and are more closely related to humans. The orangutan is a great ape that lives in Asia. The three types of African ape—the gorilla, chimpanzee, and the bonobo—are the closest living relatives of human beings (Figure 5.19).

FIGURE 5.20

An evolutionary "tree" showing the relationships among the living great apes and humans. Note that humans and the African apes are more closely related to each other than either is to the orangutan.

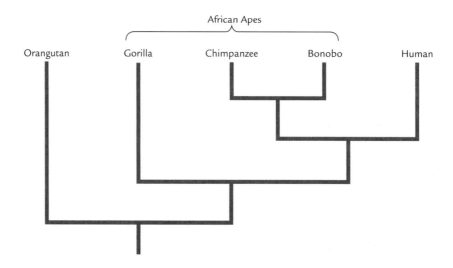

hominid A family (Hominidae) within the hominoids. In recent years, this family has been defined as including humans and the great apes (orangutan, gorilla, chimpanzee, and bonobo). Some scientists still use a more traditional definition that refers only to humans and their human-like ancestors.

hominine The subfamily of hominoids that includes humans, chimpanzees, and bonobos.

hominin Humans and their ancestors since the time of divergence from the common ancestor of humans, chimpanzees, and bonobos.

Genetic comparisons of living hominoids show a clear and consistent pattern. The African apes and humans form a closely related group, with orangutans more distant from this group, and gibbons more distant still. In addition, chimpanzees and bonobos are even more closely related to humans than either is to gorillas (Horai et al. 1995; Gagneux et al. 1999). Given these findings, we can reconstruct a family tree of the relationships of the great apes and humans. As shown in Figure 5.20, this tree suggests that the orangutan split off from the common ancestor of African apes and humans. The next split was between the line leading to the gorilla and the line leading to the common ancestor of humans and chimpanzees and bonobos, the latter two of which diverged later in time.

How should the hominoids be classified relative to one another? While it may be tempting to separate the group into apes and humans, genetic studies show us that some apes are actually more similar to humans than to other apes. As such, the term "ape" is meant as a purely descriptive term and not a formal taxonomic unit. Many argue that classification of living hominoids should take into account the close evolutionary relationship of the African apes and humans, as shown in Figure 5.21. Here, the hominoids are subdivided into two families, the hylobatids (gibbons, or lesser apes) and the **hominids,** a group consisting of the great apes and humans. The hominid family is then broken down into three subfamilies, one for orangutans, one for gorillas, and one (called **hominines**) that includes humans and our closest living relatives, the chimpanzee and bonobo.

Under the classification shown in Figure 5.21, the hominines are further broken down into two tribes (a zoological unit within the unit of subfamily). One tribe, the panins, consists of the chimpanzee and the bonobo. The other tribe, termed **hominins,** refers to humans and our ancestors since the time of divergence from the common ancestor of humans, chimpanzees, and bonobos (Figure 5.22). This system of classification is very useful because it

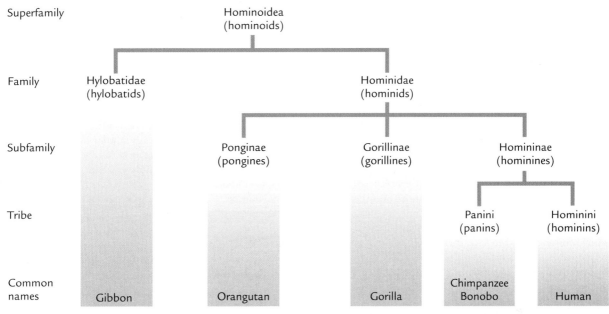

Superfamily — Hominoidea (hominoids)

Family — Hylobatidae (hylobatids) — Hominidae (hominids)

Subfamily — Ponginae (pongines) — Gorillinae (gorillines) — Homininae (hominines)

Tribe — Panini (panins) — Hominini (hominins)

Common names — Gibbon — Orangutan — Gorilla — Chimpanzee Bonobo — Human

FIGURE 5.21

Classification of hominoids to emphasize genetic and evolutionary relationships (see Figure 5.20). Humans, chimpanzees, and bonobos form a group separate from the gorilla and orangutan. (Wood and Richmond 2000.)

highlights the exact genetic and evolutionary relationships of humans and the great apes. However, as we have seen before, there are often alternative systems of classification depending on the specific purpose of the classification. For those who wish to highlight the evolutionary uniqueness of humans relative to apes, a different system is often used. This traditional system placed all of the great apes in one zoological family and humans in a separate zoological family. Details about this approach are given in Box 5.3.

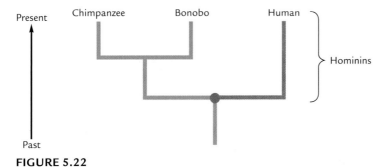

Present ← → Past

Chimpanzee — Bonobo — Human

Hominins

FIGURE 5.22

The evolutionary relationships between humans and their closest living relatives—the chimpanzee and bonobo. Humans and all their ancestors since the time of the divergence from the common ancestor (represented by the large dot) are called *hominins*.

BOX 5.3

Different Definitions of Hominids

Although the classification of living species can be informative, it can also be very confusing. It takes some time to become familiar with the various levels of classification and their names. For example, consider the classification of humans used in this chapter. Humans are simultaneously hominoids, hominids, hominines, and hominins! As shown in Table 5.1 and Figure 5.21, each of these labels corresponds to a different level of classification—superfamily, family, subfamily, and tribe. A frequent problem with learning these terms (particularly before an exam) is that they all share the same root and differ only by their suffixes: -oid, -id, -ine, and –in. I will not deny that it takes some time and effort to keep these straight, but when that is done the system is quite useful, and it tells us where we humans fit into the natural world and our relatives in order of similarity as we move from the level of tribe up to the level of superfamily.

However, as was the case with defining different suborders of primates, there are alternatives to the evolutionary classification presented in this chapter. One alternative, used for years and still with its proponents, favors basing classification considering adaptive differences. When we compare humans to apes, for example, many of the unique features of our evolution stand out—our large brains, upright walking, hairlessness, and reliance on culture and technology. From a purely cladistic point of view, such traits should not be used in classification because they are *unique* derived traits. Nonetheless, they are obviously important in defining the very nature of human evolution, and we can argue that our classification should highlight these evolutionary trends (e.g., Marks 2011).

For many, a preferred alternative is to subdivide the hominoids into three families: hylobatids (gibbons, the lesser apes), pongids (the great apes—orangutans, gorillas, chimpanzees, and bonobos), and hominids (humans). Although this scheme does not reflect the fact that some apes are actually more genetically similar to humans than to other apes, it does provide a nice classification based on overall appearance and adaptive nature, such that humans (and our fossil relatives) are given their own zoological family.

Again, the difference between this approach and the one shown in Figure 5.21 reflects philosophical differences in the function and nature of taxonomic classification. You can make up your own mind after reading the rest of this text. For the moment, you just need to keep in mind that because different people prefer different classification schemes, the word *hominid* is used differently in different contexts. In this book, the term *hominid* follows the scheme shown in Figure 5.21, which is a zoological family that includes the great apes and humans. For those who prefer the more traditional alternative, the word *hominid* refers only to humans. Most of the discussion comes down to the question of what to call humans and their fossil relatives. Those favoring the traditional alternative would use the term *hominid,* whereas those following the scheme used in this book (Figure 5.21) would use the term *hominin,* and instead use *hominid* to refer to humans and great apes. Although this undoubtedly sound very confusing, in practice it is very easy to keep things straight from context.

Summary

Humans are animals, chordates, and vertebrates. We share certain characteristics, such as a more developed nervous system, with other creatures in these categories. Humans are mammals, which means we rely a great deal on a reproductive strategy of few births and extensive parental care. This reproductive pattern is associated with higher intelligence and a greater capacity for learned behaviors. Other adaptations of mammals include differentiated teeth, a skeletal structure capable of swift movement, and the ability to maintain a constant body temperature.

Humans belong to a specific order of mammals known as primates. The primates have certain characteristics, such as skeletal flexibility, grasping hands, and keen eyesight, which evolved in order to meet the demands of life in the trees. Although many primate species no longer live in the trees, they have retained these basic primate characteristics and use them in new ways to adapt to the environment. Most humans no longer use their grasping hands to move about in trees, but use them instead for tool manufacture and use.

There is a great deal of biological and behavioral variation among the living primates. The order Primates is composed of two suborders, the strepsirhines (primitive wet-nosed primates) and the haplorhines (the dry-nosed primates). Haplorhines consist of tarsiers and anthropoids (monkeys, apes, and humans). The two major subgroups of anthropoids are the New World anthropoids (consisting of New World monkeys) and the Old World anthropoids (consisting of Old World monkeys and the hominoids, which are apes and humans). Humans belong to the subfamily of hominines, which consist of humans and our closest living relatives, the chimpanzee and bonobo, both African apes. The term *hominin* refers to humans and our fossil relatives that lived after the evolutionary split with the African apes.

Supplemental Readings

Campbell, C. J., A. Fuentes, K. C. MacKinnon, M. Panger, and S. K. Bearder, eds. 2007. *Primates in Perspective*. New York: Oxford University Press. An excellent general text on primates.

Chimpanzees, one of three groups of African apes. Chimps, along with the bonobo, another African ape, are the closest living relative of human beings. Most chimpanzee groups live in the rainforests of Africa, and have a diet heavy in fruits, but also eat leaves, nuts, and insects.

Primate Behavior and Ecology

When we visit a zoo and watch a group of monkeys or apes, we often see scenes of individual animals playing or fighting. We also see older primates holding and comforting infants, even to the extent where a mother will gently pat the back of an infant that she is holding to provide comfort and reassurance. In short, if you watch a group of nonhuman primates, you may often conclude, when considering their behavior: "How human they act." Indeed, it is not uncommon to hear people voice this exact statement in such cases. We saw in the last chapter how other primates share a number of biological traits with us. It should therefore come as no surprise that we also share a number of behavioral traits as well. As an example, consider the fact that humans live in a variety of different family units. Within the Western world, we see examples of nuclear families, extended families, single-parent families, and same-sex families. Beyond this variation, we see commonality in the fact that *all* of these are families have a common function—taking care of offspring—that is a reflection of our mammalian and primate heritage. In addition, we will see in this chapter that the nonhuman primates show variation in social structure, but all have common elements such as the close bond between mothers and infants. Such observations raise an interesting question—does behavior reflect ancestry, environment, or both? Further, we are interested in knowing which species, if any, can provide us with insights into the behavior of our ancestors. If we are to understand human behavior in an evolutionary context, we need to apply the comparative method and examine nonhuman primate behavior across a variety of different species and a range of environments. This chapter provides some basic background in the range of primate behavior, starting with a discussion of some basic principles and continuing with a series of case studies.

PRIMATE BEHAVIORAL ECOLOGY

Studies of primate behavior have often used ecological approaches to explain variation in primate behavior, both between different species and within a single species. Early ecological studies of primates focused on habitat—specifically, the contrast between species that live in the trees and species that live on the ground (DeVore 1963). This arboreal-terrestrial contrast suggested

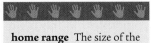

home range The size of the geographic area that is normally occupied and used by a social group.

behavioral ecology The study of behavior that focuses on the adaptive value of behavior from an ecological and evolutionary perspective.

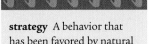

strategy A behavior that has been favored by natural selection and that increases an individual's fitness.

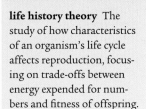

life history theory The study of how characteristics of an organism's life cycle affects reproduction, focusing on trade-offs between energy expended for numbers and fitness of offspring.

some basic relationships between habitat and social organization, territoriality, group size, and **home range** (the size of the geographic area normally occupied in a group). Additional studies showed that this simple contrast in habitats did not fully explain variation in primate behavior. Crook and Gartlan (1965) and Jolly (1972) later expanded on this idea by breaking down primate species into groups defined by habitat and diet. Other researchers began focusing on other ecological principles, such as food density, mating strategies, and predation, to help explain differences in primate behavior and social organization (e.g., Denham 1971).

By the mid-1980s, the study of primate behavior had shifted toward the field of **behavioral ecology,** the study of behavior from an ecological and evolutionary perspective. The primary concern of primate behavioral ecology is the evolutionary analysis of behaviors as strategies for adapting to specific conditions, with a focus on feeding, social, and reproductive strategies (Fedigan and Strum 1999; Strier 2011). This focus relates primate behavior to the basic problems of adaptation from an evolutionary perspective: finding food, reproducing, and getting along with others. Analysis of primate behavior needs to take into account multiple costs and benefits for various behaviors.

Consider, for example, something as basic as the nature of the social group. Why live in groups? Advantages of group living include more successful defense against predators and cooperative defense of valuable food resources (Wrangham 1987a; Fedigan and Strum 1999). Large groups, however, may be *disadvantageous* if food resources are limited. To what extent are group size and structure (or any social behavior, for that matter) a trade-off between the costs and benefits of different behavioral strategies? As used here, the term *strategy* does not imply a conscious decision. Instead, **strategy** has a very specific meaning in behavioral ecology, referring to any behavior that has been selected for because it increases an individual's overall fitness (in terms of reproduction and survival) (Strier 2011).

Reproductive Strategies

Reproduction is central to evolution. In terms of behavior, it is useful to examine the costs and benefits associated with different reproductive strategies. **Life history theory** deals with characteristics of an organism's life cycle and their effects on the quantity and quality of reproduction. These characteristics include age at maturity, age at reproduction, gestation length, the interval between births, and overall life span, among others. A central concept of life history theory is the allocation of energy. Energy is used by organisms for growth, maintenance, and reproduction, and energy expended for one function cannot be used for something else. Life history theory focuses on the trade-off between energy needs, and one of the most important trade-offs is between the number of offspring and their fitness (Hill 1993; Leigh and Blomquist 2007). This relationship has been discussed in the last chapter, noting that compared with reptiles, mammals invest a great deal of care in a relatively smaller number of offspring.

Some animal species can be described as having "fast" life histories, whereby individuals reach maturity early and have a large number of offspring during their reproductive life. Other species have "slow" life histories, whereby maturation is delayed until later in the life span, and the total number of offspring is lower (Strier 2011). In general, primates have "slow" life histories characterized by a small number of offspring and a great deal of parental care. Primates tend to mature more slowly, live longer, have larger brains, and have fewer offspring. Almost all primates have a reproductive pattern of having one offspring at a time. The next offspring is generally not born until the previous one is mature enough, biologically and socially, to survive on its own. In some primates, such as the apes, the interval between offspring may be five years or more. Humans are an exception to this rule because we have overlapping births without sacrificing the quality of parental care.

The Mother–Infant Bond Evolutionary explanations of behavior often focus on maximizing fitness. This refers to behaviors that increase the probability that an individual's DNA will be passed on to the next generation. If such behaviors are affected even partially by genetic factors, then natural selection will cause those behaviors to increase in frequency. A related concept is the idea of **parental investment,** which refers to parental behaviors that increase the probability that the offspring will survive. Mammalian (and especially primate) females invest a great deal of time and energy in care of offspring. Even though this investment reduces the number of offspring a female can have, the benefits outweigh the costs.

Primates have a strong and long-lasting bond between mother and infant. Unlike some mammals, infant primates are entirely helpless. They depend on their mothers for food, warmth, protection, affection, and knowledge, and they remain dependent for a long time (Figure 6.1). Of all the different types of social bonds in primate societies, the mother–infant bond is the strongest. In many primate species, this bond continues well past infancy. Chimpanzees,

parental investment
Parental behaviors that increase the probability that offspring will survive.

FIGURE 6.1

Female chimpanzee and her infant. The greater amount of care and attention given by the mother can be interpreted as maximizing reproductive success by increasing parental investment.

for example, regularly associate with their mothers throughout their adult lives (Goodall 1986).

The biological importance of the mother–infant bond is easy to see: The infant is dependent on the mother's milk for nourishment. Is that all there is to it? In the early twentieth century, some researchers suggested that the entire basis of "mother love" seen in primate infants arose from the infant's need for food. However, laboratory experiments and field observations soon showed that this is not the case; the social aspects of the mother–infant bond are also crucial for survival.

One of the most famous of these experiments was performed by psychologist Harry Harlow, who isolated infant rhesus monkeys from their mothers. He raised them in cages in which he placed two "surrogate mothers," the first a wire framework in the approximate shape of an adult monkey and the second the same structure covered with terry cloth. He then attached a bottle of milk to the "wire mother" (Figure 6.2). Harlow reasoned that if the need for food were stronger than the need for warmth and comfort, the infant monkeys would spend most or all of their time clinging to the "wire mother." If the need for warmth and comfort were more important, the infants would spend most or all of the time clinging to the "cloth mother." The monkeys invariably preferred the warmth and security of the "cloth mothers" to the food provided by the "wire mothers." Even when the infants needed to eat, they often kept part of their body in contact with the "cloth mother." Additional experiments showed that under the stimulus of stress or fear, the monkeys would go to the "cloth mothers" for security (Harlow 1959).

These experiments showed that motherhood was not important merely in terms of nutrition; warmth and comfort were also necessary to the infant's development. Do these experiments mean that natural mothers can be replaced by a bottle and a blanket? Definitely not. As Harlow's monkeys grew up, they showed a wide range of abnormal behaviors. They were often incapable of sexual reproduction, they did not interact normally with other

FIGURE 6.2

Harlow's maternal deprivation experiment on infant rhesus monkeys. These monkeys preferred to spend almost all of their time clinging to the cloth surrogate mother (*right*), which provided warmth, rather than to the wire surrogate mother (*left*), which provided food. Even when hungry, the infants would often remain partially attached to the cloth mother.

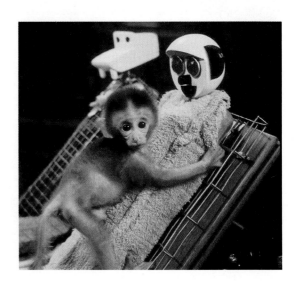

monkeys, and they often were extremely aggressive. The motherless females who later had children did not know how to care for them and frequently rejected or mistreated them.

These findings have powerful implications. We often speak of "maternal instincts," suggesting that the behaviors associated with successful mothering are somehow innate. Although the basic mother–infant bond is part of the biological basis of mammals, and maternal feelings are to some extent innate, the specific behaviors that are part of this bond are learned. Mammals, and especially primates, rely extensively on learned behaviors. As a result, variation in behavior is often great and can be influenced by a variety of other factors. Observations of the behavior of primates in their natural environments confirm that maternal behaviors are largely learned. Studies of chimpanzee mothers have shown that young females tend to model their own later parental behaviors after those of their mothers. Similar patterns are seen in humans. For example, the children of abusive parents often tend to be abusive parents themselves. Such research shows us that the study of animal behavior, especially that of other primates, is not an esoteric subject but rather helps us to understand ourselves.

Adult Males and Infant Care Maternal care is found throughout the primate order. The mother–infant bond is the strongest tie within primate groups. What role do males play in the care of infants in primate societies? Such care is variable among primate societies, in terms of both its presence and intensity. A number of **monogamous** primate species (characterized by a more or less permanent bond forming between a single male and female) show the most intensive levels of infant care by males (Whitten 1987) (Figure 6.3). From a genetic perspective, this makes sense if we assume that the male is the father, because taking care of his offspring increases his reproductive fitness. If so, then infant care may be less likely in **polygamous** species, in which a number of males could potentially be the father.

monogamy An exclusive sexual bond between an adult male and an adult female for a long period of time.

polygamy A sexual bond between an adult male and an adult female in which either individual may have more than one mate at the same time.

FIGURE 6.3

Some primate species, including humans, exhibit a close bond between fathers and offspring.

BOX 6.1

Infanticide in Nonhuman Primates

Although the basic primate pattern is for adults to care for offspring, this does not always apply. Adults in several primate species have been observed to kill infants of their own species, a behavior known as infanticide. A classic example is Sarah Hrdy's (1977) study of infanticide in langurs, a species of Old World monkey. Although it is tempting to explain such gruesome behavior as social deviance, Hrdy and others have raised the possibility that infanticide in langurs might represent a behavior that has been selected for because it increases the genetic fitness of the murderer.

How could this be? Langurs live in societies that have a single adult male and several adult females (this type of social structure is described in more detail later in the chapter). Typically, the adult male mates with all of the adult females, so that (barring infidelity) all infants in the group are his. The adult male frequently faces challenges from other adult males who attempt to take over his social group. When a male challenger successfully takes over the group, he often attempts to kill the infants fathered by the previous male. Although such behavior seems to be contrary to the survival of the group, it actually can increase the evolutionary fitness of the invading male. By killing the infants sired by the previous male, he increases his own genetic contribution to the next generation. In effect, he removes his genetic competition. In addition,

when the infants are killed, the mothers stop nursing and more quickly resume their normal pattern of ovulation, so that the invading males can more quickly father new offspring. Although this explanation might make evolutionary sense, this does not ensure that it is correct. Others have criticized the hypothesis and offered alternative explanations for the pathology, such as overcrowding and deforestation leading to stress and deviance.

There is some genetic support for the infanticide hypothesis because it predicts that there will be no genetic relationship between the killer and the victim. If we assume that infanticide increases the new male's reproductive success, then we would expect this behavior to be directed only at offspring of other males. On the other hand, if the social pathology hypothesis is correct, we might expect that a deviant male would kill his own as well as other males' infants. Borries and colleagues (1999) tested this hypothesis by examining the DNA of langur infants and attackers from fecal samples for 16 infant attacks. In all cases, the DNA analysis showed that the attacking male was *not* the infant's father. Although the sample size is relatively small, this study does suggest that infanticide is related to male reproductive success in langur monkeys. Further research will be needed to confirm this hypothesis and to see if it fits other cases and species.

The situation is more complex, however, than a simple dichotomy of monogamous versus polygamous species. For one thing, adult females in monogamous societies have been observed to have sexual relationships outside of their pair-group (Strier 2011). In addition, adult males in some monogamous species engage in very little infant care, whereas some males in polygamous species do provide such care. Infant care by adult males may be a function of females choosing mates, as a number of studies have shown that females in polygamous species are more likely to mate with males that actively care for infants (van Schaik and Paul 1996). In such cases, it would be adaptive for males to engage in infant care because it increases their chances of mating, and therefore their chances for reproductive success. There are also examples of males killing the infants of other males, which might also be related to reproductive success (Box 6.1).

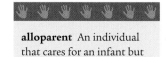

alloparent An individual that cares for an infant but is not a biological parent.

Alloparenting An **alloparent** is an individual who takes care of an infant but is not his or her biological parent. An alloparent can be another adult or a sibling. As a rule, primate females who have not given birth are more likely to engage in this behavior than females who have given birth (MacKinnon 2007). There is variation in the extent to which mothers allow others to touch and interact with their infants. Alloparent care can be potentially adaptive for both the infant and the alloparent. In cases in which a mother dies (and assuming that the infant has already been weaned), an alloparent can care for the orphan. In cases in which the mother is present, alloparents can gain valuable experience in helping to care for infants. In addition, as discussed above, if adult males help care for infants, they may increase their chances of mating with the mother.

Growing Up

The importance of the extended period of infant and juvenile growth in primates cannot be overstated. This long period is necessary for learning motor skills and social behaviors. The close bond between mother and infant provides the first important means by which an infant primate learns. It is not the only important social contact for a growing primate, however. The process of socialization in most primates depends largely on close contact with peers. Interaction with other individuals of the same age provides the opportunity to learn specific types of social behaviors, as well as how to interact socially in general.

Experiments by Harlow clearly demonstrate the importance of social contact with peers. Monkeys raised by their mothers but kept apart from other infants often grew up showing a range of abnormal behaviors. They would stare at their cages for long periods, were often self-destructive, and did not show normal patterns of sexual behavior (Harlow and Harlow 1962). Although some primate species are solitary apart from the mother–infant bond, most belong to larger social groups and require contact with peers during their growth.

Growing up as a primate, with the emphasis on learned behavior, also requires that infants and juveniles play a great deal of the time. Play behaviors had once been ignored in studies of human and nonhuman behavior because they are regarded as nonproductive. In truth, play behaviors are essential to the proper biological and social development of primates (Figure 6.4). Play

FIGURE 6.4

Monkeys playing. Play behaviors are critical to normal development in primates, promoting both physical and social skills.

behavior can serve several functions. First, physical play allows the infant to develop and practice necessary motor skills. Second, social play provides the opportunity to learn how to behave with others. Needed social skills are learned through play (Dohlinow 1999). The importance of play becomes obvious when we consider what happened to the monkeys that Harlow had separated from their peers. Without normal contact and the opportunity to develop socially, these monkeys became sociopathic.

Social Groups

Primates are essentially social creatures, but they show an amazing amount of variation in the size and structure of their primary social groups. The main social group can range in size and can vary in terms of the number of male, female, young, and old members. A social group is generally defined as a group within which there is frequent communication or interaction among members. The size and structure of a social group can vary within a species and even within a group over time. Some primates are relatively solitary, and the primary social group consists of a mother and her dependent offspring; adult males and adult females have infrequent contact, mostly for mating.

Most primate species, however, are more social and live in larger and more complex groups. The traditional labels used to describe primate social groups reflect the relative number of adult males and adult females in the social group (Fuentes 1999). The **one-male/one-female group** consists of a single adult male and single adult female in a monogamous relationship, and their offspring. Although this social group corresponds to a typical Western notion of a "family," it is not that common among nonhuman primates. It should be noted that genetic evidence shows that reproduction is not strictly monogamous in these groups.

Two types of primate social groups consist of a single adult of one sex and more than one adult of the opposite sex: the **one-male/multifemale group** and, less commonly, the **one-female/multimale group.** The most common type of social group in primates is the **multimale/multifemale group,** which consists of more than one adult of each sex and their offspring. Given multiple adult males and adult females, these complex social groups are often quite large, and members may have multiple mates. There is considerable variation in this type of social structure in terms of size, composition, and distribution.

These categories are, of course, rough labels that may not always apply to any particular primate species at all times, as there are many examples of variation *within* a species. We do not find a strict association between type of primate and social structure. Among apes, for example, we find some species that have the one-male/one-female group, some that have the one-male/multifemale group, and some that have the multimale/multifemale group. We can therefore not equate being an ape with any particular type of social structure. The same is true of other primates. Figure 6.5, for example, shows the range of variation in social structure among Old World monkey species.

one-male/one-female group A social structure in which the primary social group consists of a single adult male, a single adult female, and their immature offspring.

one-male/multifemale group A social structure in which the primary social group consists of a single adult male, several adult females, and their immature offspring.

one-female/multimale group A social structure in which the primary social group consists of a single adult female, several adult males, and their immature offspring.

multimale/multifemale group The most common type of social group in nonhuman primates, consisting of several adult males, several adult females, and their immature offspring.

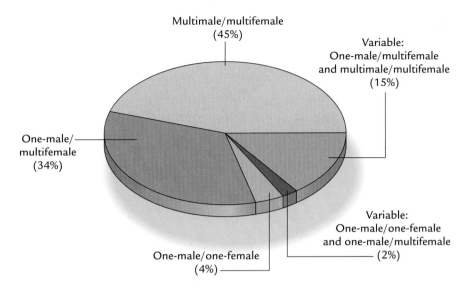

Multimale/multifemale
(45%)

Variable:
One-male/multifemale
and multimale/multifemale
(15%)

One-male/
multifemale
(34%)

One-male/one-female
(4%)

Variable:
One-male/one-female
and one-male/multifemale
(2%)

FIGURE 6.5

Variation in social structure among Old World monkeys. Numbers represent the percentage of species that have a particular social structure (species for which this information is not known have been excluded). Note that 17 percent of Old World monkey species have been observed with more than one type of social structure. (Data from Jolly 1985:129, Table 6.5a.)

Social Behaviors

As social animals who rely on learning, we should not be surprised at the range of social behaviors (interactions with others) found among primates. We see variations both within and between different species. This section focuses on a few examples of social behaviors in primates.

Affiliative and Agonistic Behaviors Social interactions between individuals can be friendly or unfriendly. As a rule, primatologists classify relationships as **affiliative,** which indicates strong and friendly bonds, or **agonistic,** which indicates unfriendly and often aggressive interactions. Affiliative bonds and behaviors are particularly important in maintaining large social groups (Ray 1999a).

One common means of developing and maintaining strong affiliative bonds that is practiced by all nonhuman primates is **grooming,** the practice of handling and cleaning another individual's fur (Figure 6.6). Although grooming has hygienic utility (the removal of dirt and parasites), it is primarily a social activity. For example, McKenna (1978) observed 1,907 cases of grooming in langur monkeys and found that 96 percent involved reciprocal social grooming; only 4 percent involved a monkey grooming itself. Grooming can function to reduce tension and conflict as well as maintain affiliative bonds.

Altruism When social relationships are analyzed from an evolutionary perspective, the bottom line is the individual's evolutionary fitness. Behaviors that increase chances of survival or reproduction will be favored by natural selection, whereas behaviors that are not conducive to survival or reproduction will be weeded out. How, then, do we explain examples of altruistic behavior that have been observed among primates? For example, Strier (2011)

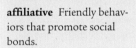

affiliative Friendly behaviors that promote social bonds.

agonistic Unfriendly social relationships.

grooming The handling and cleaning of another individual's fur. In primates, grooming serves as a form of communication and provides reassurance.

A chimpanzee grooming another chimpanzee.

kin selection The concept that altruistic behavior can be selected for if it increases the probability of survival of close relatives.

reciprocal altruism The concept that altruistic behaviors will be directed toward nonkin if they increase the probability that the recipient will reciprocate at some future time.

observed a young male baboon (an African monkey) being chased by a hyena when an adult female baboon who was not his mother attempted to intercede at risk to herself. Why would she put herself in danger?

More generally, how do we explain altruism from an evolutionary perspective? Is there an evolutionary benefit to sacrificing oneself or risking sacrifice? One evolutionary explanation involves the concept of **kin selection.** Here, altruistic behaviors may be selected for when they are directed toward biological relatives. If you die saving your own child, this act will have two genetic consequences. First, because you die, you will no longer pass alleles on to the next generation. Second, your child will live and have the opportunity to pass on his or her DNA, of which 50 percent came from you. Thus, by saving your child, you actually contribute to the survival of some of your own DNA. If your altruistic action was at least partially affected by genetic factors, this behavior will also be passed on through the survival of your child.

Studies show that primates often help those who are *not* kin (de Waal 2007). Here, the concept of **reciprocal altruism** comes into play—an extension of the adage that "one hand washes the other." The basic idea is that any altruistic action directed toward someone who is not kin can be selected for if it increases the possibility that the action will someday be rewarded. It may be useful to help others because you will, in turn, be more likely to receive help from them at some future time (assuming, of course, you do not die in the attempt). Coalitions of unrelated individuals form in a number of primate societies and provide evidence of reciprocal altruism.

Dispersal and Social Behavior   Dispersal occurs when an individual leaves the birth group and moves to another social group (or, in some cases, lives alone). Such dispersal can be voluntary or involuntary, as when an individual is kicked out of a group. In many primate species, males typically leave and move to another group. In some primate species, however, females are more typically the dispersing sex, and in some cases, both sexes disperse (Pusey and Packer 1987). Genetically, dispersal is important because it reduces inbreeding and introduces new genetic material. There are also important behavioral effects of dispersal, including a reduction in the competition of males for mates.

One of the most important effects of dispersal is that it changes social relationships based on kinship. If you move to a new group, you must develop new relationships with individuals who are not related to you. There are both costs and benefits associated with having social relationships based on kinship. Staying in one's birth group increases the chances of developing long-term relationships and coalitions, and by extension increases the probability of kin selection. Likewise, those who disperse are less likely to develop such long-term relationships. Because dispersal in most primate species is sex-based (i.e., either males or females are more likely to disperse), the act of dispersal affects the social relationships of the sexes in different ways.

Social Organization and Dominance Nonhuman primate societies rank individuals in terms of their relative dominance in the group. A **dominance hierarchy** is the ranking system within the society and reflects which individuals are most and least dominant (Figure 6.7). Dominance hierarchies are found in most nonhuman primate societies, but they vary widely in their overall importance in everyday life. The dominance hierarchy provides stability in social life. All individuals know their place within the society, eliminating to some extent uncertainty about what to do or whom to follow.

The dominance hierarchy in nonhuman primates is usually ruled by those individuals with the greatest access to food or sex or those that control social behaviors to the greatest extent. Societies with strong male-dominance hierarchies are likely to show a moderate to large difference in the sizes of adult males and adult females. The **sexual dimorphism** in body size has often been seen as the result of competition among males for breeding

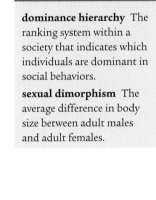

dominance hierarchy The ranking system within a society that indicates which individuals are dominant in social behaviors.

sexual dimorphism The average difference in body size between adult males and adult females.

FIGURE 6.7

An adult male baboon (an Old World monkey) opening his jaw in a threat gesture. Such gestures are used in contests of dominance.

females. The males that are larger and stronger are considered more likely to gain access to females and hence pass on their genetic potential for larger size and greater strength.

There has often been controversy over the extent to which a male's position in the dominance hierarchy is related to his reproductive success. Altmann and colleagues (1996) used DNA analysis to determine paternity of a group of baboon offspring during a four-year period. They found that the top-ranking male baboon fathered 81 percent of the surviving offspring. When they examined other periods when this baboon was not the highest-ranking male, they found that he fathered fewer offspring. Although there is a strong relationship between a male's rank and his short-term reproductive success, the fact that the ranking of adult male baboons changes so much over a short time means that the long-term relationship is weaker.

Studies of primate behavior have demonstrated a number of factors that affect dominance rank (Ray 1999b; Strier 2011). These include an individual's size, strength, age, and ability to form coalitions, among others. In some species, such as Japanese macaque monkeys, studies have found that the rank of one's mother has an influence on her son's dominance rank (Eaton 1976). Males born to high-ranking mothers have a greater chance of achieving high dominance themselves, all other factors being equal.

In a number of primate societies, the dominance hierarchy of females is more stable over time than is that of the males. Whereas the position of most dominant males can change quickly, the hierarchy among females remains more constant. Even in cases in which all males are dominant over females, the female dominance hierarchy exerts an effect on social behaviors within the group, as in the case in which mother's rank affects the rank of male offspring.

CASE STUDIES OF PRIMATE BEHAVIOR

Thus far, the discussion of primate behavior has focused on general principles. The remainder of this chapter provides selected case studies of a number of primate species to provide several comprehensive examples of primate biology, behavior, and ecology. Because of their close evolutionary relationship with us, most of the case studies focus on apes.

Strepsirhines and Monkeys

There is considerable variation among strepsirhine and monkey species in the world today. Three short examples are shown here to give a glimpse into this diversity.

The Lemurs of Madagascar   As noted in Chapter 5, the lemurs of Madagascar are different from other living strepsirhines, perhaps because of their isolation on the island. Although some lemur species have the multimale/ multifemale social structure, a large proportion (more than 25 percent) live in monogamous groups with one adult male and one adult female, a number much higher than found among other primates or mammals in general. This high proportion might reflect an adaptation to dietary sources that exist in small patches regularly distributed in the environment; in such cases, small groups might be more efficient (Wright 1999).

Another peculiar lemur trait is the prevalence of female dominance in lemur species. Among other strepsirhines, males tend to be dominant. Many lemur species, with clear female dominance, are an exception to this general pattern. Female lemurs typically win aggressive encounters with males and have priority in eating—males generally wait to feed until the females are done. Female dominance in lemurs may reflect a dietary adaptation such that females have priority access to a limited food supply in order to have sufficient food for raising offspring (Wright 1999).

Studies of ring-tailed lemurs (Figure 6.8) show the greater emphasis on smell than in the higher primates. Although they are diurnal, they retain biological adaptations for communicating via smell from a nocturnal ancestor, such as the moist nose and scent glands on the inside of their wrists. Ring-tailed lemurs use their scent glands to mark territory by rubbing them against branches. Males even challenge each other for dominance in what are known as "stink fights," where a male will rub his tail against his scent glands and then wave it toward other males in an aggressive manner (Falk 2000).

FIGURE 6.8

A group of ring-tailed lemurs.

FIGURE 6.9

A brown howler monkey.

Howler Monkeys   One interesting group of New World monkeys is the howler monkeys, consisting of 14 species in the genus *Alouatta* (Strier 2011). Howler monkeys are found in Mexico and in South America (Figure 6.9). Their name reflects their most unusual characteristic—an enlarged hyoid bone (the bone in the throat), which creates a large resonating chamber capable of making sounds that can be heard at a considerable distance. Howlers have prehensile tails and are quite at home in the trees, where they eat primarily fruit and leaves. Adult howlers weigh 13–18 pounds (6–8 kg), with males larger than females. Males are capable of making deeper and louder howls (Bramblett 1994). Howler monkeys typically live in small groups ranging from 10 to 15 individuals and consisting of between one and three adult males (Di Fiore and Campbell 2007).

The loud howling of howler monkeys serves many purposes, including warning and defense. These howls often serve to warn away competitors for food and space, and it also has been suggested that these vocalizations are a substitute for active fighting (Carpenter 1965; Crockett and Eisenberg 1987). Because groups are widely separated, fighting may be avoided, and thus the spacing may be a group defense. This spacing has also often been interpreted as evidence that howlers have specific territories, which they defend. A strict definition of **territory** is a home range that is actively defended and does not overlap with another group's home range. Actually, few primates are territorial in this sense. Carpenter (1965) noted that howlers do not defend specific and constant boundaries but rather defend wherever they are at a given time. Crockett and Eisenberg (1987) suggest that howlers cannot actually be considered territorial because the overlap in home ranges is often quite large, but they also note that others interpret the data as showing some territoriality. Perhaps the most telling observation is the variation that howlers (and many primates) show from study to study.

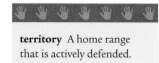

territory A home range that is actively defended.

FIGURE 6.10

Baboons on the savanna.

savanna An environment consisting of open grass-lands in which food resources tend to be spread out over large areas.

Baboons Baboons are one of the most widely studied and interesting of the Old World monkeys (technically, several different monkeys are given the general label of "baboon"; here we refer to the "savanna baboon"). Baboons live in relatively large (20–200) multimale/multifemale groups on the African **savanna** (Figure 6.10). The savanna is composed primarily of open grasslands, in which food resources tend to be spread out over large areas. Clusters of trees in the savanna provide additional opportunities for food, as well as for protection. Even though baboons are essentially terrestrial, they still have the basic primate adaptations that allow them to climb effectively, which is useful in hiding from predators and in obtaining shelter when sleeping. Because food resources are spread out over large areas of the savanna, baboons tend to have rather large home ranges, and they cover this area by foraging as a group. The baboon diet is quite diverse, including grass, leaves, fruit, and occasionally meat that has been obtained from hunting small mammals and birds. In analyzing baboon behavior, keep in mind that even among the "savanna baboons" there are groups that live in other environments, such as deserts (Jolly 2007).

Much of the focus in baboon studies has been on social organization. Adult males are dominant over adult females, and there is a constant shift in the relative position of the most dominant males. Aggressive actions play a role in this continual struggle (refer back to Figure 6.7). Adult males are considerably larger than adult females, and the largest and strongest males often have a greater chance of being the most dominant.

Size and strength are not, however, the only factors affecting male dominance in baboon society. Coalitions of two or more lower-ranking males have often been observed to displace a more dominant male who was actually larger and stronger than any of the lower-ranking males. The ability to aid others is an important determinant of dominance rank.

Environmental factors also affect patterns of dominance within baboon society. For example, Rowell (1966) found that forest-living baboons have less rigid dominance hierarchies than do groups living on the savanna. In addition, the daily life of the forest baboons is more relaxed, with a lower level of aggression. In forest environments, food is generally more available and predators are less of a threat. Quite simply, a rigid social organization is not needed in this environment.

In the initial years of baboon research, most of the attention was on the dominance hierarchies of the adult males, and less attention was given to the behaviors of adult females. We now realize that the continuity of baboon society revolves around the females and that adult males frequently move from one social group to another. The dominance hierarchy of the adult females is generally more stable over time. The importance of female continuity in baboon society must be acknowledged because females are responsible for the care of infants and provide the needed socialization prior to maturity.

The Asian Apes

The two Asian apes—the gibbon and the orangutan—are described briefly. Of these, the Asian great ape, the orangutan, is more closely related to humans.

Gibbons   Gibbons are classified into 12 species in four genera (refer back to Table 5.2). The gibbon is the smallest of the living apes. The physical characteristics of gibbons reflect adaptation to life in the trees. The climbing and hanging adaptations of hominoids have evolved in the gibbon to allow highly agile movement through trees. The gibbon's usual form of movement, known as **brachiation,** consists of hand-over-hand swinging from branch to branch. Many primates are portrayed as arm swingers, but only the gibbon can perform this movement quickly and efficiently (Figure 6.11).

A number of anatomical adaptations allow efficient arm swinging in gibbons. Body size is small, ranging from about 11 to 33 pounds (5–15 kg) (Bartlett 2007). The arms of gibbons are extremely long relative to their trunks and legs. Gibbon fingers are elongated and their thumbs are relatively short. The long fingers enable gibbons to form a hook with their hands while swinging from branch to branch. The thumb is short enough to prevent its getting in the way while swinging but still long enough to allow manipulation. On the ground, gibbons walk on two legs, though their arms are so long that they look awkward to us. Gibbons use these long arms for balance. They also walk on two legs when they move along a branch, often using their arms to grab onto overhead branches for support.

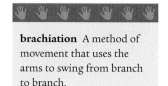

brachiation A method of movement that uses the arms to swing from branch to branch.

FIGURE 6.11

A gibbon brachiating. Gibbons are the most acrobatic of the apes and can swing by their arms easily.

Gibbons show almost no sexual dimorphism in body size. Males and females are the same size, and both have large canine teeth, with male canines slightly larger on average than females'.

Gibbons are found in the tropical rain forests of Southeast Asia—specifically, Thailand, Vietnam, Burma, and the Malay Peninsula. The rain forest environment is characterized by heavy rainfall that is relatively constant throughout the year. Rain forests have incredibly rich and diverse vegetation. The gibbons' diet consists primarily of fruits supplemented by leaves.

Gibbons have long been characterized as having a monogamous family structure—an adult male, an adult female, and their offspring—with the adult male and female forming a mating pair for long periods. Fuentes (2000) suggests that this is not always the case, and gibbon groups do not necessarily form nuclear family units. Instead, he argues that gibbons (like most other primates) originally had a multimale/multifemale social structure but now have a more variable system. Often, the small social groups result in a typical family structure, but not always. Once again, continued research has shown us the variable nature of primate social behavior.

Gibbons actively defend territories. They do this by making loud, complex sounds or songs and putting on aggressive displays to warn off other groups (Bartlett 2007). When groups come into contact in overlapping areas, the males often fight to drive the other group away. This territorial behavior may be related to the environment. In tropical rain forests, food is abundant and spread throughout the region. Because food resources are not clumped together, neither are the animal populations. Food is spread out over a large

area, so family groups come into frequent contact with one another, necessitating territorial boundaries to establish group boundaries (Denham 1971).

Orangutans   The orangutan is a large ape found only in certain areas of Southeast Asia. One of the orangutan's most obvious physical features is its reddish brown hair (Figure 6.12). Males are roughly twice the size of females;

FIGURE 6.13

Two orangutans in a tree.

an average adult male weighs roughly 190 pounds (86 kg), and an average female weighs about 86 pounds (39 kg) (Markham and Groves 1990). Males also have large pads of fat on their faces. The high degree of sexual dimorphism in orangutans has often been thought surprising because this trait occurs most often in terrestrial species. More recent evidence, however, suggests that orangutans spend more time on the ground than once thought.

Orangutans are agile climbers and hangers. In the trees, they use both arms and legs to climb in a slow, cautious manner. They will use one or more limbs to anchor themselves to branches while using the other limbs to feed (Figure 6.13). Younger orangutans occasionally brachiate, but the larger adults generally move through the trees in a different manner. A large orangutan will not swing from one tree to the next; rather, it will rock the tree it is on slowly in the direction of the next tree and then move over when the two trees are close together. The orangutan's great agility in climbing is due, in part, to its basic hominoid shoulder structure.

Orangutans are largely arboreal. Males, however, frequently descend from the trees and travel along the forest floor for long distances. On the ground, orangutans walk on all fours but with their fists partially closed. Unlike monkeys, who rest their weight on their palms, orangutans rest on their fists, a form of movement often called *fist walking*.

The orangutan is found today only in Sumatra and Borneo in Southeast Asia. Orangutans from these two regions are now classified as different species (Strier 2011). Orangutans are vegetarians, with the bulk of their diet consisting of fruit (Knott 1999). As does the gibbon, the orangutan lives in tropical rain forests.

Adult orangutans tend to be solitary, and the primary social group consists of a mother and her infant. Males are not needed for protection because there is little danger from predators. Adult males generally live by themselves, interacting only during times of mating. Orangutans are polygamous; they do not form long-term bonds with any one partner. The small group size of orangutans may be related to the nature of the environment; when food resources are widely scattered, there is not enough food in any one place to support large groups (Knott 1999).

Among nonhuman primates, a distinctive behavior of orangutans is the forced copulation of adult females by adult males, characterized by active resistance of the females. This behavior may be related to mate choice. Orangutan males have an interesting pattern of physical development whereby they first become sexually mature and capable of reproduction, and only later become socially mature and develop secondary sexual characteristics, such as cheek pads and longer fur. Females tend to resist sexual encounters with the less mature males because they prefer mating with the more socially mature males, although the reason for this mate choice is not yet clear (Knott and Kahlenberg 2007).

The African Apes

There are three kinds of African apes: gorillas, chimpanzees, and bonobos. The African apes are the closest living relatives of humans, and as such, their behavior and ecological adaptations are of key interest for us in our attempts to understand the range of possible behaviors of our ancestors (see Chapter 8). Even among this closely related group of apes, we see variation in social structure and ecology.

Gorillas   Gorillas are the largest living primates and are found only in equatorial Africa. Gorillas have recently been classified into two species, one in west-central Africa and one in east-central Africa. An adult male gorilla weighs roughly 350 pounds (159 kg) on average. Adult females weigh less but are still very large for primates (158 lbs/72 kg) (Leutenegger 1982). Besides a much larger body size, the adult males also have larger canine teeth and often have large crests of bone on top of their skulls for anchoring their large jaw muscles. Gorillas usually have blackish hair; fully mature adult males have silvery gray hair on their backs. These adult males are called *silverbacks*.

Their large size makes gorillas predominantly terrestrial. Their typical means of movement is called **knuckle walking:** They move about on all fours, resting their weight on the knuckles of their front limbs. This form of movement is different from the fist walking of orangutans. Gorilla hands have well-developed muscles and strengthened joints to handle the stress of resting on their knuckles. Because their arms are longer than their legs, gorilla spines are at an angle to the ground (Figure 6.14). In contrast, the spine of a typical quadrupedal animal, such as a monkey, is roughly parallel to the ground when walking.

Gorillas are found in only three forested areas in Africa. Their range is disappearing rapidly, primarily as the result of human poaching and of replacement (Fossey 1983). Many myths have circulated regarding the gorilla's lust for human and nonhuman flesh, but the fact is that gorillas eat a diet almost entirely made up of leaves and fruit. Diet varies by location; gorillas in the lowlands eat more fruit than the mountain gorillas.

knuckle walking A form of movement used by gorillas, chimpanzees, and bonobos that is characterized by all four limbs touching the ground, with the weight of the arms resting on the knuckles of the hands.

FIGURE 6.14

An adult female gorilla knuckle walking (with her infant riding on her back). Note the angle of the spine relative to the ground because of the longer front limbs.

Gorillas live in small social groups of typically 8–10 individuals (Robbins 2007). The social group consists of an adult male (the silverback), several adult females, and their immature offspring (Figure 6.15). Occasionally, one or more younger adult males are part of the group, but they tend not to mate with the females. Though dominance rank varies among the females and

FIGURE 6.15

A group of mountain gorillas.

subadult males, the adult silverback male is the most dominant individual in the group and is the leader. The silverback sets the pace for the rest of the group, determining when and how far to move in search of food.

A typical day for a gorilla group consists of eating and resting. Given their large body size and the limited nutritional value of leaves, it is no wonder that gorillas spend most of their day eating. Because of their size, gorillas have few problems with predators (except for humans with weapons). The life of a gorilla is for the most part peaceful, a dramatic contrast to their stereotypical image as aggressive creatures. Because gorillas are rather peaceful and slow moving, we have a tendency to think they are "slow" in a mental sense as well. This is another myth of gorilla behavior. Laboratory and field studies of gorillas have shown them to be extremely intelligent creatures. As discussed in the next chapter, they have even learned sign language.

Chimpanzees   Of all the nonhuman primates, the chimpanzee is perhaps the best known to the public. Most of our experience with chimpanzees, however, is with captive or trained animals. We like to watch chimpanzees perform "just like humans" and delight in a chimpanzee's smile (which actually signals tension, not pleasure). From a scientific perspective, chimpanzees are equally fascinating. Genetic studies during the past several decades have shown that humans and chimpanzees are even more similar than previously thought. Laboratory and field studies have shown that chimpanzees are capable of behaviors we once thought of as unique to humans, such as toolmaking and language acquisition (described in the next chapter). Any examination of the human condition must take these remarkable creatures' accomplishments into account.

Chimpanzees are found in Africa. They are smaller than gorillas and show only slight sexual dimorphism. Adult males weigh about 99 pounds (45 kilograms) on average, and adult females about 81 pounds (37 kg) on average (Leutenegger 1982). Chimpanzees have extremely powerful shoulders and arms. Like humans, chimpanzees show great variation in facial features and overall physical appearance (Figure 6.16). Chimpanzees, like gorillas, are knuckle walkers, with longer arms than legs. Chimpanzees, however, are more active and agile than gorillas. They are both terrestrial and arboreal. They spend considerable time in the trees, either sleeping or looking for food, and often hanging by their arms. On the ground, they sometimes stand on two legs to carry food or sticks.

Most chimpanzees are found in the African rain forests, although some groups are also found in the mixed forest–savanna environments on the fringe of the rain forests. The chimpanzee diet consists mainly of fruit (almost 70 percent), although they also eat leaves, seeds, nuts, insects, and meat. Chimpanzees have been observed hunting small animals, such as monkeys, and sharing the meat. Though some of the hunting occurs spontaneously when chimpanzees encounter small animals, other hunting behavior appears to be planned and coordinated.

Unlike orangutans and gorillas, chimpanzees live in multimale/multifemale societies, which might even be reflected in the male's reproductive biology (see Box 6.2). Chimpanzees live in large communities of

BOX 6.2

Why Do Male Chimpanzees Have Such Large Testes?

Although it might sound bizarre, scientists have collected data on the relative size of the testes, which is the male reproductive organ that produces sperm. As with many biological traits, there is considerable variation in the size of the testes, much of which is dependent on average body size; in general, larger primate species have larger testes. However, the relationship of body size and testes size is not consistent across all primate species. Chimpanzees have very large testes, averaging about a quarter of a pound (4 ounces), compared with the smaller average size of humans, which is about 1.4 ounces (41 grams). The large testes size of chimps is even more noticeable when comparing them with larger apes that have smaller testes—about 1 ounce in gorillas and 1.25 ounces in orangutans.

Harcourt et al. (1981) looked more closely at the relationship between body size and testes size in 33 primate species. Although they found the two were usually correlated, some species had smaller or larger testes than expected from the average mathematical relationship between body size and testes size. Humans, for example, had slightly smaller testes than expected based on body size, as did gorillas and orangutans. On the other hand, chimpanzees had testes that were 2.5 times as large as expected from their body size. Why do chimps have such large testes? Does this observation have an evolutionary explanation?

Harcourt and colleagues noticed something very interesting about the deviations of individual species from the expected relationship. Species that typically have a single adult male in their primary social group had smaller testes than expected, but species that had more than one adult male in the social group (including chimpanzees) had larger testes than expected. They reasoned that larger testes are needed in primate societies in which mating is frequent and in which many males mate with a female during her reproductive cycle. Natural selection may have favored males with large testes in such species because such males would produce more sperm and would have a greater relative chance of fathering an offspring and passing large testes on to the next generation.

FIGURE 6.16

Two chimpanzees. Chimpanzees, like people, have distinct faces.

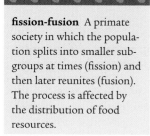

fission-fusion A primate society in which the population splits into smaller subgroups at times (fission) and then later reunites (fusion). The process is affected by the distribution of food resources.

50 or more individuals. Their social structure constantly changes, with individuals and groups fragmenting and later rejoining the main group. This type of social structure is a **fission-fusion** society, which can occur when food resources fluctuate. When food in the local area is more limited, the population breaks into smaller groups for feeding (fission) and then later comes back together. All chimpanzees recognize and interact with others in the group. Chimpanzee groups are less rigid than other multimale/multifemale primate societies, such as baboons. Although all members of the group interact to some extent, it is common for smaller subgroups to form much of the time. The actual composition of these subgroups also changes frequently (Figure 6.17).

Many social behaviors revolve around the bond between mother and infant (Figure 6.18). Chimpanzees tend to associate with their mothers and other siblings throughout their lives, even after they are fully grown. As is the case with other primates, young females watch and observe their own mothers taking care of children and learn mothering behaviors. There is no close bond between adult males and infants except for associations through the mother. Overall, chimpanzee society can be seen as a collection of smaller groups, defined in terms of mothers and siblings, forming a larger community. Other associations are also common, such as temporary all-male groups. Some chimpanzees are even solitary for periods of time.

Adult males are generally dominant over adult females, although there is much more overlap than is found in baboon societies. Some females, for example, are dominant over the lower-ranking males. Dominance is influenced by a variety of factors, such as size, strength, and the ability to form alliances. Individual intelligence also appears to affect dominance, as was revealed in Jane Goodall's study of chimpanzees in the Gombe Stream National

FIGURE 6.17

A chimpanzee group. The composition of chimpanzee groups changes frequently over time.

FIGURE 6.18

A female chimpanzee and her child. The mother–infant bond, which provides an infant chimpanzee with protection and socialization, often continues throughout life.

Park near Lake Tanganyika. In 1964, the community studied by Goodall had 14 adult males. The lowest-ranking male (Mike) replaced the most dominant male (Goliath) after displaying a particularly innovative form of dominance. There were a number of empty kerosene cans lying around Goodall's camp that the chimpanzees generally ignored. Mike would charge other males while hitting the cans in front of him, creating an unusual, noisy display. This behavior was so intimidating to other males that Mike rose from the lowest to the highest rank (Goodall 1986). This study shows not only the changing nature of dominance hierarchy but also the role of individual intelligence and initiative; all the males had access to the cans, but only Mike used them.

Although adult males are generally dominant over adult females, dominance rank among the females also has an influence on the group. Because female dominance is less noticeable, some have suggested that it is of little importance. Pusey and colleagues, however, found that female dominance rank correlated with reproductive success. Using data from 35 years of observation, they found that the higher-ranking adult female chimpanzees tended to have more offspring. In addition, they found that infants born to the higher-ranking females tended to have higher rates of survival through infancy (Pusey et al. 1997). Studies of the Gombe Stream chimpanzee community have revealed a number of other interesting features of chimpanzee social behavior and intelligence. The chimpanzees have been observed making and using tools (discussed at length in Chapter 7), hunting in cooperative groups, and sometimes engaging in widespread aggression against other groups. We examine some of these findings when we consider what behaviors may be considered uniquely human.

Bonobos   The bonobo is the third and least well known of the African apes. The bonobo is closely related to the chimpanzee and is commonly considered a separate species of chimpanzee known as the "pygmy chimpanzee" (compared to what is often termed the "common chimpanzee"). The close similarity of chimpanzees and bonobos is reflected in their assignment to the same genus—*Pan* (the scientific names are *Pan troglodytes* for the chimpanzee and *Pan paniscus* for the bonobo).

At first glance, bonobos seem quite similar to chimpanzees (Figure 6.19). On closer examination, however, we see that the bonobo has relatively longer legs, a higher center of gravity, and a narrower chest. It also tends to have a higher forehead and differently shaped face (Savage-Rumbaugh and Lewin 1994). Like gorillas and chimpanzees, bonobos are frequent knuckle walkers. Of particular interest is the fact that bonobos can walk upright more easily than other apes. This observation, combined with other evidence, suggests that the first hominids may have been quite similar in many ways to bonobos. There is some sexual dimorphism—adult males average 95 pounds (43 kg) compared with adult females, which average 73 pounds (33 kg) (de Waal 1995).

Bonobos are found only in a restricted rain forest region in Zaire in central Africa. It is estimated that there are fewer than 10,000 bonobos alive today. Their diet consists primarily of fruit, supplemented with plants. Recent studies show that bonobos also hunt and eat monkeys (Surbeck and Hohmann 2008).

As with chimpanzees, bonobos live in multimale/multifemale groups. There are, however, important differences in the social organization of these two species. In chimpanzee society, males are dominant over females, and some of the strongest bonds in the social order are between adult males. In

FIGURE 6.19

A bonobo.

bonobo society, things are quite different. Here, the strongest social bonds are between adult females (White 1996), and even though they are physically smaller, the females are sometimes the most dominant (Fruth et al. 1999). In addition, the dominance status of a male depends in large part on the dominance status of his mother (de Waal 1995).

Some of the most interesting observations of bonobo behavior have to do with how they use sexual activity in their social interactions. In addition to sexual intercourse, bonobos engage in a variety of sex play, including rubbing of genitals and oral sex. Continued observation of bonobo groups has revealed that such sex play is frequently used to reduce tension and avoid conflict. Researchers have shown repeatedly that bonobos will engage in a brief period of sex play in a tense social situation. In bonobo society, sex play is a method of peacemaking (de Waal 1995).

Summary

Primate behavior is best studied from the perspective of behavioral ecology, which looks at the ecology and evolution of traits by focusing on their adaptive value and by placing behaviors in the context of trade-offs between costs and benefits. Although there is considerable variation in specific behaviors within and between primate species, some generalities apply to all primates. Primates are highly social and have strong mother–infant bonds. All primates strengthen social bonds through grooming. Primate societies have dominance hierarchies, although their influence on social interactions is variable. Some individuals in all primate societies disperse to other groups (or to live alone), with males being more likely to disperse in some groups, and females in others. Dispersal affects social relationships that develop between kin. Studies of the behavior and ecology of individual primate species reveals a great deal of social behavior.

Supplemental Readings

Fossey, D. 1983. *Gorillas in the Mist*. Boston: Houghton Mifflin. A popular and well-written account of the late Dian Fossey's research on the behavior of the mountain gorilla. The book deals specifically with the problem of human intervention and the likely extinction of the mountain gorilla.

Goodall, J. 1986. *The Chimpanzees of Gombe: Patterns of Behavior*. Cambridge, Mass.: Harvard University Press. A comprehensive review of Jane Goodall's early research on chimpanzee behavior.

Strier, K. B. 2011. *Primate Behavioral Ecology,* 4th ed. Upper Saddle River, NJ: Prentice-Hall. An up-to-date and comprehensive text on primate behavior.

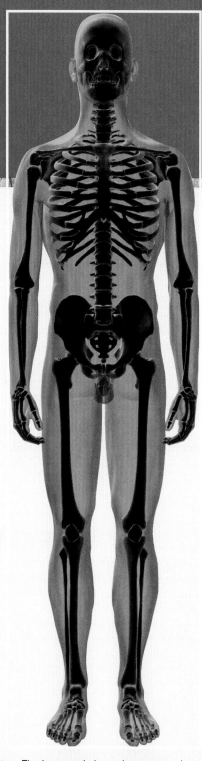

X-ray of a human skeleton. The human skeleton has many adaptations that allow us to walk upright all the time, one of our species' unique traits among living primates.

The Human Species

What does it mean to be human? This question has been a focus of science, art, and literature. Many different fields, from theology to psychology, have addressed its ultimate significance. Our perspective on ourselves is not abstract; the way we define what we are affects the way we treat others and the rest of the world.

One of the earliest written definitions of humanity is found in Psalm 8:4–6 of the Bible, where the question is put to God:

> What is man, that thou art mindful of him? And the son of man, that thou visitest him? For thou hath made him a little lower than the angels, and hast crowned him with glory and honor. Thou hast madest him to have dominion over the works of thy hands; thou hast put all things under his feet.

This brief statement reflects a long-standing belief of Western civilization that humans are inherently superior to all other life forms on the planet, ranking far above animals yet "lower than the angels." The view that humans are the supreme creatures in the natural world is also apparent in the works of many ancient Greek philosophers. Aristotle, for example, constructed an arrangement of all things with inanimate matter at the "bottom" and humans at the "top" (Kennedy 1976).

What is the scientific definition of humans? Many sciences attempt to answer this question—zoology, biochemistry, and even computer science among them. In addition, a wide range of disciplines, such as history, geography, economics, political science, sociology, psychology, and anthropology, deal almost exclusively with human beings and their behaviors. From a scientific standpoint, we are interested in a definition of humans that incorporates differences and similarities with respect to other living creatures. This is not always as simple as it sounds. For example, are humans the same as fish? Of course not, but can you explain why? Suppose you say that humans walk on two legs. Certainly, that definition separates fish and humans, but it does not separate humans and kangaroos, which also move about on two legs (albeit quite differently).

This chapter examines modern humans from the same perspective as the previous two chapters, focusing on the biological and behavioral uniqueness assigned to human beings. The final part of the chapter examines the question of how unique we are by comparing certain human behaviors (tool use, culture, language) with similar behaviors seen in some living apes.

CHARACTERISTICS OF LIVING HUMANS

This section focuses on certain key features of modern humans, particularly our brains, upright walking, teeth, reproductive patterns, and social structure.

Distribution and Environment

Humans are the most widely distributed living primate species. As later chapters will outline, humans originally evolved in a tropical environment. In fact, much of our present-day biology reflects the fact that we are tropical primates. During the course of human evolution, however, we have expanded into many different environments. Biological adaptations have aided humans in new environments, such as cold weather and high altitude. The cultural adaptations of humans have allowed even greater expansion. Today there is no place on the planet where we cannot live, given the appropriate technology. Humans can live in the frozen wastelands of Antarctica, deep beneath the sea, and in the vacuum of space. Our cultural adaptations have enabled us to range far beyond our biological limitations. These adaptations have also permitted incredible population growth. In the past, the planet could have supported no more than a few million people at a hunting-and-gathering level of existence (Weiss 1984). Today the population of the world is more than 7 billion and counting. Although the quality of life is still low for much of the world's human population, there is no doubt that our ability to learn and to develop technology has led to immense potential for population expansion.

Brain Size and Structure

One very obvious biological characteristic of the human species is the large brain. Our bulging and rounded skulls and flat faces contrast with these features in other animals, including the rest of the hominoids. Whereas an ape's skull is characterized by a relatively small brain and large face, modern humans have relatively large brains and small faces.

Figure 7.1 shows the brain size (in cubic centimeters) for a number of primate species. There is a clear relationship between taxonomic status and brain size: Monkeys have the smallest brains, followed by the lesser apes, great apes, and humans. Absolute brain size is not as useful a measure of intellectual ability because larger animals tend to have larger brains. Elephants and whales, for example, have brains that are four to five times the size of the average human brain.

Among mammals, however, the relationship between brain and body size is not linear. That is, as body size increases, brain size increases—but not at the same rate. Differences in relative size because of disparate growth rates among various parts of the body are common. The study of this phenomenon is known as **allometry.** Parts of the body grow at different rates. Brain size increases at a nonlinear rate with body size. For example, consider two species of primates, such that one species has twice the body weight of the other. If

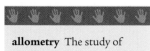

allometry The study of the change in proportion of various body parts as a consequence of different growth rates.

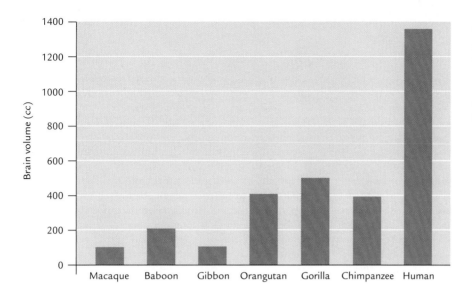

FIGURE 7.1

Average brain volume (cubic centimeters) of selected living primates. (Data from Campbell 1985 for macaques and baboons, and Tobias 1971 for all other species.)

the ratio of brain size to body size were linear, we would expect the brain size of the species with the larger body size to be twice that of the smaller species. Actually, the brain size of the larger-bodied species is on average only 1.6 times as large. Because of this relationship, larger species appear to have smaller brain/body size ratios.

This allometric relationship between brain size and body size is quite regular among almost all primates. The most notable exception is humans. We have brains that are three times the size we would expect for a primate of our body size (Figure 7.2). Human brains are not simply allometrically larger than nonhuman primate brains. Human brains also show a number of specializations not found in other primates. In particular, the human brain has a higher proportion of neocortex (part of the cerebral cortex), involved in conscious thought and language (Rilling 2006). There are also neurological differences showing the greater complexity of human brains (Premack 2007).

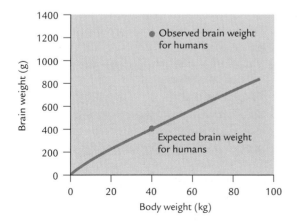

FIGURE 7.2

Relationship between body weight and brain weight in primates. The line indicates the average relationship among various primate species, excluding humans. The two dots show expected and observed brain weight for humans. Our brains are three times the weight expected if we followed the typical primate curve. (Data from Harvey et al. 1987.)

BOX 7.1

Are People with Bigger Brains Smarter?

As shown in later chapters, one of the most noticeable trends in the fossil record for human evolution is a large increase in brain size over the past two million years. As described in this chapter, the evolution of the human brain has involved structural changes as well as changes in size. However, much of our information on the past evolution of human brains comes from measures of brain size derived from fossil remains, and we see a clear increase in brain size over time. A basic assumption is that natural selection has lead to larger and more complex brains during the evolution of different human species in the past presumably because of advantages for a variety of cognitive tasks, such as planning, problem solving, and language. Given this observation, many have wondered whether there is any association between brain size and behavior *within* our species. Are people with larger brains smarter?

Historically, many people have accepted this association without any real evidence and later used it for a variety of racist and sexist agendas (Gould 1981). Several studies have since examined correlations between brain size and performance on an intelligence (IQ) test. Leaving aside for the moment the continued debate over exactly what such tests actually measure, and whether intelligence is a single attribute that we can measure with an IQ test, let us examine a different question—do people with larger brains score better on IQ tests? First, we need to qualify our definition of brain size to focus on *relative* brain size, because as noted in the text, brain size varies with body size so that bigger people tend to have bigger heads and bigger brains.

Our initial question now becomes: Do people with larger brains relative to body size score higher on IQ tests?

Several studies have looked at the correlation between brain size estimated using MRI (magnetic resonance imaging) scans and performance on IQ tests. The statistical analyses examine how much of the variation in IQ scores is explained by variation in brain size. In statistics, the amount of explained variation can range from zero (no association whatsoever) to 100 percent (complete association). On average, the brain size-IQ studies show that about 16 percent of the variation in IQ scores is explained by variation in brain size, so there is a *slight* association of larger brains with higher test scores. However, this statistic also means that 84 percent of variation in IQ scores has nothing to do with relative brain size. We could say that brain size has some relationship to IQ score, but certainly not the major one.

However, the situation is more complicated. Schoenemann and colleagues (2000) noted that the brain size-IQ studies failed to account for environmental differences adequately. That is, the correlation between brain size and IQ might be affected by environmental factors that vary from one family to the next. To get around this difficulty, they analyzed correlations *within* families and found that the correlation was close to zero. Other studies have found at best a very small genetic correlation (Schoenemann 2006). Overall, we can conclude that differences in brain size between people today show very little relationship to differences in IQ. We cannot simply extrapolate data on variation between species to make inferences within species.

Studies have also looked at the relationship among brain size, body size, and metabolism. Larger mammals have larger brains and produce greater amounts of metabolic energy. Mammals show a great deal of variation, however, in the amount of energy used by the brain. The brains of many mammals, such as dogs and cats, use from 4 percent to 6 percent of their body metabolism. Primate brains use a considerably greater proportion of energy; the Old World macaque monkey uses 9 percent, and modern humans use 20 percent (Armstrong 1983).

What does all this mean? The human brain is not merely large; it also has a different structure than the brains of other primates. This difference in structure is also probably related to the higher proportion of metabolic energy used by the human brain. The bottom line is that brain size does not tell the whole story (see also Box 7.1). Thus, the human brain is not only larger than the brain of a chimpanzee, but also structurally different. The increased convolution of the human cerebral cortex (the folding of brain tissue) means that the brain of a human child with the same volume of that of a chimpanzee has more cerebral cortex.

Bipedalism

Another striking difference between humans and apes is that humans walk on two legs. We are **bipedal** (literally, "two-footed"). This does not mean that apes cannot walk on two legs. They can, but not as well and not as often. The physical structure of human beings shows adaptations for upright walking as the normal mode of movement.

Humans are not the only animal that is routinely bipedal. The kangaroo also moves about on two legs, but in a totally different manner from humans. Consider walking in slow motion. What happens? First, you stand balanced on two legs. Then you move one leg forward. You shift your body weight so that your weight is transferred to the moving leg. As that leg touches the ground on its heel, all of your body weight has been shifted. Your other leg is then free to swing forward. As it does so, you push off with your other foot.

Human walking is more graceful than a slow-motion description sounds. The act of walking consists of legs alternately swinging free and standing still. We balance on one leg while the other leg moves forward to continue our striding motion. We tend to take these acts for granted, but they are actually quite complicated, requiring both balance and coordination. For example, when you pick up one leg to move it forward, what keeps your body from falling over?

Human bipedalism is made possible by anatomical changes involving the toes, legs, spine, pelvis, and various muscles. In terms of actual anatomy, these changes are not major. After all, no bones are added or deleted; the same bones can be found in humans and in apes. The changes involve shape, positioning, and function. The net effect of these changes, however, is dramatic. Humans can move about effectively on two legs, allowing the other limbs to be free for other activities.

The feet of human beings reflect adaptation to bipedalism. The feet of a human and a chimp are shown in Figure 7.3. The big toe of the chimp sticks

bipedal Moving about on two legs. Unlike the movement of other bipedal animals such as kangaroos, human bipedalism is further characterized by a striding motion.

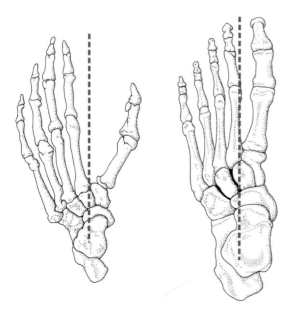

FIGURE 7.3

The skeletal structure of the feet of a chimpanzee (*left*) and a modern human (*right*). Note how the big toe of the human lies parallel to the other toes.

FIGURE 7.4

The modern human skeleton from a frontal view.

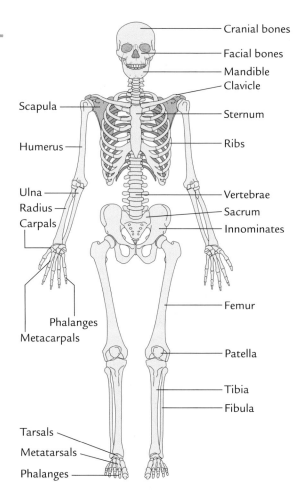

Cranial bones
Facial bones
Mandible
Clavicle
Scapula
Sternum
Humerus
Ribs
Ulna
Vertebrae
Radius
Sacrum
Carpals
Innominates
Femur
Phalanges
Metacarpals
Patella
Tibia
Fibula
Tarsals
Metatarsals
Phalanges

out in the same way that the thumb of all hominoids sticks out from the other fingers. The divergent big toe allows chimps to grasp with their feet. The big toe of the human is tucked in next to the other toes. When we walk, we use the nondivergent big toe to push off during our strides.

Our balance while we stand and walk is partly the result of changes in our legs. Figure 7.4 shows a human skeleton. Note that the width of the body at the knees is less than the width of the body at the hips. Humans are literally "knock-kneed." Our upper leg bones (the femurs) slope inward from the hips. When we stand on one leg, the angle of the femur transmits our weight directly underneath us. The result is that we continue to be balanced while one leg is moving. In contrast, the angle of an ape femur is very slight. Figures 7.5 and 7.6 provide comparative drawings of the skeletons of an ape and a monkey. Note how the legs of an ape are almost parallel from hips to feet. When an ape stands on two legs and moves one of them, the ape is off balance and tends to fall toward one side (more so than humans, because we compensate more quickly). When an ape walks on two legs, it must shift its whole body weight over the supporting leg to stay on balance. This shifting explains their characteristic waddling when apes walk on two legs.

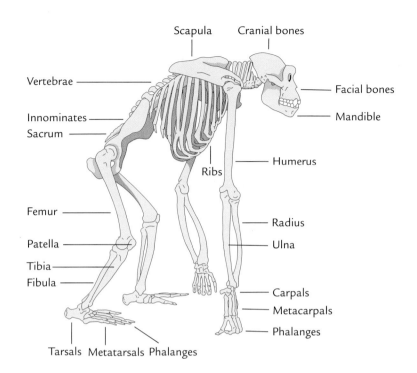

Scapula   Cranial bones

Vertebrae

Innominates
Sacrum

Facial bones

Mandible

Ribs   Humerus

Femur

Patella

Tibia
Fibula

Radius

Ulna

Carpals
Metacarpals
Phalanges

Tarsals Metatarsals Phalanges

FIGURE 7.5

Skeleton of an African ape (gorilla) shown in the typical knuckle-walking mode of locomotion. Note the longer arms and shorter legs when compared with a human (Figure 7.4) and a monkey (Figure 7.6) skeleton.

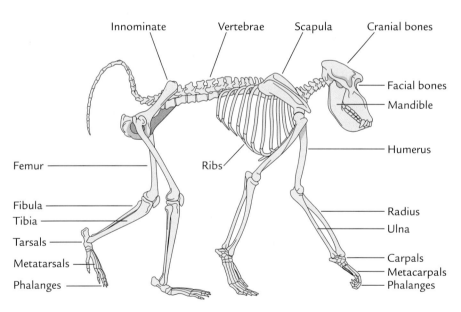

Innominate   Vertebrae   Scapula   Cranial bones

Facial bones
Mandible

Femur   Ribs

Humerus

Fibula
Tibia

Tarsals

Metatarsals

Phalanges

Radius
Ulna

Carpals
Metacarpals
Phalanges

FIGURE 7.6

Skeleton of an Old World monkey (baboon) shown in the typical quadrupedal mode of locomotion. Note the similar length of the arms and legs compared with a human (Figure 7.4) and an ape (Figure 7.5).

The human spine also promotes balance when we walk upright (Figure 7.7). The spinal column of humans is vertical, allowing weight to be transmitted down through the center of the body. In knuckle-walking apes, the spine is bent in an arc so that when the apes stand on two legs, the center of gravity is shifted to the front of the body. The ape is off balance and must compensate greatly to stay upright. What is difficult for apes is easy

FIGURE 7.7

Side view of the skeletons of a chimpanzee (*left*) and a modern human (*right*), illustrating the shape and orientation of the spine. (Adapted with permission from Bernard Campbell, *Human Evolution*, 3d ed. New York: Aldine de Gruyter. Copyright © 1985 Bernard Campbell. Reprinted by permission of Transaction Publishers.)

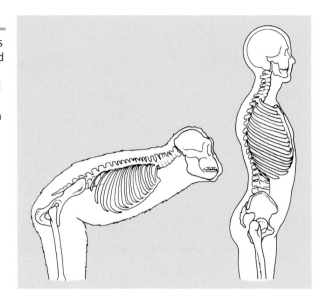

for humans. The human spine is vertical but not straight. It curves in several places, allowing it to absorb the shocks we incur while we walk.

The human pelvis is shaped differently from an ape pelvis as well (Figure 7.8). It is shorter top to bottom and wider side to side. The sides of the pelvis are broader and flair out more to the sides, providing changes in muscle attachment that permit striding bipedalism. The shortness of the human pelvis allows greater stability when we stand upright.

The changes in the human pelvis also involve changes in the positioning of various muscles. For example, certain leg muscles attach more on the sides of the pelvis. This change allows humans to maintain their balance while standing without having to bend their knees. The gluteus minimus and

FIGURE 7.8

The trunk skeletons of a chimpanzee (*left*) and a modern human (*right*) drawn to the same size. Note the proportionately shorter and wider pelvis of the human being, reflecting adaptations to upright walking. (Adapted with permission from Bernard Campbell, *Human Evolution*, 3rd ed. New York: Aldine de Gruyter. Copyright © 1985 Bernard Campbell. Reprinted by permission of Transaction Publishers.)

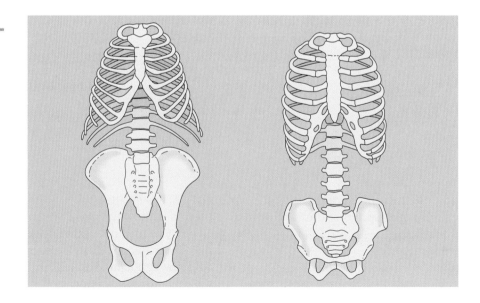

gluteus medius muscles have also shifted position relative to apes, allowing the pelvis to remain stable when one leg is lifted during walking.

Canine Teeth

Human canine teeth are different from the canines in many other mammals. Human canines are small and do not project beyond the level of the other teeth (Figure 7.9). Human canine teeth serve much the same function as the incisor teeth.

That we have small, nonprojecting canines has led to much speculation concerning causes and effects of human evolution. Given that canine teeth serve as weapons in many primate species, the lack of large canine teeth in humans seems to imply that we do not need them for weapons anymore. One scenario is that when human ancestors began using tools, they no longer required large canines. As you will see in later chapters, the uniqueness of human canine teeth is a more complex topic than we once thought.

Genetic Differences between Humans and Apes

Biochemical and genetic studies have shown that humans and the African apes are close relatives. As noted earlier in the text, humans and chimpanzees share over 98 percent of their DNA sequences (see Box 7.2 for more detail on how this is number is calculated). It is also clear from the material reviewed thus far that humans and chimpanzees have a number of anatomical differences, such as in brain size and structure, locomotion, and the size of the canine teeth. Given the close genetic relationship of humans and chimpanzees, these significant differences must reside in the remaining 2 percent or less of our genomes. Given approximately 3 billion base pairs in both species, a 2 percent difference translates to 60 million potentially different base pairs, implying a large number of different genes. However, what genes could be different, and why? These questions are the focus of ongoing research comparing the genomes of humans and apes to detect specific genetic differences. Several examples are given here to provide a glimpse at this research.

Some of the genetic changes found to date relate to some of the major unique features of human evolution. One example is the *FOXP2* gene, located on human chromosome 7, which *may* have something to do with the evolution of human language. A rare mutant allele of this gene is associated with language impairment, and two copies of the nonmutant functional form of *FOXP2* are needed for normal language acquisition. The same form of this gene is found in chimpanzees, gorillas, and rhesus monkeys, all of which differ from humans by two amino acid substitutions, a pattern that suggests that these two changes occurred after the hominin line split from the common ancestor with African apes. Statistical analysis of genetic differences suggests that this gene has been selected for during the course of human evolution within the past 200,000 years (Enard et al. 2002). Although these analyses suggest that *FOXP2* might be involved somehow in the evolution of human language acquisition, we still need to determine exactly how (and if)

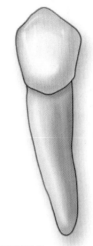

FIGURE 7.9

A human canine. The yellow part of the drawing is the root and the white part is the crown that sticks up from the jaw. Unlike other primates, human canines are small, not very sharp or pointed, and do not project beyond the level of other teeth.

BOX 7.2

How Similar Are We to Chimpanzees?

We hear frequently (including in this text) that humans and chimpanzees are over 98 percent identical genetically. This statement is heard commonly in many anthropology classes and in many books and journals. Is it accurate? The answer is yes and no.

Let us start by direct comparison of the complete genomes of humans and chimpanzees. The first thing to look at is the number of nucleotide substitutions, where the two species differ at a given single nucleotide. It turns out that 1.23 percent of all nucleotides are substitutions, which means that humans and chimpanzees are $100 - 1.23 = 98.77$ percent similar (The Chimpanzee Sequencing and Analysis Consortium 2005). The statement "over 98 percent similar" is therefore correct.

However, there are different ways to count similarities and differences. The 98 percent figure refers only to nucleotide substitutions where one nucleotide changes from one form to another in one of the species. There are other types of genetic changes, such as insertions and deletions of DNA sequences. During human evolution, some sequences have been added and some have been lost. Likewise, during chimpanzee evolution there have been sequences added and deleted. Added to the nucleotide substitutions, this means that there is about a 4 percent difference in the genetics of humans and chimpanzees (The Chimpanzee Sequencing and Analysis Consortium 2005), making the two species about 96 percent similar. There are additional differences when considering the number of copies of DNA sequences, added or lost (Cohen 2007). The genetic difference between humans and chimpanzees is close, but the exact number depends on what exactly is being counted.

the normal functioning *FOXP2* genes in humans and apes relate to differences in speech and/or language acquisition.

Some specific human traits have been traced to the loss of regulatory genes during human evolution. McLean et al. (2011) examined the genomes of humans, chimpanzees, and macaques (an Old World monkey) and identified 510 DNA sequences that had been present in chimpanzees but were lost during the course of human evolution. These sequences act to regulate the expression of genes, and two have been examined in detail. One sequence acts to regulate a gene that limits tissue growth, and the deletion of this regulatory sequence in humans may be associated with the expansion of the cerebral cortex, possibly representing a genetic mechanism associated with the rapid brain growth seen in human evolution. The other sequence affects an androgen receptor (androgen is a male sex hormone). The deletion of the regulatory gene in humans is associated with the loss of sensory whiskers and penile spines (hard spines found on the end of the penis), both of which are absent in humans but present in many other mammals. More DNA sequences need to be investigated, but it appears that a number of human characteristics may be associated with small changes in regulatory genes. This genetic information shows us how humans and chimpanzees can be (overall) very similar genetically, but still quite different physically.

Another example of gene deactivation concerns the difference between ape and human jaws. Apes have large jaws and powerful jaw muscles for chewing. By contrast, living humans have rather small, less powerful jaws. The fossil record of early hominin evolution (see Chapter 10) shows that some early hominins also had large jaws and chewing muscles, but this pattern changed over the past 2 million years with the origin of the genus *Homo*. Since then, jaws have become smaller as brain size increased. Genetic comparison of humans and other primates shows a difference in the gene for myosin (a protein in muscles). The human form of this gene that controls one of the proteins, *MYH16,* is characterized by a mutation that inactivates it, resulting in smaller jaw muscles. What is particularly interesting about these preliminary results is that the estimated date of the human mutation is 2.4 million years ago, corresponding roughly to the appearance of the genus *Homo* (with smaller jaws) in the fossil record (Stedman et al. 2004).

Sex and Reproduction

We humans consider ourselves the sexiest primates. That is, we are more concerned with sex than is any other primate. The fact that humans do not have the **estrus** cycle has often been cited as a unique aspect of human sexuality. For the most part, temperate-zone domestic animals breed only during certain seasons and mate around the time of ovulation. Human females, in contrast, cycle throughout the year and may mate at any time during the cycle. However, this distinction between humans and other primates may not be as clear as often suggested. Orangutans, for example, also lack an estrus cycle. Bonobos do have an estrus cycle but have been observed to mate outside of it to some extent.

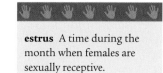

estrus A time during the month when females are sexually receptive.

The human pattern of reproduction is basically the same as that of most other primates: single births. Unlike apes, however, humans have additional infants before previous offspring have matured socially or physically. Because of cultural adaptations and an extended childhood, humans have increased reproduction without sacrificing parental care.

Childbirth in humans is more difficult and more complicated than in apes, due to our enlarged brains and the changes in pelvic anatomy that accompanied bipedalism. The pelvic anatomy of living humans means that a new baby has to rotate through a narrow and twisting birth canal. Rosenberg and Trevathan (2001) suggest that these twists and turns are unique to humans, which might explain why female humans inevitably require assistance during childbirth. This behavior may reflect an ancient adaptive practice. Childbirth is also made difficult by the fact that the baby is born backward relative to the mother (Figure 7.10), making it difficult for the mother to guide the infant from the birth canal without assistance. However, recent observations show that babies face backward during birth in chimpanzees (Hirata et al. 2011), suggesting that assistance during childbirth is not due solely to position of the baby (Milton 2011).

Social Structure

Human social structure is a topic of almost infinite complexity. One observation is obvious—there is extensive variation. Because variation in social structure is great even among monkeys and apes, it should come as no surprise that humans also show considerable variation.

A common Western assumption is that the "normal" social structure of human beings is the nuclear monogamous family group: mother, father, and children. Actually, the majority of human societies studied have a stated

FIGURE 7.10

Cross-section of a pregnant woman close to birth. Note how the fetus is facing backwards relative to the mother.

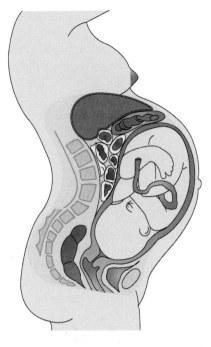

polygyny A form of marriage in which a husband has several wives.

polyandry A form of marriage in which a wife has several husbands.

preference for **polygyny**—a pattern in which one husband has several wives (Harris 1987)—and a few cultures practice **polyandry,** in which one woman has several husbands. Because of this, anthropologists have often argued that the basic human pattern is polygyny. However, it must be noted that although many societies state a *preference* for polygyny, it is still much more common for men to have a single wife. In many cases, only the wealthiest or most powerful have multiple wives. Fisher (1992) concluded that for all practical purposes monogamy is the predominant *marriage* pattern for humans (although with considerable infidelity in many societies). Clearly, it is necessary to consider the difference between stated cultural ideals and actual practices.

Humans show a great deal of variation in other aspects of their culture as well, such as economic systems, political systems, and legal systems. The dramatic changes in such institutions over the past 12,000 years—since the origin of agriculture—show exactly how variable our species' behavior can be. During this time, humans developed state-level societies, social stratification, formal legal codes, and many other aspects of culture that we take for granted today. Biological needs, such as for food and sex, place some limits on our behavior. One such limitation is the need for a family of some sort to care for dependent children. All humans live in families, although the actual structure can vary considerably depending on circumstances and tradition.

THE HUMAN LIFE CYCLE

The major stages of growth and development are prenatal (before birth) and postnatal (after birth). The general nature of these two stages is reviewed briefly, followed by consideration of what is unique about human growth.

Prenatal Growth

Prenatal life is the period from fertilization through childbirth. After fertilization, the fertilized egg, or **zygote,** develops into a cluster of identical cells deriving from the initial fertilized egg. During the first week, the fertilized egg multiplies as it travels into the uterus. By this time, there are roughly 150 cells arranged in a hollow ball that implants itself into the wall of the uterus. Cell differentiation begins. During the second week, the outer layer of this ball forms the beginning of the placenta. Some early differentiation of cells can be seen in the remainder of the ball.

The embryonic stage stretches from roughly two to eight weeks after conception. The **embryo** is very small during this time, reaching an average length of roughly 1 inch (25 mm) by the eighth week. During this time, the basic body structure is completed and many of the different organ systems develop; the embryo has a recognizably human appearance, although it is still not complete. The fetal stage lasts from this point until birth. Development of body parts and organ systems continues, along with a tremendous amount of body growth and changes in proportions. During the second trimester of pregnancy, the **fetus** shows rapid growth in overall length. During the third trimester, the fetus shows rapid growth in body weight, head size, and brain size.

zygote A fertilized egg.

embryo The stage of human prenatal life lasting from roughly two to eight weeks following conception; characterized by structural development.

fetus The stage of human prenatal growth from roughly eight weeks following conception until birth; characterized by further development and rapid growth.

The Pattern of Human Postnatal Growth

We can identify five basic stages in growth from birth until adulthood (Bogin 1999, 2001). The first stage, *infancy,* refers to the time from birth until weaning (typically up to 3 years in nonindustrialized societies) and is characterized by rapid growth. The second stage, *childhood,* refers to the time from weaning until the end of growth in brain weight, which takes place at about age 7 years (Cabana et al. 1993). The *juvenile* stage is from this point until the beginning of the fourth stage, *adolescence,* which is the time of sexual maturation and a spurt in body growth. Adolescence begins at about age 10 in females and age 12 in males, although there is considerable variation across individuals and populations. The fifth stage is labeled *adulthood.*

Human growth is usually studied by looking at growth curves. One type of growth curve, the **distance curve,** is a measure of size over time—it shows how big someone is at any given age. Figure 7.11 is a typical distance curve for human height. As we all know, until you reach adulthood, the older you get, the taller you get. However, note that this is not a straight line—you do not grow the same amount each year. This shows that the *rate* of body growth is not the same from year to year. Changes in the rate of growth are best illustrated by a **velocity curve,** which plots the rate of change over time. The difference between a distance curve and a velocity curve can be illustrated by a simple analogy—driving a car. Imagine driving a car on a highway between two cities. How *far* you have come is your distance, and how *fast* you are going is your velocity.

distance curve A measure of size over time—for example, a person's height at different ages.

velocity curve A measure of the rates of change in growth over time.

FIGURE 7.11

Typical distance curve for human height. (Adapted from *Growth and Development* by Robert M. Malina, © 1975, published by Burgess International Publishing Company. Used by permission.)

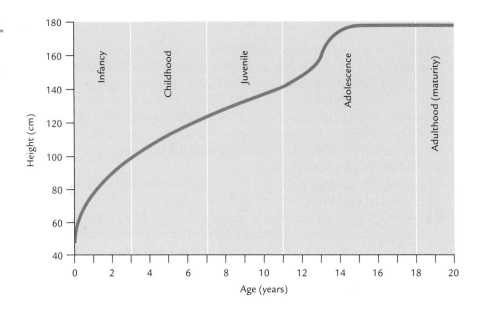

A typical velocity curve for human height is shown in Figure 7.12. The rate of growth is greatest immediately after birth, followed by a rapid deceleration during infancy. Even though the rate of growth decreases, we still continue to grow. Referring again to the car analogy, if you decelerate from 50 miles per hour to 30 miles per hour, you are still going forward, just not as fast. During childhood and the juvenile stage, height velocity decreases slightly, but then it increases rapidly for a short time during adolescence. At adulthood, the rate of growth again decreases until there is no further significant growth.

FIGURE 7.12

Typical velocity curve for human height. (Adapted from *Growth and Development* by Robert M. Malina, © 1975, published by Burgess International Publishing Company. Used by permission.)

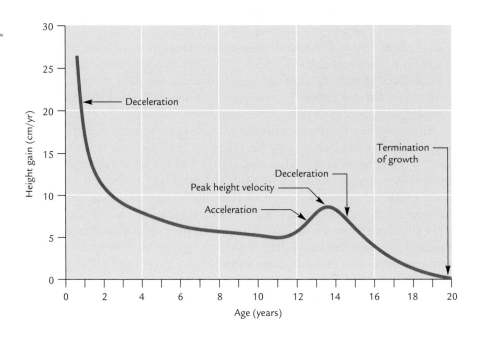

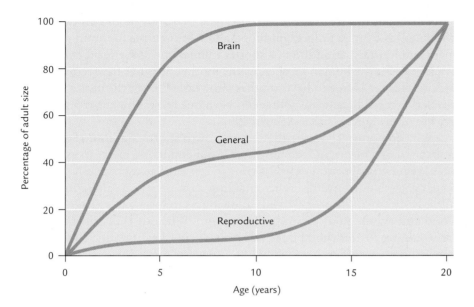

FIGURE 7.13

Distance curves for different body tissues, showing the percentage of total adult size reached at different ages. The general curve represents overall body size (height or weight). The brain curve represents brain weight. The reproductive curve represents the weight of sex organs and tissues. (From Bogin 1995, based on Scammon 1930 and updated with data on brain growth [Cabana et al. 1993].)

Comparing distance and velocity curves for human body size with other organisms has revealed two basic differences: Humans have an extended childhood and an adolescent period (Bogin 1995, 2001). In most mammals, the rate of growth decreases from childbirth, and adulthood occurs without any intervening stages. In other mammals, there is a stage of juvenile growth. Only in humans, however, do we see childhood, adolescence, and a long postreproductive period.

The discussion thus far has centered on body size. To understand the unique aspects of the human growth pattern, it is also necessary to look at changes in growth for other parts of the body, such as the head and brain tissue. Quite simply, not everything grows at the same rate. Figure 7.13 compares human distance curves for body size, brain size, and the reproductive system. All three are drawn to illustrate the percentage of total adult size attained at any given age. Note the differences in these curves—our brains and reproductive systems obviously do not grow at the same rate as our bodies. In particular, our brain grows most rapidly at first, reaching adult weight during childhood (Cabana et al. 1993). The reproductive system grows most slowly, showing hardly any growth until adolescence.

The Evolution of Human Growth

If you think about it for a moment, these differences in timing of growth make sense. Because humans are dependent on learning as a means of survival, it makes sense to have a large brain in place as soon as possible. The physical limits to the rate of brain growth while in the womb mean that the best time for extended brain growth to occur is during the first few years of life. Likewise, it makes sense to have sexual maturity postponed until later in life so that we have time to develop physically and socially enough to provide adequately for offspring.

The evolutionary advantage to delayed maturation and an extended childhood is clear—a longer childhood allows more time for brain development and learning. In addition, a shorter infancy and subsequent childhood is adaptive for the human mother. As the mother does not have to nurse the older child, she is free to have another baby earlier. Over the past 6 million years, this reproductive advantage has been one reason for the tremendous growth of the human species (Bogin 2001).

Why do humans have an adolescent growth spurt? Traditional explanations see it as a means of "catching up." If our childhood has been extended, then we have proportionately less time in our lives as reproductive adults. Rapid growth during adolescence enabling us to reach sexual maturity and adult body size more quickly, thus allowing us to have our extended childhood and an adequate reproductive period. Without this growth spurt, we would reach adulthood later and possibly not have enough time to adequately care for offspring. Bogin (2001) suggests that adolescence may also have evolved to allow time for learning adult social skills before actually reproducing.

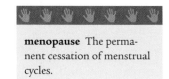

menopause The permanent cessation of menstrual cycles.

Menopause

Menopause is the permanent cessation of menstrual cycles that occurs before the aging of other body systems and before the end of the average life span. Other mammals show a decline in reproductive function with age, but this is not usually considered menopause because it occurs near the end of life or is associated with the decline in other body functions. As defined here, menopause has been found only in humans and in one species of toothed whales (Pavelka and Fedigan 1991; Peccei 2001). Menopause is universal among human societies and generally occurs at about 50 years of age (Fedigan and Pavelka 2007).

What makes humans interesting is that females live for many years after the onset of menopause, leading some to speculate on the possible evolutionary reasons for living years beyond one's reproductive life. Is it possible that natural selection could lead to postmenopausal longevity even though these women are no longer reproducing? Two different hypotheses have been offered to explain postmenopausal longevity through natural selection. The first, known as the "mother hypothesis," proposes that it is more adaptive later in life for women to expend time and energy in insuring the survival of their existing children rather than having more children. The second hypothesis, known as the "grandmother hypothesis," extends this idea another generation, by proposing that postmenopausal women can help their daughters raise their own children successfully, thus increasing their daughters' fertility. Support for these hypotheses has been mixed and inconclusive (Peccei 2001; Fedigan and Palveka 2007; Madrigal and Meléndez-Obando 2008). Other researchers have argued that menopause and postmenopausal longevity are not the result of natural selection, but instead are a by-product of the fact that humans now outlive their egg supply (Leidy 1998).

IS HUMAN BEHAVIOR UNIQUE?

Humans and apes show a great many similarities, as well as a great many differences. When we ask whether humans are unique, we do not suggest that we cannot tell an ape and a human apart. Rather, we ask what the extent of these differences is. Are the behaviors of apes and humans completely different, or are differences present only in the expression of specific behaviors? Can we say, for example, that humans make tools and apes do not? Or should we say instead that there are differences in the ways in which these two groups make and use tools?

According to the view that apes and humans show distinct and major differences, humans possess culture and apes do not. Any cultural behaviors found in apes are labeled as fundamentally different from human cultural behaviors. According to the view that ape–human differences are variations on something that is fundamentally similar, both humans and apes possess culture—the only difference being that humans rely more on culture or that humans have a more developed culture. This debate is semantic to a large extent. A more worthwhile approach is to examine some of the suggested differences between apes and humans in an effort to determine what is truly different.

Tool Use and Manufacture

Tool use has often been cited as a unique human behavior. As defined here, a tool is an object that is not part of the animal. Human tools include pencils, clothes, eating utensils, books, and houses. These are all objects that are not part of the biological organism (humans) but are used for a specific purpose. Tool use, however, does not seem to be even a unique primate characteristic. Birds use sticks for nests, and beavers use dirt in their dams. Both sticks and dirt can be considered tools by this definition.

A more common definition of modern humans focuses on humans as toolmakers. The key element of this definition is that some object is taken from the environment and modified to meet a new function. Humans take trees to make lumber to build houses. It can be argued that birds modify sticks and beavers modify dirt, but tool manufacture implies something different. Birds, for example, use sticks for building nests, but they do not use these sticks for defensive or offensive weapons. Humans, however, can take sticks and use them to make shelters, defend themselves, hunt, dig up roots, and draw pictures in the sand. When we discuss tool manufacture, we mean the new and different ways to modify an object for a task. Humans can apply the same raw materials to a variety of tasks.

In this sense, tool manufacture has long been considered a unique human activity. But research on apes, such as Jane Goodall's work on chimpanzees, has since shown that this is not true. Apes make and use tools. Though their tools are extremely simple by modern human standards, the difference between apes and humans cannot be reduced to humans making tools and apes not making tools. Differences exist in the method and use of manufactured tools, but not in the fact of toolmaking itself.

FIGURE 7.14

Chimpanzees using simple tools to "fish" for termites.

Chimpanzee Termite Fishing   In the early 1960s, Goodall reported a remarkable finding—chimpanzees were making and using tools! Though chimpanzees are predominantly fruit eaters, they also enjoy a variety of other foods, including termites. One group of chimpanzees demonstrated a method for capturing termites. They took a grass stem or a stick, went up to a termite mound, and uncovered one of the entrance holes left by the termites. They inserted the stick into the hole, twirled the stick a bit to attract termites down in the mound, and then withdrew the stick. Termites had attached themselves to the stick, and the chimpanzees ate them directly off the stick (Figure 7.14).

Close analysis of this "termite fishing" behavior shows it to be both true tool manufacture and rather complex tool use. Chimpanzees often spent a great deal of time selecting the appropriate stick. When a suitable stick was not available, they pulled a branch out of the ground or off a bush and stripped away the leaves. This is deliberate manipulation of an object in the environment—toolmaking. The act also reflects a conscious decision-making process. Termite fishing is not easy. Even finding the right kind of stick is tricky. If a stick is too flexible or too rigid, it cannot be inserted into the termite tunnel. Taking the stick out without knocking the termites off also calls for careful handling.

Termite fishing is not an innate chimpanzee behavior. It is passed on to others in the group by means of learning. Young chimpanzees watch their elders and imitate them, thus learning the methods and also developing practice. As Goodall has documented, termite fishing has become part of the local group's culture.

Other Examples of Toolmaking Termite fishing is only one of many types of tool manufacture reported among chimpanzees. Sticks are also used to hunt for ants. A chimpanzee will dig up an underground nest with its hands and then insert a long stick into the nest. The ants begin swarming up the stick, and the chimpanzee withdraws it to eat the ants. Sticks have also been used to probe holes in dead wood and to break into bee nests (Goodall 1986).

In addition, chimpanzees have been observed making sponges out of leaves. After a rainfall, chimpanzees will drink out of pools of water that collect in the holes of tree branches. Often the holes are too small for the chimps to fit their head into, so they create a tool to soak up the water: they take a leaf, put it into their mouth, and chew it slightly. (Chewing increases the ability of the leaf to absorb water.) They insert this "sponge" into the hole in the branch to soak up the water.

One of the more fascinating examples of ape toolmaking in recent years is apes making and using spears for hunting! A number of chimpanzees in Senegal have been observed selecting a loose branch, stripping off the leaves, and then trimming one or both ends of the branch with their teeth. They then climb a tree and thrust the sharpened branch into holes, spearing bushbabies (a type of loris) inside the tree (Pruetz and Bertolani 2007). Although there have been many other observations of chimpanzees hunting, this is the first example of a chimp making and using a weapon.

Other examples of chimpanzee toolmaking and tool use include using leaves as napkins and toilet paper, using branches and rocks to crack open nuts, and using a bone pick to dig out marrow from a bone (Goodall 1986; McGrew 1992). Excavations in the African rain forest have provided archaeological evidence of chimpanzee tool use. Stones were transported to places where they were used to process food, suggesting some antiquity of chimpanzee tool use (Mercader et al. 2002). Although most observations of tool use in the wild have been made on chimpanzees, there are reports of occasional tool use by bonobos, gorillas, and orangutans (Breuer et al. 2005).

Do Apes Have Culture?

Observations of ape toolmaking have narrowed the perceived gap between humans and apes. Our understanding of the ways in which these behaviors develop and are passed on from one generation to the next through learning (recall the young chimpanzee watching the adults fish for termites) has led to an interesting question: Is this cultural behavior?

It has been argued, however, that such cases are not conclusive demonstrations of culture because they concern only a single behavior, whereas human culture is characterized by a combination of behavior patterns (de Waal 1999).

Whiten et al. (1999) published a landmark review of cultural behavior in chimpanzees based on observations of seven chimpanzee communities. They examined 65 different behaviors in an effort to find behaviors that were specific to some, but not all, communities. Their goal was to identify a set of behaviors in some communities that were not seen species-wide. Of the 65 behaviors, 26 were excluded because they were rare in all communities, could be explained by local ecological conditions (e.g., no termites to fish), or were present in all communities, suggesting species-wide behaviors best explained by genetic rather than cultural transmission. The remaining 39 behaviors were found in high frequencies in some, but not all, communities and were therefore likely to be examples of local culture. For example, antfishing using a probe was found in four communities but was absent in the other three. Picking marrow out of bones was found in one community but not in the other six.

This study confirmed earlier work (e.g., McGrew 1992) showing that many chimpanzee behaviors are *not* species-wide but are confined to specific communities and passed on to each generation culturally. Further, some behaviors were found to be unique to a single community, whereas others were found in two or more communities. In addition, the cultural profiles of each community were distinct from others, a pattern typical of human cultures and unlike that found in other species. Similar results have since been reported in a comparative study of orangutan behavior (van Schaik et al. 2003), providing additional support for cultural ability in apes.

The answer to the question of whether apes have culture now appears to be yes. As noted by primatologist Frans de Waal (1999) in a commentary on the Whiten et al. paper, "The 'culture' label befits any species, such as the chimpanzee, in which one community can readily be distinguished from another by its unique suite of behavioral characteristics. Biologically speaking, humans have never been alone—now the same can be said of culture" (p. 636).

Language Capabilities

Language has long been considered a unique human property. Language is not merely communication but is also a symbolic form of communication. The nonhuman primates communicate basic emotions in a variety of ways. Chimpanzees, for example, use a large number of vocalizations to convey emotional states such as anger, fear, or stress (Figure 7.15). Humans, however, rely on language, which is more complex than simple communication.

What Is Language?   Primate communication through vocalizations, grooming, or other methods does not constitute language. Language, as a symbolic form of communication, has certain characteristics that distinguish it from simple communication. Language is an *open system;* that is, new ideas can be expressed that have never been expressed before. Chimpanzee vocalizations, on the other hand, form a closed system capable of conveying only a few basic concepts or emotions. Human language uses a finite number of sounds to create an infinite number of words, sentences, and ideas.

FIGURE 7.15

A chimpanzee screeching.

Another important characteristic of language is *displacement.* Language allows discussion of objects and events that are displaced—that is, not present—in time and/or space. For example, you can say, "Tomorrow I am going to another country." This sentence conveys an idea that is displaced in both time (tomorrow) and space (another country). We can discuss the past, the future, and faraway places. Displacement is very important to our ability to plan future events—imagine the difficulty in planning a hunt several days from now without the ability to speak of future events!

Language is also arbitrary. The actual sounds we use in our languages need not bear any relationship to reality. Our word for "book" could just as easily be "gurmf" or some other sound. The important point is that we understand the relationship of sounds to objects and ideas. This, in turn, shows yet another important feature of language—it is learned.

Apes and American Sign Language   Can apes learn a human language? Early efforts at teaching them were stymied by the fact that apes lack the vocal anatomy to speak a human language. In the 1960s, two scientists, Allen and Beatrice Gardner, began teaching American Sign Language to a young female chimpanzee named Washoe. Devised for the deaf, American Sign Language (ASL) is a true symbolic language that does not require vocalization but instead uses hand and finger gestures (Figure 7.16). Because chimpanzees are capable of making such signs, ASL was considered the most suitable medium to determine whether they were capable of using language. Washoe quickly learned many signs and soon developed an extensive vocabulary.

Washoe also demonstrated the ability to generalize—to take a concept learned in one context and apply it to another. For example, she would use the sign meaning *open* to refer to boxes as well as doors. This suggests that Washoe truly understood the general concept of *open* and not just the use of the sign in one specific context. Washoe also invented new signs and "talked" to herself while playing alone, an act human children perform when learning language.

A young couple talking in American Sign Language (ASL). Sign language is a full symbolic language that makes use of gestures and facial expressions instead of vocalizations.

As Washoe grew older, it became natural to wonder whether she would some day have an infant who would then learn ASL from her, thus showing cultural transmission of language. During the 1970s, Washoe's adopted infant, Loulis, began using ASL, learning two dozen signs within 18 months. Because care was taken to ensure that Loulis was not exposed to *humans* signing, the results of the study suggest strongly that chimpanzees can learn ASL from each other (Fouts and Mills 1997). Washoe died in 2007.

Washoe was the first ape taught ASL. Since then there have been many experiments into the nature of the language capabilities of apes (Figure 7.17). Gorillas, as well as chimpanzees, have been taught ASL. Other languages were

A chimpanzee using American Sign Language.

also invented, including one based on plastic tiles and another using a computer keyboard.

Human and Ape Language Abilities The purpose of the original research with Washoe was to determine what was unique about the way in which human children learn language. It was suggested that a comparison of human and chimpanzee language acquisition would reveal at what point human abilities surpassed those of the ape. Washoe's abilities exceeded early expectations, and soon the research focus shifted to the language capabilities of the apes themselves. The ability of Washoe and other apes to learn a symbolic language suggested that language acquisition could no longer be regarded as a uniquely human feature.

Over the past several decades, there has been considerable debate over the meaning of these studies. It is clear that apes can learn and use words, using either ASL or computer symbols, but is that actually using language? One of the major criticisms was that apes did not understand grammar and could not construct sentences, and that observations suggesting such behavior actually resulted from apes responding to unconscious clues (Terrace 1979). Premack (2007) lists other reasons that apes are not actually using language. For one thing, chimpanzee sentences are relatively simple and are not the complex and recursive forms that humans use. For example, a chimp might sign, "Tickle me," but only a human could construct a complex recursive sentence where some ideas are embedded in others, such as "Tickle your friend, the one with the bright green earrings that she bought at the new store downtown, that replaced the old deli after it went out of business." Premack (2007) also argues that a key component of human language acquisition that makes it different from what apes do is that human language is actively taught, and not just mimicked.

Other researchers note that such critiques ultimately boil down to arguments about the specific definition of language, and by focusing on unique features of human language, we are not paying sufficient attention to the things that the apes *can* do (Cohen 2010), many of which are beyond what we might have once expected. We see some capability for language and other mental concepts in apes, but they are still different from humans. These differences raise an interesting question: At what point did our own pattern of language acquisition begin? Did human language abilities evolve suddenly (and, if so, when and where?), or did they evolve gradually over a long period of time? We will return to such questions, as well as the related questions of the origin and evolution of tools and culture, in later chapters.

Summary

Humans share many features with the other hominoids, but also exhibit a number of differences. The main biological characteristics of humans are a large and complex brain, three times its expected value; bipedalism; and small canine teeth. In addition, humans have a growth pattern that differs from other primates in its extended childhood and adolescent growth spurt. Behaviorally, humans are quite variable.

Past behavioral definitions of humans have often focused on humans as toolmakers. However, studies of apes in their native habitat show that they also make and use simple tools. Accumulated data on chimpanzee behavior in the wild show that chimpanzees, like humans, possess culture. Another oft-cited human characteristic is the use of symbolic language. Although apes are unable physically to speak a human language, studies of American Sign Language and other symbolic, visually oriented languages show that apes have some limited language acquisition capabilities. Modern humans remain unique in the specific ways they use tools and language and in their reliance on these behaviors for survival. The capabilities shown by apes provide us with possible clues regarding human origins.

Supplemental Readings

Bogin, B. 2001. *The Growth of Humanity*. New York: John Wiley & Sons. Includes a detailed review of the human life cycle with particular attention to the evolution of human growth.

Fisher, H. 1992. *Anatomy of Love: A Natural History of Mating, Marriage, and Why We Stray*. New York: Ballantine. A well-written and fascinating account of evolutionary explanations of human marriage and mating.

Savage-Rumbaugh, S., and R. Lewin. 1994. *Kanzi: The Ape at the Brink of the Human Mind*. New York: John Wiley. An excellent popular account of the studies of ape language acquisition.

OUR ORIGINS

What is the evidence for human evolution? This question can be answered in a number of ways because our knowledge of past human evolution comes from several sources—the fossil record, the archaeological record, and genetic evidence. In addition to trying to understand the biological evolution of human beings, we need to understand how our cultural adaptations have changed over time. It is important to keep in mind that our present state, biologically and culturally, did not come about all at once and that different human characteristics evolved at different times. Chapter 8 provides some background on the methods of research used to study human evolution, as well as on the history of life on our planet up to 65 million years ago. Chapter 9 reviews the fossil record of primate origins and evolution from their initial appearance to the split of ape and human lines roughly 6 million years ago. Chapter 10 examines the evidence of the first hominins and the evolution of bipedalism. Chapter 11 looks at the origin and initial geographic dispersion of the genus *Homo*. Chapter 12 deals with the further evolution of archaic humans, specifically *Homo heidelbergensis* and the Neandertals. Chapter 13 discusses the origin of anatomically modern humans (*Homo sapiens*).

Robert Pleyer excavating the skeleton of a 4,500-year-old man from a tomb near Altdorf in southern Germany.

The Fossil Record

CHAPTER

8

- Dating the Past
- Reconstructing the Past
- Life before the Primates

You may have already heard about "Lucy," the nickname for one of the most famous fossils in human evolution. You will read more about Lucy in Chapter 10, but for the moment here is a summary of the facts that you would hear about Lucy in lecture or from a museum display. Lucy is a specimen of a hominin species different from our own, one that walked on two legs but had a small ape-sized brain. Lucy was an adult female and was a little less than 3.5 feet tall when she died. Lucy lived a bit over three million years ago in Africa.

When hearing this, the most appropriate question you can ask is "How do we know?" How do we know how this species is different from ours? How do we know Lucy was a female and not a male, or that she was an adult instead of a child? How can we tell how old she was when she died, and how can we tell that she lived three million years ago? All of these (and others) are necessary questions when examining the fossil record. We will be looking more closely at the fossil record for primate evolution (Chapter 9) and human evolution (Chapters 10–13) and encountering data on our ancestors. Before we do so, we need to know exactly how we can make estimates on when they lived and what they were. We derive clues about past evolution from the fossil record. When looking at human evolution, we will also need to consider clues from the archaeological record, which provides us with evidence of past behaviors (such as toolmaking and hunting).

Not all information on human evolution comes from what can be dug out of the ground. Studies of the genetics of living humans and living nonhuman primates can help us create "family trees" showing the patterns of relationship and estimates of the dates of the origin of new evolutionary lines. Studies of the behavior of living humans and of living nonhuman primates give us clues about possible patterns of behavior of our ancestors.

All of these avenues of research, and others, make up the field of **paleoanthropology,** the study of primate and human evolution in the broadest possible sense. Although the focus is anthropology, the field of paleoanthropology necessarily involves contributions from other disciplines, including geology, chemistry, and physics. This multidisciplinary approach, using information from *all* relevant fields, is critical for current research on human evolution. No one person can possibly become an expert in all of the

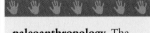

paleoanthropology The study of primate and human evolution.

areas and methods used to extract information about our past. The study of human evolution requires a team approach, tapping the strengths of different fields, all focused on the question of our origins. This chapter provides some basic background on methods of paleoanthropological research and on the history of vertebrate evolution up until the origin of the primates, setting the stage for discussion of primate and human evolution in subsequent chapters.

DATING THE PAST

Evolution is a process that occurs over time. Therefore, if we are analyzing information from either the fossil or the archaeological records, we need to know *when* a particular organism lived or *when* a particular tool was used. We need a way to determine the time sequence of fossil and archaeological remains in order to make sense of what changed over time, and how.

Two basic classes of methods are used to date fossil and archaeological sites and specimens. **Relative dating** determines the *sequence* in time by showing which specimen is older, but not its exact date. **Chronometric dating** determines an "exact" date for a specimen, subject to statistical fluctuation.

Different nomenclature has been used to refer to geological and historical dates. The abbreviation **B.P.,** meaning "Before Present," is often used. (The "Present" has been set arbitrarily as the year 1950.) Some people have used the term B.C., meaning "Before Christ," but because not all peoples share a belief in Christ, the term B.P. is preferable and has been agreed upon internationally. A date of 800,000 years B.P. would therefore mean 800,000 years before the year 1950. The term "years ago" is sometimes used instead of "Before Present." Two abbreviations are commonly used in paleontology and throughout this book: ka (thousands of years ago) and Ma (millions of years ago).

Relative Dating Methods

If we have two sites containing fossil or archaeological material, relative dating methods can tell us which is older, but not by how much. Relative dating methods can tell us the basic time sequence of fossil and archaeological sites. Other relative dating methods can provide us with a range of possible dates based on comparison of the fossils or geology with other sites of known age.

Stratigraphy   **Stratigraphy** makes use of the geologic process of superposition, which refers to the cumulative buildup over time of the earth's surface (Figure 8.1). When an organism dies or a tool is discarded on the ground, it will ultimately be buried by dirt, sand, mud, and other materials. Winds move sand over the site, and water can deposit mud on it. In most cases, the older a site is, the deeper it is. That is, if you find one fossil 3 feet deep and another 6 feet deep, the principle of stratification allows you to infer that the latter fossil is older. You still do not know the age of the fossils or the exact amount of time between the two, but you have established which is older in geologic time.

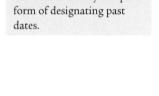

relative dating A comparative method of dating the older of two or more fossils or sites, rather than providing a specific date.

chronometric dating The method of estimating the specific date of fossils or sites.

B.P. Before Present (1950), the internationally accepted form of designating past dates.

stratigraphy A relative dating method based on the fact that older remains are found deeper in the earth because of cumulative buildup of the earth's surface over time.

FIGURE 8.1

Example of strata in the geologic record. Grand Canyon National Park, Arizona.

In some situations, stratigraphy is more difficult to use. Where the earth's crust has folded and broken through the surface of the ground, the usual stratigraphic order is disturbed. This does not invalidate the method, however, for careful geological analysis can reconstruct the patterns of disturbance and allow relative dates to be determined.

Other Relative Dating Methods   A number of other methods can provide relative dates. One example is a form of chemical analysis known as **fluorine dating,** which measures the accumulation of fluorine levels in bone. When an organism dies, its bones absorb fluorine from water. The more time that has passed since the organism died, the more fluorine has accumulated. Unfortunately, the rate of this process varies from site to site, so we cannot tell exactly how old a bone is by using this method. The method does allow us, however, to determine if two bones found at the same site are the same age by comparing their fluorine levels, which should be the same if the fossils are the same age. Sometimes bones from different ages can be found at the same location because of geological factors affecting deposition, and fluorine dating can help in such cases to determine if the bones are from the same time.

Other relative dating methods can provide, with comparative data, an approximate age of a site. One example is **biostratigraphy,** which involves

fluorine dating A relative dating method, based on the accumulation of fluorine in a bone, that tells if two bones from a site are of the same age.

biostratigraphy A relative dating method in which sites can be assigned an approximate age based on the similarity of animal remains to those from other dated sites.

comparison of animal remains found at different sites to determine similarity in time levels. Imagine that you have discovered a site that contains a fossil of a certain species of pig. Suppose you know from previous studies that this species of pig has always been dated to between 2.0 million and 1.5 million years ago wherever it has been found (using chronometric dating methods discussed below). Logically, this suggests that your newly discovered site is also between 2.0 million and 1.5 million years old. Plant pollens can sometimes be used in a similar manner.

Another relative dating method involves **paleomagnetic reversals.** At present, a compass will point toward the North Pole, but there have been times in earth's history when this was reversed, and the magnetic pole was near the South Pole! The magnetic field of the earth runs between the North and South Poles, and the polarity of this field (which direction a compass would point) changes at irregular intervals over long periods of time. The last time a reversal occurred was approximately 780,000 years ago, known as the Brunhes-Matuyama Reversal, which separated the current period of normal polarity (Bruhnes) from the previous time of reversed polarity (Matuyama). Sedimentary rocks preserve a record of these past changes in polarity. Past changes in polarity have been calibrated using other dating methods (covered in the next section) that give an estimate of an exact date (Figure 8.2). By comparing a

paleomagnetic reversal A method of dating sites based on the fact that the earth's magnetic field has shifted back and forth from the north to the south in the past at irregular intervals.

FIGURE 8.2

The paleomagnetic record for the past 6 million years. The different colors correspond to periods of normal polarity (magnetic north) and reversed polarity. The four polarity epochs (Brunhes, Matuyama, Gauss, and Gilbert) refer to periods when the polarity is primarily normal or reversed. Note that these epochs include intervals (polarity events) when the polarity is reversed for a short time. (Data from Conroy 2005.)

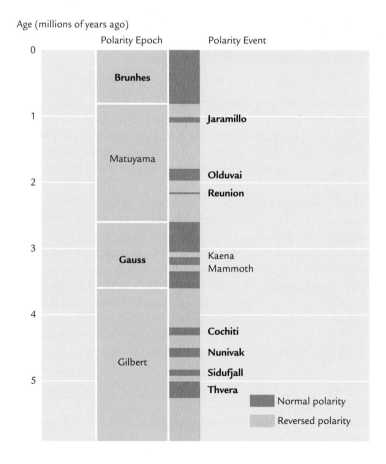

sample with this calibrated record, we can sometimes get a range of possible dates. For example, if we find that a fossil is found right above the Brunhes-Matuyama Reversal, we know that the fossil was close to (but no older than) 780,000 years old.

Chronometric Dating Methods

Chronometric dating methods provide an "exact" date, subject to statistical variation. Chronometric dating relies on physical and chemical processes in the universe that remain constant. Many of these methods utilize the fact that the average rate of radioactive decay is constant for a given radioactive atom no matter what chemical reaction it might be involved in. If we know that a certain element decays into another at a constant rate, and if we can measure the relative proportions of the original and new elements in some object, then we can mathematically determine the age of the object. Radioactive decay is a probabilistic phenomenon, meaning that we know the average time for decay for many atoms. Such processes allow us to specify an average date within the limits of statistical certainty.

Carbon-14 Dating   Living organisms take in the element carbon (C) throughout their lives. Ordinary carbon, carbon-12 (^{12}C), is absorbed by plants, which take in carbon dioxide gas from the air, and by animals, which eat the plants (or animals that eat the animals that eat the plants). Because of cosmic radiation, some of the carbon in the atmosphere is a radioactive isotope known as carbon-14 (^{14}C). An organism takes in both ^{14}C and ^{12}C, and the proportion of ^{12}C to ^{14}C is constant during the organism's life because the proportion is constant in the atmosphere. When an organism dies, no additional ^{14}C is ingested, and the accumulated ^{14}C begins to decay. The rate at which ^{14}C decays is constant; it takes 5,730 years for one-half of the ^{14}C to decay into ^{14}N (nitrogen-14). Carbon-14 is therefore said to have a **half-life** of 5,730 years (Figure 8.3). The half-life is the time it takes for half of a radioactive substance to decay.

Carbon-14 dating uses this constant rate of decay to determine the age of materials containing carbon. The process of the decay of ^{14}C results in the emission of radioactive particles that can be measured. We look at the rate of radioactive emissions for a sample and compare it to the rate of emissions expected in a living organism (a rate of 15 particles per minute per gram of carbon). For example, suppose a sample is analyzed and is found to emit 3.75 particles per minute per gram of carbon. Compared to a living organism, two half-lives have elapsed (one half-life results in 7.5 particles, and a second half-life results in half of this number, or 3.75 particles). Because the half-life of ^{14}C is 5,730 years, the age of our sample is 5,730 × 2 = 11,460 years old. If the sample were analyzed in 2012, its carbon-14 date would be 11,398 years ago (or 11.4 ka in abbreviated form). This date was computed by noting that 62 years have passed since the reference year of 1950 (the "Present"), giving 11,460 − 62 = 11,398.

half-life The average length of time it takes for half of a radioactive substance to decay into another form.

carbon-14 dating A chronometric dating method based on the half-life of carbon-14 that can be applied to organic remains, such as charcoal, dating back over the past 50,000 years.

FIGURE 8.3

The process of radioactive decay. The half-life of ^{14}C (carbon-14) is 5,730 years, which is the time it takes for *half* of ^{14}C to decay into ^{14}N (nitrogen-14). After 5,730 years, 50 percent of the ^{14}C remains. It then takes another 5,730 years for half of the remaining ^{14}C to decay, such that after two half-lives, 75 percent of the ^{14}C has decayed into ^{14}N, leaving 25 percent ^{14}C.

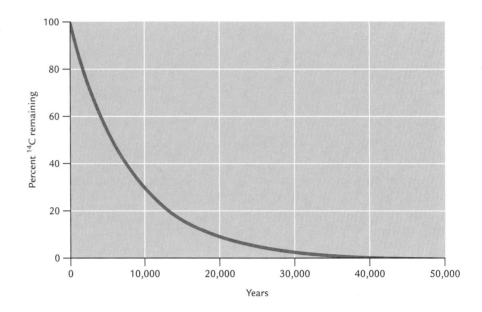

In theory, any sample containing carbon can be used. In practice, however, bone tends not to be reliable in all cases because of chemical changes during fossilization, in which carbon is replaced. In most circumstances, charcoal is the best material to use. If we find that a fire occurred at a certain site, either naturally or human-made, we can use the charcoal for carbon-14 dating. But careful attention must be given to possible contaminants at any given site. Another problem with carbon-14 dating is that the level of ^{14}C in the atmosphere has not been constant in the past due to climatic change, human activity, and other factors. Consequently, the radiocarbon date derived from carbon-14 dating needs to be adjusted using a calibration curve to give an estimate of the actual calendar age of a specimen.

Carbon-14 dating is useful only for sites dating back over the past 50,000 years at most. Any older samples would contain too little ^{14}C to be detected. Though carbon-14 dating is extremely valuable in studies of recent hominin evolution, it is not useful for dating most of earth's geological history.

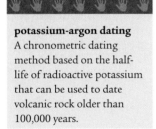

potassium-argon dating
A chronometric dating method based on the half-life of radioactive potassium that can be used to date volcanic rock older than 100,000 years.

Argon Dating   Two related chronometric dating methods make use of radioactive decay of isotopes into argon gas using samples of volcanic rock. One method, known as **potassium-argon dating** (abbreviated as $^{40}K/^{40}Ar$ dating), makes use of the decay of an isotope of potassium (^{40}K) into argon gas (^{40}Ar) with a half-life of roughly 1.25 billion years. This slow rate of radioactive decay means that this method works best on samples older than 100,000 years.

Potassium-argon dating requires rocks that did not possess any argon gas to begin with. The best material for this method is volcanic rock, because the heat generated by volcanic eruptions removes any initial argon gas. Thus,

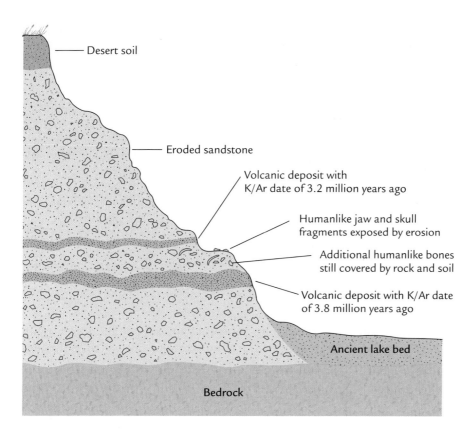

— Desert soil

— Eroded sandstone

Volcanic deposit with
K/Ar date of 3.2 million years ago

Humanlike jaw and skull
fragments exposed by erosion

Additional humanlike bones
still covered by rock and soil

Volcanic deposit with K/Ar date
of 3.8 million years ago

Ancient lake bed

Bedrock

FIGURE 8.4

Hypothetical example of the use of potassium-argon dating. Hominin remains are found between two layers of volcanic ash, one dating to 3.8 million years ago and the other dating to 3.2 million years ago. The hominin can therefore be dated at between 3.8 million and 3.2 million years ago. (From *Human Antiquity: An Introduction to Physical Anthropology and Archaeology,* 4d ed., by Kenneth Feder and Michael Park, Fig. 7.7. © 2001 by Mayfield Publishing Company. Reprinted by permission of The McGraw-Hill Companies.)

we can be sure that any argon gas we find in a sample of volcanic rock is the result of radioactive decay. By looking at the proportions of ^{40}K and ^{40}Ar, we can determine the number of elapsed half-lives and therefore the age of the volcanic rock.

Though we cannot date a fossil directly with this method, we can assign a date based on the relationship of a fossil find to different levels of volcanic ash (Figure 8.4). If we find a fossil halfway between two layers of volcanic rock with dates of 4.6 million and 4.5 million years ago, we can then assign the fossil an age of roughly 4.55 million years ago. Potassium-argon dating is best applied in areas with frequent volcanic eruptions. Fortunately, much of hominin evolution in East Africa took place under such conditions, allowing us to date many fossil sites.

Potassium-argon dating has largely now been replaced with a more accurate and useful variant, known as **argon-argon dating** ($^{39}Ar/^{40}Ar$ dating). Here, the sample is first irradiated to convert the ^{39}K isotope of potassium into the ^{39}Ar isotope of argon. Because the amount of the ^{39}Ar isotope is a function of potassium content, the method allows estimation of the ratio of potassium and argon. The argon-argon method is more accurate because the final estimates can be calculated from a single extraction of argon gas, whereas the potassium-argon dating method requires

argon-argon dating A variation of potassium-argon dating that can be applied to very small samples of volcanic rock.

FIGURE 8.5

Tree rings, which can be dated by the method of dendrochronology.

dendrochronology A chronometric dating method based on the fact that trees in dry climates tend to accumulate one growth ring per year.

fission-track dating A chronometric dating method based on the number of tracks made across volcanic rock as uranium decays into lead.

thermoluminescence A chronometric dating method that uses the fact that certain heated objects accumulate trapped electrons over time, which allows the date when the object was initially heated to be determined.

two separate samples for assessing potassium and argon. The argon-argon method can be accurately applied to small samples—even a single crystal (Brown 2000).

Other Chronometric Dating Methods   Many other types of chronometric dating methods can be used in certain circumstances. Some utilize radioactive decay and some use other constant effects for determining age. Archaeologists working on the relatively recent past (within the last 10,000 years) often use a method known as **dendrochronology,** or tree ring counting (Figure 8.5). We know that a tree will accumulate a new ring for every period of growth. The width of each ring depends on available moisture and other factors during that specific period. In dry areas, there is usually only one growth period in a year. By looking at the width of tree rings, archaeologists have constructed a master chart of tree ring changes. Any new sample, such as a log from a prehistoric dwelling, can be compared to this chart to determine its age.

In addition to radioactive decay, other physical constants allow an estimate of age to be assigned to a sample. **Fission-track dating** relies on the fact that when uranium decays into lead in volcanic glass (obsidian) and other igneous rocks, it leaves small "tracks" across the surface of the glass. We can count the number of tracks and determine the age of the obsidian from the fact that these tracks occur at a constant rate. Fission-track dating is useful for dates from several hundred thousand years to billions of years ago (Schwarcz 2000).

Thermoluminescence is a dating method that relies on the fact that certain heated objects accumulate trapped electrons over time, thus allowing us to determine, in some cases, when the object was initially heated. This method has been applied to pottery, bronze, and burned flints. Thermoluminescence can be used to date objects as far back as 1 million years.

Electron spin resonance (ESR) is a method that provides an estimate of dating from observation of radioactive atoms trapped in the calcite crystals present in a number of materials, such as bones and shells. Although this method can be used for sites over a million years old, it works best for dates under 300,000 years (Grün 1993).

RECONSTRUCTING THE PAST

In addition to dating fossil and archaeological sites, paleoanthropologists use a variety of methods to reconstruct the past and provide a more complete picture of human evolution.

Interpreting Fossils

Imagine that you have uncovered the fossil remains of some hominin ancestors. What can you tell from these fossil remains? To what species do they belong? What is the level of variation within the species?

Identifying Species   As described in Chapter 4, the biological species concept provides a test to determine if individuals from two populations belong to the same species—they must be capable of reproducing naturally and giving rise to fertile offspring. Application of the biological species concept to the fossil record is particularly problematic because we will never have any direct evidence on interbreeding. Instead, we must make our species assignments for fossils based on inferences from the physical appearance, or morphology, of the fossils. Here, we compare the physical structure of the fossils with other fossils and living organisms, keeping in mind the ranges of variation. When we find two specimens that exceed the normal range of variation of similar organisms, we can make a stronger case for assigning the two specimens into different species. We also look for unique characteristics not found in other recognized species.

Because direct evidence of interbreeding is not possible, we often refer to species identified from the fossil record as **paleospecies** and note that the relationship of a paleospecies to the biological species can be subjective. In this sense, some scientists treat paleospecies as convenient labels of physical characteristics and recognize that the question of interbreeding is complex and not easily resolved from fossil evidence alone.

Species identification is also complicated by philosophical differences among scientists regarding the nature of species and speciation. Some feel that the range of variation within species is often rather large and suggest that it therefore makes more sense to assign fossils to species already known and described than to create new categories. Scientists with this view are often called "lumpers" because of the preference for lumping new fossils into a small number of preexisting categories. Lumpers view much of evolutionary change as taking place within lineages (anagenesis). Others take a different approach, seeing the fossil record as evidence of frequent speciation

electron spin resonance (ESR) A chronometric dating method that estimates dates from observation of radioactive atoms trapped in the calcite crystals present in a number of materials, such as bones and shells.

paleospecies Species identified from fossil remains based on their physical similarities and differences relative to other species.

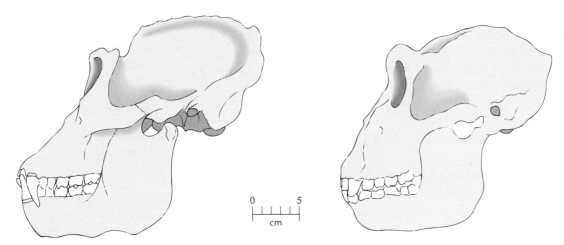

0 |||||| 5
cm

FIGURE 8.6

Sexual dimorphism in gorilla skulls. The skull of a male gorilla (*left*) is larger than that of the female gorilla (*right*) and also shows heavy crests of bones on top of the skull for muscle attachment. Such sex differences must be taken into account in analyzing fossil remains and assigning such remains to different species.

(cladogenesis). In this case, they anticipate numerous species at any point in time and tend to call any new fossil that is somewhat different a new species. Scientists with this view are often referred to as "splitters."

Variation within Species   Any description of the characteristics of a species should provide lists of traits that are common to all members in that species but are different from those of other species. This is easy enough when dealing with very different types of organisms, such as grasshoppers and elephants, but is more difficult when comparing closely related species. In such cases, we must be aware of the amount of variation that exists *within* a species and make sure that we do not confuse differences arising within a species with differences *between* species.

One source of variation within a species is the difference between males and females. As noted in Chapter 6, some primate species show a great deal of sexual dimorphism. Consider, for example, the skulls of male and female gorillas (Figure 8.6). Adult male and female gorillas are quite different in size and other features. If we were to encounter such specimens in the fossil record without knowing beforehand that they represented male and female from the same species, we might be tempted to place them in different species based on size differences. Thus, if we find fossils that differ in overall size or in the size of certain features, we must consider what we know about levels of sexual dimorphism before drawing any conclusions about species status.

How do we know whether a particular specimen is male or female? A number of methods exist to identify sex from the skeletal remains of humans and other primates. These methods are often very accurate, depending on what part of the body we have for analysis. Sometimes we can estimate sex from skulls. Overall size and the size of certain features on the skull can be used to separate males and females, because males are generally larger. The best source of information on sex (for adult specimens) comes from the pelvis, which shows a number of differences between male and female because females are capable of childbearing. Collectively, these differences provide a high level of accuracy in assigning sex to a human skeleton. Additional details on determining sex from skeletal remains are provided in Appendix 2 (Human Skeletal Biology) at the end of the book.

Another factor that must be considered when looking at anatomical variation within a species is age. Age can be determined from a variety of skeletal measures. One method involves looking at the closure of bones in the skull, some of which close early in life and some of which close in adulthood. Bone growth provides another means of age determination, because of variation in the age at which cartilage fuses into bone throughout the body. For example, growth of the femur (the lower leg bone) typically happens between 17 and 20 years of age. Another example of age estimation is the teeth—as mammals, humans have two sets of teeth during their lifetime, and the age at which the permanent adult teeth come in varies from tooth to tooth. For example, the third molar tooth (the "wisdom" tooth) typically comes in the late teens or early 20s. Any skeleton that has all of their third molars is dentally an adult. Further details on age determination are found in Appendix 2.

Interpreting Behavior

In addition to interpreting the fossil remains of our ancestors, we are interested in their behavior and the environment they lived in. Paleoanthropology employs a number of methods that allow inferences of behavior to be made.

Taphonomy When describing the behavior of early hominins or other organisms, we rely on a wide variety of data to reconstruct their environment and to provide information on population size, diet, presence or absence of predators, and other ecological characteristics. Often, we rely on what is found at a given site other than the fossil. For example, the presence of animal bones, particularly those that are fractured, might indicate hunting. The distribution of animal bones might also give us clues regarding behavior. The types of animal bones found at human hunting sites are different from those found at carnivore sites. A major problem is figuring out how animal bones and other objects got there and what happened to them. Imagine finding the leg bone of a fossil antelope and the leg bone of a fossil hominin at the same site. How did these bones wind up in the same place? Did the hominin hunt and kill the antelope? Did a predator hunt and kill both the antelope and the hominin? Did both bones wash down a river and land at the same place even though they might have originally been separate in time and space?

Some of these questions can be answered by methods developed within the field of **taphonomy,** the study of what happens to plants and animals after they die. This field provides us with valuable information about which bones are more likely to fossilize, which bones are more likely to wash away, the distribution of bones left by a predator, the likely route of pollen dispersal in the air, and many other similar topics. Taphonomic studies also provide us with ways of finding out whether objects or fossils have been disturbed or whether they have stayed where they were first deposited. Such studies can

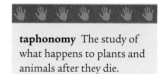

taphonomy The study of what happens to plants and animals after they die.

help us distinguish between human and natural actions as well. A fractured leg bone of a deer might result from normal wear and tear on a fossil or might reflect the action of a prehistoric hunter. By understanding what happens to fossils in general, we are in a better position to infer what happened to *specific* fossils.

Paleoecology   When reconstructing the past, we need to know more than just what early organisms looked like. We also need to know about the environment in which they lived. What did they eat? Were they predators or prey? What types of vegetation were available? Where were water sources? These questions, and many others, involve **paleoecology,** the study of ancient environments.

One example of the many methods used in reconstructing ancient environments is **palynology,** the study of fossil pollen. By looking at the types of pollen found at a given site, experts can identify the specific types of plants that existed at that time. They can then make inferences about annual and seasonal changes in temperature and rainfall based on the relative proportion of plant species. Further information on vegetation can be extracted from analysis of fossil teeth. Microscopic analysis of scratch patterns on teeth can tell us whether an organism relied more heavily on leaves, fruits, or meat.

Diet can also be inferred using **stable isotope analysis** of fossil remains. Stable isotopes are nonradioactive isotopes and so remain stable over time and are preserved in fossil remains. Ratios of different isotopes can provide information on diet. In carbon isotope analysis, for example, the ratio of ^{13}C to ^{12}C in animal bones is different depending on the type of plant predominantly eaten, such as grasses versus trees and other plants. If the animal eats other animals, then this analysis could tell us about the diet of the animal being eaten and, by extension, the type of animal. Other stable isotope ratios make use of nitrogen, hydrogen, oxygen, and strontium (Schoeninger 1995; Conroy 2005). Each type of analysis can add to the picture of ancient diets and environments.

Another aspect of ancient environments of interest is climate. This is particularly important when studying global climate changes over the past 2 million years of human evolution. At some points, average global temperatures dropped, leading to the spread of glaciers, whereas at other times, the glaciers receded as average temperatures increased. Past temperature can be studied by looking at the ratio of two isotopes of oxygen, ^{16}O and ^{18}O, which are found in the skeletal structure of small marine organisms. When water evaporates, water that contains ^{16}O evaporates more quickly because ^{16}O is lighter than ^{18}O. During glacial times, much of the water that evaporates is trapped as snow or ice and does not return to the sea. Consequently, sea levels drop and the relative amount of ^{16}O decreases and the relative amount of ^{18}O increases. The changes in this ratio over time have allowed us to plot global temperature changes for much of human evolution (Figure 8.7).

Experimental Archaeology   Humans are toolmakers and tool users. Given that many ape species, particularly the chimpanzee, are also capable of

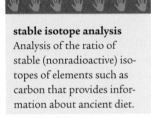

paleoecology The study of ancient environments.

palynology The study of fossil pollen.

stable isotope analysis Analysis of the ratio of stable (nonradioactive) isotopes of elements such as carbon that provides information about ancient diet.

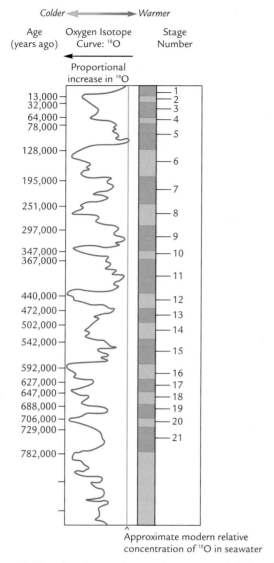

Colder ◄——————► Warmer

Age (years ago)   Oxygen Isotope Curve: ^{18}O Stage Number

◄—— Proportional increase in ^{18}O

Approximate modern relative concentration of ^{18}O in seawater

Odd-numbered stages (in orange) = warmer periods, less glacial ice cover
Even-numbered stages (in blue) = colder periods, more glacial ice cover

FIGURE 8.7

Changes in global temerature as inferred from the ratio of oxygen isotope ^{18}O to oxygen isotope ^{16}O. (From *Human Antiquity: An Introduction to Physical Anthropology and Archaeology,* 5th edition, by Kenneth Feder and Michael Park, p. 276. Copyright © 2007 by Mayfield Publishing Company. Reprinted by permission of The McGraw-Hill Companies.)

toolmaking and tool use, it seems reasonable to assume that the ability to make and use tools was also present in the last common ancestor of humans and African apes, and therefore present throughout hominin evolution. When reconstructing the past, however, we are limited to what kinds of material remain intact over thousands and millions of years. A hominin from 4 million years ago might have used a stick to dig termites out of a mound or some other task, but we will not find that stick 4 million years later. Instead, our record of early toolmaking and tool use is necessarily limited to stone tools, which can remain intact over time.

There is therefore a justifiable interest in the remains of stone tools used by our ancestors and discovered by archaeologists. The function of such tools

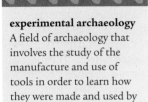

experimental archaeology
A field of archaeology that involves the study of the manufacture and use of tools in order to learn how they were made and used by people in the past.

is less clear. Were they used to butcher animals? Were they used to break open bone? There is also the question of how they were made. **Experimental archaeology** involves learning how to make and use tools in the present in order to shed some light on toolmaking and tool use in ancient times. For example, by attempting to re-create a stone tool, the experimental archaeologist can learn about the kinds of materials that work best, possible methods of manufacture, and potential uses. Likewise, if a question comes up regarding the efficiency of a small stone blade for butchering, the experimental archaeologist can test the idea by trying to butcher an animal with such a tool to see if it can be done, and how. Experimental archaeology can provide insight into other aspects of behavior as well. For example, Schick and Toth (1993) found that the pattern of flaking of a stone tool core was different in right- and left-handed people, an observation that was then extended to past remains to discover similar proportions of right- and left-handed people in the past.

Nonhuman Primate Models for Behavior   What can we say about the social behavior of our distant ancestors? Can we make any inferences about mating patterns or social structure or dispersal patterns, among other behaviors? Paleoanthropology relies on insights into behavior during human evolution by using comparative data from studies on nonhuman primates. As shown in Chapters 5 and 6, primate behavior is quite variable, and that leaves us with the question of *which* primate species, if any, should be used to provide insights into early hominin evolution.

There have been several approaches to this question. Some early studies of baboons focused on aspects of their society and behavior, such as large multimale/multifemale societies with strong male dominance hierarchies, as potential models for early hominin behavior (Figure 8.8a). The reason for the baboon analogy was environmental; many baboon groups live in the savannas of Africa, the same type of environment thought to have been inhabited by the earliest hominins. If certain behaviors represented adaptations to the

FIGURE 8.8

Primate species that have been used as models for early hominin behavior. (a) Savanna baboons, (b) Chimpanzees. Although early studies focused on baboons as possible models, chimpanzees (and bonobos) are preferred today.

(a)

(b)

savanna-particular environment, then we might expect that our earliest ancestors also shared such behaviors. The recognition that baboon societies, environments, and behaviors were more variable than first thought led to the baboon's falling out of favor as a possible model for hominin behavior, in light of the difficulty of making generalizations even within a species, let alone predictions about ancestors (Strum and Mitchell 1987). In addition, we now know that the earliest hominins did not live on the savanna (see Chapter 10).

Many paleoanthropologists now argue that a better choice of model would be one of the African apes because they are most closely related to us (Figure 8.8b). Chimpanzees have long served as possible models for early hominin behavior, but some scholars have also argued for using the bonobo. However, the choice of chimpanzee or bonobo is problematic because these species split from each other *after* the hominin line diverged. As such, they are equally related to us. Which one should serve as the common ancestor for a given behavior? In some cases, we would get different answers—for example, when looking at patterns of dominance, given that bonobos tend to show strong patterns of female dominance, whereas chimpanzees do not.

Primatologist Richard Wrangham (1987b) has suggested an alternative approach—comparing human behaviors to those of the three African apes (gorillas, chimpanzees, and bonobos). He argues that since all four species share a common ancestor, any behaviors that are shared at present in all four species likely have been inherited from that common ancestor. Using this logic, he has suggested that the common ancestor lived in societies in which males mated with more than one female. Males also engaged in hostile relationships between social groups, and some males lived alone outside of a social group. Females dispersed from their birth group and tended not to form alliances (Wrangham 1987b; Lewin and Foley 2004).

LIFE BEFORE THE PRIMATES

The next five chapters outline the fossil record for primate and human evolution. Before moving on, it is important to understand two points about primate and human evolution. First, *all* of the events covered in the next five chapters took place within a relatively short time, geologically speaking. The first primates appeared about 50 million years ago, and the first hominins about 6+ million years ago. These dates seem incredibly remote, but when we compare them to the 4.6-*billion*-year history of the planet, they are recent events (Box 8.1). The second point is that primates and humans did not appear out of nowhere, but instead evolved from earlier mammals. Therefore, in order to place primates and humans in evolutionary perspective, we need to review some basic features of mammalian evolution, which in turn requires that we look more generally at vertebrate evolution, and so forth back into the past. Although the focus of the next five chapters is on primate and human evolution, it is useful to review briefly some of the major events that preceded these events.

BOX 8.1

Deep Time and the Recent Nature of Human Evolution

When we study human evolution, we focus on the last 6 million years or so of earth's history, which (as will be discussed in Chapter 10) corresponds to the origin of the first hominins. Given that written history is only about 5,000 years old (which we refer to as "ancient" history), a date of 6 million seems incredibly old. However, this date pales when considering the age of the earth, which is 4.6 *billion* years. The long history of our planet was recognized in the concept of "deep time" argued by James Hutton (see Chapter 1) and other early geologists, but it is still a difficult concept to grasp. It is difficult for us to fathom the enormity of numbers that lie so far beyond our own personal lifespan.

It is important to realize that these dates are relative. Although the 6-million-year age of the human line seems very long relative to our own lifespan, it is but a blink of the eye relative to the much longer history of the planet. Because such large numbers are beyond our daily experience (unless you are a millionaire or a billionaire), the late astronomer Carl Sagan used an analogy he called the "Cosmic Calendar," which expressed geologic time relative to a calendar year (Sagan 1977). Here, I use a similar analogy by relating the 4.6 billion-year history of the earth to a 100-yard football field. Imagine that one end of the field corresponds to the origin of the earth and the other end corresponds to today. Now, as you walk from one end to the other, visualize the distance traveled as relative to key events in evolution. On this scale, you would have to travel almost 25 yards to get to the origin of the first single-celled organisms, and almost 87 yards to get see some of the first forms of multicelled life. The first vertebrates, which in real time appeared about 500 million years ago, appear at 89 yards.

You have now travelled almost 90 percent of the field and nothing close to humans has yet appeared. Mammals do not appear until 96 yards, and the dinosaurs become extinct at over 98.5 yards. In terms of human evolution, the first hominins appear at about 99 yards, 2 feet, 7 inches. This means that the material you will read about in Chapters 10–13 correspond to the last 5 inches or so of the football field.

Consider all that happens in these last 5 inches. The first stone tools are found at 99 yards, 2 feet, and 10 inches. The first modern humans appear at 99 yards, 2 feet, and 11.9 inches. The origin of agriculture, which takes place about 12,000 years ago in real time, occurs at 99 yards, 2 feet, and 11.995 inches. All of history since then took place within the last five-thousandths of an inch, which is slightly more than the average thickness of a human hair. This simple exercise shows that although time is deep, our own history is extremely recent. Humans are a new form of life on our planet.

eon A major subdivision of geologic time.

era A subdivision of a geologic eon.

period A subdivision of a geologic era.

Precambrian A term that refers to earth's history before the Cambrian period of the Paleozoic era. Precambrian time includes the Hadean, Archean, and Proterozoic eons, and lasted from 4,600 million to 542 million years ago.

The Origin of Life

Geologists and paleontologists divide the history of the earth into four **eons,** which are further broken down into **eras,** which are still further broken down into **periods.** Each of these units of time is defined by geologic and/or biological events observed in the fossil record and dated with long-range dating methods.

Almost 90 percent of the earth's 4.6-billion-year history is often referred to as the **Precambrian,** a period that includes the first three of four eons. The **Hadean eon** (4,600–3,850 Ma) covers the time from the origin of the earth prior to any fossil evidence for life. The **Archean eon** (3,850–2,500 Ma) is characterized by fossil evidence for the first forms of life, which were simple single-celled organisms. In the **Proterozoic eon** (2,500–542 Ma), there was a transition to an oxygen atmosphere, and the first simple multicelled organisms appeared.

Although the fossil record preserves some of the earliest life in the Archean and Proterozoic eons, we lack direct evidence for the initial origin

of life, generally thought to be a period of prebiological chemical evolution. We must rely instead on knowledge of the early conditions of the planet and combine these observations with laboratory evidence suggesting possible origins of life (Schopf 1999).

Vertebrate Evolution

The fourth geologic eon is the **Phanerozoic eon,** which covers the last 542 million years of earth's history and is characterized by the rapid origin and continued evolution of more complex life forms. In the beginning of this eon, the first vertebrates appeared, which eventually evolved into the five classes of vertebrates that live today—fish, amphibians, reptiles, birds, and mammals. The Phanerozoic eon is broken down into three geologic eras: Paleozoic, Mesozoic, and Cenozoic. Table 8.1 lists the eras and periods of the Phanerozoic eon and the major evolutionary events that occurred during each.

The Paleozoic Era The **Paleozoic era** is the term given for the period between 542 million and 251 million years ago. At the Cambrian period at the beginning of the Paleozoic era, there was a rapid diversification of many complex multicelled organisms, sometimes referred to as the "Cambrian explosion." As we have fossil evidence of life before this time, the "explosion" marks a time of rapid evolution and not a sudden origin (Ridley 2004). Of particular interest is the origin of the first vertebrates, the primitive jawless fish. Over time, some of these early vertebrates adapted to living partially on land—the first primitive amphibians. The fossil vertebrate *Tiktaalik* documents the transition from early fish to tetrapods (vertebrates with limbs)

Hadean eon The first geologic eon, dating from 4,600 to 3,850 Ma, which occurred before the oldest fossil evidence of life.

Archean eon The second geologic eon, dating from 3,850 to 2,500 Ma, characterized by the appearance of the first single-celled organisms.

Proterozoic eon The third geologic eon, dating from 2,500 to 542 Ma, characterized by the appearance of the first simple multicelled organisms.

Phanerozoic eon The fourth geologic eon, covering the past 542 million years.

Paleozoic era The first era of the Phanerozoic eon, dating from 542 to 251 Ma, when the first vertebrates appeared.

TABLE 8.1	Geologic Eras and Periods of the Phanerozoic Eon		
Era	*Period*	*Millions of Years Ago*	*Major Evolutionary Events*
Cenozoic	Neogene	23.0–today	Origin and evolution of hominoids and hominins
	Paleogene	65.5–23.0	Origin and evolution of many mammals, including first prosimians and anthropoids
Mesozoic	Cretaceous	145.5–65.5	Extinction of dinosaurs; first birds and placental mammals
	Jurassic	201.6–145.5	Dinosaurs dominate; first birdlike reptiles
	Triassic	251–201.6	First dinosaurs; first egg-laying mammals
Paleozoic	Permian	299–251	Radiation of reptiles; first mammal-like reptiles
	Carboniferous	359–299	Radiation of amphibians; first reptiles and insects
	Devonian	416–359	Many fish; first amphibians; first forests
	Silurian	444–416	First fish with jaws; first land plants
	Ordovician	488–444	Early vertebrates, including jawless fish; trilobites and many other invertebrates
	Cambrian	542–488	"Explosion" of life; marine invertebrates

Source: Dates from Walker and Geissman (2009).

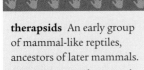

therapsids An early group of mammal-like reptiles, ancestors of later mammals.

Mesozoic era The second geologic era of the Phanerozoic eon, dating from 251 to 65.5 Ma, when the dinosaurs were dominant and when mammals and birds appeared.

FIGURE 8.9

Reconstruction of two dinosaurs. (a) Drawing of *Tyrannosaurus,* (b) Sculpture of *Diplodochus.* Dinosaurs were the dominant form of life on land during the Mesozoic era. The extinction of the dinosaurs (and other life forms) 65 million years ago created new opportunities for the evolution of mammals.

(Daeschler et al. 2006). Later in the Paleozoic era, complete adaptation to living on land occurred in the first primitive reptiles.

Mammals and birds eventually evolved from reptiles. The first primitive reptiles split into two major evolutionary lines. One line ultimately led to modern-day reptiles, as well as dinosaurs and birds. The other group was the **therapsids,** often referred to as the "mammal-like reptiles." The therapsids had many anatomical features that were reptilian. They also possessed certain characteristics that were mammalian, such as different types of teeth and greater emphasis on chewing food. The therapsids are accordingly labeled as "mammal-like" reptiles, and they represent the beginning of transitions that eventually led to later mammals. Therapsids underwent an adaptive radiation in the Permian period of the Paleozoic era, exhibiting a wide variety of shapes and sizes. Dental adaptations made the therapsids well suited to life on land, allowing them to forage and hunt. Although this group was highly successful for a time, they ultimately declined following the adaptive radiation of dinosaurs in the Mesozoic era.

The Mesozoic Era   The **Mesozoic era,** lasting from 251 million to 65.5 million years ago, is often called the "Age of Dinosaurs" because it was a time when dinosaurs were the dominant form of life on land (Figure 8.9). The major characteristic of the dinosaurs was the modification of the leg and pelvic structures. Many dinosaurs were bipedal, and some appear to have

(a)

(b)

BOX 8.2

Where Do They Get Those Dates?

You may be wondering why the various geologic units such as eons, eras, and periods have such odd starting and ending points. Wouldn't it make more sense to divide geologic time into even units, such as we do for time on an everyday basis, using units such as minutes, hours, and days? After all, all hours are the same length (60 minutes) and all days are the same length (24 hours). Why then are geologic eons, eras, and other units all different?

The difference is simple. When we use hours and days, the purpose is to have standard measures of time. When we look at the history of the earth, we are focused instead on events, such as major biologic and geologic changes that occurred in the past. For example, we have long known that a mass extinction took place in the past resulting in the disappearance of the dinosaurs (among other species). We knew this from the fossil record, and geologists have identified this time as the boundary between the Cretaceous Period of the Mesozoic Era and the Tertiary Period of the Cenozoic Era (a boundary usually abbreviated as the "K–T boundary"). What we did not know until the second half of the twentieth century was *when* this event took place. By dating the K–T boundary with argon-argon dating, we assign the date of this event at 65.5 Ma.

As dating methods have improved, we have been able to become more precise in our assignment of dates to the geologic time scale. That is why you can sometimes look up a geologic event, such as a mass extinction, and find differences in the date.

been extremely quick movers and efficient walkers and runners. As the dinosaurs became more dominant, the therapsids declined and eventually became extinct. Before they died out, however, some therapsids evolved to become the first "true mammals," by roughly 200 million years ago.

During the Triassic period, the monotremes, or egg-laying mammals, evolved. Some, such as the platypus of Australia, have survived until the present day. The first placental mammals evolved during the Jurassic period, which was the heyday of the dinosaurs. Birdlike reptiles also evolved during this time. The end of the Cretaceous period is marked by a mass extinction, when the dinosaurs and many other organisms became extinct.

What caused this mass extinction? The most accepted hypothesis is that an asteroid or comet hit the earth with tremendous force, kicking up vast clouds of dust and blocking the sun. Temperatures dropped, and many plant forms became extinct. As plants died, so did the plant eaters and those who ate the plant eaters. As such, the entire ecology of the planet shifted following this mass extinction. There is considerable geologic evidence to support the hypothesis of an extraterrestrial impact (e.g., Sheehan et al. 1991).

The Cenozoic Era   When the dinosaurs died out, a variety of opportunities opened up for the mammals, which underwent a series of adaptive radiations that filled vacant environmental niches. The last 65.5 million years of earth's history is known as the **Cenozoic era,** often called the "Age of Mammals" because of the rise of mammals in the wake of the extinction of the dinosaurs. During this time, all modern groups of mammals evolved, including the primates. The earliest primates appeared by 50 million years ago, the early primitive apes by 20 million years ago, and the first hominins by around 6 million years ago. The history of primate and hominin evolution is covered in the next five chapters (also, see Box 8.2 for an explanation of the dates used to define different eras).

Cenozoic era The third and most recent geologic era of the Phanerozoic eon, dating to the last 65.5 Ma. Primate and human evolution occurs during the Cenozoic era.

Summary

Paleoanthropology is a multidisciplinary approach to the analysis of primate and human evolution, relying primarily on information from the fossil record (and the archaeological record for human evolution). Dating methods provide the means by which to place fossils and other ancient data in sequence over time. Relative dating methods provide information on which samples are older or younger, but not the exact age. A commonly used relative dating method is stratigraphy, which makes inferences about age from a specimen's position in geologic strata—the deeper the specimen, the older it is. Chronometric dating methods make use of radioactive decay and other physical phenomena to provide an estimate of the actual age of a specimen. Commonly used methods of chronometric dating include carbon-14 dating for relatively "recent" specimens (less than 50,000 years old) and argon dating for very ancient specimens.

The fossil record provides a direct view on what our ancestors looked like and how they adapted. Analysis of fossil remains involves considering the relationships of a given specimen to known species in order to classify it into a known species or to designate a new species. Anatomical variation within species, such as due to sex and age, is important in distinguishing between fossil remains. Reconstruction of our ancestor's behavior makes use of information we can obtain from ancient environments including diet. Analysis of the archaeological record helps us understand human evolution over the past 2.5 million years, following the origin of stone tool technology. Our understanding of the creation and function of stone tools is enhanced through experimental archaeology. Attempts to reconstruct behavior can also benefit by inferences made from the behavior of living primates, particularly our closest living relatives, the African apes.

The earth is 4.6 billion years old. Roughly half a billion years ago, the first vertebrates appeared, followed by the first amphibians, and then the first reptiles. The therapsids, or mammal-like reptiles, were one of the first groups of reptiles. The therapsids eventually died out under competition from the dinosaurs, but some evolved into primitive mammals. When the dinosaurs and other organisms died in a mass extinction over 65 million years ago, the mammals had the opportunity to expand, and they underwent a series of adaptive radiations. One group of mammals, the primates, appeared about 50 million years ago.

Supplemental Readings

Futuyma, D. J. 2009. *Evolution,* 2d edition. Sunderland, MA: Sinauer Associates. A comprehensive source on evolution that includes a good review of the fossil record of evolution since the origin of the earth.

Klein, R. G. 2009. *The Human Career: Human Biological and Cultural Origins.* Chicago: University of Chicago Press. A comprehensive account of human evolution that includes a thorough discussion of dating methods used in paleoanthropology.

Schick, K. D., and N. Toth. 1993. *Making Silent Stones Speak: Human Evolution and the Dawn of Technology.* New York: Simon and Schuster. A very readable discussion of life during the Stone Age that includes many examples of experimental archaeology.

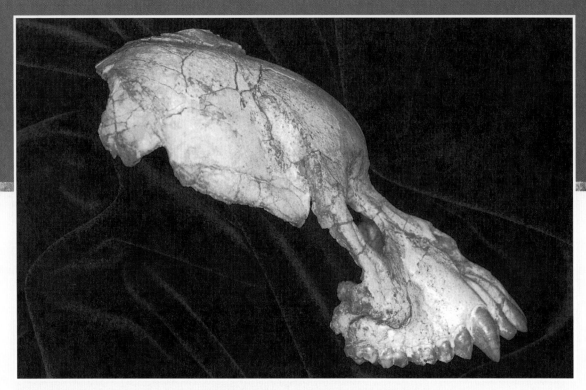

Proconsul heseloni, the smallest of several species of *Proconsul,* a genus of extinct African ape likely to be related to the common ancestor of all later hominoids, including humans.

Primate Origins and Evolution

Despite what we often see in cartoons and movies, humans and dinosaurs did not live at the same time. In fact, they did not even come close to overlapping in time. The dinosaurs died out, along with many other species, in a mass extinction over 65 million years ago. Modern humans (us) did not appear until about 200,000 years ago. The first bipeds appeared only 6+ million years ago. Although the mass extinction 65.5 million years ago marks the boundary between the "Age of Reptiles" (the Mesozoic Era) and the "Age of Mammals" (the Cenozoic Era), we should not think that this boundary marked the instantaneous appearance of all *modern* mammals. True, there were many species of more primitive mammals, but the first appearance of more modern forms, such as horses and whales, had yet to take place. The disappearance of the dinosaurs offered the opportunity for later forms of mammals to evolve, but this all took time.

Keep in mind that at the beginning of the Cenozoic Era there were no humans. Nor were there any monkeys, apes, or true primates for that matter. The diversity of primates that we see in the world today represents the totality of all that has happened over the last 65 million years. This chapter reviews some of the more basic trends in primate evolution in order to see where our own line of primates began. We begin with the origin of the first primitive primates and sketch in broad terms the overall evolution of later primates, ending with the branching of the African ape and human lines. The classification of primates that you reviewed in Chapter 5 comes into play here, reflecting the major branches in the family tree of primates.

However, reconstructing this family tree is not as simple as connecting the dots between fossils and living species. Over the past several decades, we have uncovered a rich fossil record of primate evolution that shows us that there had been considerable diversity in the past. We now know that many species of ancient primates have no living counterpart—they became extinct without leaving any descendants.

EARLY PRIMATE EVOLUTION

Primates evolved during the Cenozoic era, which is the past 65.5 million years. (The **epochs** of this era are listed in Table 9.1.) Primate evolution should not be thought of as a simple evolutionary "tree" with a few branches. A better

epoch A subdivision of a geologic period.

TABLE 9.1	**Epochs of the Cenozoic Era**	

Epoch	Millions of Years Ago	Major Events in Primate Evolution
Holocene	0.01–present	Humans develop agriculture and civilization; all of recorded history
Pleistocene	2.6–0.01	Origin and extinction of *Paranthropus*; origin and evolution of the genus *Homo*; development of stone tools; expansion out of Africa; increase in brain size; origin of modern humans
Pliocene	5.3–2.6	Adaptive radiation of first hominins, including *Ardipithecus* and *Australopithecus*
Miocene	23.0–5.3	Adaptive radiations of first hominoids; the origin of hominins (bipedal ancestors)
Oligocene	33.9–23.0	Adaptive radiation of anthropoids; divergence of New World monkeys
Eocene	55.8–33.9	Adaptive radiation of the first true primates; first anthropoids
Paleocene	65.5–55.8	Adaptive radiation of primate-like mammals

Source: Dates from Walker and Geissmann (2009), reflecting the new change in the boundaries of the Pleistocene.

analogy would be a series of "bushes" with many different branches at each stage of primate evolution. One or more adaptive radiations of primate forms occurred during each epoch. Many of the new forms became extinct, some evolved to become present-day representatives, and some moved into the next phase of primate evolution.

Overview of Early Primate Evolution

Before getting into the details of primate origins and evolution, it is useful to summarize some of the major events that took place. An adaptive radiation of primate-like mammals led to the origin of what we would call "true primates." The primate-like mammals showed evidence of an initial adaptation to life in the trees. Most of these species died out, but some evolved into primitive primates, which were fully adapted to living in the trees. These early primates then underwent another adaptive radiation. Although many of these early primate species became extinct, some species survived to ultimately evolve into the different lines of modern strepsirhines. Some of the early primates evolved into early haplorhines, including the anthropoids. Subsequent adaptive radiations led to separate groups of New World monkeys, Old World monkeys, and the first primitive apes.

FIGURE 9.1

A colugo, a gliding mammal also known as a "flying lemur" even though it does not fly and is not a lemur. Cologus, along with tree shrews, are genetically very similar to primates.

Primate Origins

Living primates are most closely related to a group of mammals known as colugos (Figure 9.1) and the insect-eating tree shrews (Janečka et al. 2007; Zischler 2007). Fossil evidence for the appearance of the primate-like mammals that led to more modern looking primates is found in the early Cenozoic era.

Continental Drift and Primate Evolution Most of the fossil evidence on primate origins comes from deposits over 55 million years ago in North America and Europe of a group of insectivores known as the primate-like mammals. This widespread distribution may seem strange given the fact that North America and Europe are now separated by the Atlantic Ocean. This was not, however, the configuration at that time. The continents continually move about on large, crusted plates on top of a partially molten layer of the earth's mantle—a process known as **continental drift.** This process continues today: North America is slowly drifting away from Europe and toward Asia. The expansion of the South Atlantic has even been measured from satellites. The placement of the different continents at various times in the past is shown in Figure 9.2.

continental drift The movement of continental land masses on top of a partially molten layer of the earth's mantle that has altered the relative location of the continents over time.

FIGURE 9.2

Continental drift. More than 200 million years ago, all of the continents formed a single land mass (called Pangea). By 180 million years ago, two major land masses had formed (Laurasia and Gondwana). By 65 million years ago (the beginning of primate evolution), South America had split from Africa, but North America and Europe were still joined. (From *Human Antiquity: An Introduction to Physical Anthropology and Archaeology,* 4th ed., by Kenneth Feder and Michael Park, Fig. 3.6. Copyright © 2001 by Mayfield Publishing Company. Reprinted by permission of The McGraw-Hill Companies.)

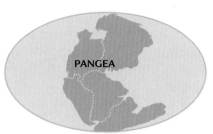

More than 200 million years ago

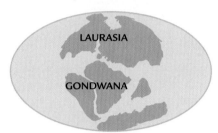

180 million years ago

65 million years ago

Present

An understanding of past continental drift is crucial in interpreting the fossil evidence for primate evolution. As continents move, their environments change. When continents separate, populations become isolated; when continents join, there is an opportunity for large-scale migrations of populations. Roughly 230 million years ago, all the continents were joined together as one large land mass. By 180 million years ago, this large mass had split in two: one containing North America, Europe, and Asia, and the other containing South America, Africa, Australia, and Antarctica. By the time of the primate-like mammals, South America had split off from Africa, but North America and Europe were still joined. Thus, it is no surprise to find fossils of primate-like mammals on both continents—they represent part of the group's range on a single land mass.

The Primate-like Mammals During the **Paleocene epoch** (66–56 million years ago), we find evidence of what are referred to as "primate-like mammals" (technically known as *plesiadapiforms*), which were small creatures, usually no larger than a cat and often smaller. They were quadrupedal (four-footed) mammals whose arms and legs were well adapted for climbing. Within this general group, there was considerable diversity. Gunnell and Silcox (2010) note that there are more than 120 species that have been discovered. Most of this extensive variation was in body size and dental specializations. Some of the primate-like mammals had large incisors for heavy gnawing, others had teeth better adapted for slicing, and still others had teeth adapted for eating nectar and insects. Such variation is expected from an adaptive radiation. These small insectivores had some ability to climb and thus were able to exploit many different types of food.

In spite of their arboreal adaptations, these creatures are not considered true primates. A picture of the skull of one of these creatures (Figure 9.3) shows why. The front teeth are far apart from the rest of the teeth, a feature not found in primates. The eyes are located more toward the sides of the skull, unlike the forward-facing eyes of primates. In addition, the primate-like mammals lack a post-orbital bar.

One important discovery relating to primate origins was the discovery of a skeleton belonging to the species ***Carpolestes simpsoni,*** a primate-like mammal that lived in Wyoming between 56 million and 55 million years ago (Bloch and Boyer 2002). This species was a small, arboreal fruit eater. Although it lacked certain primate traits, such as stereoscopic vision, it had a foot adapted for grasping and an opposable big toe, as well as a nail rather than a claw on its big toe (Figure 9.4). Thus, it is intermediate in many ways between more primitive primate-like mammals and true primates, and serves as a model for the primate origins.

Carpolestes provides us with evidence on the nature of primate origins. There have been debates over the sequence of origin of primate traits. Living primates have stereoscopic vision and grasping hands, and the question has been raised as to which of these evolved first or whether these traits evolved simultaneously. Because *Carpolestes* shows grasping hands but *not* stereoscopic vision, it appears clear that grasping hands came first in the evolutionary sequence of primate origins. The fact of grasping hands, combined with dental evidence pointing to a diet of fruit, supports a model of primate origins whereby *Carpolestes* evolved grasping hands to allow successful feeding on fruits and flowers at the ends of branches, an activity that would require the ability to anchor oneself on small branches (Susmann 1991). Although other mammals, such as squirrels, take food back to the main trunk of a tree to eat it safely, grasping hands would have allowed *Carpolestes* to eat more food in less time and to do so more safely.

The First Primates The first "true" primates appeared roughly 50 million to 55 million years ago at the beginning of the **Eocene epoch** (56–34 million

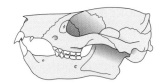

FIGURE 9.3

Side view of a skull of a Paleocene primate-like mammal. (Redrawn from John Fleagle, *Primate Adaptation and Evolution,* 1988, Academic Press, Inc., with permission from Elsevier. Stephen D. Nash, Illustrator.)

Paleocene epoch The first epoch of the Cenozoic era, dating between 65.5 million and 55.8 million years ago. The primate-like mammals appeared during the Paleocene.

Carpolestes simpsoni A species of primate-like mammal that had some derived primate traits, such as a grasping foot and an opposable big toe. This species is intermediate in many respects between primitive primate-like mammals and true primates.

Eocene epoch The second epoch of the Cenozoic era, dating between 55.8 million and 33.9 million years ago. The first true primates, primitive prosimians, appeared during the Eocene.

FIGURE 9.4

Reconstruction of *Carpolestes*, a fruit-eating, primate-like mammal that possessed a grasping foot. (Courtesy of Doug Boyer.)

FIGURE 9.5

Side view of the skull of an Eocene primate. (Redrawn from John Fleagle, *Primate Adaptation and Evolution,* 1988, Academic Press, Inc., with permission from Elsevier. Stephen D. Nash, Illustrator.)

years ago). The climate during this time was warm and humid, and the predominant land environment was tropical and subtropical. Initially, the continents of Europe and North America were still joined, resulting in migration and similarity among the fossils we find in this region. Many orders of modern-day mammals first appeared during this time, including aquatic mammals (whales, porpoises, and dolphins), rodents, and horses.

Fossil primates from the Eocene epoch have been found both in North America and in Europe. During the Eocene, there was an adaptive radiation of the first true primates—early primitive species. This adaptive radiation was part of the general increase in the diversity of mammals associated with the warming of the climate and related environmental changes, and almost 200 different primate species have been discovered (Fleagle 1999).

The Eocene forms possessed stereoscopic vision, grasping hands, and other anatomical features characteristic of primates. A picture of the skull of an Eocene primate (Figure 9.5) shows many of these changes. Compared to the Paleocene primate-like mammals, the snout is reduced and the teeth are closer together. These forms possessed a postorbital bar and had larger brain cases and features of cerebral blood supply similar to that of modern primates. The large size of the eyes of some of the Eocene primates suggests that they were still nocturnal. It is not clear why stereoscopic vision evolved, although it seems possible that depth perception would have increased the ability to move quickly in the trees.

Although there are numerous species of early Eocene primates, they tend to fall into two groups that resemble, in some ways, primitive forms of modern primates. One group shows similarity to later strepsirhines, some of which may have been ancestral to modern-day lemurs and lorises. The other group may be ancestral to later haplorhines, including anthropoids. Others argue that the situation may be more complex. More fossils will be needed to sort out these evolutionary relationships.

Anthropoid Origins

What of the anthropoids? Although living anthropoids are more similar to tarsiers than to lemurs or lorises, identification of the first anthropoids, and their relationship to other fossil primates, is not as clear. A continuing debate is whether the first anthropoids evolved in Africa or Asia. There is evidence of early African anthropoids close to 40 million years ago that shows considerable diversity. It is not clear whether this diversity means that anthropoids had been in Africa for some time prior to these finds, or that it represents colonization from Europe alongside known movements of other mammals from Asia during the Eocene (Jaeger et al. 2010).

It is possible that the first anthropoids did not develop from either of the two main groups of primates in the Eocene, but instead from a third, independent line in early primate evolution. It is too soon to determine which of these ideas (if any) is correct. The main lesson we have learned from recent fossil discoveries is that past diversity was much greater than we once thought, and even given our recent accumulation of data, we are unlikely to have sampled more than a fraction of early primate diversity.

Old World Anthropoids   We have evidence of anthropoid fossils from the start of the **Oligocene epoch** (34–23 million years ago) at several locations in the Old World and the New World. The climate cooled during this time, and there was an expansion of grasslands and a reduction in forests. This change in climate seems to have resulted in the southward movement of primate populations, and we find little evidence of further evolution in North America or Europe. Most of the fossil evidence for anthropoid evolution is found in Africa and South America and in parts of eastern Asia.

The Oligocene primates show the continued radiation of anthropoid forms in both the Old World and the New World. The Oligocene anthropoids show continued reduction of the snout and nasal area, indicating greater reliance on vision than on smell. The Oligocene anthropoids have a fully enclosed eye socket, characteristic of modern anthropoids. All of the Oligocene anthropoids were small and arboreal and were generalized quadrupeds; none show signs of specialized locomotion. Their diet appears to have consisted primarily of fruit supplemented with insects and leaves.

The smaller eye orbits of many early anthropoids suggests that these forms were diurnal (Figure 9.6). The transition from a nocturnal lifestyle to a diurnal lifestyle was extremely important in the later evolution of the anthropoids. Given the variation in the daily schedule of living creatures, we can imagine a situation in which some ancestral primates began feeding during daylight hours. As this new environmental niche was exploited, natural

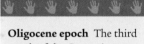

Oligocene epoch The third epoch of the Cenozoic era, dating between 33.9 million and 23.0 million years ago. Anthropoids underwent an adaptive radiation during the Oligocene.

FIGURE 9.6

Three-quarters view of the Oligocene anthropoid *Aegyptopithecus,* which lived about 33 million years ago. The smaller eye orbit, relative to the size of the skull, shows that this form was diurnal (nocturnal creatures have bigger eyes). *Aegyptopithecus* was once considered a possible early ape but is now recognized as an anthropoid that lived prior to the split of the Old World monkey and ape lines.

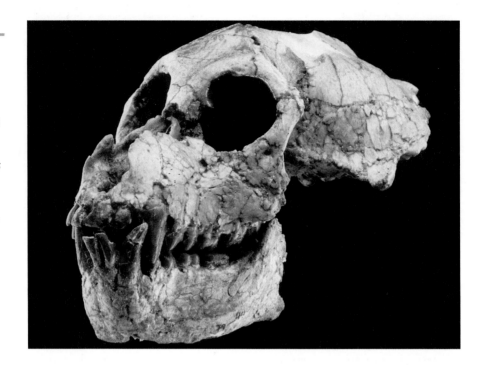

selection would act to favor individuals that possessed the abilities needed for such a way of life, such as improved vision. Daylight living also offers increased opportunities for social interactions because animals can see one another at greater distances. As a result, we would expect the development of larger social groups and an increase in social behaviors.

Evolution of the New World Monkeys   What about the New World monkeys? The earliest fossil record of New World monkeys dates back over 25 million years (Rasmussen 2007). Most of this evidence consists of fragmentary dental remains. Many of these fossils resemble living New World monkeys. Other forms have unusual features, such as narrow jaws and protruding incisors, and do not appear to have any living counterparts.

Where did the New World monkeys come from? Decades ago, it was thought that New and Old World monkeys represented a good example of parallel evolution from prosimians. However, current evidence points to enough similarities between the two groups of monkeys to make it more reasonable to assume a single origin for anthropoids somewhere in the Old World. How did the New World monkeys get to the New World? By this time, continental drift had resulted in the separation of the Old and New Worlds.

One explanation is that anthropoids reached South America by "rafting." (Figure 9.7) No, this does not mean that these early primates built rafts and paddled to South America! Ocean storms often rip up clumps of land near the shore, which are then pulled out into the ocean. Sometimes these "floating islands" contain helpless animals. Often they drown, but occasionally, they will be washed up on an island or continent. Based on what we know of

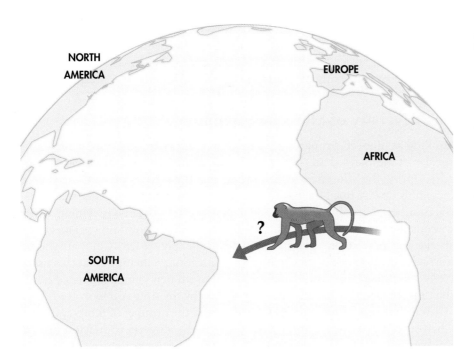

FIGURE 9.7

The "rafting" hypothesis for the origin of New World monkeys. In the past, when Africa and South America were closer together, African ancestors of New World monkeys could have reached South America on floating islands, consisting of large clumps of land and vegetation.

Atlantic Ocean currents and winds, Houle (1999) has calculated that small populations of monkeys could have survived long enough on these floating islands to complete a trans-Atlantic trip.

Present geological evidence supports this rafting hypothesis, with some researchers advocating that the monkeys rafted from North America to South America and others suggesting that they rafted from Africa to South America. At present, the evidence supports an African origin for three reasons. First, no early anthropoid ancestors have been discovered in North America. Second, there is evidence of other animals (rats) rafting from Africa (Fleagle 1995). Third, New World fossil evidence points to a close similarity to African anthropoids (Flynn et al. 1995).

EVOLUTION OF THE MIOCENE HOMINOIDS

Continued evolution of the Old World anthropoids led to two major branches, one line leading to the modern Old World monkeys, and the other to the modern hominoids (apes and humans). The oldest evidence for fossil hominoids is based primarily on dental remains and comes from Old World sites dating to the **Miocene epoch** (23.0–5.3 million years ago). Most Miocene mammals are fairly modern in form, and roughly half of all modern mammals were present during this time. South America and Australia were isolated due to continental drift. The land mass of **Eurasia** (a term given to the combined land masses of Europe and Asia) and Africa joined during part of the Miocene, roughly 16 million to 17 million years ago.

Miocene epoch The fourth epoch of the Cenozoic era, dating between 23.0 million and 5.3 million years ago. Several adaptive radiations of hominoids occurred during the Miocene, and the oldest known possible hominins appeared during the Late Miocene.

Eurasia The combined land masses of Europe and Asia.

The Early and Middle Miocene (before 16 million years ago) was a time of dense tropical forests, particularly in Africa. Subsequently, the climate became cooler and drier, and there was an increase in open grasslands and mixed environments consisting of open woodlands, bushlands, and savannas.

The Diversity of Miocene Hominoids

Looking at modern primates, it is apparent that there are more genera and species of monkeys than there are of apes. Monkeys are more diverse than apes. During the Miocene epoch, however, just the reverse was true—apes were incredibly diverse until the past 5 million to 10 million years. Since that time, the number of ape species has been declining. This decline is evident when we consider the diversity of fossil Miocene hominoids now known. Dozens of species are known from Africa, Asia, and Europe (Figure 9.8). Compare this to the few apes alive today (see Chapter 5). In addition, remember that this list is likely incomplete—we find new fossils, and often new genera and species, all the time. In fact, this list could be out of date by the time you look at it!

Why have the number of apes declined and the number of monkeys flourished since the Miocene? One possibility is the slow reproduction rate of modern apes. If Miocene apes were as nurturing of their offspring as modern

FIGURE 9.8

The distribution of Miocene hominoids in space and time. Notes: *Possible hominin (see Chapter 10). **Some consider some specimens of *Dryopithecus* to belong to the genera *Pierolapithecus* and *Anoiapithecus*. (Data from Begun 2010).

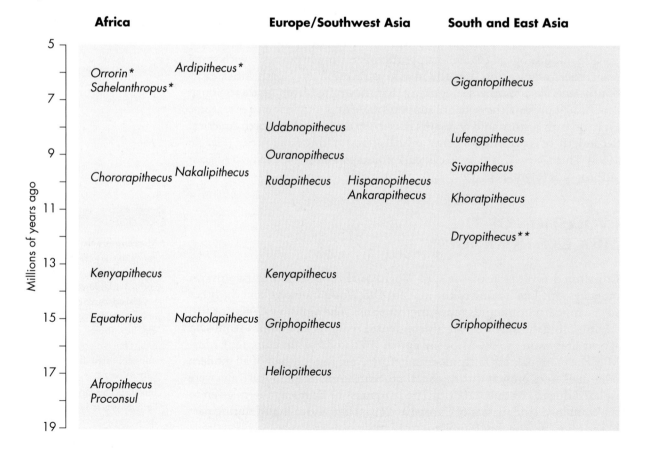

apes are, then they may have reproduced too slowly and died out. This problem would have been exacerbated by environmental changes over time.

For the purpose of reconstructing the evolution of the apes, this past diversity creates a problem. Given that there were more species in the past than are alive today, this means that many fossil species have no living descendants. Decades ago, when the fossil record was less complete, it was tempting to identify any newly discovered fossil ape as the Miocene ancestor of one of the living apes, such as the chimpanzee or gorilla. Today we have evidence of greater diversity in the past, but we now realize that evolution often produces initial diversity followed by later extinction of many branches. It therefore becomes more difficult to find the ancestors of modern apes. We can certainly recognize fossil apes in a general sense and see general evolutionary trends, but it is much more difficult to arrange the known fossils into a definitive evolutionary tree.

The Fossil Evidence

In general, the identification of the Miocene forms shown in Figure 9.8 as *hominoid* is based on dental and cranial features. In most cases, much less is known about the **postcranial** skeleton (the skeleton below the skull), and such evidence as does exist shows characteristics different from those of modern apes. Overall, it appears that the postcranial structure of Miocene hominoids was often more generalized than that of modern apes, whose particular adaptations (e.g., knuckle walking) may be more recent. In light of the great diversity of Miocene hominoids, only a few selected forms are discussed here. Keep in mind that many other forms existed.

Proconsul One early Miocene hominoid that appears to have evolutionary significance is the genus *Proconsul,* which lived in Africa between 21 million and 14 million years ago (Walker and Shipman 2005). Specimens placed in this genus show considerable variation, particularly in overall size, making assignment to specific species somewhat difficult. The skeletal structure of *Proconsul* shows a mixture of monkey and ape features (Figure 9.9). Like modern apes and humans, *Proconsul* did not have a tail (Ward et al. 1991). The

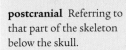

postcranial Referring to that part of the skeleton below the skull.

Proconsul A genus of fossil hominoid that lived in Africa between 21 million and 14 million years ago and that shows a number of monkey characteristics.

FIGURE 9.9

Reconstructed skeleton of *Proconsul.* (Redrawn from John Fleagle, *Primate Adaptation and Evolution,* 1988, Academic Press, Inc., with permission from Elsevier. Stephen D. Nash, Illustrator.)

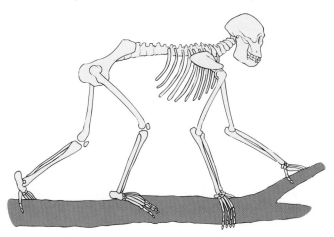

FIGURE 9.10

Two upper jaws of *Proconsul* specimens. Note the size and shape of the canine teeth.

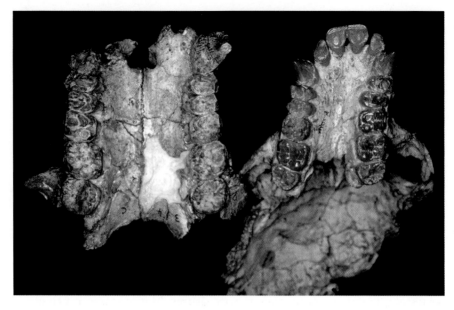

diastema A gap next to the canine tooth that allows space for the canine on the opposing jaw.

limb proportions, however, are more like that of a monkey than an ape, with limbs of roughly the same size. In a modern ape, the front limbs are generally longer than the rear limbs. The arms and hands of *Proconsul* are monkey-like, but the shoulders and elbows are more like those of apes. Analyses of the limb structure suggest that *Proconsul* was an unspecialized quadruped that lived in the trees and ate fruit (Pilbeam 1984; Walker and Teaford 1989).

The skull of a typical *Proconsul* specimen (refer back to the picture at the beginning of the chapter) is more like that of an ape in that it is large relative to overall body size. The teeth also demonstrate that these forms were hominoid (Figure 9.10). The shape of the lower premolar is like that of modern apes, with a single dominant cusp rather than two more or less equal-sized cusps, as found in humans. In apes, the single large cusp rubs against, and sharpens, the upper canine tooth. Ape jaws also have a noticeable gap, called a **diastema,** next to the canine teeth, which allows the jaws to close. Imagine the problem you would have if your canines were long and protruding and you did not have a gap between the teeth in the opposite jaw for them to fit into. You would not be able to close your mouth or chew!

Overall, the teeth and jaws of *Proconsul* are similar enough to those of modern African apes that they were once thought to be direct ancestors of the chimpanzee and gorilla. Today we realize that the situation is more complex than this. Environmental reconstructions show that *Proconsul* lived in the Miocene forests and ate primarily fruits. The mixture of monkey and ape traits points to them as typical of a transitional form from early generalized anthropoid to what we think of as an ape. Though definitely not identical to a modern ape, their overall structure is more like that of an ape than a monkey; hence, we refer to them as an early form of hominoid. Overall, *Proconsul* or some related form seems likely to be a common ancestor of later hominoids.

Proconsul was adapted to forest living and was a successful group for millions of years. As the climate cooled and became drier in certain regions during the Miocene, their habitat shrank. As competition for dwindling resources increased, other hominoids developed that were more successful in dealing with the new environments.

Later Miocene Hominoids   As seen in Figure 9.8, there were many more species of hominoids alive during the Miocene than exist today. It is also clear that the geographic distribution of fossil hominoids was greater than it is today (excluding humans). Whereas apes are found today in small pockets in Africa and Southeast Asia, during the Miocene they lived in both Africa and across a large part of Eurasia. Since the Miocene, the number of apes has declined, as has their geographic distribution, and it is within these broad evolutionary changes that we find some clues as to the origin of the first hominins.

As noted earlier, it seems likely that *Proconsul* or a related form in the early Miocene was a common ancestor of later apes (and ultimately, humans). What happened next? Between 17 and 14 million years ago, the climate in Africa became drier and differences between seasons became more pronounced. The fossil record provides evidence (Figure 9.8) of a number of new ape species arising at this time. After the time that Africa and Eurasia joined as a result of continental drift (17–16 Ma), a number of fossil apes spread out throughout Eurasia, ranging from Europe to Southeast Asia (Harrison 2010).

The number of hominoid species began to decline about 10 million years ago, and many Eurasian species were extinct by 5 million years ago, excepting those that were living in Southeast and East Asia, including the ancestors of the modern-day orangutan. One such form, ***Sivapithecus*** (Figure 9.11), lived in Indian and Pakistan between 12.5 and 7 million years ago (Begun 2010).

Sivapithecus A genus of fossil ape that lived in Asia between 12.5 million and 7 million years ago, possibly an ancestor to modern orangutans.

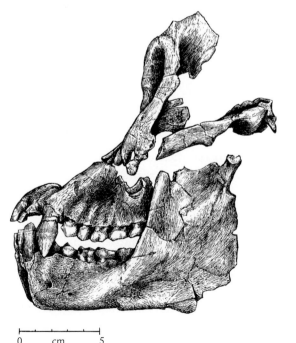

FIGURE 9.11

Side view of a *Sivapithecus* specimen from Pakistan. (From Clark Spencer Larsen, Robert M. Matter, and Daniel L. Gebo, *Human Origins: The Fossil Record,* 3d ed. Copyright © 1998 by Waveland Press, Inc., Long Grove, IL. All rights reserved. Reprinted with permission from the publisher.)

0   cm   5

FIGURE 9.12

Comparison of the *Sivapithecus* specimen GSP 15000 (*left*) with a modern orangutan (*right*).

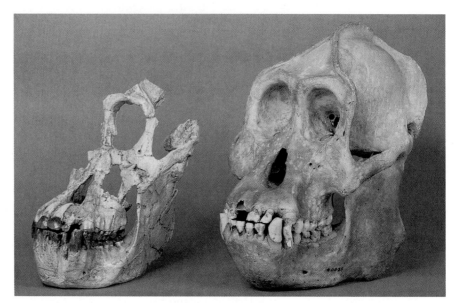

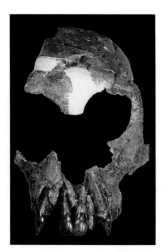

FIGURE 9.13

Frontal view of a *Dryopithecus* specimen RUD 200 from Rudabánya, Hungary. (Copyright David Begun 2003.)

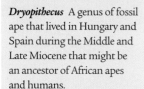

Dryopithecus A genus of fossil ape that lived in Hungary and Spain during the Middle and Late Miocene that might be an ancestor of African apes and humans.

Ouranopithecus A genus of fossil ape that lived in Greece during the Late Miocene that might be an ancestor of African apes and humans.

The skull and teeth of *Sivapithecus* are very similar to modern-day orangutans (Pilbeam 1982). The overall shape of the skull, particularly when viewed from the side, is different from African apes but similar to the orangutan (Figure 9.12). The eye orbit of *Sivapithecus* has an oval shape, and the orbits are close together, both features that are also found in orangutans. The post-cranial anatomy of *Sivapithecus* is different from orangutans, but the overall similarity in cranial and dental anatomy shows it to be within the group of Miocene apes that was ancestral to orangutans. The orangutan is a thus a survivor of what had once been a widespread group of Asian apes, including some very unusual forms such as the giant ape, *Gigantopithecus* (see Box 9.1).

What about the common ancestor of African apes and humans? Some anthropologists argue that a common ancestor was one of the Eurasian apes that subsequently dispersed back into Africa (e.g., Begun 2010). Two European Miocene apes, ***Dryopithecus*** and ***Ouranopithecus,*** lived about 10 to 12 million years ago, and have been suggested to be possible ancestors of African apes and humans, as they share a number of cranial features with living African apes and early hominins, including a long, low brain case and a lower face that tilts downward (Figure 9.13) (Kordos and Begun 2002; Begun 2003). Another possible common ancestor is a fossil ape known as *Pierolapithecus,* who lived in Spain 13 million years ago (Moyà-Solà et al. 2004). Some have suggested that this fossil ape is actually *Dryopithecus* (Begun 2010). Either way, the specimen consists of both a cranium and a partial skeleton (Figure 9.14). The post-cranial anatomy shows a mixture of monkey and ape traits, suggesting a form that was a climber but still walked on all fours on tree branches, rather than hang underneath them like modern apes.

It is interesting that these suggested common ancestors of African apes and humans are all European fossil apes. According to Begun (2010), the most likely explanation is that as the climate changed and Eurasian apes

BOX 9.1

The Giant Ape

The fossil record of Miocene apes shows us that the living hominoids (apes and humans) represent a fraction of the hominoid diversity that once existed. This means that we sometimes see fossils that appear strange given our more restricted idea of hominoid variation based on living creatures. One interesting example of an extinct hominoid species that continues to capture the imagination of the public and the scientific community is a Miocene fossil ape known as *Gigantopithecus*; here, the genus name translates literally as "giant ape," which gives you a good idea of what sets this ape apart from others. *Gigantopithecus* was an Asian ape, with remains having been found in China, India, and Vietnam. Some of these date back as far as 9 million years old, although the Chinese specimens may date only to about 500,000 years ago, which means these creatures may have lived at the same time as some of our own ancestors in the genus *Homo* (Ciochon et al. 1990). Although the name conjures up many images, in reality almost everything that we know about *Gigantopithecus* is from teeth and jaws—we do not have a skeleton or even a skull.

Although it sounds strange, *Gigantopithecus* was first found in a drugstore! Throughout much of Asia, fossil teeth and bones are ground into powder and used in various potions that are said to have healing properties. The teeth are often called "dragon's teeth" and are sold in apothecary shops. In 1935, the anthropologist Ralph von Koenigswald discovered huge teeth in one such store and later named the fossil remains *Gigantopithecus*. Since then, additional teeth and jaws have been recovered from fossil sites.

The major characteristic of *Gigantopithecus* is that it had huge molar and premolar teeth set in a massive jaw. Another interesting feature is that although the canine teeth are large, they are not that large relative to the rest of the teeth. The *relatively* smaller canines and the thick enamel on the molar teeth suggested to some that *Gigantopithecus* might have been related to humans, who have the same characteristics. We now realize that Miocene ape evolution is a lot more complicated than once thought. *Gigantopithecus* is in some ways similar to *Sivapithecus* and probably represents a side branch in Asian ape evolution. It is likely an extinct relative of the orangutan.

The large molars, thick molar enamel, small canines, and large jaws all suggest an ape that was well adapted for a diet consisting of items that were very hard to chew. In fact, the tips of the canines are worn down in a manner consistent with heavy chewing. The large teeth and jaws have always captured people's imagination. Based on the size of the teeth, some have suggested that *Gigantopithecus* might have stood over 9 feet tall! Unless we can find parts of the rest of the skeleton, such estimates will remain uncertain. Some have suggested that *Gigantopithecus* is somehow related to the mythical "Abominable Snowman," presumably because of its geographic location and possible size. There is no support for this idea (or for the existence of the Snowman). What *Gigantopithecus* really shows us is yet another example of the diversity of Miocene apes.

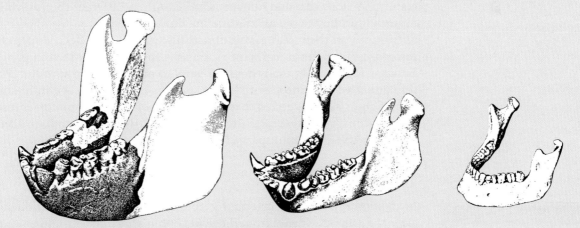

Comparison of the lower jaws of *Gigantopithecus* (*left*), a modern gorilla (*middle*), and a modern human (*right*). *Gigantopithecus* has the largest overall size but relatively small canines compared to the gorilla. (Illustrations by Tom Prentiss from *Gigantopithecus,* by E. L. Simons and P. C. Ettel, *Scientific American,* January 1970. Copyright © 1970 by Scientific American, Inc. Used with permission of Nelson H. Prentiss.)

FIGURE 9.14

Pierolapithecus, a Miocene ape that might be a common ancestor of African apes and hominins. Some consider this a form of *Dryopithecus.*

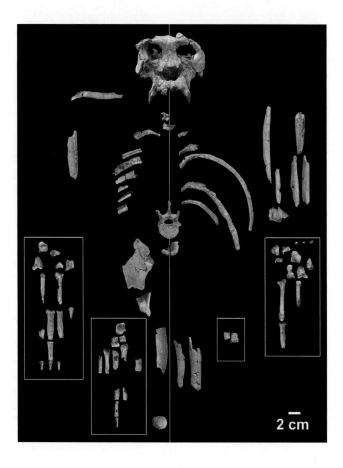

2 cm

became extinct, some dispersed back into Africa, including the common ancestor of African apes and humans. Once in Africa, different species evolved ultimately leading to the African ape and human lines. At the risk of oversimplifying, we can then see the evolutionary history of many Miocene apes as an initial dispersion from Africa into Eurasia, a subsequent extinction of most Eurasian forms other than those ancestral to modern Asian apes and those that dispersed back into Africa before splitting into African ape and human lines. Others have suggested that the ancestors of the last common ancestor evolved from forms already in Africa (Harrison 2010), although the evidence still favors the Eurasian dispersal (Begun 2010).

The Genetic Evidence

In addition to fossil evidence, our interpretations of Miocene evolution must also take genetic evidence from the living hominoids into account. Since the 1960s, a comparison of the genetics of living organisms using a set of methods known as **molecular dating** has shed new light on hominoid evolution.

Comparison of genetic data from different species can give us a picture of the evolutionary relationships between them. If certain assumptions are made, these methods can also be used to provide an estimate of the date at

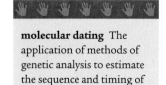

molecular dating The application of methods of genetic analysis to estimate the sequence and timing of divergent evolutionary lines.

BOX 9.2

How Does Molecular Dating Work?

We have seen in previous chapters how genetic comparisons between species can tell us which species are the most closely related. In addition, we have seen (Chapter 5) how an evolutionary tree can be reconstructed from these patterns of similarity. We can go one step further and estimate *when* different species branched off from each other. All of these analyses are possible given the basic premise that genetic similarity reflects common ancestry. The more similar the genetics of two species, the more closely related they are.

There are a variety of different ways of expressing the genetic similarities and differences between species. Here, we will use a simple measure of genetic distance, where the higher the number, the more different the two species. Imagine we are looking at the genetics of three different species (A, B, and C) and find the following genetic distances:

The distance between species A and species B is 2.
The distance between species A and species C is 6.
The distance between species B and species C is 6.

Again, we need not concern ourselves with the specific measures of genetic distance, but their values relative to each other. We see clearly that the distance between A and B is much lower than between A and C, or between B and C. This means that species A and B are more closely related. Given this information, we might infer the following evolutionary tree:

Here, we see a pattern where common ancestor 1 splits into two lines, one leading to species C, and the other line later splitting to form species A and B. This reconstruction is based on the observed patterns of genetic differences between the species—species C is the most different, and therefore branched off earlier in time.

Molecular dating allows us to estimate when common ancestors lived if we know from fossil data when at least one other common ancestor lived. In this hypothetical case, let us assume that we have a good idea from the fossil record that the common ancestor of all three species (common ancestor 2) lived about 12 million years ago. We also know from the genetic distances that the difference between species A and B (= 2) is one-third the difference between either A and C or B and C (= 6). Assuming that the time elapsed since the origin of a new species is proportional to genetic distance, we can infer that the time when species A and B split is one-third the time when species C split. Because we know in this case from the fossil record that species C split 12 million years ago, our estimate for the time when species A and B split from common ancestor 1 is $12 \times 1/3 = 4$ million years ago.

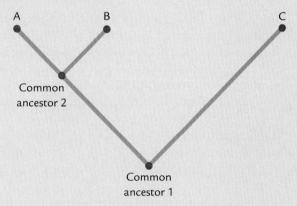

which two species split from a common ancestor. When two species separate, mutations occur, and neutral mutations accumulate in each line independently. If the rate of accumulation is constant in both lines, then a comparison of molecular differences in living forms will provide us with a relative idea of how long the two species have been separated (see Box 9.2).

Estimates from molecular dating vary due to the type and number of genes analyzed, differences in statistical estimation, and different calibration

FIGURE 9.15

Suggested evolutionary
relationship and dates for
common ancestors (shown
by dots) between great apes
and humans based on genetic
data. Dates in parentheses
represent the range of
likely dates. Estimates
are based on nuclear and
mitochondrial DNA except
for the chimpanzee-bonobo
split, which is based only on
mitochondrial DNA. (Data from
Glazko and Nei 2003, and Gagneux
et al. 1999 for the chimpanzee-
bonobo split.)

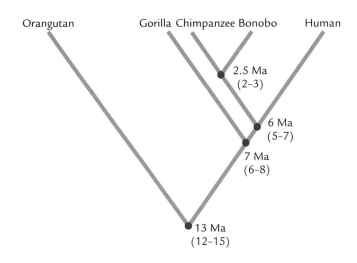

FIGURE 9.15

Suggested evolutionary relationship and dates for common ancestors (shown by dots) between great apes and humans based on genetic data. Dates in parentheses represent the range of likely dates. Estimates are based on nuclear and mitochondrial DNA except for the chimpanzee-bonobo split, which is based only on mitochondrial DNA. (Data from Glazko and Nei 2003, and Gagneux et al. 1999 for the chimpanzee-bonobo split.)

points from the fossil record (Glazko and Nei 2003). Even taking all of these factors into account, there is some general consensus for the evolution of the great apes and humans. Figure 9.15 shows one summary. The first divergence was geographic, with the line leading off to the Asian great ape, the orangutan, splitting about 13 million years ago. The other line consisted of the African hominoids (as shown in the next chapter, the first hominins arose in Africa). The gorilla line split off next, at roughly 7 million years ago, followed by the split between the hominin and chimpanzee–bonobo lines at roughly 6 million years ago. The chimpanzee and bonobo lines then split roughly 2.5 million years ago.

As noted above, there is variation in estimates depending on the specific genetic comparisons and methods used, among other factors. In general, however, the estimates of the divergence of the gorilla line fall between 7 and 10 million years ago, and the divergence of the human line fall between 6 and 7 million years ago (Glaszko and Nei 2003; Steiper and Young 2006; Fabre et al. 2009).

The estimates from genetics agree with what we know from the fossil record. Based on genetic data, we would expect to see evidence of the first hominins in Africa at about 6 million to 7 million years ago. As we will see in the next chapter, this is exactly when the fossil record shows the first fossil evidence of the hominins—our ancestors following the split from the African apes.

Summary

Following the extinction of the dinosaurs 65.5 million years ago, early mammal forms dispersed to new environments. Some early insectivores began to adapt more and more to life in the trees, developing grasping hands and binocular stereoscopic vision. These changes may have begun in response to the needs of insect predation and later been used to exploit additional food resources in a three-dimensional environment. The origins of primates can be traced to the primate-like mammals of the Paleocene epoch and the ancient primates of the Eocene. Primitive anthropoids evolved from a group of

Eocene primates. The early Oligocene anthropoids ultimately gave rise to the separate lines of Old World monkeys and hominoids.

The Miocene epoch is characterized by two major adaptive radiations. In the Early Miocene, primitive hominoid forms appeared in Africa. These forms, placed in the genus *Proconsul,* were similar in some ways to later apes but were also monkey-like in a number of features. They had jaws and teeth like those of later apes and lacked a tail. Their postcranial skeleton was generalized and primitive in a number of features.

During the Middle Miocene, several new genera of hominoids evolved. These hominoids include the ancestors of present-day great apes and humans, although the specific evolutionary relationships between Miocene species and modern species are not clear at present.

We are currently not able to identify precisely the common ancestor of the African apes and humans. Evidence from molecular dating supports a fairly recent split, roughly 6 to 7 million years ago. Although several genera of fossil apes could be a common ancestor (or related to a common ancestor), we cannot be definitive at this time. What is clear, however, is that there was extensive diversity in hominoids during the Miocene.

Supplemental Readings

Beard, C. 2004. *The Hunt for the Dawn Monkey: Unearthing the Origins of Monkeys, Apes, and Humans.* Berkeley: University of California Press.

Walker, A., and P. Shipman. 2005. *The Ape in the Tree: An Intellectual and Natural History of Proconsul.* Cambridge, MA: Belknap Press. Two well-written accounts of primate evolution.

Fossil footprints at the site of Laetoli, Tanzania. These footprints, dating over 3.7 million years ago, were most likely made by the species *Australopithecus afarensis,* an early hominin.

The First Hominins

How old are humans? Anthropologists are frequently asked this question, and it seems simple enough. But in fact we have no simple answer. The answer depends on how we define human beings. If we limit our question to humans who are more or less anatomically the same as living humans, the answer is roughly 200,000 years. If we include all large-brained humans, even those with a somewhat different skull shape, the answer would be several hundred thousand years. If we focus on all members of the genus *Homo,* with some significant cranial expansion and a dependence on stone tools, the answer is more than 2 million years. If we include all bipedal hominins, the answer may be more than 6 million years.

Past human evolution was not a one-step process. Humans did not emerge instantaneously from an apelike ancestor. What we are, biologically and culturally, is the product of many different evolutionary changes occurring at different times. The fossil record of human evolution is complete enough to show that the characteristics of *living* humans have evolved over time in a mosaic fashion. Fossil evidence now suggests that bipedalism first arose close to 6 to 7 million years ago, around the time of the divergence of hominins and African apes as estimated from genetic data. A number of dental changes took place over the next few million years. The first major increase in brain size, and the first use of stone tool technology, took place between 2.5 million and 2 million years ago (and possibly earlier). Brain size roughly equivalent to that of living humans appeared within the past few hundred thousand years, and modern cranial shape within the past 200,000 or so years. Many of our current cultural patterns appeared even more recently. It was only 12,000 years ago that humans began relying on agriculture and only 6,000 years ago that the first civilizations and complex state-level societies appeared. Many of the things we take for granted in our own lives today, such as automobiles, nuclear energy, and computer technology, are even more recent, many developing only in the last generation or two.

This chapter examines the beginning of the story of human evolution, focusing on the earliest hominins prior to the appearance of the genus *Homo.* The fossil species discussed in this chapter all lived in Africa between 6+ million and 1.4 million years ago.

OVERVIEW OF HUMAN EVOLUTION

The study of human evolution is fascinating but often confusing the first time around. To follow the evolutionary history of the first hominins, you must become familiar with a multitude of names, places, and events. Just as rereading a book often yields more insight because you now have a framework within which to integrate the information, it is useful to consider the general picture of human evolution before absorbing the details.

A Timeline of Human Evolution

Let us look at the broad story of human evolution (Figure 10.1 provides a graphic representation of this review). As discussed in the previous chapter, our best estimates from molecular dating suggest that the hominin line split

FIGURE 10.1

Simplified summary of hominin evolution emphasizing major evolutionary events.

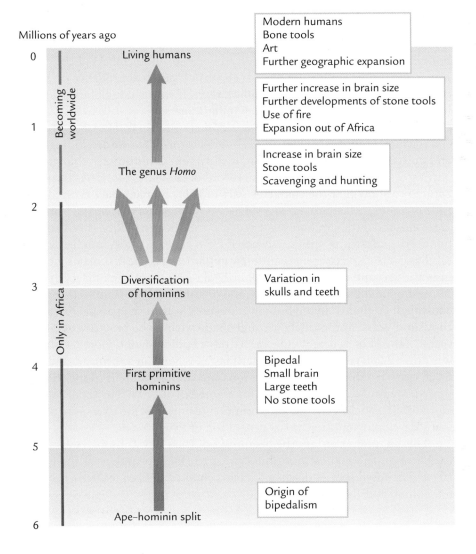

Millions of years ago

Modern humans
Bone tools
Art
Further geographic expansion

Further increase in brain size
Further developments of stone tools
Use of fire
Expansion out of Africa

Increase in brain size
Stone tools
Scavenging and hunting

Variation in
skulls and teeth

Bipedal
Small brain
Large teeth
No stone tools

Origin of
bipedalism

0 — Living humans

Becoming worldwide

1

The genus *Homo*

2

Diversification
of hominins

Only in Africa

3

4 — First primitive
hominins

5

6 — Ape–hominin split

from the African apes about 6 to 7 million years ago. At present, there is fossil evidence of several possible candidates for the earliest known hominin, all dating to about 6 million years ago. One or more species of primitive hominins lived in Africa over the next few million years, most classified in the genus *Australopithecus,* and they retained apelike features in some teeth and had ape-sized brains. These early hominins were bipedal, but they may have spent time climbing in the trees as well as walking on the ground. They foraged for food, primarily fruit, in the woodlands and savanna. By 3 million years ago, a rapid diversification had led to at least two distinct lines of hominin evolution. One line led to several species in the genus *Paranthropus,* also known as the "robusts," so named for their large back teeth and powerful chewing muscles. The robusts were well adapted to a diet that was hard to chew, such as seeds, nuts, and hard-skinned fruits. They became extinct by 1.4 million years ago. The other line of hominins began to rely more and more on learned behavior and perhaps began using the first stone tools.

One species of *Australopithecus* evolved into the first members of the genus *Homo* sometime between 2.5 million and 2 million years ago. The species known as *Homo erectus* had appeared in Africa by 2 million years ago, having an essentially modern skeleton, full bipedal adaptations, and a brain much larger than earlier hominins (roughly 70 percent the size of a modern human, on average). *Homo erectus* was the first hominin to expand out of Africa, moving into parts of Asia and Europe. *Homo erectus* hunted, used fire, and invented a new form of general-purpose stone tool known as the hand axe.

Around 800,000 years ago, a new species, *Homo heidelbergensis,* began to appear. This species occupied parts of Africa, Europe, and Asia, and had a large brain, almost the same size as living humans, but still with a large face and low skull. Hunting skills had increased by this time, and new methods of making stone tools had developed by 300,000 years ago. In Europe and the Middle East, humans known as Neandertals evolved, with distinctive facial traits and a large brain. Anatomically modern humans (*Homo sapiens*) had appeared in Africa by 200,000 years ago, spreading out across the Old World over the past 100,000 years. There is still debate over whether these expanding humans interbred with preexisting humans such as the Neandertals.

Modern humans dispersed even farther geographically, reaching Australia by 60,000 years ago and the New World 15,000–20,000 years ago. Starting 12,000 years ago, human populations in several different places developed agriculture, and the human species began to increase rapidly in number. Cities and state-level societies began about 6,000 years ago. Subsequent cultural developments took place at an ever-increasing pace. The Industrial Revolution began only 250 years ago. The use of electricity as a power source became common only during the twentieth century. Finally, it has been only about 50 years since the exploration of outer space began, another step in the geographic expansion of human beings.

This brief review shows one thing very clearly—what we are today as modern humans came about not all at the same time but at different times over millions of years. Thus, we should speak not of a single origin but rather of multiple origins.

BOX 10.1

The Piltdown Hoax

The fossil record shows us that bipedalism is the oldest unique human trait. Another unique human trait, our large brain, did not appear until much later in our evolution. However, at the beginning of the twentieth century, many thought that the reverse was true, and that brain size evolved first. Because there were few fossils to show otherwise at that time, this popular hypothesis could not then be rejected. In addition, the idea was supported for a time by fossil evidence for the great antiquity of the large human brain!

Between 1911 and 1915, primate fossils were discovered at Piltdown, England, alongside stone tools and the fossils of prehistoric animals such as mastodons. A primary specimen ("Piltdown Man") consisted of a large human skull and an apelike jaw. The teeth, however, were worn flat, more closely resembling the condition of human teeth than ape teeth. The specimen showed a mixture of ape and human traits and had a modern human brain size. It offered clear proof that large brains came first in human evolution.

Because of Piltdown, any fossils that had human characteristics but did not have the large brain were rejected by many as possible human ancestors. Indeed, this helps explain the reluctance of scientists to accept an early hominin discovered by Raymond Dart in South Africa in 1924. This specimen consisted of the face, teeth, and cranial fragments (including a cast of the brain case) of a young child. Dart named the specimen *Australopithecus africanus* (you will read more about *Australopithecus* later in this chapter). Based on cranial evidence relating to the angle at which the spinal cord entered the skull, he claimed that it was an upright walker.

The brain size was apelike, as was the protruding face. The teeth, however, were more like those of humans, particularly the small canines. Here was another specimen that had a mixture of ape and human traits, but one suggesting that the large brain evolved *after* bipedalism and humanlike teeth. However, at that time, more people tended to support Piltdown and the idea that large brains came first.

Some scientists, however, were more skeptical about Piltdown Man. Eventually, continuing investigation showed that Piltdown Man was a fake. In 1953, a fluorine analysis (see Chapter 8) confirmed that the jaw bones and skull bones did not come from the same time period. Closer inspection showed that the skull was that of a modern human and the jaw that of an orangutan. The teeth had been filed down, and all of the bones had been chemically treated to simulate age. Who was responsible for the Piltdown hoax? Over the years, many different suspects have been suggested.

The story of Piltdown Man is often offered up as evidence that anthropologists (and other scientists) do not know what they are talking about and are easily fooled. This criticism misses the point altogether. Science and scientists make mistakes, and sometimes they commit outright fraud. It would be foolish to expect otherwise. Science does not represent truth per se but rather a means of arriving at the truth. When Piltdown was discovered, scientific investigation did not stop. Instead, scientists kept looking at the evidence, questioning it and various assumptions, and devising new ways of testing. As a result, the hoax was uncovered. This is how science is supposed to work.

The Origin of Bipedalism

The major event discussed in the remainder of this chapter is the origin of the first hominins, characterized as being bipeds. As discussed in Chapter 7, there are some obvious unique physical characteristics of modern humans. We walk on two legs, we have large brains, and we have small faces and canine teeth. Before enough fossils had been discovered, scientists wondered whether these traits evolved at the same time or if one or more traits evolved first. One dominant idea at the beginning of the twentieth century was that large brains evolved early in human evolution, presumably because the great complexity of the human brain would have taken the longest amount of time to evolve. This expectation led to acceptance of a fossil hoax known as "Piltdown Man," that appeared to have a large human brain and an ape-like lower jaw (see Box 10.1 for a history of this hoax).

We now have a fossil record complete enough to show that the expectation of an early evolution of a large brain is incorrect. It turns out that of all the unique human anatomical traits discussed in Chapter 7, bipedalism is the oldest. The origin of the human line appears to be literally "feet first." As seen from the rough summary of human evolution that you just read, we can see that bipedalism evolved millions of years before the beginning of significant brain expansion. All of the early hominin species described in this chapter can be characterized as small-brained bipeds. Bipedalism goes back at least 4.2 million years and most likely existed in one or more species around 6 million years ago. On the other hand, expansion of the brain and widespread stone tool use do not begin until about 2.5 to 2 million years ago. Our ancestors therefore went through a time when they were likely very apelike in behavior, but spent much time walking on two legs. The key question here is why? Although apes are sometimes bipedal (Figure 10.2), humans are bipeds all the time. What makes us different is that our anatomy has evolved to make bipedalism more efficient and effective, such that today we are "obligate bipeds." Whereas bipedalism is one of a number of options for locomotion in apes, it is the only option for us. This fact raises the question of whether bipedalism evolved initially as obligate bipedalism, or if some of our ancestors spent only *part* of the time on two legs. Either way, we are faced with trying to explain why natural selection would have favored the evolution of bipedalism. Here, we examine some ideas on the origin of bipedalism so that we can see how well different hypotheses are supported by fossil data of the earliest hominins.

FIGURE 10.2

Baby gorilla standing upright while playing with a stick.

Locomotion in the Common Ancestor The origin of bipedalism raises an interesting question: How did the ancestor of the first hominins move? To answer this, we have to consider the likely locomotion of the common ancestor of African apes and hominins. Two suggestions have typically been offered. The first is that the common ancestor was a generalized climber, and the second is that the common ancestor was a knuckle-walker. Figure 10.3 shows these two hypotheses. Under the view that the common ancestor was a climber, there were two evolutionary shifts: bipedalism in the hominin line, and knuckle walking in the African ape lines. However, this hypothesis requires that knuckle walking evolved twice, once in the line leading to the gorilla and again in the chimpanzee–bonobo line.

The alternative idea is that the common ancestor was a knuckle walker. Here, all of the African apes retained the knuckle-walking adaptation of the common ancestor, and the only evolutionary change occurred in the hominin line, a transition from knuckle walking to bipedalism. Although this model may appear more parsimonious, we must keep in mind that parallel evolution does occur, and consider both hypotheses as we examine the fossil record.

The Environmental Context To evaluate hypotheses regarding the origin of bipedalism, it is necessary to consider the environmental context within which bipedalism arose. The earth had been changing during the Late Miocene, resulting in a cooler, drier climate in Africa. Over time, the large forests began to shrink, leading to smaller patches of forest and woodlands

FIGURE 10.3

Possible evolutionary changes in locomotion based on the evidence that humans are more closely related to chimpanzees and bonobos than to gorillas. Locomotion: KW = knuckle walking, B = bipedalism, C = generalized suspensory climber. Two models are shown, one in which the common ancestor of African apes and humans was a generalized climber (C), and the other in which the common ancestor was a knuckle walker (KW). Note that if the common ancestor was a climber, then knuckle walking would have evolved twice.

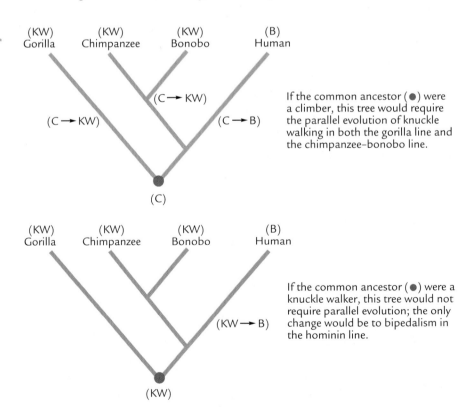

If the common ancestor (●) were a climber, this tree would require the parallel evolution of knuckle walking in both the gorilla line and the chimpanzee–bonobo line.

If the common ancestor (●) were a knuckle walker, this tree would not require parallel evolution; the only change would be to bipedalism in the hominin line.

surrounded by increasing grassland (savanna). Traditional explanations for the origin of bipedalism have considered the savanna environment critical in understanding hominin origins. For many years, the oldest known fossil hominins were found in environments that were grasslands or a mix of grasslands and woodlands. These explanations are now being questioned based on new evidence for the environment of the earliest possible hominins. Prior to 4.4 million years ago, hominins did not occupy the open grasslands but lived in relatively wet forests and woodlands (Pickford and Senut 2001; WoldeGabriel et al. 2001).

Why Bipedalism? Ever since Darwin's time, hypotheses have been proposed to account for the origin of bipedalism. Darwin offered one of the first hypotheses, focusing on the link between bipedalism and tool use. By standing up, early hominins had their hands free to carry tools. This basic model was later expanded by a number of anthropologists to consider the evolution of a number of human characteristics. The model proposed that as tool use increased and became more important, natural selection led to larger brains and enhanced learning abilities. As larger brains evolved along with longer periods of infant and child dependency, tools became even more important for survival. Thus, tool use affected brain size, which in turn affected tool use. Tool use would benefit from walking upright, such that the model predicted a simultaneous evolution of bipedalism, larger brains, and tool use. Although popular for many years, the tool use model has been rejected because fossil evidence from the past several decades has shown that bipedalism evolved millions of years before significant increases in brain size and the emergence of a stone tool technology.

Although the idea of a simultaneous evolution of hominin traits has been rejected, the basic idea that bipedalism offers an evolutionary advantage by freeing the hands to carry things may still have some merit. Wooden tools, such as digging sticks, could be carried. As the early hominins were at least as smart as chimpanzees, which make and use simple tools, it is possible that environmental changes prompted an increase in simple tool use that led to a selective advantage for bipedalism. Tools are not the only items that can be carried effectively if the hands are free. A hominin could also have carried food and infants, which, under the right conditions, could promote increased survival and reproduction. Lovejoy (1981) has suggested that bipedalism evolved as a strategy to increase the survival of infants and other dependent offspring by having some group members forage for food and then carry it back to the group. Consequently, more infants could be cared for, allowing an increase in reproduction and potential population growth. According to Lovejoy, bipedalism is the way in which hominins got around the basic problem faced by apes—a long period of infant dependency, resulting in slow rates of population growth. Bipedalism might have altered the situation and allowed more infants to be cared for at the same time. The specifics of Lovejoy's model have been rather controversial, as he proposed that the social structure that evolved along with bipedalism was of monogamous family groups, whereby the male foraged for food and the female stayed with the dependent offspring. It is also possible that a group of adult females could have shared the care and feeding of offspring, thus producing the same result—selection for bipedalism.

Bipedalism has also been linked to food acquisition and energy efficiency, which refers to the amount of energy expended relative to the task being performed. Bipedalism is more energy-efficient in traveling long distances in search of food. Increased energy efficiency means using less energy to move about looking for and gathering food. Rodman and McHenry (1980) looked at the energy efficiency of bipedal humans and knuckle-walking chimpanzees at normal walking speeds. The results, shown in Figure 10.4, indicate that bipedalism is more energy-efficient at speeds of both 2.9 km per hour (the normal walking speed of a chimpanzee) and 4.5 km per hour (the normal walking speed of a human). Leonard and Robertson (1995) confirmed these observations and compared the expected daily energy costs for an early hominin with a knuckle walker of similar size, finding that bipedalism could save more than 50 percent of the expected daily expenditure of calories. Energy efficiency is often considered in terms of an adaptation to open savanna environments and long distances to travel, but the earliest hominins may have spent most of their time in the forests and woodlands. Still, these environments were shrinking and they may have needed to travel more between shrinking clusters to find enough food. As the forests and woodlands continued to shrink, the energy-efficient advantage of bipedalism may have continued to increase.

Another explanation for the origin of bipedalism comes from observations of chimpanzees practicing bipedalism in the wild. One way that chimps are bipedal is when they stand upright in order to forage for fruits from lower branches. Another way is when chimps in trees stand upright on branches to reach food (Hunt 1996; Stanford 2006). Bipedalism may have first evolved as a feeding posture and secondarily as a way of moving around on the ground in the forests and woodlands. As we will see, the foraging model fits nicely

FIGURE 10.4

The relative energy cost of movement for chimpanzees and humans compared with a quadruped of similar size (set equal to 1.0 in this graph). The knuckle-walking chimpanzee uses more energy for movement (values >1), and the bipedal human uses less (<1). These comparisons have been made at two speeds: 2.9 km per hour (the normal speed of a chimpanzee) and 4.5 km per hour (the normal speed of a human). These results show that bipedalism is more energy efficient at normal walking speeds. (Data from Rodman and McHenry 1980.)

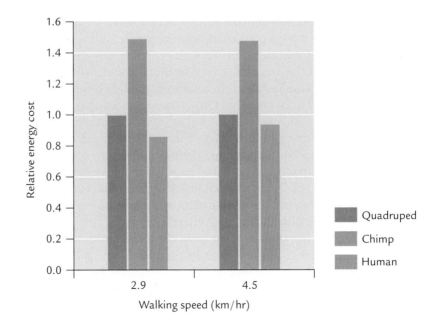

FIGURE 10.5

An orangutan walking bipedally on a tree branch.

with the fossil evidence for bipedalism of the earliest hominins, which suggests a life spent partially on the ground and partially in the trees.

Another hypothesis based on observations of living apes is the idea that bipedalism first arose in the trees and not on the ground. Thorpe and colleagues (2007) note that orangutans often walk bipedally on tree branches, with full extension of their legs, while using their hands to hang onto other branches for balance (Figure 10.5). This behavior is adaptive in the trees, as it helps orangutans move across small, flexible branches. Thorpe et al.'s model suggests that, because of this adaptation, the common ancestor was *already* bipedal when it moved to the ground. Here, human bipedalism is the further development of a behavior that was inherited from a common ancestor, and the African apes changed more, becoming knuckle walkers. Under this model, the common ancestor of African apes and hominins was not likely a knuckle walker.

It is important to keep in mind that there was likely not a *single* cause for the initial origin of bipedalism. Carrying ability, energy efficiency, and bipedal foraging might have all played a role in this initial selection, as well as predisposition for bipedal behavior in the trees. In addition, we need to consider that once bipedalism was in place it may have been further selected for as our ancestors moved increasingly into the savanna. Here, there are further advantages for bipedalism. For one thing, walking upright would have allowed for better detection of predators on the savanna (where there are fewer places to hide) because an upright hominin could see farther. In addition, we have evidence that being bipedal reduces heat stress on the savanna during the hottest times of the day (Wheeler 1991).

THE EARLIEST HOMININS

The time span of the hominins covered in this chapter ranges from more than 6 million years ago to roughly 1.5 million years ago. This period includes portions of the Miocene epoch, the **Pliocene epoch** (5.3–2.6 Ma), and the

Pliocene epoch The fifth epoch of the Cenozoic era, dating from 5.3 million to 2.6 million years ago.

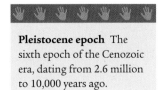

Pleistocene epoch The sixth epoch of the Cenozoic era, dating from 2.6 million to 10,000 years ago.

Pleistocene epoch (2.6–0.01 Ma). All of the early hominins described in this chapter have been found only in Africa, supporting Darwin's idea that Africa was the birthplace of human evolution. It also means that early hominins were limited to a specific environment—woodlands and tropical grasslands for the most part. Not until later in hominin evolution do we see evidence for movement out of Africa, as discussed in the next chapter.

Figure 10.6 shows the location of some of the major sites of hominins discussed in this chapter. Most of the early hominin species have been found at sites in South Africa and East Africa. Chronometric dating has been difficult at many of the South African sites, and for many years, we were not sure

FIGURE 10.6

Location of some of the major sites in Africa where early hominin specimens have been found.

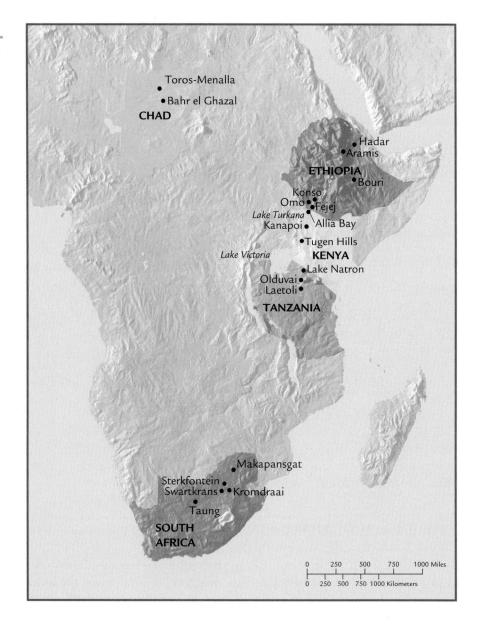

exactly how old the early South African sites were. Sites in East Africa are better dated; extensive volcanic activity in East Africa millions of years ago allows us to use argon dating at these sites.

The hominins described in this chapter are generally classified into a number of different species. The evidence of such diversity shows us that early human evolution cannot be described in terms of a simple "family tree" with one species evolving into the next in a linear fashion, but instead in terms of a "bush" with many branches. Although there is only one hominin species alive today (us!), the situation was different in the past—at a number of times, more than one species existed. One of our challenges is to figure out how these different species were related to each other and to us.

Despite the diversity in species of early hominins, we do see some general characteristics that are shared by all of the early hominins discussed in this chapter. All are classified as hominin because they show evidence, direct or indirect, of being bipedal (although, as noted below, some of this evidence for the earliest possible hominins is being debated). The first hominins had small, ape-sized **cranial capacities,** a measure of the interior volume of the brain case measured in cubic centimeters (cc). Cranial capacities tend to average about 400–500 cc for most early hominin species, which is, on average, only slightly larger than that of chimpanzees and much smaller than that of living humans (who average 1350 cc). The average estimated body weight tends to be less than 100 pounds for most species, roughly the same as that of chimpanzees. The average adult height is less than that of living humans, ranging from about 3.5 to almost 5 feet (McHenry 1992).

cranial capacities A measurement of the interior volume of the brain case measured in cubic centimeters (cc) and used as an approximate estimate of brain size.

Sahelanthropus and Orrorin

The oldest evidence of hominins dates back to around 6+ million years ago in Africa. Three different forms have been proposed as early hominins because of suggestive evidence of bipedalism. All three have been discovered since the mid-1990s and remains to date are very fragmentary.

Sahelanthropus At present, the oldest species thought to be hominin is *Sahelanthropus tchadensis,* discovered in Chad in central Africa. Comparison of associated fossil animal remains with other firmly dated sites using biostratigraphy indicates that *Sahelanthropus* lived between 7 million and 6 million years ago (Brunet et al. 2002). More recent finds suggest that the older date is more appropriate (Brunet et al. 2005), although chronometric dating is needed for confirmation. The fossil remains consist of a number of jaws and teeth, but the major specimen discovered to date is a distorted partial cranium (Figure 10.7). The back of this specimen resembles an ape, and it had a small, ape-sized brain, but the face does not protrude and as such is more comparable in appearance to later hominins. The teeth also show a number of hominin traits, including a small canine.

No postcranial bones have yet been found, but the structure of the base of the skull suggests bipedalism, including the position of the **foramen magnum,** the large hole in the base of the skull where the spinal cord enters.

Sahelanthropus tchadensis An early possible hominin species from Africa, dating between 6 million and 7 million years ago, that has a number of hominin dental traits and may have been bipedal.

foramen magnum The large opening at the base of the skull where the spinal cord enters. This opening is located more toward the center of the skull in hominins, who are bipeds, so that the skull sits atop the spine.

FIGURE 10.7

Side view of cranial specimen TM 266-01-060-1 (*Sahelanthropus tchadensis*).

The foramen magnum in quadrupeds is located more toward the rear of the skull, whereas in bipeds it is located more toward the center. This position of the foramen magnum in *Sahelanthropus* has been debated, with resolution difficult given the distorted nature of the specimen. In 2005, advanced medical-imaging and computer technology was used to create a "virtual" reconstruction of the cranium to account for deformation after death. The reconstruction shows that the angle between the front part of the face and the base of the cranium is more like that in humans than in apes, and therefore likely to have been a biped (Zollikofer et al. 2005). Postcranial remains will be needed to resolve the hominin status of *Sahelanthropus*.

Orrorin tugenensis An early, primitive hominin species from Africa, dating to the Late Miocene (6 Ma).

Ardipithecus ramidus An early primitive hominin species from Africa, dating between 5.8 million and 4.4 million years ago.

Ardipithecus kadabba An early primitive hominin from Africa with very apelike teeth, dating between 5.8 million and 5.2 million years ago.

Orrorin   The species ***Orrorin tugenensis*** is known from fragmentary remains of several individuals found in the Tugen Hills of Kenya in East Africa, dating to 6 million years ago. The fossils include a number of dental remains and some leg and arm bone fragments. According to the discoverers, the leg bone (Figure 10.8) indicates that this species was a bipedal hominin, although the arm bone suggests that it still spent a fair amount of time in the trees (Senut et al. 2001). The femur has a groove for muscle attachment that is consistent with bipedalism, and analysis of the shape of different parts of the femur show that it is not apelike, but instead looks like femurs from other early hominins (Richmond and Jungers 2008). Although the evidence at this point suggests strongly that *Orrorin* was a biped, further fossils are needed to confirm this.

Ardipithecus

The genus **Ardipithecus** (the name translates as "ground ape") is known from the Middle Awash site in Ethiopia. Two species have been named: ***Ardipithecus ramidus,*** dating back 4.4 million years ago, and the more primitive species ***Ardipithecus kadabba,*** dating back 5.2 to 5.8 million years ago (White et al. 1994, 1995; Haile-Selassie et al. 2004). The species name *ramidus* translates as "root" and the species name *kadabba* translates as "basal family ancestor." Remains of the earlier species are very fragmentary, consisting mostly of

FIGURE 10.8

Paleoanthropologist Brigette Senut holding the *Orrorin* femur.

teeth and a few other skeletal remains. The difference between the two species is thus defined based on the teeth—the earlier species has more primitive, ape-like canine teeth.

When the genus *Ardipithecus* was first discovered, there were a few clues that it was bipedal, including the position of the foramen magnum. Much of what we know about *Ardipithecus,* including its bipedalism, comes from a partial skeleton of *Ar. ramidus* first discovered in the mid-1990s (the abbreviation "*Ar*" stands for *Ardipithecus*—it is conventional to use genus abbreviations after the first full mention of a species complete name, such as *H. sapiens* being an abbreviation of *Homo sapiens*). The partial skeleton, specimen *ARA-VP-6/500* but better known by its nickname "Ardi," was in very poor condition and required extensive care in its excavation, reconstruction, and analysis. In 2009, the reconstruction was complete, and revealed a number of interesting findings about *Ar. ramidus* (White et al. 2009). Figure 10.9 shows all of the cranial, dental, and post-cranial bones of "Ardi." Ardi was an adult female, with an estimated height of about 4 feet and an estimated weight of more than 110 pounds (Lovejoy, Suwa, Simpson et al. 2009). Although this single individual has added much to our knowledge of *Ar. ramidus,* we also have information on more than 100 other specimens including teeth and post-cranial fragments.

As with all early hominins, *Ar. ramidus* had a small, ape-sized brain and was bipedal. The cranial capacity is between 300 and 350 cubic centimeters, which is about the size of a female chimpanzee. Although the middle face

FIGURE 10.9

The *ARA-VP-6/500* skeleton of *Ardipithecus ramidus,* nicknamed "Ardi."

does protrude like that of an ape, the lower face does not protrude as much (Suwa, Asfaw et al. 2009). The molar teeth of *Ar. ramidus* are smaller than the later hominins to be described in this chapter, and have thin enamel like those of African apes (unlike later hominins, including modern humans, that have thicker enamel). The canine teeth show a reduction in size and apelike features from the earlier species, *Ar. kadabba*. Wear patterns on the teeth suggest that *Ar. ramidus* had an omnivorous diet with a lot of fruit (Suwa, Kono et al. 2009).

Perhaps the most interesting aspect of *Ar. ramidus* is the evidence for bipedalism shown in the reconstruction of Ardi. Although fragments of other specimens of *Ar. ramidus* had suggested bipedalism, such as the position of the foramen magnum in a cranial fragment, the analysis of Ardi shows the greatest amount of evidence, although in surprising ways (Figure 10.10). The pelvis shows a mixture of ape and hominin traits. The upper part of the pelvis is shaped like that of humans, but the lower part retains some primitive ape structure. Taken together, the pelvis shows that *Ar. ramidus* was a biped, but was likely also a frequent climber (Lovejoy, Suwa, Spurlock et al. 2009). The limb proportions are neither like those of a human (long legs) or like those of an ape (long arms), but instead have arms and legs of similar length (Lovejoy, Suwa, Simpson et al. 2009). The hand and wrist bones do not show any special adaptation for vertical climbing, but instead suggest that *Ar. ramidus* supported itself on all fours resting on its palms while in the trees (Lovejoy, Simpson et al. 2009). Finally, the feet are unusual, as Ardi's big toe is divergent, unlike the big toes of later hominins (including modern humans) that are used for propulsion. The divergent big toe suggests an adaptation to

FIGURE 10.10

Reconstructed frontal and side views of *ARA-VP-6/500, Ardipithecus ramidus,* This reconstruction shows a pelvis adapted for some bipedalism, but other traits associated with careful climbing along the tops of branches in the trees, such as front and rear limbs of equal size, the structure of the bottom part of the pelvis, and a divergent big toe.

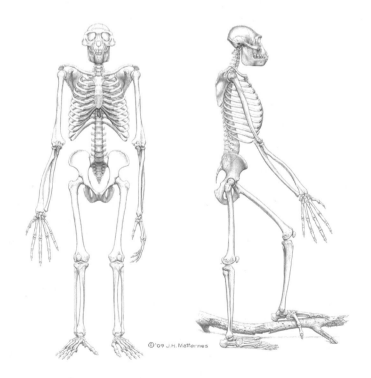

climbing, although not of the same type of vertical climbing seen in living apes; instead, the toe structure is consistent with climbing on top of branches (Lovejoy, Latimer et al. 2009).

What does this all mean? *Ar. ramidus* appears to have spent a lot of time in the trees, but did not have the kind of suspensory adaptations and vertical climbing found in living apes. Instead, *Ar. ramidus* likely walked on the tops of branches resting on its palms (like a monkey) and moved about as a very careful climber. When it descended to the ground, it walked on two legs, although not the same way or as efficiently as did later hominins. In sum, *Ar. ramidus* appears to be a species that existed close to the beginning of bipedalism, and was not yet an obligate biped. *Ar. ramidus* gives us perhaps a glimpse at a unique combination of terrestrial and arboreal adaptations associated with the initial origin of bipedalism.

Ar. ramidus also provides clues about the type of locomotion seen in the common ancestor of African apes and hominins. If *Ar. ramidus* represents the typical pattern of early hominin bipedalism, it does not seem likely that hominins and African apes evolved from a knuckle-walking common ancestor because the hand and wrist bones of *Ar. ramidus* do not show any evidence of a knuckle-walking ancestry, but instead show a creature that supported itself on its palms (Lovejoy, Simpson et al. 2009). As noted earlier in Figure 10.3, this would mean that knuckle-walking evolved independently in the African apes. Does this mean that the common ancestor of African apes and humans was a climber? To some extent, the answer would be yes, although the fossil evidence suggests that *Ar. ramidus* was a different kind of climber. More fossils will be needed to sort this out, but it does appear that we can no longer use living African apes, such as chimpanzees, as direct representatives of a common ancestor. Instead of the simpler model held by many in the past that the common ancestor was basically similar to a chimp (complete with knuckle-walking), it now seems as though *both* African apes and hominins have diverged considerably from a common ancestor (White et al. 2009).

Another question that remains is the evolutionary relationship between *Ar. ramidus* and earlier possible hominins. Although the discoverers of the *Ardipithecus* fossils have made a convincing case that the two species of *Ardipithecus* are related, it is still not clear what the relationship is between *Ardipithecus* and *Sahelanthropus* and/or *Orrorin*. Do these different fossils represent different lines of early hominins? If so, which is ancestral to later hominins? On the other hand, is it possible that these different forms are variations on the same thing? As always, we will need more fossils to test these hypotheses.

AUSTRALOPITHECUS

What happens after *Ardipithecus*? Between 4.2 and 1.4 million years ago, there are a variety of hominin species that lived in Africa. Most (if not all) can be placed into one of three genera—*Homo, Australopithecus,* and *Paranthropus.* The genus *Homo* is, of course, the one that we belong to, characterized by (among other traits) an expanded brain. The next three chapters examine

Australopithecus A genus of fossil hominin that lived between 4.2 million and 1.8 million years ago and is characterized by bipedal locomotion, small brain size, large face, and large teeth.

different species in the genus *Homo*. Here, we focus on the genus *Australopithecus*, which is the ancestor of both the genus *Homo* and the genus *Paranthropus* (discussed later in this chapter).

The genus name **Australopithecus** literally translates as "southern ape," so named because the first species discovered in this genus was found in *South* Africa and had certain apelike traits, such as a small brain (Dart 1925). This may sound confusing when you see that since then we have found other species of *Australopithecus* that actually lived in *East* Africa! The reason for this confusion is that scientists have agreed to an international system of naming species in which the *first* name given takes precedence even if the name is no longer the most descriptive.

Characteristics of Australopithecus

The genus *Australopithecus* is characterized by being a biped with a small brain and large face, and with relatively small canines and large molars with thick enamel. Overall, *Australopithecus* is less primitive than *Ardipithecus*. At least five species of *Australopithecus* are generally recognized, and all lived in Africa. These species span between 4.2 million and 1.8 million years ago, and comparison of the different species shows evolutionary trends over time. For example, the teeth become less and less apelike over time.

Brain size is a bit larger than *Ardipithecus*, but still much smaller than in modern humans. Depending on the species, the cranial capacity ranges from about 400 to 450 cc on average (Aiello and Dunbar 1993; Falk et al. 2000). The back teeth (molars and premolars) are large relative to the front teeth with considerable surface area, a condition showing great chewing ability. Over time, the canine teeth of *Australopithecus* became more similar to that of later humans, although the earlier species still tended to have somewhat larger canines than do modern humans.

In general, *Australopithecus* is smaller than are modern humans. We can estimate both weight and height from statistical formulas that predict these values from different measures of the skeleton (some of these methods are discussed in Appendix 2). McHenry (1992) compiled estimates for the two best-known species of *Australopithecus* (*Au. afarensis* and *Au. africanus*) and finds that, on average, adult males weighed about 95 pounds (43 kilograms) and adult females weighed about 65 pounds (30 kg). He also estimated adult height, finding an average of about 4 feet, 9 inches for males (145 cm), and 3 feet, 7 inches (110 cm) for females. Such estimates are of course only approximations, but they do show that *Australopithecus* was small compared with modern humans.

Of course, the major reason we count *Australopithecus* as a hominin ancestor is that they were bipedal. There is a great deal of evidence for bipedalism in *Australopithecus*, including pelvic bones, leg bones, knee joints, and toe bones. Collectively, the post-cranial evidence for *Australopithecus* shows that they were less primitive than *Ardipithecus*. The pelvis, for example, lacks the apelike features seen in *Ardipithecus*. Overall, the bipedal anatomy of *Australopithecus* is more similar to that of *Homo*.

Early Species of Australopithecus

Now that we have seen some general characteristics of *Australopithecus* as a group, it is useful to examine some of the variation between different species of *Australopithecus*. Because of the history of discovery, some species are very well known, whereas others are newer discoveries with less data and analysis. One of the major distinguishing features between the different species of *Australopithecus* is the size and structure of different teeth. In general, the earlier species tend to have somewhat more primitive teeth.

Australopithecus anamensis The species ***Australopithecus anamensis*** has been found at sites in Kenya and Ethiopia in East Africa dating back 4.2 million to 3.9 million years ago (Leakey et al. 1995, 1998; White et al. 2006). The first discoveries were made on the western shores of Lake Turkana in Kenya. The species name is based on the word for lake (*anam*) among the local people, the Turkana. The fossil evidence consists mostly of dental remains, as well as some pieces of arm and leg bones. Though fragmentary, the remains of *Au. anamensis* ("*Au.*" is an abbreviation for *Australopithecus*) clearly show biped with evidence of primitive traits, particularly in the teeth.

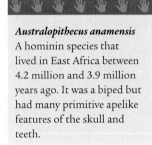

Australopithecus anamensis A hominin species that lived in East Africa between 4.2 million and 3.9 million years ago. It was a biped but had many primitive apelike features of the skull and teeth.

The evidence for bipedalism is clear from the lower portion of the tibia (the larger of the two lower leg bones). The lower portion of the tibia fits together with the ankle and has a different appearance in humans and in apes. As shown in Figure 10.11, if you orient the tibia so that the bottom surface is parallel with the ground, the inclination of the shaft of the bone in a human is close to perpendicular. In an ape, however, there is a definite angle. Note from Figure 10.11 that the tibia of *Au. anamensis* shows essentially the same angle as in a human being, providing definite evidence (along with evidence from other arm and leg bone remains) that this species was bipedal (Ward et al. 1999).

Au. anamensis shows a number of primitive, apelike characteristics in the teeth (Figure 10.12). The canines tend to be fairly large, and the back teeth are in parallel rows, a feature typical of apes and unlike the more parabolic jaw shape of humans (see Figure 10.15 for comparative pictures). Overall, the mixture of primitive and derived traits in *Au. anamensis,* along with its date, makes it an excellent transition between *Ardipithecus* and later hominin species (White et al. 2006). This transition is particularly clear when we look at the teeth, which become less apelike over time.

Australopithecus afarensis The best-known species of early *Australopithecus* is the species ***Australopithecus afarensis,*** which lived in East Africa between 3.7 million and 3.0 million years ago. *Au. afarensis* was first discovered by Donald Johanson in the 1970s at the site of Hadar in Ethiopia. The fossils collected by Johanson and colleagues date between about 3.4 million and 3.0 million years old. Additional fossils collected by Mary Leakey at the site of Laetoli in Tanzania date to 3.7 million years ago (Kimbel et al. 2006). Johanson and colleagues (1978) noted the close similarity between the Hadar and Laetoli finds, and placed them together in their newly proposed species *Australopithecus afarensis*. The species name *afarensis* derives from the Afar region in Ethiopia

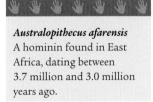

Australopithecus afarensis A hominin found in East Africa, dating between 3.7 million and 3.0 million years ago.

FIGURE 10.11

Evidence of bipedalism in *Australopithecus anamensis*. (*top*) Specimen KNM-KP 29285, the bottom portion of the right tibia. As shown, the joint surface at the bottom of the tibia is oriented horizontally, and the shaft of the tibia is close to perpendicular. (*bottom*) The same specimen is shown in comparison with human and chimpanzee tibias. The *Au. anamensis* tibia shows the same angle of the shaft as the modern human and not like that of the chimpanzee. (Modified from Ward et al. 1999, 2001. Courtesy of Carol Ward.)

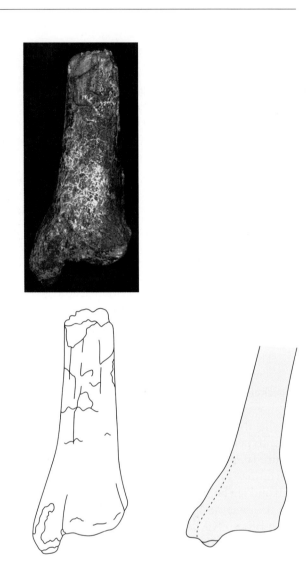

Human   *Australopithecus anamensis*   Chimpanzee

where the Hadar site is located. Additional fossils of *Au. afarensis* have been discovered at a number of other sites, mostly in Ethiopia. The abundance of data on this species gives us a detailed picture of its anatomy.

There is considerable evidence for bipedalism in *Au. afarensis,* including a knee joint from Ethiopia and footprints found at the Laetoli site (see the picture at the opening of this chapter). Perhaps the clearest evidence of bipedalism, and the most famous fossil of *Au. afarensis,* is the partial skeleton nicknamed "Lucy," a rather complete skeleton of an adult female (Figure 10.13). The pelvic anatomy shows that Lucy was a female. Lucy's third molar tooth had erupted, which means that she was an adult when she died (see Appendix 2). Despite her adult status, Lucy was a small individual—she probably weighed only about 60 pounds (27 kg) and was about 3 feet, 5 inches (105 cm) in height (McHenry 1992). The pelvis and post-cranial bones all

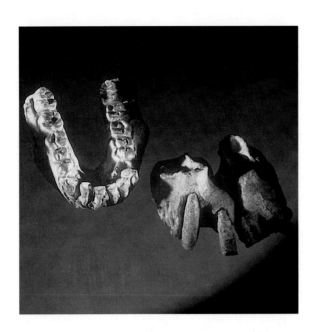

FIGURE 10.12

Some fossil specimens of *Australopithecus anamensis:* lower jaw (*left*) and upper jaw (*right*). *Australopithecus anamensis* was a biped but still had very apelike features in the jaws and teeth.

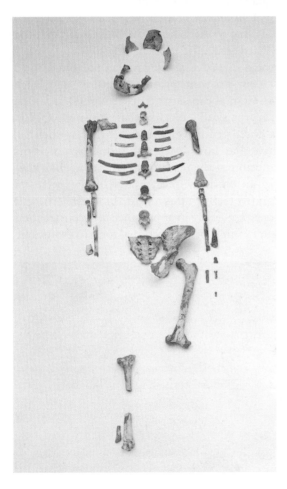

FIGURE 10.13

The skeletal remains of "Lucy," a 40 percent complete specimen of *Australopithecus afarensis.*

show that Lucy was a biped, although she did have somewhat longer arms proportionately.

Au. afarensis was definitely a biped. However, there are some differences, such as a tendency for somewhat longer arms and slightly curved finger and toe bones in some specimens. Although not as primitive as *Ardipithecus,* such traits do suggest that some apelike traits persisted in *Australopithecus.* The important question here is what such traits mean. These apelike traits could be interpreted in two ways. First, they might simply be retentions from a recent apelike ancestor—that is, evolutionary "leftovers" reflecting ancestry but having no functional significance. Second, these traits might reflect the retention of considerable climbing ability.

Thus, the question is the type of bipedalism in *Au. afarensis.* Was it an obligate biped, such as all species in the genus *Homo,* or did it combine some mixture of bipedalism and climbing as was the case for *Ardipithecus*? Debate continues, with some favoring the view that *Au. afarensis* was not yet a fully committed obligate biped, and still spent a lot of time climbing (e.g., Stern and Susman 1983). The discovery of the more primitive features in *Ardipithecus* and the possible evolution of bipedalism has suggested to others than *Au. afarensis* was indeed an obligate biped (White et al. 2009). This view has been supported by the discovery of *Au. afarensis* foot bones that show the presence of foot arches similar to those of modern humans, suggesting that *Au. afarensis* was an obligate biped (Ward et al. 2011).

Like other early hominins, the skull of *Au. afarensis* has a small brain and a face that juts out (Figure 10.14), as well as some primitive features on its back and bottom (Kimbel et al. 1994). Cranial capacity ranges from 400 to 500 cc (Aiello and Dunbar 1993). Overall, the skull looks like that of a small ape.

The teeth of *Au. afarensis* are less primitive than the earlier species *Au. anamensis,* but still more primitive than later species of *Australopithecus.* This makes sense in terms of the evolution of the teeth from a more apelike condition to a more humanlike condition over time. As such, early species of *Australopithecus* have the more primitive teeth. In this regard, *Au. afarensis* shows a number of characteristics that are intermediate in appearance between apes and humans, and provides an excellent example of a transitional form in evolution.

FIGURE 10.14

Side view of a cranium of *Australopithecus afarensis.*

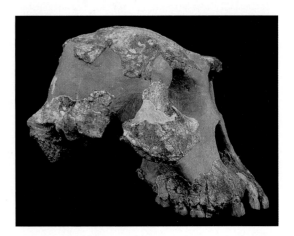

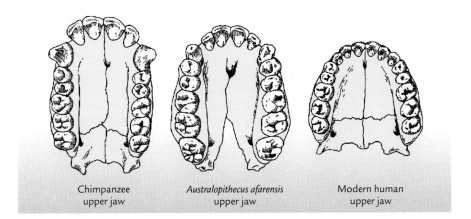

Chimpanzee
upper jaw

Australopithecus afarensis
upper jaw

Modern human
upper jaw

FIGURE 10.15

Comparison of the teeth
and upper jaws of a modern
chimpanzee, *Australopithecus
afarensis,* and a modern
human. In most features,
the teeth and jaws of
Australopithecus afarensis
are intermediate between
those of modern apes and
modern humans. (From *Lucy: The
Beginnings of Humankind* by Donald
C. Johanson and Maitland A. Edney.
Drawings © 1981 Luba Dmytryk
Gudz/Brill Atlanta.)

As noted in earlier chapters, the teeth of modern apes and modern humans can be easily distinguished (Figure 10.15). The canines of apes are generally large and protrude past the surface of the other teeth, whereas modern humans have small, non-projecting, rather puny canines. The canines of *Au. afarensis,* however, are intermediate in appearance; they are larger and more projecting than those of modern humans, but smaller than those of most modern apes. An ape's upper jaw has a diastema (gap) between the canine and the adjacent incisor. This space is needed for the large lower canine to fit into when the ape closes its jaw. Modern humans do not have a diastema. In fact, we are often lucky to be able to get a piece of dental floss between our front teeth! The jaws of *Au. afarensis* show an intermediate condition. They have a diastema, but it is smaller than that of modern apes.

Another dental difference between humans and apes is the anatomy of the lower premolar behind the canine. In apes, this lower premolar is pointed and has one cusp, which serves to sharpen the upper canine when the ape's jaw is closed. Modern humans do not have this feature (because we do not have large canines); instead, we have two cusps of the same size (which is why your dentist calls the premolar teeth "bicuspids"). In *Au. afarensis,* this lower molar shows an intermediate state with two cusps, but one cusp is more developed, representing a transition from the ape condition to the human condition. Overall, most dental features of *Au. afarensis* show a state that is transitional between apelike teeth and humanlike teeth. As such, *Au. afarensis* is a good link between earlier and later hominins in the time between 4 and 3 million years ago (but also, see Box 10.2).

Later Species of Australopithecus and the Ancestry of *Homo*

Beginning about 3 million to 2.5 million years ago, there is a noticeable increase in the number of hominin species. Current thinking is that *Au. afarensis* was the ancestor of two major lines in human evolution. One line lead to a genus known as **Paranthropus**, characterized by massive back teeth and jaws, which became extinct about 1.5 million years ago. The other line led to several

Paranthropus A genus of fossil hominin that lived in Africa from 2.5 to 1.4 million years ago, at which time it became extinct. They differ from *Australopithecus* by having even larger back teeth, and robust jaws, cheekbones, and faces, all adaptations to heavy chewing.

BOX 10.2

The Flat-Faced Man from Kenya

As noted in the text, the species *Australopithecus afarensis* lived in East Africa between roughly 4 and 3 million years ago and appears to be a link between earlier and later hominins. For many years, it has been suggested that *Au. afarensis* was the only hominin species that lived during this time. This view was challenged in 2001 when Meave Leakey and colleagues (Leakey et al. 2001) discovered a fossil hominin skull that they proposed as a new species—*Kenyanthropus platyops*, which translates literally as "Kenyan man with flat face" or "the flat-faced man from Kenya." The reason for this name is the fact that the skull had a flat face with a tall cheek region, making it look different from *Au. afarensis*.

The skull has a small cranial capacity and lived 3.5 million years ago, the same time as *Au. afarensis*.

The evolutionary status of *Kenyanthropus* is not clear. Most anthropologists see it as a side branch of early hominin evolution and still consider *Au. afarensis* the ancestor of later hominins. The status of this *K. platyops* as a separate species has also been challenged. White (2003) has suggested that the fact that the skull has been fragmented and is distorted makes it look different. In other words, the distinctive flat face might be a function of distortion. Further cranial remains are needed to resolve this debate.

species of later *Australopithecus,* one of which evolved into the genus *Homo* (Figure 10.16).

By around 3 million years ago, the major change in *Australopithecus* was that the apelike characteristics of the teeth found in the earlier species had disappeared, although teeth still tended to be larger than in modern humans. Later *Australopithecus* was bipedal, had small brains, and are not associated directly with stone tools (although see Box 10.3 for some indirect evidence of tool use by *Australopithecus*).

FIGURE 10.16

Simplified family tree of human evolution focusing on major stages.

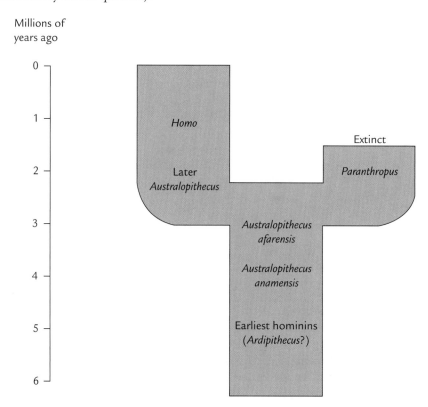

BOX 10.3

Did Australopithecus Make and Use Stone Tools?

As discussed in Chapter 7, toolmaking is something that is not confined to humans, as we have much evidence for chimpanzees making and using simple tools, such as the preparation of sticks for termite fishing. It seems logical to assume that our early ancestors, such as *Australopithecus*, would have acted similarly. It is not a stretch to imagine *Australopithecus* using a stick to "fish" for termites or to dig in the ground. The problem here is that we would have no direct record of such behavior, as the stick would have decomposed millions of years ago. When we look for evidence of early toolmaking, our focus is generally on the association of an ancestor with deliberately manufactured stone tools.

Stone tools have been found in Africa dating back 2.5 million years ago, and (as shown in the next chapter) associated with fossils most often classified in the genus *Homo*. In general, there has not been much support for the idea that *Australopithecus* was an early toolmaker, but recent finds have reopened this debate with the association of butchered animal bones with *Australopithecus*. When stone tools are used to butcher, they leave distinct cut marks that are often different from the types of scratches made by other actions, such as animals stepping on bones and grinding them into the dirt, or carnivores chewing on the bones.

Butchered animal bones showing these distinct cut marks have been found near the discovery of *Australopithecus garhi* in Ethiopia (de Heinzelin et al. 1999), which suggests that *Au. garhi* was using stone tools 2.5 million years ago. This is strong suggestive evidence that later *Australopithecus* did use stone tools (assuming we find no fossils of early *Homo* nearby). The date fits in nicely with the fact that the oldest known stone tools are also 2.5 million years ago (at another site). This is the time period when we think the transition to *Homo* may have begun, so the idea that some of the later groups of *Australopithecus* were beginning to make stone tools is reasonable.

There has been the more controversial suggestion that stone tool use goes back even further in time. McPherron et al. (2010) found animal bones with evidence of butchering dating back at least 3.39 million years ago. The only hominin species found in this location at this time was *Australopithecus afarensis*, suggesting that it was the toolmaker. A problem with this date is that no stone tools have ever been found this far back in time, which seems to some to be unlikely if early *Australopithecus* was actually using stone tools on a regular basis. Another problem is that in some cases stone tool cut marks can be mimicked by other events, such as when bones are chewed on by crocodiles, which were abundant near this site in the past (Shipman 2010). More supporting evidence will be needed to confirm the suggestion that stone tools were being used this far back in the past.

Three species of later *Australopithecus* have been suggested as possible ancestors of the genus *Homo*. One of these is the South African species **Australopithecus africanus**, which was the first species of *Australopithecus* ever discovered and lived between about 3.3 and 2.5 million years ago (Figure 10.17) (the species name *africanus* translates as "African"). For many years, the default position was that *Au. africanus* was the direct ancestor of the genus *Homo* because it was the only suitable species that lived right before the first appearance of *Homo*, somewhat earlier than 2 million years ago. Physically, it appeared that little change would be needed for *Au. africanus* to evolve into the earliest specimens in the genus *Homo*, which had somewhat larger brains and somewhat smaller faces and teeth.

In 1979, Johanson and White questioned the view that *Au. africanus* was the direct ancestor of *Homo* because they felt that the large back teeth of *Au. africanus* meant it was too specialized to be an ancestor of *Homo*. Instead, they proposed that *Homo* evolved directly from *Au. afarensis*. The problem with this hypothesis was that it left a large gap in the fossil record between the last appearance of *Au. afarensis* and the first appearance of *Homo*. Some have suggested that this gap has been filled by the discovery in the late 1990s of the species **Australopithecus garhi** (Figure 10.18) that lived in Ethiopia in East Africa 2.5 million years ago and has been associated with the possible use of stone tools (see Box 10.3). *Au. garhi* (the species name *garhi* means "surprise" in the local

Australopithecus africanus
A species of early hominin, dating between 3.3 million and 2.5 million years ago and found in South Africa. It may be an ancestor of the genus *Homo*.

Australopithecus garhi An early hominin, dating to 2.5 million years ago in East Africa. It had large front and back teeth.

FIGURE 10.17

Skull of *Australopithecus africanus*, specimen STS 5, Sterkfontein, Republic of South Africa.

FIGURE 10.18

Side view of *Australopithecus garhi* skull, specimen BOU-VP-12/130.

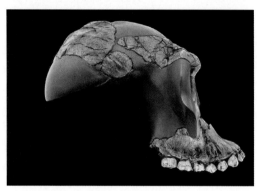

Australopithecus sediba
A species of *Australopithecus* found in South Africa 2 million years ago, that has a number of characteristics linking earlier hominins and *Homo.*

Afar language) is similar in many ways to *Au. afarensis,* and although it has large front and back teeth, they do not appear to be specialized. Because of its similarity in some ways to both *Au. afarensis* and *Homo,* it has been proposed as the link between early *Australopithecus* and the genus *Homo* (Asfaw et al. 1999).

A third possible direct ancestor of *Homo* was discovered in 2008 at the Malapa site in South Africa. Specimens of this species, ***Australopithecus sediba***, have been found in deposits that date to 2 million years old (Pickering et al. 2011). The species name *sediba* means "fountain" or "wellspring" in the local Sesotho language (Figure 10.19). This species shows a number of characteristics similar to the other South African species, *Au. africanus,* including a small brain (420 cc), cusp structure of some teeth, certain cranial features, and long upper limbs. On the other hand, *Au. sediba* also shares a number of characteristics with early *Homo,* such as dental anatomy, certain aspects of brain structure, pelvic shape, and features of the hands and feet (Carlson et al. 2011; Kibii et al. 2011; Kivell et al. 2011; Zipfel et al. 2011). This mixture of primitive and derived traits suggests that *Au. sediba* is an evolutionary link between *Au. africanus* and *Homo* (Berger et al. 2010). Under this hypothesis, *Au. africanus* evolved into *Au. sediba,* who then evolved into the first members of the genus *Homo.* Thus, *Au. africanus* is still our ancestor, but not our *direct* ancestor.

If confirmed, the transitional nature of *Au. sediba* suggests some interesting trends. For example, the combination of such a small brain with some

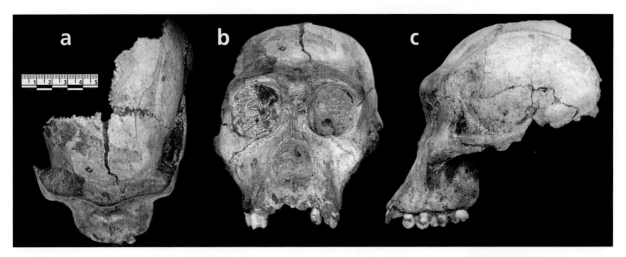

FIGURE 10.19

Australopithecus sediba skull, specimen MH1. (a) Top view, (b) Frontal view, (c) Side view.

shifts towards *Homo* in frontal lobe anatomy suggests that a certain amount of brain reorganization took place before the expansion of the brain in the genus *Homo* (discussed in the next chapter) (Carlson et al. 2011). Likewise, the transitional nature of the pelvis of *Au. sediba* suggests that the pelvis had begun to evolve before the evolution of larger brains, a change often felt to have affected the evolution of the pelvis because of the physical demands of giving birth to larger-brained babies (Kibii et al. 2011). Further fossils and analysis will be needed to address the transitional nature of *Au. sediba*.

Figure 10.20 summarizes the debate over a possible ancestor of the genus *Homo*. At present, three species are possible candidates—*Au. africanus*, *Au. garhi*, and *Au. sediba*. A fourth possibility is that there is another, as yet undiscovered, species of *Australopithecus* that connects *Au. afarensis* with *Homo*. As is often the case, the fossil record allows us to see general connections of relationship, but drawing more intricate family trees with greater certainty will require more data. Despite this debate, it is clear that the origin of the genus *Homo* lies somewhere in the genus *Australopithecus* after 3 million years ago.

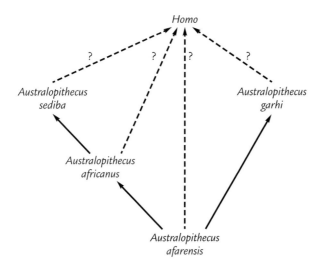

FIGURE 10.20

Possible evolutionary relationships between later species of *Australopithecus* and the genus *Homo*. Solid lines indicate evolutionary relationships that are supported better; dashed lines with question marks indicate different hypotheses about the origin of the genus *Homo*.

PARANTHROPUS

Hominin evolution cannot be described as a simple straight line from *Ardipithecus* to *Australopithecus* to *Homo*. As was shown in Figure 10.16, the time between 3 and 2 million years ago was marked by hominin diversity that included a number of species that were "side branches" in human evolution. These species are typically placed in the genus *Paranthropus*, which translates as "beside humans." Because these early bipeds share a number of characteristics with *Australopithecus*, such as small brain size, some anthropologists classify them in the genus *Australopithecus* and distinguish them from other species by using the adjective "robust," calling them "robust australopiths." It is also common to see these forms labeled simply as "the robusts."

The label "robust," which means "strongly constructed" is apt, because *Paranthropus* show very large and robust back teeth, jaws, and faces relative to other hominins. Despite the name "robust," these species were not that large in overall body size. The average weight was about 100 pounds (45 kg) for males and a bit more than 70 pounds (33 kg) for females. Like *Australopithecus*, the species of *Paranthropus* were not that tall, and both males and females were less than 4.5 feet tall (McHenry 1992). Like other early hominins, *Paranthropus* had a small brain size, averaging 450 cc (Falk et al. 2000).

The distinguishing feature of *Paranthropus* is their large back teeth and relatively small front teeth. Apart from size, the overall structure of the teeth is quite human: The canines are nonprojecting, there is no diastema, and the lower premolar has two cusps. In terms of size, however, the teeth of *Paranthropus* are quite different from those of modern humans. The front teeth are small, both in absolute size and in relationship to the rest of the teeth. The back teeth (premolars and molars) are huge, more than four times the size of modern human back teeth in some cases (Figures 10.21 and 10.22). Note how massive the jaws are and how large the back teeth are, especially compared to

FIGURE 10.21

Lower jaw of *Paranthropus boisei* from the Lake Natron site in Tanzania. Note the small front teeth (incisors and canines) and the massive back teeth (premolars and molars). (From Clark Spencer Larsen, Robert M. Matter, and Daniel L. Gebo, *Human Origins: The Fossil Record*, 3d ed., p. 72. Copyright © 1998 Waveland Press, Inc., Long Grove, IL. All rights reserved. Reprinted with permission from the publisher.)

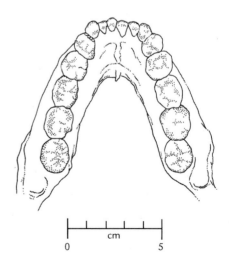

0   cm   5

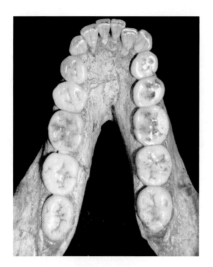

FIGURE 10.22

Lower jaw of *Paranthropus robustus,* specimen SK 23, Swartkrans, Republic of South Africa. Because of distortion, the rows of the jaw are closer than they should be. Note the small front teeth and the large back teeth.

FIGURE 10.23

Side, frontal, and top views of a *Paranthropus boisei* skull, specimen KNM-ER 406, from Lake Turkana, Kenya.

the front teeth. Also note that the premolars are larger side to side than front to back. All of these features indicate heavy chewing.

The skulls of *Paranthropus* also reflect heavy chewing (Figures 10.23 and 10.24). These skulls show massive dished-in faces, large flaring cheekbones, and a bony crest running down the top. All of these anatomical features are related to large jaws and back teeth and to powerful chewing muscles. As shown in Figure 10.25, two muscles are responsible for closing the mouth during chewing. One, the masseter muscle, runs from the back portion of the jaw to the forward portion of the **zygomatic arch** (the cheekbone, which connects the zygomatic and temporal bones). The zygomatic arch and facial skeleton anchor the masseter muscle. In hominins with large jaws and large masseter muscles, the face and zygomatic arch must be massive to withstand the force generated by chewing. The other muscle, the temporalis, runs from the jaw up under the zygomatic arch and attaches to the sides and top of the skull. The larger the temporal muscle is, the more the zygomatic arch must flare out from the side of the skull. To anchor the temporalis muscle on the sides and top of the skull, a ridge of bone sometimes develops down the center of the skull, called a **sagittal crest.** All these cranial and facial features indicate powerful chewing activity.

zygomatic arch The cheekbone, formed by the connection of the zygomatic and temporal bones on the side of the skull.

sagittal crest A ridge of bone running down the center of the top of the skull that serves to anchor chewing muscles.

FIGURE 10.24

Skull of *Paranthropus robustus,* specimen SK 48, Swartkrans, Republic of South Africa.

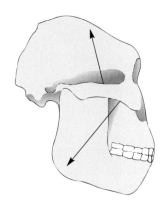

FIGURE 10.25

Skull of *Paranthropus,* with arrows indicating the action of chewing muscles: (*top*) temporalis, (*bottom*) masseter.

Paranthropus aethiopicus The oldest species of *Paranthropus,* dating to 2.5 million years ago in East Africa. It combines derived features seen in other species of *Paranthropus* with primitive features seen in *Au. afarensis.*

Paranthropus robustus A species of *Paranthropus,* dating between roughly 2 million and 1.4 million years ago and found in South Africa.

Paranthropus boisei A very robust species of *Paranthropus,* dating between 2.4 million and 1.4 million years ago and found in East Africa.

As noted previously, three species of *Paranthropus* are generally recognized. The oldest, dating from 2.5 million years ago, is ***Paranthropus aethiopicus*** (named after Ethiopia). *P. aethiopicus* is very robust but also shows a number of primitive cranial traits, such as the anatomy of the base of the cranium, that link it to *Au. afarensis* (Figure 10.26). The later two species, ***Paranthropus robustus*** and ***Paranthropus boisei,*** differ in terms of geography and size. *P. robustus* (named after its robust nature) was found in South Africa, and *P. boisei* (named after Charles Boise, who provided funding for excavation) was found in East Africa. Of the two, *P. boisei* is the more robust.

What does the dental morphology of *Paranthropus* tell us about how they lived? The massive jaws and back teeth show powerful chewing ability, which suggests a diet that was hard to chew, such as nuts, seeds, and hard fruits. Isotope

FIGURE 10.26

Specimen KNM-WT 17000 from Lake Turkana, Kenya, also known as the "Black Skull" because of the color of the mineral staining. This skull dates to 2.5 million years ago. It is classified as *Paranthropus aethiopicus* by some and as an early example of *Paranthropus boisei* by others. It shows a mixture of specialized robust features (e.g., the sagittal crest) and primitive features (e.g., the forward jutting of the jaw).

analysis of their teeth, however, reveals that they had a more diverse diet (Sponheimer et al. 2006). In addition, microscopic analysis of wear on their teeth shows that they did not regularly eat hard objects but often had a softer diet typical of other hominins (Ungar et al. 2008). These results suggest that the powerful chewing ability of *Paranthropus* evolved to enable them to eat harder foods in times of limited resources, which served as "fallback" foods, and not as daily staples.

Although they appear to have been successfully adapted to changing diets, *Paranthropus* ultimately became extinct by 1.4 million years ago, perhaps in competition from the genus *Homo*. Although *Paranthropus* is not our direct ancestor, it does show the breadth of early hominin diversity. Such diversity also shows us that there was no single path of human evolution leading inexorably and directly to us.

Summary

The origin of the hominins takes place in Africa. The earliest possible hominins date back 6 to 7 million years ago (*Sahelanthropus, Orrorin, Ardipithecus kadabba*), coinciding with the suggested time for hominin divergences based on genetic studies. From this time until the origin of the genus *Homo* at about 2+ million years ago, hominins were bipeds with small, ape-sized brains and larger faces and teeth than found in *Homo*. More information on early bipedalism comes from fossil remains of *Ardipithecus ramidus,* who lived 4.4 million years ago in East Africa. *Ar. ramidus* has bipedal adaptations in the pelvis and legs, but also has a number of primitive features including front and hind limbs of roughly equal size and a divergent big toe. The anatomy of *Ar. ramidus* suggests that it was not yet an obligate biped, but combined bipedalism on the ground with careful climbing on all fours in the trees.

A number of species in the genus *Australopithecus* lived in Africa between 4.2 and 1.8 million years ago and were definite bipeds. The earlier species of *Australopithecus* had some primitive apelike characteristics in their teeth, but became more humanlike over time. It is likely that the species *Au. afarensis* was the common ancestor of two lines of hominin evolution. One line is ancestral to the genus *Homo* and consists of three species, although it is not yet clear which species was the direct ancestor of *Homo*. The other line consists of three species in the genus *Paranthropus* (also known as "the robusts") who had very large back teeth and jaws reflecting adaptation to a diet that was hard to chew. *Paranthropus* went extinct about 1.4 million years ago.

Supplemental Readings

Cartmill, M., and F. H. Smith. 2009. *The Human Lineage.* Hoboken, NJ: Wiley-Blackwell. A comprehensive introduction to human evolution that includes a large section focusing on early hominin evolution.

Johanson, D., B. Edgar, and D. L. Brill. 2006. *From Lucy to Language.* Revised, updated, and expanded edition. New York: Simon & Schuster. An excellent introduction to human evolution with spectacular photographs of many of the key fossil hominin specimens.

The site of Olduvai Gorge in Tanzania. This site, worked on for many decades by the famous Leakey family, has proven to be a gold mine for hominin fossil studies. The early excavations at Olduvai uncovered many species, including *Homo erectus*, the first hominin species to move outside of Africa.

The Origin of the Genus *Homo*

Homo A genus of hominins characterized by large brain size and dependence on culture as a means of adaptation.

The history of the first hominins, discussed in the previous chapter, provides us with some insight into the *beginning* of human evolution and the origin of one of the unique characteristics of humankind—bipedalism. Although bipedalism may be 6 million or more years old, it is not until about 2.5 million to 2 million years ago that we begin to see the origin of other human characteristics, such as an increase in brain size and the development of stone tool technology. The genus **Homo** is usually defined in terms of an increased brain size, a reduction in the size of the face and teeth, and increased reliance on cultural adaptations. Keep in mind that the origin of the genus *Homo* does not correspond to the origin of modern humans. The evolutionary changes leading to modern humans did not occur all at once, but took place over almost 2 million years. This chapter focuses on the origin of the genus *Homo* in Africa, including the species *Homo erectus,* and the expansion of this species into Asia and Europe. The following two chapters continue examining the evolution of the genus *Homo*.

Hominin fossils are assigned to the genus *Homo* partly, but not exclusively, based on brain size. The range of brain size overlaps slightly between early hominins and *Homo*. For example, the cranial capacity of *Australopithecus* fossils ranges from 400 cubic centimeters (cc) to 515 cc, whereas the cranial capacity of *Homo* fossils, regardless of species, ranges from 509 cc to 1,880 cc (see Figure 11.1 for references). The point here is that although brain size is an important defining characteristic, it is not the only one. Other characteristics of cranial shape, facial shape, dental size, and postcranial anatomy are also important in assigning fossils to different species within the genus *Homo*.

The genus *Homo* also shows an increase in brain size over the past 2 million years. Figure 11.1 plots the cranial capacity of a number of *Australopithecus, Paranthropus,* and *Homo* crania dating from roughly 10,000 years ago to more than 3 million years ago. This figure shows clearly that brain size in *Homo* has increased over time. Whereas *Australopithecus* and *Paranthropus* show no major increase in brain size over time, the genus *Homo* shows rapid increase over time, particularly after about 750,000 years ago.

Another key characteristic of the genus *Homo* is reliance on cultural behaviors, including increasing sophistication in stone tool technology. Sometime during the course of human evolution, our ancestors became completely

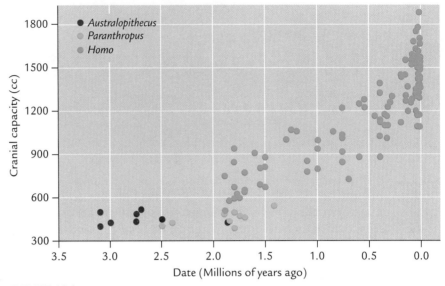

FIGURE 11.1

Evolution of *hominin* brain size. This figure is a plot of cranial capacity (in cubic centimeters) over time for specimens of *Australopithecus, Paranthropus,* and *Homo* from 3.1 million years ago to 10,000 years ago. (Data for *Australopithecus* from Aiello and Dunbar (1993), Asfaw et al. (1999), Falk et al. (2000), and Berger et al. (2010); for *Paranthropus* from Suwa et al. (1997) and Falk et al. (2000); for *H. habilis* and *H. rudolfensis* from Aiello and Dunbar (1993); for *Homo erectus* from Ruff et al. (1997), Gabunia et al. (2000), Vekua et al. (2002), Rightmire (2004), Lordkipanidze et al. (2006), Spoor et al. (2007), and Wu et al. (2011), with revisions for dating from Shen et al. (2009) for the Zhoukoudian site and Indriati et al. (2011) for the Ngandong site; for *Homo heidelbergensis* from Ruff et al. (1997) and Rightmire (2004), including the Ceprano specimen; Neandertals from Ruff et al. (1997); *Homo sapiens* from Ruff et al. (1997) and White et al. (2003), with revision for dating for the Omo site from McDougall et al. (2005). The specimen known as *Homo floresiensis* [see Chapter 13] is not included here.)

dependent on toolmaking. Keep in mind, however, that the cultural evolution of the genus *Homo* was not simply confined to technological invention and development. As shown in this and the next two chapters, different species in the genus *Homo* also used fire, developed hunting and gathering strategies, expanded into new and diverse environments, and developed various types of symbolic expression, including intentional burial and art.

There is ample fossil evidence for the genus *Homo* in Africa almost 2 million years ago. The initial origin of *Homo* is less clear, as the few fossils found dating prior to 2 million years ago are more fragmentary and difficult to assign to any particular species. By a little less than 2 million years ago, however, there is evidence of two (and perhaps three) species in the genus *Homo* existing in Africa. These two species, *Homo habilis* and *Homo erectus,* are both characterized by an increase in brain size relative to earlier hominins and by the widespread manufacture and use of stone tools. Of these two, *Homo erectus* is more similar to later humans, has a larger brain, and is our ancestor. The relationship of *Homo habilis* and *Homo erectus* is less clear, and will be discussed later.

HOMO HABILIS

The species known as **Homo habilis** lived in Africa between at least 1.9 and 1.44 million years ago (Spoor et al. 2007). Some fossil material, particularly a partial jaw dating to 2.33 million years ago, suggest that *H. habilis* existed earlier (Kimbel et al. 1996), but this is not yet conclusive.

The first discovered specimens of *Homo habilis* were found at Olduvai Gorge in Tanzania in East Africa. Starting in the 1930s, Louis and Mary Leakey conducted fieldwork at this site. Among their early finds were the remains of the then-oldest stone tools. For many years, the Leakeys searched Olduvai Gorge for the makers of these tools. In 1960, they found a jaw, two cranial fragments, and several postcranial bones dating to 1.75 million years ago. This specimen represented a hominin with a larger brain and smaller teeth than that of *Australopithecus* (Figure 11.2). Continued work led to the discovery of several more specimens, and in 1964, Louis Leakey and colleagues proposed a new species based on this material: *Homo habilis* (Leakey et al. 1964). The species, whose name translates as "able man" or "handy man," was found in association with stone tools. Since that time, additional specimens have been found elsewhere in East Africa.

Physical Characteristics

Overall, *H. habilis* has a larger brain than *Australopithecus,* although still much smaller than in living humans, and a primitive postcranial skeleton similar in some ways to earlier hominins.

Brain and Teeth Size   The most noticeable difference between *H. habilis* and earlier hominins is the larger brain size of *H. habilis*. The average cranial capacity of *H. habilis* is 612 cc (Aiello and Dunbar 1993), which is over

Homo habilis An early species of *Homo* that lived in Africa between 1.9 million and 1.44 million years ago (and perhaps earlier), with a brain size roughly half that of modern humans and a primitive postcranial skeleton.

FIGURE 11.2

Skull of *Homo habilis,* specimen KNM-ER 1813, Lake Turkana, Kenya.

35 percent larger than the average cranial capacity of *Australopithecus*. The brain size of *H. habilis* is still small relative to other species within the genus *Homo*. For example, the average brain size of *H. habilis* is roughly half that of the average for living humans. The teeth of *H. habilis* are generally smaller than those of *Australopithecus*, but still somewhat larger than for most living humans.

The Postcranial Skeleton   For many years, very little was known about the anatomy of *H. habilis* from the neck down. The fossil evidence had been limited to a foot, a hand, and a few other bones. In 1987, Donald Johanson and colleagues reported the discovery of a partial adult skeleton from Olduvai Gorge in Tanzania. Although fragmentary, the skeleton contains many clues about the postcranial anatomy of *H. habilis*. The species was definitely bipedal, and it was similar to earlier hominins in being relatively small—about 4 feet tall (McHenry 1992). The arms were relatively long, a primitive trait that has led some anthropologists to propose reclassifying *H. habilis* into the genus *Australopithecus* (Wood and Collard 1999; Gibbons 2011).

Cultural Behavior

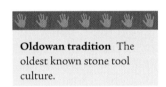

Oldowan tradition The oldest known stone tool culture.

Simple stone tools have been found in association with *H. habilis*. These tools, referred to as the **Oldowan tradition,** are relatively simple chopping tools made by striking several flakes off a rounded stone to give it a rough cutting edge (Figure 11.3). These tools were normally made from materials such as flint, obsidian, or quartz. The stone core was held steady and was then struck with another stone at a certain angle to remove a flake of stone. Several such strikes would produce a rough edge capable of cutting through animal flesh. Proper tool manufacture requires skill in finding the right materials and using the right amount of force.

These tools could have been used for a variety of purposes. For many years, the emphasis in archaeological investigation was on the stone cores produced by flaking. The small flakes, often found in great abundance, were considered garbage—waste material left over from making the stone tool. Analysis of wear on these flakes, however, has shown that they were often used for a variety of tasks, such as cutting meat, scraping wood, and cutting grass stems (Ambrose 2001).

Stone tools are often associated with butchered animal bones that show clear evidence of cut marks. There is also evidence that stone tools were used to crack open animal bones for the marrow inside. Stone tools were thus important in expanding the dietary base of early hominins. It is less clear, however, to what extent *H. habilis* relied on hunting, and it has been argued that *H. habilis* relied instead on scavenging the remains of carnivore kills. More than half the cut marks left by stone tools are found on bones with little meat, such as the lower legs. This suggests that *H. habilis* was taking what was left over from carnivores. In addition, there is no evidence of complete carcasses of larger animals brought to the Olduvai sites, only portions—and these are most often the bones left by carnivores (Potts 1984).

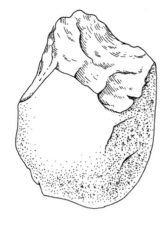

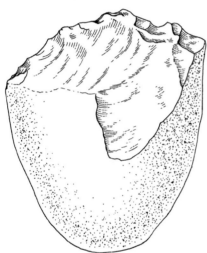

FIGURE 11.3

Oldowan tools. (From *The Old Stone Age* by F. Bordes, 1968, Weidenfeld and Nicolson, Ltd. Reprinted by permission of The McGraw-Hill Companies.)

More Than One Species?

As with any species, *H. habilis* shows a certain amount of variability. Some anthropologists, however, suggest that the levels of variability in fossils traditionally assigned to *H. habilis* are too great to fit within a single species, and that therefore another species is represented. Under this view, some of the fossils classified as *H. habilis* should instead be classified into a different species known as **Homo rudolfensis.** This species name comes from the site of Lake Turkana in Kenya, which had, at one time, been named Lake Rudolf (as mentioned in the previous chapter, the history behind species names can often be confusing). The major specimens assigned to *H. rudolfensis* lived in Africa about 1.9 million years ago.

The cranial capacity of fossils assigned to *H. rudolfensis* is somewhat larger than that of *H. habilis*. Figure 11.4 shows the most famous fossil assigned to *H. rudolfensis*—a cranium with a cranial capacity of 752 cc (Holloway et al. 2004). An **endocast**—a cast of the interior brain case—of this specimen reveals that this specimen has fissures and other features typical of *Homo* and unlike

Homo rudolfensis A species of early *Homo* from Africa that lived 1.9 million years ago, with a brain size somewhat larger than *H. habilis* but with larger back teeth and a broader face.

endocast A cast of the interior of the brain case used in analyzing brain size and structure.

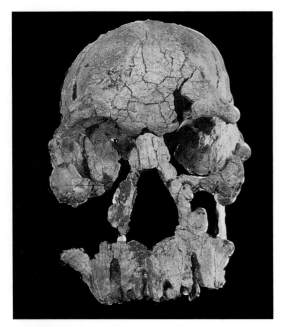

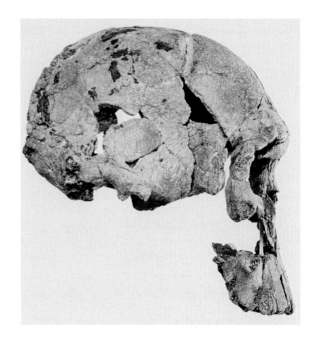

FIGURE 11.4

Frontal and side views of specimen KNM-ER 1470, Lake Turkana, Kenya, dating to 1.9 million years ago. This specimen has sometimes been assigned to the species *Homo habilis,* although a number of anthropologists now advocate placing it in a different species, *Homo rudolfensis.*

that of apes or *Australopithecus* (Falk 1983; Holloway et al. 2004). In some dental and facial measures, however, *H. rudolfensis* appears more primitive than *H. habilis.* The back teeth of *H. rudolfensis* are larger than those of *H. habilis,* and the midfacial region of the skull is broader (Wood 1996).

Debate continues over whether the fossil material discussed above represents a single species (*H. habilis*) or two species (*H. habilis* and *H. rudolfensis*). Several statistical analyses of the skull and teeth suggest two species (e.g., Kramer et al. 1995; Wood 1996), although others disagree (e.g., Miller 2000; Blumenschine et al. 2003). Those advocating two species generally see *H. habilis* as more similar to later humans than *H. rudolfensis,* which appears more primitive despite the slightly larger cranial capacity.

Evolutionary Relationships

How is *H. habilis* (and *H. rudolfensis*) related to earlier and later hominins? In an evolutionary sense, *H. habilis* represents a transition from *Australopithecus* to later, larger-brained species in the genus *Homo.* This transition consisted of a slight increase in brain size and a slight reduction in dental and facial size. Based on the postcranial skeleton, *H. habilis* retained the more primitive bipedal anatomy seen in *Australopithecus.*

One model of evolutionary change sees a species of *Australopithecus,* evolving into *H. habilis,* which in turn evolved into *H. erectus.* The actual situation, however, may be more complicated. For one thing, both *H. habilis* and *H. erectus* are present at the same time (1.9 million years ago), and it is possible that some other, earlier species evolved into *both* of them. More fossils are needed in the critical period between 2.5 million and 2 million years ago to answer these questions.

Regardless of the origin of these species, the fossil evidence to date shows that there was a long time of overlap of *H. habilis* and *H. erectus*—both species lived in Africa between 1.9 million and 1.44 million years ago (after which time *H. habilis* became extinct and *H. erectus* continued). This means that *if H. habilis* evolved into *H. erectus,* it was a case of cladogenesis, with one species splitting off while the parental species continued, rather than one species evolving directly into the next (Spoor et al. 2007). The situation may be even more complex if further evidence confirms *H. rudolfensis* as a separate species. Perhaps the most interesting implication of this overlap in time is that it is evidence that at least two toolmaking hominin species coexisted in the same place for almost half a million years.

HOMO ERECTUS

The species name **Homo erectus** literally means "upright walking human." This may seem odd given the fact that earlier hominin species also walked upright. When the first specimens of *H. erectus* were found in the late nineteenth century, they were the oldest evidence of bipedalism at that point (Box 11.1). This section reviews the biological and behavioral evidence for *Homo erectus.*

Homo erectus A species of the genus *Homo* that arose 1.9 million years ago in Africa and then spread to parts of Asia and Europe.

Distribution in Time and Space

The distribution of some key *H. erectus* sites is shown in Figure 11.5. The oldest known specimens of *H. erectus* have been found in East Africa, dating back 1.9 million years (Spoor et al. 2007). What is perhaps most significant about *H. erectus* is that it appears to be the first hominin species to move out of Africa, and current dating suggests that some *H. erectus* populations migrated out of Africa very quickly after their initial African origin. Fossils of *H. erectus* have been found in Indonesia in Southeast Asia dating back as far as 1.8 million to 1.6 million years ago (Swisher et al. 1994). The movement of *H. erectus* into Indonesia might seem puzzling given the fact that today the islands that make up Indonesia are separated from the Asian mainland. In the past, however, the sea level was lower during glacial times, and there was a direct land connection between mainland Asia and Indonesia. This happened because water was trapped in ice during glacial times and did not return to the sea, which resulted in a lowering of the sea level. Thus, *H. erectus* could have walked to Indonesia directly from the southeastern coast of Asia.

Further evidence for the early dispersal of *H. erectus* comes from the easternmost fringes of Europe. Several *H. erectus* specimens have been discovered at Dmanisi in the country of Georgia dating to 1.75 million years ago (Gabunia et al. 2000; Vekua et al. 2002). There has not been definitive evidence for the expansion of *H. erectus* farther west into Europe. A skull

BOX 11.1

The Discovery of Homo erectus

When Charles Darwin published his famous book, *On the Origin of Species*, the fossil record for human evolution was virtually nonexistent. For the next several decades, the oldest known record of human evolution consisted of some early discoveries of Neandertals, a group of early humans discussed in the next chapter. The lack of fossils did not stop scientists with speculating on the evolutionary connection that must have existed between ape and human. One anatomist, Ernst Haeckel (1834–1919), felt that our ancestors must have arisen in Southeast Asia. He further postulated that the "missing link" between apes and humans would have been an apelike human that could not talk, and assigned the name "*Pithecanthropus alali*," which means the "ape-man without speech," to this hypothetical ancestor, even though there was no fossil evidence at all! (Shipman and Storm 2002).

A young Dutch anatomist, Eugène Dubois (1858–1940), was interested in human evolution and influenced by the works of both Darwin and Haeckel. Whereas many scientists of his day were focusing on the evidence for human evolution through the study of comparative anatomy, Dubois was interested in finding fossil evidence of human evolution. Dubois reasoned that Indonesia would be a logical place to start for several reasons. Living apes live in the tropics, and it would therefore be likely that fossil apes providing a link to humans would also live in the tropics. At this time, fossil apes had been found in India, and fossil fauna similar to that found in India had been found in Indonesia, suggesting that fossil apes would also be found in Indonesia. In order to test his ideas, and against much advice, Dubois quit his job and joined the Dutch army as a physician to be posted in Indonesia (then known as the Dutch East Indies), where he could spend part of his time in his search for human origins (Shipman 2001). By doing so, Dubois became the first scientist to look actively for a human ancestor using a definite research plan (Shipman and Storm 2002).

In 1891, Dubois found the top part of a skull along the shores of the Solo River in Java, at a site named Trinil. This skull was low, had very large brow ridges, and had a cranial capacity that was much larger than that of any ape, but still smaller than that of a modern humans. The following year, Dubois found a femur (upper leg bone) that was virtually the same as the femur of a modern human. Dubois had found what he was looking for, a creature that had both human and apelike characteristics. Dubois named this new species "*Pithecanthropus erectus*," taking the genus name "*Pithecanthropus*" from Haeckel and using the species name *erectus* to designate his "bipedal ape-man." Later discoveries of bipedal fossils that had smaller brain size and larger brow ridges were made in Indonesia and in China, and eventually scientists realized that they were dealing with different populations of the same species. At this point, the species was transferred to the genus *Homo*, giving us the name *Homo erectus*. (Note: this is why we place quotation marks around the genus name "*Pithecanthropus*," to indicate that we no longer use the name).

Although we now have even more ancient bipedal ancestors, Dubois's discovery of *Homo erectus* marked the oldest known ancestors at the beginning of the twentieth century. At the time, Dubois's ideas that "*Pithecanthropus*" was a human ancestor were not well received, and it took much more fossil evidence to vindicate his views. Many stories have been told about Dubois's reaction to such criticism, including one where he hid his fossils so that no one could look at them, or the story where he decided that "*Pithecanthropus*" was actually a species of giant gibbon. Neither story is true (Shipman 2001).

---

from Ceprano, Italy, dates back 850,000 years and was originally classified as *H. erectus*, but further analysis suggests that it may belong to a later species (Antón 2003; Manzi 2004).

How long was *H. erectus* in existence? As shown in the next chapter, the fossil record shows a change from *H. erectus* to another species of *Homo* beginning about 800,000 years ago. There is evidence in Asia, however, that some populations of *H. erectus* lived on until more recent times. Some *H. erectus* at the famous site at Zhoukoudian, China (discussed later), survived until about 400,000 years ago (Shen et al. 2009). In Southeast Asia, populations of *Homo erectus* may have survived a bit longer. The most recent dating of the

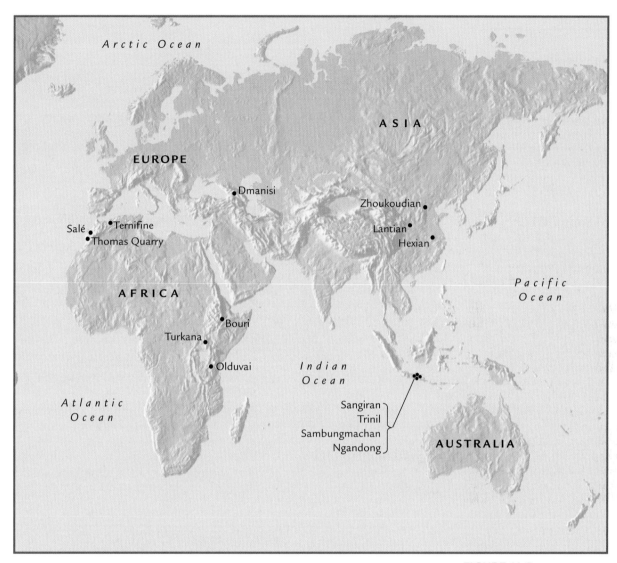

FIGURE 11.5

Location of some major *Homo erectus* sites.

Ngandong site in Indonesia shows that *Homo erectus* lived there until at least 546,000 years ago, and may have been there as recently as 143,000 years ago (Indriati et al. 2011).

Physical Characteristics

The following section focuses on the physical characteristics of *Homo erectus*—specifically, those of the skull, teeth, and postcranial skeleton. Following this general review, variation within the species, and the question of whether what we have traditionally called *Homo erectus* is actually two species, will be considered.

FIGURE 11.6

FIGURE 11.6

Comparison of the cranial capacity of *Australopithecus, Paranthropus, Homo habilis,* and *Homo erectus.* The dots indicate the average cranial capacity (in cubic centimeters) for each group. The lines indicate the range from minimum to maximum. (Data from sources listed in Figure 11.1.)

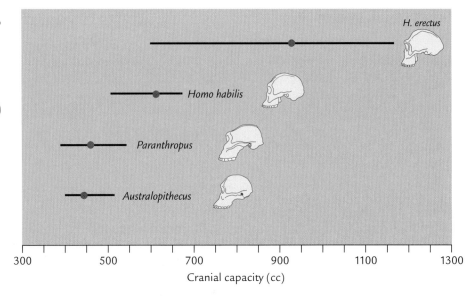

Brain Size   The most obvious characteristic of *H. erectus* compared to earlier hominins is its larger brain size (Figure 11.6). The average cranial capacity of *H. erectus* is 929 cc, which is 69 percent that of the average of living humans. On average, the brain size of *H. erectus* is more than 50 percent larger than that of *H. habilis* (excluding the *H. rudolfensis* specimen). There is an increase in cranial capacity over time in *H. erectus* specimens (Figure 11.7).

Cranial and Dental Characteristics   One of the earliest *H. erectus* skulls, from Lake Turkana in Kenya, is shown in Figure 11.8. Examples of Asian

FIGURE 11.7

Plot of cranial capacity (in cubic centimeters) over time for *Homo erectus.* The solid line indicates the statistical trend, showing an increase over time (Data from sources listed in Figure 11.1.)

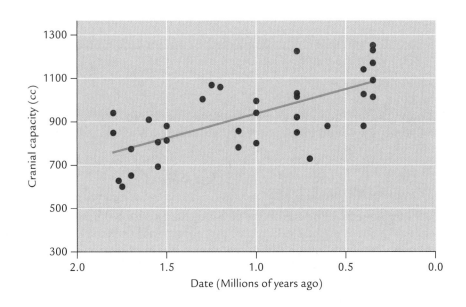

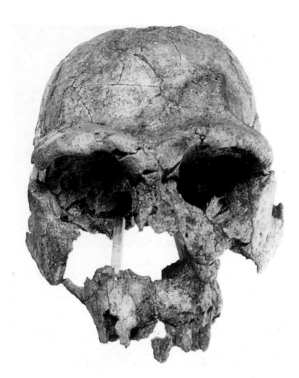

FIGURE 11.8

Homo erectus skull, specimen KNM-ER 3733, Lake Turkana, Kenya. Dated at 1.8 million years ago, this is one of the oldest known specimens of *Homo erectus* (some anthropologists consider this specimen a different species, *Homo ergaster*).

H. erectus are shown in Figure 11.9 (China) and Figure 11.10 (Indonesia). One of the crania from the Dmanisi site in the country of Georgia is shown in Figure 11.11. Overall, the brain case of *H. erectus* is larger than that of earlier hominins, but it is still smaller than that of modern *H. sapiens*. The skull of *H. erectus* is lower, and the face still protrudes more than in modern humans. Neck muscles are attached to a ridge of bone along the back side of the skull. The development of this bony ridge shows that *H. erectus* had powerful neck muscles.

FIGURE 11.9

Frontal and side views of *Homo erectus* from the site of Zhoukoudian, China. The specimens from this site are sometimes referred to as "Peking Man" in older literature.

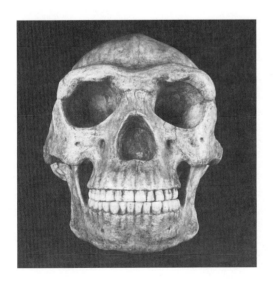

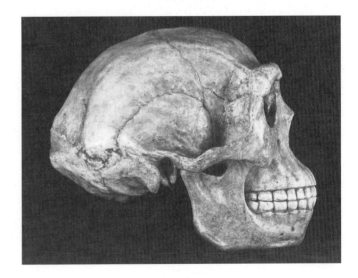

FIGURE 11.10

Homo erectus skull, specimen Sangiran 17, from Sangiran, Indonesia.

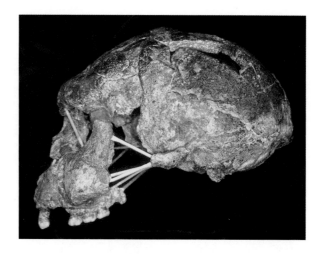

postorbital constriction
The narrowness of the skull behind the eye orbits, a characteristic of early hominins and *Homo erectus*.

Figure 11.12 shows a *H. erectus* skull and a *H. sapiens* skull from a top view. The frontal region of the *H. erectus* skull is narrower than *H. sapiens*, due to **postorbital constriction,** suggesting less development in the frontal and temporal lobes of the brain relative to modern humans. Figure 11.13 shows an *H. erectus* skull and a *H. sapiens* skull from the rear. Note that the *H. erectus* skull is much broader toward the base of the skull, whereas the *H. sapiens* skull is broadest near the top of the skull.

FIGURE 11.11

Views of *Homo erectus* specimen D2282 from the Dmanisi site in Georgia, Eastern Europe: (a) Frontal view, (b) top view, (c) rear view, (d) side view.

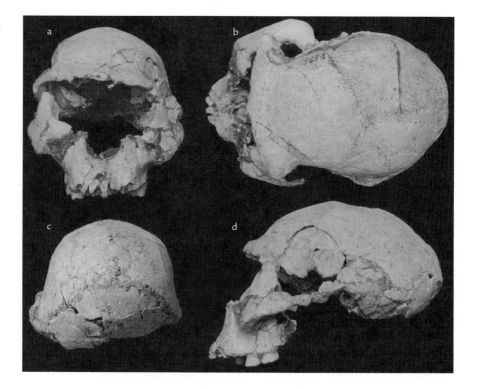

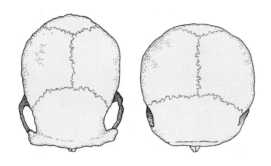

FIGURE 11.12

Top views of the skulls of *Homo erectus* (*left*) and modern *Homo sapiens* (*right*). Note the greater constriction behind the eyes in *Homo erectus.*

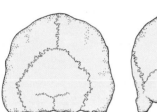

FIGURE 11.13

Rear views of the skulls of *Homo erectus* (*left*) and modern *Homo sapiens* (right). Note the broader brain case of *Homo sapiens* and how the maximum width is higher on the skull.

The face of *H. erectus* protrudes, but not as much as in earlier hominins. One noticeable characteristic of the *H. erectus* face is the development of a large ridge of bone above the eyes—**brow ridges.** Different explanations have been offered for the development of large brow ridges in *H. erectus,* including structural support for forces exerted by chewing and protection of the eyes and face (Wolpoff 1999; Boaz and Ciochon 2004). The jaws and teeth of *H. erectus* are still large compared to those of modern humans but smaller than those of earlier hominins, particularly the back teeth. Microscopic analysis of the teeth shows wear patterns characteristic of extensive meat eating.

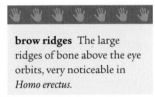

brow ridges The large ridges of bone above the eye orbits, very noticeable in *Homo erectus.*

The Postcranial Skeleton   For many years, however, the postcranial evidence for *H. erectus* was rather limited—a femur here, a pelvic bone there. In 1984, this situation changed with the discovery of a nearly complete *H. erectus* skeleton at Lake Turkana, dating to 1.6 million years ago (Brown et al. 1985) (Figure 11.14). The skeleton is that of a young male. The pattern of dental eruption suggests that he was about 11 to 12 years old at the time of his death. This age estimate depends, of course, on the extent to which his growth pattern was similar to that of living humans; some have suggested that his actual age was somewhat less, perhaps between 8 and 10 years old (Gibbons 2008).

The estimated height of the "Turkana Boy" (as the specimen is known) has been controversial. The initial estimate of height at death was 5 feet, 3 inches (160 cm), and other estimates were a bit shorter. However, the Turkana Boy had died before he underwent the adolescent growth spurt (see Chapter 7), and studies have suggested that had he lived, he would have reached 6 feet, 1 inch (185 cm) (Ruff and Walker 1993). Of course, this estimate is based on the assumption that *H. erectus* had the same type

FIGURE 11.14

Homo erectus skeleton, specimen KNM-WT 15000, Lake Turkana, Kenya. This skeleton of perhaps a 12-year-old boy, dating to 1.6 million years ago, is the most complete specimen of *Homo erectus* yet found.

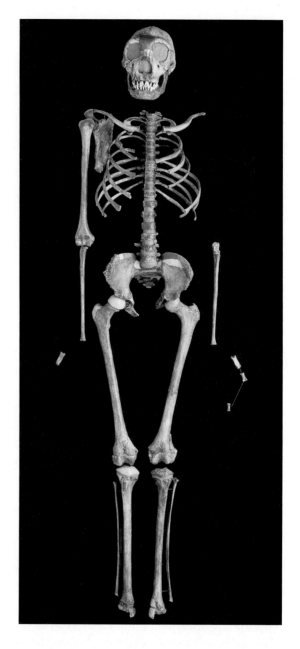

of growth pattern as modern humans do, and as noted above, this may not be the case. After considering different growth models and different ages at death, Graves et al. (2010) have suggested that the Turkana Boy might have only reached a height of 5 feet, 4 inches (163 cm) had he lived until adulthood. The idea that *H. erectus* as a species was tall has also been questioned based on estimates of height from the Dmanisi site in the country of Georgia. Estimated height for these specimens ranges from 4 feet, 9 inches to 5 feet, 5 inches (145–166 cm) (Lordkipanidze et al. 2007). This does not rule out taller populations in Africa, as there was likely regional variation, but additional specimens from Africa will be needed to confirm the original hypothesis of tall *H. erectus* populations in Africa.

The Turkana Boy shows body proportions that are very similar to those of modern humans, and unlike *Australopithecus* and *H. habilis,* who had longer arms. The modern limb proportions of *H. erectus* reflect that its bipedalism was modern in form, including improvements allowing for more efficient long-distance walking. Close examination of the postcranial skeleton of *H. erectus* also suggests that it was capable of endurance running, just like modern humans. We are not very good at sprinting, but we can run at slower speeds for long distances because of certain features of our skeletal and muscular anatomy, such as springlike tendons in our legs, a well-developed arch in the foot, a long stride length, and anatomical specializations that allow stabilization of the neck and trunk while running. Based on the fossil evidence, *H. erectus* could do the same, an ability that could have been very helpful in scavenging and hunting (Bramble and Lieberman 2004).

The modern body proportions shown by the Turkana Boy also have implications for diet and brain growth. As noted in Chapter 7, the human brain is metabolically expensive. The same is true for other organ systems, including the digestive system. We humans tend to have larger brains and smaller guts than expected for a primate our size, observations that Aiello and Wheeler (1995) have argued are related in their "expensive tissue hypothesis." They propose that during human evolution an increase in brain size would need a corresponding reduction in gut size, since both are metabolically expensive. The reduction in gut size would allow more energy for brain metabolism. Smaller gut size would have been possible with the addition of high-quality, easy-to-digest food, such as meat and other animal products, to the diet. Thus, a change in diet would have allowed further brain growth. Aiello and Wheeler suggest that this change occurred in *H. erectus,* because the shape of the thoracic region and the width of the pelvis of the Turkana Boy are more like those of modern humans, marking a change from earlier hominins and reflecting a reduction in gut size.

The discovery of an adult female *H. erectus* pelvis in 2008 (Simpson et al. 2008) has provided us with some insight regarding the evolution of human growth patterns discussed in Chapter 7. This pelvic specimen is broad and would have been capable of giving birth to a baby with a relatively large brain, suggesting that the rate of *prenatal* brain growth in *H. erectus* was high, just like in modern humans. However, the adult brain size of *H. erectus* is smaller than ours, suggesting a rate of *postnatal* brain growth less than ours. Consequently, it appears that the unique extended childhood of modern humans may not have yet evolved by the time of *H. erectus.*

More Than One Species?

There is disagreement among anthropologists as to whether the fossils of *Homo erectus* described here constitute one species or two. Although some favor the single species idea, others have suggested that the African fossils be placed in the species ***Homo ergaster*** (a name that translates as "working

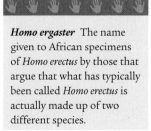

Homo ergaster The name given to African specimens of *Homo erectus* by those that argue that what has typically been called *Homo erectus* is actually made up of two different species.

human") and the species name *H. erectus* be used specifically for the Asian fossils. Part of the difficulty in classifying the fossils is the fact that *Homo erectus* was the first hominin species to have lived on several different continents. As is typical with species that are spread out geographically across different regions and environments, *H. erectus* shows some geographic differences between the African, Western Eurasian (Dmanisi), and East/Southeast Asian specimens. The crania of the early African and Dmanisi specimens tend to have smaller cranial capacities and less rugged brow ridges. There are some differences in cranial shape between the regional samples as well (Antón 2003), although there is some overlap too, with traits typically found in one region also found in another (Spoor et al. 2007). The postcranial skeletons of the *H. erectus* fossils from Dmanisi tend to be shorter (Lordkipanidze et al. 2007).

What does this variation mean? Some anthropologists see the variation as consistent with a geographically widespread species (e.g., Rightmire 1992). Others disagree, viewing the differences between geographic samples as evidence of different species incapable of interbreeding (e.g., Tattersall 1997). The debate over the number of species reflects different views on variation and speciation, and whether one tends to be a "lumper" or a "splitter" (refer back to Chapter 8). How one views this debate influences one's ideas on the relationship of the Asian specimens to later human evolution. If *H. erectus* is a single species, the Asian specimens are part of a widely dispersed species that is part of our ancestry. Proponents of the two-species model argue that the species *H. ergaster* appeared first in Africa and ultimately led (through one or more other species) to modern humans, with some populations moving into Asia to become the species *H. erectus,* which then became extinct.

The question of the number of species continues to be debated. The approach taken in this text is a more conservative one that sees a single, geographically widespread species—*H. erectus*. Although this chapter has stressed the general characteristics of the entire species, it would not be useful to consider the different samples from Africa and Eurasia as identical. There is certainly geographic variation, and only further research will determine if the extent of this variation is best described by different species.

The Evolution of Larger Brains

The fossil record shows clearly that *H. erectus* had a larger brain than any earlier hominin and that it was larger than the species *H. habilis*. Statistical comparisons show that the larger brain of *H. erectus* is a substantial increase even accounting for the larger body size of that species. Changes in brain size were also accompanied by changes in brain organization (Holloway et al. 2004).

Although we (as large-brained living humans) tend to take our large brains for granted, we need to consider this trait in evolutionary perspective, noting that there are a number of potential *disadvantages* to having large brains. As noted above, large brains are metabolically expensive. In addition, larger heads lose heat more quickly than do smaller heads, posing a problem with heat stress. Finally, larger heads can complicate childbirth. For relative brain size to have increased in *H. erectus* means that the *advantages* of larger brains must have outweighed the potential disadvantages.

What are the advantages of a larger and more complex brain relative to body size? Intelligence is the most often cited general explanation, but the term *intelligence* can encompass a wide variety of behaviors. One factor that seems to be linked with the evolution of larger and more complex brains is toolmaking and tool use, including new tools and behaviors (discussed in the next section). Technological skill and, more generally, problem-solving ability would provide an evolutionary advantage. Other aspects of intelligence, such as spatial awareness and memory, would also be useful in a variety of environments, providing maximum adaptability. Some anthropologists have suggested that the development of enhanced language abilities is also related to the origin of a larger brain (Schoenemann 2006), although, as will be discussed in the next chapter, the fossil evidence relating to language acquisition is difficult to evaluate conclusively. Another potential advantage of larger brains is "social intelligence," the ability to keep track of a large number of individuals and the social relationships between them (Dunbar 1998). As with the origin of bipedalism, selection for larger reorganized brains probably was the net result of a number of advantages that outweighed any disadvantages.

THE CULTURE OF *HOMO ERECTUS*

The archaeological and fossil evidence shows us that *Homo erectus* developed a new form of stone tool technology and added significant amounts of meat in their diet.

Stone Tool Technology

Major changes in stone tool technology did not take place immediately with the origin of *H. erectus*. Early *H. erectus* in Africa made tools similar to, but somewhat more sophisticated than, the Oldowan tools used by *H. habilis*. *H. erectus*, however, went further to invent a new type of stone tool.

The Invention of New Tools   *H. erectus* developed a new type of stone tool technology referred to as the **Acheulean tradition** (also often spelled 'Acheulian'). A key feature of this stone tool culture was a new way of manufacture known as the **soft hammer technique.** Here, flakes are removed from the stone core by using a piece of bone, antler, or wood. Softer materials absorb much of the shock in flake removal, allowing greater precision and control, and the ability to remove smaller flakes (Figure 11.15). The Acheulean tool kit includes **bifaces,** which are stone tools that have been worked on both sides, producing a symmetric tool. These tools are flatter and have straighter, sharper sides than Oldowan tools. The oldest known Acheulean tools have been found in Kenya, East Africa, and date back almost 1.8 million years (Lepre et al. 2011).

Acheulean tradition The stone tool culture that appeared first with *Homo erectus* and was characterized by the development of hand axes and other bifacial tools.

soft hammer technique A method of removing flakes from a stone core by striking it with a softer material, such as bone, antler, or wood.

biface A stone tool with both sides worked, producing greater symmetry and efficiency.

FIGURE 11.15

Making an Acheulean tool. Nicholas Toth uses a piece of antler to remove small flakes from both sides of the flint, producing a symmetric hand axe (*left*). Shown are flint hand axes and a cleaver (*right*).

The basic Acheulean tool is the hand axe (Figures 11.15 and 11.16a), which could be used for a variety of purposes, including meat preparation. Other tools were made for different purposes, such as scrapers and cleavers (Figure 11.16). The use of different tools for different purposes marked an important step in the cultural evolution of humans. Increased specialization allowed for more efficient tool use and required greater mental sophistication in design and manufacture.

Geographic Variation in Toolmaking   There are distinct differences in the type of stone tools found in different geographic regions. Whereas Acheulian hand axes are found in Africa and Europe, they are absent in Asia, where a large number of less sophisticated chopping tools have been found (see Figure 11.16d and 11.16e). Stone tools that show Acheulean-like technology have been found in China, dating to the time of *H. erectus* (Hou et al. 2000), but no hand axes. One explanation for this difference is that there were cultural differences between *H. erectus* populations. Another is that it might reflect differences in available natural resources. For example, Pope (1989) suggested that Asian *H. erectus* might have been using bamboo for making sharp implements, something that would not preserve in the archaeological record.

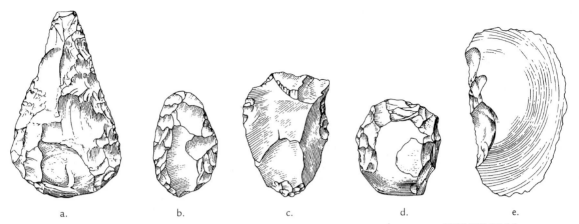

a.   b.   c.   d.   e.

FIGURE 11.16

Examples of tools made by *Homo erectus:* (a) hand axe, (b) side scraper, (c) small chopping tool, (d) chopper, (e) cleaverlike tool. (From *The Old Stone Age* by F. Bordes, 1968, Weidenfeld and Nicolson, Ltd. Reprinted by permission of The McGraw-Hill Companies.)

Hunters or Scavengers?

Homo erectus ate meat; this is clear from butchered animal bones with stone tool cut marks. The change in the body shape of *H. erectus* discussed previously is also evidence that the diet of *H. erectus* included a substantial amount of meat. An important question is, Where did this meat come from? There are two possibilities—hunting and scavenging. Early investigations of *H. erectus* produced evidence that was consistent with a hunting and gathering lifestyle. *H. erectus* was found with stone tools, butchered animal bones, and artifacts indicating the control and use of fire. Together, this evidence seemed to point to an easy explanation—*H. erectus* hunted animals and then butchered and cooked them. As such, the culture of *H. erectus* was interpreted as equivalent to that of later (and living) hunter-gatherers. With *H. erectus,* the emphasis on hunting rather than gathering is in part a consequence of the archaeological record, as bones and stones preserve better than do plants or wooden containers.

Although all agree that *H. erectus* butchered animals, the assumption that they *hunted* these animals has been questioned. An alternative explanation is that *H. erectus* was a scavenger, using stone tools to obtain meat from animals that had already been killed by predators. Electron microscopes have been used to look at animal bones from *H. erectus* sites. A number of these bones have both the characteristic marks left by stone tools and bite marks from other animals. In some cases, the stone tool cut marks overlaid the bite marks, showing that the stone tools were used *after* a predator had eaten part of the animal's flesh, which in turn suggests that *H. erectus* was likely a scavenger (Boaz and Ciochon 2004). Although such studies have challenged the older view of *H. erectus* as a big-game hunter, it is still possible that *H. erectus* hunted small game.

Fire

The use of fire as a source of energy is a significant human activity. Fire provides heat and light and is used for cooking, keeping warm, scaring off animals, and seeing at night. The control of fire marked an important step in the evolution of human culture, and so it is of interest to know when and where fire was first used. *Homo erectus* has long been associated with the first use of fire in human evolution. Documenting the earliest evidence of controlled fire is problematic, however, because it is difficult to distinguish between naturally occurring fire and controlled fire. There are some possible cases of controlled fire dating back 1.5 million years ago in Africa, but these are not conclusive (Klein 2009). The oldest conclusive use of fire comes from Israel, dating back 790,000 years ago (Goren-Inbar et al. 2004). Although Acheulean tools were found at this site, there are no fossil hominin remains. Although the date fits with the time range of *H. erectus,* it also fits with a later species (see Chapter 12) that also used Acheulean tools and fire.

The case for *H. erectus* being the first hominin species to use fire is strengthened by evidence from the Zhoukoudian cave site in China, where redating now shows inhabitation between 400,000 and 780,000 years ago (Shen et al. 2009). Some of this evidence has been questioned, such as the presence of ash that had initially been interpreted as resulting from accumulations of campfires over time. More recent studies have shown that the ash was deposited by water flowing into the cave (Weiner et al. 1998). There is evidence, however, of both fire-cracked stones and burned animal bones at Zhoukoudian that support the use of fire by *H. erectus* (Boaz and Ciochon 2004). Of course, the fact that *H. erectus* used fire does not mean that they knew how to *make* fire. We have no evidence of such ability, and it may be that *H. erectus* had to rely instead on finding naturally occurring fire and keeping it smoldering for long periods of time.

Summary

The genus *Homo,* characterized by a larger brain, smaller teeth and face, and increased reliance on stone tool technology, appeared first in Africa by 2.3 million years ago. Fossils from two species, *Homo habilis* and *Homo erectus,* date to at least 1.9 million years ago, although *H. habilis* may be older. Some anthropologists argue that the fossil material assigned to *H. habilis* includes a third species, *Homo rudolfensis. H. habilis* is associated with a simple stone tool technology known as the Oldowan tradition.

The species *Homo erectus* is the ancestor of later humans. It appeared first in Africa by 1.9 million years ago and rapidly spread to parts of Southeast Asia and the fringes of Europe between 1.8 million and 1.6 million years ago. *H. erectus* showed signs of cranial expansion (the average brain size was roughly 69 percent that of modern humans). The skull of *H. erectus* is lower than that of modern humans and protrudes more. The postcranial skeleton of *H. erectus* is similar to that of modern humans in having relatively long legs capable of long-distance walking.

The cultural adaptations of *H. erectus* included development of more sophisticated tools (the Acheulian tradition) and the addition of significant amounts of meat to the diet, although it appears that more of the meat came from scavenging than from hunting. *H. erectus* is associated with the use of fire at some sites and appears to have cooked its food. It is not clear, however, whether *H. erectus* could actively *make* fire.

Supplemental Readings

Boaz, N. T., and R. L. Ciochon. 2004. *Dragon Bone Hill: An Ice-Age Saga of* Homo Erectus. New York: Oxford University Press. A highly readable account of the history of discoveries at Zhoukoudian, China, and the anatomy and culture of *Homo erectus*.

Stringer, C., and P. Andrews. 2005. *The Complete World of Human Evolution*. New York: Thames and Hudson. A well-illustrated review of human evolution, with many sections on the evolution of *Homo* species.

The Evolution of Archaic Humans

A typical image of early human evolution is that of the cave man (and cave woman). Such images often incorporate stone tools, spears for hunting, fire building, hunting, wearing animal skins, and living in social groups as major themes (in addition to a cave in the background!) (Figure 12.1). Although such representations are often simplified, they are based on archaeological evidence, and collectively form an image of what many of us consider being "human," as opposed to just being a "hominin."

As noted in the previous chapter, there is still debate over which of these typical features of life among cave people apply to *Homo erectus*. Although they certainly lived in caves, we are not sure how often they used fire, or how much they scavenged rather than hunted (Boaz and Ciochon 2004). The fossil record shows us that during the middle part of the Pleistocene epoch, human evolution had reached a point where these behaviors are all represented. The **Middle Pleistocene** (often referred to as the Ionian stage of the Pleistocene) is the term used to refer to the period of time between 781,000 and 126,000 years ago. This time period marks the evolution of some *H. erectus* (or *H. ergaster*) populations into humans that had a larger brain but retained a large face and a long and low skull shape. Many anthropologists classify these early humans in the species *Homo heidelbergensis*. By the end of the Middle Pleistocene, some populations had evolved into modern humans (*Homo sapiens*) and others had evolved into a group known as the Neandertals. Both groups continued into the **Upper Pleistocene** (also known as the Late Pleistocene or the Tarantian stage). Both *Homo heidelbergensis* and the Neandertals are sometimes referred to as "archaic" humans as a way of contrasting them with ourselves, who are also large-brained humans. This chapter focuses on these archaic humans, and the next chapter examines the evolution of modern humans.

Middle Pleistocene A geological stage of the Pleistocene epoch that lasted from 781,000 to 126,000 years ago.

Upper Pleistocene A geological stage of the Pleistocene epoch that lasted from 126,000 to 11,700 years ago.

◀ The La Chapelle-aux-Saints skeleton, found in France, is a Neandertal, an archaic human whose relationship with modern humans is still being debated. The La Chapelle discovery showed that Neandertals, like modern humans, buried their dead.

An artist's representation of cave people.

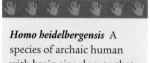

Homo heidelbergensis A species of archaic human with brain size close to that of modern humans but a larger, less modern face that lived in Africa, Europe, and Asia between 800,000 and 200,000 years ago.

HOMO HEIDELBERGENSIS

The species known as ***Homo heidelbergensis*** is named for the city of Heidelberg, Germany, near the location of a fossil site. *H. heidelbergensis* is considered a species linking *H. erectus* and *H. sapiens,* and is thus ancestral to us.

Distribution in Time and Space

Even though *Homo heidelbergensis* is named after a European site, its fossils have been found across the Old World at a number of sites in Europe, Africa, and Asia, dating to between roughly 800,000 and 200,000 years ago. As noted in Chapter 8, this was a time of alternating glacial and interglacial periods, showing that *H. heidelbergensis* had to cope in some places with colder

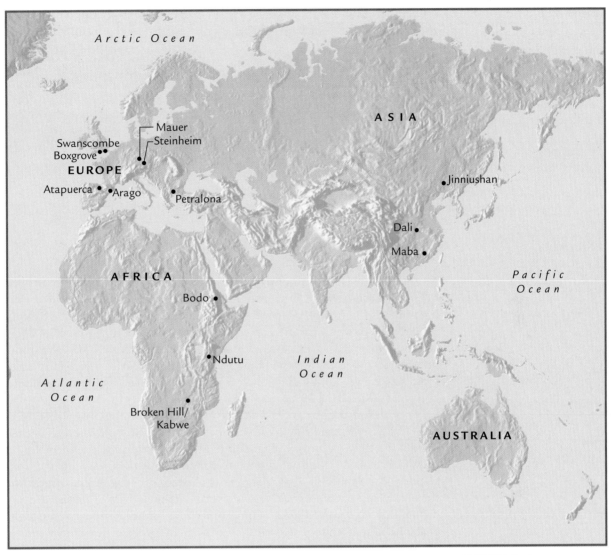

FIGURE 12.2

Location of major *Homo heidelbergensis* sites.

temperatures than are found today and with a pattern of changing climate over many millennia.

The distribution of some *H. heidelbergensis* sites is shown in Figure 12.2. Some of the earliest assigned specimens come from the Gran Dolina Cave site in the Atapuerca hills of Spain, dating to 800,000 years ago (and, in fact, some have argued that the early Atapuerca remains should be considered a separate species). A cranial remain from Ceprano, Italy, dating to 850,000 years ago, may be another early example of a transitional form between *H. erectus* and *H. heidelbergensis* (Manzi 2004). A jaw dating to over 1 million years ago in Spain is the oldest known fossil hominin in Europe and may represent an ancestor of *H. heidelbergensis* (Carbonell et al. 2008).

FIGURE 12.3

Comparison of the cranial capacity of *Homo habilis*, *Homo erectus*, and *Homo heidelbergensis*. The lines indicate the range from minimum to maximum. (Data from sources listed in Figure 11.1).

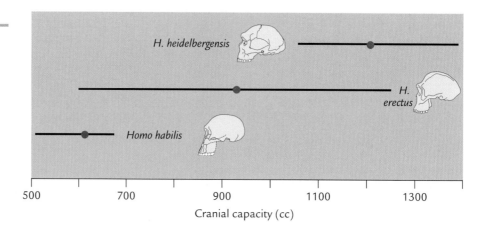

Physical Characteristics

Although there is a fair amount of overlap in brain size, the average brain size of *Homo heidelbergensis* is larger than *H. erectus,* and almost as large as in living humans (Figure 12.3). The average cranial capacity of *H. heidelbergensis* is roughly 1,200 cubic centimeters (cc) with a range of about 1,100 to 1,400 cc. The average brain size is almost 30 percent larger than that of *H. erectus* and only about 10 percent less than that of living humans on average. The relative brain size, however, was a bit smaller given that *H. heidelbergensis* had a larger body mass (Ruff et al. 1997).

In addition, the skull of *H. heidelbergensis* is higher and more well rounded than in *H. erectus,* and the face does not protrude as much. Brow ridges remain large, but the brows are more separated with thinner sides, unlike the brow ridges of *H. erectus,* which tend to be more continuous. Compared with *H. sapiens,* the skull of *H. heidelbergensis* is lower and is less well rounded in the back. The face of *H. heidelbergensis* is still large relative to *H. sapiens.* In addition, *H. heidelbergensis* lacks a chin, something found in modern *H. sapiens.* Overall, the anatomy of the skull shows a form intermediate in many ways between *H. erectus* and *H. sapiens* but with larger brain size. Postcranial remains suggest that *H. heidelbergensis* was often tall and powerfully built (Stringer and Andrews 2005).

An example of *H. heidelbergensis* is shown in Figure 12.4. This skull was found in Zambia, Africa, and dates to between 700,000 and 400,000 years ago. This skull has a large cranial capacity (1,280 cc). The face is rather large, as are the brow ridges, and the skull is higher than in *H. erectus* but lower than in *H. sapiens.* Figure 12.5 shows an example of *H. heidelbergensis* from Europe; this skull, from Petralona in Greece, dates to between 400,000 and 250,000 years ago. Its cranial capacity is about average for *H. heidelbergensis* (1,230 *cc*). Another example of *H. heidelbergensis,* shown in Figure 12.6, is the skull from Dali, China, which dates to 200,000 year ago and has a cranial capacity of 1,120 cc. All three of these examples show the high cranial capacity of *H. heidelbergensis* relative to *H. erectus* but with a cranial shape different from modern *H. sapiens.*

FIGURE 12.4

The Broken Hill skull, Kabwe, Zambia—an example of *Homo heidelbergensis* from Africa.

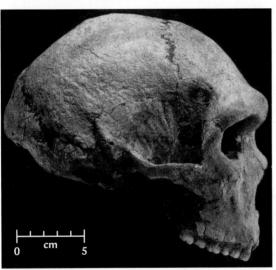

FIGURE 12.5

The Petralona skull, Greece—an example of *Homo heidelbergensis* from Europe.

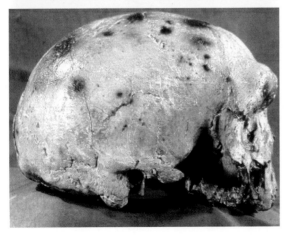

FIGURE 12.6

The Dali skull, Dali County, People's Republic of China—an example of *Homo heidelbergensis* from Asia.

The Culture of *Homo Heidelbergensis*

The archaeological record of *Homo heidelbergensis* shows that they used the same sort of tools as earlier hominins but also developed a new method of stone tool manufacture. The evidence also shows that *H. heidelbergensis* was actively involved in hunting. Some fossils suggest that *H. heidelbergensis* was capable of language.

Stone Tool Technology   Many *H. heidelbergensis* sites show that they continued to use the same sorts of stone tools (chopping tools and Acheulean tools) as earlier hominins. New stone tool technologies do not emerge in step with the origin of new species. Just as *H. erectus* continued using Oldowan tools prior to the invention of Acheulean tools, *H. heidelbergensis* continued using earlier tools as well. Then, about 300,000 years ago, the situation changed in some populations, and we see the origin of stone tools using a new method of manufacture—the **Levallois technique,** named after a site in France and also known as the prepared-core method (Stringer and Andrews 2005). As shown in Figure 12.7, a flint nodule is first chipped around the edges, shaping the core into the desired shape. Small flakes are then removed from the top

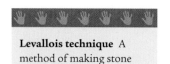

Levallois technique A method of making stone tools in which a stone core is prepared in such a way that finished tools can be removed from it by a final blow. Also known as the prepared-core method.

FIGURE 12.7

Manufacture of a stone tool, using the Levallois technique or prepared-core method. First, the core is shaped by removing small flakes from the sides and top (a–d). Then the finished tool is removed from the core (e). (From *Archaeology: Discovering Our Past,* 2d ed., by Robert Sharer and Wendy Ashmore, Fig. 10.3. Copyright © 1993 by Mayfield Publishing Company. Reprinted by permission of The McGraw-Hill Companies.)

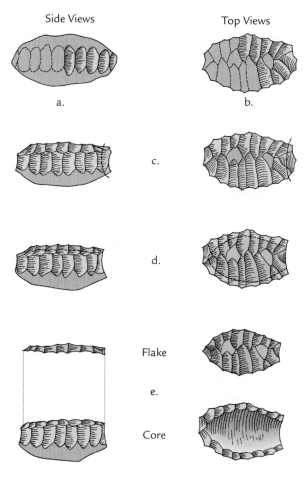

surface of the core. In the final step, the core is struck precisely at one end, and the final finished tool is removed.

The Levallois technique produces very sharp and efficient tools. It is also a way of maximizing the utilization of stone cores. Once a finished flake is removed, the core can be prepared again and another tool, identical to the first, can be produced. More tools can be prepared out of a single core, which saves time and effort spent looking for and transporting raw material. The use of the Levallois technique also shows us how skilled these archaic humans were. Their precise toolmaking implies an excellent knowledge of flaking methods and the structural characteristics of stone. It also shows how they were able to visualize the final desired product in their minds while making the tool.

Hunting   As noted previously, there is some debate over the extent to which *H. erectus* was a hunter as well as a scavenger. The evidence that *H. heidelbergensis* was a hunter is more definitive. A number of sites suggest or show evidence of hunting. Many butchered animal bones have been found at the Gran Dolina Cave site in Spain. The representation of skeletal parts shows that entire carcasses were brought into the cave for butchering, which indicates that humans had the first access to meat. In addition, in those cases where stone tool cut marks and carnivore bite marks overlapped, the pattern shows that humans had first access (Díez et al. 1999). Although it is possible that these archaic humans were scavenging complete carcasses, hunting seems more likely. An interesting side note is that some human bones were found with cut marks indicating removal of flesh, although it is not clear whether this would have been for ritualistic or cannibalistic reasons.

Additional evidence of hunting by *H. heidelbergensis* comes from the Boxgrove site in England. Analysis of animal bones shows that here too humans had access to complete carcasses. Although it is possible that complete carcasses came from animals that were already dead, which would indicate that *H. heidelbergensis* scavenged them, the presence of several butchered rhino adults is more consistent with hunting. To be scavenged, the rhinos would have had to die of natural causes or to be killed but then abandoned by a predator. These rhinos were adults in good health, and it is doubtful that they had any natural predators. Although not conclusive, this evidence argues strongly that the rhinos were hunted (Stringer et al. 1998).

Strong evidence for hunting also appears in wooden spears found at an archaeological site in Schöningen, Germany, dating to 400,000 years ago (Thieme 2000). Although wood generally decomposes, occasionally, when conditions are just right, wooden objects can be preserved over many thousands of years. Several wooden spears have been recovered from the Schöningen site. One was made of spruce and was relatively short—31 inches (78 cm)—and had both ends sharpened. Others were longer, ranging from roughly 6 to 8 feet in length (1.8–2.5 m). The overall appearance and weight balance was very similar to a modern-day javelin. The site also contains numerous butchered animal bones, and the spears were found among the butchered remains of as many as 19 horses. The inference from these remains is that hominins hunted an entire herd at one time. Although no hominin remains were found, the location and date of the site are most consistent with *H. heidelbergensis* being the hunter, as *H. erectus* has not been found in this part of Europe at this late date.

Language?   Did *H. heidelbergensis* use language, and if so, did they do so to the same extent as living humans? Did modern language abilities emerge with this species, or were they present in early forms, such as *H. erectus*? Or did modern language abilities emerge only with the origin of modern humans? There is a wide range of views among anthropologists, with some arguing for language abilities in *H. erectus* or earlier hominins, some arguing for language by the time of *H. heidelbergensis,* and others claiming that language emerged only in the past 50,000 years or so of human evolution.

The question of language origins is complicated in part by differing views on how language evolved. Some argue that the origin of language was a rapid and qualitatively different change that would have taken place very quickly. Others suggest that the evolution of complex language was more gradual, building upon previous capacity (Schepartz 1993). Studies of language acquisition in apes (Chapter 7) show that some capacity for language exists in these closest relatives and, by extension, would have been present in a common ancestor. If so, then all subsequent hominins had *some* language abilities, and these were elaborated upon over time. So, the question becomes, What level of language development existed in *H. heidelbergensis*?

One approach to studying the evolution of language is to look at clues about brain structure from fossil endocasts, such as brain surface structure and the relative size of different parts of the brain. Holloway and colleagues (2004) reviewed the data on fossil hominin endocasts and concluded that language development was underway for *H. erectus* and was mostly complete by the time of *H. heidelbergensis.*

Another clue about the origin of spoken language comes from considering anatomical differences between apes and modern humans. Our species' linguistic ability rests in part in our ability to make a wider number of sounds, and to do so faster, than apes. During infancy, two components of our vocal anatomy, the larynx and the hyoid bone, are positioned high in the throat as they are in other mammals. In both apes and humans, the larynx descends in the throat, but in humans alone, the hyoid bone continues to descend, thus forming our unique vocal anatomy (Nishimura et al. 2003). Although these changes lead to a clear-cut anatomical difference between humans and apes, most of the vocal anatomy consists of soft tissue that decomposes, so we cannot detect this anatomy in fossil specimens. We can get clues about vocal anatomy, however, by looking at the base of the cranium. In apes, the lower profile of the cranium is fairly straight, whereas it is more flexed in modern humans, reflecting changes in the position of the larynx (Figure 12.8).

What do studies of the cranial base of fossil skulls tell us? Laitman and colleagues (1979) investigated the crania of a number of fossil hominins and concluded that whereas *Australopithecus* had the ape pattern of flexing, the crania of many archaic humans were more similar to those of modern humans. One *H. erectus* cranium has been found that has a modernlike amount of cranial

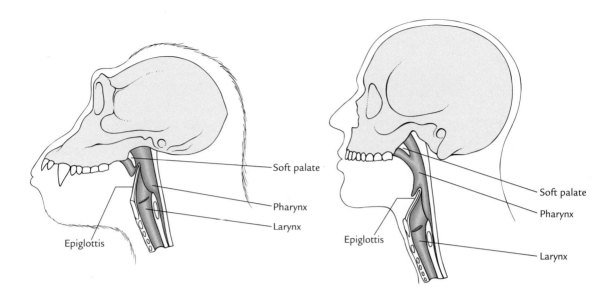

FIGURE 12.8

Side views of the cranium
and vocal anatomy of an ape
(*left*) and a modern human
(*right*). Note that the lower
profile of the cranium is fairly
straight in apes, whereas it
is flexed in modern humans.
(From Roger Lewin, *In the Age of
Mankind: A Smithsonian Book
of Human Evolution,* 1989:181,
Smithsonian Institution Press. Used
by permission.)

flexing (Baba et al. 2003). Although these studies suggest that the anatomical changes leading to spoken language began with *H. erectus* and were in place with *H. heidelbergensis,* the issue is not yet settled; studies have also suggested that the flexing of the cranial base is not a good indication of the dimensions of the vocal tract (Lieberman and McCarthy 1999). Overall, the increased technological skill and hunting ability of *H. heidelbergensis,* combined with the fossil evidence, is suggestive but not conclusive (Campbell et al. 2006). The debate over the evolution of language is likely to continue for some time.

Classification and Evolutionary Relationships

As noted previously, debate continues regarding the appropriate classification of the Middle Pleistocene hominins. This text uses the species name *Homo heidelbergensis* as a label for a paleospecies that may or may not correspond to the biological species concept. Part of the debate is over whether evolution within the genus *Homo* was through anagenesis (evolution within a lineage over time) or cladogenesis (speciation and separation of species at one point in time). Some use the species name *H. heidelbergensis* to represent a stage in the evolution from *H. erectus* to modern *H. sapiens.* As such, the species names represent different chronospecies in a single line, and the boundaries between them are viewed as arbitrary (see Figure 12.9a). Others would use the label "archaic *H. sapiens*" or "early *H. sapiens*" to represent the Middle Pleistocene stage (Bräuer 2001). Still others view the transition in the Middle Pleistocene as a true speciation and *H. heidelbergensis* as a reproductively isolated species (Rightmire 1998) (see Figure 12.9b). There are also advocates of a more complex system, placing some of what are referred to here as *H. heidelbergensis* into different species. For example, some have suggested that the Gran Dolina hominins should be placed into their own species—*Homo antecessor* (Bermúdez de Castro et al. 2004).

FIGURE 12.9

Different interpretations of the evolutionary status of *Homo heidelbergensis*. (a) *Homo erectus* evolves through anagenesis into *Homo sapiens,* and the species name *"Homo heidelbergensis"* is simply a label for this transitional stage, (b) *Homo heidelbergensis* represents a new species arising from *Homo erectus* via cladogenesis, and later evolving into Neandertals and modern humans. XXX = extinction.

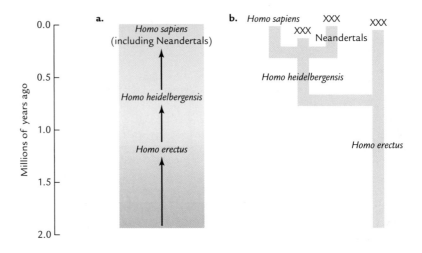

Regardless of the name used for these Middle Pleistocene hominins, clearly they are descended from *H. erectus* (although some would argue that this is true only of the African forms of *H. erectus*). It is also widely thought that some population(s) of *H. heidelbergensis* evolved into modern humans, a topic covered in the next chapter. It turns out as well that later populations of *H. heidelbergensis* in Europe show a number of physical similarities to a later group of European hominins that lived at the same time as modern humans—the Neandertals.

THE NEANDERTALS

The **Neandertals** are a group of large-brained hominins with particular physical characteristics that lived in Europe and the Middle East. Named after the site of the first discovery (Box 12.1), the Neandertals have always been a subject of intense interest because of their similarities to and differences from us, and the question of whether they are part of our ancestry.

Distribution in Time and Space

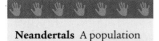

Neandertals A population of humans that lived in Europe and the Middle East between about 130,000 and 28,000 years ago. Debate continues as to whether they are a subspecies of *Homo sapiens* or a separate species and to what extent they contributed to the ancestry of modern humans.

The distribution of major Neandertal sites is shown in Figure 12.10. Although the majority of Neandertal sites are in Europe and the Middle East, some evidence suggests that their range extended into Central Asia and Siberia (Krause, Orlando, et al. 2007). Neandertals appeared in Europe around 130,000 years ago (McKee et al. 2005), although some Neandertal traits can be seen in earlier (*Homo heidelbergensis*) populations at Atapuerca in Spain dating to 400,000 years ago. Some Neandertal populations *may* have survived in isolated parts of Europe until about 28,000 years ago (Smith et al. 1999). If so, then Neandertals and modern humans may have both lived in the same part of the world at the same time. However, some of the younger dates are in question and the amount of overlap might have been

BOX 12.1

Neandertal Names and Images

The word "Neandertal" comes from the site in the Neander Valley where Neandertals were first found. In German, "tal" means "valley." Hence, "Neandertal" translates as "Neander Valley." You may be more familiar with an alternative spelling—"Neanderthal"—and an alternative pronunciation (emphasizing the "THAL" sound). However, the *h* is silent in German so that "thal" is actually pronounced "tal." Because of this characteristic of German pronunciation, many (although not all) anthropologists simply drop the *h* in the spelling as well. Note, however, that the *h* is retained in the original spelling in the species (or subspecies) name *neanderthalensis*, because even though the *h* is silent, the word for valley was spelled "thal" in the nineteenth century, the time when the taxonomic name *neanderthalensis* was established. According to the rules of biological nomenclature, the original spelling must be retained even though modern German no longer uses the *h* in spelling.

In addition to their name, Neandertals also present a confusing array of images about their very nature. The very mention of Neandertals usually invokes a number of images and preconceptions. For example, you may conjure up one of many images of the Neandertals as crude and simple subhumans with limited intelligence that walked bent over. These images have become such a part of our popular culture that a typical dictionary definition includes "Neandertal" as an adjective meaning "suggesting primitive man in appearance or behavior (Neandertal ferocity)"

and "extremely old-fashioned or out-of-date," as well as a noun meaning "a rugged or uncouth person" (*Webster's Third International Dictionary*). It is no wonder that many people use "Neandertal" as an insult.

Why do Neandertals have such a bad reputation? Regardless of whether we view Neandertals as a separate species or as a subspecies of *Homo sapiens*, we know that they had large brains, walked upright, and possessed a sophisticated culture, including use of stone tools and fire, hunting, and cave burial. Part of the image problem comes from an inaccurate reconstruction of a Neandertal skeleton in the early 1900s. Because of certain physical features, such as curved thigh bones, scientists of the time believed that Neandertals did not walk completely upright, but instead moved about bent over. It was discovered later that the curved bones and other features were simply a reflection of the poor health, including severe arthritis, of that particular Neandertal. Other features once taken to indicate mental inferiority, such as large brow ridges, are now recognized as biomechanical in nature. Even though the scientific interpretation has changed, the popular images of Neandertals unfortunately remain to this day, and the term "Neandertal" is still used as an insult. More information on the history of Neandertals, including further discussion of their image, can be found in Trinkaus and Shipman (1992) and Stringer and Gamble (1993).

---

less (Pinhasi et al. 2011). Neandertal populations lived in the Middle East at different times in the past; they may have been present before 100,000 years ago, and appear again between 70,000 and 45,000 years ago (Cartmill and Smith 2009). The Middle Eastern finds are particularly interesting, as they fall near a time when modern humans also lived in the Middle East, although here too it is difficult to tell how much, if any, the two groups overlapped (Finlayson 2009). We will return to this issue in the next chapter.

Physical Characteristics

The Neandertals had very large brains, averaging about 1,450 cc. Although Neandertals on average had larger brains than living humans do, they also had large body mass. Relative to body size, Neandertal cranial capacity is slightly lower than that of living humans (Ruff et al. 1997). According to Holloway (1985), the structural organization of Neandertal brains, as assessed from endocasts, is no different from that of modern humans.

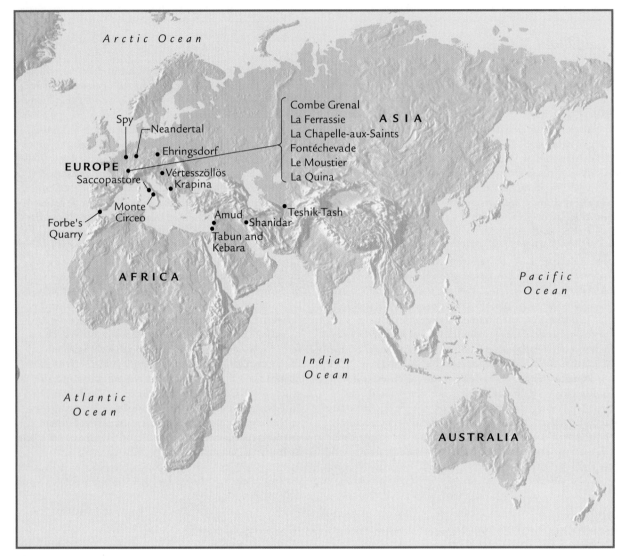

FIGURE 12.10

Location of some major
Neandertal sites.

Cranial Features Neandertals shared many characteristics with earlier hominins, such as a low skull, sloping forehead, lack of chin, and large brow
ridges. Neandertals also possessed a number of features that were unique to
them, or found in lower frequencies in other populations. Figure 12.11 show
a Western European Neandertals from France dating to roughly 70,000 years
ago. Neandertal faces are generally long and protrude more than those of
modern humans. The nasal region is large, suggesting large, protruding
noses, and the sinus cavities to the side of the nose expand outward. As such,
the entire midfacial region protrudes from the skull. The large nasal and
midfacial areas on Neandertals have often been interpreted as some type of

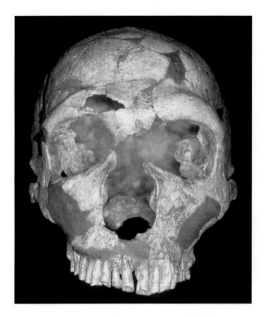

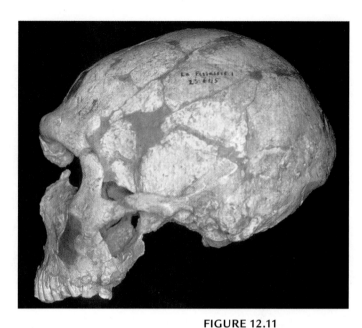

FIGURE 12.11

Frontal and side views of the La Ferrassie skull, a Neandertal from France.

adaptation to a cold climate (see the discussion on nasal size and shape in relation to climate in Chapter 16). Others have suggested that these features reflect some sort of biomechanical adaptation. It is also quite possible that the distinctive cranial anatomy of Neandertals does not have anything to do with adaptation through natural selection, but instead reflects genetic drift (Weaver et al. 2007).

The front teeth of Neandertals are large relative to their back teeth and often show considerable wear, suggesting that they were used as tools. Neandertals tend to have large brow ridges that form double arches over the eyes. The cheekbones of Neandertals tend to be swept back, and the back of the skull is rather puffed out, a feature called an **occipital bun.** Cranial differences between Neandertals and modern humans appear to develop early in life (Ponce de León and Zollikofer 2001).

occipital bun The protruding rear region of the skull, a feature commonly found in Neandertals.

There is also regional variation within Neandertals. Figure 12.12 shows the skull of a Middle Eastern Neandertal. Though the Middle Eastern forms possess the general characteristics of Neandertal, they are not as morphologically extreme. The skulls are a bit more well rounded than most Western European Neandertals.

The Postcranial Skeleton Neandertal postcranial remains show that Neandertals were relatively short and stocky (Figure 12.13). The limb bones farthest from the body (the lower arm and lower leg) are relatively short, most likely reflecting cold adaptation (Trinkaus 1981). The limb and shoulder bones are more rugged than those of modern humans, and the areas of muscle attachment show that the Neandertals were very strong. The pelvic bones are also rather robust compared with those of modern humans, with the

FIGURE 12.12

The Shanidar I skull, Iraq.

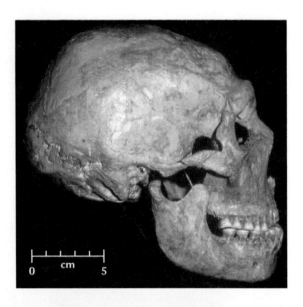

FIGURE 12.13

A reconstructed Neandertal skeleton (*left*) compared to a modern human skeleton (*right*). The reconstruction shows clearly the stockier physique of the Neandertals. See Sawyer and Maley (2005) for details on this reconstruction, based largely on a specimen from the La Ferrassie site in France.

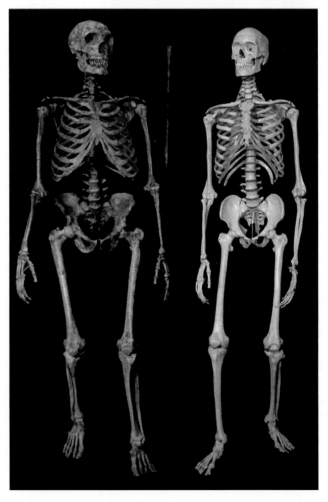

exception of the upper portion of the pubis (at the front of the pelvis), which is actually thinner and longer than in modern humans. The uniqueness of the Neandertal pelvis may reflect some biomechanical function of posture and locomotion (Rak and Arensberg 1987).

Neandertal DNA

In the summer of 1997, an article in the journal *Cell* announced to the world an amazing technological breakthrough—the extraction of a DNA sequence from a Neandertal fossil at the Feldhofer site in Germany (Krings et al. 1997). This marked the first time human DNA had been successfully extracted from such an old specimen; the site dates to about 40,000 years ago (Schmitz et al. 2002). Since then, a number of other Neandertal specimens have been used for ancient DNA analysis.

Mitochondrial DNA   As discussed in Chapter 3, mitochondrial DNA is inherited solely from one's mother. Mitochondrial DNA preserves better than nuclear DNA and is commonly used in studies of ancient DNA. The first Neandertal mitochondrial DNA sequence that was extracted consisted of 379 base pairs (bp). Since that time, partial mitochondrial DNA sequences of varying lengths (31–357 bp) have been extracted from an additional 14 Neandertal fossils (Hodgson and Disotell 2008). These sequences are all from a section of mitochondrial DNA known as the hypervariable region, an area marked by frequent mutation. All of the Neandertal mitochondrial DNA sequences are more similar to each other than to any living humans.

These extracted Neandertal sequences are all small relative to the total size of the mitochondrial DNA genome, which is over 16,000 base pairs. In 2008, however, using new techniques of ancient DNA analysis, researchers were able to sequence the *entire* mitochondrial DNA sequence from a 38,000-year-old Neandertal fossil from Croatia (Green et al. 2008). This sequence was 16,568 bp in length. Compared with a standard reference for living humans, the Neandertal DNA showed 206 base pair differences, as well as a deletion of 4 bases and an insertion of 1 base not found in living humans. This number of DNA differences is quite large and outside the range of variation found among living humans—the authors found that the sample of living humans differed from each other by only between 2 and 118 bases. The number of mutational differences between the mitochondrial DNA of the Neandertal specimen and living humans translates to a divergence of the two lines about 660,000 years ago.

These mitochondrial DNA analyses have shown a number of DNA substitutions found in all Neandertals that are not found in any living humans. Further, the analysis of mitochondrial DNA in two modern human skeletons dating between 24,000 and 28,000 years ago likewise shows no trace of Neandertal mitochondrial DNA (Caramelli et al. 2003, 2008). For many, these findings have suggested that the simplest explanation for this finding is

BOX 12.2

Neandertal Skin Color

One of the advantages of ancient DNA analysis is that we are sometimes able to learn about the phenotypes of ancient humans. Analysis of skeletal remains can tell us a lot about body and cranial size and shape, but other aspects of an ancestor's appearance, such as their skin color, cannot be determined directly. In some cases, ancient DNA analysis can help us fill in the gaps.

One such study was conducted by Carles Lalueza-Fox and colleagues, who sequenced pieces of a gene known as *MC1R* (melanocortin 1 receptor gene) from two Neandertals dating between 40,000 and 50,000 years ago, one from Italy and one from Spain. This gene is one of several that have been found to affect human skin color (Mielke et al. 2011). They found a mutation from nucleotide A to nucleotide G in the *MC1R* gene at position 319, which would have changed an amino acid and modified the balance between different forms of melanin. These changes meant that these two Neandertals had very light skin and red hair (Lalueza-Fox et al. 2007).

The fact that Neandertals had light skin is not surprising given that they lived at northern latitudes in Europe and light skin is an adaptation that occurs at these latitudes and is shared with living Europeans (see Chapter 15 for more information on the evolution of human skin color). What makes these results particularly fascinating is that the specific light-skinned mutation found in these two Neandertals is *not* the same as that found in living Europeans. It appears that light skin evolved independently from different initial mutations.

that Neandertals were a separate species and there was *no* interbreeding with modern humans. However, we must always remember that mitochondrial DNA is but a small fraction of our entire genome, and as such might not give us the complete history of a group. Thus, it is possible that Neandertals and modern humans *did* interbreed to some extent, but the mitochondrial DNA does not show it because of genetic drift.

Even though we now have one complete mitochondrial DNA sequence and a number of partial sequences from Neandertals, you should not think of ancient DNA analysis as a routine matter. Not all fossil samples are usable, and preservation of DNA tends to occur more often in certain environments (such as caves). There is no guarantee of being able to extract DNA from any given fossil. In addition, we need to be cautious of problems of contamination from people that have handled the fossil. Major advances have been made in the field of ancient DNA analysis, but it is not as easy as it might sound!

Nuclear DNA Because mitochondrial DNA samples only a tiny fraction of a person's genome, analysis of the nuclear DNA sequences is preferred. At one time, the idea that we could sequence ancient nuclear DNA seemed doubtful, but new technologies have allowed this. Several studies have been able to isolate specific sequences, providing us with some specific information on aspects of Neandertal biology, such as their skin color (Box 12.2).

Following several preliminary studies, a draft of the entire Neandertal genome was sequenced using DNA from the bones of three female Neandertals in Vindija Cave in Croatia, dating to 38,000 to 44,000 years ago (Green et al. 2010). The entire DNA sequence was compared with several living humans; we share 99.84 percent of our genome with them (Gibbons 2010). The

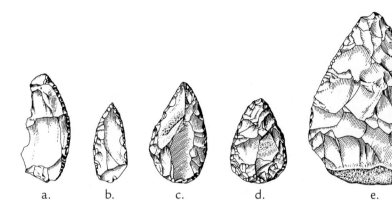

FIGURE 12.14

Examples of Mousterian tools: (a) scraper, (b) point, (c) scraper, (d) point, (e) hand axe. (From *The Old Stone Age* by F. Bordes, 1968, Weidenfeld and Nicolson, Ltd. Reprinted by permission of The McGraw-Hill Companies.)

number of genetic differences means that Neandertals and modern humans diverged from a common ancestor between 270,000 and 440,000 years ago. Given this date, the geographic distribution of Neandertals, and patterns of physical similarity, this common ancestor was likely *Homo heidelbergensis.* Analysis of the Neandertal genome also suggests that there was some interbreeding of Neandertals and modern humans later in time. Current estimates suggest that between 1 and 4 percent of the ancestry of living humans outside of Africa derives from Neandertals (Green et al. 2010). We will explore the implications of this finding in Chapter 13.

The Culture of the Neandertals

As with later *Homo heidelbergensis,* the Neandertals made tools using the Levallois technique. The specific stone tool culture of the Neandertals is known as the **Mousterian tradition.** The Mousterian culture, named after the site of Le Moustier in France, produced a wide variety tools, including a preponderance of scrapers (Figure 12.14). Wooden spears used for hunting have also been found at Neandertal sites, including one found in an elephant skeleton (Stringer and Andrews 2005).

Mousterian tradition The prepared-core stone tool culture of the Neandertals.

Cave Burial   The archaeological record shows that Neandertals were capable of some symbolic thought, perhaps holding beliefs in an afterlife. Neandertals buried their dead intentionally, as did early modern humans. Burial is a more recent behavior; no earlier hominins buried their dead. Deliberate burial is apparent from the condition of the bodies, with skeletons found intact and arranged carefully in graves (Figure 12.15). Evidence of cave burial is found at a number of European and Middle Eastern sites. This intentional burial of the dead has suggested a ritualistic purpose to some researchers. At the Shanidar Cave site in Iraq, flowers had been placed all over the bodies, an event that was reconstructed based on the presence of fossil pollen in the graves, although some have suggested that the pollen was introduced by

FIGURE 12.15

A Neandertal burial from the La Ferrassie site in France.

rodents burrowing into the grave after burial. In any case, deliberate burial suggests the evolution of symbolic expressions and the possibility of supernatural beliefs.

Health The physical condition of Neandertal fossils provides us with information on their behavior and lifestyle. By looking at bone fractures, the condition of teeth, and other features, we can get an idea of the health status of Neandertals. The fossil evidence shows that Neandertals lived a hard life; few of them lived past 30 years of age (Caspari 2011).

Their skeletal remains show a variety of traumatic injuries. In particular, they suffered from a very high proportion of head and neck injuries and a high proportion of shoulder and arm injuries. Berger and Trinkaus (1995) found that the anatomical distribution of Neandertal injuries was very similar to the distribution found in modern humans who are professional rodeo athletes; these two groups both deal with animals at close range. For Neandertals, this dangerous contact would have come about when they hunted, as the types of weapons they had, such as thrusting spears, necessitated close (and dangerous) contact with their prey.

Language?   Did Neandertals have language? Could they speak as well as modern humans? These questions have long been asked. Lieberman and Crelin (1971), who reconstructed the vocal anatomy of Neandertals, concluded that they were incapable of vocalizing certain vowel sounds. The implication was that Neandertals did not possess as wide a range of sounds as modern humans and perhaps had limited language abilities. This hypothesis was criticized, however, because of differences of opinion on vocal anatomy reconstruction. The lack of direct fossil evidence at the heart of the debate was ultimately resolved with the discovery of the first Neandertal hyoid bone, a bone lying in the neck that can be used to provide information on the structure of the respiratory tract. That this specimen is almost identical in size and shape to the hyoid bone of modern humans suggests that there were *no* differences in vocal ability between Neandertals and modern humans (Arensberg et al. 1990). In addition, no evidence exists from brain anatomy to show that Neandertals lacked speech centers (Holloway 1985).

Language ability of Neandertals is also suggested from ancient DNA analysis. As noted in Chapter 7, studies comparing humans and other primates suggest that the *FOXP2* gene might be involved, to some extent, in language acquisition. Humans differ from the other primates by having two mutations. Ancient DNA analysis of two fossils from Spain shows that Neandertals shared these mutations with modern humans (Krause, Lalucza-Fox, et al. 2007). Again, the relationship of *FOXP2* to normal language acquisition needs to be confirmed, but these results do add to the suggestion that Neandertals had speech, although debate continues on the nature of their speech relative to our species'.

Classification and Evolutionary Relationships

Available fossil evidence shows strong similarities among Middle Pleistocene populations in Europe, which likely represent a large part of Neandertal ancestry. What is less clear, and is a long-term controversy, is the relationship of the Neandertals to modern humans. In the nineteenth century, anatomist William King (1864) assigned the first-known Neandertal remains to a separate species, *Homo neanderthalensis,* because of the physical differences, from modern humans. By the mid-twentieth century, many anthropologists had begun to focus more on the similarities, such as the large brain, than the differences and to consider Neandertals as a separate subspecies known as *Homo sapiens neanderthalensis,* set apart from living humans, who are classified in the subspecies *Homo sapiens sapiens.* As more data on anatomical differences have accumulated since the last part of the twentieth century, some anthropologists have advocated returning to the practice of placing Neandertals in a separate species. The debate continues over whether to consider Neandertals a species or a subspecies.

Underlying discussion of what to call Neandertals is the more significant question of their evolutionary relationship to us. Were they a part of our ancestry, or did they contribute nothing to the current gene pool of our species? The fossil evidence shows that Neandertals as a group were last seen about 28,000 years ago. Toward the end of their existence, anatomically modern humans also lived in Europe, but it appears that they moved there from elsewhere (see the next chapter). Although the amount of time that Neandertals and modern humans may have coexisted in Europe is still being debated, it is clear that after 28,000 years ago, the only fossil hominins in Europe are modern humans. Where did the Neandertals go? Did they become extinct as a species, and if so, why? Or were their genes absorbed into the gene pool of modern humans, as suggested by ancient DNA evidence? These questions will be discussed in more detail in the next chapter.

Summary

Close to 800,000 years ago, at the beginning of the Middle Pleistocene, hominins had evolved a larger brain, close in size to that of modern humans, but still retained a fairly large face and brow ridges and a less well-rounded skull. These hominins, classified as *H. heidelbergensis,* lived in Africa, Europe, and Asia until about 200,000 years ago. These Middle Pleistocene hominins were definitely hunters and, by 300,000 years ago, had invented the Levallois technique of making stone tools, a process by which a core is shaped and a finished tool is removed with a single blow. Archaeological evidence shows that *H. heidelbergensis* was an efficient hunter. The fossil evidence also suggests that this species may have developed near-modern language capability.

Two groups of hominins appear to have descended from the Middle Pleistocene hominins. One group was anatomically modern *H. sapiens,* whose origins are discussed in detail in the next chapter. The other group was the Neandertals, large-brained humans with large noses and midfaces, as well as other anatomical differences. Neandertals lived in Europe and the Middle East. Some anthropologists suggest that the Neandertals were a separate species that became extinct by 28,000 years ago. Other anthropologists argue that Neandertals mixed genetically with modern humans but made little contribution to our gene pool over time, perhaps because of their small numbers. In any event, the Neandertals were skilled toolmakers and hunter-gatherers who buried their dead.

Supplemental Readings

Stringer, C., and C. Gamble. 1993. *In Search of the Neanderthals: Solving the Puzzle of Human Origins.* New York: Thames and Hudson. Somewhat dated, but still an excellent review of Neandertal (and other human) biology and culture.

A prehistoric cave painting from Chad, Africa, showing people and animals. Cave art is one of several behaviors that either originated with or became much more common with the advent of modern humans.

The Origin of Modern Humans

Would you notice if a prehistoric ancestor, dressed in modern clothes and with a modern hairstyle, walked in the door of your classroom? (This hypothetical question assumes a time machine). The answer depends on *which* ancestor. I think *Homo erectus* would be immediately noticed as being different from the rest of us. The larger-brained early humans, such as *Homo heidelbergensis* and the Neandertals, might not elicit the same immediate reaction, but closer inspection would likely reveal their differently shaped skulls and tremendous brow ridges, among other characteristics. At what point in our prehistory do we see people that fall within the range of modern human variation in terms of their physical appearance?

The fossil record suggests that this happens in some populations about 200,000 years ago with the first appearance of what we call **anatomically modern humans** (*Homo sapiens*), evolving from an earlier population (or populations) of Middle Pleistocene hominins. We use the term "anatomically modern" to refer to fossils that are the same as we are today, possessing certain physical characteristics such as a well-rounded skull and a noticeable chin. The origin of modern humans is an area of considerable debate among anthropologists today.

At the heart of this debate is a series of basic questions: What is the nature of this change? When and where did it occur? Did it occur in only one place, or was it widespread? Why did it occur? What cultural changes took place, and how are they related to the biological changes? In short, our questions concern the recent history of the human species.

CHAPTER OUTLINE

- Anatomically Modern Humans
- The Modern Human Origins Debate
- Recent Biological and Cultural Evolution in *Homo sapiens*

anatomically modern humans The modern form of the human species, which dates back 200,000 years.

ANATOMICALLY MODERN HUMANS

Though it is clear that earlier humans evolved into anatomically modern humans, the exact nature of this evolution is less certain. This section deals with the biological and cultural characteristics of anatomically modern humans, followed by consideration of the nature of their evolution.

Distribution in Time and Space

Anatomically modern humans are found in many sites across both the Old World and the New World. Some of these sites are shown in Figure 13.1.

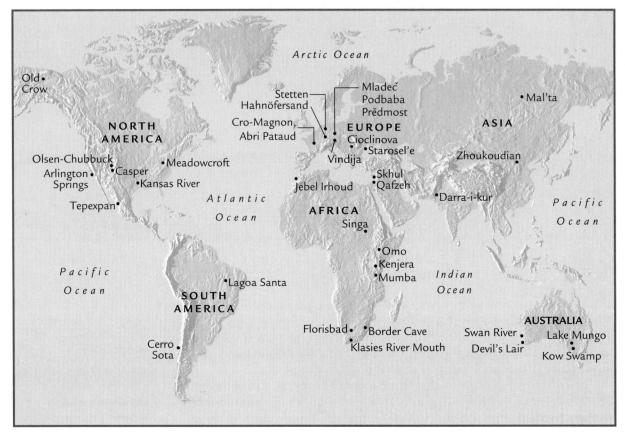

FIGURE 13.1

Location of some anatomically modern *Homo sapiens* sites.

As noted in the previous chapter, modern *H. sapiens* likely evolved from *Homo heidelbergensis*. The fossil evidence shows the earliest appearance of anatomically modern humans in Africa almost 200,000 years ago. At present, the oldest known modern human fossils come from the Omo site in Ethiopia, which dates to 195,000 years ago (McDougall et al. 2005). Though fragmentary, the Omo 1 skull shows a number of modern traits, such as a well-rounded rear of the skull, a high skull, and the presence of a chin (Figure 13.2). Several crania from the Middle Awash area of Ethiopia, dating to almost 160,000 years ago, show a number of modern human traits, including a high, well-rounded cranium (White et al. 2003) (Figure 13.3). And cranial remains from the Border Cave site in southeastern Africa are fragmentary but show typically modern features (Figure 13.4). The dating for this site is not definite but ranges from 115,000 to 90,000 years ago. In addition, modern humans may have occupied Klasies River Mouth in South Africa as early as 90,000 years ago (Grün et al. 1990). All of these data show a clear presence of anatomically modern humans in Africa between 100,000 and 200,000 years ago.

Modern humans are not found outside of Africa until later in time. The next appearance of modern humans is in the Middle East at the Qafzeh and Skhul sites in Israel, dating to 92,000 years ago (Grün et al. 1991).

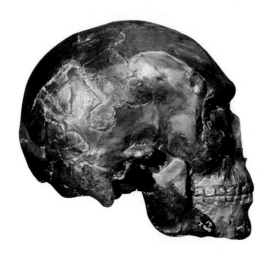

FIGURE 13.2

The Omo 1 skull from Omo, Ethiopia. This skull shows modern human characteristics such as a high, well-rounded cranium and a chin. The Omo site dates to 195,000 years ago, making this specimen the earliest example of anatomically modern *Homo sapiens*.

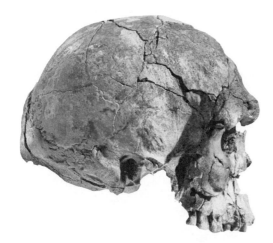

FIGURE 13.3

Side view of specimen BOU-VP-16/1, an early *Homo sapiens* cranium from the Middle Awash area of Ethiopia.

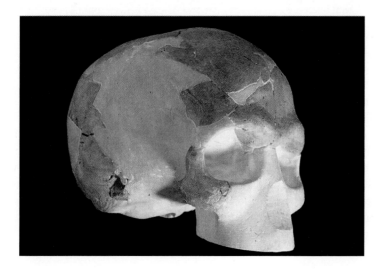

FIGURE 13.4

The Border Cave skull, South Africa. The fragmentary remains are clearly those of anatomically modern *Homo sapiens* (note the vertical forehead). Dating is not precise, but current estimates suggest an age of more than 100,000 years ago.

BOX 13.1

What Is the "Hobbit"?

As noted in the main text, the fossil record has long shown *Homo sapiens* as the only hominin species for the last 25,000 years or so. This view has been challenged with the discovery of fossil remains that might represent a different hominin species that lived very recently. In 2003, a skull and parts of a skeleton of an adult hominin dating to 18,000 years ago were discovered at the Liang Bua Cave site on the island of Flores in Indonesia (Brown et al. 2004). This find was quite startling because of the specimen's size. Even though it was an adult, it was only about 3.5 feet (106 cm) tall and had a cranial capacity of only 417 cc (Falk et al. 2005). The specimen's small size has led to its being nicknamed the "Hobbit," after the diminutive characters in J. R. R. Tolkien's book of the same name and his Lord of the Rings trilogy. The combination of small height and cranial capacity resembled that of *Australopithecus,* but cranial and dental features were more similar to the genus *Homo,* so it was classified as a new species, ***Homo floresiensis*** (Brown et al. 2004). The species initially was found in association with stone tools and animal bones (Morwood et al. 2004), and additional postcranial bones have since been discovered (Morwood et al. 2005). All of the finds of *H. floresiensis* date to between 12,000 and as long as 94,000 years ago.

One explanation of this find is that it represents a dwarf species of some earlier hominin. A process known as island dwarfism has been observed for a number of animal species. When a population of large animals is trapped on an island with limited resources, natural selection favors smaller body size, ultimately leading to species that are much smaller than their ancestors were. This process has been documented for a variety of animals, including some creatures that were related to elephants that lived on Flores.

Another suggestion is that the Hobbit is *not* a different species, but instead is a pathological modern human from a short population. Short populations are found throughout the world, so the height of the Hobbit is not that unusual. The most unusual characteristic is the small brain size, much smaller than expected for its height. Although it is possible that the small brain size of the Hobbit is the result of some disease, such as microcephaly (which leads to a small brain), other aspects of the specimen's morphology do not fit with such diagnoses. Although more fossil evidence will be needed to resolve the identity of the Hobbit, at present the evidence does *not* support the pathology argument (Aiello 2010). In turn, this means that future research is needed to determine the origins of *H. floresiensis,* including who they are descended from, how they got to Flores, and what happened to them.

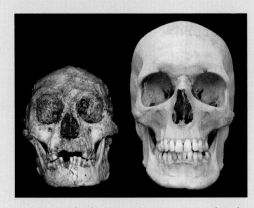

The LB1 skull (left) and a modern human skull (right). The LB1 specimen has been classified by some anthropologists as *Homo floresiensis.*

Homo floresiensis The species name given to a very small hominin that lived in Indonesia in recent times, and thought by some to be a dwarf species of *Homo erectus.*

Modern humans first appeared in Australia sometime between 60,000 and 46,000 years ago. The fossil record from East Asia is less clear but suggests a date of perhaps 60,000 years ago (Stringer and McKie 1996). Modern humans are relative newcomers in Europe. Although it has long been believed that modern humans reached different parts of Europe between 40,000 and 30,000 years ago, estimates (including recalibration to account for fluctuations in atmospheric carbon-14) now suggest that modern humans may have dispersed across Europe between 46,000 and 41,000 years ago (Mellars 2006).

As noted in the last chapter, Neandertals disappeared in Europe by 28,000 years ago. Conventional wisdom holds that *Homo sapiens* has been the only hominin species that was alive after 25,000 years ago, although this idea has been questioned with the discovery of a possible small-brained dwarf species of hominin from Indonesia that lived 18,000 years ago (see Box 13.1).

Physical Characteristics

Figure 13.5 shows a skull from one of the more famous anatomically modern sites—Cro-Magnon, France, dating to between 27,000 and 23,000 years ago. This skull shows many of the characteristics of anatomically modern *Homo sapiens*. It is high and well rounded. There is no occipital bun; the back of the skull is rounded instead. The forehead rises vertically above the eye orbits and does not slope, as in archaic humans. The brow ridges are small, the face does not protrude very much, and a strong chin is evident.

Another example of anatomically modern *H. sapiens* is shown in Figure 13.6, a skull from the Skhul site at Mount Carmel, Israel. This skull also has a high, well-rounded shape without an occipital bun and with a small chin. Compared to the Cro-Magnon skull, the brow ridges are larger and the face protrudes slightly. The differences between the Skhul and the Cro-Magnon skulls are typical of variation within a species, particularly when we consider that they existed at different times in separate places.

FIGURE 13.5

Side and frontal views of the Cro-Magnon skull, France. This specimen is one of the best-known examples of anatomically modern *Homo sapiens*.

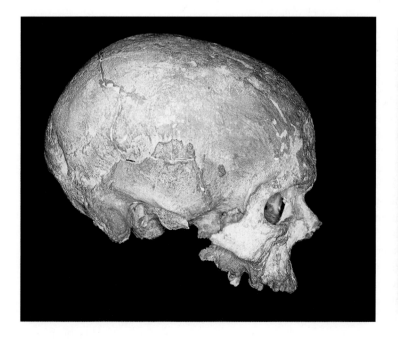

FIGURE 13.6

An early anatomically modern *Homo sapiens* skull from Skhul, Israel.

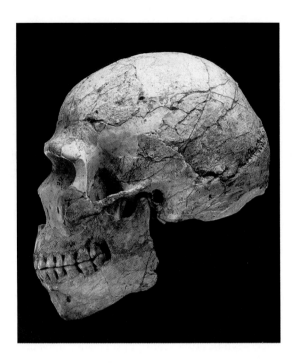

Cultural Behavior

Discussing the cultural adaptations of anatomically modern *Homo sapiens* is difficult because they include both prehistoric technologies and more recent developments, such as agriculture, generation of electricity, the internal combustion engine, and nuclear energy. So that we may provide a comparison with the culture of earlier hominins, this section is limited to prehistory before the development of agriculture (roughly 12,000 years ago).

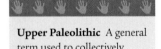

Upper Paleolithic A general term used to collectively refer to the stone tool technologies of anatomically modern *Homo sapiens*.

Lower Paleolithic A general term used to collectively refer to the stone tool technologies of *Homo habilis/Homo rudolfensis* and *Homo erectus*.

Middle Paleolithic A general term used to refer collectively to the stone tool technologies of *Homo heidelbergensis* and the Neandertals.

Tool Technologies   There is so much variation in the stone tool technologies of anatomically modern *H. sapiens* that it is impossible to define a single tradition. Earlier populations of anatomically modern *H. sapiens* are found with earlier types of tools, but by about 90,000 years ago, newer technologies appeared. For the sake of discussion, these types of new stone tool industries are often lumped together under the term **Upper Paleolithic** (which means "Upper Old Stone Age"). **Lower Paleolithic** consists of the stone tool traditions of *H. habilis* and *H. erectus,* and **Middle Paleolithic** includes the stone tool traditions of *Homo heidelbergensis* and the Neandertals. Even though we use a single label to describe common features of Upper Paleolithic tool industries, do not be misled into thinking that all traditions were the same. Variation, both within and among sites, is even greater in the Upper Paleolithic than in earlier cultures. This variation demonstrates the increasing sophistication and specialization of stone tools.

Figure 13.7 shows some examples of Upper Paleolithic stone tools. These tools are much more precisely made than the stone tools of earlier hominins

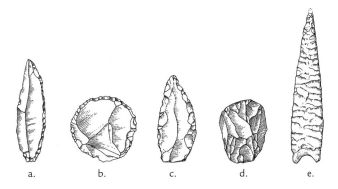

FIGURE 13.7

Examples of Upper Paleolithic stone tools: (a) knife, (b) scraper, (c) point, (d) scraper, (e) point. Tools a, b, and c are from the Perigordian culture; tool d is from the Aurignacian culture; tool e is from the Solutrean culture. (From *The Old Stone Age* by F. Bordes, 1968, Weidenfeld and Nicolson, Ltd. Reprinted by permission of The McGraw-Hill Companies.)

and are also quite a bit more diverse in function and styles. One notable characteristic of the Upper Paleolithic is the development of **blades,** stone tools defined as being at least twice as long as they are wide (Figure 13.8). Blade tools are made by removing long, narrow flakes off a prepared core. The core is struck by a piece of antler or bone, which in turn is struck by a stone. That is, the core is not hit directly by the hammerstone; rather, the force of the blow is applied through the antler. This method allows very thin and sharp blade tools to be made (Figure 13.9).

Upper Paleolithic tools were also used to make tools out of other resources, such as bone. A small stone tool called a **burin** has an extremely

blade A stone tool characteristic of the Upper Paleolithic, defined as being at least twice as long as it is wide.

burin A stone tool with a sharp edge that is used to cut and engrave bone.

FIGURE 13.8

Example of a flint blade tool. (From *Human Antiquity: An Introduction to Physical Anthropology and Archaeology,* 4th ed., by Kenneth Feder and Michael Park, Fig. 13.3. Copyright © 2001 by Mayfield Publishing Company. Reprinted with permission of The McGraw-Hill Companies.)

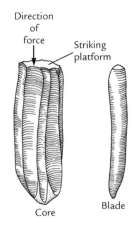

FIGURE 13.9

Method of blade tool manufacture. A striking platform is formed, and a blade tool can then be made by flaking off a long vertical piece from the side. (From *Discovering Anthropology* by Daniel R. Gross, Fig. 7.10. Copyright © 1993 by Mayfield Publishing Company. Reprinted by permission of The McGraw-Hill Companies.)

sharp edge that is used to cut, whittle, and engrave bone. Bone was used to make needles, awls, points, knives, and harpoons, as well as art objects. Bone tools and elaborate art objects first appeared with modern *H. sapiens;* they are not found in the culture of earlier hominins (although there are suggestions of art objects associated with earlier humans, these finds are controversial). For years, it appeared that bone tools were fairly recent, dating back roughly 40,000 years. Research in Zaire, however, has produced a much earlier age of 90,000 years (Brooks et al. 1995; Yellen et al. 1995).

Shelter   Like early humans, modern *H. sapiens* lived in caves and rock shelters where available. The archaeological evidence also shows definite evidence of manufactured shelter—huts made of wood, animal bone, and animal hides. Although much of this material decomposes, we can still find evidence of support structures. One example of hut building comes from the 18,000-year-old site of Mal'ta in south-central Russia (Figure 13.10). This hut is particularly interesting because people used mammoth ribs and leg bones for structural support. Other sites, such as the 15,000-year-old site of Mezhirich in the Ukraine, contain evidence of shelters built almost entirely from mammoth bones.

Art   Another form of symbolic behavior is artistic expression, including cave art, sculptures, and engravings. Although some archaeologists consider art to be unique to modern humans, beginning 50,000 to 40,000 years ago, others have suggested that art began earlier in Africa and gradually increased in frequency in later modern humans. Engravings have been found in Africa dating to 77,000 years ago, which supports the latter view (Henshilwood et al. 2002). In either case, artistic expression became more pronounced in modern humans.

Perhaps the best example of prehistoric art is cave art, which dates back more than 30,000 years in Europe, Africa, and Australia. Some of the

FIGURE 13.10

Reconstruction of a hut at the Mal'ta site in Russia. This site dates to 18,000 years ago. (From *Human Antiquity: An Introduction to Physical Anthropology and Archaeology,* 4th ed., by Kenneth Feder and Michael Park, Fig. 13.5. Copyright © 2001 by Mayfield Publishing Company. Reprinted by permission of The McGraw-Hill Companies.)

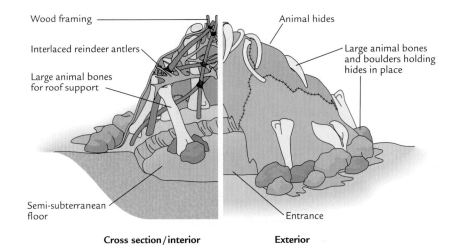

Cross section/interior   Exterior

FIGURE 13.11

Cave painting of a running horse from Lascaux Cave, France.

best-known cave art, primarily paintings of large game animals and hunting, comes from sites in Europe (Figure 13.11). These paintings are anatomically correct and are well executed. Painting is a human activity that is spiritually rewarding but has no apparent function in day-to-day existence. Why, then, did early humans paint images on the walls of caves? Several interpretations have been offered, including sympathetic magic (capturing the image of an animal to improve hunters' chances of actually killing it). Other interpretations focus on cultural symbolism or a means of communicating ideas and images. We will never know exactly *why* early humans made these paintings. What is clear, however, is that they did something that serves a symbolic purpose. Although we cannot know the reason for these behaviors, the art shows us that humans by this time had developed a need to express themselves symbolically. To these early moderns, life was not just eating and surviving—something else was important to them as well.

Cave paintings are not the only form of art associated with early modern *H. sapiens*. We also find evidence of engravings, beads and pendants, and

FIGURE 13.12

A Venus figurine.

ceramic sculpture. One of the best-known examples is the "Venus" figurines found throughout parts of Europe. These figures are pregnant females with exaggerated breasts and buttocks (Figure 13.12). Although these figurines are often interpreted as fertility symbols (fertility would have been critical to survival), we are not sure of their exact meaning or function. However, as with cave paintings, the Venus figurines show us that symbolism was fully a part of the life of early modern *H. sapiens.*

Geographic Expansion   The archaeological evidence shows that humans became more and more successful over time in adapting to their environment, and consequently, populations grew and expanded into new areas. Although *H. erectus* and archaic humans lived in parts of Africa, Asia, and Europe, it is only with the appearance of modern humans that we see expansion into Australia and the New World.

Australia was first occupied by modern humans at least 46,000 years ago (Bowler et al. 2003) and perhaps as early as 60,000 years ago (Thorne et al. 1999). As mentioned in the previous chapter, during times of glaciation, sea levels drop, extending the land mass of continents, which meant that humans could have reached Southeast Asia. However, Australia was not connected to the mainland, and the only way modern humans could have reached that continent was by crossing many kilometers of sea using some sort of raft or boat. Modern humans probably reached the New World between 20,000 and 15,000 years ago, either by crossing the Bering Land Bridge or by boat, or both (see Chapter 15).

***First Appearance of the Culture of Early Modern* Homo Sapiens**   There is debate over the speed of the emergence of the culture of early modern humans, with some favoring a model of rapid development and others a more gradual accumulation of these behaviors over time. For many years, the archaeological record of early modern humans was interpreted as supporting a rapid "creative explosion" of new technologies and behaviors that first appeared about 40,000 to 50,000 years ago. This interpretation was based in part on the first appearance of modern behaviors in the European archaeological record and did not take into account changes happening elsewhere. In recent decades, archaeological research from Africa has suggested that many of these behaviors actually appeared tens of thousands of years earlier, and the emergence of modern human culture did not take place all at once but instead cumulatively over time in Africa (McBrearty and Brooks 2000; Henshilwood et al. 2002).

THE MODERN HUMAN ORIGINS DEBATE

Where, when, how, and why did anatomically modern humans evolve? The general trend in the fossil record shows that modern humans evolved from *Homo heidelbergensis*. Details of this evolutionary transition are the focus of the debate over modern human origins. The debate revolves around two key issues: the location of the transition and the nature of the transition (Relethford 2001). In terms of location, where (and when) did modern humans first appear? Did the initial transition take place in one part of the Old World, or did the transition involve the entire Old World? In terms of the nature of the transition, were modern humans a new species, or did they arise through anagenesis from an earlier species?

Where Did Modern Humans Begin?

During the Middle Pleistocene, *Homo heidelbergensis* was spread out over parts of Africa, Europe, and Asia. One or more of these populations evolved into

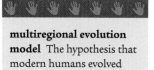

multiregional evolution model The hypothesis that modern humans evolved throughout the Old World as a single species after the first dispersion of *Homo erectus* out of Africa.

modern humans. Some have argued that the transition to modern humans was a worldwide phenomenon; others have argued that modern humans originated in Africa. According to the **multiregional evolution model,** human evolution over that past 2 million years took place within a single evolving lineage, from *H. erectus,* to *H. heidelbergensis,* to *H. sapiens.* According to some proponents of this model, modern human anatomy did not appear in any single place, but instead took place piecemeal across the Old World, with some changes occurring in different places at different times, and with modern humans eventually arising through the mixing of these changes through gene flow (Wolpoff et al. 1994).

The alternative to a worldwide transition to modern humans is the hypothesis of an African origin. In this view, modern human anatomy appeared *first* in Africa and then spread across the Old World. This view has been supported by both fossil and genetic evidence.

The Fossil Evidence   The question of *where* modern humans first appeared is related to the question of *when* modern humans first appeared. We need to look to see when modern humans appear in different parts of the world. This is not always as easy as it sounds, as individual fossil specimens show variation and sometimes present a mix of modern and archaic features. Nonetheless, sufficient fossil evidence has accumulated to support the idea of an initial African origin. As noted earlier in the chapter, we see the first examples of anatomically modern humans in Africa between about 200,000 and 100,000 years ago, a time when no modern humans are present elsewhere in the world. We do not see any evidence of modern humans outside of Africa until about 90,000 years ago in the Middle East, 50,000 years ago in Australia, and less than 40,000 years ago in Europe. The greater antiquity of modern humans in Africa is best explained by an initial African origin, followed by the spread of modern human populations and genes throughout the Old World later in time.

The Genetic Evidence   In addition to the fossil evidence, we can make inferences about the origin of modern humans from information on genetic variation in living populations. We observe patterns of genetic variation in the present day and work backwards in time, asking what models of evolutionary change could have produced the patterns of variation that we see. Whereas with fossils we work from the past to the present, genetic studies start with the present in an effort to reconstruct the past.

One way of reconstructing the past is to use DNA sequences from living people to make inferences about their **most recent common ancestor (MRCA).** In essence, we use genetic data to trace common ancestry. These methods use DNA sequences that do not recombine, such as mitochondrial DNA, which is inherited only through the mother's line. Consider your relationship with a sibling. Assuming your sibling and you have the same mother, your mother is the MRCA for mitochondrial DNA for you and your sibling. Now consider your relationship with your first cousin. You have to go back an additional generation (your mother's mother) for the MRCA for you,

most recent common ancestor (MRCA) The most recent individual from which a set of organisms are descended. MRCAs are estimated from genetic data and are different for different loci.

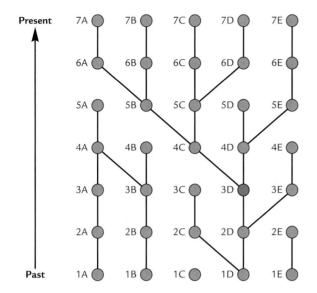

Present

7A	7B	7C	7D	7E
6A	6B	6C	6D	6E
5A	5B	5C	5D	5E
4A	4B	4C	4D	4E
3A	3B	3C	3D	3E
2A	2B	2C	2D	2E

Past 1A 1B 1C 1D 1E

FIGURE 13.13

Example of a gene tree. This tree represents the inheritance of mitochondrial DNA over seven generations. Only females are shown, and each dot represents a different woman. Going from the past forward, some women left more female descendants than others. For example, in the first generation, woman 1A had one daughter (2A) and woman 1D had two daughters (2C and 2D). If we start at the present and work backwards, we can identify common ancestors. For example, the most recent common ancestor of woman 7A and 7B is two generations earlier—woman 5B. Likewise, the most recent common ancestor of woman 7C and 7D is woman 5C. The most recent common ancestor of *all* women in the present-day generation is woman 3D (marked in red). Gene tree analysis can estimate when and where the most recent common ancestor lived based on comparing their DNA sequences.

your sibling, and your first cousin. Mathematically, it is a certainty that any set of people will have an MRCA for a given gene or DNA sequence (see Figure 13.13 for an example). Genetic analysis can be used to estimate when and where the MRCA for a group of people lived. These estimates are obtained from mitochondrial DNA, Y-chromosome DNA, or small nuclear DNA sequences that are not affected by recombination.

Any group of people has a specific MRCA for a particular DNA sequence. Consider, for example, your anthropology class. If we could trace back everyone's ancestry, we would find a number of ancestors in the past that everyone in the class had in common. Genetic data can be used to estimate when and where the most recent of these ancestors lived. This raises an interesting question: Who was the MRCA of all of humanity? We can address this question by examining DNA sequences from a representative sample of humanity. In essence, DNA sequences are used to build a "gene tree" of relationships that shows the evolutionary history of that particular DNA sequence.

Gene tree analysis was first applied to mitochondrial DNA sequences from around the world. The gene tree produced showed two major clusters of related individuals. One cluster consisted solely of people of African ancestry, and the other cluster consisted of people who had different ancestries, both African and non-African. Because both clusters contained individuals of African ancestry, the MRCA for mitochondrial DNA was therefore African. By considering the mutation rate of the mitochondrial DNA segment, researchers were able to estimate when this common ancestor lived, which was about 200,000 years ago (Cann et al. 1987; Vigilant et al. 1991; Penny et al. 1995). The location of this MRCA matched the fossil evidence, thus providing support for African origin. Gene tree analysis has also been applied to a number of different DNA sequences, including Y-chromosome DNA and other nuclear DNA. The problem with gene tree analysis is that each gene or

DNA sequence may have a different evolutionary history, and the only way we can get at information about the history of a population carrying these genes is to look at a number of them. These studies (Takahata et al. 2001; Templeton 2005) show that most, although not all, gene trees have African roots, supporting the initial African origin of modern humans.

Replacement or Assimilation?

What happened when modern humans expanding out of Africa met other populations? Did they interbreed, or were they too genetically different to do so?

There are two commonly held models of how modern humans spread following their initial origin in Africa. According to the **African replacement model,** modern humans emerged as a new species in Africa, splitting off from *H. heidelbergensis* roughly 200,000 years ago. Some populations began leaving Africa by 100,000 years ago and spread throughout the Old World, replacing preexisting human populations outside of Africa (Cann et al. 1987). In this model, any humans outside of Africa (such as the Neandertals in Europe) became extinct and are not part of the ancestry of living humans (Figure 13.14).

An alternative view is the **assimilation model,** which proposes that the initial change to modern humans took place in Africa, as in the African replacement model, but that these changes then spread to other populations outside of Africa through gene flow (Eswaran 2002; Smith 2002). The genes of the non-African populations were assimilated into the gene pool of the expanding modern human population rather than being replaced. Another way of looking at the difference between the African replacement model and the assimilation model is to consider the two models in terms of the ancestry of living humans (Relethford 2003). Where did our ancestors live 200,000

African replacement model The hypothesis that modern humans evolved as a new species in Africa 200,000 years ago and then spread throughout the Old World, replacing preexisting human populations.

assimilation model The hypothesis that modern human anatomy arose first in Africa as a change within a species and then spread through gene flow to populations outside of Africa. The gene pool of the non-African populations was thus assimilated into an expanding population of modern humans out of Africa.

FIGURE 13.14

The African replacement model. Modern humans (*Homo sapiens*) arose as a new species in Africa about 200,000 years ago. This species then spread out across the Old World, replacing other species, such as *Homo heidelbergensis* and *Homo erectus,* outside of Africa.

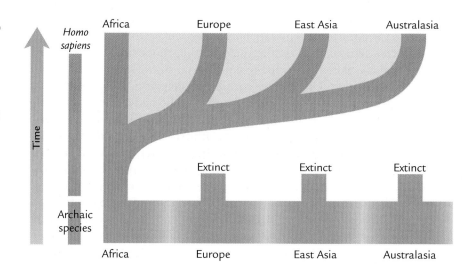

years ago? In the African replacement model, they *all* lived in Africa. In the assimilation model, many lived in Africa, but not all. What is the evidence for these two models?

The Fossil Evidence   The assimilation model predicts some ancestry from populations outside of Africa, which would lead to a pattern of **regional continuity** in the fossil record—the appearance of similar traits within the same geographic region over time. For example, some humans, past and present, have a particular dental trait known as shovel-shaped incisors, which have a ridge on the outer margins of the incisor teeth. Although this trait is found across the world today, it is found most frequently in both living *and* ancient populations in East Asia. The fact that this trait is most common throughout time in the same geographic region suggests some genetic contribution over time; that is, earlier hominin populations contributed some of their genes to living Asian populations. Another example is the high angle of the nose, a trait found frequently in both European Neandertals and living Europeans. Even though gene flow will reduce the frequency of regional differences, such that some regional traits will be lost over time, others will persist because of genetic drift and selection (Wolpoff and Caspari 1997; Relethford 2001).

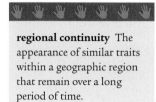

regional continuity The appearance of similar traits within a geographic region that remain over a long period of time.

The regional continuity of traits is perhaps best explained by the genetic continuity over time predicted by the assimilation model. The presence of regional continuity is difficult to explain under the African replacement model because it would require traits to reappear independently. There is debate over which traits, if any, show continuity and in which regions. Many anthropologists have argued that the evidence for continuity is strong in the fossil records of East Asia and Australasia (e.g., Hawks et al. 2000; Wolpoff et al. 2001). Others (e.g., Lahr 1996) find little evidence of regional continuity and argue further that the few indications of continuity can be explained by common evolutionary trends.

The issue of continuity is more complicated in Europe, where the coexistence of Neandertal and modern human populations for perhaps several thousand years, followed by the disappearance of the Neandertals, has often been considered evidence of replacement. This pattern, combined with the distinct morphology of the Neandertals, has led some anthropologists to support the idea that Neandertals were a separate species that became extinct, which supports the replacement model. Not everyone agrees, and some suggest that there is fossil evidence for regional continuity in Europe. One example is the skeleton of a 4-year-old child from 25,000 years ago that was found at the Lagar Velho site in Portugal. Although the child is considered an anatomically modern human, the cranium shows a mix of modern and Neandertal characteristics, and the postcranial skeleton shows Neandertal features (Duarte et al. 1999). This find may represent an example of Neandertal ancestry in modern humans that came about when the two populations encountered each other in Western Europe (Trinkaus and Zilhão 2002). Further evidence of Neandertal ancestry in modern humans comes from Trinkaus's (2007) analysis of a number of early modern human fossils in Europe; he found that these modern human fossils show a number of characteristic Neandertal traits, a pattern best explained by the moderns having some Neandertal ancestry. Wolpoff (1999) found similar results and noted that the frequency of such Neandertal traits declined over time, which would happen if Neandertals were absorbed into a larger gene pool of modern humans. Thus, the Neandertals might have become extinct through assimilation, and not replacement (Smith et al. 2005).

Genetic Evidence of Interbreeding with Neandertals   As noted earlier, data on genetic variation in modern human populations shows that many gene trees reflect a recent African origin. However, some gene trees point to non-African ancestors further back in time, which is consistent with the idea that there has been some mixture with other populations as modern humans expanded out of Africa. Although suggestive, the most compelling genetic evidence to date comes from ancient DNA analysis, specifically the sequencing of the Neandertal nuclear genome.

The Neandertal genome has been compared with the genomes of several living humans living in different parts of the world. The vast size of a genome allows statistical analysis of genetic similarity on a massive scale. One surprising result was that living Europeans and Asians are more similar to Neandertals than are Africans (Green et al. 2010). If the Neandertals were a separate line that became extinct with no mixture, then we would expect that *all* human populations would be equally distant from the Neandertals, as the replacement model has the Neandertals splitting off *before* modern humans evolved and left Africa. The closer similarity of Europeans and Asians to Neandertals suggests instead that there was some degree of interbreeding with Neandertals *after* some modern humans left Africa.

Where and when did this interbreeding take place? It would have to be somewhere when both Neandertals and modern humans were in the same place at the same time. As discussed in Chapter 13, there are two possible examples of such coexistence—the Middle East as early as 70,000 years ago, and Europe as early as 40,000 years ago. The Neandertal DNA evidence supports the first of these alternatives. If there were significant interbreeding resulting from contact in Europe, then Neandertal DNA would be more similar to living Europeans than to living Asians, which is not what we see. Instead, the fact that Neandertal DNA is equally similar to living Europeans and living Asians suggests that the contact took place before modern humans leaving Africa dispersed across Europe and Asia, which suggests that the mixture took place in the Middle East (Figure 13.15).

Given that there was interbreeding of modern humans and Neandertals, the next question is how much of our ancestry is from the Neandertals. Based on comparisons of the genomes of Neandertals and modern humans, Green et al. (2010) developed methods of estimating this quantity and conclude that between 1 and 4 percent of the ancestry of living Europeans and Asians is from the Neandertals. There has not been sufficient gene flow into Africa to produce any detectable sign of Neandertal ancestry in living Africans.

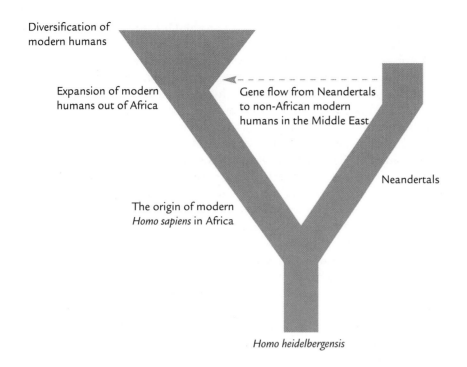

Diversification of modern humans

Expansion of modern humans out of Africa

Gene flow from Neandertals to non-African modern humans in the Middle East.

Neandertals

The origin of modern *Homo sapiens* in Africa

Homo heidelbergensis

FIGURE 13.15

A possible model explaining the genetic relationship of Neandertals and living humans. The species *Homo heidelbergensis* gives rise to both *Homo sapiens* and the Neandertals. Later in time, modern human populations expand out of Africa, at which point there is gene flow from Neandertals into the modern human gene pool during a time when both groups were living in the Middle East. Because this interbreeding took place after the expansion out of Africa but before modern humans spread further into Europe and Eastern Asia, all of these non-African populations are equally related to Neandertals.

These results have significant evolutionary implications. Regardless of whether one considers Neandertals a separate species or not, there is strong evidence of some mixture (not uncommon among mammalian species, showing again that the strict definition of species as reproductively isolated groups does not always work). Although 1 to 4 percent Neandertal ancestry is not a large amount, it is not a trivial amount. These results suggest that *complete* replacement of earlier human populations outside of Africa did not happen, and some degree of assimilation with Neandertals occurred, at least once, in the Middle East.

The Denisovans   Ancient DNA analysis has helped us unravel the evolutionary relationships between modern humans and Neandertals. In 2010, ancient DNA analysis also gave us a glimpse into a previously unknown line of archaic humans. This ancient DNA comes from Denisova Cave in southern Siberia. In addition to Upper Paleolithic tools, excavations at this site have uncovered a human molar tooth and finger bone dating between 50,000 and 30,000 years ago. Normally, not a lot can be told from such fragmentary remains, but in this case, preservation was excellent and allowed the DNA genome to be sequenced from the finger bone. This sequence is more closely related to Neandertals than to modern humans, but is still different enough that it cannot be considered a Neandertal, but rather a member of a group that split from the Neandertals about 200,000 years ago. This evolutionary line has been named after the cave site, and is referred to as the "Denisovans." (Reich et al. 2010).

The genetic comparisons show that the Denisovans split from the Neandertals before the contact between Neandertals and modern humans. The Denisovans did not go extinct; the genetic data show that although there was no interbreeding of Denisovans and most Eurasian populations, there *is* evidence of Denisovan ancestry among living Melanesians (a group of living humans that lives in the Pacific Ocean regions to the northeast and east of Australia for the last 45,000 years). Here, about 5 percent of the ancestry of living Melanesians is from the Denisovans. The connection between tropical Melanesians and the inhabitants of Denisova Cave might seem strange, but likely reflects a process where the Denisovans were once widespread across much of Eastern Asia, including areas where the ancestors of Melanesians lived. Today, we see only a fraction of this history surviving in Melanesia, just as earlier history of Neandertal contact survives in human populations outside of Africa (Bustamante and Henn 2010; Reich et al. 2010; Gibbons 2011).

Given the information on Neandertal and Denisovan DNA, we see evidence that although most of our ancestry is from Africa, there have been cases of interbreeding. Some human populations have ancestry from Neandertals (Europeans and Asians), some have ancestry from *both* Neandertals and Denisovans (Melanesia), and some have no ancestry from either ancient population (Africa). Further ancient DNA studies might show us even more examples of small levels of interbreeding with different archaic populations. If confirmed, modern human origins might best described as a process of dispersion out of Africa with bits and pieces of interbreeding taking place in different times and places.

Why Did Modern Humans Evolve?

The different models for the origin of modern humans are fascinating, as are debates over whether Neandertals could interbreed with modern humans. Despite all of these debates, however, we all agree on the basic fact that only modern humans live on our planet today, and there are no archaic humans. In addition to explaining the nature of the transition from archaic to modern anatomy, we must ask ourselves *why* this transition occurred. Was this an example of genetic drift, or did modern humans have an evolutionary advantage? If the latter, then what was this advantage?

Modern humans differ from earlier humans in several features, including a more well rounded skull, smaller brow ridges, and a prominent chin. It is also clear that the changes from archaic to modern humans were larger than changes that took place beforehand in human evolution (Trinkaus 2006; Lieberman 2008). Whereas the change from *H. erectus* to *H. heidelbergensis* was primarily one of an increase in both brain and facial size, the transition to *H. sapiens* involved a more complex set of anatomical changes (Lieberman 2008). What could have caused these later changes?

As with ideas on the origin of bipedalism (Chapter 10) and the origin of increased brain size (Chapter 11), a number of explanations have been offered for the origin of modern human craniofacial anatomy, and these are not mutually exclusive. Lieberman (2008) reviews five basic explanations.

First is the hypothesis that changes in the cranium followed from an increase in size in the temporal lobe of the brain, which was selected for due to increased cognitive ability. Second is the hypothesis that the increase in cooked food changed the nature of selection for the anatomy of chewing, resulting in changes in craniofacial shape. A third hypothesis proposes that anatomical changes, particularly a reduction in facial size, resulted from the need for better stabilization of the head during endurance running. The fourth suggestion involves changes in craniofacial anatomy that would accompany a shortened pharynx, making for more efficient breathing in hot and arid environments. A fifth idea, which has long been popular among anthropologists, is that craniofacial changes resulted from selection for improved vocal language skills. Lieberman notes that all of these models need further testing, particularly of key anatomical assumptions, but suggests that some combination of these forces was probably responsible for selection for modern human anatomy.

RECENT BIOLOGICAL AND CULTURAL EVOLUTION IN *HOMO SAPIENS*

Human evolution did not end with the origin of modern *Homo sapiens*. Biologically, we have continued to change in subtle ways even over the past 10,000–20,000 years or so. Cranial capacity has declined somewhat (Henneberg 1988; Ruff et al. 1997), probably a reflection of a general decrease in size and ruggedness. Teeth have also become somewhat smaller (Brace et al. 1987), most likely reflecting the changing costs and benefits of larger teeth.

Within the very recent past (10,000–15,000 years), many changes in human evolution have been cultural. One major change in human existence—the invention of agriculture—began roughly 12,000 years ago. Up to this point, humans had been exclusively hunters and gatherers. Agriculture changed the entire ecological equation for human beings. Humans began manipulating the environment to increase the availability of food through the domestication of plants and animals. Many explanations are offered as to why agriculture developed, including that it was a solution to the increased population size that had resulted from more efficient hunting and gathering. In any case, the effects of agriculture were and continue to be quite dramatic—the human population grew and continues to do so today (see Chapter 17).

Agriculture did not have a single origin but rather developed independently in many parts of both the Old World and the New World. Over the next several thousand years, the use of agriculture became increasingly dominant around the world (Figure 13.16). Today there are very few hunters and gatherers left. Our current focus on agriculture often blinds us to the reality that we have changed so much culturally in so short a time. Biologically, we are still hunters and gatherers.

Cultural change continued at an even faster rate following the origin of agriculture and rapid population growth. Cities and state-level societies

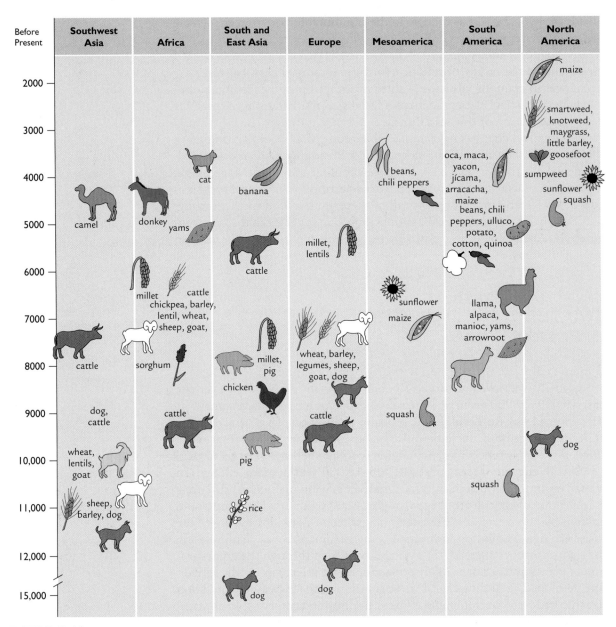

FIGURE 13.16

Chronological outline of the origins of domestication and agriculture. (From *Human Antiquity: An Introduction to Physical Anthropology and Archaeology,* 4th ed., by Kenneth Feder and Michael Park, Fig. 14.1. Copyright © 2001 by Mayfield Publishing Company. Reprinted by permission of The McGraw-Hill Companies.)

developed. Exploration brought the inhabitants of the Old World and the New World back into contact, and industrialization spread rapidly. Today, only 12,000 years after the time our ancestors survived by hunting and gathering, we are able to explore and live in every environment on earth and beyond (Figure 13.17). However one feels about the rapid cultural changes of *H. sapiens,* these changes can be viewed as a continuation of the basic adaptations of culture and learning that have been apparent for at least the past 2.5 million years of human evolution.

FIGURE 13.17

Travel into outer space represents our species' continuing exploration and utilization of new environments.

Summary

Among other features, anatomically modern *Homo sapiens* is characterized by a higher, more well-rounded skull and a smaller face than most archaics and by the presence of a noticeable chin. Modern humans appeared first 200,000 years ago in Africa and by about 90,000 years ago in the Middle East. By 50,000 years ago, the culture of *H. sapiens* had begun to change rapidly; the use of more sophisticated stone tools (especially blade tools) and bone tools spread, burials of the dead became more elaborate, and art appeared. Modern humans had colonized Australia by 60,000 years ago and the New World by at least 15,000 years ago.

Different models have been proposed to explain the origin of modern humans. The African replacement model proposes that modern humans arose as a new species around 200,000 years ago in Africa and then spread across the Old World, replacing preexisting archaic humans. The assimilation model proposes that modern human anatomy did appear first in Africa, but that there was genetic mixing with the expanding African population and populations outside of Africa. Current fossil and genetic evidence appears to better support the assimilation model, particularly given strong evidence from ancient DNA analysis that living Europeans and Asians have 1 to 4 percent Neandertal ancestry.

Human evolution did not end after the initial appearance of modern humans. Although there have been some biological changes during our recent past, most of our species' evolution over the past 10,000 years has been cultural. Perhaps the single most important event was the development of agriculture, which changed our entire way of life. Predicting the specifics of future human evolution is problematic, but our future will no doubt involve more and more cultural change, which occurs at a far greater rate than biological evolution. This does not mean that biological evolution has stopped; rather, our fate is becoming increasingly affected by cultural change.

Supplemental Readings

Morwood, M., and P. van Oosterzee. 2007. *A New Human: The Startling Discovery and Strange Story of the "Hobbits" of Flores, Indonesia*. New York: HarperCollins. An interesting popular account of the discovery and debate over the "Hobbit."

Stringer, C., and R. McKie. 1996. *African Exodus: The Origins of Modern Humanity*. New York: Henry Holt.

Wolpoff, M. H., and R. Caspari. 1997. *Race and Human Evolution*. New York: Simon and Schuster. These two books are somewhat dated, but otherwise excellent reviews of the modern human origins debate from different perspectives.

OUR DIVERSITY

How and why are human beings similar to and different from each other? We all encounter biological variation (diversity) every day of our lives. Some people are taller than others are or have rounder heads or lighter skin color. Additional diversity exists in many genetic traits that are not visible to the naked eye, such as blood groups and DNA sequences. Biological anthropologists are interested in describing and explaining such variation, particularly in terms of the recent evolution of our species. Many people consider human biological variation from the perspective of the classification of human races. Chapter 14 examines the history and use of the biological race concept for describing human variation and presents an evolutionary alternative to analyzing variation. Chapter 15 explores a number of case studies of recent human microevolution, including studies of genetics and population history and of recent natural selection. Chapter 16 examines biological diversity from the perspective of biocultural adaptations. Chapter 17 concludes with an examination of the biological impact of our species' rapid cultural changes over the past 12,000 years, since the origin of agriculture.

The human species exhibits genetic and physical variation. Biological anthropologists study variation within and between populations from an evolutionary perspective.

Race and Human Variation

Every day, we encounter human biological diversity in physical characteristics such as skin color, hair color, and hair form (Figure 14.1), but these observable variations are only the tip of the iceberg. Variation also exists in less easily observed characteristics such as teeth and fingerprints. Still more variation exists at the molecular level, which is not directly visible to the naked eye.

One of the tasks of biological anthropology is to make sense out of this variation. It should be no surprise by this point in the book that we take an evolutionary approach to human variation, seeking to explain the patterns of similarities and differences that we see in terms of the interaction of the evolutionary forces. What we see in the world today is a reflection of what happened in the past, so biological variation in any species (including humans) is best understood in terms of evolutionary history. As recounted in the previous chapter, modern humans arose in Africa about 200,000 years ago, later dispersing across the Old World some 70,000 years or so ago. In some places, there was interbreeding with earlier human populations, such as the Neandertals. This history is the backdrop against which we need to view contemporary human variation. Specifically, we want to know how much of modern human variation reflects our past history of migrations and changing population size, and how much reflects past adaptation to different environments. We also need to consider the effects of the continuing evolution of our species, as human evolution did not end with the advent of modern humans.

This chapter and the ones that follow it provide views into the evolution of human biological variation. For the moment, we need to contrast this evolutionary view on human variation with a more common, less precise approach to human variation—race. Many of us typically describe human variation in terms of the race concept, a concept that many anthropologists and geneticists find imprecise. Race is used for classification, both in everyday use as well as in medicine and forensics. Race is used to describe biological characteristics but is also used in many cases to ascribe aspects of human behavior and social status. Although much of the anthropological world conducts research on human variation, the term "race" is seldom used. How can there be such a gap between the scientific study of human variation and some everyday conceptions? What exactly is race, and why have a number of researchers abandoned the concept? In order to answer these questions,

FIGURE 14.1

Human biological variation in external physical traits. Human beings vary considerably in terms of skin color, hair color, and some craniofacial measures.

it is necessary to examine the concept of biological race and its history, and examine how well the concept helps us understand the nature and causes of human variation.

THE BIOLOGICAL RACE CONCEPT

What is race? One of the major problems with using race as a focus of analysis is that the term has multiple definitions, and these definitions are not always in agreement (Graves 2001). **Race** has been used to refer to everything from skin color (the "white" race), to nationality (the "Japanese" race), to religion (the "Jewish" race). In everyday terms, there is an unfortunate tendency to use "race" to refer to everything from a biological unit, to an ethnic group, to one's nationality. When two of us talk about "race," how do we know we are talking about the same thing?

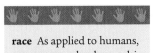

race As applied to humans, a vague term that has multiple meanings, both cultural and biological, referring to group membership.

Biological and Cultural Definitions of Race

Problems arise because the two different approaches to race—cultural and biological—do not always match up or even overlap with each other. In many state and federal government reports, race refers to some aspect of nationality or ethnic identity that may not connect directly to any specific biological population. For example, "black" refers to someone with African or African American ancestry, which in turn could include individuals who also have some European ancestry, and in some cases more European than African ancestry (see Chapter 15). "Hispanic" refers to Spanish speakers but actually encompasses a wide variety of people from Mexicans to Bolivians. Such classifications have their use, particularly in defining social groups that have suffered inequities, but they should not be construed as necessarily reflecting biological reality. We must understand the context to know whether someone is talking about a cultural or a biological definition of race. For our purposes, the question is whether the biological meaning of race has value in describing human variation.

Biological Race   Historically, there have been a number of different definitions of **biological race** (Feldman et al. 2003). A taxonomic definition equates race with the concept of a subspecies, a division of a species into distinct and distinguishable types. Subspecies rank is usually given to sets of populations that appear to represent a species in the early stages leading to speciation, which can form very distinct populations. The subspecies approach does not work for humans because there are no clearly distinct types of humanity (Graves 2001). There is generally less genetic variation within the human species relative to species such as chimpanzees, and virtually all scientists agree that living humans belong to a single subspecies. Humans are widespread geographically and are constantly moving across population boundaries. Although human variation does exist, it does not fall neatly into biologically discrete groups. Taxonomic race (subspecies) works fine with some species but not with humans.

Geography and Biological Race   Another approach to biological race is based on geography—identifying clusters of populations similar to each other that differ from other clusters in terms of allele frequencies and physical characteristics. This approach essentially equates geographic regions, such as sub-Saharan Africa, East Asia, or Polynesia, with different races. The focus here is on distinguishing distinct groups of populations that are genetically similar. A typical definition of biological race based on geography is "a division of a species that differs from other divisions by the frequency with which certain hereditary traits appear among its members" (Brues 1977:1). Although scientists agree that the subspecies view of race does not apply to humans, they are more mixed on the utility of geographic races.

A Brief History of the Race Concept

In order to understand how the race concept has been used to describe human biological variation, it is useful to examine the historical roots of the concept of race.

Early Views   In Chapter 1, you read about the history of the development of evolutionary thought, a discussion which started with the impact of ancient Greek philosophy on how people viewed the natural world as unchanging. These ideas dealt with variation, the focus of race. Greek philosophers such as Plato (427?–347 B.C.E.; B.C.E. means "Before Common Era," an alternative to "B.C." for historical dates used across the world). Plato viewed the real world as an imperfect representation of an ideal world. In his view, variation was a nuisance and the goal of philosophers was to see beyond variations in

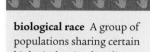

biological race A group of populations sharing certain biological traits that distinguish them from other groups of populations. In practice, the biological concept of race has been difficult to apply to human populations.

order to perceive the ideal "type." Thus, Plato would view human variation as we perceive it of less interest than the abstraction of the ideal image of a human (Kennedy 1976). This may sound rather abstract, but such ideas had a substantial and lasting influence on how Western civilization viewed race. Here, the search for races was directed in large part by the idea that we should minimize consideration of variation and focus instead on the "type," which would provide a valid description of the general tendencies of the group. This happens, for example, when people rely on stereotypes—the emphasis is on a type, and not on variation within the group. The problem here is that an emphasis on looking for types (races in this case) makes the assumption that there are a fixed number of types to begin with. As we shall see, this approach does not fit certain aspects of human biological variation.

Another Greek philosopher who made a lasting impact was Plato's student, Aristotle (384–322 BCE), who focused on arranging the types of living creatures in a "ladder of life" that ranked living organisms by different criteria, such as complexity. Aristotle placed plants at the bottom of this ladder and humans at the top, showing his bias that the natural order led to humans being on the top (Kennedy 1976). Of course, viewing the world in this manner, combined with the idea that there exists a fixed number of different types of humans, leads to the idea that the different types of humans (races) can be themselves ranked. Needless to say, adherence to such views have led to considerable human suffering at the hands of those who view one group of humans as inherently superior to another.

Racial Classifications   As discussed in Chapter 1, in the eighteenth century Linnaeus organized species into a classification system that was very much influenced by the ideas of the ancient Greeks, with an emphasis on the concept of "type" (Kennedy 1976). In the second edition of his compilation of species, Linnaeus added four subdivisions of humanity, which he called "varieties" but are equivalent to later uses of "race." Linnaeus's four groups were based primarily on geography and skin color—Europeans, Africans, Asians, and Americans (the last referring to Native Americans). Linnaeus also attributed different personality traits to each group based on cultural stereotypes, such as Europeans being regulated by laws while Americans are regulated by custom (Kennedy 1976; Marks 1995). As with the ancient Greeks, Linnaeus focused on typological ideas and did not emphasize the role of variation within groups.

An alternative approach was taken by the French naturalist Georges-Louis Leclerc, Comte de Buffon (1708–1788). Although Buffon discussed human variation in terms of race, his approach was different from that of Linnaeus. Buffon did not try to classify humans into a set number of discrete races but instead took a more descriptive approach to human variation; rather than trying to place a particular population into a fixed classification of races, he merely identified them by their place of origin, such as Japanese or Egyptians. He recognized the arbitrary nature of trying to delineate races and rejected classification as the goal of studying human variation (Marks 1995; Anemone 2011).

TABLE 14.1	Some Different Racial Classification Schemes				
Linnaeus (1740)	*Blumenbach (1781)*	*Cuvier (1790)*	*Boyd (1950)*	*Coon (1962)*	*Garn (1965)*
African	American Indian	Caucasoid	American Indian	Australoid	African
American	Caucasoid	Mongoloid	African	Capoid	Amerindian
Asian	Ethiopian	Negroid	Australoid	Caucasoid	Asiatic
European	Malay		Asiatic	Congoid	Australian
	Mongoloid		Early European	Mongoloid	European
			(Basque)		Indian
			European		Melanesia-Papuan
					Micronesian
					Polynesian

Source: Boyd (1950), Coon (1962), Garn (1965), Marks (1995), Molnar (2006).

Although Buffon's approach is more similar to that used by anthropologists today, the typological approach favored by Linnaeus had greater impact historically, and scholars over the next two centuries spent considerable time debating the number of human races and the best way to distinguish among them. This effort did not produce any real consensus, as different researchers came up with different numbers of races. Table 14.1 shows a sample of the different approaches to human race that have developed in the last several centuries. Here, the number of human races ranges from 3 to 9. Although there is some agreement among these classifications in that they all recognize large continental regions such as Africa, Asia, and Europe, there is disagreement over the composition of these groups as well as the identity of other groups. For example, Boyd's classification splits Europeans into two races, but indentifies a single African race. On the other hand, Coon's classification advocates one European race but two African races (Capoid and Congoid). Some researchers classify Native Americans as a separate race, while others include them in an Asian race. It should be clear from even the few examples shown in Table 14.1 that the race concept is arbitrary, and one can choose to recognize a varying number of races.

Rethinking the Race Concept It is important to remember that the race concept developed out of pre-Darwinian ideas of a static world. Human variation was looked at from the perspective of the ideal types of ancient Greek philosophy and later integrated with biblical views of creation (see, for example, Box 14.1). Human races were considered fixed and unchanging over time, and variation was of little consequence. Of course, this view began to change with Darwin's observations about the central importance of variation in the natural world. Rather than follow the ancient Greek ideas about ignoring variation, the focus shifted to stress the analysis of variation. In the twentieth century, the development of evolutionary theory resulted in a shift of biological studies away from such earlier views. By the

BOX 14.1

Monogenism and Polygenism

Before the development of modern evolutionary thought, the history of species was typically interpreted using a biblical framework. This is also true of speculations on the nature and origin of human races. Using the book of Genesis as a guide, humans were created once, and therefore all living humans are descended from Adam and Eve. Under this view, known as *monogenism* (= single origin), the differences among races were thought to have arisen from the effects of living in different environments, but all humans ultimately traced their ancestry back to a single creation event.

To some, however, there was simply not enough time for racial differences to have come about given the then-accepted young age of the earth (typically considered to be about 6,000 years old based on biblical genealogies). By the sixteenth century, an alternative view, known as *polygenism* (= many origins), developed that proposed different creation events for each race. This view was popular with those that saw huge differences between human groups, and

sometimes served as pseudo-scientific justification for differential treatment. However, polygenism ran counter to the biblical view in Genesis that stated a single origin. Advocates of polygenism argued that there had been other creations before Adam, and that these separate creations corresponded to different racial groups. Because this view ran counter to religious teachings, it was heretical, and several proponents of polygenism were jailed; two were burned at the stake. By the nineteenth century, some advocates of polygenism had attempted to provide scientific "proof," but these attempts obviously failed (Kennedy 1976; Anemone 2011). The rise of evolutionary theory and the rejection of a simplistic view of race and racial classification led to a demise of the monogenism–polygenism debate. We are still interested in the description of human biological variation and explaining the origins of such variation, but we now pursue these questions using an evolutionary, not a racial, model.

1950s, such new views had begun to influence anthropology, and biological anthropology continued to shift away from descriptive studies of human variation that emphasized racial classification to studies that incorporated evolutionary theory and explanation (Relethford 2010). As a consequence, the concept of race and racial classification was examined in detail. This reconsideration of race was also influenced by historical factors, such as the horrors of misuse of racial thinking during World War II and the Holocaust, as well as the rise of the Civil Rights Movement in the United States during the 1960s, which helped move people beyond simple stereotypes and racial rankings. Human biological variation was being looked at in new ways, and problems with a simplistic application of the biological race concept to humans emerged.

Problems with the Biological Race Concept

Many anthropologists argue that the biological race concept does not fit the observed pattern of human biological variation and that it is, at best, a crude description of that variation. It is not uncommon to hear people argue against this critique. After all, we can obviously see human variation all around us. We can easily identify people who have dark skin and those who have light skin. We can also easily identify people who have different facial features. Are not these observations evidence for the existence of human races?

It is important to remember that a criticism of the biological race concept is *not* a rejection of the obvious reality of human biological variation.

Nor do opponents of the race concept deny the fact that people in different parts of the world are more likely to be more biologically different from their neighbors. Human variation exists, and it is geographically structured. The argument has to do with the best way to describe this variation. The race concept is associated with the idea that there are discrete and easily identifiable groups of human populations, and proponents of this idea assume that our species can be categorized into races. If this is the case, then how many human races are there?

The Number of Races   As noted earlier, scientists attempting racial classification of humans have never agreed on how many races exist. For example, some have suggested that there are three human races: Europeans, Africans, and Asians (often referred to by the archaic terms "Caucasoid," "Negroid," and "Mongoloid," which are almost never used in scientific research today). But many populations do not fit neatly into one of these three basic categories. What about native Australians (aborigines)? As shown in Figure 14.2, these are dark-skinned people who frequently have curly or wavy (and, in some cases, blond) hair. On the basis of skin color, we might be tempted to label these people as African, but on the basis of hair shape, they might be considered a different race. Another approach is to place them into their own race—"Australoid."

As we travel around the world, we find more and more populations that do not fit a three- or four-race system. Consequently, some authors added more races to their lists, but over time there has never been any consensus on the number of human races. The fact that there has never been clear consensus illustrates that the race concept does not fit human biological variation very well.

The Nature of Continuous Variation   The failure to agree on the number of races is partly the result of trying to divide a continuous range of variation into a number of discrete units; the decision is often arbitrary. For example, consider human height. No one would deny that there is variation in human height; clearly, some people are shorter and some people are taller. The question is how best to describe this variation. If you asked a large number of adults to line up from shortest to tallest, you would see that height has a continuous distribution, ranging from one extreme to the other with virtually every value in between. Could you then divide this range up into a number of distinct groups? Yes, but any such division would be arbitrary. How many groups would you use? Three? Ten? Some other number? The decision would be arbitrary because there are no naturally occurring distinct groups.

Many of the traits that historically have been used to define human races suffer from the same problem of trying to subsume continuous variation into a small number of discrete groups. Human skin color is a good example. Our everyday language describing skin color implies discrete groups: "white," "brown," and "black." In reality, human skin color does *not* come in 3 or 5 or even 10 different shades. Instead, when we consider the full range

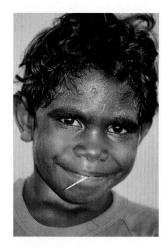

FIGURE 14.2

An Australian aborigine with dark skin and curly hair.

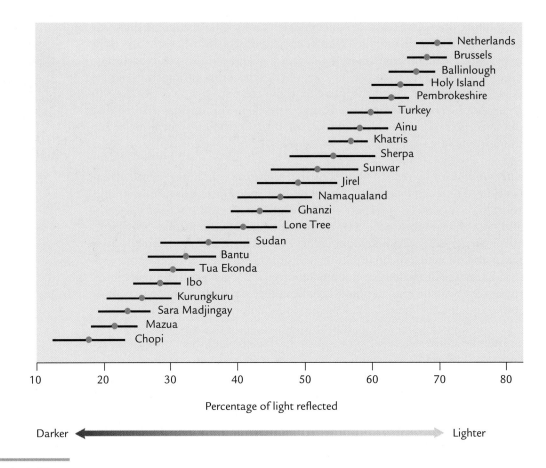

Percentage of light reflected

Darker ← ——————————————————————— → Lighter

FIGURE 14.3

Variation in skin color in 22 human populations (males). Skin color is measured using a device that tells the amount of light reflected back at a given wavelength. Dots indicate the mean skin reflectance measured at a wavelength of 685 nanometers; lines indicate one standard deviation on each side of the mean, an interval that includes 68 percent of the cases within each sample. Clearly, there is overlap between different populations, and there are no abrupt breaks in the distribution from dark to light. Human skin color does not come in a finite number of shades but varies continuously from darkest to lightest. (All data from published literature. Original references listed in Relethford 1997.)

of humanity, human skin color varies from the darkest to the lightest people without any breaks in the distribution (Figure 14.3).

We could acknowledge this arbitrariness of classification but still come up with some grouping based on geography. For one reason or another, we sometimes find it convenient to represent a range of variation in terms of a small number of discrete groups. Course grades are a good example. Instead of representing a student's course grade as a number between 0 and 100 percent, most schools divide this range into a number of discrete categories, such as "A," "B," "C," and so forth. Other schools use more categories (such as "B+"), but the principle is the same. Likewise, there might be times when it is convenient to refer to someone's height as "short," "medium," or "tall." When we refer to geographic groupings as races, aren't we doing the same thing?

Yes, but there is a vital difference. Because of the historical origin and development of the race concept, there is a tendency to consider races as naturally occurring discrete groups rather than definitional groups. This does not occur with the height example. Although variation in height is real, and you can crudely describe it in terms of height groups (short, medium, tall), you know that human height does not naturally cluster this way and that humans do not come in only three different heights. Again, the debate over the existence of human races is a debate not over the existence of human differences but instead over the best way to describe them—as discrete groups or as part of a range of variation.

Variation between and within Groups Even if we accept a definition of biological race that is synonymous with geographic region, the reality of most human variation is that the level of genetic variation is far greater within than between human populations. Racial classifications focus on differences between groups. This is apparent in the use of group stereotypes (e.g., "they are short" or "they have broad heads"). Such statements provide information about the average in a group but say nothing about variation within the group. For example, consider the statement that adult males in the United States tend to be taller than adult females in the United States. No one can argue with this basic fact regarding the average height of adult men and women. However, does it imply that all males are taller than all females? Of course not. There is variation within both sexes and a great deal of overlap.

A number of studies have quantified the relative amount of genetic variation within and between different groupings of humanity. We start by acknowledging that genetic variation exists within our species. The question is how this variation is partitioned. Imagine a species consisting of only two populations (Figure 14.4). We wish to examine genetic variation within and between the two populations. In terms of population genetics, genetic variation within populations refers to the relative numbers of different alleles. If all the alleles are the same within a population, then there is no genetic variation in that population. Genetic variation between populations refers to the differences in allele frequencies. If the two populations have the same allele frequency, there is no genetic variation between the populations. If everyone is genetically the same within each population but the two populations are genetically different from each other, then by definition there is no genetic variation within populations, and all of the genetic variation in the species exists between populations (case 1 in Figure 14.4). To put this numerically, we would say that the variation within populations is 0 percent and that the variation between populations is 100 percent. This scenario is consistent with the most extreme view of races—"they all look alike" (0 percent variation within populations) and "they look different from others" (100 percent variation between populations). Now, consider a completely different scenario in which there are genetic differences between individuals within each population, but the allele frequencies are the same in both populations (case 2 in Figure 14.4). Here, there is no difference between the two populations, and all of the genetic variation exists within populations. Numerically, this means that the variation within populations is 100 percent and the variation between populations is 0 percent.

Which pattern does human genetic variation look like? Anthropologists and geneticists have computed these percentages based on data from native populations in various large geographic regions of the world, such

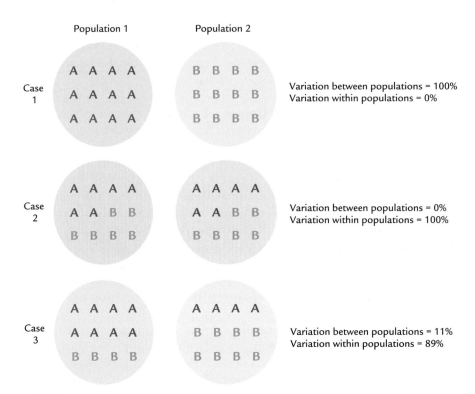

FIGURE 14.4

Three different examples showing how variation is partitioned between and within populations. The circles each enclose a population with a specific number of two alleles, *A* and *B*. In case 1, population 1 consists entirely of *A* alleles and population 2 consists entirely of *B* alleles. There is no variation *within* either population, but the two populations are completely different in terms of the frequencies of the *A* and *B* alleles. As such, 100 percent of the variation is *between* the populations and 0 percent is *within* populations. Case 2 shows the opposite pattern. The genetic composition of both populations is the same—50 percent *A* alleles and 50 percent *B* alleles. There is therefore no variation *between* the populations, and all of the variation occurs *within* populations. Case 3 shows a less extreme condition, where the frequency of the *A* allele is 8/12 = 0.67 in population 1 and 4/12 = 0.33 in population 2. There is variation *within* each population, and there is some variation *between* the populations. The actual partitioning of variation (11 percent between populations and 89 percent within populations) is of the magnitude seen among major geographic regions of humans (see text)—most genetic variation exists *within* populations. Both populations have *A* and *B* alleles but differ in their relative frequency. The percentage of variation within and between populations was computed using a measure known as F_{ST}, which relates allele frequencies to the proportion of variation between populations.

as sub-Saharan Africa, Europe, East Asia, and North America. Studies of blood groups and other genetic markers show that roughly 10 percent of the total variation in the human species exists between geographic regions, with the remaining 90 percent existing within geographic regions (Brown and Armelagos 2001; Relethford 2001). The same pattern has been found for DNA markers (Barbujani et al. 1997) and craniometric traits (Relethford 1994). Further, most of the variation within regions is due to variation within local populations (85 percent) and far less between local populations (5 percent) (Barbujani et al. 1997; Relethford 2002). Skin color, on the other hand, shows more variation between regions than within regions (Relethford 2002). The large difference in skin color is expected because it has been affected by natural selection in different parts of the world (see Chapter 15). Although skin color has been a primary means of racial classification, its global distribution is atypical; thus, one should not extrapolate from skin color variation to genetic variation on the whole.

Classification and Racial Identification   If the biological concept of race does not apply to humans, how is it that we can accurately identify people's ancestry from different parts of the world based on their genetic or physical makeup? Or, to quote the title of a paper by forensic anthropologist Norman Sauer (1992), "If races don't exist, why are forensic anthropologists so good at identifying them?" Some have argued that even though the concept of subspecies does not fit human variation, the presence of clear geographic differences in many traits means that the geographic race concept, while limited and somewhat arbitrary, does have some utility. In many cases, forensic studies of the human skeleton are able to correctly assign individuals to a given geographic region, such as Europe or Africa, based on a combination of measurements (e.g., Gill 1998). Recent studies of DNA markers have also shown high accuracy in classification by geographic region (Rosenberg et al. 2002; Bamshad et al. 2003). Because we can accurately classify individuals according to different geographic regions, one could argue that these regions must be equivalent to different geographic races.

Does this mean that geographic races are real in the sense of being distinct groups? Although the ability to classify individuals accurately by region is strong in some studies, this does not mean that the race concept, with its focus on discrete groupings of humanity, is a logical consequence of these studies. As Sauer (1992) notes, the ability to "identify a person as having ancestors from, say, Northern Europe, does not identify a biological race of Northern Europeans" (p. 110). The ability to place an individual within a range of variation does not mean that this variation is best represented by discrete groups.

An example of this principle is provided by Relethford's (2009) analysis of cranial differences for human populations from six geographic regions: sub-Saharan Africa, Europe, East Asia, Australasia, Polynesia, and the New World (Native Americans). Based on 57 different cranial measures, a computer program was able to classify accurately individual specimens into their correct geographic region 97 percent of the time. To many, this high level of accuracy would imply that these six geographic regions correspond to six different races. However, these groupings can be changed, and the level of classification accuracy remains the same. For example, when the New World sample was split into two groups (North America and South America), the classification accuracy for the seven "races" was still 97 percent. The same occurred with other alternative numbers of races, ranging from five to eight. All produced the same accuracy. If using different numbers of geographically defined races all produce the same accuracy in classification, then why should one number be preferred over another? As noted earlier, the number of races is a subjective decision. What the cranial analyses do show us is that human variation is largely structured geographically; populations that are far from each other tend, on average, to be more different. This variation is noticeable, but it does not correspond to the race concept, which implies something else—that populational differences can be assigned to discrete and discontinuous races.

What Use Is the Biological Race Concept?   Those who argue both for and against the validity of geographic races agree on the geographic pattern of human biological variation. Instead, the debate is over whether race is a particularly useful way of describing this variation. If you choose to use "race" as a unit of analysis, you have to remember that the definition (and number) of races is arbitrary and somewhat subjective. We use categories of classification all the time, such as socioeconomic status, but as convenient labels for describing continuous variation (in the case of socioeconomic status, no one thinks that we have only three distinct levels—lower, middle, and upper class; we realize that there is variation within these groups and the boundaries between them are arbitrary).

However, what is the harm in using racial categories as long as we acknowledge their limitations? Some would argue that the very term *race* has so many meanings and such heavy historical baggage that its use tends to confuse more than to clarify, and that we should perhaps use different terms. In any case, *race* is a purely descriptive term that does not tell us anything about the underlying *causes* of variation. There are better ways to understand and analyze the geographic distribution of human genetic variation than race, as shown in the next section.

The Race-IQ Debate

Perhaps the most controversial topic when looking at human biological variation is the relationship between genetics, race, and IQ test scores. IQ stands for "intelligence quotient" and is a measure derived by dividing a person's mental age by her or his chronological age; it is designed so that the average score for a reference population is 100. The IQ test was developed in France by Alfred Binet, who sought a means by which to identify children with learning disabilities. The purpose of the test was not to measure intelligence per se, but rather to identify those children who would most likely require special education. The test was not meant to provide a ranking of intelligence among the rest of the students, although it has often been used that way. There continues to be controversy over the extent to which IQ tests measure innate intelligence, or if intelligence is even a single quantity that can be measured (Gould 1981). Therefore, we need to keep in mind that variation in IQ scores may not correspond to our usual conceptions of variation in intelligence.

Are there differences in IQ test scores and do they correspond to typical views on race? In the context of the United States, this debate focuses on average IQ scores of individuals of African, Asian, and European descent. Differences have been found, with the test scores being on average highest in those of Asian ancestry and lowest in those of African ancestry. The debate is over the cause of these differences. Do they reflect genetics, environment, or both? A common argument that genetics is at least part of the explanation for these group differences goes as follows:

1. Differences in IQ scores are partly due to genetic differences.
2. The races have different average IQ scores.
3. Therefore, because races are by definition genetically different, the racial differences in IQ scores are due to genetic differences.

It is worthwhile to examine briefly each of these claims. There is evidence for both genetic (Bouchard et al. 1990) and environmental components for IQ (Gould 1981). The latter include diet, education, social class, and health, among others. The exact heritability of IQ has been widely debated. Some have suggested that 60–80 percent of the variation in IQ scores may be due to genetic variation, while others suggest heritability might be closer to 34–48 percent (Devlin et al. 1997). In any case, we can make a case that the heritability of IQ is moderate to high.

The second claim is that there are racial differences in IQ test scores. In the United States, for example, European Americans tend to score, on average, roughly 15 points higher than African Americans. Asian Americans tend to score, on average, several points higher than European Americans. What exactly is being compared? Categories such as "European American," "African American," and "Asian American" are broad groupings based on ethnicity and national origin, but they are not by any stretch of the imagination homogeneous populations, in terms of either genetics or environment. People within any of these broad ancestral groupings can come from a wide variety of countries and environments. The problem with using races as the unit of analysis is that it obscures much of the variation *within* groups, which makes comparative analysis difficult at best.

The next problem is the third claim in the list. We assume that any group differences in a trait that has a genetic basis must themselves be genetic in nature. This is not a valid assumption, however, as group differences could be the result of genetics, environment, or both. As noted in Chapter 2, heritability is a measure of genetic variation *within* groups and not *between* groups. If we estimate the heritability of IQ as x percent, this does not mean that x percent of the difference between groups in IQ scores is due to genetics.

We have no way of telling beforehand the causes of group differences; this requires testing. In terms of racial comparisons, we know that these groups show average differences in environmental conditions that affect performance on IQ tests, such as education and income. To date, the bulk of the evidence supports an environmental explanation of racial difference in IQ test scores (Loehlin et al. 1975; Gould 1981; Mackintosh 1998). One of the most revealing studies, reviewed by Mackintosh (1998), looked at the IQ scores of German female children fathered by African American soldiers after World War II. The IQ scores of these children, who were raised by their mothers or foster parents, were no different from those of white German children when matched for other characteristics. In this study, the ancestry of the two groups was different, but the environment was the same, as were the IQ scores.

Another test of the hypothesis that group differences in IQ test scores are genetic involves comparing scores by individual ancestry. If IQ differences reflect genetics, then test scores among African Americans should vary proportionately according to the degree of European admixture; those with greater European ancestry should score higher. However, analyses have shown no relationship between amount of European ancestry and IQ score (Flynn 1980; Mackintosh 1998). Finally, we have ample evidence that IQ scores in many nations have changed over the past few decades, changes that are too fast to explain in terms of genetics, but which make sense in terms of changes in environmental conditions (Flynn 1987). All of these studies (and others) support the view that group differences in IQ scores reflect environmental differences.

PATTERNS OF GLOBAL GENETIC VARIATION

For centuries, the primary way of looking at human biological variation was from a racial perspective, with emphasis on enumerating and describing human races. The description of human variation was made primarily on the basis of physical measures, such as skin color and cranial shape. Today, we still use such measures (see Box 14.2) but have also added to our understanding of human variation through the collection of numerous genetic markers (see Box 14.3). We not only have more information on human variation, but we also use a different approach than in past centuries; the growth of evolutionary thought led to a new focus on human variation that considers the evolution of populations over time. Here, humanity is not viewed as a set of discrete races, but rather a set of interconnected populations over time. Instead of tabulating a list of races, the goal here is to understand the present in terms of the past. This section of the chapter examines some basic findings about patterns of human biological variation. The focus here is on *overall* trends in genetic diversity for our entire species. Subsequent chapters will provide case studies of specific human populations (such as Native Americans) as well as the evolution and variation of specific traits (such as skin color).

Genetic Variation in Our Species

Even though living humans are spread out across the planet, the overall level of genetic variation of humans is low relative to other primate species. For

BOX 14.2

Physical Measures of Human Variation

When we walk down the street, we notice some outward aspects of human biological variation. We might note a person's height, body build, skin and hair color, and other aspects of physical appearance. Biological anthropologists are interested in many such physical characteristics but rely on objective measurements rather than imprecise estimates, such as "he is tall" or "she has light skin."

Measurements of the human body, including the head and face, are known as *anthropometrics*. Two of the most commonly used anthropometrics are height and weight. Other measurements of the body include the length of limbs and limb segments and the width of the body at different places, such as the shoulders and the hips. Skinfold measures—the thickness of a section of skin and fat that have been pinched together—provide a useful means of assessing body fat and nutritional status. Numerous methods have been developed to measure the human face and skull. These include measures of the length and width of the skull and face at various locations (notably, near the eyes, cheekbones, and lower jaw). Similar measures are used on skeletal remains.

Another physical measure is skin color. In the past, skin color was often measured by comparing a person's skin to a set of tiles, but this was too subjective and inaccurate. Today, the most common method of measuring skin color involves using a reflectance spectrophotometer—a device that measures the percentage of light reflected back from a given source at different wavelengths. Lighter skin reflects more light and has a higher reading than darker skin does. This type of device was used for collecting the data on skin color that you saw in Figure 14.3. Instead of arbitrarily dividing people into imprecise categories such as "light," "medium," and "dark," we can measure skin color exactly.

Anthropologists use many other physical measurements. These include measures of the size of teeth (length and width) as well as observations of dental variations, such as extra cusps, or shovel-shaped incisors, in which individuals have ridges on the inside margins of their incisor teeth. Some anthropologists study fingerprints, measuring variations in the number of ridge lines on each finger, as well as the different types of fingerprints (loops, whorls, arches). Although we all have unique fingerprints, families and related populations tend to have similar ridge counts and frequencies of different types of prints.

The author measuring his son's height. Height and weight are two of the most common anthropometric measures.

example, as a species we show levels of genetic diversity that are about half the amount found in chimpanzees, who are much less geographically widespread (Hawks 2009). In other words, there is less genetic difference between humans from across the world than between chimpanzees within a restricted range in West Africa. Our reduced genetic variation is likely the consequence of our species' origin in African and subsequent dispersal. Each new group would give rise to a smaller founding group as our species spread out from Africa. This pattern would produce a lot of genetic drift through the founder

BOX 14.3

Genetic Measures of Human Variation

In 1900, the ABO blood group system was discovered. In addition to its medical significance (problems can result if you get a transfusion of blood with an incompatible blood type), the discovery of this blood group opened up the use of genetic markers in anthropological research. Unlike physical measures such as body measures, genetic markers are not affected by the environment or by aging; you will live and die with the same blood type you were born with. The ABO blood group is an example of a genetic marker characterized by the types of molecules present on the surface of your red blood cells, and different phenotypes are detected by observing whether there is a reaction between these molecules (antigens) and selected antibodies. There are many different types of blood groups, inherited separately, such as Rhesus, MN, Diego, Kell, and others. Most of these have no medical significance, but all have proven valuable for analyzing allele frequency variation in human populations. By the 1960s, the study of genetic markers of the blood had expanded further with the analysis of different blood cell proteins and enzymes. These discoveries led to hundreds of genetic markers.

Due to advances in genetic technology over the past several decades, we now have many different types of DNA markers (some studies routinely use hundreds of thousands of loci). DNA is easily obtained from samples of hair or cheek swabs. One type of DNA marker that is routinely used in human population studies is **microsatellite DNA**, which consists of repeated short sections of DNA (2–5 bases). For example, the DNA sequence CACACACACA contains five repeats of the CA sequence, while the DNA sequence CACACACA contains four repeats. The number of such repeats is quite variable, making these markers valuable in detecting genetic relationships between populations. Hundreds of microsatellite DNA loci have been detected in a number of human populations. Another useful type of DNA marker is a **single-nucleotide polymorphism** (known as **SNPs**). These are loci characterized by differences at one base of a DNA sequence. For example, consider the following two DNA sequences:

> Sequence # 1: GAACCTTA
> Sequence # 2: GAATCTTA

These two sequences differ at the fourth position; sequence # 1 has a C and sequence # 2 has a T. To date, millions of SNPs have been detected in human populations (International HapMap Consortium 2007). The existence of so many SNPs provides geneticists with the ability to map the genome and look for linkages with a number of traits, including genes that might influence disease susceptibility.

In many genetic analyses, we look at different combinations of DNA markers, known as **haplotypes**, which are inherited as a single unit. For example, a haplotype might be defined based on the presence of a set of SNPs and a certain number of repeats for a set of microsatellite DNA loci. As an example, consider Foster et al.'s (1998) analysis that looked for Y-chromosome DNA that was linked to Thomas Jefferson in an attempt to determine if Jefferson had fathered a child with an enslaved African American woman, Sally Hemings. This analysis used a combination of seven SNPs, 11 microsatellite DNA markers, and one longer repeated unit of DNA known as a minisatellite. This combination of different markers on the Y chromosome is a haplotype and was unique to the Jefferson family (the results showed that one of Sally Heming's

microsatellite DNA Repeated short sequence of DNA; the number of repeats is highly variable.

single-nucleotide polymorphisms (SNPs) Specific positions in a DNA sequence that differ at one base. For example, the DNA sequences CCTGAA and CCCGAA differ in the third position—one sequence has the base T, and the other the base C.

effect (see Chapter 3), which would reduce our species' overall level of genetic variation (Relethford 2012b).

Regional Differences in Genetic Variation

When we look at genetic variation within populations from around the world, we see an interesting pattern—Africa tends to be more genetically diverse than other geographic regions, such as Europe or Asia (Figure 14.5). Higher levels of African diversity can be explained in terms of our species' African origin. The older a population, the more time it has had to accumulate mutations, which will make the population more genetically diverse. When some human

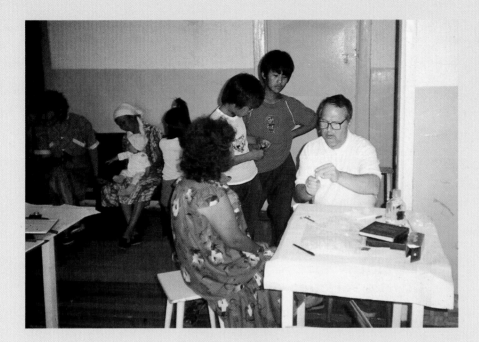

Dr. Michael Crawford collecting hair samples from the Evenki, a group of reindeer herders in Siberia. DNA can be extracted from hair samples and cheek swabs.

sons did have the Jefferson haplotype, but this does not necessarily mean that Jefferson was the father; it could have been another male in the Jefferson line). Geneticists and anthropologists often examine different haplotypes and determine how they are related evolutionarily by finding groups of haplotypes that share common mutations; these related haplotypes are known as **haplogroups**.

Different types of DNA are useful in different types of studies depending on the pattern of inheritance. As discussed in Chapter 2, almost all of the DNA a person has is nuclear DNA, which is inherited from both parents and subject to recombination. Mitochondrial DNA, inherited solely from the mother, is not subject to recombination. The same is true of almost all of the DNA on a male's Y chromosome, which is inherited solely from the father, and almost none of which is subject to recombination.

populations moved out of Africa, they lost diversity because of genetic drift (due to small founding populations), and they have had less time to accumulate more diversity.

The dispersion out of Africa resulted in two other interesting features of African diversity. Not only is genetic diversity outside of Africa less than within Africa, but the level of genetic diversity is less the farther away a population is from Africa. This decrease in diversity with distance is what we would expect when new populations split off from older ones over and over again as humans expanded across the planet (Ramachandran et al. 2005). In addition, studies of DNA markers show that genetic diversity outside of Africa is often a subset of the diversity within Africa (Tishkoff and Gonder 2007). In other words, alleles have been lost due to genetic drift as populations moved out of Africa.

haplotype A combination of gene or DNA sequences that are inherited as a single unit.

haplogroup A set of related haplotypes that share similar mutations.

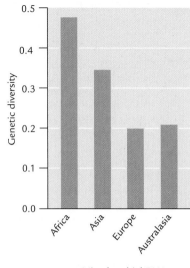

a. Mitochondrial DNA

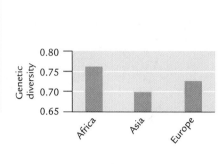

b. Microsatellite DNA

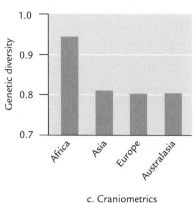

c. Craniometrics

FIGURE 14.5

Comparison of genetic diversity among different geographic regions of living humans based on (a) mitochondrial DNA variation, (b) microsatellite DNA variation, and (c) craniometric variation. In each case, different measures of "diversity" are used so that the scales (vertical axes) cannot be compared directly. Instead, simply note that in each case Africa is the most diverse region genetically. (Data from Cann et al. 1987; Relethford and Harpending 1994; Jorde et al. 1997.)

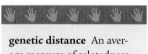

genetic distance An average measure of relatedness between populations based on a number of traits.

Geographic Distance and Genetic Variation

As noted above, much of human genetic variation is geographically structured, so that the farther apart different populations are geographically, the more genetically dissimilar they tend to be. Average genetic differences between populations are typically described using a measure known as **genetic distance,** which is a relative measure of genetic dissimilarity. A variety of methods exist to compute genetic distance measures, but discussion of how this is done is beyond the scope of this book; simply realize that genetic distances represent relative similarity. Suppose, for example, that you computed the genetic distance between three populations (A, B, and C) and found the following:

Distance between A and B = 0.007

Distance between A and C = 0.090

Distance between B and C = 0.139

These distances are relative: the larger the number, the greater the genetic difference. In this case, it is clear that populations A and B are relatively similar to each other, whereas population C is more different.

In practical terms, if we want to know how closely related populations are, we need to focus on genes or traits that have not been affected strongly by natural selection because we want to know about shared ancestry and gene flow. Traits that have been affected by natural selection could give us an inaccurate estimate. For example, both central African and Australian native populations have dark skin color. If we used this physical similarity to infer a recent common ancestry or gene flow between the groups, we would be making a mistake. In this case, the two populations are similar in skin color because of adaptation to a similar environment (see Chapter 15).

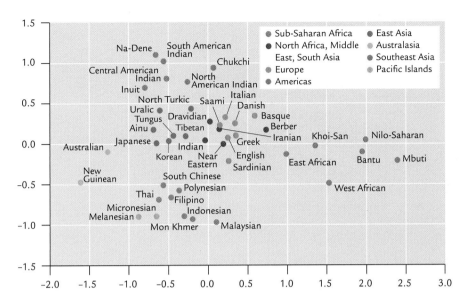

FIGURE 14.6

Genetic distance map showing the genetic relationships among 42 native human populations around the world. The genetic distances are based on 120 allele frequencies. This map was constructed using a method known as *multidimensional scaling.* The scales correspond to positions in genetic space and are dependent on the method used to construct the map. European and many Asian populations plot near the center of the map, with Native American, sub-Saharan African, Southeast Asian, and Pacific Island populations plotting farther away. Overall, this map reproduces the geographic distances between human populations to a large extent. (Data from Cavalli-Sforza et al. 1994.)

Genetic Distance between Human Populations A number of studies have examined genetic distance between native populations across the world using a variety of genetic and physical traits. One of the most comprehensive studies looked at the genetic distance between 42 human populations worldwide using data on 120 allele frequencies (mostly red blood cell polymorphisms and HLA markers) (Cavalli-Sforza et al. 1994). It is important in genetic distance studies to use a large number of traits to avoid statistical bias. Because genetic distances are computed between each population and all others, this study generated a total of 861 distances between the 42 populations, a number much too large to list in a table, let alone make any sense! The usual method of analysis is to construct a **genetic distance map,** which gives a graphic representation of the genetic differences between populations. Genetic distance maps are easy to interpret—the closer two populations are on the "map," the more similar they are, and the farther apart two populations are on the map, the less similar they are. This is analogous to a road map—towns and cities that are close to each other geographically are close to each other on the map.

The genetic distance map for the 42-population analysis is shown in Figure 14.6. The overall picture corresponds well to geography and known history. Many of the populations in Europe and Asia plot near the center of the map, with native populations in sub-Saharan Africa, the Pacific Islands, and the Americas plotting farther away. Native American populations plot closer to populations in Northeast Asia than elsewhere in the world, consistent with their origin there (see Chapter 15). Populations in the Pacific (Melanesia, Micronesia, Polynesia) plot closest to Southeast Asian populations, which is consistent with geography and history.

The Correspondence of Genetics and Geography Figure 14.7 shows the geographic structure of human genetic variation even more clearly. Here, the genetic and geographic distances were averaged together for pairs of

genetic distance map A graphic representation that shows the genetic relationships between populations, based on genetic distance measures.

FIGURE 14.7

The global relationship between geographic distance and genetic distance between human populations. The genetic distances between all 42 populations in Figure 14.6 were averaged within different groups depending on the geographic distance between them. Geographic distances were computed from the longitude and latitude of each population, with some restrictions based on past migration paths. Each dot represents the average genetic distance for all pairs of populations within a given geographic distance group. (Adapted from Relethford 2003.)

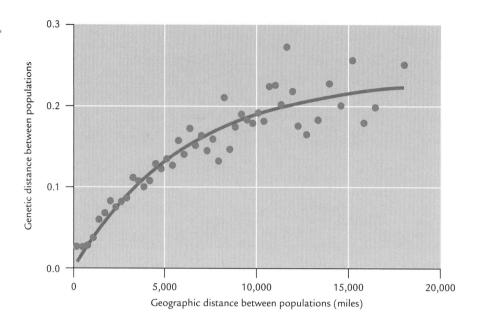

populations at different classes of geographic distance. This plot clearly shows that the farther two populations are apart from each other, the greater their genetic distance. This pattern has also been found for DNA markers and cranial measures (Relethford 2004b).

Overall, the picture of genetic relationships in Figures 14.6 and 14.7 shows a strong relationship to the geographic distances between populations. This correspondence is to some extent a reflection of the sequential founding of populations as modern humans expanded out of Africa (Ramachandran et al. 2005). Under this scenario, a population is most related to its neighbor, and less related to populations farther away. Over time, gene flow between populations would reduce genetic differences, but this too would depend on distance—the farther two populations are apart from each other, the less likely they are to exchange genes. The close correspondence of genetics and geography in the human species argues against a view of humanity as geographically dispersed separate races. The average difference between human populations (Figure 14.7) is gradual over geographic space.

Summary

Throughout much of history, human biological variation has been discussed in terms of race and racial classification, with an emphasis on identifying discrete groups of human populations that differ widely in genetics. In the past, race was used as a crude means by which to describe patterns of human variation. A major problem in using race as a concept is that distinct "races" take on a reality of their own in people's minds. The race concept has limited use in analyses of biological variation, particularly for widespread species such as human beings, because it uses arbitrary classifications of predominantly continuous traits.

Studies of genetic variation in the human species do not produce results consistent with the race concept. Instead, we find evidence of geographic differences between human groups, but with no clear boundaries between them. Genetic variation is greatest within local human populations, such that for many traits only 10 percent of the total genetic variation is found between major geographic groups. The pattern of genetic distances between human populations is strongly related to geography and its effect on gene flow.

Supplemental Readings

Brace, C. L. 2005. *"Race" Is a Four-Letter Word: The Genesis of the Concept*. New York: Oxford University Press. A detailed discussion of the history of the biological race concept.

Cavalli-Sforza, L. L. 2000. *Genes, Peoples, and Languages*. New York: North Point Press. A short, readable introduction to genetic variation in the human species.

Cavalli-Sforza, L. L., P. Meonozzi, and A. Piazza. 1994. *The History and Geography of Human Genes*. Princeton, NJ: Princeton University Press. Similar in focus to the above book, but with much greater, and exceptional, detail.

A herd of dairy cattle. Dairy farming is one of many cultural adaptations of modern humans over the past 12,000 years. Some of these cultural changes have led to genetic changes in some human populations. In the case of dairy farming, some human populations have evolved higher frequencies of alleles that allow them to digest milk products into adulthood.

Recent Human Evolution

A re we still evolving? This is a common question in introductory anthropology classes. The short answer is "yes." Humans did not stop evolving once they reached the status of anatomically modern humans. It is true that we look more or less very similar to the first modern humans that appeared in Africa. It is also true that we have not changed to be a different species in the recent past. However, these observations do not mean we are not evolving at all. There are considerable data showing examples of recent evolutionary changes, some of which will be touched upon in this chapter. Our focus here is on "recent" evolutionary changes, some of which occurred since our species' dispersal from Africa, some of which occurred only within the past few 10,000 years, and some of which have taken place only in the last few centuries. As we will see, many of these recent changes in human evolution have been brought about by our species' cultural adaptations. As we developed agriculture and grew dramatically in size, we changed our interactions with the environment, which has led to a number of genetic changes in human populations. We will continue to change in the future.

This chapter provides a number of case studies that show how our species' recent history can be examined using data on biological variation. The questions we examine are historical in nature. The first part of the chapter focuses on questions concerning the history of *populations,* looking at the origins of genetic diversity in different parts of the world. The focus here is on gene flow and genetic drift, and how they have shaped differences between groups. The remainder of the chapter examines the history of different *traits* and the influence of natural selection.

GENETICS AND POPULATION HISTORY

Some questions about population history focus on the origin of populations. For example, where did a given population come from? Did it form as a splinter group from another population? Did it result from the movement of some group of initial colonizers or settlers? Did it form from the genetic merging of two or more groups? Other questions about population history focus on the relationship between historical events and genetic outcomes.

For example, if a population was invaded from elsewhere, did the invaders introduce any genes, and if so, how much of an effect was there?

Human populations are constantly interacting with each other, and we are interested here in the genetic effects of such events. In general, we look at genetic relationships between populations in terms of common ancestry and gene flow, both of which are expected to result in populations being more similar genetically to each other. We assume that, for the most part, common ancestry and gene flow affect all genes and DNA sequences to the same extent (an exception is a possible difference between mitochondrial DNA and Y-chromosome polymorphisms because of differences in female and male gene flow). However, other evolutionary forces do not always have the same impact on all of our genomes. Genetic drift, for example, could make the allele frequencies in two closely related populations different by chance (or make two less-related populations appear more similar). Natural selection could also have this effect. As noted in the previous chapter, it is for these reasons that we try to use averages based on a large number of traits and to limit analysis to traits that appear to have little or no relationship to natural selection.

The Origin of Native Americans

One example of population origins and history is the case of Native American populations. Europeans became aware of the existence of the New World (the Americas) and Native Americans following the initial exploration of Christopher Columbus in 1492, when he attempted to circumnavigate the globe to find an alternate route from Europe to Asia. Indeed, when Columbus arrived in the New World, he thought he had succeeded in reaching the "Indies," the term then used for Asia. Consequently, the native peoples found in the New World became known as "Indians." A number of people contemplated exactly where these people had originated. For those who interpreted the natural world from a strict biblical perspective, Native Americans were seen as one of the lost tribes of Israel (Crawford 1998).

As discussed previously, humans first evolved in Africa, later spreading throughout the Old World (Africa, Asia, Europe, and Australia), and later still into the New World. All human fossils found in the New World are modern; no earlier species of humans lived here. In the late sixteenth century, some argued that Asia was the place of origin for Native Americans, and the dominant view since then has been that Asians moved into the Americas across the Bering Land Bridge (Figure 15.1). During periods of glaciation, sea levels fell, exposing a stretch of land connecting Asia and North America that was almost 1,000 miles wide. This "land bridge" did not appear or disappear suddenly but developed slowly over thousands of years as sea levels dropped. Under this model, groups of humans following game herds moved across this region and eventually down into North, Central, and South America. In recent years, some archaeologists have suggested that humans may have used boats to migrate to the New World (Nemecek 2000). Either way, the archaeological record shows a connection between Asia and the New World.

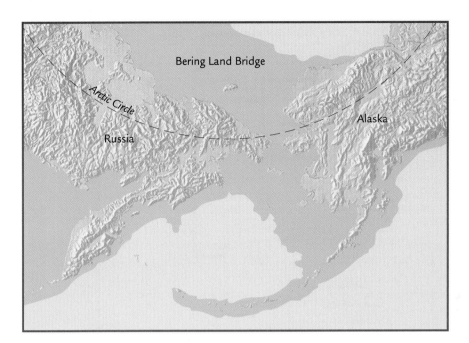

FIGURE 15.1

The Bering Land Bridge. Today Siberia and Alaska are separated by water. During the "Ice Ages," water was trapped in glaciers, producing a drop in the sea level that exposed the land known as the Bering Land Bridge.

When did this happen? For many years, it was thought that humans moved into the New World roughly 12,000 years ago. These dates were consistent with the dates of sites containing the first examples of the Clovis stone tool culture, which dates back over 12,000 years ago. Over time, archaeologists have found evidence of a number of more ancient pre-Clovis sites, some dating back as far as 15,000 years ago (Waters et al. 2011). Allowing for different estimates of the speed at which the New World was settled, a range of initial entry from 15,000 to 20,000 years ago seems reasonable.

The Genetic Evidence for an Asian Origin A number of physical traits, such as the presence of shovel-shaped incisors, tend to support a genetic connection between Asians and Native Americans. These traits tend to be more common in both groups and are found at lower frequencies in other populations. The best evidence, however, comes from analysis of genetic markers and DNA analysis. These studies have consistently found that Native Americans are more similar to populations in Asia, particularly Northeast Asia, than to other human populations.

An example of the closer genetic link to Asia is presented in Figure 15.2, which shows the genetic relationships between nine geographic regions based on 120 allele frequencies (Cavalli-Sforza et al. 1994). Native Americans are most similar genetically to Northeast Asians than to other geographic regions, which is consistent with archaeological evidence that the first migrants to the New World came from Northeast Asia.

Even greater insight into genetic relationships with Native American populations has been provided through the analysis of mitochondrial DNA haplogroups. Mitochondrial DNA from Native Americans (both living and from ancient skeletal material) belongs to one of five different haplogroups, labeled

FIGURE 15.2

Genetic relationships between nine regions of the world based on an analysis of 120 allele frequencies for red and white blood cell polymorphisms. The lower the genetic distance, the more similar the populations. This diagram shows clearly that Native Americans are the most similar to Northeast Asians and Arctic Northeast Asians. (Data from Cavalli-Sforza et al. 1994.)

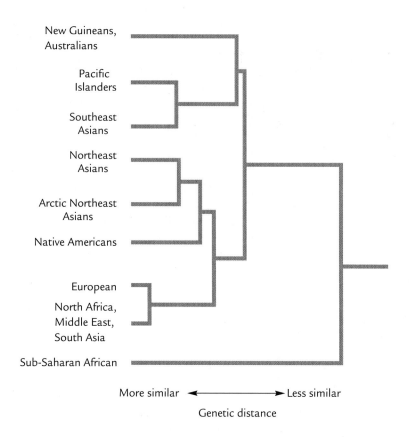

New Guineans, Australians

Pacific Islanders

Southeast Asians

Northeast Asians

Arctic Northeast Asians

Native Americans

European

North Africa, Middle East, South Asia

Sub-Saharan African

More similar ←——————→ Less similar

Genetic distance

A, B, C, D, and X (Schurr 2000). Four of these haplogroups (A, B, C, D) are found in Northeast Asian populations and are absent or rare in other parts of the world (Schurr 2000; Derenko et al. 2001). The fifth haplogroup, X, is found in both Northeast Asian populations and parts of Europe, the latter likely suggesting migration between Asia and Europe. Collectively, the mitochondrial DNA haplogroup distributions support the connection between Asia and North America, confirming that Native Americans are the descendants of migrants from Northeast Asia. The distribution of Y-chromosome DNA shows the same pattern. Most Native American males have Y-chromosome haplogroup C or Q, both of which trace their origins to Siberia (Zegura et al. 2004).

How Many Migrations?   Although virtually everyone agrees with an Asian origin of Native Americans, there remains considerable debate over the number of major migration events. Did humans move into the New World only once, or were there two, three, or more separate migration events, perhaps each from a different region of Asia? New methods of molecular analysis of DNA markers have potential for answering this question. Based on patterns of diversity in DNA markers, it seems clear that Native Americans came from a single source of ancestors in Siberia (Goebel et al. 2008). Further, an analysis of complete mitochondrial DNA genomes revealed patterns of diversity that suggest that the initial founders spent some time in isolation in the region of the Bering Straits, rather than a quick migration through the area (Tamm et al. 2007).

The Population History of Ireland

From the perspective of genetic variation, the population history of Ireland is fascinating because of the numerous possibilities for gene flow in Ireland's past. ("Ireland" refers here to the entire island, which is currently made up of two countries—the Republic of Ireland and Northern Ireland.) Through the years, Ireland has seen many different invasions and settlements from England, Scotland, Wales, and Scandinavia. What was the genetic impact of these different sources of gene flow?

Several studies have looked at patterns of biological variation among Irish populations and their relationship to history through the analysis of a large data set of anthropometric measurements originally collected on thousands of Irish men during the 1930s (Relethford and Crawford 1995; Relethford 2008). Although body, facial, and cranial measures are affected by environmental factors, a number of studies have shown that they can also be used to unravel genetic differences between populations.

Genetic Impact of Gene Flow from England and Wales One approach has been to look at how different traits vary across space and to use these spatial patterns as clues about population history. Relethford (2008) looked at a number of composite measures of anthropometric size and shape in 197 Irish populations. One measure, associated with overall body size, showed a distinctive gradient from the east coast to the west coast of Ireland, with an average pattern of larger body size in the west (Figure 15.3). This east-west

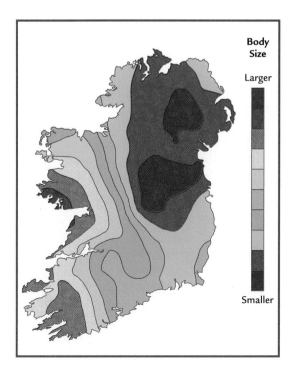

FIGURE 15.3

Spatial variation in body size in Ireland. The colors represent different levels of a composite measure of body size taking height, weight, and other body measurements into account. The contours represent the average trends in body size variation. The gradient from east to west corresponds to the impact of differential settlement from England and Wales in the east. (Adapted from Relethford 2008.)

difference has also been seen in studies of blood groups and Y-chromosome DNA, and is generally interpreted as being a reflection of past immigration into Ireland. Historically, we know that much immigration from England and Wales began in the early 1600s, and these immigrants settled predominantly in the eastern parts of Ireland. Comparative analysis supports this hypothesis, as populations in the eastern part of Ireland are more similar in their anthropometrics to the English than those in the west (Relethford and Crawford 1995).

Genetic Impact of Viking Invasion   Not all measurements show the same east-west gradient. Measures of craniofacial height (from the chin to the top of the head) show a much different pattern, as shown in Figure 15.4. Here, there is a distinct pattern of shorter faces and heads in the middle of the island. What accounts for the distinctiveness of the midlands? One possibility is gene flow from Viking invasion and settlement. Irish history reveals that the Vikings first came to Ireland in 794 and that contact continued through the early thirteenth century. Although some Viking settlements were on the coast, substantial numbers of Vikings moved into the Irish midlands, which are accessible by river from the Atlantic Ocean. At least one of these invasions involved as many as 12,000 men, which would be expected to have a noticeable genetic impact. Comparative analysis shows that the Irish midland populations are the most similar anthropometrically to Norse and Danish populations, who are representative of the place of origin of the Vikings (Relethford and Crawford 1995).

FIGURE 15.4

Spatial variation in craniofacial height in Ireland. The colors represent different levels of a composite measure of craniofacial height, including measurements of height from the chin to the top of the head. Although much of the variation shows no particular spatial pattern, there is a clear distinction of smaller-sized individuals in the midlands of Ireland, likely corresponding to Viking invasion. (Adapted from Relethford 2008.)

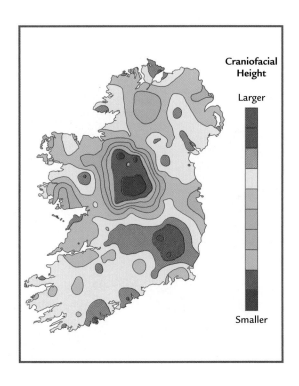

Genetic Ancestry of African Americans

The genetics of African Americans provides an example of the potential confusion between genetic ancestry and cultural identity. Between the early 1600s and the early 1800s, an estimated 380,000–570,000 Africans, primarily from West and West-Central Africa, were brought to the United States as part of the slave trade. Over time, there has been gene flow from Europeans into the African American gene pool, mostly from European men who fathered children with enslaved African women (Chakraborty 1986; Parra et al. 1998). As a result, allele frequencies in African Americans tend to be between those of Europeans and Africans but remain closer to those of Africans.

Analysis of allele frequency differences between Africans, Europeans, and African Americans allows us to estimate the overall proportion of African and European ancestry in different African American populations. Figure 15.5 reports the results of one study using DNA markers; the estimated amount of European ancestry varies from 4 percent in parts of South Carolina to 23 percent in New Orleans. These numbers represent *average* patterns of ancestry of the different populations, and the amount of European ancestry of individuals within each group varies. For example, the average amount of European ancestry in the African American population in Columbia, South Carolina, is 18 percent, but researchers have found that the amount of European ancestry for any given *individual* in that population varies from less than 10 percent to more than 50 percent (Parra et al. 2001).

Differences have also been found when comparing maternal and paternal ancestry. Parra and colleagues (1998, 2001) have used mitochondrial DNA to estimate maternal European ancestry in African Americans and Y-chromosome polymorphisms to estimate paternal European ancestry. In

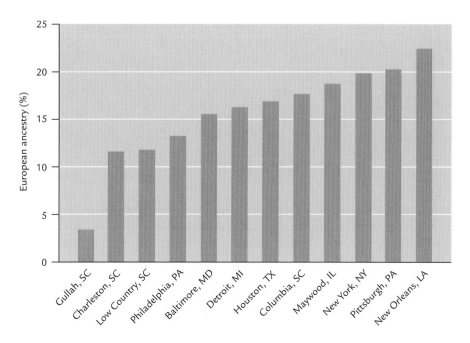

FIGURE 15.5

Estimates of European ancestry in African American populations in the United States based on DNA markers. (Data from Parra et al. 1998, 2001.)

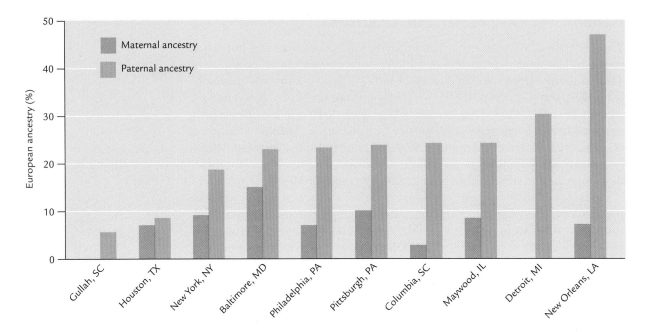

FIGURE 15.6

Estimate of European maternal and paternal ancestry in African American populations in the United States. Maternal ancestry is estimated from mitochondrial DNA, and paternal ancestry from Y-chromosome DNA. (Data from Parra et al. 1998, 2001.)

each of their samples, the amount of European ancestry was greater on the father's side than on the mother's side (Figure 15.6). This means that it was more common for European men to father children with African American women than for European women to have the children of African American men, which is consistent with the history of slavery in the United States. Male slaveholders often fathered children with enslaved African American women.

These studies illustrate the confusion between genetic ancestry and cultural identity (see Box 15.1). All of the individuals in these studies classified themselves culturally as African American even though some had a large proportion of European ancestry. Further, these studies show that African Americans are genetically diverse in their ancestral makeup and cannot be treated as a single homogeneous biological population, which is sometimes done in studies of health and disease. In addition, individuals with a mixed genetic ancestry often use a single grouping for cultural identity despite genetic differences.

NATURAL SELECTION IN HUMAN POPULATIONS

Natural selection has been operating throughout hominin evolution, resulting in a number of major anatomical changes, such as the origin of bipedalism and the increase in brain size and complexity. Natural selection did *not* end with the origin of anatomically modern humans, and it continues to operate on our species today. Several examples of the evolutionary history and natural selection in recent human evolution are presented in this section.

BOX 15.1

Who Are the Lemba?

Although genetic data can reveal much about a person's genetic ancestry, it should be remembered that ancestry is also defined culturally and sometimes genetic ancestry and cultural identity do not correspond. An example is the Lemba of South Africa, a group that has often been referred to as the "black Jews." The Lemba have an oral tradition of Jewish ancestry that claims to come from an influx of Jewish traders more than 2,000 years ago. Although the Lemba do practice certain traditions associated with Judaism, such as circumcision and certain food rituals, these cultural traits are also practiced by some other African and Middle Eastern societies. Genetic data support this oral history, as Y-chromosome DNA haplotypes are found among the Lemba that are found most often in males in Jewish populations (Thomas et al. 2000). Mitochondrial DNA (transmitted from the mother) in the Lemba are African. Thus, the genetic evidence is consistent with the oral histories suggesting gene flow from Jewish men.

However, this genetic connection does not make the Lemba Jewish, because being Jewish is a condition of cultural identity. According to Jewish tradition, there are two ways an individual can be considered Jewish—their mother was Jewish, or they converted to Judaism (some practitioners of Reform Judaism also consider the children of a Jewish father and a non-Jewish mother to be Jewish, but this is not accepted by all Jews). The cultural identify of being Jewish is transmitted through the mother's line, whereas the genetic connection with Jews among the Lemba is through the father's line. Although the Lemba are genetically related to Jewish populations, this does not make them Jewish, because they cannot show matrilineal descent or evidence of conversion. The relationship between genetic ancestry and cultural identity is often complex.

Hemoglobin, Sickle Cell, and Malaria

Perhaps the best-known example of natural selection operating on a discrete genetic trait is the relationship of hemoglobin variants to malaria. One of the proteins in red blood cells is hemoglobin, which functions to transport oxygen to body tissues (see Chapter 2). The normal structure of the beta chain of hemoglobin is coded for by an allele usually called hemoglobin *A*. In many human populations, the *A* allele is the only one present, and as a result everyone has the *AA,* or normal adult hemoglobin, genotype.

Hemoglobin Variants   Many hemoglobin variants are produced by the mutation of an *A* allele to another form. The most widely studied mutations include hemoglobin *S, C,* and *E.* The *S* allele is also known as the sickle cell allele. A person who has two *S* alleles (genotype *SS*) has **sickle cell anemia,** a condition whereby the structure of the red blood cells is altered and oxygen transport is severely impaired (Figure 15.7). Untreated, few people with sickle cell anemia survive to adulthood.

If the *S* allele is harmful in homozygotes, we expect natural selection to eliminate *S* alleles from the population in such a way that the frequency of *S* should be relatively low. Mutation introduces the *S* allele, but natural selection eliminates it. Indeed, in many parts of the world, the frequency of *S* is extremely low, fitting the model of mutation balanced by selection. In a number of populations, however, the frequency of *S* is much higher—often between 5 and 20 percent. Such high frequencies seem paradoxical given the harmful effect of the *S* allele in the homozygous genotype. Why does *S* reach such high frequencies?

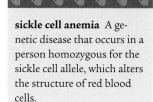

sickle cell anemia A genetic disease that occurs in a person homozygous for the sickle cell allele, which alters the structure of red blood cells.

FIGURE 15.7

Sickle cell anemia. The blood cell on the left is twisted and deformed compared to the round, normal red blood cells.

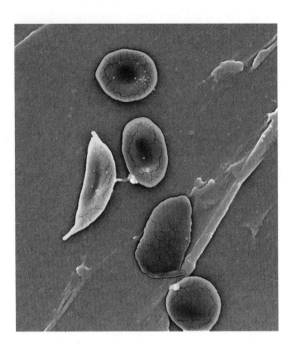

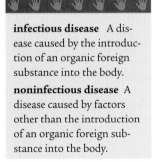

infectious disease A disease caused by the introduction of an organic foreign substance into the body.

noninfectious disease A disease caused by factors other than the introduction of an organic foreign substance into the body.

Distribution of the Sickle Cell Allele and Malaria   The distribution of the sickle cell allele is related to the prevalence of a certain form of malaria. Malaria is an **infectious disease**—that is, a disease caused by the introduction into the body of an organic foreign substance, such as a virus or parasite. (A disease that is not caused by an organic foreign substance is a **noninfectious disease.**) Malaria is caused by a parasite that enters an organism's body, and four different species of the malarial parasite can affect humans. Malaria remains one of the major infectious diseases in the world today. There are an estimated 300 million to 500 million cases of malaria each year and between 1 million and 3 million deaths (Sachs and Malaney 2002).

The Old World shows a striking correspondence between higher frequencies of the *S* allele (Figure 15.8) and the prevalence of malaria caused by the parasite *Plasmodium falciparum* (Figure 15.9). This parasite is spread through the bites of certain species of mosquitoes. Except through blood transfusions, humans cannot give malaria to one another directly. Those areas with frequent cases of malaria, such as Central Africa, also have the highest frequencies of the sickle cell allele. The falciparum form of malaria, which is the most serious, is often fatal.

The strong geographic correspondence suggests that sickle cell anemia and malaria are both related to the high frequencies of the *S* allele. Further experimental work has confirmed this hypothesis. Because the *S* allele affects the structure of the red blood cells, it makes the blood an inhospitable place for the malaria parasite.

The Evolution of the S Allele   In a malarial environment, people who are heterozygous (genotype *AS*) actually have an advantage. The presence of one

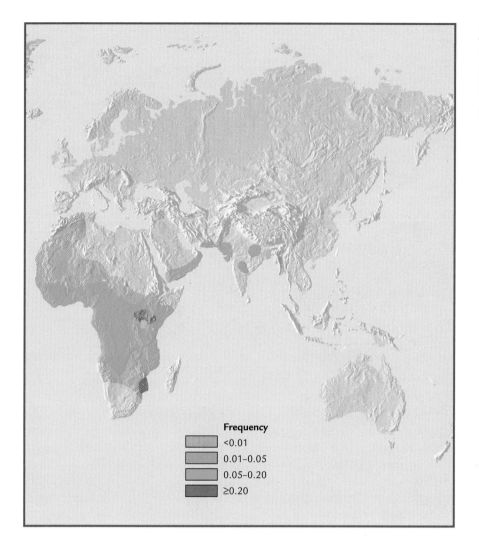

FIGURE 15.8

Distribution of the sickle cell allele in the Old World. Compare high-frequency areas with the high-frequency areas of malaria in Figure 15.9.

S allele does not give the person sickle cell anemia, but it does change the blood cells sufficiently so that the malaria parasite does not have as serious an effect. Overall, the heterozygote has the greatest fitness in a malarial environment. As discussed in Chapter 3, this is a case of balancing selection, in which selection occurs for the heterozygote (*AS*) and against both homozygotes (*AA* from malaria and *SS* from sickle cell anemia).

If the effects of sickle cell anemia and malaria were equal, then we would expect the frequencies of the normal allele (*A*) and the sickle cell allele (*S*) ultimately to reach equal frequencies. The two diseases, however, are not equal in their effects. Sickle cell anemia is much worse. The balance between these two diseases is such that the maximum fitness of an entire population occurs when the frequency of *S* is somewhere between 10 and 20 percent (Figure 15.10).

The sickle cell example clearly shows the importance of the specific environment on the process of natural selection. In a nonmalarial environment, the *AS* genotype has no advantage in terms of differential survival, and the

FIGURE 15.9

Regions where falciparum malaria is common (shown in green).

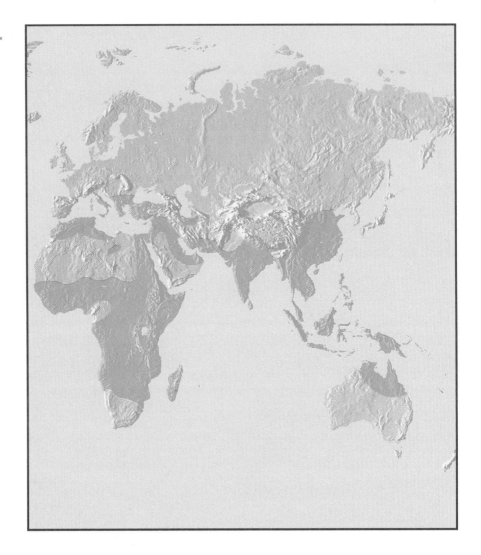

AA genotype has the greatest evolutionary fitness. In such cases, the frequency of the *S* allele is very low, approaching zero. In a malarial environment, however, the situation is different and the heterozygote has the advantage. Clearly, we cannot label the *S* allele as intrinsically "good" or "bad"; it depends on circumstances.

The example of sickle cell also shows that evolution has a price. The equilibrium is one in which the fitness for the entire population is at a maximum. The cost of the adaptation, however, is an increased proportion of individuals with sickle cell anemia, because the frequency of *S* has increased. People with the heterozygous genotype *AS* have the greatest fitness, but they also carry the *S* allele. When two people with the *AS* genotype mate, they have a 25 percent chance of having a child with sickle cell anemia. This is not advantageous from the perspective of the individual with the disease. From the perspective of the entire population, however, it is the most adaptive outcome. Every benefit in evolution is likely to carry a price.

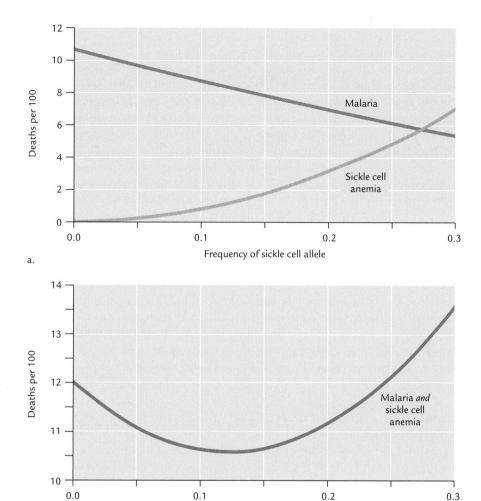

a.

b.

FIGURE 15.10

Illustration of balancing selection for the hemoglobin *S* allele. Selection was modeled using these estimates of fitness from Bodmer and Cavalli-Sforza (1976): 88 percent of individuals with the genotype *AA* survive, but 12 percent die due to malaria; 14 percent of individuals with the genotype *SS* survive, but 86 percent die due to sickle cell anemia; everyone with genotype *AS* survives. Figure 15.10a shows the expected number of deaths due to malaria and sickle cell anemia for every 100 people in the population. As the frequency of *S* increases, the number of deaths due to malaria declines because more people now have the genotype *AS* and fewer people have the genotype *AA*. At the same time, however, the number of deaths due to sickle cell anemia increases because there are more people with genotype *SS* in the population. The result is a trade-off. Figure 15.10b shows what happens when we consider the *total* number of deaths due to malaria *and* sickle cell anemia. The total number of deaths declines at first because of increased resistance to malaria. The total number of deaths reaches a minimum point for a frequency of 0.122 for the *S* allele. If *S* were to increase further, the increased number of sickle cell anemia deaths would offset the decrease in malaria deaths. Natural selection will lead to an optimal balance corresponding to the minimum number of total deaths.

The *CCR5* Gene

The *CCR5* gene is located on chromosome 3 and codes for a chemical receptor. A mutant allele, known as *CCR5-Δ32,* is characterized by a deletion of 32 base pairs. This allele has been found in moderate frequencies (0.03–0.14) in Europeans but is absent in Africans, East Asians, and Native Americans. The mutation has been linked to resistance to HIV (human immunodeficiency virus), the virus that causes AIDS. Individuals homozygous for the *CCR5-Δ32* allele are almost completely resistant to HIV-1 infection.

At first glance, this association might suggest selection for the allele due to HIV infection. However, the allele is found at low frequencies in some populations and not at all in others, and does not account for much of the difference in risk of AIDS between individuals or populations (Bamshad et al. 2002). More important, it is unlikely that differences in HIV resistance led to variation in allele frequencies because AIDS has not been around long enough to have had any evolutionary impact. Instead, it appears that there was selection for the *CCR5-Δ32* allele for resistance to *some other* infectious disease in the past, and the HIV resistance seen today is a by-product of that previous selection. In other words, the *CCR5-Δ32* allele arose as a mutation and was then selected for because of its impact on the susceptibility to an infectious disease in Europeans, resulting in an increase in the frequency of the allele in Europe. Once established, this allele now provides resistance to HIV infection.

What might this earlier selection involve? Bubonic plague in the fourteenth century (the "Black Death") had initially been suggested as a possibility, but the finding of the *CCR5-Δ32* allele in Bronze Age skeletons in Germany dating back 2,900 years shows that the allele has been around much longer (Hummel et al. 2005). A case has also been made for selection due to resistance to smallpox (Galvani and Slatkin 2003), a disease that caused many deaths until a vaccine became widespread in the nineteenth century. It is also possible that another infectious disease might have been involved. Whatever the actual cause(s), the *CCR5-Δ32* allele provides an excellent example of how past selection can affect future selection. As often happens in evolution, a trait that evolves by selection for one reason can be adaptive for some other reason later in time.

Skin Color

Human skin color is a complex trait. It has a strong genetic component (Williams-Blangero and Blangero 1992) and is also affected by the environment, particularly the amount of direct sunlight.

The Biology of Skin Color   One pigment, melanin, is responsible for the majority of variation in lightness and darkness in skin color. Melanin is a brown pigment secreted by cells in the bottom layer of the skin. Variation in human skin color is affected by at least six genes which influence melanin production (Norton et al. 2007; Parra 2007). Molecular analysis also shows light skin in Europeans and Asians might be due to different genes,

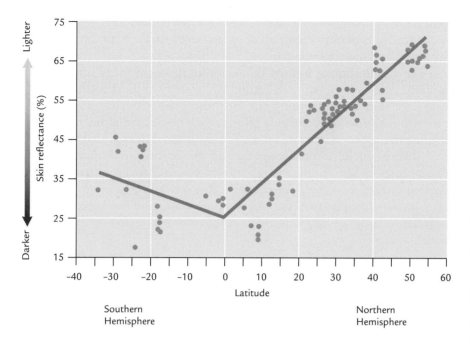

FIGURE 15.11

Geographic distribution of human skin color for 102 male Old World samples. Circles indicate the mean skin reflectance measured at a wavelength of 685 nanometers plotted against latitude. Negative values of latitude correspond to the Southern Hemisphere (below the equator), and positive values of latitude correspond to the Northern Hemisphere (above the equator). The solid line indicates the best-fitting curve relating skin color and latitude. Closer analysis shows that skin color is darker in the Southern Hemisphere than in the Northern Hemisphere at an equivalent distance from the equator. (Adapted from Relethford 1997.)

suggesting that natural selection for light skin may have occurred independently in different parts of the world (Norton et al. 2007).

Another pigment affecting skin color is hemoglobin, which gives oxygenated blood cells their red color. Light-skinned people have little melanin near the surface of the skin, and so the red color shows through. Because of this effect, "white" people are actually "pink."

Skin color is also affected to a certain extent by sex and age. In general, males are darker than females, probably because of differential effects of sex hormones on melanin production. Age also produces variation. The skin darkens somewhat during adolescence, particularly in females.

The Distribution of Skin Color As mentioned in Chapter 14, human skin color is measured by the percentage of light reflected off the skin at a given wavelength of light. Figure 15.11 shows the worldwide distribution of human skin color based on data from 102 male samples from the Old World. Skin color is darkest at the equator and tends to be lighter with increasing distance from the equator, north or south. Closer investigation shows that there is also a hemispheric difference—skin color tends to be darker in the Southern Hemisphere (below the equator) than in the Northern Hemisphere, even at equivalent latitudes (Relethford 1997). The distribution of skin color and latitude corresponds to the amount of ultraviolet radiation received at the earth's surface. Because of the way sunlight strikes the earth, ultraviolet radiation is strongest at the equator and diminishes in strength as we move away from the equator. Further, ultraviolet radiation tends to be greater in the Southern Hemisphere than in the Northern Hemisphere due to a number of astronomical and meteorological factors (McKenzie and Elwood 1990; Relethford 1997). Jablonski and Chaplin (2000) have confirmed that human skin color is correlated with ultraviolet radiation; populations living in areas with high levels of ultraviolet radiation tend to be darker than those living in areas with less ultraviolet radiation.

The distribution of human skin color in the world today suggests past evolutionary events relating to natural selection. Current thinking suggests that dark skin evolved among our early ancestors in Africa as a means of protection against the damaging effects of ultraviolet radiation, most likely relating to the loss of hair and increase in sweat gland density that we suspect took place as our ancestors became increasingly adapted to the hot climate in Africa. Later, as some humans began moving out of Africa, lighter skin color evolved farther away from the equator. This scenario poses two questions: (1) What were the selective effects of ultraviolet radiation leading to dark skin near the equator? and (2) Why did light skin evolve in regions with less ultraviolet radiation?

The Evolution of Dark Skin   Ultraviolet radiation can have several harmful effects. In sufficient amounts, ultraviolet radiation can lead to skin cancer. The greater the intensity of ultraviolet radiation, the greater the risk for skin cancer at any given level of pigmentation. Among the European American populations of the United States, skin cancer rates are much higher in Texas than in Massachusetts (Damon 1977). Dark-skinned individuals have lower rates of skin cancer because the heavy concentration of melanin near the surface of the skin blocks some of the ultraviolet radiation. Some have suggested that dark skin evolved in human populations near the equator to protect against skin cancer (Robins 1991). Others have rejected skin cancer as a significant factor in the evolution of human skin color because it tends to affect primarily individuals past their reproductive years (Jablonski and Chaplin 2000). If someone dies from skin cancer after reproducing, his or her death does not affect the process of natural selection.

Sunburn has also been suggested as a potential factor in natural selection. Severe sunburn can lead to infection and can interfere with the body's ability to sweat effectively. Dark skin could protect from these effects and thus be selected for in areas of high ultraviolet radiation (Robins 1991), although the exact magnitude of this selection is not clear.

Jablonski and Chaplin (2000) argue that the potential selective effects of skin cancer and sunburn are minimal and that the most significant factor leading to darker skin in equatorial populations was the damaging effect of ultraviolet radiation on folate levels in the body. Folic acid, a necessary nutrient, is converted into folate in the body. Ultraviolet radiation can destroy folate, leading to several serious consequences. Folate deficiency has been linked to disorders in developing fetuses, including an increase in neural tube defects, which reduces survivability. Folate levels also affect reproductive capabilities; folate deficiency can disrupt the production of sperm and lead to male infertility. Jablonski and Chaplin suggest that photodestruction of folate has serious consequences for both mortality and fertility and that dark skin evolved for protection in areas with high levels of ultraviolet radiation.

The Evolution of Light Skin   As some humans moved farther from equatorial regions, they lived in areas with lower levels of ultraviolet radiation, and consequently, the risks from ultraviolet radiation decreased. Lighter-skinned individuals would be at less risk from folate deficiency (as well as sunburn and skin cancer if they are indeed selective factors). This does not explain *why* light skin evolved farther from the equator, however, only that it *could* evolve. To construct a complete model for the evolution of human skin color variation, we need to have one or more reasons *why* light skin would have been adaptive farther from the equator. In the absence of such reasons, we would not expect a strong correlation with latitude. Factors that explain the evolution of dark skin near the equator do not explain light skin farther from the equator.

The most widely accepted model for the evolution of light skin focuses on the synthesis of vitamin D. As noted earlier, the major source of vitamin D throughout human history and prehistory has been the sun because ultraviolet radiation stimulates vitamin D synthesis. Today, we may receive vitamin D through vitamin supplements or through the injection of vitamin D into our milk. Both of these dietary modifications are recent human inventions, however. Formerly, humans had to obtain their vitamin D through diet or through stimulation of chemical compounds by ultraviolet radiation. Some foods, such as fish oils, are high in vitamin D but are not found in all environments. For most human populations in the past, the major source of vitamin D was the sun.

Vitamin D deficiency can cause a number of problems relating to poor bone development and maintenance, including diseases such as rickets, which leads to deformed bones. Such health hazards can affect fertility as well as mortality. One frequent consequence of childhood rickets is the deformation of a woman's pelvis, an effect that can hinder or prevent successful childbirth. In one U.S. study, only 2 percent of European American women had such pelvic deformities as compared to 15 percent of African American women (Molnar 1998). This difference presumably relates to skin color; darker women are unable to absorb enough vitamin D for healthy bone growth.

Vitamin D deficiency can be linked to the evolution of light skin. As discussed previously, dark skin protects against the harmful effects of ultraviolet radiation in populations near the equator, where ultraviolet radiation is the most intense. As human populations moved away from the equator, these risks declined and the risk for vitamin D deficiency increased because darker skin blocked too much ultraviolet radiation. Natural selection thus produced a change toward lighter skin color that would be adaptive in such environments.

There has been considerable debate over causal factors in the evolution of human skin color and their relative importance. As noted by Jablonski and Chaplin (2000), current evidence suggests that the primary reason for the evolution of human skin color is the balance between the need for darker skin to protect against photodestruction of folate and the need for lighter skin to facilitate vitamin D synthesis. At any given latitude, the optimal skin color reflects the balance between these risks. Near the equator, the primary

FIGURE 15.12

Schematic diagram of the relationship between latitude, ultraviolet radiation, and the relative risks of folate deficiency and vitamin D deficiency. Near the equator, dark skin is selected for to block the photodestruction of folate due to high levels of ultraviolet radiation. Farther away from the equator, this risk decreases and the risk for vitamin D deficiency increases, facilitating the evolution of lighter skin color to allow sufficient vitamin D synthesis.

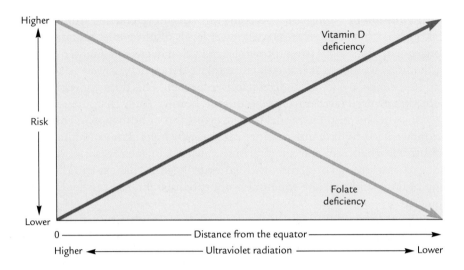

risk is folate deficiency, leading to darker skin for protection. As we go farther from the equator, this risk decreases and the risk for vitamin D deficiency increases, thus leading to lighter and lighter skin color farther and farther from the equator (Figure 15.12). It is possible that other factors, such as protection against sunburn near the equator, also contribute to the observed correspondence between skin color and latitude.

NATURAL SELECTION AND CULTURE CHANGE

Natural selection acts on individuals in a specific environment. In humans, the interaction with the environment is often strongly affected by cultural practices and culture change. The general issue of the interaction between human biology and culture change is discussed further in Chapter 17. Here, we look at two examples of how culture change has affected natural selection in human populations. Genetic evidence shows that we are still experiencing natural selection (Box 15.2).

Horticulture and the Sickle Cell Allele in Africa

Sickle cell anemia provides an excellent example of the interaction of biology and culture. Livingstone (1958) and others have taken information on the distribution and ecology of the malaria parasite and the mosquito that transmits it, along with information on the prehistory and history of certain regions in Africa, and presented a hypothesis about changes in the frequency of the sickle cell allele. Several thousand years ago, the African environment was not conducive to the spread of malaria. Large areas of the continent were covered in dense forests, and the mosquito that spreads malaria thrives best

BOX 15.2

Are We Still Experiencing Natural Selection?

When we compare ourselves with the African apes, we see many traits that have been selected for during the course of human evolution, including habitual bipedalism, an enlarged brain relative to body size, and development of vocal anatomy for language. We have also changed culturally, including the origins of agriculture and civilization. Over the past 12,000 years, our species' cultural evolution has been very rapid, particularly relative to the much slower pace of biological change (see Chapter 17). As we increasingly adapt to new challenges culturally, does this mean that the biological process of natural selection no longer operates in human populations? Some scientists have argued that there is now little selection pressure operating in human populations because of our technology and medical advances, but others disagree and note that selection still operates on the human genome (Balter 2005).

Some of the examples given in this chapter should convince you that much of natural selection in human populations has been recent. Changes in sickle cell allele frequency in malarial environments (as well as other genetic adaptations to malaria) are likely to be relatively recent in human evolution because only with the development of agriculture, which led to larger population sizes, have epidemic diseases been widespread among humanity (see Chapter 17 for further discussion). Culture change has altered the trajectory of genetic change in human evolution. Given our species' proclivity for culture change and its effect on us, there is no reason to expect natural selection to stop. New diseases, such as AIDS and the Ebola virus, continue to emerge and will affect differences in survival and reproduction.

Indeed, new research in molecular genetics suggests that there are many examples of recent and ongoing natural selection in human populations. Our ability to sequence our genome has helped in our search for DNA sequences affected by natural selection. There are a number of statistical tests for selection. These tests examine the frequency of different SNPs and DNA haplotypes (see Box 14.3), and compare observed patterns of genetic diversity with those expected under a balance between mutation and genetic drift; any differences from the expected numbers are potential clues to natural selection (Sabeti et al. 2006; Voight et al. 2006). Hawks and colleagues (2007) found evidence of considerable potential for natural selection in their analysis of 3.9 million SNPs from the human genome. As noted in Chapter 2, they argue that the potential for natural selection has actually increased in recent human history because of population growth; the larger the species, the more potentially adaptive mutations will arise each generation.

---

in ample sunlight and pools of stagnant water. Neither condition then existed in the African forests, where extensive foliage prevented much sunlight from reaching the forest floor. In addition, the forest environment was highly absorbent, so water did not tend to accumulate in pools. In other words, the environment was not conducive to large populations of mosquitoes. Consequently, the malaria parasite did not have a hospitable environment either. This situation changed several thousand years ago when prehistoric African populations brought horticulture to the area. **Horticulture** is a form of farming employing only hand tools and no animal labor or irrigation. As the land was cleared for crops, the entire ecology shifted. Without the many trees, it was easier for sunlight to reach the land surface. Continued use of the land changed the soil chemistry, allowing pools of water to accumulate. Both changes led to an environment ideal for the growth and spread of mosquito populations, and therefore the spread of the malaria parasite. The growth of the human population also provided more hosts for the mosquitoes to feed on, thus increasing the spread of malaria.

Before the development of horticulture in Africa, the frequency of the sickle cell allele was probably low, as it is in nonmalarial environments today.

horticulture A form of farming in which only simple hand tools are used.

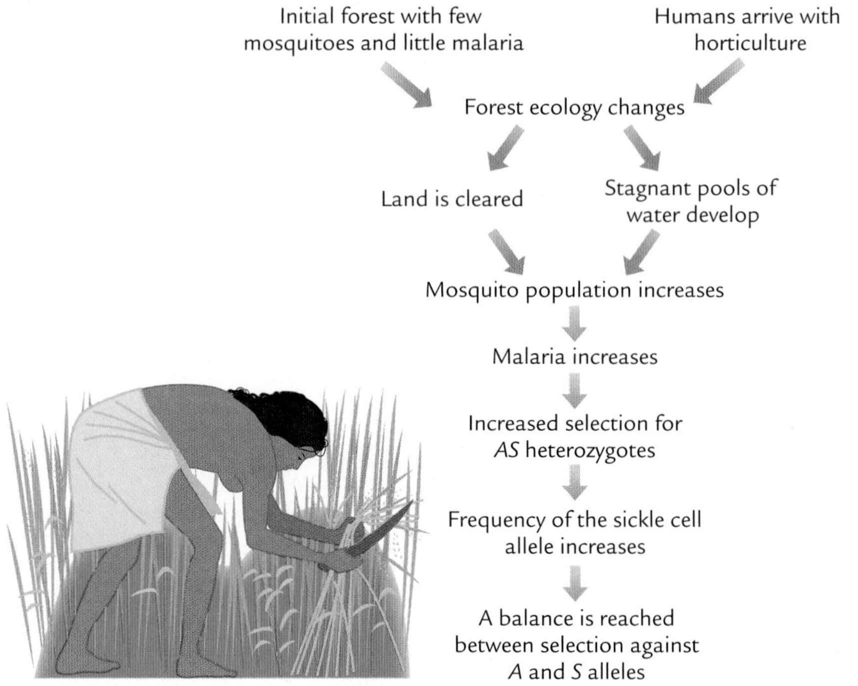

FIGURE 15.13

Sequence of cultural and environmental changes leading to changes in the frequency of the sickle cell allele in malarial Africa.

Initial forest with few mosquitoes and little malaria

Humans arrive with horticulture

Forest ecology changes

Land is cleared

Stagnant pools of water develop

Mosquito population increases

Malaria increases

Increased selection for AS heterozygotes

Frequency of the sickle cell allele increases

A balance is reached between selection against A and S alleles

When the incidence of malaria increased, it became evolutionarily advantageous to have the heterozygote *AS* genotype because those who had it would have greater resistance to malaria without suffering the effects of sickle cell anemia. As shown earlier, this change could have taken place in a short period of time, roughly 100 generations, because of the large differences in fitness among hemoglobin genotypes. The initial introduction of the sickle cell allele, *S*, through mutation or gene flow was followed by a rapid change, reaching an equilibrium point in which the fitness of the entire human population was at a maximum.

This scenario shows that human cultural adaptations (horticulture) can affect the ecology of other organisms (the mosquito and malaria parasite), which can then cause genetic change in the human population (an increase in the frequency of the sickle cell allele). This sequence of events is summarized in Figure 15.13.

Of course, we cannot observe these events directly because they occurred in the past. Nonetheless, all available evidence supports this hypothesis. We know the physiological differences between different hemoglobin types. We also know that low frequencies of the *S* allele occur in nonmalarial environments and higher frequencies occur where there is malaria. Archaeological evidence shows when and where the spread of horticulture took place in Africa. From studies of modern-day agriculture, we also know that malaria spreads quickly following the clearing of land. Taking all this information together, the scenario for changes in the frequency of the sickle cell allele in Africa seems most reasonable.

Lactase Persistence and Lactose Intolerance

As mammals, human infants receive nourishment from mothers' milk. Infants produce an enzyme, lactase, which allows milk sugar to be digested. In most human populations, lactase production stops by around 5 years of age. Lactase production is related to a gene on chromosome 2 that has two alleles (Mielke et al. 2011). The *LCT*R* allele causes lactase to stop being produced after several years of age. The *LCT*P* allele is dominant and causes lactase to be produced throughout life, a condition known as **lactase persistence.** Individuals with the recessive homozygote (*LCT*R/LCT*R*) will not produce lactase later in life and have difficulty digesting milk, a condition known as **lactose intolerance,** which can lead to diarrhea, cramps, and other digestive problems (Beall and Steegmann 2000).

Figure 15.14 shows the frequency of lactose intolerance in a number of human populations. In general, the frequency of lactose intolerance is high in most African and Asian populations and tends to be lower in European populations. A noticeable exception to this rule is the Fulani in Africa, who have a much lower prevalence (22 percent) of lactose intolerance than the rest of Africa. A number of analyses have found that the frequency of lactose intolerance is lowest in populations that have a history of dairy farming (Holden and Mace 1997; Leonard 2000).

This correspondence is clearest in Africa, where populations such as the Ibos and Bantus—known agricultural populations that did not practice dairy farming—typically have high rates of lactose intolerance. The Fulani, however, are nomadic cattle herders who rely extensively on milk in their diet. The correspondence of lactase persistence and dairy farming provides a powerful example of convergent evolution, whereby natural selection has led to the same outcomes in different parts of the world depending on a cultural trait—dairy farming. There are several advantages for those able to digest milk. In addition to providing overall nutrition, milk can be an important source of

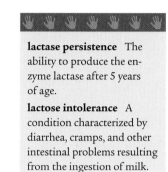

lactase persistence The ability to produce the enzyme lactase after 5 years of age.

lactose intolerance A condition characterized by diarrhea, cramps, and other intestinal problems resulting from the ingestion of milk.

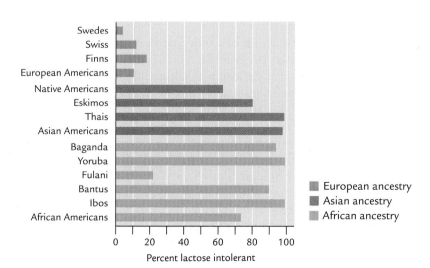

FIGURE 15.14

Frequencies of lactose intolerance in some human populations. (Data from Lerner and Libby 1976:327 and Molnar 1998:133. Data for African Americans, Asian Americans, Thais, Eskimo, Native Americans, and European Americans are the midpoints of a range of values given in the data sources.)

water. Molecular analysis shows that several different mutations are associated with lactase persistence that have been selected for among dairy farmers, and these date back an estimated 7,000 years (Tishkoff et al. 2007). Lactase persistence thus provides an excellent example of recent and rapid evolution in human populations.

Studies of lactase persistence illustrate that we need to consider biological variation and evolutionary change when making policy decisions. In the United States, which has a large dairy economy, milk is regarded as an essential part of a "normal" diet. We think of milk as intrinsically good and in the past have sent milk to people in less developed nations in the belief that what was good for us must be good for them. It soon became clear, however, that many of these people were lactose intolerant and that milk was not good for them. Health and dietary policies must always consider biological and cultural diversity.

Summary

Biological anthropologists use information on biological variation to make inferences concerning the evolutionary history of populations and of specific traits. Many studies have used biological data to examine questions about a population's history, such as where they came from and how they interacted with other populations. Case studies in this chapter focus on the Asian origin of Native Americans, the genetic impact of population settlement and invasion in Ireland, and the biological history of African Americans.

Data on biological variation can also inform us about natural selection in recent human history. Perhaps the best-documented example of natural selection in human populations is the relationship between hemoglobin alleles and two selective forces: sickle cell anemia and malaria. In environments where malaria is common, selection has led to an increase in the sickle cell allele because the heterozygotes are the most fit—they show greater resistance to malaria but do not suffer from the adverse effects of sickle cell anemia. Studies of blood groups and other genetic markers also suggest a role for natural selection in human variation.

Skin color is another example of a trait that shows a strong environmental correlation, in this case with latitude. This distribution, combined with other evidence, suggests that dark skin is selected for near the equator primarily to protect against the harmful effects of excess ultraviolet radiation (photodestruction of folate). Light skin may have evolved farther from the equator to facilitate sufficient vitamin D synthesis.

Natural selection in human populations is often affected by culture change. In the case of the evolution of the sickle cell allele in Africa, the introduction of horticulture by humans altered the physical environment, making it a more hospitable environment for the reproduction of mosquitoes that transmit malaria. As a consequence, higher frequencies of the sickle cell allele were selected for. The distribution of lactase persistence in human populations also shows the impact of culture change; higher frequencies are found in populations that have a long history of dairy farming.

Supplemental Readings

Jablonski, N. G., and G. Chaplin. 2000. The evolution of human skin coloration. *Journal of Human Evolution* 39:57–106. A long article that provides the best current review and synthesis regarding the evolution of human skin color.

Jobling, M. A., M. E. Hurles, and C. Tyler-Smith. 2004. *Human Evolutionary Genetics: Origins, Peoples and Disease.* New York: Garland Science. A comprehensive survey of human population genetics, with a number of chapters on population history.

Olsen, S. 2002. *Mapping Human History: Discovering the Past through Our Genes.* Boston: Houghton Mifflin.

Relethford, J. H. 2003. *Reflections of Our Past: How Human History Is Revealed in Our Genes.* Boulder, CO: Westview Press. Two books, written for a general audience, that show how genetic data can provide information on history and ancestry.

Stinson, S., B. Bogin, R. Huss-Ashmore, and D. O'Rourke. 2000. *Human Biology: An Evolutionary and Biocultural Perspective.* New York: John Wiley. A comprehensive volume consisting of review chapters on a variety of topics relating to human population biology. Many chapters include valuable summaries of topics considered here, including population history, genetic polymorphisms, lactase persistence, and skin color.

A Sherpa walking across a bridge in Nepal. The Sherpa are an example of a population that has adapted, both biologically and culturally, to the stresses of living at high altitudes.

Human Biocultural Adaptation

How do humans adapt? Thus far, we have focused on genetic adaptation through natural selection. However, this is one of several ways of adapting. In this chapter, we examine a broader perspective of adaptation. Central to the study of adaptation is the concept of **stress,** broadly defined as any factor that interferes with the normal limits of operation of an organism. Organisms maintain these limits through an ability known as **homeostasis.** As ways of dealing with the stresses that alter your body's functioning, adaptations restore homeostasis. For example, within normal limits, your body maintains a relatively constant body temperature. When you stand outside in a cold wind, you may shiver. This is your body's way of adapting to cold stress. You might also choose to put on a jacket.

As human beings, we can adapt both biologically and culturally. It is important to note, however, that our biocultural nature can work against us. In adapting to stresses culturally, we can introduce other stresses as a result of our behavior. Pollution, for example, is a consequence of cultural change that has had a negative impact on our physical environment in numerous ways.

Key to the interaction between human biology and culture, human adaptation operates on a number of levels—physiologic, developmental, genetic, and cultural—all of which are interrelated, for better or for worse. Thus, countering a biological stress such as disease with the cultural adaptation of medicine can lower the death rate for human populations but can also increase population size, which in turn can lead to further stresses, such as food shortages and environmental degradation.

Besides genetic and cultural adaptation, humans are capable of three other forms of adaptation that are physiologic in nature: acclimation, acclimatization, and developmental acclimatization. **Acclimation** refers to short-term changes that occur very quickly after exposure to a stress, such as sweating when you are hot. **Acclimatization** refers to physiologic changes that take longer, from days to months, such as an increase in red blood cell production after moving to a high-altitude environment. When a change occurs during the physical growth of any organism, it is known as **developmental acclimatization.** An example (covered later in the chapter) is the increase in chest size that occurs when a person grows up in high altitudes. The ability of organisms to respond physiologically or developmentally to environmental stresses is often referred to as **plasticity.**

stress Any factor that interferes with the normal limits of operation of an organism.

homeostasis In a physiologic sense, the maintenance of normal limits of body functioning.

acclimation Short-term physiologic responses to a stress, usually within minutes or hours.

acclimatization Long-term physiologic responses to a stress, usually taking from days to months.

developmental acclimatization Changes in organ or body structure that occur during the physical growth of any organism.

plasticity The ability of an organism to respond physiologically or developmentally to environmental stress.

CLIMATE AND HUMAN ADAPTATION

Though originally tropical primates, we humans have managed to expand into virtually every environment on our planet. Such expansion has been possible largely because of multiple adaptations to the range of temperatures around the world.

Physiologic Responses to Temperature Stress

As warm-blooded creatures, humans have the ability to maintain a constant body temperature. This homeostatic quality works well only under certain limits.

vasoconstriction The narrowing of blood vessels, which reduces blood flow and heat loss.

vasodilation The opening of blood vessels, which increases blood flow and heat loss.

Cold Stress When you are cold, your body is losing heat too rapidly. One response is to increase heat production temporarily through shivering, which also increases your metabolic rate. This response is not very efficient and is costly in terms of energy. A more efficient physiologic response to cold stress is minimization of heat loss through alternate constriction and dilation of blood vessels. **Vasoconstriction,** the narrowing of blood vessels, reduces blood flow and heat loss. **Vasodilation,** the opening of the blood vessels, serves to increase blood flow and heat loss. These responses are examples of acclimation to cold stress.

When a person is first subjected to cold stress, vasoconstriction acts to minimize the loss of heat from the body to the extremities (i.e., the hands, feet, and face). As a result, skin temperature drops. This response becomes dangerous, however, if it continues too long. Should this start to happen, vasodilation begins, causing blood and heat to flow from the interior of the body to the extremities. The increased blood flow prevents damage to the extremities, but now the body is losing heat again! Neither vasoconstriction nor vasodilation by itself provides an effective physiologic response to cold stress. *Both* must operate, back and forth, to maintain a balance between heat loss and damage to the extremities.

An interesting phenomenon occurs after initial exposure to cold stress. The cycles of alternating vasoconstriction and vasodilation, accompanied by alternating cycles of cold and warm skin temperatures, begin to level out, becoming more frequent and less extreme. Skin temperature changes more quickly, but the increases and decreases are not as great. This pattern, called the *Lewis hunting phenomenon,* demonstrates how effective the body's ability is to adapt. The smaller and more frequent cycles are more efficient (Figure 16.1).

Heat Stress When experiencing heat stress, your body is not removing heat quickly enough. There are four ways in which heat is lost from the body, three of which can also increase heat (Frisancho 1993). *Radiation* is heat flow from objects in the form of electromagnetic radiation. The body removes heat

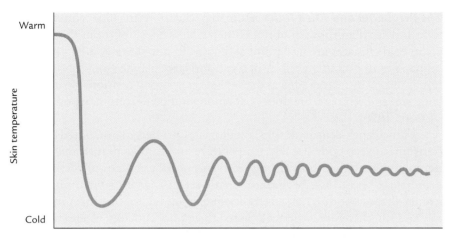

Warm

Skin temperature

Cold

Time after exposure to ice water

FIGURE 16.1

The Lewis hunting phenomenon. Initial immersion of a finger in ice water produces a decrease in skin temperature, caused by vasoconstriction. After a while, this response gives way to vasodilation, which causes skin temperature to increase. The cycles continue over time but become more frequent and less extreme, thus providing more efficient adaptation. (Modified after Frisancho 1993:85.)

through radiation but also picks up heat radiated by other objects. *Convection* refers to the removal or gain of heat through air molecules. Heat flows from a warm object to a cooler object. *Conduction* is heat exchange through physical contact with another object, such as the ground or clothes. Conduction generally accounts for a very small proportion of heat exchange. *Evaporation* is the loss of heat through the conversion of water to vapor. In the process of sweat evaporation, heat energy is consumed. Evaporation is the only one of these four mechanisms that results in heat loss without heat gain.

The amount of heat loss through these mechanisms varies according to both temperature and humidity. As the temperature increases, the only way your body can cope is to increase the amount of evaporation (your body can't amplify any of the other three mechanisms). As a result, evaporation is the most effective mechanism for heat removal in excessively hot temperatures. At comfortable temperatures, most heat is lost through radiation, and evaporation accounts for only 23 percent of the total lost. At hot temperatures (95°F), evaporation accounts for 90 percent. Vasodilation is also important in heat loss. The opening of the blood vessels moves internal heat to the outside skin. The heat can then be transferred to the environment through radiation, convection, and evaporation.

Evaporation has its drawbacks. The removal of too much water from the body can be harmful and even fatal. The efficiency of evaporation is also affected by humidity. In humid environments, evaporation is less efficient, making heat loss more difficult under hot and humid conditions than under hot and dry conditions.

Climate and Morphological Variation

Differences in physiologic responses and certain morphological variations— most notably, the size and shape of the body and head—affect people's ability to handle temperature stress. Nose size and shape are related to temperature and humidity.

The Bergmann and Allen Rules Human populations in colder climates tend to be heavier than those in hotter climates. This does not mean that all people in cold climates are heavy and all people in hot climates are light. Every human group contains a variety of small and large people. Some of this variation is caused by factors such as diet. However, a strong relationship of *average* body size and temperature does exist among indigenous human populations (Roberts 1978).

A nineteenth-century English zoologist, Carl Bergmann, noted the relationship between body size and temperature in a number of mammal species. Bergmann explained his findings in terms of mammalian physiology and principles of heat loss. **Bergmann's rule** states that if two mammals have similar shapes but different sizes, the smaller animal will lose heat more rapidly and will therefore be better adapted to warmer climates, where the ability to lose heat is advantageous. Larger mammals lose heat more slowly and are therefore better adapted to colder climates.

The reason for these relationships is that heat loss is a function of the total surface area of a mammal, whereas heat production is a function of total volume. A larger mammal has greater surface area and volume than a smaller mammal, but the *ratio* of surface area to volume is less (this is because surface area increases with the *square* of a dimension, whereas volume increases with the *cube* of a dimension). The net effect is that the larger the mammal, the slower the rate of heat loss. Consequently, larger body size is more adaptive in a cold climate, where heat loss would be a problem. Small body size, on the other hand, is more adaptive in a hot climate, because it would be beneficial to lose heat more quickly.

Bergmann's rule also deals with body shape. Because of the biophysical principles of heat production and loss, mammals that have a more linear body shape lose heat more rapidly and are better adapted to hot climates. Mammals whose body shape is less linear and more stocky lose heat less rapidly and are better adapted to cold climates. Another zoologist, J. Allen, applied these principles to body limbs and other appendages. **Allen's rule** predicts that mammals in cold climates will have shorter, bulkier limbs, whereas mammals in hot climates will have longer, narrower ones.

Body Size and Shape Do the Bergmann and Allen rules hold for human body size and shape? Figure 16.2 shows several Masai cattle herders from Africa and an Inuit (Eskimo) child. Note the thinness and length of the Masai's body and limbs compared to those of the Inuit. These physiques do in fact conform to Bergmann's and Allen's predictions. Analysis of data from many human populations has found the rules to be accurate in describing the *average* trends among populations in the world today and in the past (Ruff 1994). Again, don't forget that extensive variation exists within populations. Also, some populations are exceptions to the general rule. African pygmies, for example, are short and have short limbs, yet they live in a hot climate. The pygmy's short size appears to be due to a hormonal deficiency (Shea and Gomez 1988).

The Bergmann and Allen rules apply to adult human body size and shape. Are these average patterns the result of natural selection (i.e., genetic

Bergmann's rule States that among mammals of similar shape, the larger mammal loses heat less rapidly than the smaller mammal, and that among mammals of similar size, the mammal with a linear shape will lose heat more rapidly than the mammal with a nonlinear shape.

Allen's rule States that mammals in cold climates tend to have short, bulkier limbs, allowing less loss of body heat, whereas mammals in hot climates tend to have long, slender limbs, allowing greater loss of body heat.

FIGURE 16.2

An Inuit (*left*) and Masai cattle herders (*right*) illustrate the relationship between body size, body shape, and climate predicted by the Bergmann and Allen rules. The shorter and stockier build of the Inuit is better adapted for a cold climate, and the taller and thinner body of the Masai is better adapted for a hot climate.

adaptation) or changes in size and shape during the growth process (i.e., developmental acclimatization)? Do infants born elsewhere who move into an environment attain the same adult size and shape as native-born infants? If so, this suggests a direct influence of environment on growth. If not, then the growth pattern leading to a certain adult size and shape may be genetic in nature and determined by natural selection. If the growth pattern is entirely genetic, then we can expect to see the same ultimate size and shape regardless of environment. That is, an infant born in a cold climate but raised in a hot climate will still show the characteristic size and shape of humans born in cold climates. Of course, if *both* environmental and genetic factors are responsible for adult size and shape, then the expected pattern is more complex. Unraveling the potential genetic and climatic effects is a difficult process because other contributing influences, such as nutrition, also vary with climate.

The evidence to date suggests that both genetic and environmental factors influence the relationship among climate, growth, body size, and body shape. When children grow up in a climate different from that of their ancestors, they tend to grow in ways the indigenous children do (Malina 1975; Roberts 1978). Changes in nutritional patterns also have an effect. Katzmarzyk and Leonard (1998) examined the relationship between body size and shape and average annual temperature using data collected from 1953 to 1996, and compared their results with previous studies. They found that although the more recent data still showed the patterns expected from the Bergmann and Allen rules, this relationship was not as strong as in previous decades, suggesting

BOX 16.1

Cranial Plasticity—Did Boas Get it Wrong?

Franz Boas (1858–1942) is often referred to as the father of American anthropology; he promoted the four-field approach described in this book's introduction, where anthropology is made up of the subfields of archaeology, biological anthropology, cultural anthropology, and linguistics. One of his major contributions to biological anthropology was a study of the effect of environment on the cephalic index, a measure of cranial shape described in the man text of this chapter. Up until Boas' time, many viewed the cephalic index as a racial characteristic that was overwhelmingly inherited, with little environmental influence. Boas compared the cephalic index of children born in the United States to immigrant parents to that of immigrant children born in Europe. He found that the cephalic indices of various groups (Italians, Polish, etc.) changed, and therefore the cephalic index of the children depended on the environment in which they grew up. This study became

a classic example of the kind of plasticity that can occur during one's growth and development. The key finding was that physical traits were not solely a function of genetics; the environment also has an effect.

In the 2000s, Boas' original data were reanalyzed using modern statistical methods to determine if Boas was correct. Two sets of researchers initially came to somewhat different conclusions. Sparks and Jantz (2002) argued that Boas' data showed only minimal evidence for cranial plasticity, whereas Gravlee and colleagues (2003b) argued that Boas had gotten it right and that the data did show evidence of cranial plasticity. Although some of the media portrayed this as a major debate, careful reading of these papers, as well as subsequent comments (Gravlee et al. 2003a; Sparks and Jantz 2003), suggests that there is an element of truth to both groups' claims—it depends on the specific questions being asked (Relethford 2004a).

---

that other factors, such as changes in nutrition and health care, have obscured the relationship between climate and morphology to some extent.

cephalic index A measure of cranial shape, defined as the maximum width of the skull divided by the maximum length of the skull.

Cranial Size and Shape The size and shape of the human head has long been of interest to anthropologists. In past times, the shape of the head was the focus of studies of racial classification. In the nineteenth century, the Swedish anatomist Anders Retzius developed a measure of cranial shape called the **cephalic index.** This index is derived from two measurements: the total length of the head and its maximum width. To compute the index, you simply divide the width of the head by the length of the head and multiply the result by 100. For example, if a person has a head length of 182 mm and a head width of 158 mm, the cephalic index is $(158/182) \times 100 = 86.8$. That is, the person's head width is almost 87 percent of head length. Among human populations today, the cephalic index ranges from roughly 70 percent to 90 percent.

At first, cranial shape was felt to be a measurement capable of determining racial groupings. For example, African skulls were found to have lower cephalic indices than European skulls. Further study showed *rough* agreement but also produced many examples of overlap and similar values in different populations. For example, both Germans and Koreans have average cephalic indices of about 83 percent. Likewise, both African pygmies and Greenland Eskimos have average cephalic indices of approximately 77 percent (Harrison et al. 1988). These values do not correspond to any racial classification; they represent *averages* for each population. There is also considerable variation *within* each population (see also Box 16.1).

As more data were obtained and compared geographically, a different pattern emerged—a correspondence was found to exist between cranial shape

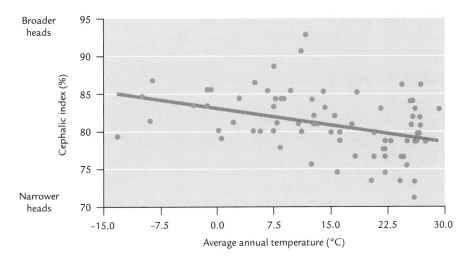

FIGURE 16.3

Relationship between cranial shape (cephalic index) and average annual temperature across the world. The solid line indicates the best-fitting linear equation. The cephalic index is greater (broader head) in colder climates because a round shape has a lower surface area/volume ratio, which minimizes heat loss. (Data from Kenneth Beals, unpublished.)

and climate. Beals (1972) examined the cephalic index and climate around the world. He found a direct relationship: Populations in colder climates tend to have wider skulls relative to length than those in hot climates (Figure 16.3). In particular, he found the average cephalic index for populations that experienced winter frost to be higher than for those in tropical environments.

This correspondence makes sense in terms of the Bergmann and Allen rules. The shape of the upper part of the skull is related to heat loss. Rounded heads (those with a high cephalic index) lose heat slowly and therefore are at an advantage in cold climates. Narrow heads lose heat more quickly and are therefore at an advantage in hot climates. It appears that as human populations moved into colder climates, natural selection led to a change in the relative proportions of the skull. Beals and colleagues (1983) have extended this analysis to fossil human crania over the past 1.5 million years and found similar results.

Nasal Size and Shape The shape of the nasal opening in the skull is another morphological variation that has a strong relationship to climate. The **nasal index** is the width of the nasal opening divided by the height of the nasal opening, multiplied by 100. Typical values of the nasal index range from roughly 64 percent to 104 percent (Molnar 1998). Stereotypic racial views associate wide noses (large nasal indices) with African peoples. Although it is true that some African populations have very wide noses, others have long, narrow noses.

Numerous studies have found positive associations between the average nasal index of populations and average temperature. Populations in cold climates tend to have narrow noses; those in hot climates tend to have wide noses. Relationships have also been found between average nasal index and average humidity. Populations in dry climates tend to have narrow noses; those in humid climates tend to have wide noses (Franciscus and Long 1991; Noback et al. 2011). The mucous membranes of the nose serve to warm and moisten incoming air. High, narrow noses can warm air to a greater extent than low, wide noses and therefore may be more adaptive in cold climates.

nasal index A measure of the shape of the nasal opening, defined as the width of the nasal opening divided by the height.

High, narrow noses also have a greater internal surface area with which to moisten air and are thus more adaptive in dry climates.

Cultural Adaptations

In Western societies, we tend to take cultural adaptations to temperature stress for granted. Housing, insulated clothing, heaters, air conditioners, and other technologies are all around us. How do people in other cultures adapt to excessive cold or heat?

Cold Stress The Inuit, or Eskimo people, of the Arctic have realized effective cultural adaptations to cold stress—most notably, in their clothing and shelter. It is not enough just to wear a lot of clothes to stay warm; if you work hard, you tend to overheat. The Inuit wear layered clothing, trapping air between layers to act as an insulator. Outer layers can be removed if a person overheats. Also, the Inuit design their clothing with multiple flaps that can be opened to prevent buildup of sweat while working.

While out hunting or fishing, the Inuit frequently construct temporary snow shelters, or igloos, that provide quite efficient protection from the cold. The ice is an excellent insulator, and its reflective surface helps retain heat (Figure 16.4, top). More permanent shelters also provide ample protection from the cold. Inuit houses have an underground entry, which is curved to reduce incoming wind. Inside, the main living area lies at a higher level than the fireplace; this architectural feature serves to increase heat and minimize drafts (Moran 1982).

Not all cold-weather housing is as effective as the types constructed by the Inuit. Among the Quechua Indians of the Peruvian highlands, the temperature inside temporary houses is often not much warmer than it is outside. However, these shelters do provide protection against rain and to some extent the cold. The bedding used by the Quechua is their most effective protection against heat loss (Frisancho 1993).

Heat Stress Human populations live in environments that are dry and hot (i.e., deserts) and that are humid and hot (i.e., tropical rain forests). Moran (1982) has summarized some basic principles of clothing and shelter that are used in desert environments, where the objectives are fourfold: to reduce heat production, to reduce heat gain from radiation and from conduction, and to increase evaporation. Clothing is important because it protects from both solar radiation and hot winds. Typical desert clothing is light and loose, thus allowing circulation of air to increase evaporation. The air between the clothing and the body also provides excellent insulation.

Shelters are frequently built compactly to minimize the surface area exposed to the sun. Light colors on the outside help reflect heat. Doors and windows are kept closed during the day to keep the interior cool. Building materials are also adaptive. Adobe, for example, is efficient in absorbing heat during the day and radiating it at night (see Figure 16.4, bottom); nighttime temperatures may drop precipitously in desert environments.

FIGURE 16.4

Forms of human shelter such as igloos (*top*) and Pueblo houses (*bottom*) reflect adaptation to a wide range of climatic conditions.

Heat stress in tropical environments is often a problem because the extreme humidity greatly reduces the efficiency of evaporation through sweating. Cultural adaptations to tropical environments are similar throughout the world. Clothing is minimal, helping to increase the potential for evaporation. In some cultures, shelters are built in an open design, without walls, to augment cooling during the day; in others, shelters are built closed to increase warmth at night. The combination of high heat and high humidity obviously affects daily routines. Generally, people start work early in the day, taking long midday breaks to keep from overheating.

In sum, humans have adapted to a number of environments that produce temperature stress. They have managed to adapt to extremes of hot and cold through physiologic changes, long-term genetic adaptations, and adaptive behaviors, particularly those manifested in clothing and shelter technology and in the pace of daily life.

HIGH-ALTITUDE ADAPTATION

Some human populations have lived for long periods of time at elevations of over 8,200 feet (2,500 m).

High-Altitude Stresses

High-altitude environments produce several stresses, including oxygen starvation, extreme cold, and sometimes poor nutrition. Studies of high-altitude populations have provided insight into how humans cope with multiple stresses.

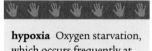

hypoxia Oxygen starvation, which occurs frequently at high altitudes.

Hypoxia   Oxygen starvation, or **hypoxia,** is more common at high altitudes because of the relationship of barometric pressure and altitude. Although the percentage of oxygen in the atmosphere is relatively constant up to almost 70 miles above the earth, barometric pressure decreases quickly with altitude. Because air is less compressed at high altitudes, its oxygen content is less concentrated, and less oxygen is thus available to the hemoglobin in the blood. The percentage of arterial oxygen saturation decreases rapidly with altitude. For persons at rest, hypoxia generally occurs around 10,000 feet; for active persons, it can occur as low as 6,000 feet (Frisancho 1993).

Other Stresses   Because the air is thinner at high altitudes, the concentration of ultraviolet radiation is greater, and the air itself offers less protection against it. The thinner air also causes considerable heat loss from the atmosphere, resulting in cold stress. In many high-altitude environments, conditions are also extremely dry because of high winds and low humidity. In addition, hypoxia affects plants and animals; for lack of oxygen, trees cannot grow above 13,000 feet. The limited availability of plants and animals means that nutritional stress is likely in many high-altitude environments.

Numerous studies have compared the physiology, genetics, and morphology of high-altitude and low-altitude populations. Early research tended to attribute any differences to the effects of hypoxia on the human body. More recent studies have shown that other stresses of high altitude are significant factors as well (Frisancho 1990). When dealing with human adaptation, we do best to consider the effect and interaction of *multiple* stresses.

Physiologic Responses to High-Altitude Stress

People who live at low altitudes experience several physiologic changes when they enter a high-altitude environment and suffer hypoxia. Some of these happen immediately; others occur over several months to a year. Such physiologic responses help to maintain sufficient oxygen levels. Respiration increases initially but returns to normal after a few days. Red blood cell production increases for roughly 3 months. The weight of the right ventricle of the heart is greater than the weight of the left ventricle in individuals who have grown up at high altitudes. Other changes include possible hyperventilation, higher hemoglobin concentration in the blood, loss of appetite, and weight loss. Memory and sensory abilities may be affected, and hypoxia may influence hormone levels. These changes are not all necessarily adaptive, and some (such as weight loss) can be harmful.

The physiologic differences between high-altitude and low-altitude natives are primarily acquired during the growth process. Studies of children who were born at low altitudes but moved into high altitudes during childhood clearly substantiate this phenomenon. In terms of aerobic capacity, for example, the younger the age of migration, the higher the aerobic capacity (Frisancho 1993). In other words, the longer a child lives in a high-altitude environment, the greater the developmental response to that environment. Age at migration has no effect on the aerobic capacity of adults, however, further indicating that most physiologic changes are the result of developmental acclimatization.

Genetic Adaptations to High-Altitude Stress

Because some human populations have lived at high altitude for many generations, there is the possibility that some features of high-altitude adaptation have been shaped by natural selection. Genetic studies of high-altitude populations have revealed evidence of such selection, and have further shown that selection has been different in different high-altitude populations. Many of these studies have involved comparisons of two different groups, one living in the Andean Plateau of South America and the other living in the Tibetan Plateau. These populations are both adapted to living at high altitude, but in different ways. Differences have been found in the level of blood oxygen, the level of oxygenation saturation, and the level of hemoglobin saturation (Beall 2007; Storz 2010). Preliminary research suggests genetic differences underlying these different responses to hypoxic stress. Such studies provide an interesting example of how there are often different paths to genetic adaptation, perhaps reflecting the nature of the initial genetic variation and different types of mutations.

Physical Growth in High-Altitude Populations

Studies conducted by Paul Baker and colleagues of high-altitude and low-altitude Indian populations in Peru found two peculiarities in growth. Chest dimensions and lung volume were greater at all ages in the high-altitude group (Figure 16.5), and high-altitude populations were also shorter at most ages than low-altitude populations (Figure 16.6) (Frisancho and Baker 1970).

FIGURE 16.5

Chest circumference for high-altitude and low-altitude Peruvian Indian populations. At all ages, the high-altitude population has the greatest chest circumference. (Courtesy A. R. Frisancho.)

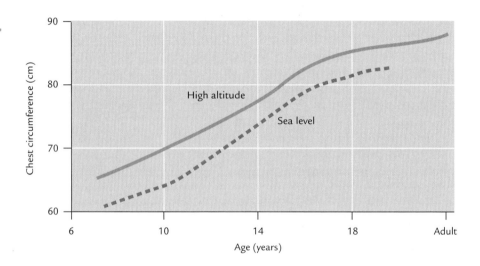

FIGURE 16.6

Stature for high-altitude and low-altitude Peruvian Indian populations. At most ages, the low-altitude population is taller. (Courtesy A. R. Frisancho.)

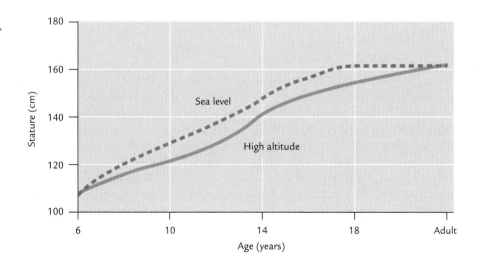

The shorter stature is related to delayed maturation, whereas the increase in chest size is due to growth acceleration during childhood.

Initially, the researchers interpreted both patterns of physical growth as direct developmental responses to hypoxia and cold stress at high altitude. Larger chests and larger lung volumes relative to body size would be better able to provide sufficient oxygen levels. More energy devoted to the growth of oxygen transport systems, however, would leave less energy available for growth in other organ systems, especially the skeletal and muscle systems. Compounded by cold stress at high altitudes, this energy deficit would lead to an increase in basal metabolic rates and further reduction in energy available for body growth. As discussed later, this view is now being questioned.

Studies in high-altitude environments around the world have shown a similar pattern of growth in chest dimensions, although the extent of growth varies. Migrants to high-altitude populations also show an increase in chest dimensions, particularly among those who migrate at an early age. Increased growth of oxygen transport systems appears to be a developmental response to hypoxia.

Are the developmental changes in chest and lung growth in high-altitude populations genetic in nature? Were they shaped by natural selection? Most research to date assigns a relatively minor role to genetic factors. One study examined high-altitude and low-altitude populations of European ancestry in Bolivia (Greksa 1990). Because these groups do not have a long history of residence at high altitude, they would not possess any genetic predisposition for high-altitude adaptations. The study showed that there was an increased capacity of the oxygen transport system in these populations at high altitude even though they were not of high-altitude ancestry. The observed changes were instead direct effects of a chronic hypoxic stress. Weitz and colleagues (2000) did not find any such effect in low-altitude Han Chinese who had migrated to a high-altitude environment, however, suggesting that there might be genetic differences between populations that underlie their differential response to hypoxia. It appears that chest dimensions and lung size are affected by both developmental and genetic factors that interact differently in different human populations (Greksa 1996).

The delayed maturation and small stature of the Peruvians have not been found in all studies of growth in high-altitude populations. As a result, some researchers have questioned the initial premise that hypoxia and cold stress have necessarily led to these characteristics, suggesting instead that other causal factors might be at work. A study undertaken in Peru has in fact shown that nutrition is a major influence on stature (Leonard et al. 1990). Though high altitude may play a role in nutritional stress in the Peruvian highlands, income levels and access to land are of greater consequence. Also, other high-altitude populations, such as those found in Ethiopia, have a higher standard of living and do not show the growth deficits observed in Peru. Thus, it appears that although increased chest growth is a functional adaptation to hypoxia, the smaller body size is not necessarily related to high altitude. These results amply illustrate the complexity in assessing the relative value of stresses in any given environment.

NUTRITIONAL ADAPTATION

The previous examples of human adaptation have focused on adaptive responses to the stresses imposed by the physical environment—specifically, temperature and high-altitude stress. This section examines adaptation to nutritional needs and differences in the availability of food resources.

Basic Nutritional Needs

Proper nutrition is needed for body maintenance, growth, and the energy needs of daily activity. Ingested nutrients provide the energy for these. During infancy, childhood, and adolescence, a greater proportion of nutrient energy goes into physical growth. Too little energy can result in a reduction in overall size and speed of maturation. Too much nutrient energy can result in accumulation of fat and acceleration of maturation. Inadequate amounts of certain critical nutrients can also affect basic biological processes, such as insufficiency in vitamin A or C, both of which can increase susceptibility to certain diseases.

Ingested energy (measured in calories) comes from carbohydrates, proteins, and fats. Dietary proteins are also necessary for certain metabolic functions. Proteins provide amino acids, of which 20 are needed by the body for synthesis and repair of body tissues. Although the body synthesizes some amino acids, adult humans require 8 amino acids available only through diet (children need 9). Without adequate sources of protein in the diet, lack of these amino acids can lead to growth retardation, illness, and death. The major sources of proteins in Western human populations are animal products, including meat, eggs, fish, and milk. Plants provide proteins, but they are lacking in one or more amino acids and must be eaten in combination with other plants to ensure adequate nutrition.

Dietary requirements in the United States are referred to as Dietary Reference Intakes (DRIs) and are published by the Institute of Medicine of the National Academies (www.iom.edu). Energy needs (caloric intake) vary by sex, height, weight, and average level of activity, with larger and more active individuals having greater energy needs. Energy needs decline with age. Protein needs are generally higher in men than women, unless the woman is pregnant or nursing, in which case her protein needs are, on average, over 25 percent higher than those of a man, and over 50 percent higher than those of a woman who is not pregnant or nursing (Figure 16.7).

Our bodies also require other nutrients, such as fatty acids, vitamins, and minerals. A diet lacking in one or more of these nutrients can lead to medical problems. A lack of iodine, for example, can lead to thyroid problems, and a lack of vitamin C can lead to the disease scurvy.

Variation in Human Diet

Human nutritional needs have been shaped by evolution. In a general sense, the nutritional needs of humans are similar to those of other omnivorous

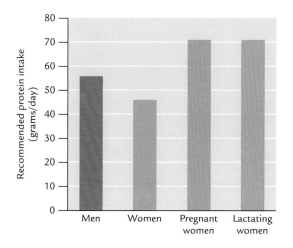

FIGURE 16.7

Recommended daily protein intake (grams per day) for different groups. Note the increased protein needs for women who are pregnant or breast-feeding. (Data from Institute of Medicine of the National Academies 2005.)

primate species. Our physiology reflects the general primate adaptation to a diet comprised of large amounts of fruit and vegetation, such as our shared inability to synthesize vitamin C, forcing us to acquire it from our diet (Leonard 2000). Humans, however, have a considerably more diverse diet, reflecting the broad range of environments we have adapted to and the diversity in cultural adaptations developed to acquire food.

As is discussed elsewhere, the primary means of acquiring food throughout most of human evolution has been hunting and gathering. This way of life began close to 2 million years ago and was the only way humans obtained food until about 12,000 years ago, when an increasing number of human populations became reliant on agriculture. As discussed further in Chapter 17, this shift in subsistence has had a noticeable biological impact on our health as we frequently eat a diet quite unlike that which we adapted to in the past.

Hunting and Gathering It is important for us to understand the diet of hunting and gathering societies because most of our biological evolution took place in this type of environment. Hunting and gathering populations do not all have the same type of diet; their specific patterns of resource utilization are shaped by their specific environments. For example, you cannot fish if there are no fish around, and you will have fewer plant foods in colder environments. Early studies of living hunter-gatherer societies such as the San of South Africa suggested that the bulk of their caloric intake came from gathering activities rather than animal proteins (Lee 1968). It is now recognized that this is not the case. In a review of data from hunting-gathering societies, Cordain et al. (2000) found that 73 percent of these societies obtained more than half of their energy needs from animal foods (hunting and/or fishing) and only 14 percent obtained more than half of their energy needs from gathered plant foods. They also found that while there is not a single hunting and gathering population that was primarily dependent on gathering, one out of five populations were almost entirely dependent on animal foods. Relative to contemporary Westernized societies, hunting-gathering societies have diets that are much higher in proteins, lower in carbohydrates, and as high, or higher, in fats (although the type of fat is different from that typically found in Western diets).

Agriculture   There is also variation among agricultural populations, dependent largely on available resources and the level of technology. Some populations practice simple horticulture, such as slash-and-burn agriculture; other populations rely on intensive agriculture. The specific food crop(s) exploited depends on the environment; rice is a main crop in Southeast Asia, wheat in Europe, and corn in the Americas.

Different ways of processing food can improve its quality. Leonard (2000) discusses one example—corn among Native American populations. Corn (maize) has advantages and disadvantages; it is high in protein but lacks two amino acids (lysine and tryptophan) and niacin. Many Native American populations use alkali substances, such as ash or lime, when cooking corn, which act to increase amino acid and niacin concentrations. Comparative research has shown that the more a society relies on corn, the more it uses such methods.

Malnutrition

malnutrition Poor nutrition, from either too much or too little food or from the improper balance of nutrients.

We tend to equate the term **malnutrition** with a diet deficient in calories, proteins, or other nutrients, but it literally means "bad nutrition." Malnutrition often does refer to having too little food (quantity and/or quality), but it can also refer to having too much. If you ingest more calories than are needed for growth, body maintenance, or physical activity, the excess is deposited as fat in your body. Obesity can lead to medical problems such as high blood pressure, heart disease, and diabetes. Obesity is a growing problem in industrialized nations such as the United States.

Throughout much of the world, however, the major nutritional problem is the lack of food, or at least the lack of a balanced diet. Poor nutrition acts to slow down the growth process, leading to small adult body size. In one sense, this change in growth is adaptive, because a smaller adult will require fewer nutrients. By focusing on this relationship, however, we ignore the problem that the slowing of growth is an indication of potential harm. Severe undernutrition, especially in infancy and childhood, can have serious effects. Not only is physical growth stunted but mental retardation also may result, and susceptibility to infectious disease increases. Severe undernutrition is common in much of the Third World, compounded by problems of poverty, overpopulation, inadequate sewage disposal, contaminated water, and economic and political conflicts.

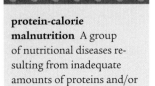

protein-calorie malnutrition A group of nutritional diseases resulting from inadequate amounts of proteins and/or calories.

A number of nutritional problems, collectively known as **protein-calorie malnutrition,** result from an inadequate amount of proteins and/or calories in the diet. Protein-calorie malnutrition is the most serious nutritional problem on the planet. Its various forms have different physical symptoms, but all stem from the basic problems of an inadequate diet and have the same ultimate effects, ranging from growth retardation to death.

The most severe types of protein-calorie malnutrition are **kwashiorkor** (a severe deficiency in proteins but not calories) and **marasmus** (severe deficiencies in *both* proteins and calories). Kwashiorkor occurs most often in infants and young children who are weaned from their mother's breast onto a diet lacking in proteins. The infant suffers growth retardation, muscle wasting, and lowered resistance to disease. One of the symptoms of kwashiorkor is the swelling of the body due to water retention (Figure 16.8). Marasmus is also most prevalent during infancy and similarly leads to growth retardation, muscle wasting, and death. A child suffering from marasmus typically looks emaciated (Figure 16.9).

Although the physical appearance of children with kwashiorkor and marasmus differs, both suffer from an inadequate diet. Population pressure and poverty certainly play a major role in much of protein-calorie malnutrition, but they are not the only factors. Some researchers, such as anthropologist Katherine Dettwyler, have argued that cultural beliefs regarding nutrition are at least as important. Such beliefs include stressing quantity over quality, postponing the age at which children eat solid foods, and following other practices that compromise proper nutrition. Thus, the elimination of protein-calorie malnutrition will require more than an attack on population growth and the reduction of poverty and disease; it will also require nutritional education (Dettwyler 1994). Dettwyler's work also shows us the folly of assuming that all cultural behaviors are necessarily adaptive.

The devastating impact of malnutrition should not be underestimated. Worldwide, 26 percent of children under the age of 5 are classified as moderately or severely undernourished (this is 160 *million* people). And more than 5.5 million children under the age of 5 die each year for reasons linked to malnutrition (UNICEF 2005).

Biological Costs of Modernization and Dietary Change

Increasingly, formerly "traditional" societies have undergone economic and technological development. Compared to rates of change in historical and prehistoric times, modernization in many parts of the world today is occurring almost instantaneously. Such rapid modernization has produced many new biological stresses due to rapid population growth, economic and

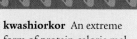

kwashiorkor An extreme form of protein-calorie malnutrition resulting from a severe deficiency in proteins but not calories.

marasmus An extreme form of protein-calorie malnutrition resulting from severe deficiencies in both proteins and calories.

FIGURE 16.8

A child with kwashiorkor in Mali, West Africa.

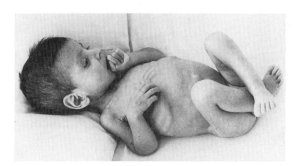

FIGURE 16.9

A child with marasmus, a severe protein and calorie deficiency.

political change, increased use of natural resources, and increased levels of pollution, to name but a few. With these rapid changes, populations face new stresses. One of these changes is the impact of modernization on traditional diets.

Modernization and Obesity There is a tendency for populations undergoing modernization to show increased height and weight. Weight gain, in particular, has often been quite dramatic in recently modernized populations, resulting in part from dietary changes and a more sedentary lifestyle. These populations show high rates of obesity, which in turn predisposes them to serious health problems (Figure 16.10).

A number of studies of the biological impact of modernization have been conducted in Samoa, a Polynesian island group in the southern Pacific Ocean. Samoa had been relatively homogeneous in both genetics and lifestyle until the beginning of the twentieth century, at which time dramatic socio-economic development took place. At present, Samoa is divided into two groups: Western Samoa, characterized by traditional diet and lifestyle, and American Samoa, characterized by a shift to modern employment patterns and diet. Bindon and Baker (1985) found that adult males and females from modernized islands weighed more and had greater amounts of subcutaneous fat. They concluded that modernization has led to a rapid increase in the frequency of obesity. In the traditional sample, for example, 14 percent of adult males older than 45 years of age were obese, whereas 25 percent were obese on one modernized island and 41 percent on another. This study illustrates how

FIGURE 16.10

Comparison of average weight (in kilograms) for adult males in traditional and modernized groups within various populations. In each case, adult males in modernized groups weigh more. (Data from Harrison et al. 1988:536.)

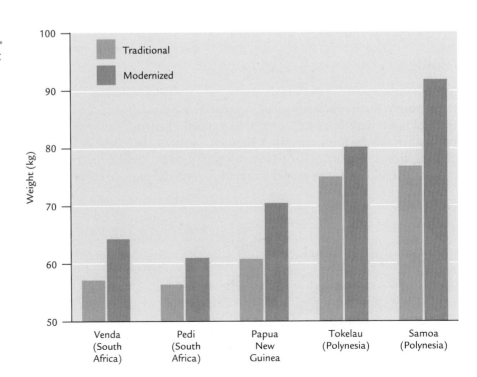

quickly some aspects of human biology can change in response to a changing environment—and the dramatic cost of modernization in much of the world.

Modernization and Blood Pressure   Blood pressure provides a measure of health. Excessive blood pressure, or hypertension, is a serious condition, both in itself and as a risk factor for other diseases. Blood pressure is measured using two readings: *systolic* blood pressure, measured during ventricular contractions, and *diastolic* blood pressure, measured during ventricular relaxation. Blood pressure tends to be higher in modernized societies and increases with age in these populations (Little and Baker 1988). In traditional societies, blood pressure tends to be lower and does not increase with age. Changes in blood pressure patterns in modernized societies reflect a number of factors, including changes in diet, lifestyle, physical activity, and overall level of stress.

Figure 16.11 presents the results of a study of modernization and blood pressure conducted by Lewis (1990) in the Gilbert Islands of the Republic of Kiribati in the central Pacific Ocean. Measurements collected during two time periods were compared: the first in 1960, when the islands had a more traditional economy, and the second in 1978, by which point the islands had undergone extensive modernization. There is a clear increase in blood pressure over time; blood pressure is higher in the 1978 sample than in the 1960 sample for all but one age group. There is also a noticeable increase in blood pressure with age in the 1978 sample, characteristic of a modernized population, but there is no apparent age-related pattern in the 1960 traditional sample. Culture change significantly affects human biology, and there is a biological cost to modernization.

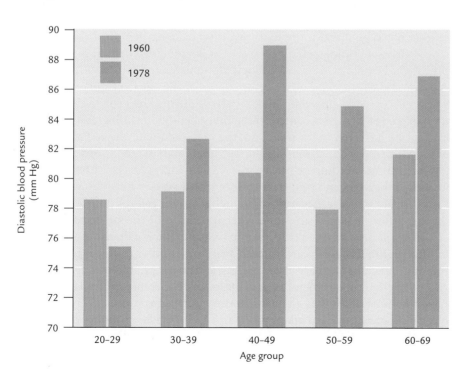

FIGURE 16.11

Effects of modernization on adult male diastolic blood pressure (mm Hg) in the Gilbert Islands. From 1960 to 1978, the area underwent modernization. Note that the average blood pressures in 1978 are higher than in 1960 and that they show an increase with age. These observations are common findings in studies of modernization and blood pressure. (Data from Lewis 1990:146.)

Summary

Studies of adaptation focus on the many ways in which organisms respond to environmental stresses. Human adaptation is particularly interesting because humans not only adapt both biologically and culturally but also must deal with stresses from their physical and cultural environments. Biological adaptation includes physiologic responses and genetic adaptation (natural selection). Cultural adaptation includes aspects of technology, economics, and social structure. In any study of human adaptation, we must look at multiple stresses and multiple adaptive (or nonadaptive) mechanisms.

Many studies of human adaptation have focused on cold and heat stress. Though as mammals, humans have the capacity for maintenance of body temperature, they must still cope with extremes in temperature. Physiologic responses of the human body to temperature stress include changes in peripheral blood flow and evaporation. Studies have shown that general relationships exist worldwide between body size and shape and temperature. These observed trends agree with the predictions of the Bergmann and Allen rules. In hot climates, small body size and linear body shape maximize heat loss. In cold climates, large body size and less linear body shape minimize heat loss. Cranial studies show that worldwide the shape of the skull also varies predictably, according to the principles of differential heat loss and the Bergmann and Allen rules. Although some of these biological features are the result of genetic adaptation, studies of children have revealed that response to temperature stress can affect growth. Cultural adaptations, especially those involving clothing, shelter, and physical activity, are also important in climatic adaptation.

Millions of people around the world live at high altitudes. The major stresses of a high-altitude population are hypoxia (oxygen shortage) and cold stress. Many physiologic changes have been documented in high-altitude peoples, including short-term physiologic responses and long-term increases in the size of the lungs and other components of the oxygen transport system. These changes are caused by hypoxic stress during the growth period, and their degree of change is related to the time spent living at high altitudes: the longer one has lived there as a child, the more adapted one is. Early studies of high-altitude populations also noted small body size that, along with delayed maturation, could be due to insufficient energy levels for body growth because of hypoxia and cold stress. More recent studies have shown that this is not always the case, because some high-altitude groups do not show this growth deficit. Instead, variation in diet appears to be the key factor.

Humans have adapted culturally to basic nutritional demands in a variety of ways. For millions of years, human ancestors utilized different methods of hunting and gathering to feed themselves, and about 12,000 years ago, humans adopted agriculture as their primary means of subsistence. Although humans have a number of ways of adapting to their nutritional needs, there are some basic biological limits to adaptation, and an increasing number of children are malnourished. Modernization has altered traditional diets as well as other aspects of lifestyle, resulting in an increased biological cost in many cases.

Supplemental Readings

Frisancho, A. R. 1993. *Human Adaptation and Accommodation.* Ann Arbor: University of Michigan Press. A thorough review of adaptation studies, focusing on physiologic adaptation.

Stinson, S., B. Bogin, R. Huss-Ashmore, and D. O'Rourke. 2000. *Human Biology: An Evolutionary and Biocultural Perspective.* New York: John Wiley. A comprehensive volume consisting of review chapters on a variety of topics relating to human population biology. Several chapters deal with climatic, high-altitude, nutritional, and infectious disease adaptation.

Chinese farmers working in rice paddies. The transition to agriculture began in the human species 12,000 years ago. This major cultural event has led to many changes in human biology, including shifts in rates of disease, death, and fertility.

The Biological
Impact of Agriculture
and Civilization

CHAPTER

17

D uring the past 12,000 years, we have changed from being hunters and gatherers to being agriculturalists; an increasing portion
of humanity lives in or near large urban centers; and our population has ex-
ploded from 5 million to 10 million people to more than 7 billion. In many
ways, we live in a world very unlike that of our ancestors.

These cultural changes have happened much faster than biological
change. As a result, biologically, we are still hunters and gatherers to some extent, but we live in conditions that are often quite different from those under
which our ancestors evolved. We live in larger groups, eat different foods,
and structure our societies in different ways. The disparity between rates of
cultural change and biological evolution has had serious consequences for
our biology. An example of this type of change was described briefly in the
section on nutritional adaptation in the previous chapter, which noted the
biomedical impact of a changing diet and lifestyle on Samoan populations.
This example is only one of many that show how rapid cultural changes have
affected our biology—not always to our benefit. This chapter considers the
impact of culture change on human biology by focusing on some major cultural changes in human evolution over the past 12,000 years.

THE BIOLOGICAL IMPACT
OF AGRICULTURE

A major shift in human adaptation was the transition from hunting and
gathering to agriculture. Human populations began relying increasingly
on agriculture starting 12,000 years ago. Although a small proportion of
human populations today still rely on hunting and gathering, most are agricultural. The reasons for this change are still widely debated, and there
was probably no single overriding cause. Feder (2007) notes that there is a
general pattern in the archaeological record showing that human populations became more **sedentary** (settled in one place) *before* agriculture developed. Human populations might have been able to settle down because
of increased efficiency at hunting and gathering and/or changes in the

CHAPTER OUTLINE

- The Biological Impact
of Agriculture

- The Biological Impact
of Civilization

- Changes in Modern
Times

sedentary Settled in one
place throughout most or
all of the year.

environment resulting from the warming climate near the end of the Pleistocene. Some archaeologists suggest that the shift to a sedentary life led to population growth, which in turn led to the need for more food resources. Under such conditions, sedentary populations would shift their methods of acquiring food and adopt a variety of agricultural strategies to increase the food supply, such as weeding, protecting plant resources, and clearing forests. Over time, human populations became more reliant on such methods, and the domestication of plants and animals became their primary means of feeding themselves.

The study of the biological impact of the transition to agriculture relies extensively on the field of **bioarchaeology,** the study of human skeletal remains from archaeological sites. These remains provide a variety of information on health and disease, including age at death, cause of death, nutritional status, growth patterns, and trauma (Cohen 1989; Larsen 2000; see also Appendix 2). Diseases such as osteoarthritis may affect bones directly (Figure 17.1). Other diseases, such as syphilis and tuberculosis, may leave indications of their effects on the skeletal system (Figure 17.2). Physical trauma due to injury or violence often leaves detectable fractures. Signs of healing or infection tell us the long-term effects of such trauma (Figure 17.3). X-ray and chemical analysis can provide us with information about nutrition and growth patterns. Collectively, these methods and others provide us with a view of the health of prehistoric populations.

bioarchaeology The study of human skeletal remains from archaeological sites that are used to provide information on the health and lifestyle of prehistoric people.

FIGURE 17.1

Osteoarthritis. The head of the femur is deformed.

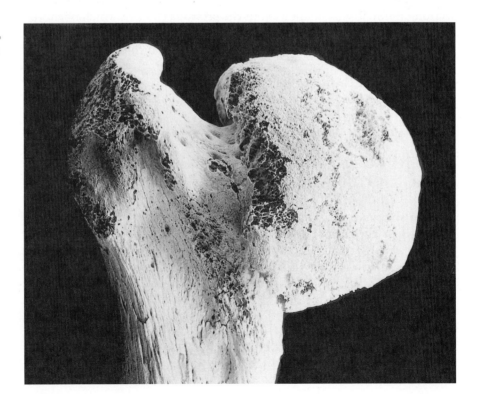

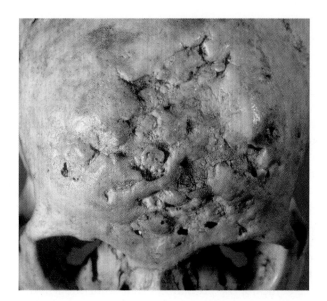

FIGURE 17.2

Skull showing signs of treponemal infection. The marks on the top of the skull are typical of a long-term syphilitic infection.

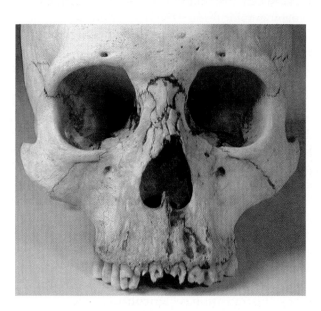

FIGURE 17.3

Nasal fracture.

Population Growth

The shift to agriculture led to many changes in human populations. A major change was the increase in population size, which in turn led to a greater reliance on agriculture, and ultimately to further population growth. The relationship between population size and agriculture is clear when considering the maximum size, or **carrying capacity,** of human populations. Hunting and gathering populations tend to be small, usually no more than a few dozen people, because there would not be enough food for more. Agriculture can support much larger populations.

carrying capacity The maximum population size capable of being supported in a given environment.

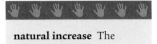

natural increase The number of births minus the number of deaths.

life expectancy at birth A measure of the average length of life for a newborn child.

life table A compilation of the age distribution of a population that provides an estimate of the probability that an individual will die by a certain age, used to compute life expectancy.

Why did agricultural populations become larger? Population growth results from the net effects of fertility, mortality, and migration. Births increase the population size, and deaths decrease the population size. Migration can either increase or decrease the population size, depending on whether more people move into a population or leave it. Ignoring migration for the moment, the change in population size because of **natural increase** is the number of births minus the number of deaths. If the number of births exceeds the number of deaths, then the population grows. If the number of births is less than the number of deaths, then the population declines.

The fact that the human species grew in numbers following the rise of agriculture suggests that this growth was due to an increase in fertility (more births per year), a decrease in mortality (fewer deaths per year), or both. There does not appear to have been a reduction in overall mortality, as assessed by estimates of **life expectancy at birth,** a measure of the average length of life for a newborn child. Life expectancy at birth is derived by looking at a population's **life table,** which is the age distribution of members of a population that is used to compute the probability that someone will die by a certain age based on the current distribution of the age at death. Life tables are routinely used in demographic research (and by the insurance industry) and can be compiled for prehistoric populations by estimating from skeletal remains the age at death.

Hunting and gathering populations typically have a low life expectancy at birth—roughly 20–40 years (Cohen 1989). Keep in mind that the life expectancy at birth is an *average* length of life. The value of 20–40 years does *not* mean that everyone lives only 20–40 years total. Some live much longer, and others do not live this long. This average provides a crude index of overall health in a population. Skeletal evidence suggests that, in general, agricultural populations did not improve on this figure; in fact, in some cases, mortality rates actually increased and life expectancy at birth declined somewhat following the transition to agriculture. For example, analysis of skeletal remains from Dickson Mound, a prehistoric Native American site in Illinois, shows that life expectancy at birth was 26 years at a time when the people at Dickson Mound were exclusively hunter-gatherers but decreased to 19 years following the transition to agriculture (Cohen 1989). Such studies focus on *overall* mortality, however, and there is evidence for a reduction in *childhood* mortality during the transition to agriculture, which could contribute to population growth without having much impact on overall life expectancy (Pennington 1996; Sellen 2001).

The population growth that accompanied the agricultural revolution is often attributed to an increase in fertility. The traditional explanation is that the shift to a sedentary life and diet resulted in improved ovarian function and shorter intervals of breast-feeding. Studies of living hunter-gatherers have shown that breast-feeding has a contraceptive effect. When a woman nurses her child, hormonal changes take place that reduce the probability of ovulation (Wood 1994). Among some contemporary hunting-gathering populations, the women breast-feed for several years, contributing to a long interval between births—44 months on average among the !Kung of the

Kalahari Desert in Africa (Potts 1988). The shift to agriculture resulted in foods being available to infants, which allowed for earlier weaning, and hence shorter intervals between children, leading to an increase in population size. In addition, there would be less need to carry dependent children. In nomadic populations, the need to carry children limits the number of dependent children; it is not easy to care for another child until the earlier children can walk on their own. The sedentary nature of agricultural populations may have allowed short birth intervals (Livi-Bacci 1997).

Disease

A popular myth is that life improved across the board when humans developed agriculture. Clearly, this is not the case. The transition to agriculture resulted in major shifts in the leading causes of disease and death, including an increase in infectious diseases and nutritional diseases.

Disease in Hunting-Gathering Populations   Before considering the effect of the transition to agriculture on disease, it is necessary to review briefly general patterns of health and disease in hunting-gathering populations. Information on health and disease in hunting-gathering populations has been obtained by studying the few remaining hunting-gathering societies and from studying prehistoric hunter-gatherers using the methods of paleopathology.

The two most common types of infectious disease in hunting-gathering populations are those due to parasites and those due to **zoonoses,** diseases that are transmitted from other animals to humans. Parasitic diseases may reflect the long-term evolutionary adaptation of different parasites to human beings. Among hunting-gathering societies, these parasites include lice and pinworms. The zoonoses are introduced through insect bites, animal wounds, and ingestion of contaminated meat. These diseases include sleeping sickness, tetanus, and schistosomiasis, among others (Armelagos and Dewey 1970). The prevalence of various parasitic and zoonotic diseases varies among different hunting-gathering environments. The disease microorganisms found in arctic or temperate environments are generally not found in tropical environments.

The spread of infectious diseases is often classified as being either epidemic or endemic. An **epidemic** pattern is one in which new cases of a disease spread quickly. A typical epidemic starts with a few new cases of a disease, increases geometrically (exponentially) in a short period of time as more people are infected, and then declines rapidly as the number of susceptible individuals declines. An **endemic** pattern shows a low but constant rate; a few cases are always present, but no major spread occurs. In general, hunting-gathering populations do not experience epidemics because of two ecological factors associated with a hunting-gathering way of life: small population size and a nomadic lifestyle (Figure 17.4). Hunter-gatherers live in small groups of roughly 25–50 people that interact occasionally with other small groups in their region. Under such conditions, infectious diseases tend not to spread rapidly. There are simply not enough people to become infected to keep the disease

zoonose A disease transmitted directly to humans from other animals.

epidemic A pattern of disease rate when new cases of a disease spread rapidly through a population.

endemic A pattern of disease rate when new cases of a disease occur at a relatively constant but low rate over time.

FIGURE 17.4

!Kung women gathering vegetables. The small size and nomadic nature of hunting-gathering populations mean that infectious disease is endemic, not epidemic.

going at high rates. Without enough people to infect, the disease microorganisms die off. This does not apply to chronic infectious diseases, whose microorganisms can stay alive long enough to infect people coming into the group. Certain diseases caused by parasitic worms fall into this category. In such cases, the prevalence of infectious diseases does not increase rapidly. Although infectious diseases are the leading cause of death in some hunting-gathering populations (Howell 2000), the rate is *endemic,* not epidemic. The difference has to do with whether the deaths are concentrated in a short interval of time (epidemic) or not (endemic).

The noninfectious diseases common in industrial societies, such as heart disease, cancer, diabetes, and high blood pressure, are rare in hunting-gathering societies. Part of the reason for these low rates may be the diet and lifestyle of hunter-gatherers, but it is also because fewer individuals are likely to live long enough to develop these diseases. The diet of hunting-gathering populations is well balanced, low in fat and high in fiber. In fact, some researchers have suggested that people in Western society should emulate this diet to improve their health (Eaton et al. 1988). A major nutritional problem in hunting-gathering societies is the scarcity of food during hard times, such as droughts. The rate of malnutrition and starvation in most hunting-gathering groups is usually very low (Dunn 1968).

Apart from endemic infectious disease, what accounts for the major causes of death in hunting-gathering societies? Injury deaths are one factor. In most environments, death can result from hunting injuries and burns. Depending on the specific environment, death can result from drowning, cold exposure, or heat stress. In some hunting-gathering populations, injuries are the leading cause of death (Dunn 1968). For females, an additional factor is death during childbirth.

FIGURE 17.5

Farmers planting rice. The larger size and sedentary nature of agricultural populations contribute to epidemics of infectious disease.

Infectious Disease in Agricultural Populations   The pattern of disease is different in agricultural populations. Agriculture allows larger population size and requires a sedentary life. The increased size and lack of mobility have certain implications for the spread of disease (Figure 17.5). Large populations with many susceptible individuals allow for rapid spread of short-lived microorganisms. Such conditions exist in agricultural populations because of increased population size and the increased probability of coming into contact with someone who has the disease. As a result, agricultural populations have often experienced epidemics of diseases such as smallpox, measles, and mumps. The size of a population needed to sustain an epidemic varies according to the disease. Some infectious diseases, such as measles, require very large populations for rapid spread.

A sedentary lifestyle increases the spread of infectious disease in other ways. Large populations living continuously in the same area accumulate sewage. Poor sanitation and contamination of the water supply increase the chance for epidemics.

Agricultural practices also cause ecological changes, making certain infectious diseases more likely. The introduction of domesticated animals adds to waste accumulation and provides the opportunity for further exposure to diseases carried by animals. Cultivation of the land can also increase the probability of contact with insects carrying disease microorganisms. For example, standing pools of water are created when forests are cleared for agriculture, creating an opportunity for an increase in the mosquito population that transmits malaria.

The use of feces for fertilization can also have an impact on rates of infectious disease. In addition to potential contamination from handling these waste products, the food grown in these fertilizers can become contaminated. This problem was so acute in South Korea that steps had to be taken to reduce the use of feces as fertilizer (Cockburn 1971). In addition, irrigation can lead to an increase in the spread of infectious disease. One of the major problems in tropical agricultural societies is the increased snail population that lives in irrigation canals and carries schistosomiasis. Irrigation can pass infectious microorganisms from one population to the next.

Nutritional Disease in Agricultural Populations   Although agriculture provides populations with the ability to feed more people, this way of life does not guarantee an improvement in nutritional quality. Extensive investment in a single food crop, such as rice or corn, may provide too limited a diet, and certain nutritional deficiency diseases can result. For example, populations relying extensively on corn as a prime food source may show an increase in pellagra (a disease caused by a deficiency in niacin), as well as protein deficiency. Dependency on highly polished (white) rice is often associated with protein and vitamin deficiencies.

Perhaps the greatest problem associated with reliance on a single crop is that if that crop fails, starvation can result. A population may become so dependent on a major crop that if a drought or plague wipes it out, not enough food is left to feed the people. An example of this is the Great Famine in Ireland between 1846 and 1851. The population of Ireland had grown rapidly since the introduction of the potato in the early 1700s, which provided a nutritious food that was easy to grow. Marriage in Ireland was linked to land inheritance; owning land was often a prerequisite for marriage, and only one son tended to inherit. However, the introduction of the potato provided more efficient use of the land, which allowed families to subdivide their property and give more sons the opportunity to start a family. The population of Ireland grew rapidly, but this resulted in a precarious ecology. The potato crop was often destroyed by blight, and during the Great Famine, there were five continuous years of blight with no relief (Connell 1950). Roughly 1.5 million people died and another million left the country (Woodham-Smith 1962), starting a pattern of population decline that continued into the twentieth century (Figure 17.6).

An agricultural diet can also lead to dental problems. The increased amount of starches in an agriculturalist's diet, combined with an increase in dirt and grit in the food, can lead to an increase in dental wear and cavities. Such changes are readily apparent in many bioarchaeological studies (Cohen 1989; Larsen 2000).

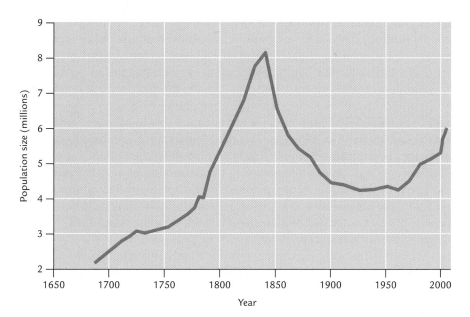

FIGURE 17.6

Population growth in Ireland, 1687–2006. Data from the two currently separate nations, the Republic of Ireland and Northern Ireland, have been pooled. (Data for 1687–1971 from Vaughan and Fitzpatrick 1978; for 1981–2006, from the Central Statistics Office, Ireland, www.cso.ie/, and the Northern Ireland Statistics and Research Agency, www.nisra.gov.uk/; 2002 and 2006 data for Northern Ireland are projections based on the 2001 census.)

THE BIOLOGICAL IMPACT OF CIVILIZATION

Following the origin and spread of agriculture in different parts of the world, a number of human populations began to develop urban centers and civilization as much as 6,000 years ago. As defined by archaeologists, a **civilization** is a large, state-level society that has a number of specific characteristics including large population size, high population density, urbanization, social stratification, food and labor surpluses, monumental architecture, and a system of record keeping (Feder 2007).

civilization A large, state-level society characterized by large population size, high population density, urbanization, social stratification, food and labor surpluses, monumental architecture, and record keeping.

Urbanization and Disease

Preindustrial cities date back several thousand years. Such cities often developed as market or administrative centers for a region, and their increased population size and density provided many opportunities for epidemics of infectious disease. In addition, a number of early cities had inadequate sewage disposal and contaminated water, both major factors increasing the spread of epidemics. To feed large numbers of people, food had to be brought in from the surrounding countryside and stored inside the city. In Europe during the Middle Ages, grain was often stored inside the house. Rats and other vermin had easy access to these foods and their populations increased, furthering the spread of disease. In preindustrial cities located in arid regions, grain was stored in ceramic containers, which limited the access of vermin.

Perhaps the best-known example of an epidemic disease in preindustrial cities is the bubonic plague in Europe during the fourteenth century. Bubonic plague, also known as the Black Death, is caused by a bacterium spread by

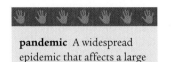

pandemic A widespread epidemic that affects a large geographic area, such as a continent.

fleas among field rodents. With the development of large urban areas and the corresponding large indoor rat populations, the disease spread to rats in the cities. As the rats died, the fleas jumped off them to find a new host, which was frequently a human being. The spread of bubonic plague during this time was **pandemic,** a widespread epidemic affecting large continental areas. Up to 20 million Europeans may have died from bubonic plague between 1346 and 1352 (McEvedy 1988). A major factor in the spread of plague was trade; rats would board ships sailing across the Mediterranean Sea and disembark at distant ports, infecting more rats and, ultimately, the human population. The ecological changes accompanying the development of urbanization in Europe provided an opportunity for the rapid spread of fleas and rats, and therefore the disease. Bubonic plague is still around today, including in the American Southwest, although treatment with antibiotics has kept the incidence of death close to zero.

Industrialization, which began more than 250 years ago, accelerated population growth in urban areas. Technological changes provided more efficient methods of agriculture and the means to support more people than in previous eras. Increased urbanization was accompanied initially by further spread of infectious diseases, compounded by problems in waste disposal. By the end of the nineteenth century, however, some populations had begun a transition wherein the rate of infectious disease declined and the rate of noninfectious disease increased. This shift in disease patterns was accompanied by a reduction in mortality, especially infant mortality, and an increase in life expectancy. In evolutionary terms, all of these changes are very recent.

Culture Contact

One consequence of expanding civilizations was an increase in long-distance contact with other societies through exploration, colonization, trade, and conquest. With the rise of European exploration in the 1500s, many previously separate human populations met one another. In addition to the vast cultural, economic, and political problems resulting from such contact, infectious diseases could now spread into populations that had no prior immune experience. The results were generally devastating.

The epidemiologic effects of culture contact have been documented for a number of populations, particularly Native Americans and Pacific Islanders. Many infectious diseases, such as smallpox, measles, and mumps, were introduced into the New World at this time, leading to massive loss of life in many populations (McNeill 1977; Cohen 1989). The actual impact of infectious disease varied across populations—some were hit much harder than others, and at different times (Larsen 1994). The overall impact was a severe reduction in population size across the Americas (Crawford 1998).

The flow of disease seems to have been primarily in one direction, from the Old World to the New World. The reason for this might have to do with the fact that there were fewer domesticated animals in the New World. These animals are often the initial source of diseases that infect humans (Wolfe et al. 2007). One possible exception to this one-way flow of human disease is treponemal diseases, including venereal syphilis. Venereal syphilis (spread by sexual contact) increased rapidly in Europe after 1500, a date that coincides with the initial contact between New World and Old World populations. Following European settlement in the Americas, it was also noted that many Native Americans had syphilis. Did the disease evolve in Europe and then spread to the Americas? Or did it first appear in the New World and then spread to Europe? Or did it evolve independently in both the New World and the Old World? Bioarchaeological studies have shown that cases of treponemal disease occurred in the New World before European contact, suggesting a New World origin for venereal syphilis (Baker and Armelagos 1988). However, some research has suggested venereal syphilis in two English skeletons *before* European contact (von Hunnius et al. 2006), providing possible support for the hypothesis that syphilis evolved in *both* the New World and the Old World, prior to contact.

CHANGES IN MODERN TIMES

The past hundred years has seen dramatic shifts in our species. Industrialization and economic development have spread throughout much (but not all) of the world, resulting in major biological impacts on disease, mortality, fertility, and population growth. The exact changes experienced by a society are in part a reflection of its economic status. Demographers routinely classify nations into two groups: more developed countries (MDCs) and less developed countries (LDCs). Over much of the past century, the MDCs have seen a reduction in death rates and birth rates, a shift from infectious disease to noninfectious disease as the leading causes of death, a slowing (and in some cases a reversal) of population growth, and an aging population. The LDCs have seen some reduction in mortality and fertility, although infectious disease still dominates and birth rates remain high in parts of the world. Population growth continues at a high rate in many LDCs.

The Epidemiologic Transition

In the MDCs, life expectancy at birth has increased more than 50 percent, and the leading causes of death have shifted from infectious to noninfectious diseases. The increase in life expectancy and the shift from infectious to noninfectious diseases as the primary cause of death are a feature of the **epidemiologic transition** that has been observed in the MDCs and that is under way, to varying degrees, in the LDCs.

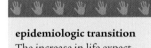

epidemiologic transition
The increase in life expectancy and the shift from infectious to noninfectious disease as the primary cause of death.

The Nature of the Epidemiologic Transition According to the model developed by Omran (1977), a pretransition population has high death rates, particularly because of epidemics of childhood infectious disease. As public health, sanitation, and medical technologies improve, epidemics become less frequent and less intense. The overall death rate declines, and life expectancy at birth increases. Following the transition, the leading causes of death are primarily noninfectious rather than infectious diseases.

FIGURE 17.7

Life expectancy at birth in the United States, 1900–2009. Life expectancy at birth increased over time, with the major exception of 1918, the year of an influenza pandemic. (Data for 1900–2006 from Arias 2010; for 2007 from Xu et al. 2010; for 2008 and 2009 from Kochanek et al. 2011.)

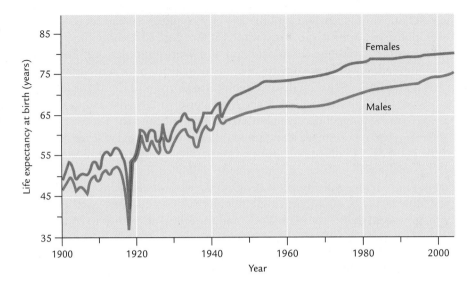

A major characteristic of the epidemiologic transition is the increase in life expectancy at birth. Figure 17.7 shows life expectancy at birth for males and females in the United States from 1900 through 2009. In the United States in 1900, life expectancy at birth was 47.3 years (Arias 2010), but by 2009, it had risen to 78.2 years (Kochanek et al. 2011). Except for a major dip in 1918 (the year of a worldwide influenza pandemic), life expectancy has continued to rise since 1900. Females tend to live longer, as reflected in their higher life expectancies at birth; in 2009, the life expectancy of a newborn girl in the United States was 80.6 years, compared with 75.7 years for a newborn boy (Kochanek et al. 2011).

Not all parts of the world have the same life expectancy. Variation reflects differences in health care, infant mortality, poverty, economic development, warfare, and many other factors influencing the overall health of a population. Overall, the global life expectancy at birth is 70 years, but with an average of 59 in the least economically developed nations and an average of 78 in the most economically developed nations. The lowest life expectancies are found in Afghanistan (44 years), Zimbabwe (46 years), and the Democratic Republic of the Congo and Zambia (both 49 years). The highest life expectancy is 83 years, found in Hong Kong, Japan, and San Marino (Population Reference Bureau 2011). Although life expectancies have risen in many parts of the world over the past century, it is not clear how far this trend could continue (see Box 17.1).

The increase in life expectancy is related to a dramatic decline in deaths due to infectious diseases. Infants and young children are at greater risk for such diseases, and a large number of deaths in this age group lowers the average length of life in a population. As infectious disease death rates decline, the average length of life increases. A consequence of people living longer is that the death rate from degenerative noninfectious diseases, such as cancer and heart disease, begins to rise. Thus, there was a shift from infectious to noninfectious diseases as the primary causes of death. In the United States in

BOX 17.1

Will Life Expectancy Continue to Increase?

For countries that have undergone the epidemiologic transition, the increase in life expectancy has been astounding; the United States, for example, has risen from 47 to 78 years since 1900, an 81 percent increase (see Figure 17.7). The same is true of a number of other nations. Will this upward trend continue? If so, how far? Will the average life expectancy at birth reach 100? The topic of future life expectancy is controversial, and difficult to address because of problems in extrapolating past trends into the future. Most predictions suggest that a life expectancy at birth of 85 for the United States seems possible (Wilmouth 2011). Could life expectancy go beyond that?

It is true that there have been major increases in life expectancy at birth in recent times; in developed nations roughly 0.2 years have been added to life expectancy each

year, leading some to predict that most babies born in certain countries at the beginning of the twentieth century will live to 100 (Christensen et al. 2009). Others argue that such predictions are overly simplistic and inaccurate (Olshansky and Carnes 2010). Some have noted that past increases in life expectancy are largely due to the reduction of infant and childhood mortality, and reductions in mortality among the elderly will have less impact on average life expectancy (Couzin-Frankel 2011). It has even been suggested that life expectancy in the United States might actually *decrease* because of an increase in health problems such as obesity (Olshansky et al. 2005). As with many demographic phenomena, the prediction of long-term trends is difficult at best because of the large number of potential influences.

1900, the top three causes of death were all infectious diseases: pneumonia/influenza, tuberculosis, and diarrheal diseases. In 2009, the top three causes of death were all degenerative diseases: heart disease, cancer, and chronic lower respiratory diseases (Kochanek et al. 2011).

Figure 17.8 illustrates this dramatic shift by comparing the mortality rate (deaths per 100,000 people) for selected diseases in the United States in 1900 and in 2009. Note the tremendous decline in infectious disease mortality

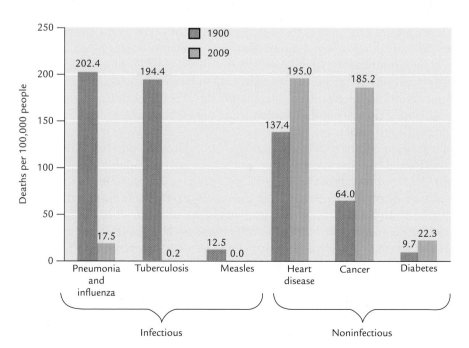

FIGURE 17.8

Death rates (per 100,000 people) for selected infectious and noninfectious diseases in the United States, 1900 and 2006. Note the decrease in infectious disease and the increase in noninfectious disease. (Data for 1900 from Centers for Disease Control and Prevention, www.cdc.gov/nchs/data/dvs/lead1900_98.pdf, and Molnar 1998 for measles and diabetes; for 2006 from Kochanek et al. 2011.)

FIGURE 17.9

The 10 leading causes of death
in the United States, 2009.
(Data from Kochanek et al. 2011.)

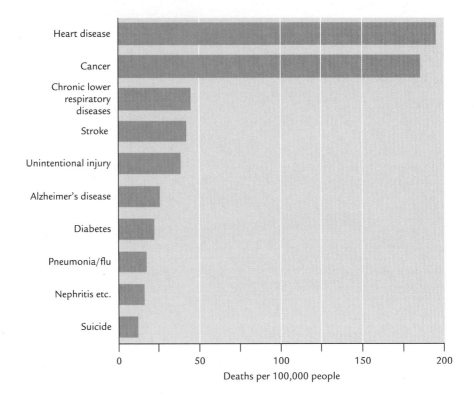

FIGURE 17.9

The 10 leading causes of death in the United States, 2009. (Data from Kochanek et al. 2011.)

and the increase in noninfectious diseases. As we continue to live longer, we are more likely to die from a degenerative noninfectious disease. The major health problems today are quite different from what they were only several generations in the past, when infectious diseases were the primary cause of death. Figure 17.9 shows the 10 leading causes of death in the United States in 2009. Heart disease and cancer are the two major causes of death, accounting for almost half of all deaths. Only one of the top 10 causes of death is an infectious disease: pneumonia/influenza. Heart disease and cancer are likely to remain the major causes of death in the near future, but the other leading causes may change rapidly, primarily due to new technologies and aggressive public health measures.

It is important to remember that these figures for the United States are also typical of other nations that have undergone the epidemiologic transition, but not typical of the entire world. Infectious disease remains a leading cause of death in many human populations, particularly among the LDCs. Figure 17.10 shows the leading causes of death worldwide in 2002, illustrating that infectious disease is still a leading cause of death in the human species. HIV infection, which has dropped in the United States, remains high elsewhere in the world and is the sixth-leading cause of death in our species. The magnitude of infectious disease is even more apparent when we consider the leading causes of death in the LDCs. For example, Figure 17.11 shows that the leading cause of death in Africa is HIV/AIDS, accounting for more than 20 percent of all deaths in Africa, compared with less than 0.4 percent of

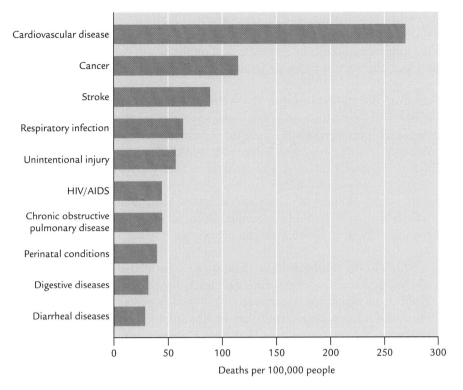

FIGURE 17.10

The 10 leading causes of death in the world, 2002. (Data from World Health Organization 2004.)

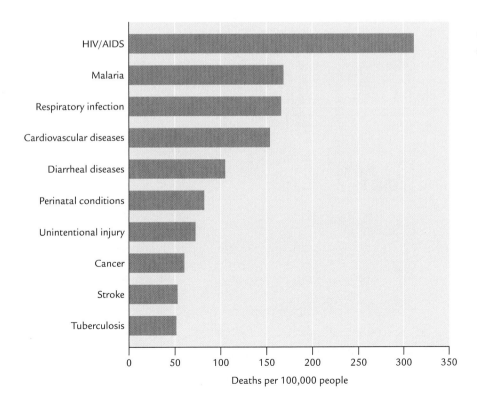

FIGURE 17.11

The 10 leading causes of death in Africa, 2002. (Data from World Health Organization 2004.)

all deaths in the United States (World Health Organization 2004; Kochanek et al. 2011). Population differences in disease and death are due to differences in the level of economic development and public health measures, and different populations are at different points in the epidemiologic transition.

Causes of the Epidemiologic Transition   What has caused these rapid changes in disease rates and life expectancy? Cultural changes in industrial societies have often resulted in major improvements in health care, public sanitation, and water quality. These factors aid in reducing the spread and effect of infectious diseases, particularly in infancy. Advances in medical technology, such as antibiotics and vaccination, have continued to help reduce the death rate due to infectious diseases, but the main reason for the initial decline was a cleaner environment brought about by civil engineering—particularly sewers and water treatment systems.

Case Study of the Epidemiologic Transition   The relationship between cultural change and disease rates emerges clearly in specific case studies of the epidemiologic transition. Omran (1977) looked at overall death rates in his study of the epidemiologic transition in New York City. Figure 17.12 shows the changes in total mortality in New York City over time. Before the 1860s, the overall death rate was high and had frequent spikes, primarily because of epidemics of cholera. Following the mid-1860s, both the overall death rate and the intensity of epidemics declined. This decrease corresponds to the establishment of the Health Department. After the 1920s, the continued incorporation of better sanitation and a clean water supply, along with an

FIGURE 17.12

Changes in the death rate in New York City during the nineteenth and twentieth centuries. (*Source:* Omran 1977:12. Courtesy Population Reference Bureau, Inc., Washington, D.C.)

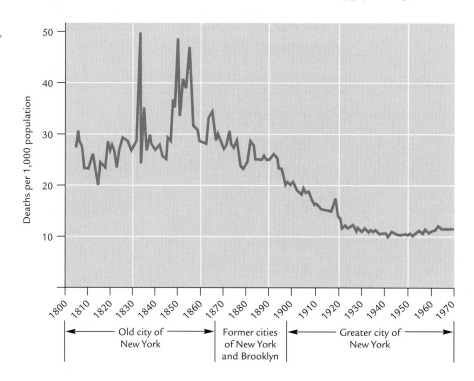

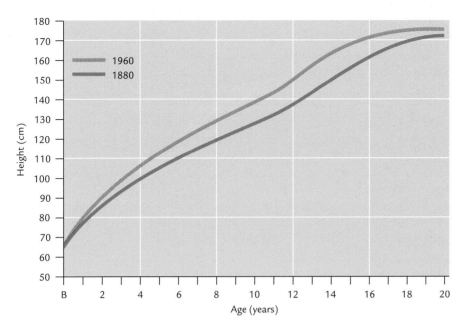

FIGURE 17.13

Secular change in European American males in North America. At all ages, the males living in 1960 had greater height than those who lived in 1880. (Adapted from *Growth and Development* by Robert M. Malina, © 1975, publisher Burgess International Publishing Company. Used by permission.)

improvement in drugs and health care and the introduction of pasteurized milk, caused the death rates to decline even more.

Secular Changes in Human Growth

The epidemiologic transition affects more than disease and death rates; its effects have also been observed in studies of child growth. Since the turn of the twentieth century, many industrialized nations have shown several secular changes in child growth. A **secular change** is simply a change in the pattern of growth across generations.

Types of Secular Change   Three basic secular changes have been observed over the past century: an increase in height, an increase in weight, and a decrease in the age of sexual maturation. Children in many industrialized nations are taller and heavier today than children the same age were a century or so ago. Figure 17.13 shows the average distance curve for height of North American males of European ancestry in 1880 and 1960. There is no noticeable difference in body length at birth. Note, however, that at all postnatal ages the 1960 males are consistently taller than the 1880 males. This difference is most noticeable during adolescence. Comparison of distance curves for weight shows the same pattern.

Another secular change is a decrease in the age of maturation. This is most apparent in a specific measure of human development—the **age at menarche,** the age at which a female experiences her first menstrual period. Figure 17.14 plots the average age at menarche for the United States and several Western European nations over time. The general trend is one of earlier biological maturation.

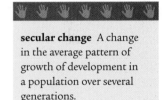

secular change A change in the average pattern of growth of development in a population over several generations.

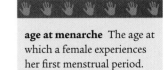

age at menarche The age at which a female experiences her first menstrual period.

FIGURE 17.14

Secular change in age at menarche (the age of a female's first menstrual period) in the United States and several Western European countries. (Adapted from *Growth and Development* by Robert M. Malina, © 1975, publisher Burgess International Publishing Company. Used by permission.)

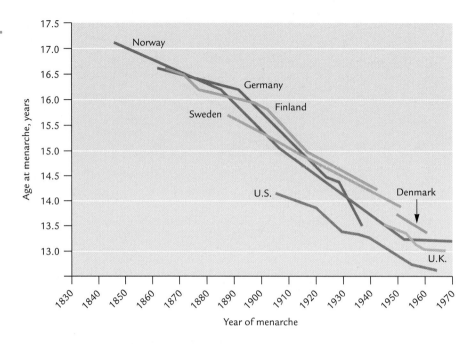

Causes of Secular Change   The basic secular changes observed in industrialized nations during the past century reflect environmental change. These changes came too fast and were too pervasive to be due to genetic change; rather, environmental changes have enabled more people to reach their genetic potential for growth. These trends, however, should not be projected indefinitely into the future. Future environmental improvements could enable more and more children to reach their genetic potential for growth, but we should not expect average heights of 8 feet or more in another hundred years!

Many environmental factors have been suggested as being responsible for these secular changes, including improved nutrition, reduction of childhood infectious disease, improved availability of health care, improved standard of living, and reduction of family size. Many of these factors are interrelated, making precise identification of causes difficult. Malina (1979) has noted that improved nutrition is often cited as a primary cause of the observed secular changes. Though nutritional intake has improved for many people, especially during infancy, Malina does not think it is solely responsible for secular changes and argues that one of the most important factors was an improvement in health conditions resulting in the reduction in childhood infectious diseases. Thus, the epidemiologic transition appears to be related to secular changes in human growth as well.

The Reemergence of Infectious Disease

The success in reducing infectious disease in developed nations during the first half of the twentieth century gave rise to an overly optimistic view that *all* infectious diseases would be eliminated by the year 2000. Smallpox, once a killer of millions, had been eliminated by 1977, and polio and tuberculosis were close behind. This view is now known to be incorrect; despite our efforts, new infectious diseases are emerging, and old ones are coming back in new forms (Garrett 1994). A dramatic example occurred in May 1995 with the outbreak of a frequently fatal disease, Ebola, in the Democratic Republic of the Congo (then known as Zaire) in Africa. Although the Ebola virus was discovered only in 1976, previous epidemics had killed hundreds of people in Zaire and Uganda (Cowley et al. 1995).

Emergent Infectious Disease   This outbreak was not an isolated event. There are many other examples of **emergent infectious diseases,** newly evolved diseases that have appeared only in the past few decades, including Legionnaire's disease, Korean hemorrhagic fever, Hantavirus, and HIV (Armelagos et al. 1996).

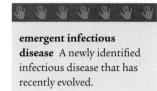

emergent infectious disease A newly identified infectious disease that has recently evolved.

The emergence of new diseases shows the evolution of microorganisms, a process often exacerbated by environmental changes brought about by human populations. New environments are created by rapid deforestation and conversion of land for cultivation and industrialization. Conversion of remote and isolated habitats provides the opportunity for previously rare microorganisms to encounter the human species. Continued pollution can increase the mutation rate of microorganisms in addition to interfering with ecosystems. New forms of quick travel, such as jet planes, and international commerce increase the amount of contact between human groups, enabling diseases to spread quickly and to new populations, many of which have no prior immune experience. New technologies often lend themselves to the emergence of infectious diseases by creating new microenvironments conducive to bacterial spread. Air conditioning, for example, has been implicated in the origin and spread of Legionnaire's disease. Cultural and environmental changes have provided new opportunities for the evolution of microorganisms (Garrett 1994; Levins et al. 1994).

Reemergent Infectious Disease   An additional problem is **reemergent infectious diseases,** which are infectious diseases that have evolved resistance to antibiotics. Tuberculosis, for example, is a respiratory disease that had been treated very successfully with antibiotics in the last half of the twentieth century, but tuberculosis rates began to increase in the 1980s and 1990s. Figure 17.15 shows tuberculosis rates in New York, a state hard hit by an increase in tuberculosis in the early 1990s. This increase was due to a number of factors, including the outbreak of antibiotic-resistant strains of the bacterium. Aggressive public health measures have reversed this trend, but it remains a problem for many residents and illustrates the danger of bacteria evolving resistance to antibiotics.

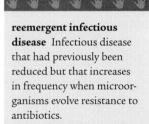

reemergent infectious disease Infectious disease that had previously been reduced but that increases in frequency when microorganisms evolve resistance to antibiotics.

Antibiotic resistance illustrates the principle of natural selection applied to disease-causing microorganisms. Sometimes a mutant form of bacteria exists that is resistant to a specific antibiotic. Although most bacteria are killed, the mutant form will multiply and become more common in successive generations of bacteria. Because bacteria have short life spans, an antibiotic-resistant form of bacteria can spread very quickly. The problem of reemergence

FIGURE 17.15

Tuberculosis rates in New York State, 1984–2009. (Data from New York State Department of Health, www.health.ny.gov/statistics/diseases/communicable/)

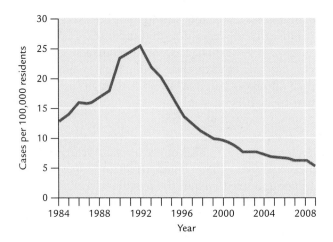

of infectious diseases is linked to indiscriminate use of antibiotics for treating illness in humans and the increasing use of antibiotics in animal feed (Armelagos et al. 1996). As these practices have increased, so have antibiotic-resistant forms of bacteria. This problem has required development of new antibiotics, which in turn leads to new forms of antibiotic resistance.

The problems of emergent and reemergent infectious diseases show us that infectious disease is not gone, and is unlikely ever to be gone. We will always have to deal with infectious disease, but the nature of this threat will change over time as the microorganisms continue to evolve and as we continue to change our environment. The ongoing struggle against infectious disease will require increased funding, global coordination, and a holistic approach to cultural, environmental, and technological factors affecting the spread of infectious disease (Binder et al. 1999).

Demographic Change

The reduction in death rates and the increase in life expectancy in much of the world have obvious implications for population growth. The natural increase of our species reflects the difference between the rate of births and deaths. If death rates drop but birth rates remain the same, a population will grow in size. This is what happened to our species during the twentieth century, when the world population more than tripled in size from less than 2 billion to 7 billion by 2011 (Figure 17.16).

demographic transition theory A model of demographic change stating that as a population becomes economically developed, a reduction in death rates (leading to population growth) will take place, followed by a reduction in birth rates.

The Demographic Transition   What led to such high rates of population growth in our species and to the variability in growth rates among nations today? As death rates dropped, there was a lag before birth rates also declined, resulting in a time of significant population growth. Observations of these demographic patterns in a number of European countries led to the development of **demographic transition theory.** The utility of this model to explain and predict demographic shifts in all human populations has been questioned (e.g., Cohen 1995), but it does provide a convenient summary of some basic demographic trends.

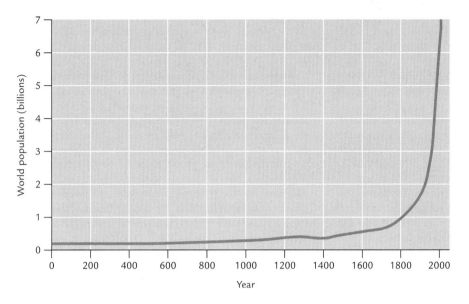

FIGURE 17.16

World population growth over the past 2,000 years. Rapid growth began after the eighteenth century. (Data for 1–1940 from Weeks 2005; for 1950-2010 from U.S. Census Bureau, www.census.gov/population/international/data/idb/worldpoptotal.php, September 1, 2011; for 2011 from Population Reference Bureau (2011).)

Demographic transition theory states that as a population becomes more economically developed, a reduction in death rates will take place first, followed by a reduction in fertility rates. Three stages are usually identified in this model (Swedlund and Armelagos 1976). Stage 1 populations are those of undeveloped areas with high mortality and high fertility rates. Because the high number of births is balanced by the high number of deaths, the overall population size remains more or less stable. In stage 2, the transitional stage, demographic and economic factors are changing rapidly, and there is high fertility but lowered mortality. The transition to lowered mortality, especially in childhood, is a consequence of improvements in public health and medical technology. Because fertility rates remain high, there are more births than deaths, and the population grows quickly in size. Stage 3 populations have completed the transition with a reduction in fertility rates. Because of technological, social, economic, and education changes, people in the MDCs have more of a desire and opportunity to control family size, and the birth rate declines. Because the rates of both births and deaths are low, such populations tend to show little growth (ignoring migration).

The demographic transition model does describe the experience seen in some of the MDCs today, but it has a number of problems. Although it serves as a rough description of the types of changes that tend to take place as populations become more economically developed, there is considerable variation in the timing of these events, with some populations having less of a lag between falling death rates and falling birth rates than others. The model is less accurate in predicting the timing of fertility declines, and the assumption that economic development must occur before a decline in mortality rate does not fit all cases (Cohen 1995). There are also cases of the basic trends reversing, such as in the United States in the twentieth century, when fertility rates declined at first and then increased rapidly for a short time following World War II before falling again (see Box 17.2).

BOX 17.2

The Baby Boom

A classic example of how changing social and economic factors affect population growth is the "Baby Boom" in the United States. At the beginning of the twentieth century, fertility rates in the United States had begun to decline, as expected under a demographic transition. In 1909, the fertility rate (the number of births per 1,000 women of reproductive age, 15–44 years) was 127. By the end of World War II, this number had declined to 85 per 1,000. After World War II, the fertility rate increased dramatically, peaking at 123 in 1957, after which there was a subsequent decline.

This temporary increase in fertility is labeled the Baby Boom, a term for the generation of children born between 1946 and 1964, a period of high fertility relative to prewar years. Several social and economic factors account for the Baby Boom. It was not simply that men returning from the war made up for lost time with their wives. Such an effect often accompanies the end of a war, but the Baby Boom lasted much longer. The economic growth of the United States continued following World War II. As economic growth increases, so does the demand for labor. This demand is often met by new immigrants in a population. In the United States, however, restrictive laws had reduced the number of immigrants. The pool of available labor was also reduced by the fact that there had been fewer births during the 1920s and 1930s, perhaps in part due to the Great Depression. Thus, fewer men were available to meet the increased demand for labor. Women tended to

be locked out of many occupations because of sex bias. Though it is true that women took the place of men in the workforce during the war, afterward the preference for women to remain at home raising children prevailed.

The relative lack of available labor meant that young men returning from the war often had excellent opportunities for employment. A good income meant that men could afford to marry and raise families earlier than they could under different circumstances. The economic conditions prevailing after World War II meant that a couple could have several children without lowering their standard of living (Weeks 2005). People married earlier, and the spacing between births was shorter than in previous times, both of which contributed to an increase in the birth rate. Of course, not everyone married or had larger families or even shared in economic growth. On average, however, these changes were sufficient to affect the birth rate, and therefore the rate of population growth.

After 1958, the fertility rate in the United States began to decline. By the mid-1960s, the Baby Boom was over. From this point on, changing economic conditions and greater educational and economic opportunities contributed to delayed marriage and childbirth, as well as the desire for smaller families. By the mid-1980s, the fertility rate had dropped to 65 per 1,000, and the average number of children per couple was less than replacement (i.e., fewer than 2 children per couple).

World Population Growth In mid-2011, the world numbered almost 7 billion people and had a rate of natural increase of 1.2 percent per year. Projections based on the decline in rate of growth in recent years suggest that there will be 8 billion people by 2025 and 9.6 billion by 2050. The MDCs, with roughly 18 percent of the world's population, have low birth and death rates. In mid-2011, the annual rate of natural increase in the MDCs was a very low 0.2 percent, and their total population is expected to increase by only 4 percent by 2050. The LDCs, with 82 percent of the world's population, have higher fertility rates and a rate of natural increase of 1.4 percent per year, and their total population size is expected to increase by 44 percent by 2050 (Population Reference Bureau 2011).

There is variation in growth rates around the world. For example, China (an LDC) has a rate of natural increase of 0.5 percent per year, whereas sub-Saharan Africa has a rate of 2.6 percent per year. This rapid growth is due in large part to high fertility; the average woman in sub-Saharan Africa will have 5.2 children in her lifetime. On the other hand, some countries in Europe have negative growth rates and are actually losing population due to low fertility rates (Population Reference Bureau 2011).

Implications of Changing Age Structure The demographic transition of decreasing mortality and fertility rates affects not only the size of human populations but also their composition. A major effect of a transition is on the age structure of a population. Most demographic studies look at the number of males and females in different age groups in a population—the **age-sex structure** of a population. A device known as a **population pyramid** is the best way to describe a population's age-sex structure at a particular point in time. The population pyramid is a graph showing the percentage of both sexes in different age groups, normally at five-year intervals (e.g., 0–4 years of age, 5–9 years of age, and so forth).

The population pyramid looks different in less developed and more developed countries. Figure 17.17 shows the population pyramid (age structure) of Chad, an LDC in Africa in 2010. The bottom axis of the graph shows the percentage of males on the left and the percentage of females on the right. The vertical axis represents different age groups, from 0–4 years of age at the bottom to 80+ years of age at the top. The population pyramid has a true pyramid shape, broad on the bottom and tapering to a small point at the top. Note that the largest segment of society is infants and young children, which is characteristic of a population with high fertility rates. Because the majority of the population in Chad are infants and children, with fewer elderly people, the median age is 17 years (i.e., half the population is younger than 16 and

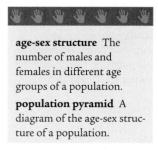

age-sex structure The number of males and females in different age groups of a population.

population pyramid A diagram of the age-sex structure of a population.

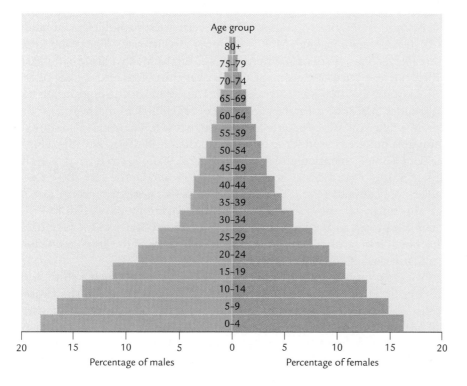

FIGURE 17.17

The age-sex structure of Chad in 2010, drawn to the same scale as Figures 17.18 and 17.19 for comparison. (Data from U.S. Census Bureau International Database, www .census.gov/population/international/ data/idb/informationGateway.php, database revision of September 2, 2011.)

FIGURE 17.18

The age-sex structure of
the United States in 2010,
drawn to the same scale
as Figures 17.17 and 17.19
for comparison. (Data from
U.S. Census Bureau International
Database, www.census.gov/
population/international/data/idb/
informationGateway.php, database
revision of September 2, 2011.)

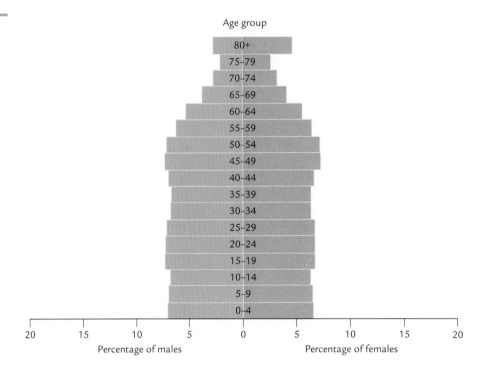

half is older than 16). Only 3 percent of the population are 65 years of age or older.

By contrast, Figure 17.18 shows the age-sex structure of the United States in 2010 as an example of an MDC with lower fertility rates. The graph looks more like a rectangle than a pyramid. Fewer births mean a decreasing base, which carries over to the next age group over time. The median age of the United States in 2010 was 37 years, with 13 percent of the population age 65 or older. Note the greater proportion of females than males among the elderly, a reflection of the greater longevity of women. The graph also shows a noticeable bulge corresponding to people in their mid-30s to late 40s. This is the Baby Boom generation discussed in Box 17.2. A rise in the birth rate in the United States occurred between 1946 and 1964, and by the year 2000, these babies were between 36 and 54 years of age. As this generation continues to age, this bulge will move upward on the population pyramid. Figure 17.19 shows the projected age-sex structure for the United States in the year 2025. The lower birth rates will continue to make the shape of the graph even more rectangular in appearance over time.

We can expect many cultural changes to accompany such a shift to an older population. Many of these shifts are apparent today in the United States. For example, if we assume current average ages for retirement, there will be fewer people of working age in the future. Such a shift might be seen as having both advantages and disadvantages. A smaller labor pool might mean better economic opportunities for working-age people. On the other

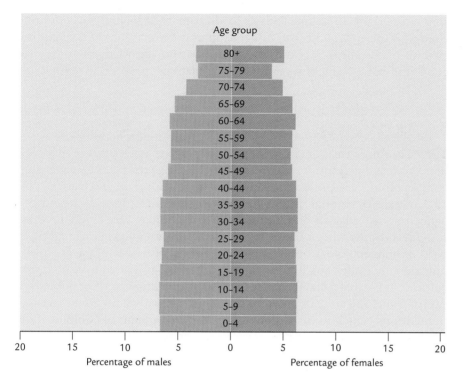

FIGURE 17.19

The projected age-sex structure of the United States in 2025, drawn to the same scale as Figures 17.17 and 17.18 for comparison. (Data from U.S. Census Bureau International Database, www.census.gov/population/international/data/idb/informationGateway.php, database revision of September 2, 2011.)

hand, we may also expect greater taxation to help provide for the well-being of the retired portion of the population.

Many questions are being asked by those concerned with social and economic shifts. For example, how well will our Social Security system function when more people are drawing from it? What changes need to be made in the insurance industries? How can we provide adequate health and other care to an aging population?

Economic shifts can also be examined. Perhaps one of the best examples of the effects of changing age structure is in our system of higher education. During the 1960s and early 1970s, as more and more Baby Boomers reached college age, the demand for colleges and universities increased. This demand was accompanied by an increased desire for a college education, in part because of a changing economy and the value of a college degree in terms of earning potential. As college enrollments increased, more schools were built, and more faculty and staff were hired. By the mid-1970s, the effects of the Baby Boom were over, and enrollments began to diminish at many institutions. How, then, can we afford to maintain our colleges? Increases in tuition and taxes are remedies, but they are generally not popular. Should schools be closed? If so, what happens to the local economies, which are often highly dependent on these schools? What about the future? If we cut back on programs now, will we need to start them up again in a few years?

These questions have no easy answers. Awareness of the problems and their connections to a variety of economic, social, and political factors is a step in the right direction. Today's world is marked by high level of rapid change. A society's successful integration of demographic change requires analysis of current trends and, above all, a basic acknowledgment that, for good or ill, these changes are indeed taking place.

Summary

The evolution of the human species continues to the present day. Although biological change continues in human populations, the rate of such change is most often exceeded by the rapid rate of culture change. Over the past 12,000 years, the human species has moved from hunting and gathering to agriculture to feed itself, and the total size of the human species has increased roughly a thousandfold. These rapid cultural changes have influenced aspects of human biology by affecting our patterns of health, physical growth, nutrition, mortality, and fertility, among other things. The transition to agriculture represented a major change in human adaptation, and the domestication of plants and animals provided the opportunity to maintain much larger populations, which in turn allowed for the development of complex state-level societies. Larger sedentary populations led to many epidemics of infectious disease. Although more food could be produced, many people in early agricultural societies suffered from nutritional stress. Overall, life expectancy did not increase with the origins of agriculture.

The subsequent rise of state-level societies with large urban populations was accompanied by further epidemics and nutritional problems. Exploration, trade, and conquest led to contact between cultures that had been isolated previously, resulting in catastrophic epidemics and social upheaval. By the end of the nineteenth century, modernization had begun the epidemiologic transition, whereby improvements in public health and civil engineering, later supplemented by improvements in medical science, led to a reduction in deaths from infectious diseases and a dramatic increase in life expectancy at birth.

As people lived longer on average, the death rate due to noninfectious degenerative diseases increased. In the more developed countries, children mature faster and grow larger because of changes in disease and diet. Recent decades have seen a resurgence in infectious diseases, in part due to the evolution of new diseases and in part due to the reemergence of diseases as microorganisms evolve resistance to antibiotics. The world's population tripled in size during the twentieth century as death rates declined. Many populations have since seen a reduction in fertility rates, such that the rate of population growth has declined somewhat. Even given this trend, most projections suggest a global population of roughly 9 to 10 billion by the middle of the twenty-first century. Another consequence of recent demographic change is the changing age structure of the more developed countries. As birth rates decline, populations become older on average. All of these demographic changes are interrelated with many contemporary social, economic, and political problems.

Supplemental Readings

Cohen, J. E. 1995. *How Many People Can the Earth Support?* New York: W. W. Norton. A comprehensive discussion of the demographic history of the human species, population projection, and global carrying capacity.

Howell, N. 2000. *Demography of the Dobe !Kung,* 2d ed. New York: Aldine de Gruyter. An extensive description of the demography of a hunting-gathering society focusing on mortality and fertility.

Larsen, C. S. 2000. *Skeletons in Our Closet: Revealing Our Past through Bioarchaeology.* Princeton, N.J.: Princeton University Press. A detailed survey of the field of bioarchaeology and what it can tell us about disease and life in prehistoric times, focusing on the transition to agriculture and on culture contact among prehistoric Native Americans.

Weeks, J. R. 2005. *Population: An Introduction to Concepts and Issues,* 9th ed. Belmont, Calif.: Wadsworth. A comprehensive review of the field of demography.

THE FUTURE
OF OUR SPECIES

This book has focused on human biological variation and evolution, past and present. What about the future? Can biological anthropology, or indeed any science, make predictions about the future of our species? What directions might our biological and cultural evolution take?

One thing is certain—we continue to evolve both biologically and culturally, and will do so in the future. Human evolution is increasingly complex because of our biocultural nature. Much of our adaptive nature is culturally based. We can adapt to a situation more quickly through cultural evolution than through biological evolution. Theoretically, we can also direct our cultural evolution. We can focus our efforts on solutions to specific problems, such as finding a vaccine for AIDS or developing ways to further reduce dental decay. Biological evolution, however, has no inherent direction. Natural selection works on existing variation, not on what we might desire or need.

Our success with cultural adaptations should not lead us to conclude that we do not continue to evolve biologically. Regardless of our triumphs in the field of medicine, many incurable diseases still carry on the process of natural selection. Biological variation still takes place in potential and realized fertility. As many as a third to half of all human conceptions fail to produce live births. We still live in a world in which many children have an inadequate diet. Even if all inhabitants of the world were raised to an adequate standard of living tomorrow, we would still be subject to natural selection and biological evolution. The fact that we are cultural organisms does not detract from the fact that we are also biological organisms. Scholars in various fields throughout history have argued about whether humans and human behavior should be studied biologically, as products of nature, or culturally, as products of nurture. Both sides were wrong. Humans must be studied as *both* biological and cultural organisms.

Given that we will continue to evolve, *how* will we evolve? This question cannot be answered. Evolution has many random elements that cannot be predicted. Also, the biocultural nature of humans makes prediction even harder. The incredible rate of cultural and technological change in the past century was not predicted. What kinds of cultural evolution are possible in the next hundred years? We may be able to forecast some short-term changes, but we know nothing about the cultural capabilities of our species hundreds or thousands of years in the future.

Another problem is that our own viewpoint can influence our predictions. An optimistic view might focus on the success of past cultural adaptations and the rate of acquisition of knowledge, and then develop a scenario including increased standard of living for all, cheap energy sources, and an elevated life expectancy. A pessimistic view might consider all the horrors of the past and present, and project a grim future. A pessimist might envisage widespread famine, overcrowding, pollution, disease, and warfare. Most likely, any possible future will be neither pie-in-the-sky nor doom-and-despair, but rather a combination of positive and negative changes. If the study of evolution tells us one thing, it is that every change has potential costs and benefits. We need to temper our optimism and pessimism with a sense of balance.

In any consideration of the future, we must acknowledge change as basic to life. Many people find it tempting to suggest that we would be better off living a "simpler" life. Others argue that we should stop trying to deal with our problems and let nature take its course or that we should trust in the acts of God. This is unacceptable—indeed, our understanding of human evolution argues for the reverse. Our adaptive pattern has been one of learning and problem solving. More than that, this is our primate heritage. Our biology has allowed us to develop the basic mammalian patterns of learned behavior to a high degree. We have the capability for rational thought, for reason, and for learning. Even if many of our cultural inventions have led to suffering and pain, our *potential* for good is immense. In any case, we must continue along the path of learning and intelligence; it is our very nature. Good or bad, the capabilities of the human mind and spirit may be infinite.

CELL BIOLOGY

This section, which focuses on the structure of the cell and on the processes of mitosis and meiosis, can be used as a supplement for students wishing to review the basic biology necessary for an understanding of the fundamental principles of Mendelian genetics.

THE CELL

All living creatures are made up of cells. Humans, like many organisms, are multicelled. Figure A1.1 shows some of the components of a typical cell. Two major structures are the *nucleus* and the *cytoplasm;* the latter contains a number of other structures. The entire body of the cell is enclosed by a *cell membrane.*

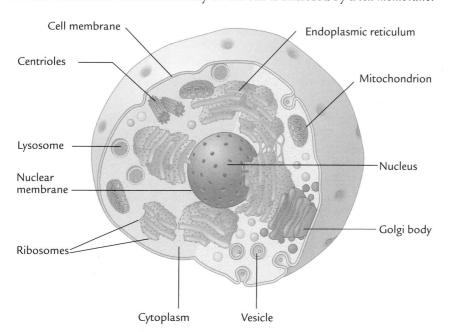

Cell membrane

Centrioles

Lysosome

Nuclear membrane

Ribosomes

Cytoplasm

Vesicle

Endoplasmic reticulum

Mitochondrion

Nucleus

Golgi body

FIGURE A1.1

Schematic diagram of a cell.

Within the cytoplasm, *mitochondria* convert some cellular material into energy that is then used for cellular activity. *Ribosomes* are small particles that are frequently attached to a larger structure known as the *endoplasmic reticulum*. Composed of RNA and proteins, ribosomes serve as sites for the manufacture of proteins.

As discussed in Chapter 2, the DNA sequences that make up the genetic code are bound together by proteins in long strands known as *chromosomes*. In body cells, chromosomes come in pairs; humans have 23 pairs of chromosomes. The chromosomes within the nucleus of the cell contain all of the DNA, with the exception of mitochondrial DNA.

DNA has the ability to make copies of itself. This ability is vital for transmitting genetic information from cell to cell and for transmitting genetic information from generation to generation. The replication of DNA is part of the process of cell replication. We will examine two basic processes: mitosis, the replication of body cells, and meiosis, the replication of sex cells.

MITOSIS

Mitosis produces two identical body cells from one original. Between cell divisions, each chromosome produces an exact copy of itself, resulting in two pairs with two chromosomes each. When a cell divides, each part contains one of each of the pairs of chromosomes. Thus, two identical body cells, each with the full number of chromosome pairs, are produced. As outlined in Figure A1.2, five stages compose the process of mitosis: interphase, prophase, metaphase, anaphase, and telophase. (Some people do not refer to interphase as a stage.)

During *interphase*, the chromosomes that are dispersed throughout the nucleus duplicate. During *prophase*, the chromosomes, each of which is attached to its copy, become tightly coiled and move toward one another in the nucleus. Each of the two copies is called a *chromatid*, and their point of attachment is called the *centromere*. Small structures located outside the nuclear membrane, known as *centrioles* (see Figure A1.1), move toward opposite ends of the cell, and *spindle fibers* form between the centrioles. The nuclear membrane then dissolves.

During *metaphase*, the duplicated chromosomes line up along the middle of the cell, and the spindle fibers attach to the centromeres. During *anaphase*, the centromere divides, and the two strands of chromatids (original and duplicate) split and move toward opposite ends of the cell. During *telophase*, new nuclear membranes form around each of the two clusters of chromosomes. Finally, the cell membrane pinches in the middle, creating two identical cells.

MEIOSIS

Meiosis, the production of sex cells (gametes), differs from mitosis in several ways. The main difference is that sex cells contain only half of an organism's DNA—one chromosome from each pair. Thus, when a new zygote, or

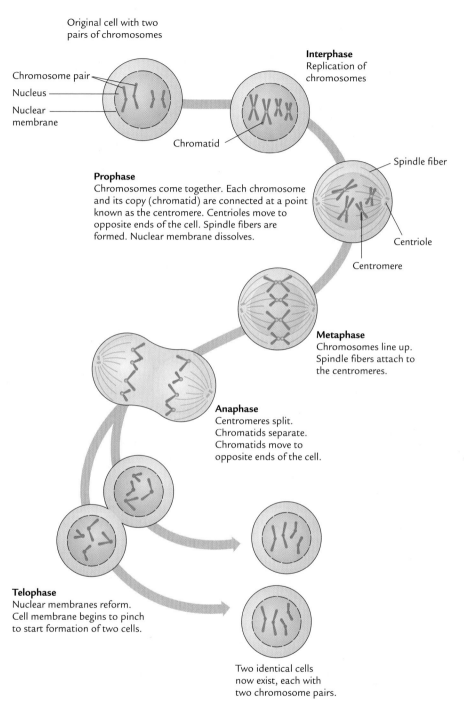

Original cell with two pairs of chromosomes

Chromosome pair
Nucleus
Nuclear membrane

Chromatid

Interphase
Replication of chromosomes

Prophase
Chromosomes come together. Each chromosome and its copy (chromatid) are connected at a point known as the centromere. Centrioles move to opposite ends of the cell. Spindle fibers are formed. Nuclear membrane dissolves.

Spindle fiber

Centriole

Centromere

Metaphase
Chromosomes line up. Spindle fibers attach to the centromeres.

Anaphase
Centromeres split. Chromatids separate. Chromatids move to opposite ends of the cell.

Telophase
Nuclear membranes reform. Cell membrane begins to pinch to start formation of two cells.

Two identical cells now exist, each with two chromosome pairs.

FIGURE A1.2

The five phases of mitosis. In this example, the original body cell contains two pairs of chromosomes. Mitosis produces two identical body cells, each containing two chromosome pairs (a total of four chromosomes each).

fertilized egg, is formed from the joining of egg and sperm, the offspring will have 23 chromosome pairs. One of each pair comes from the mother, and one of each pair comes from the father.

Meiosis involves two cycles of cell division (Figure A1.3). The total sequence of events following the initial duplication of chromosomes

FIGURE A1.3

The phases of meiosis for a sperm cell. In this example, the original cell contained two chromosome pairs. As a result of meiosis, four sperm cells were produced, each with two chromosomes. The process is similar for egg cells, except that one egg cell and three polar bodies are produced.

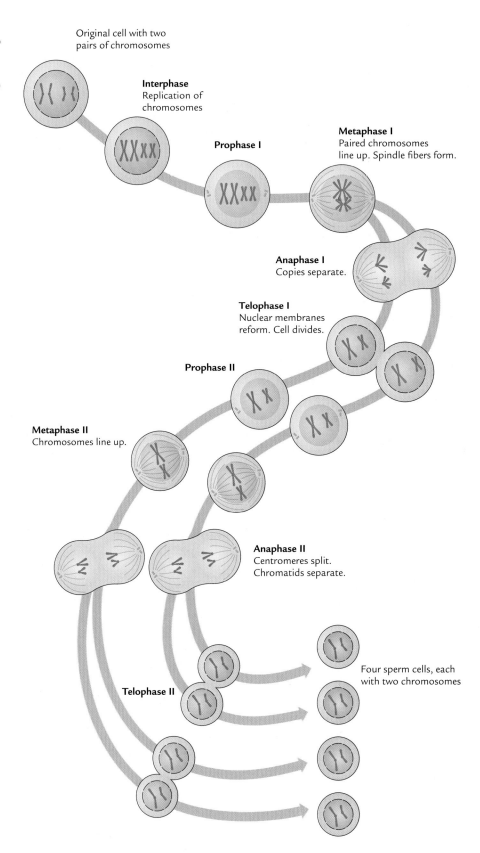

Original cell with two pairs of chromosomes

Interphase
Replication of chromosomes

Prophase I

Metaphase I
Paired chromosomes line up. Spindle fibers form.

Anaphase I
Copies separate.

Telophase I
Nuclear membranes reform. Cell divides.

Prophase II

Metaphase II
Chromosomes line up.

Anaphase II
Centromeres split. Chromatids separate.

Telophase II

Four sperm cells, each with two chromosomes

(interphase) involves eight stages: prophase I, metaphase I, anaphase I, telophase I, prophase II, metaphase II, anaphase II, and telophase II. Figure A1.3 presents a diagram of this process for the production of sperm cells, for a hypothetical organism with two chromosome pairs. Each of the two pairs of chromosomes has replicated itself by the start of prophase I, leading to eight chromatids: the two chromosomes of each pair duplicate, giving a total of $2 \times 2 \times 2 = 8$ chromatids, each pair of which attaches to one of the centromeres through a process known as *synapsis*. At the end of prophase I, the nuclear membrane dissolves. Then, during metaphase I, the paired chromosomes line up and spindle fibers form. The copies separate during anaphase I. During telophase I, the nuclear membranes reform and the cell divides. The realization of two cells, each containing eight chromatids, constitutes prophase II. During metaphase II, the chromosomes line up, after which the centromeres split and the chromatids separate, completing anaphase II. The nuclear membranes reform during telophase II, and the cell divides. The net result of this sequence of two cell divisions is four sperm cells, each with two chromosomes—half of the genetic material of the father. The process is similar for the production of egg cells from the female, except that the net result is one egg cell and three structures known as *polar bodies* that do not function as sex cells.

Meiosis thus allows half of a parent's genetic material to be passed on to the next generation. When a sperm cell fertilizes an egg cell, the total number of chromosomes is restored. For humans, the resulting zygote contains $23 + 23 = 46$ chromosomes, or 23 chromosome pairs.

Sex cells may also contain genetic combinations not present in the parent. When synapsis occurs during prophase I, and the chromosomes pair with their copies, becoming attached to one another at several places, the potential exists for genetic material to be exchanged, in a process known as *crossing over*. The resulting genetic combinations allow for variation in each sex cell from its source.

Independent assortment also enhances genetic variability. As discussed in Chapter 2, according to this principle, the segregation of any pair of chromosomes does not affect the probability of segregation of any other pair of chromosomes. If you have two chromosome pairs, A and B, with two chromosomes each (A1 and A2, and B1 and B2), only one of each pair will be found in any sex cell. However, you might have one sex cell with A1 and B1, and another sex cell with A1 and B2. Whichever member of the first pair of chromosomes is found in any given sex cell has no bearing on whichever member of the second pair is also found in that sex cell. Independent assortment results from processes occurring during metaphase I. When the paired chromosomes line up, they do so at random and are not influenced by whether they originally came from the person's mother or father. This process allows for tremendous genetic variability in potential offspring.

HUMAN SKELETAL BIOLOGY: FORENSIC ANTHROPOLOGY AND BIOARCHAEOLOGY

The study of human skeletal biology is a major part of biological anthropology. Throughout this book, aspects of human skeletal biology have been touched upon when examining ape-human differences (Chapter 7), the analysis of fossils (Chapter 8), issues of race and classification (Chapter 14), and studies of health and disease (Chapter 17), among others. This appendix provides a bit more insight into some of the methods of analyzing human skeletal remains (including those of our ancestors). Because skeletal biology touches upon many topics throughout the book, a somewhat more focused examination is presented here rather than trying to squeeze in different topics in different places throughout the book. This appendix serves both as a single point of reference on selected topics in skeletal biology, but can also stand as a separate chapter should your instructor prefer to cover these topics all at one time.

The primary emphasis in this appendix is on selected topics that are useful in the related fields of forensic anthropology and bioarchaeology. As noted in the book's introduction, forensic anthropology is concerned with issues of identification, such as sex, age, physical characteristics, and ancestry. These issues are often clues to determining the identity of a given specimen, such as in a criminal or missing person investigation. Such traits are also of interest to studies of bioarchaeology. As noted in Chapter 17, bioarchaeology is concerned with using skeletal remains to inform us about the health and lifestyle of a past population. Here, the focus is more on the population than the individual. Although the purpose of forensic and bioarchaeological studies may be different, they share a number of methods.

SEX DETERMINATION

Perhaps the most basic aspect of identification is sex. Is a given specimen male or female? There are a number of ways to estimate sex from human skeletal remains with varying degrees of accuracy. Cranial measures and observations often provide a high degree of accuracy, and measures and observations using the pelvis provide even more accuracy (hardly surprising, given the differences in adult pelvic anatomy that accompany child-bearing by females). The more observations that can be made, the higher the degree of accuracy.

As noted in Chapter 8, the size of the human skull is a clue to sex because males are larger on average. Certain parts of the skull are particularly informative, such as the ridge of bone above the eyes (the brow ridge, or *supraorbital torus*). As shown in Figure A2.1, the brow ridges of males are generally larger and more prominent than in females.

Another key diagnostic feature is the size of the mastoid process, which is the large bump behind your ear (see Figure A2.2). The mastoid process of males is typically larger than that of females. The brow ridges and mastoid process are but two of a number of features used to sex cranial remains. Other diagnostic features are also related to the greater size and robusticity of males, including the fact that males generally have larger palates, larger teeth, larger muscle markings, and squarer chins (Bass 1995; White et al. 2012). A potential problem here is variation in size from one population to another. Because of size variation, sexing based on crania is best done using a large sample or comparison to a similar reference sample (White et al. 2012), and ancestry should be taken into account.

Although the human skull can be used for accurate estimation of sex, the best part of the body to use, if available, is the pelvis. There are a number of anatomical differences between the pelvis of adult males and females (these methods do not work for children). Differences between the adult male and

FIGURE A2.1

Adult male (*left*) and female (*right*) human skulls. Brow ridges tend to be larger and more prominent in males than in females.

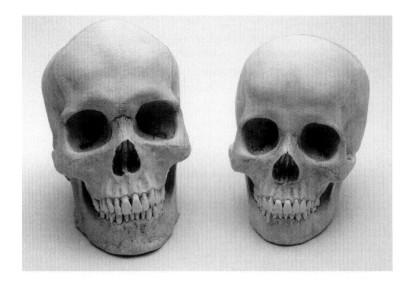

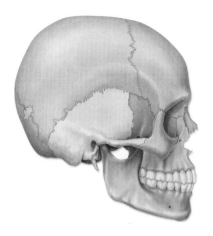

FIGURE A2.2

Color-coded lateral view of the human skull. The temporal bone is shown in yellow, and includes the mastoid process, immediately to the left of the ear hole. The mastoid process is one of a number of characteristics used to sex a human skull, as males typically have a larger mastoid process.

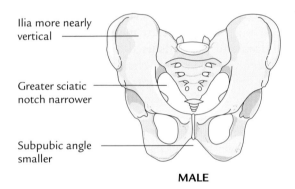

Ilia more nearly vertical

Greater sciatic notch narrower

Subpubic angle smaller

MALE

FIGURE A2.3

Comparison of the pelvic anatomy of modern human males and females. (From *Human Antiquity: An Introduction to Physical Anthropology and Archaeology*, 4d ed., by Kenneth Feder and Michael Park, Fig. 7.17. Copyright © 2001 by Mayfield Publishing Company. Reprinted by permission of The McGraw-Hill Companies.)

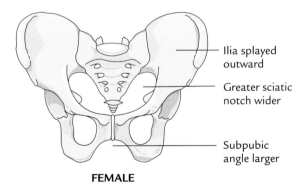

Ilia splayed outward

Greater sciatic notch wider

Subpubic angle larger

FEMALE

adult female pelvis relate to childbirth in the latter. As shown in Figure A2.3, adult females have a larger subpubic angle and a wider sciatic notch. In addition, the side blades of the pelvis (the ilia) are not as vertical as in adult males. These and other differences provide a means of sexing pelvic remains with high accuracy (see Bass 1995 and White et al. 2012 for further details).

AGE DETERMINATION

Another basic question is age—how old was someone when they died? Age is an important characteristic in any forensic identification. Age at death also provides us with important information in a bioarchaeological study of a population. If we have a large enough sample that includes individuals of all ages, we can use the estimated ages at death to estimate various mortality statistics, including life expectancy at birth. This number in turn tells us something about the overall health of a population, particularly in terms of infant mortality, as the more frequently that infants and young children die, the lower the average age at death and the life expectancy of a newborn child. Examples of such studies have been mentioned in Chapter 17 regarding the biological impact of the transition to agriculture during prehistory.

There are a variety of ways to determine age at death from skeletal remains. These methods are based on the fact that certain aspects of skeletal and dental anatomy change over one's lifetime in a regular manner, allowing us to compare the presence/absence or the extent of development of selected traits with a reference standard. In general, there are methods that can be used for estimating age of children and methods used for estimating age in adults. Because many of the dental and skeletal changes occur early in life, age estimation is generally more precise for children, often allowing us a narrow range of ages (e.g., 11–12). For adults, age estimates are often less precise.

One of the more commonly used measures of age estimation is based on patterns of dental eruption. As mammals, humans have two sets of teeth—the *deciduous teeth* ("baby teeth") and the *permanent teeth* ("adult teeth"). During an individual's lifetime, the deciduous teeth erupt first. Over time, the permanent teeth erupt and the baby teeth are lost. Different teeth, both deciduous and permanent, erupt at different ages, allowing us to estimate how old someone was when they died based on which teeth had erupted. This method works only up to the time of young adulthood, when all permanent teeth have erupted.

Figure A2.4 shows the average age of eruption for permanent teeth in the upper jaw (maxilla) and lower jaw (mandible). As an example, note that the last permanent tooth to erupt is the third molar tooth (often known as the "wisdom tooth"), which typically erupts between ages 17 and 21. If we find a jaw where the second molar has erupted but the third molar has not, this suggests that the individual is likely between 13 and 17 years of age. Note that since the last tooth to erupt (the third molar) does so by age 21 on average, looking at eruption times is only useful for subadults; you cannot distinguish a 25-year-old from a 35-year-old based on what teeth have erupted. For older adults, we would examine the amount of *wear* of the different teeth. Tooth wear can provide information on age of older adults when compared to a set of standards, because the older you are, the more worn teeth will be on average (see White et al. 2012 for more details). However, such methods are very much dependent on other factors that influence tooth wear, such as diet, which makes comparisons across populations difficult.

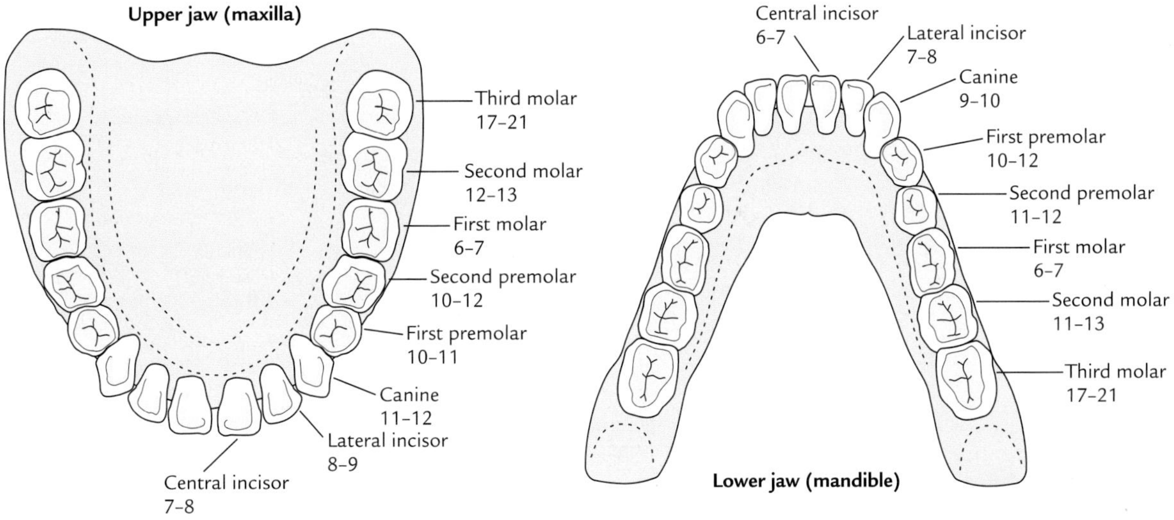

Upper jaw (maxilla)

Third molar
17–21

Second molar
12–13

First molar
6–7

Second premolar
10–12

First premolar
10–11

Canine
11–12

Lateral incisor
8–9

Central incisor
7–8

Central incisor
6–7

Lateral incisor
7–8

Canine
9–10

First premolar
10–12

Second premolar
11–12

First molar
6–7

Second molar
11–13

Third molar
17–21

Lower jaw (mandible)

FIGURE A2.4

Average age (in years) of dental eruption for adult human teeth. (Data from Ash and Nelson 2003.)

Bones of the arms, legs, hands, and feet also provide clues to an individual subadult's skeletal age. As these bones grow, the cartilage fuses between the two ends of the bone, known as *epiphyses*. This fusion is complete at different ages for different bones, and for the different ends of the bone. Thus, by examining the bones of a subadult to see which bones have closed and which have not can give us an estimate of the age at death. Figure A2.5 shows the average ages of epiphyseal closure for various bones based on a European sample. If, for example, we find that all arm and leg bones show closure, but the clavicle (collarbone) has not, we would estimate that the individual was about 20 years of age.

There are also some methods that can be used to estimate age for adult specimens where dental eruption and epiphyseal closure are not applicable. One such source of information on age is the *pubic symphysis,* which is the point where the two hip bones join at the pubis (refer back to Figure A2.3). In young adults, the surface of the bones is very rough, with many grooves and ridges. As a person ages, these rough feature smooth out, and a rim develops at around age 35. By comparing a specimen to a standard sample, the age can be estimated (see White et al. 2012 for more details).

ESTIMATING HEIGHT

Another important characteristic in forensic investigation is an individual's height. Estimates of height can also be useful in bioarchaeological analyses of population health, as trends in average height might provide clues as to trends in nutrition and infectious disease, both of which act to reduce height.

Height is normally estimated using a series of equations, many based on studies of decreased soldiers from World War II and the Korean War. Here, the soldier's height was known during their life, and the arm and leg bones

FIGURE A2.5

Average age (in years) of the closure of some epiphyses in long bones based on a European sample (males and females pooled). Different standards may apply to males and females and to different populations. (Data from Schwarz 2007.)

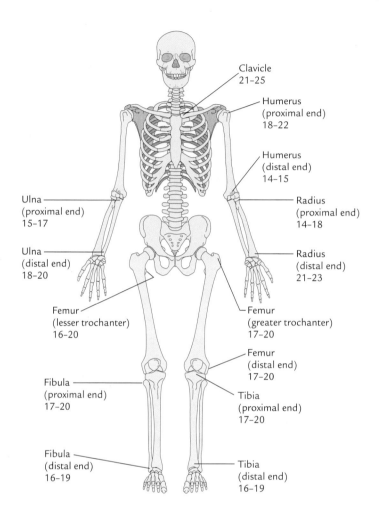

Clavicle
21–25

Humerus
(proximal end)
18–22

Humerus
(distal end)
14–15

Ulna
(proximal end)
15–17

Radius
(proximal end)
14–18

Ulna
(distal end)
18–20

Radius
(distal end)
21–23

Femur
(lesser trochanter)
16–20

Femur
(greater trochanter)
17–20

Femur
(distal end)
17–20

Fibula
(proximal end)
17–20

Tibia
(proximal end)
17–20

Fibula
(distal end)
16–19

Tibia
(distal end)
16–19

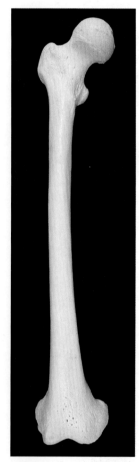

FIGURE A2.6

The femur, the upper leg bone, is one of several long bones that can be used to estimate height.

were known from skeletal analysis after their death, such that height and bone length could be compared for the same individuals. Height estimation is based on the fact that on average the taller someone is, the longer their bones are. A statistical method known as regression analysis is used to develop a predictive equation from this relationship. The bones typically used in height estimation are the femur (upper leg bone), tibia (larger of the two lower leg bones), humerus (upper arm bone), and the ulna and radius (lower arm bones).

The most commonly used equations were developed by Trotter and Gleser (1952, 1958) separately for males and females as well as individuals of European and African ancestry. As an example, this is the equation used for the femur (Figure A2.6) of males of European ancestry:

Height (in centimeters) = 65.53 + 2.32 (femur length in centimeters).

Using standard methods (see Bass 1995), the length of the femur is measured in centimeters and plugged into this equation. For example, suppose we have a femur that is 45 centimeters in length. The estimated height is

65.53 + 2.32 (45) = 169.93 centimeters, which is 67 inches, or 5 feet, 7 inches. Because this is a statistical estimation, any prediction would also include a margin of error. In an ideal case, you would estimate height from a number of bones from the same individual in order to get a more accurate prediction.

ANCESTRY

Forensic investigators are often called upon to estimate the ancestry of an individual. Ancestry is typically labeled as "race," even though as noted in Chapter 14 the concept of biological race is not that useful in describing human variation. However, as noted by forensic anthropologist Norman Sauer (1992), what we are really doing is estimating what general part of the world someone's ancestry derives from, which is not really the same thing as the pre-Darwinian notion of separate and distinct races. We might be able to detect African ancestry, but this does not mean there is a separate African race, or a set of African races. Basically, ancestry identification is trying to locate an individual roughly within a geographically dispersed species.

Because human biological variation is continuous, and the race concept is discrete, identification of ancestry works best in cases where the most likely ancestral groups originated in geographically different parts of the world. The United States is a good example of this, where a primary concern is classifying individuals as European, African, Asian, or North American. In reality, these large racial groupings typically refer to more specific ancestral groups; for example, "Asians" typically mean people from East Asia, as historically there have been fewer immigrants to the United States from other parts of Asia (White et al. 2012). Thus, the forensic anthropologist in the United States can use history as a guide for determining ancestry, as the choices of possible ancestries within the human species are more limited. For example, we typically do not have to worry about identifying someone of native Australian ancestry because there are relatively few immigrants from that part of the world.

As noted in Chapter 14, human biological variation is continuous, which makes it difficult to sort out populations that are very similar to their neighbors. However, when we are choosing between possible ancestries that represent populations from far distances (as in the case of Northwestern Europe and Western Africa), there are clues from skeletal, cranial, and dental anatomy.

Ancestry can be estimated from the presence of a number of traits. As with classification by sex and age, it is best to look at a number of traits. For example, shovel-shaped incisors (mentioned in Chapters 13 and 14) are found in very high frequencies in populations of East Asian and Native American ancestry, but are occasionally found in European and African samples as well (Bass 1995). The presence of shovel-shaped incisors is a good clue for East Asian/Native American ancestry, but it is not perfect by itself. If we look at a number of traits, the probability of making a correct identification increases (see White et al. 2012 for more examples). In some cases, skeletal assessment can be supplemented by DNA analysis.

FIGURE A2.7

Forensic scientist using calipers to take a measurement on a human skull.

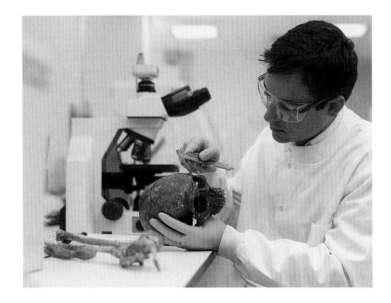

Ancestry can also be estimated by taking a large number of measurements of the skull (such as length and breadth of the skull, height of the nasal cavity, width across the cheekbones, and many others) and comparing these measurements statistically to reference samples of known ancestry (Figure A2.7). Results are good when using a large number of cranial measures and choosing between broad ancestral groups (e.g., Europe, Africa) that are widely separated in space (Ousley et al. 2009; Relethford 2009).

DISEASE, DIET, AND HEALTH

As noted in Chapter 17, examination of skeletal remains allows us in many cases to make statements regarding the health status of an individual when they died. Some diseases affect directly the bone tissue, such as osteoarthritis (Figure A2.8, as well as Figure 17.1 in Chapter 17). Other diseases affect other tissues and organs primarily, but have effects on the bones, such as syphilis (see Figure 17.2 in Chapter 17), tuberculosis, and leprosy. However, only a small percentage of individuals with such diseases will show any impact in their skeletal remains.

Disease or nutritional stress in general leaves its mark on the human skeleton by disrupting patterns of growth. For example, incisor teeth can show the presence of *enamel hypoplasias*, which are horizontal grooves that form on the front side of the teeth. These grooves represent that the individual experienced some degree of disease and/or nutritional stress during their growth. Such stresses can also be seen in pathological lines (Harris lines) forming in long bones when growth is disrupted by disease or nutrition. Even if a specific cause of disease or poor nutrition cannot be identified, such markers do indicate some problem with health. The prevalence of such stress markers allows us to make comparisons of overall health among populations, such as comparing a hunting-gathering group to an early agricultural group.

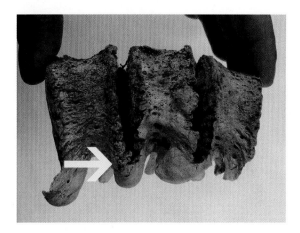

FIGURE A2.8

Osteoarthritis of the vertebrae. Osteoarthritis fuses the vertebrae, producing immobility.

Aspects of diet can also be determined from skeletal and dental evidence, which is particularly useful in bioarchaeological analyses of changing dietary patterns over time. Some nutritional deficiencies are seen in skeletal remains. One example is a condition known as *cribra orbritalia*, which is when the bone inside the eye orbit becomes more porous. This condition is considered to be due to some nutritional deficiency; some argue that it represents iron deficiency and others argue that it reflects vitamin-B deficiency (Walker et al. 2009). Another measure of diet is *stable isotope analysis*, discussed in Chapter 8, which looks at the ratio of the stable (nonradioactive) isotopes of different elements in bones. For example, different carbon isotopes provide clues about what kind of plants were eaten. In archaeological sites in Eastern North America for example, the carbon isotope associated with corn shows that corn became a major part of the diet in this region after about the year 900 (Larsen 2000).

Another aspect of health—physical trauma—can also be determined from skeletal analysis, as well as an indication of whether the trauma has had time to heal or become infected. If neither healing nor infection is present, we might be able to correlate the trauma with the time of death, which might in turn reflect cause, such as a major cranial blow with no signs of healing or post-traumatic infection.

The above examples are not meant to give a full review of the ways in which health can be studied using skeletal and dental remains, but rather simply a flavor of the types of analyses that are possible. As with issues of sex, age, height, and ancestry, the analysis of health and disease shows us the wide range of questions that can be answered by looking at human skeletal biology.

acclimation   Short-term physiologic responses to a stress, usually occurring within minutes or hours.

acclimatization   Long-term physiologic responses to a stress, usually taking from days to months.

Acheulean tradition   The stone tool culture that appears first with *Homo erectus* and is characterized by the development of hand axes and other bifacial tools.

adaptation   The process of successful interaction between a population and an environment. Cultural or biological traits that offer an advantage in a given environment are adaptations.

adaptive radiation   The formation of many new species following the availability of new environments or the development of a new adaptation.

affiliative   Friendly behaviors that promote social bonds.

African replacement model   The hypothesis that modern humans evolved as a new species in Africa 200,000 years ago and then spread throughout the Old World, replacing preexisting human populations.

age at menarche   The age at which a human female experiences her first menstrual period.

age-sex structure   The number of males and females in different age groups of a population.

agonistic   Unfriendly social relationships.

allele   The alternative form of a gene or DNA sequence that occurs at a given locus. Some loci have only one allele, some have two, and some have many alternative forms. Alleles occur in pairs, one on each chromosome.

Allen's rule   States that mammals in cold climates tend to have shorter and bulkier limbs, allowing less loss of body heat, whereas mammals in hot climates tend to have long, slender limbs, allowing greater loss of body heat.

allometry   The study of the change in proportion of various body parts as a consequence of their growth at different rates.

alloparent   An individual that cares for an infant but is not a biological parent.

anagenesis   The transformation of a single species over time.

anatomically modern humans   The modern form of the human species, which dates back 200,000 years.

anthropoids   A group of haplorhine primates consisting of monkeys, apes, and humans.

anthropology   The science that investigates human biological and cultural variation and evolution.

arboreal   Living in trees.

archaeology   The subfield of anthropology that focuses on cultural variations in prehistoric and historic populations by analyzing the culture's remains.

Archean eon   The second geologic eon, dating from 3,850 to 2,500 Ma, characterized by the appearance of the first single-celled organisms.

Ardipithecus   A genus of fossil hominin that lived between 5.8 and 4.4 million years ago in Africa that shows primitive bipedalism.

Ardipithecus kadabba   An early primitive hominin with very apelike teeth from Africa dating between 5.8 million and 5.2 million years ago.

Ardipithecus ramidus   An early primitive hominin species from Africa dating between 5.8 million and 4.4 million years ago.

argon-argon dating   A variation of potassium-argon dating that can be applied to very small samples of volcanic rock.

assimilation model   The hypothesis that modern human anatomy arose first in Africa as a change within a species, and then spread through gene flow to populations outside of Africa. The gene pool of the non-African archaic populations was thus assimilated into an expanding population of modern humans out of Africa.

Australopithecus   A genus of fossil hominin that lived between 4.2 million and 1.8 million years ago and is characterized by bipedal locomotion, small brain size, large face, and large teeth.

Australopithecus afarensis   A hominin found in East Africa, dating between 3.7 million and 3.0 million years ago. The teeth show a number of primitive and apelike features.

Australopithecus africanus   An early hominin, dating between 3.3 million and 2.3 million years ago and found in South Africa. It may be an ancestor of the genus *Homo*.

Australopithecus anamensis   An early hominin that lived in East Africa between 4.2 million and 3.9 million years ago. It was a biped but had many primitive, apelike features of the skull and teeth.

Australopithecus garhi   An early hominin, dating to 2.5 million years ago in East Africa. It had large front and back teeth.

Australopithecus sediba   A species of *Australopithecus* found in South Africa 2 million years ago that has a number of characteristics linking earlier hominins and *Homo*.

balancing selection   Selection for the heterozygote and against the homozygotes (the heterozygote is most fit). Allele frequencies move toward an equilibrium defined by the fitness values of the two homozygotes.

base   Chemical units (adenine, thymine, guanine, cytosine) that make up part of the DNA molecule and specify genetic instructions.

behavioral ecology   The study of behavior that focuses on the adaptive value of behavior from an ecological and evolutionary perspective.

Bergmann's rule   States that (1) among mammals of similar shape, the larger mammal loses heat less rapidly than the smaller mammal and that (2) among mammals of similar size, the mammal with a linear shape will lose heat more rapidly than the mammal with a nonlinear shape.

biface   A stone tool with both sides worked, producing greater symmetry and efficiency.

bilateral symmetry   Symmetry in which the right and left sides of the body are approximately mirror images, a characteristic of vertebrates.

binocular stereoscopic vision   Overlapping fields of vision (binocular), with both sides of the brain receiving images from both eyes (stereoscopic), thereby providing depth perception.

bioarchaeology   The study of human skeletal remains from archaeological sites that are used to provide information on the health and lifestyle of prehistoric people.

biocultural approach   A method of studying humans that looks at the interaction between biology and culture in evolutionary adaptation.

biological anthropology   The subfield of anthropology that focuses on the biological evolution of humans and human ancestors, the relationship of humans to other organisms, and patterns of biological variation within and among human populations. Also referred to as *physical anthropology*.

biological race   A group of populations sharing certain biological traits that distinguish them from other groups of populations. In practice, the biological concept of race has been difficult to apply to human populations.

biological species concept   A definition of species that focuses on reproductive capabilities, whereby organisms from different populations are considered to be in the same species if they naturally interbreed and produce fertile offspring.

biostratigraphy   A relative dating method in which sites can be assigned an approximate age based on the similarity of animal remains to those from other dated sites.

bipedal   Moving about on two legs. Unlike the movement of other bipedal animals such as kangaroos, human bipedalism is further characterized by a striding motion.

blade   A stone tool characteristic of the Upper Paleolithic, defined as being at least twice as long as it is wide. Blade tools were made using an efficient and precise method.

B.P.   "Before Present" (1950), the internationally accepted form of designating past dates.

brachiation   A method of movement that uses the arms to swing from branch to branch. Gibbons are brachiators.

breeding population   A group of organisms that tend to choose mates from within the group.

brow ridges   The large ridges of bone above the eye orbits, very noticeable in *Homo erectus*.

burin   A stone tool with a sharp edge that is used to cut and engrave bone.

canine   One of four types of teeth found in mammals. The canine teeth are located in the front of the jaw behind the incisors. Mammals normally use these teeth for puncturing and defense. Unlike most mammals, humans have small canine teeth that function like incisors.

carbon-14 dating   A chronometric dating method based on the half-life of carbon-14 that can be applied to organic remains such as charcoal dating back over the past 50,000 years or so.

Carpolestes simpsoni   A species of primate-like mammal that had some derived primate traits, such as a grasping foot and an opposable big toe. This species is intermediate in many respects between primitive primate-like mammals and true primates.

carrying capacity   The maximum population size capable of being supported in a given environment.

catarrhines   Anthropoids native to the Old World that have narrow noses with downward facing nostrils. This group consists of Old World monkeys, apes, and humans.

Cenozoic era   The third and most recent geologic era of the Phanerozoic eon, dating to the last 65.5 Ma. Primate and human evolution occurred during the Cenozoic era.

cephalic index   A measure of cranial shape, defined as the maximum width of a skull divided by the maximum length of the skull.

cerebrum   The area of the forebrain that consists of the outermost layer of brain cells. The cerebrum is associated with memory, learning, and intelligence.

Chordata   A vertebrate phylum consisting of organisms that possess a notochord at some period during their life.

chromosome   A long strand of DNA sequences.

chronometric dating   A method of dating fossils or sites that provides an estimate of the specific date (subject to probabilistic limits).

chronospecies   Labels given to different points in the evolutionary lineage of a single species over time. As a species changes over time, the different stages are labeled as chronospecies to recognize the biological changes that have taken place.

civilization   A large, state-level society characterized by large population size, high population density, urbanization, social stratification, food and labor surpluses, monumental architecture, and record keeping.

cladistics   A school of thought that stresses evolutionary relationships between organisms based on shared derived traits.

cladogenesis   The formation of one or more new species from another over time.

codominant   Both alleles affect the phenotype of a heterozygous genotype, and neither is dominant over the other.

comparative approach   Comparing human populations to determine common and unique behaviors or biological traits.

continental drift   The movement of continental land masses on top of a partially molten layer of the earth's mantle. Because of continental drift, the relative location of the continents has changed over time.

convergent evolution   Independent evolution of a trait in rather distinct evolutionary lines. The development of flight in birds and certain insects is an example of convergent evolution.

cranial capacity   A measurement of the interior volume of the brain case measured in cubic centimeters (cc) and used as an approximate estimate of brain size.

crossing over   The exchange of DNA between chromosomes during meiosis.

cultural anthropology   The subfield of anthropology that focuses on variations in cultural behaviors among human populations.

culture   Behavior that is shared, learned, and socially transmitted.

cusp   A raised area on the chewing surface of a tooth.

demographic transition theory   A model of demographic change stating that as a population becomes economically developed, a reduction in death rates (leading to population growth) will take place, followed by a reduction in birth rates.

dendrochronology   A chronometric dating method based on the fact that trees in dry climates tend to accumulate one growth ring per year. The width of the rings varies according to climate, and a sample can be compared with a master chart of tree rings over the past 10,000 years.

dental formula   A shorthand method of describing the number of each type of tooth in half of one jaw of a mammal. The dental formula consists of four numbers: I-C-P-M, where I is the number of incisors, C is the number of canines, P is the number of premolars, and M is the number of molars. When a mammal has a different number of teeth in the upper and lower jaws, two dental formulae are used.

derived trait   A trait that has changed from an ancestral state. The large human brain is a derived trait relative to the common ancestor of humans and apes.

developmental acclimatization   Changes in organ or body structure that occur during the physical growth of any organism.

diastema   A gap next to the canine teeth that allows space for the canine on the opposing jaw.

directional selection   Selection against one extreme in a continuous trait and/or selection for the other extreme.

distance curve   A measure of size over time, for example, a person's height at different ages.

diurnal   Active during the day.

DNA (deoxyribonucleic acid)   The molecule that provides the genetic code for biological structures and the means to translate this code.

dominance hierarchy   The ranking system within a society that indicates which individuals are dominant in social behaviors.

dominant allele   An allele that masks the effect of the other allele (which is recessive) in a heterozygous genotype.

Dryopithecus   A genus of fossil ape that lived in Hungary and Spain during the Middle and Late Miocene that might be an ancestor of African apes and humans.

electron spin resonance (ESR)   A chronometric dating method that estimates dates from observation of radioactive atoms trapped in the calcite crystals present in a number of materials, such as bones and shells. This method is useful for dating sites back to roughly 1 million years.

embryo   The stage of human prenatal life lasting from roughly two to eight weeks following conception, characterized by structural development.

emergent infectious disease   A newly identified infectious disease that has recently evolved.

endemic   A pattern of disease rate when new cases of a disease occur at a relatively constant but low rate over time.

endocast   A cast of the interior of the brain case used in the analysis of brain size and structure.

Eocene epoch   The second epoch of the Cenozoic era, dating between 55.8 million and 33.9 million years ago. The first true primates, primitive prosimians, appeared during the Eocene.

eon   The major subdivision of geologic time.

epidemic   A pattern of disease rate when new cases of a disease spread rapidly through a population.

epidemiologic transition   The increase in life expectancy and the shift from infectious to noninfectious disease as the primary cause of death.

epoch   Subdivision of a geologic period.

era   Subdivision of a geologic eon.

estrus   A time during the month when females are sexually receptive.

Eurasia   The combined land masses of Europe and Asia.

evolution   The transformation of species of organic life over time.

evolutionary forces   Four mechanisms that can cause changes in allele frequencies from one generation to the next: mutation, natural selection, genetic drift, and gene flow.

evolutionary systematics   A school of thought that stresses the overall similarity of all (primitive and derived) homologous traits in classification.

exon   A section of DNA that codes for the amino acids that make up proteins. It is contrasted with an intron.

experimental archaeology   A field of archaeology that involves the study of the manufacture and use of tools in order to learn how they were made and used in the past.

fetus   The stage of human prenatal growth from roughly eight weeks following conception until birth, characterized by further development and rapid growth.

fission-fusion   A primate society in which the population splits into smaller subgroups at times (fission) and then later reunited (fusion). The process is affected by distribution of food resources.

fission-track dating   A chronometric dating method based on the number of tracks made across volcanic rock as uranium decays into lead.

fitness   An organism's probability of survival and reproduction. Fitness is generally measured in terms of the different genotypes for a given locus.

fluorine dating   A relative dating method based on the accumulation of fluorine in a bone that tells if two bones from a site are of the same age.

foramen magnum   The large opening at the base of the skull where the spinal cord enters. This opening is located more toward the center of the skull in hominins, who are bipeds, so that the skull sits atop the spine.

founder effect   A type of genetic drift caused by the formation of a new population by a small number of individuals. The small size of the sample can cause marked deviations in allele frequencies from the original population.

gene   A DNA sequence that codes for a functional polypeptide or RNA product.

gene flow   A mechanism for evolutionary change resulting from the movement of genes from one population to another. Gene flow introduces new genes into a population and also acts to make populations more similar genetically to one another.

generalized structure   A biological structure adapted to a wide range of conditions and used in very general ways. For example, the grasping hands of humans are generalized structures allowing climbing, food gathering, toolmaking, and a variety of other functions.

genetic distance   An average measure of relatedness between populations based on a number of traits.

genetic distance map   A graphic representation that shows the genetic relationships between populations, based on genetic distance measures.

genetic drift   A mechanism for evolutionary change resulting from the random fluctuations of gene frequencies from one generation to the next, or from any form of random sampling of a larger gene pool.

genome   The total DNA sequence of an organism.

genotype   The genetic endowment of an individual from the two alleles present at a given locus.

genus   Groups of species with similar adaptations.

gradualism   A model of macroevolutionary change whereby evolutionary changes occur at a slow, steady rate over time.

grooming   The handling and cleaning of another individual's fur. In primates, grooming serves as a form of communication that soothes and provides reassurance.

Hadean eon   The first geologic eon, dating from 4,600 to 3,850 Ma, which occurred before the oldest fossil evidence of life.

half-life   The average length of time it takes for half of a radioactive substance to decay into another form.

haplogroup   A set of related haplotypes that share similar mutations.

Haplorrhini (haplorhines)   One of two suborders of primates (the other is the strepsirhines). Haplorhines are primates without a moist nose (tarsiers, monkeys, apes, and humans).

haplotype   A combination of genes or DNA sequences that are inherited as a single unit.

Hardy-Weinberg equilibrium   A mathematical statement whereby in the absence of nonrandom mating and evolutionary forces, genotype and allele frequencies will remain the same from one generation to the next.

hemoglobin   The molecule in blood cells that transports oxygen.

heritability   The proportion of total variance in a trait due to genetic variation. This measure is not always the same; the actual value depends on the degree of environmental variation in any population.

heterodontic   Having different types of teeth. Mammals have four different types of teeth: incisors, canines, premolars, and molars.

heterozygous   The two alleles at a given locus are different.

holistic   Refers to the viewpoint that all aspects of existence are interrelated and important in understanding human variation and evolution.

homeobox gene   A group of regulatory genes that encode a sequence of 60 amino acids that regulate embryonic development. Homeobox genes subdivide from head to tail a developing embryo into different regions, which then form limbs and other structures. These genes are similar in many organisms, such as insects, mice, and humans.

homeostasis   In a physiologic sense, the maintenance of normal limits of body functioning.

homeotherm   An organism capable of maintaining a constant body temperature under most circumstances. Mammals are homeotherms.

home range   The size of the geographic area that is normally occupied and used by a social group.

hominid   A family (Hominidae) within the hominoids. In recent years, this family has been defined as including humans and the great apes (orangutan, gorilla, chimpanzee, and bonobo). Some scientists still use a more traditional definition that refers only to humans and their humanlike ancestors.

hominin   Humans and their ancestors since the time of divergence from the common ancestor of humans, chimpanzees, and bonobos.

hominine   The subfamily of hominoids that includes humans, chimpanzees, and bonobos. Some include gorillas in this group as well, whereas others place gorillas in their own subfamily of gorillines.

hominoid   A superfamily of anthropoids consisting of apes and humans. Hominoids have a shoulder structure adapted for climbing and hanging, lack a tail, are generally larger than monkeys, and have the largest brain to body size ratio among primates.

Homo   A genus of hominins characterized by large brain size and dependence on culture as a means of adaptation.

homodontic   All teeth are the same.

Homo erectus   A species of the genus *Homo* that arose 1.9 million years ago in Africa and then spread to parts of Asia and Europe.

Homo ergaster   The name given to African specimens of *Homo erectus* by those who argue that what has typically been called *Homo erectus* is actually made up of two different species.

Homo floresiensis   The species name given to a very small hominin that lived in Indonesia in recent times, and is suggested by some to be a dwarf species of *Homo erectus*.

Homo habilis   An early species of *Homo* that lived in Africa between 1.9 million and 1.44 million years ago (and perhaps earlier), with a brain size roughly half that of modern humans and a primitive postcranial skeleton.

Homo heidelbergensis   A species of archaic human, with a brain size close to that of modern humans but a larger, less modern face, that lived in Africa, Europe, and Asia between 800,000 and 200,000 years ago.

Homo rudolfensis   A species of early *Homo* from Africa that lived about 1.9 million years ago, with a brain size somewhat larger than *Homo habilis* but with larger back teeth and a broader face.

Homo sapiens   Modern humans.

homology   Similarity due to descent from a common ancestor.

homoplasy   Similarity due to independent evolution.

homozygous   Both alleles at a given locus are identical.

horticulture   A form of farming in which only simple hand tools are used.

hypothesis   An explanation of observed facts. To be scientific, a hypothesis must be testable.

hypoxia   Oxygen starvation, which occurs frequently at high altitudes.

inbreeding   Mating between biologically related individuals.

incisor   One of four types of teeth found in mammals. The incisors are the chisel-shaped front teeth used for cutting, slicing, and gnawing food.

infectious disease   A disease caused by the introduction of an organic foreign substance into the body. Such substances include viruses and parasites.

intelligent design creationism   The idea that the biological world was created by an intelligent entity and did not arise from natural processes.

intron   A section of DNA that does not code for the amino acids that make up proteins. It is contrasted with an exon.

kin selection   The concept that altruistic behavior can be selected for if it increases the probability of survival of close relatives.

knuckle walking   A form of movement used by chimpanzees and gorillas that is characterized by all four limbs touching the ground, with the weight of the arms resting on the knuckles of the hands.

kwashiorkor   An extreme form of protein-calorie malnutrition resulting from a severe deficiency in proteins but not calories.

lactase persistence   The ability to produce the enzyme lactase after age 5.

lactose intolerance   A condition characterized by diarrhea, cramps, and other intestinal problems resulting from the ingestion of milk.

lemur   A strepsirhine found today on the island of Madagascar. Lemurs include both nocturnal and diurnal species.

Levallois technique   A method of making stone tools in which a stone core is prepared in such a way that finished tools can be removed from it by a final blow. Also known as the *prepared-core method*.

life expectancy at birth   A measure of the average length of life for a newborn child.

life history theory   The study of how characteristics of an organism's life cycle affect reproduction, focusing on trade-offs between energy expended for numbers and fitness of offspring.

life table   A compilation of the age distribution of a population that provides an estimate of the probability that an individual will die by a certain age, used to compute life expectancy.

linguistic anthropology   The subfield of anthropology that focuses on the nature of human language, the relationship of language to culture, and the languages of nonliterate peoples.

linkage   Alleles on the same chromosome are inherited together.

locus   The specific location of a gene or DNA sequence on a chromosome.

loris   A nocturnal strepsirhine found today in Asia and Africa.

Lower Paleolithic   A general term used to refer collectively to the stone tool technologies of *Homo habilis/ Homo rudolfensis* and *Homo erectus*.

macroevolution   Long-term evolutionary change. The study of macroevolution focuses on biological evolution over many generations and on the origin of higher taxonomic categories, such as species.

malnutrition   Poor nutrition, from either too much or too little food, or from the improper balance of nutrients.

marasmus   An extreme form of protein-calorie malnutrition resulting from severe deficiencies in both proteins and calories.

mass extinction   Many species becoming extinct at about the same time.

meiosis   The creation of sex cells by replication of chromosomes followed by cell division. Each sex cell contains 50 percent of an individual's chromosomes (one from each pair).

Mendelian genetics   The branch of genetics concerned with patterns and processes of inheritance. This field was named after Gregor Mendel, the first scientist to work out many of these principles.

Mendel's Law of Independent Assortment   A law stating that the segregation of any pair of chromosomes does not affect the probability of segregation for other pairs of chromosomes.

Mendel's Law of Segregation   A law stating that sex cells contain one of each pair of alleles.

menopause   The permanent cessation of menstrual cycles.

Mesozoic era   The second geologic era of the Phanerozoic eon, dating from 251 to 65.5 Ma, when the dinosaurs were dominant and when mammals and birds appeared.

messenger RNA   The form of RNA that transports the genetic instructions from the DNA molecule to the site of protein synthesis.

microevolution   Short-term evolutionary change. The study of microevolution focuses on changes in allele frequencies from one generation to the next.

microsatellite DNA   Repeated short sequences of DNA; the number of repeats is highly variable.

Middle Paleolithic   A general term used to refer collectively to the stone tool technologies of *Homo heidelbergensis* and the Neandertals.

Middle Pleistocene   A geologic stage of the Pleistocene epoch that lasted from 781,000 to 126,000 years ago.

Miocene epoch   The fourth epoch of the Cenozoic era, dating between 23.0 million and 5.3 million years ago. Several adaptive radiations of hominoids occurred during the Miocene, and the oldest known possible hominins appeared during the Late Miocene.

mitochondrial DNA   A small amount of DNA that is located in the mitochondria of cells. Mitochondrial DNA is inherited only through the mother.

mitosis   The process of replication of chromosomes in body cells. Each cell produces two identical copies.

molar   One of four types of teeth found in mammals. The molars are back teeth used for crushing and grinding food.

molecular dating   The application of methods of genetic analysis to estimate the sequence and timing of divergent evolutionary lines.

molecular genetics   The branch of genetics concerned with the structure and function of genes and DNA sequences at the molecular level.

monogamy   An exclusive sexual bond between an adult male and an adult female for a long period of time.

monosomy   A condition in which one chromosome rather than a pair is present in body cells.

most recent common ancestor (MRCA)   The most recent individual from which a set of organisms are descended. MRCAs are estimated from genetic data and are different for different loci.

Mousterian tradition   The prepared-core stone tool technology of the Neandertals.

multimale/multifemale group   The most common type of social group in nonhuman primates; it consists of several adult males, several adult females, and their immature offspring.

multiregional evolution model   The hypothesis that modern humans evolved throughout the Old World as a single species after the first dispersion of *Homo erectus* out of Africa. According to this view, the transition from *Homo erectus* to archaic humans to modern *Homo sapiens* occurred within a single evolutionary line throughout the Old World.

mutation   A mechanism for evolutionary change resulting from a random change in the genetic code; the ultimate source of all genetic variation. Mutations must occur in sex cells to cause evolutionary change.

nasal index   A measure of the shape of the nasal opening, defined as the width of the nasal opening divided by the height.

natural increase   The number of births minus the number of deaths.

natural selection   A mechanism for evolutionary change favoring the survival and reproduction of some organisms over others because of their biological characteristics.

Neandertals   A population of humans that lived in Europe and the Middle East between about 130,000 and 28,000 years ago. Debate continues about whether they are a subspecies of *Homo sapiens* or a separate species and to what extent they contributed to the ancestry of humans today.

nocturnal   Active during the night.

noninfectious disease   A disease caused by factors other than the introduction of an organic foreign substance into the body.

nonrandom mating   Patterns of mate choice that influence the distributions of genotype and phenotype frequencies. Nonrandom mating does not lead to changes in allele frequencies.

notochord   A flexible internal rod that runs along the back of an animal. Animals possessing a notochord at some period in their life are known as *chordates*.

nuclear DNA   The DNA that is contained in the nucleus of the cell.

occipital bun   The protruding rear region of the skull, a feature commonly found in Neandertals.

Oldowan tradition   The oldest known stone tool culture.

Oligocene epoch   The third epoch of the Cenozoic era, dating between 33.9 million and 23.0 million years ago. Anthropoids underwent an adaptive radiation during the Oligocene.

one-female/multimale group   A social structure in which the primary social group consists of a single adult female, several adult males, and their immature offspring.

one-male/multifemale group   A social structure in which the primary social group consists of a single adult male, several adult females, and their immature offspring.

one-male/one-female group   A social structure in which the primary social group consists of a single adult male, a single adult female, and their immature offspring.

Orrorin tugenensis   An early primitive, possibly hominin, species from Africa, dating to the late Miocene (6 Ma).

orthogenesis   A discredited idea that evolution would continue in a given direction because of some vaguely defined "force."

Ouranopithecus   A genus of fossil ape that lived in Greece during the Late Miocene that might be an ancestor of African apes and humans.

outgroup   A group used for comparison in cladistic analyses to determine whether the ancestral state of a trait is primitive or derived.

paleoanthropology   The study of primate and human evolution.

Paleocene epoch   The first epoch of the Cenozoic era, dating between 65.5 million and 55.8 million years ago. The primate-like mammals appeared during the Paleocene.

paleoecology   The study of ancient environments.

paleomagnetic reversal   A method of dating sites based on the fact that the earth's magnetic field has shifted back and forth from the north to the south in the past at irregular intervals.

paleospecies   Species identified from fossil remains based on their physical similarities and differences relative to other species.

Paleozoic era   The first era of the Phanerozoic eon, dating from 542 to 299 Ma, when the first vertebrates appeared.

palynology   The study of fossil pollen. Palynology allows prehistoric plant species to be identified.

pandemic   A widespread epidemic that affects a large geographic area, such as a continent.

parallel evolution   Independent evolution of a trait in closely related species.

Paranthropus   A genus of fossil hominin that lived in Africa from 2.5 to 1.4 million years ago, at which time it became extinct. They differ from *Australopithecus* by having even larger back teeth, and robust jaws, cheekbones, and faces, all adaptations to heavy chewing.

Paranthropus aethiopicus   The oldest species of *Paranthropus*, dating to 2.5 million years ago in East Africa. It combines derived features seen in other species of *Paranthropus* with primitive features seen in *Au. afarensis*.

Paranthropus boisei   A very robust species of *Paranthropus*, dating between 2.4 million and 1.4 million years ago and found in East Africa.

Paranthropus robustus   A species of *Paranthropus*, dating between roughly 2 million and 1.4 million years ago and found in South Africa.

parental investment   Parental behaviors that increase the probability that offspring will survive.

period   Subdivision of a geologic era.

Phanerozoic eon   The fourth geologic eon, covering the last 542 million years.

phenotype   The observable appearance of a given genotype in the organism. The phenotype is determined by the relationship of the two alleles at a given locus, the number of loci, and often environmental influences as well.

phylogenetic tree   A diagram showing the evolutionary relationships between species (a "family tree").

placenta   An organ that develops inside a pregnant placental mammal that provides the fetus with oxygen and food, and helps filter out harmful substances.

plasticity   The ability of an organism to respond physiologically or developmentally to environmental stress.

platyrrhines   Anthropoids native to the New World that have broad and flat noses with nostrils on the side. This group consists of New World monkeys.

pleiotropy   A single allele that has multiple effects on an organism.

Pleistocene epoch   The sixth epoch of the Cenozoic era, dating from 2.6 million to 11,700 years ago.

Pliocene epoch   The fifth epoch of the Cenozoic era, dating from 5.3 million to 2.6 million years ago.

polyandry   In humans, a form of marriage in which a wife has several husbands. In more general terms, it refers to an adult female having several mates.

polygamy   A sexual bond between an adult male and an adult female in which either individual may have more than one mate at the same time.

polygenic   A complex genetic trait affected by two or more loci.

polygyny   In humans, a form of marriage in which a husband has several wives. In more general terms, it refers to an adult male having several mates.

polymorphism   A discrete genetic trait in which there are at least two alleles at a locus having frequencies greater than 0.01.

population genetics   The branch of genetics concerned with the changes in the frequency of genes and DNA sequences in populations over time.

population pyramid   A diagram of the age-sex structure of a population.

postcranial   Referring to that part of the skeleton below the skull.

postnatal   The period of life from birth until death.

postorbital bar   The bony ring that separates the eye orbit from the back of the skull. The postorbital bar is a primate characteristic.

postorbital constriction   The narrowness of the skull behind the eye orbits, a characteristic of early hominins and *Homo erectus*.

potassium-argon dating   A chronometric dating method based on the half-life of radioactive potassium (which decays into argon gas) that can be used to date volcanic rock older than 100,000 years.

Precambrian   A term that refers to earth's history before the Cambrian period of the Paleozoic era. Precambrian time includes the Hadean, Archean, and Proterozoic eons, and lasted from 4.6 billion to 542 million years ago.

prehensile   Capable of grasping. Primates have prehensile hands and feet, and some primates (certain New World monkeys) have prehensile tails.

premolar   One of four types of teeth found in mammals. The premolars are back teeth used for crushing and grinding food.

prenatal   The period of life from conception until birth.

prepared-core method   An efficient method of stone tool manufacture in which a stone core is prepared and then finished tools are removed from it.

primates   The order of mammals that has a complex of characteristics related to an initial adaptation to life in the trees, including binocular stereoscopic vision and grasping hands. The primates include lemurs, lorises, tarsiers, monkeys, apes, and humans.

primitive trait   A trait that has not changed from an ancestral state.

Proconsul   A genus of fossil hominoid that lived in Africa between 21 million and 14 million years ago. Though classified as apes, this genus also shows a number of monkey characteristics. It most probably represents one of the first forms to evolve following the divergence of the monkey and ape lines.

protein-calorie malnutrition   A group of nutritional diseases resulting from inadequate amounts of protein and/or calories. Protein-calorie malnutrition is a severe problem in less developed countries today.

Proterozoic eon   The third geologic eon, dating from 2,500 to 542 Ma, characterized by the appearance of the first simple multicelled organisms.

punctuated equilibrium   A model of macroevolutionary change in which long periods of little evolutionary change (stasis) are followed by relatively short periods of rapid evolutionary change.

quadrupedal   A form of movement in which all four limbs are of equal size and make contact with the ground, and the spine is roughly parallel to the ground. Monkeys are typical quadrupedal primates.

race   As applied to humans, a vague term that has multiple meanings, both cultural and biological, referring to group membership.

recessive allele   An allele whose effect is masked by the other allele (which is dominant) in a heterozygous genotype.

reciprocal altruism   The concept that altruistic behaviors will be directed toward nonkin if they increase the probability that the recipient will reciprocate at some future time.

recombination   The production of new combinations of DNA sequences caused by exchanges of DNA during meiosis.

reemergent infectious disease   Infectious disease that had previously been reduced but that increases in frequency when microorganisms evolve resistance to antibiotics.

regional continuity The appearance of similar traits within a geographic region that remain over a long period of time.

regulatory gene A gene that acts as a genetic switch to turn protein-coding genes on or off.

relative dating Comparative method of dating fossils and sites that provides an estimate of the older find but not a specific date.

reproductive isolation The genetic isolation of populations that may render them incapable of producing fertile offspring.

RNA (ribonucleic acid) The molecule that functions to carry out the instructions for protein synthesis specified by the DNA molecule.

sagittal crest A ridge of bone running down the center of the top of the skull that serves to anchor chewing muscles.

Sahelanthropus tchadensis An early possible hominin species from Africa dating between 6 million and 7 million years ago that has a number of hominin dental traits and may have been bipedal.

savanna An environment consisting of open grasslands in which food resources tend to be spread out over large areas.

secular change A change in the average pattern of growth or development in a population over several generations.

sedentary Settled in one place throughout most or all of the year.

sexual dimorphism The average difference in body size between adult males and adult females. Primate species with sexual dimorphism in body size are characterized by adult males being, on average, larger than adult females.

sickle cell allele An allele of the hemoglobin locus. Individuals homozygous for this allele have sickle cell anemia.

sickle cell anemia A genetic disease that occurs in a person homozygous for the sickle cell allele, which alters the structure of red blood cells.

single-nucleotide polymorphisms (SNPs) Specific positions in a DNA sequence that differ at one base. For example, the DNA sequences CCTGAA and CCCGAA differ in the third position—one sequence has the base T and the other the base C.

Sivapithecus A genus of fossil ape that lived in Asia between 14 million and 7 million years ago, possibly an ancestor to modern orangutans.

soft hammer technique A method of removing flakes from a stone core by striking it with a softer material, such as bone, antler, or wood.

specialized structure A biological structure adapted to a narrow range of conditions and used in very specific ways. For example, the hooves of horses are specialized structures allowing movement over flat terrain.

speciation The origin of a new species.

species A group of populations whose members can interbreed naturally and produce fertile offspring.

stabilizing selection Selection against extreme values, large or small, in a continuous trait.

stable isotope analysis Analysis of the ratio of stable (nonradioactive) isotopes of elements, such as carbon, that provides information about ancient diet.

strategy A behavior that has been favored by natural selection and increases an individual's fitness.

stratigraphy A relative dating method based on the fact that older remains are found deeper in the earth (under the right conditions). This method makes use of the fact that a cumulative buildup of the earth's surface takes place over time.

Strepsirrhini (strepsirhines) One of two suborders of primates (the other is the haplorhines). Strepsirhines are primates that have a moist nose (lemurs and lorises).

stress Any factor that interferes with the normal limits of operation of an organism.

subspecies Groupings within a species that are quite physically distinct from one another but capable of fertile interbreeding. When used, subspecies are often listed as a third name in a taxonomic classification, such *Homo sapiens sapiens,* the subspecies to which all living humans belong.

suspensory climbing The ability to raise the arms above the head and hang on branches and to climb in this position. Hominoids are suspensory climbers.

taphonomy The study of what happens to plants and animals after they die. Taphonomy helps in determining reasons for the distribution and condition of fossils.

tarsier A nocturnal haplorhine found today in Indonesia.

taxonomy The science of describing and classifying organisms.

terrestrial Living on the ground.

territory A home range that is actively defended.

theistic evolution The belief that God operates through the natural process of evolution.

theory   A set of hypotheses that have been tested repeatedly and that have not been rejected. This term is sometimes used in a different sense in social science literature.

therapsids   An early group of mammal-like reptiles and the ancestors of later mammals.

thermoluminescence   A chronometric dating method that uses the fact that certain heated objects accumulate trapped electrons over time, which allows the date when the object was initially heated to be determined.

transfer RNA   A free-floating molecule that is attracted to a strand of messenger RNA, resulting in the synthesis of a protein chain.

trisomy   A condition in which three chromosomes rather than a pair occur. Down syndrome is caused by trisomy by the addition of an extra chromosome to the 21st chromosome pair.

uniformitarianism   The observation that the geologic processes that operate in the world today also operated in the past.

Upper Paleolithic   A general term used to collectively refer to the stone tool technologies of anatomically modern *Homo sapiens*.

Upper Pleistocene   A geological stage of the Pleistocene epoch that lasted from 126,000 to 11,700 years ago. Also referred to as the Late Pleistocene and also as the Tarantian stage.

variation   The differences that exist among individuals or populations. Anthropologists study both cultural and biological variation.

vasoconstriction   The narrowing of blood vessels, which reduces blood flow and heat loss.

vasodilation   The opening of blood vessels, which increases blood flow and heat loss.

velocity curve   A measure of the rates of change in growth over time.

Vertebrata   A subphylum of the phylum Chordata, defined by the presence of an internal, segmented spinal column and bilateral symmetry.

zoonose   A disease transmitted directly to humans from other animals.

zygomatic arch   The cheekbone, formed by the connection of the zygomatic and temporal bones on the side of the skull.

zygote   A fertilized egg.

Aiello, L. 2010. Five years of *Homo floresiensis. American Journal of Physical Anthropology* 142:167–179.

Aiello, L. L., and R. Dunbar. 1993. Neocortex size, group size, and the evolution of language. *Current Anthropology* 34:184–193.

Aiello, L. C., and P. Wheeler. 1995. The expensive-tissue hypothesis: The brain and the digestive system in human and primate evolution. *Current Anthropology* 36:199–221.

Altmann, J., S. C. Alberts, S. A. Haines, J. Dubach, P. Muruthi, T. Coote, E. Geffen, D. J. Cheesman, R. S. Mututua, S. N. Saiyalel, R. K. Wayne, R. C. Lacy, and M. W. Bruford. 1996. Behavior predicts genetic structure in a wild primate group. *Proceedings of the National Academy of Sciences, USA* 93: 5797–5801.

Ambrose, S. H. 2001. Paleolithic technology and human evolution. *Science* 291:1748–1753.

Anemone, R. L. 2011. *Race and Human Diversity: A Biocultural Approach.* Boston: Prentice-Hall.

Antón, S. C. 2003. Natural history of *Homo erectus. Yearbook of Physical Anthropology* 46:126–170.

Arensberg, B., L. A. Schepartz, A. M. Tillier, B. Vandermeersch, and Y. Rak. 1990. A reappraisal of the anatomical basis for speech in Middle Paleolithic hominids. *American Journal of Physical Anthropology* 83:137–146.

Arias E. 2010. United States life tables, 2006. *National Vital Statistics Reports,* vol. 58, no. 21. Hyattsville, MD: National Center for Health Statistics.

Armelagos, G. J., K. C. Barnes, and J. Lin. 1996. Disease in human evolution: The re-emergence of infectious disease in the third epidemiologic transition. *AnthroNotes, National Museum of Natural History Bulletin for Teachers* 18(3) (Fall 1996). Washington: Smithsonian Institution.

Armelagos, G. J., and J. R. Dewey. 1970. Evolutionary response to human infectious diseases. *BioScience* 157:638–644.

Armstrong, E. 1983. Relative brain size and metabolism in mammals. *Science* 220:1302–1304.

Asfaw, B., T. White, O. Lovejoy, B. Latimer, S. Simpson, and G. Suwa. 1999. *Australopithecus garhi:* A new species of early hominid from Ethiopia. *Science* 284:629–635.

Ash, M. M., and S. J. Nelson. 2003. *Wheeler's Dental Anatomy, Physiology, and Occlusion,* 8th ed. Philadelphia: W. B. Saunders.

Baba, H., F. Aziz, Y. Kaifu, G. Suwa, R. T. Kono, and T. Jacob. 2003. *Homo erectus* calvarium from the Pleistocene of Java. *Science* 299:1384–1385.

Baker, B. J., and G. J. Armelagos. 1988. The origin and antiquity of syphilis: Paleopathological diagnosis and interpretation. *Current Anthropology* 29:703–737.

Balter, M. 2005. Are humans still evolving? *Science* 309:234–237.

Bamshad, M. J., S. Mummidi, E. Gonzalez, S. S. Ahuja, D. M. Dunn, W. S. Watkins, S. Wooding, A. C. Stone, L. B. Jorde, R. B. Weiss, and S. K. Ahuja. 2002. A strong signature of balancing selection in the 5' *cis*-regulatory region of *CCR5. Proceedings of the National Academy of Sciences, USA* 99: 10539–10544.

Bamshad, M. J., S. Wooding, W. S. Watkins, C. T. Ostler, M. A. Batzer, and L. B. Jorde. 2003. Human population genetic structure and inference of group membership. *American Journal of Human Genetics* 72:578–589.

Barbujani, G., A. Magagni, E. Minch, and L. L. Cavalli-Sforza. 1997. An apportionment of human DNA diversity. *Proceedings of the National Academy of Sciences, USA* 94:4516–4519.

Barnosky, A. D., N. Matzke, S. Tomiya, G. O. U. Wogan, B. Swartz, T. B. Quental, C. Marshall, J. L. McGuire, E. L. Lindsey, K. C. Maguire, B. Mersey, and E. A. Ferrer. 2011. Has the Earth's sixth mass extinction already arrived? *Nature* 471:51–57.

Bartlett, T. Q. 2007. The Hylobatidae: Small apes of Asia. In *Primates in Perspective,* eds. C. J. Campbell, A. Fuentes, K. C. MacKinnon, M. Panger, and S. K. Bearder, pp. 274–289. New York: Oxford University Press.

Bass, W. M. 1995. *Human Osteology: A Laboratory and Field Manual,* 4th ed. Columbia: Missouri Archaeological Society.

Beall, C. M. 2007. Two routes to functional adaptation: Tibetan and Andean high-altitude natives. *Proceedings of the National Academy of Sciences* 104:8655–8660.

Beall, C. M., and A. T. Steegmann Jr. 2000. Human adaptation to climate: Temperature, ultraviolet radiation, and altitude. In *Human Biology: An Evolutionary and Biocultural Perspective,* eds. S. Stinson, B. Bogin, R. Huss-Ashmore, and D. O'Rourke, pp. 163–224. New York: John Wiley.

Beals, K. L. 1972. Head form and climatic stress. *American Journal of Physical Anthropology* 37:85–92.

Beals, K. L., C. L. Smith, and S. M. Dodd. 1983. Climate and the evolution of brachycephalization. *American Journal of Physical Anthropology* 62:425–437.

Begun, D. R. 2003. Planet of the apes. *Scientific American* 289(2):75–83.

——. 2010. Miocene hominids and the origins of African apes and humans. *Annual Review of Anthropology* 39:67–84.

Berger, L. R., D. J. de Ruiter, S. E. Churchill, P. Schmid, K. J. Carlson, P. H. G. M. Dirks, and J. M. Kibii (2010) *Australopithecus sediba*: A new species of *Homo*-like australopith from South Africa. *Science* 328:195–204.

Berger, T. D., and E. Trinkaus. 1995. Patterns of trauma among the Neandertals. *Journal of Archaeological Science* 22:841–852.

Bermúdez de Castro, J. M., M. Martinón-Torres, E. Carbonell, S. Sarmiento, A. Rosas, J. van der Made, and M. Lozano. 2004. The Atapuerca sites and their contributions to the knowledge of human evolution in Europe. *Evolutionary Anthropology* 13:25–41.

Binder, S., A. M. Levitt, J. J. Sacks, and J. M. Hughes. 1999. Emerging infectious diseases: Public health issues for the 21st century. *Science* 284:1311–1313.

Bindon, J. R., and P. T. Baker. 1985. Modernization, migration and obesity among Samoan adults. *Annals of Human Biology* 12:67–76.

Bird, A. 2007. Perceptions of epigenetics. *Nature* 447:396–398.

Bloch, J. I., and D. M. Boyer. 2002. Grasping primate origins. *Science* 298:1606–1610.

——. 2003. Response to comment on "Grasping primate origins." *Science* 300:741c.

Blumenschine, R. J., C. R. Peters, F. T. Masao, R. J. Clarke, A. L. Deino, R. L. Hay, C. C. Swisher, I. G. Stanistreet, G. M. Ashley, L. J. McHenry, N. E. Sikes, N. J. van der Merwe, J. C. Tactikos, A. E. Cushing, D. M. Deocampo, J. K. Njau, and J. I. Ebert. 2003. Late Pliocene *Homo* and hominid land use from western Olduvai Gorge, Tanzania. *Science* 299:1217–1221.

Boaz, N. T., and R. L. Ciochon. 2004. *Dragon Bone Hill: An Ice-Age Saga of* Homo erectus. New York: Oxford University Press.

Bodmer, W. F., and L. L. Cavalli-Sforza. 1976. *Genetics, Evolution, and Man.* San Francisco: W. H. Freeman.

Bogin, B. A. 1995. Growth and development: Recent evolutionary and biocultural research. In *Biological Anthropology: The State of the Science,* eds. N. T. Boaz and L. D. Wolfe, pp. 49–70. Bend, Ore.: International Institute for Human Evolutionary Research.

——. 1999. *Patterns of Human Growth,* 2d ed. Cambridge: Cambridge University Press.

——. 2001. *The Growth of Humanity.* New York: John Wiley.

Borries, C., K. Launhardt, C. Epplen, J. T. Epplen, and P. Winkler. 1999. DNA analyses support the hypothesis that infanticide is adaptive in langur monkeys. *Proceedings of the Royal Society of London B* 266:901–904.

Bouchard, T. J., D. T. Lykken, M. McGue, N. L. Segal, and A. Tellegen. 1990. Sources of human psychological differences: The Minnesota study of twins reared apart. *Science* 250:223–228.

Bowler, J. M., H. Johnston, J. M. Olley, J. R. Prescott, R. G. Roberts, W. Shawcross, and N. A. Spooner. 2003. New ages for human occupation and climatic change at Lake Mungo, Australia. *Nature* 421:837–840.

Boyd, W. C. 1950. *Genetics and the Races of Man.* Boston: Little, Brown and Co.

Brace, C. L., K. R. Rosenberg, and K. D. Hunt. 1987. Gradual change in human tooth size in the Late Pleistocene and Post-Pleistocene. *Evolution* 41:705–720.

Bramble, D. M., and D. E. Lieberman. 2004. Endurance running and the evolution of *Homo. Nature* 432:345–352.

Bramblett, C. A. 1976. *Patterns of Primate Behavior.* Palo Alto, Calif.: Mayfield.

——. 1994. *Patterns of Primate Behavior,* 2d ed. Prospect Heights, Ill.: Waveland Press.

Bräuer, G. 2001. The KNM-ER 3884 hominid and the emergence of modern anatomy in Africa. In *Humanity from African Naissance to Coming Millennia,* eds. P. V. Tobias, M. A. Raath, J. Moggi-Cecchi, and G. A. Doyle, pp. 191–197. Firenze, Italy: Firenze University Press; and Johannesburg, South Africa: Witwatersrand University Press.

Breuer, T., M. Ndoundou-Hockemba, and V. Fishlock. 2005. First observation of tool use in gorillas. *PLoS Biology* 3(11):e380. doi:10.1371/journal.pbio.0030380.

Brooks, A. S., D. M. Helgren, J. S. Cramer, A. Franklin, W. Hornyak, J. M. Keating, R. G. Klein, W. J. Rink, H. Schwarcz, J. N. L. Smith, K. Stewart, N. E. Todd, J. Verniers, and J. E. Yellen. 1995. Dating and context of three Middle Stone Age sites with bone points in the Upper Semliki Valley, Zaire. *Science* 268:548–553.

Brown, F. H. 2000. Potassium-argon dating. In *Encyclopedia of Human Evolution and Prehistory,* 2d ed., eds. E. Delson, I. Tattersall, J. A. Van Couvering, and A. S. Brooks, pp. 582–584. London: Routledge.

Brown, F., J. Harris, R. Leakey, and A. Walker. 1985. Early *Homo erectus* skeleton from west Lake Turkana, Kenya. *Nature* 316:788–792.

Brown, P., T. Sutikna, M. J. Morwood, R. P. Soejono, Jatmiko, E. Wahyu Saptomo, and Rokus Awe Due. 2004. A new small-bodied hominin from the Late Pleistocene of Flores, Indonesia. *Nature* 431:1055–1061.

Brown, R. A., and G. J. Armelagos. 2001. Apportionment of racial diversity: A review. *Evolutionary Anthropology* 10:34–40.

Brues, A. M. 1977. *People and Races.* New York: Macmillan.

Brunet, M., F. Guy, D. Pilbeam, D. E. Lieberman, A. Likius, H. T. Mackaye, M. S. Ponce de León, C. P. E. Zollikofer, and P. Vignaud. 2005. New material of the earliest hominid from the Upper Miocene of Chad. *Nature* 434:752–755.

Brunet, M., F. Guy, D. Pilbeam, H. T. Mackaye, A. Likius, D. Ahounta, A. Beauvilain, C. Blondel, H. Bocherens, J. R. Boisserie, L. De Bonis, Y. Coppens, J. Dejax, C. Denys,

P. Duringer, V. Eisenmann, G. Fanone, P. Fronty, D. Geraads, T. Lehmann, F. Lihoreau, A. Louchart, A. Mahamat, G. Merceron, G. Mouchelin, O. Otero, P. P. Campomanes, M. Ponce de Leon, J-C. Rage, M. Sapanet, M. Schuster, J. Sudre, P. Tassy, X. Valentin, P. Vignaud, L. Virlot, A. Zazzo, and C. Zollikofer. 2002. A new hominid from the Upper Miocene of Chad, Central Africa. *Nature* 418:145–151.

Bustamante, C. D., and B. M. Henn. 2010. Shadows of early migration. *Nature* 468:1044–1045.

Cabana, T., P. Jolicoeur, and J. Michaud. 1993. Prenatal and postnatal growth and allometry of stature, head circumference, and brain weight in Québec children. *American Journal of Human Biology* 5:93–99.

Campbell, B. G. 1985. *Human Evolution,* 3d ed. New York: Aldine.

Campbell, B. G., J. D. Loy, and K. Cruz-Uribe. 2006. *Humankind Emerging,* 9th ed. Boston: Pearson.

Cann, R. L., M. Stoneking, and A. C. Wilson. 1987. Mitochondrial DNA and human evolution. *Nature* 325:31–36.

Caramelli, D., C. Lalueza-Fox, C. Vernesi, M. Lari, A. Casoli, F. Mallegni, B. Chiarelli, I. Dupanloup, J. Bertranpetit, G. Barbujani, and G. Bertorelle. 2003. Evidence for a genetic discontinuity between Neandertals and 24,000-year-old anatomically modern humans. *Proceedings of the National Academy of Sciences, USA* 100:6593–6597.

Caramelli, D., L. Milani, S. Vai, A. Modi, E. Pecchioli, M. Girardi, E. Pilli, M. Lari, B. Lippi, A. Ronchitelli, F. Mallegni, A. Casoli, G. Bertorelle, and G. Barbujani. 2008. A 28,000 years old Cro-Magnon mtDNA sequence differs from all potentially contaminating modern sequences. *PLoS One* 3(7):e2700. doi:10.1371/journal.pone.0002700.

Carbonell, E., J. M. Bermúdez, J. M. Parés, A. Pérez-González, G. Cuenca-Bescós, A. Ollé, M. Mosquera, R. Huguet, J. van der Made, A. Rosas, R. Sala, J. Vallverdú, N. García, D. E. Granger, M. Martinón-Torres, X. P. Rodríguez, G. M. Stock, J. M. Vergès, E. Allué. F. Burjachs, I. Cáceres, A. Canals, A. Benito, C. Diez, M. Lozano, A. Mateos, M. Navazo, J. Rodriguez, J. Rosell, and J. A. Arsuaga. The first hominin of Europe. *Nature* 452:465–469.

Carlson, K. J., D. Stout, T. Jashashvii, D. J. de Ruiter, P. Tafforeau, K. Carlson, and L. R. Berger. 2011. The endocast of MH1, *Australopithecus sediba. Science* 333:1402–1407.

Carpenter, C. R. 1965. The howlers of Barro Colorado Island. In *Primate Behavior: Field Studies of Monkeys and Apes,* ed. I. DeVore, pp. 250–291. New York: Holt, Rinehart and Winston.

Carroll, S. B., B. Prud'homme, and N. Gompel. 2008. Regulating evolution. *Scientific American* 298(5):61–67.

Cartmill, M., and F. H. Smith. 2009. *The Human Lineage.* Hoboken, NJ: Wiley-Blackwell.

Caspari, R. 2011. The evolution of grandparents. *Scientific American* 305(2):45–49.

Cavalli-Sforza, L. L., and W. F. Bodmer. 1971. *The Genetics of Human Populations.* San Francisco: W. H. Freeman.

Cavalli-Sforza, L. L., P. Menozzi, and A. Piazza. 1994. *The History and Geography of Human Genes.* Princeton, N.J.: Princeton University Press.

Cavalli-Sforza L. L., A. Moroni, and G. Zei. 2004. *Consanguinity, Inbreeding, and Genetic Drift in Italy.* Princeton: Princeton University Press.

Chakraborty, R. 1986. Gene admixture in human populations: Models and predictions. *Yearbook of Physical Anthropology* 29:1–43.

Chapman, C. A., and C. A. Peres. 2001. Primate conservation in the new millennium: The role of scientists. *Evolutionary Anthropology* 10:16–33.

Chimpanzee Sequencing and Analysis Consortium. 2005. Initial sequence of the chimpanzee genome and comparison with the human genome. *Nature* 437:69–87.

Christensen, K., G. Doblhammer, R. Rau, and J. W. Vaupel. 2009. Ageing populations: The challenges ahead. *The Lancet* 374:1196–1208.

Ciochon, R., J. Olsen, and J. James. 1990. *Other Origins: The Search for the Giant Ape in Human Prehistory.* New York: Bantam Books.

Cockburn, T. A. 1971. Infectious diseases in ancient populations. *Current Anthropology* 12:45–62.

Cohen, J. 2007. Relative differences: The myth of 1%. *Science* 316:1836.

Cohen, J. 2010. Boxed about the ears, ape language research is still standing. *Science* 328:38–39.

Cohen, J. E. 1995. *How Many People Can the Earth Support?* New York: W. W. Norton.

Cohen, M. N. 1989. *Health and the Rise of Civilization.* New Haven, Conn.: Yale University Press.

Collins, F. S., E. D. Green, A. E. Guttmacher, and M. S. Guyer. 2003. A vision for the future of genomics research. *Nature* 422:835–847.

Connell, K. H. 1950. *The Population of Ireland 1750–1845.* Oxford: Clarendon Press.

Conroy, G. C. 2005. *Reconstructing Human Origins,* 2d ed. New York: W. W. Norton.

Cook, L. M. 2000. Changing views on melanic moths. *Biological Journal of the Linnean Society* 69:431–441.

Cook, L. M., R. L. H. Dennis, and G. S. Mani. 1999. Melanic morph frequency in the peppered moth in the Manchester area. *Proceedings of the Royal Society of London B* 266: 293–297.

Coon, C. S. 1962. *The Origin of Races.* New York: Alfred A. Knopf.

Cordain, L., J. B. Miller, S. B. Eaton, N. Mann, S. H. A. Holt, and J. D. Speth. 2000. Plant-animal subsistence ratios and macronutrient energy estimations in worldwide hunter-gatherer diets. *American Journal of Clinical Nutrition* 71:682–692.

Couzin-Frankel, J. 2011. A pitched battle over life span. *Science* 333:549–550.

Cowley, G., J. Contreras, A. Rogers, J. Lach, C. Dickey, and S. Raghavan. 1995. Outbreak of fear. *Newsweek,* May 22.

Crawford, M. H. 1998. *The Origins of Native Americans: Evidence from Anthropological Genetics.* Cambridge: Cambridge University Press.

Crockett, C. M., and J. F. Eisenberg. 1987. Howlers: Variations in group size and demography. In *Primate Societies,* eds. B. B. Smuts, D. L. Cheney, R. M. Seyfarth, R. W. Wrangham, and T. T. Struhsaker, pp. 54–68. Chicago: University of Chicago Press.

Crook, J. H., and J. S. Gartlan. 1966. Evolution of primate societies. *Nature* 210:1200–1203.

Daeschler, E. B., N. H. Shubin, and F. A. Jenkins, Jr. 2006. A Devonian tetrapod-like fish and the evolution of the tetrapod body plan. *Nature* 440:757–763.

Dalton, R. 2006. Decoding our cousins. *Nature* 442: 238–240.

Damon, A. 1977. *Human Biology and Ecology.* New York: W. W. Norton.

Dart, R. A. 1925. *Australopithecus africanus:* The man-ape of South Africa. *Nature* 115:195–199.

Dawkins, R. 1987. *The Blind Watchmaker: Why the Evidence of Evolution Reveals a Universe without Design.* New York: W. W. Norton.

de Heinzelin, J., D. Clark, T. White, W. Hart, P. Renne, G. WoldeGabriel, Y. Beyene, and E. Vrba. 1999. Environment and behavior of 2.5-million-year-old Bouri hominids. *Science* 284:625–629.

Denham, W. W. 1971. Energy relations and some basic properties of primate social organization. *American Anthropologist* 73:77–95.

Derenko, M. V., T. Grzybowski, B. A. Malyarchuk, J. Czarny, D. Miścicka-Śliwka, and I. A. Zakharov. 2001. The presence of mitochondrial haplogroup X in Altaians from south Siberia. *American Journal of Human Genetics* 69:237–241.

De Robertis, E. M., G. Oliver, and C. V. E. Wright. 1990. Homeobox genes and the vertebrate body plan. *Scientific American* 263(1):46–52.

Dettwyler, K. A. 1994. *Dancing Skeletons: Life and Death in West Africa.* Prospect Heights, Ill.: Waveland Press.

Devlin, B., M. Daniels, and K. Roeder. 1997. The heritability of IQ. *Nature* 388:468–471.

DeVore, I. 1963. A comparison of the ecology and behavior of monkeys and apes. In *Classification and Human Evolution,* ed. S. L. Washburn, pp. 301–309. Chicago: Aldine.

de Waal, F. B. M. 1995. Bonobo sex and society. *Scientific American* 272(3):82–88.

———. 1999. Cultural primatology comes of age. *Nature* 399:635–636.

———. 2007. With a little help from a friend. *PLoS Biology* 5(7):e190. doi:10.1371/journal.pbio.0050190.

Dickson, J. H., K. Oeggl, and L. L. Handley. 2003. The Iceman reconsidered. *Scientific American* 288(5):70–79.

Díez, J. C., Y. Fernández-Salvo, J. Rosell, and I. Cáceres. 1999. Zooarchaeology and taphonomy of Aurora Stratum (Gran Dolina, Sierra de Atapuerca, Spain). *Journal of Human Evolution* 37:623–652.

Di Fiore, A., and C. J. Campbell. 2007. The atelines: Variation in ecology, behavior, and social organization. In *Primates in Perspective,* eds. C. J. Campbell, A. Fuentes, K. C. MacKinnon, M. Panger, and S. K. Bearder, pp. 155–185. New York: Oxford University Press.

Dohlinow, P. 1999. Play: A critical process in the developmental system. In *The Nonhuman Primates,* eds. P. Dohlinow and A. Fuentes, pp. 231–236. Mountain View, Calif.: Mayfield.

Duarte, C., J. Maurício, P. B. Pettitt, P. Souto, E. Trinkaus, H. van der Plicht, and J. Zilhão. 1999. The early Upper Paleolithic human skeleton from the Abrigo do Lagar Velho (Portugal) and modern human emergence in Iberia. *Proceedings of the National Academy of Sciences, USA* 96: 7604–7609.

Dunbar R. I. M. 1998. The social brain hypothesis. *Evolutionary Anthropology* 6:178–190.

Dunn, F. L. 1968. Epidemiological factors: Health and disease among hunter-gatherers. In *Man the Hunter,* eds. R. B. Lee and I. DeVore, pp. 221–228. Chicago: Aldine.

Eaton, G. G. 1976. The social order of Japanese macaques. *Scientific American* 235(4):96–106.

Eaton, S. B., M. Shostak, and M. Konner. 1988. Stone agers in the fast lane: Chronic degenerative diseases in evolutionary perspective. *American Journal of Medicine* 84:739–749.

Eldredge, N., and S. J. Gould. 1972. Punctuated equilibria: An alternative to phyletic gradualism. In *Models in Paleobiology,* ed. T. J. M. Schopf, pp. 82–115. San Francisco: Freeman, Cooper.

Enard, W., M. Przeworski, S. E. Fisher, C. S. L. Lal, V. Wiebe, T. Kitano, A. P. Monaco, and S. Pääbo. 2002. Molecular evolution of *FOXP2,* a gene involved in speech and language. *Nature* 418:869–872.

Ereshefsky, M., ed. 1992. *The Units of Evolution: Essays on the Nature of Species.* Cambridge, Mass.: MIT Press.

Eswaran, V. 2002. A diffusion wave out of Africa. *Current Anthropology* 43:749–774.

Fabre, P-H., A. Rodrigues, and E. J. P. Douzery. 2009. Patterns of macroevolution among primates inferred from a supermatrix of mitochondrial and nuclear DNA. *Molecular Phylogenetics and Evolution* 53:808–825.

Falk, D. 1983. Cerebral cortices of East African early hominids. *Science* 221:1072–1074.

———. 2000. *Primate Diversity.* New York: W.W. Norton.

Falk, D., C. Hildebolt, K. Smith, M. J. Morwood, T. Sutikna, P. Brown, Jatmiko, E. Wayhu Saptomo, B. Brunsden, and F. Prior. 2005. The brain of LB1, *Homo floresiensis. Science* 308:242–245.

Falk, D., J. C. Redmond Jr., J. Guyer, G. C. Conroy, W. Recheis, G. W. Weber, and H. Seidler. 2000. Early hominid brain evolution: A new look at old endocases. *Journal of Human Evolution* 38:695–717.

Feder, K. L. 2007. *The Past in Perspective: An Introduction to Human Prehistory.* 4th ed. New York: McGraw-Hill.

——. 2008. *Frauds, Myths, and Mysteries: Science and Pseudoscience in Archaeology,* 6th ed. New York: McGraw-Hill.

Fedigan, L. M., and M. S. M. Pavelka. 2007. Reproductive cessation in female primates: Comparisons of Japanese macaques and humans. In *Primates in Perspective,* eds. C. J. Campbell, A. Fuentes, K. C. MacKinnon, M. Panger, and S. K. Bearder, pp. 437–447. New York: Oxford University Press.

Fedigan, L. M., and S. C. Strum. 1999. A brief history of primate studies: National traditions, disciplinary origins, and stages in North American field research. In *The Nonhuman Primates,* eds. P. Dolhinow and A. Fuentes, pp. 258–269. Mountain View, Calif.: Mayfield.

Feldman, M. W., R. C. Lewontin, and M.-C. King. 2003. A genetic melting-pot. *Nature* 424:374.

Finlayson, C. 2009. *The Humans Who Went Extinct: Why Neanderthals Died Out and We Survived.* Oxford: Oxford University Press.

Fisher, H. 1992. *Anatomy of Love: A Natural History of Mating, Marriage, and Why We Stray.* New York: Ballantine Books.

Fleagle, J. G. 1995. The origin and radiation of anthropoid primates. In *Biological Anthropology: The State of the Science,* eds. N. T. Boaz and L. D. Wolfe, pp. 1–21. Bend, Ore.: International Institute for Human Evolutionary Research.

——. 1999. *Primate Adaptation and Evolution,* 2d ed. San Diego: Academic Press.

Flynn, J. J., A. R. Wyss, R. Charrier, and C. C. Swisher. 1995. An early Miocene anthropoid skull from the Chilean Andes. *Nature* 373:603–607.

Flynn, J. R. 1980. *Race, IQ and Jensen.* London: Routledge.

——. 1987. Massive IQ gains in 14 nations: What IQ tests really measure. *Psychological Bulletin* 101:171–191.

Fossey, D. 1983. *Gorillas in the Mist.* Boston: Houghton Mifflin.

Foster, E. A., M. A. Jobling, P. G. Taylor, P. Donnelly, P. de Knijff, R. Mieremet, T. Zerjal, and C. Tyler-Smith. 1998. Jefferson fathered slave's last child. *Nature* 396:27–28.

Fouts, R., and S. T. Mills. 1997. *Next of Kin: What Chimpanzees Have Taught Me about Who We Are.* New York: William Morrow.

Franciscus, R. G., and J. C. Long. 1991. Variation in human nasal height and breadth. *American Journal of Physical Anthropology* 85:419–427.

Frisancho, A. R. 1990. Introduction: Comparative high-altitude adaptation. *American Journal of Human Biology* 2:599–601.

——. 1993. *Human Adaptation and Accommodation.* Ann Arbor: University of Michigan Press.

Frisancho, A. R., and P. T. Baker. 1970. Altitude and growth: A study of the patterns of physical growth of a high altitude Peruvian Quechua population. *American Journal of Physical Anthropology* 32:279–292.

Fruth, B., G. Hohmann, and W. C. McGrew. 1999. The *Pan* species. In *The Nonhuman Primates,* eds. P. Dohlinow and A. Fuentes, pp. 64–72. Mountain View, Calif.: Mayfield.

Fuentes, A. 1999. Variable social organization: What can looking at primate groups tell us about the evolution of plasticity in primate societies? In *The Nonhuman Primates,* eds. P. Dohlinow and A. Fuentes, pp. 183–188. Mountain View, Calif.: Mayfield.

——. 2000. Hylobatid communities: Changing views on pair bonding and social organization in hominoids. *Yearbook of Physical Anthropology* 43:33–60.

Futuyma, D. J. 1983. *Science on Trial: The Case for Evolution.* New York: Pantheon Books.

——. 1986. *Evolutionary Biology,* 2d ed. Sunderland, Mass.: Sinauer.

——. 2009. *Evolution,* 2d ed. Sunderland, MA: Sinauer Associates.

Gabunia, L., A. Vekua, D. Lordkipanidze, C. C. Swisher III, R. Ferring, A. Justus, M. Nioradze, M. Tvalchrelidze, S. C. Antón, G. Bosinski, O. Jöris, M. A. de Lumley, G. Majsuradze, and A. Mouskhelishvili. 2000. Earliest Pleistocene hominid cranial remains from Dmanisi, Republic of Georgia: Taxonomy, geological setting, and age. *Science* 288: 1019–1025.

Gagneux, P., C. Wills, U. Gerloff, D. Tautz, P. A. Morin, C. Boesch, B. Fruth, G. Hohmann, O. A. Ryder, and D. S. Woodruff. 1999. Mitochondrial sequences show diverse evolutionary histories of African hominoids. *Proceedings of the National Academy of Science, USA* 96:5077–5082.

Galdikas, B. M. F., and J. W. Wood. 1990. Birth spacing patterns in humans and apes. *American Journal of Physical Anthropology* 83:185–191.

Galvani, A. P., and M. Slatkin. 2003. Evaluating plague and smallpox as historical selective pressures for the *CCR5-* $\Delta 32$ HIV-resistant allele. *Proceedings of the National Academy of Sciences, USA* 100:15276–15279.

Garn, S. M. 1965. *Human Races,* 2d ed. Springfield, IL: Charles C. Thomas.

Garrett, L. 1994. *The Coming Plague: Newly Emerging Diseases in a World Out of Balance.* New York: Farrar, Straus and Giroux.

Gibbons, A. 2008. The birth of childhood. *Science* 322: 1040–1043.

——. 2010. Close encounters of the prehistoric kind. *Science* 328:680–684.

——. 2011 A new view on the birth of *Homo sapiens. Science* 331:392–394.

Gill, G. W. 1998. The beauty of race and races. Reprinted in *Taking Sides: Clashing Views on Controversial Issues in Anthropology,* eds. K. M. Endicott and R. Welsch, pp. 45–50. Guilford, Conn.: McGraw-Hill.

Gingerich, P. D., B. H. Smith, and E. L. Simons. 1990. Hind limbs of Eocene *Basilosaurus:* Evidence of feet in whales. *Science* 249:154–157.

Glass, H. B. 1953. The genetics of the Dunkers. *Scientific American* 189(2):76–81.

Glazko, G. V., and M. Nei. 2003. Estimation of divergence times for major lineages of primate species. *Molecular Biology and Evolution* 20:423–434.

Goebel, T., M. R. Waters, and D. H. O'Rourke. 2008. The Late Pleistocene dispersal of modern humans in the Americas. *Science* 319:1497–1502.

Goodall, J. 1986. *The Chimpanzees of Gombe: Patterns of Behavior.* Cambridge, Mass.: Harvard University Press.

Goren-Inbar, N., N. Alperson, M. E. Kislev, O. Simchoni, Y. Melamed, A. Ben-Nun, and E. Werker. 2004. Evidence of hominin control of fire at Gesher Benot Ya'aqov, Israel. *Science* 304:725–727.

Gould, S. J. 1981. *The Mismeasure of Man.* New York: W. W. Norton.

———. 1991. *Bully for Brontosaurus.* New York: W. W. Norton.

———. 1999. Non-overlapping magisterial. *Skeptical Inquirer* 23(4):55–61.

———. 2002. *The Structure of Evolutionary Thought.* Cambridge, MA: Harvard University Press.

Gould, S. J., and N. Eldredge. 1977. Punctuated equilibria: The tempo and mode of evolution reconsidered. *Paleobiology* 3:115–151.

Gould, S. J., and R. C. Lewontin. 1979. The spandrels of San Marco and the Panglossian paradigm: A critique of the adaptationist programme. *Proceedings of the Royal Society of London* (Series B), 205:581–598.

Grant, V. 1985. *The Evolutionary Process: A Critical Review of Evolutionary Theory.* New York: Columbia University Press.

Graves, L. L., Jr. 2001. *The Emperor's New Clothes: Biological Theories of Race at the Millennium.* New Brunswick, N.J.: Rutgers University Press.

Graves, R. R., A. C. Lupo, R. C. McCarthy, D. J. Wescott, and D. L. Cunningham. 2010. Just how strapping was KNM-WT 15000? *Journal of Human Evolution* 59:542–554.

Gravlee, C. C., H. R. Bernard, and W. R. Leonard. 2003a. Boas's *Changes in Bodily Form:* The immigrant study, cranial plasticity, and Boas's physical anthropology. *American Anthropologist* 105:326–332.

———. 2003b. Heredity, environment, and cranial form: A reanalysis of Boas's immigrant data. *American Anthropologist* 105:125–138.

Green, R. E., J. Krause, A. W. Briggs, T. Maricic, U. Stenzel, M. Kircher, N. Patterson, H. Li, W. Zhai, M.H-Y Fritz, N. F. Hansen, E.Y. Durand, A-S Malaspinas, J. D. Jensen, T. Marques-Bonet, C. Alkan, K. Prüfer, M. Meyer, H. A. Burbano, J. M. Good, R. Schultz, A. Aximu-Petri, A. Butthof, B. Höber, B. Höffner, M. Siegemund, A. Weihmann, C. Nusbaum, E.S. Lander, C. Russ, N. Novod, J. Affourtit, M. Egholm, C. Verna, P. Rudan, D. Brajkovic, Z. Kucan, I. Gušic, V. B. Doronichev, L. V. Golovanova, C. Lalueza-Fox, M. de la Rasilla, J. Fortea, A. Rosas, R.W. Schmitz, P. L. F.

Johnson, E. E. Eichler, D. Falush, E. Birney, J. C. Mullikin, M. Slatkin, R. Nielsen, J. Kelso, M. Lachmann, D. Reich, and S. Pääbo. 2010. A draft sequence of the Neandertal genome. *Science* 328:710–722.

Green, R. E., A.-S. Malaspinas, J. Krause, A. W. Briggs, P. L. F. Johnson, C. Uhler, M. Meyer, J. M. Good, T. Maricic, U. Stenzel, K. Prüfer, M. Siebauer, H. A. Burbano, M. Ronan, J. M. Rothberg, M. Egholm, P. Rudan, D. Brajković, Z. Kućan, I. Gušic, M. Wikström, L. Laakkonen, J. Kelso, M. Slatkin, and S. Pääbo. 2008. A complete Neanderthal mitochondrial genome sequence determined by high-throughput sequencing. *Cell* 134:416–426.

Greksa, L. P. 1990. Developmental responses to high-altitude hypoxia in Bolivian children of European ancestry: A test of the developmental adaptation hypothesis. *American Journal of Human Biology* 2:603–612.

———. 1996. Evidence for a genetic basis to the enhanced total lung capacity of Andean highlanders. *Human Biology* 68:119–129.

Groves C. P. (2005) Order Primates. In *Mammal Species of the World: A Taxonomic and Geographic Reference,* 3d ed., eds. D. E. Wilson and D. M. Reeder, pp. 111–184. Baltimore: Johns Hopkins University Press.

Grün, R. 1993. Electron spin resonance dating in paleoanthropology. *Evolutionary Anthropology* 2:172–181.

Grün, R., N. J. Shackleton, and H. J. Deacon. 1990. Electron-spin-resonance dating of tooth enamel from Klasies River Mouth. *Current Anthropology* 31:427–432.

Grün, R., C. B. Stringer, and H. P. Schwartz. 1991. ESR dating of teeth from Garrod's Tabun cave collection. *Journal of Human Evolution* 20:231–248.

Gunnell, G. F., and M. T. Silcox. 2010. Primate origins: The early Cenozoic fossil record. In *A Companion to Biological Anthropology,* ed. C.S. Larsen, pp. 275–294. Chichseter, UK: Wiley-Blackwell.

Haile-Selassie, Y., G. Suwa, and T. D. White. 2004. Late Miocene teeth from Middle Awash, Ethiopia, and early hominid dental evolution. *Science* 303:1503–1505.

Harcourt, A. H., P. H. Harvey, S. G. Larson, and R. V. Short. 1981. Testis weight, body weight, and breeding system in primates. *Nature* 293:55–57.

Harlow, H. F. 1959. Love in infant monkeys. *Scientific American* 200(6):68–74.

Harlow, H. F., and M. K. Harlow. 1962. Social deprivation in monkeys. *Scientific American* 207(5):136–146.

Harris, M. 1987. *Cultural Anthropology,* 2d ed. New York: Harper and Row.

Harrison, G. A., J. M. Tanner, D. R. Pilbeam, and P. T. Baker. 1988. *Human Biology: An Introduction to Human Evolution, Variation, Growth, and Adaptability,* 3d ed. Oxford: Oxford University Press.

Harrison, T. 2010. Apes among the tangled branches of human origins. *Science* 327:532–534.

Harvey, P. H., R. D. Martin, and T. H. Clutton-Brock. 1987. Life histories in comparative perspective. In *Primate Societies,* eds. B. B. Smuts, D. L. Cheney, R. M. Seyfarth, R. W. Wrangham, and T. T. Struhsaker, pp. 181–196. Chicago: University of Chicago Press.

Harvey, P. H., and M. D. Pagel. 1991. *The Comparative Method in Evolutionary Biology.* Oxford: Oxford University Press.

Hawks, H. 2009. Update to Eller et al.'s "Local extinction and recolonization, species effective size, and modern human origins (2004). *Human Biology* 81:825–828.

Hawks, J., S. Oh, K. Hunley, S. Dobson, G. Cabana, P. Dayalu, and M. H. Wolpoff. 2000. An Australasian test of the recent African origin model using the WLH-50 calvarium. *Journal of Human Evolution* 39:1–22.

Hawks, J., E. T. Wang, G. M. Cochran, H. C. Harpending, and R. K. Moyzis. 2007. Recent acceleration of human adaptive evolution. *Proceedings of the National Academy of Sciences, USA* 104:20753–20758.

Henneberg, M. 1988. Decrease of human skull size in the Holocene. *Human Biology* 60:395–405.

Henshilwood, C. S., F. d'Errico, R. Yates, Z. Jacobs, C. Tribolo, G. A. T. Duller, N. Mercier, J. C. Sealy, H. Valladas, I. Watts, and A. G. Wintle. 2002. Emergence of modern human behavior: Middle Stone Age engravings from South Africa. *Science* 295:1278–1280.

Hill, K. 1993. Life history theory and evolutionary anthropology. *Evolutionary Anthropology* 2:78–88.

Hirata S., K. Fuwa, K. Sugama, K. Kusunoki, and H. Takeshita. 2011. Mechanism of birth in chimpanzees: Humans are not unique among primates. *Biology Letters,* online publication of April 20, 2011. doi:10.1098.rsbl.2011. 0214.

Hodgson, J. A., and T. R. Disotell. 2008. No evidence of a Neanderthal contribution to modern human diversity. *Genome Biology* 9:206. doi:10.1186/gb-2008-9-2-206.

Holden, C., and R. Mace. 1997. Phylogenetic analysis of the evolution of lactose digestion in adults. *Human Biology* 69:605–628.

Holloway, R. L. 1985. The poor brain of *Homo sapiens neanderthalensis:* See what you please. In *Ancestors: The Hard Evidence,* ed. E. Delson, pp. 319–324. New York: Alan R. Liss.

Holloway, R. L., D. C. Broadfield, and M. S. Yuan. 2004. *The Human Fossil Record,* vol. 3: *Brain Endocasts—The Paleoneurological Evidence.* Wilmington, Del.: Wiley-Liss.

Horai, S., K. Hayasaka, R. Kondo, K. Tsugane, and N. Takahata. 1995. Recent African origin of modern humans revealed by complete sequences of hominoid mitochondrial DNAs. *Proceedings of the National Academy of Sciences, USA* 92:532–536.

Hou, Y., R. Potts, B. Yuan, Z. Gou, A. Deino, W. Wang, J. Clark, G. Xie, and W. Huang. 2000. Mid-Pleistocence Acheulian-like stone technology of the Bose Basin, South China. *Science* 287:1622–1626.

Houle, A. 1999. The origin of the Platyrrhines: An evaluation of the Antarctic scenario and the floating island model. *American Journal of Physical Anthropology* 109:541–559.

Howell, N. 2000. *Demography of the Dobe !Kung,* 2d ed. New York: Aldine de Gruyter.

Hrdy, S. B. 1977. *The Langurs of Abu.* Cambridge, Mass.: Harvard University Press.

Hummel, S., D. Schmidt, B. Kremeyer, B. Herrmann, and M. Oppermann. 2005. Detection of the *CCR5-Δ32* HIV resistant gene in Bronze Age skeletons. *Genes and Immunology* 6:371–374.

Hunt, K. D. 1996. The postural feeding hypothesis: An ecological model for the evolution of bipedalism. *South African Journal of Science* 92:77–90.

Indriati, E., C. C. Swisher III, C. Lepre, R. L. Quinn, R. A. Suriyanto, A. T. Hascaryo, R. Grün, C. S. Feibel, B. L. Pobiner, M. Aubert, W. Lees, and S. C. Antón. 2011. The age of the 20 meter Solo River Terrace, Java, Indonesia and the survival of *Homo erectus* in Asia. *PLoS One* 6(6):e21562. doi:10.1371/journal/pone.0021562.

Institute of Medicine of the National Academies. 2005. Dietary Reference Intakes for Energy, Carbohydrate, Fiber, Fat, Fatty Acids, Cholesterol, Protein, and Amino Acids. Washington, DC: The National Academies Press. Available online at: http://www.nap.edu/catalog.php?record_id=10490

International HapMap Consortium. 2007. A second generation human haplotype map of over 3.1 million SNPs. *Nature* 449:851–861.

Jablonski, N. G., and G. Chaplin. 2000. The evolution of human skin coloration. *Journal of Human Evolution* 39:57–106.

Jaeger, J-J., K. C. Beard, Y. Chaimanee, M. Salem, M. Benammi, O. Hlal, P. Coster, A. A. Bilal, P. Duringer, M. Schuster, X. Valentin, B. Marandat, L. Marivaux, E. Métais, O. Hammuda, and M. Brunet. 2010. Late middle Eocene epoch of Libya yields earliest known radiation of African anthropoids. *Nature* 467:1095–1099.

Janečka, J. E., W. Miller, T. H. Pringle, F. Weins, A. Zitzmann, K. M. Helgen, M. S. Springer, and W. J. Murphy. 2007. Molecular and genomic data identify the closest living relative of primates. *Science* 318:792–794.

Jobling, M. A., M. E. Hurles, and C. Tyler-Smith. 2004. *Human Evolutionary Genetics: Origins, Peoples and Disease.* New York: Garland Science.

Johanson, D. C., F. T. Masau, G. G. Eck, T. D. White, R. C. Walter, W. H. Kimbel, B. Asfaw, P. Manega, P. Ndessokia, and G. Suwa. 1987. New partial skeleton of *Homo habilis* from Olduvai Gorge, Tanzania. *Nature* 327:205–209.

Johanson, D. C., and T. D. White. 1979. A systematic assessment of early African hominids. *Science* 203:321–330.

Johanson, D. C., T. D. White, and Y. Coppens. 1978. A new species of the genus *Australopithecus* (Primates: Hominidae) from the Pliocene of Eastern Africa. *Kirtlandia* 28:1–14.

Jolly, A. 1972. *The Evolution of Primate Behavior.* New York: Macmillan.

———. 1985. *The Evolution of Primate Behavior,* 2d ed. New York: Macmillan.

Jolly, C. J. 2007. Baboons, mandrills, and mangabeys: Afro-Papionin socioecology in a phylogenetic perspective. In *Primates in Perspective,* eds. C. J. Campbell, A. Fuentes, K. C. MacKinnon, M. Panger, and S. K. Bearder, pp. 240–251. New York: Oxford University Press.

Jorde, L. B., A. R. Rogers, M. Bamshad, W. S. Watkins, P. Krakowiak, S. Sung, J. Kere, and H. C. Harpending. 1997. Microsatellite diversity and the demographic history of modern humans. *Proceedings of the National Academy of Sciences, USA* 94:3100–3103.

Karn, M. N., and L. S. Penrose. 1951. Birth weight and gestation time in relation to maternal age, parity, and infant survival. *Annals of Eugenics* 15:206–233.

Katzmarzyk, P. T., and W. R. Leonard. 1998. Climatic influences on human body size and proportions: Ecological adaptations and secular trends. *American Journal of Physical Anthropology* 106:483–503.

Kennedy, K. A. R. 1976. *Human Variation in Space and Time.* Dubuque, Iowa: Wm. C. Brown.

Kibii, J. B., S. E. Churchill, P. Schmid, K. J. Carlson, N.D. Reed, D. J. de Ruiter, and L. R. Berger. 2011. A partial pelvis of *Australopithecus sediba. Science* 333:1407–1411.

Kimbel, W. H., D. C. Johanson, and Y. Rak. 1994. The first skull and other new discoveries of *Australopithecus afarensis* at Hadar, Ethiopia. *Nature* 368:449–451.

———. 1996. Systematic assessment of a maxilla of *Homo* from Hadar, Ethiopia. *American Journal of Physical Anthropology* 103:235–262.

Kimbel, W. H., C. A. Lockwood, C. V. Ward, M. G. Leakey, Y. Rak, and D. C. Johanson. 2006. Was *Australopithecus anamensis* ancestral to *A. afarensis*? A case of anagenesis in the hominin fossil record. *Journal of Human Evolution* 51:134–152.

King, W. 1864. The reputed fossil man of the Neanderthal. *Quarterly Journal of Science* 1:88–97.

Kitzmiller et al. v. Dover Area School District. Case No. 04cv2688, United States District Court for the Middle District of Pennsylvania, December 20, 2005. Text available at www.pamd.uscourts.gov/kitzmiller/kitzmiller_342.pdf.

Kivell, T. L., J. M. Kibii, S. E. Churchill, P. Schmid, and L. R. Berger. 2011. *Australopithecus sediba* hand demonstrates mosaic evolution of locomotor and manipulative abilities. *Science* 333:1411–1417.

Klein, R. G. 2009. *The Human Career: Human Biological and Cultural Origins.* Chicago: University of Chicago Press.

Knott, C. 1999. Orangutan behavior and ecology. In *The Non human Primates,* eds. P. Dohlinow and A. Fuentes, pp. 50–57. Mountain View, Calif.: Mayfield.

Knott, C. D., and S. M. Kahlenberg. 2007. Orangutans in perspective: Forced copulations and female mating resistance. In *Primates in Perspective,* eds. C. J. Campbell, A. Fuentes, K. C. MacKinnon, M. Panger, and S. K. Bearder, pp. 290–305. New York: Oxford University Press.

Kochanek, K. D., J. Xu, S. L. Murphy, A. M. Miniño, and H-C. Kung. 2011. Deaths: preliminary data for 2009. *National Vital Statistics Reports,* vol. 59, no. 4. Hyattsville, MD: National Center for Health Statistics.

Kordos, L., and D. R Begun. 2002. Rudabánya: A Late Miocene subtropical swamp deposit with evidence of the origin of the African apes and humans. *Evolutionary Anthropology* 11:45–57.

Kramer, A., S. M. Donnelly, J. H. Kidder, S. D. Ousley, and S. M. Olah. 1995. Craniometric variation in large-bodied hominoids: Testing the single-species hypothesis for *Homo habilis. Journal of Human Evolution* 29:443–462.

Krause, J., C. Lalueza-Fox, L. Orlando, W. Enard, R. E. Green, H. A. Burbano, J.-J. Hublin, C. Hänni, J. Fortea, M. de la Rasilla, J. Bertranpetit, A. Rosas, and S. Pääbo. 2007. The derived *FOXP2* variant of modern humans was shared with Neandertals. *Current Biology* 17:1908–1912.

Krause, J., L. Orlando, D. Serre, B. Viola, K. Prüfer, M. P. Richards, J.-J. Hublin, C. Hänni, A. P. Derevianko, and S. Pääbo. 2007. Neanderthals in Central Asia and Siberia. *Nature* 449:902–904.

Krings, M., A. Stone, R. W. Schmitz, H. Krainitzki, M. Stoneking, and S. Pääbo. 1997. Neandertal DNA sequences and the origin of modern humans. *Cell* 90:19–30.

Lahr, M. M. 1996. *The Evolution of Modern Human Diversity: A Study of Cranial Variation.* Cambridge: Cambridge University Press.

Laitman, J. T., R. C. Heimbuch, and E. S. Crelin. 1979. The basicranium of fossil hominids as an indicator of their upper respiratory systems. *American Journal of Physical Anthropology* 51:15–34.

Lalueza-Fox, C., H. Römpler, D. Caramelli, C. Stäbert, G. Catalano, D. Hughes, N. Rohland, E. Pilli, L. Longo, S. Condemi, M. de la Rasilla, J. Fortea, A. Rosas, M. Stoneking, T. Schöneberg, J. Bertranpetit, and M. Hofreiter. 2007. A melanocortin 1 receptor allele suggests varying pigmentation among Neanderthals. *Science* 318:1453–1455.

Larsen, C. S. 1994. In the wake of Columbus: Native population biology in the postcontact Americas. *Yearbook of Physical Anthropology* 37:109–154.

———. 2000. *Skeletons in Our Closet: Revealing Our Past through Bioarchaeology.* Princeton, N.J.: Princeton University Press.

Larson, E. J. 1997. *Summer for the Gods: The Scopes Trial and America's Continuing Debate over Science and Religion.* Cambridge, Mass.: Harvard University Press.

Leakey, L. S. B., P. V. Tobias, and J. R. Napier. 1964. A new species of the genus *Homo* from Olduvai Gorge. *Nature* 202:7–9.

Leakey, M. G., C. S. Feibel, I. McDougall, and A. Walker. 1995. New four-million-year-old hominid species from Kanapoi and Allia Bay, Kenya. *Nature* 376:565–571.

Leakey, M. G., C. S. Feibel, I. McDougall, C. Ward, and A. Walker. 1998. New specimens and confirmation of an early age for *Australopithecus anamensis. Nature* 393:62–66.

Leakey, M. G., F. Spoor, P. N. Gathogo, C. Kiarie, L. N. Leakey, and I. McDougall. 2001. New hominin genus from eastern Africa shows diverse middle Plioecene lineages. *Nature* 410:433–440.

Lee, R. B. 1968. What hunters do for a living, or, how to make out on scarce resources. In *Man the Hunter,* eds. R. B. Lee and I. DeVore, pp. 30–48. Chicago: Aldine.

Leidy, L. E. 1998. Accessory eggs, follicular atresia, and the evolution of human menopause. *American Journal of Physical Anthropology,* Supp. 26:148–149 (abstract).

Leigh, S. R., and G. E. Blomquist. 2007. Life history. In *Primates in Perspective,* eds. C. J. Campbell, A. Fuentes, K. C. MacKinnon, M. Panger, and S. K. Bearder, pp. 396–407. New York: Oxford University Press.

Leonard, W. R. 2000. Human nutritional evolution. In *Human Biology: An Evolutionary and Biocultural Perspective,* eds. S. Stinson, B. Bogin, R. Huss-Ashmore, and D. O'Rourke, pp. 295–343. New York: John Wiley.

Leonard, W. R., T. L. Leatherman, J. W. Carey, and R. B. Thomas. 1990. Contributions of nutrition versus hypoxia to growth in rural Andean populations. *American Journal of Human Biology* 2:613–626.

Leonard, W. R., and M. L. Robertson. 1995. Energetic efficiency of human bipedality. *American Journal of Physical Anthropology* 97:335–338.

Lepre, C. J., H. Roche, D. V. Kent, S. Harmand, R. L. Quinn, J-P. Brugal, P-J. Texier, A. Lenoble, and C. S. Feibel. 2011. An earlier origin for the Acheulian. *Nature* 477:82–85.

Lerner, I. M., and W. J. Libby. 1976. *Heredity, Evolution, and Society.* San Francisco: W. H. Freeman.

Leutenegger, W. 1982. Sexual dimorphism in nonhuman primates. In *Sexual Dimorphism in* Homo sapiens: *A Question of Size,* ed. R. L. Hall, pp. 11–36. New York: Praeger.

Levins, R., T. Awerbuch, U. Brinkman, I. Eckardt, P. Epstein, N. Makhoul, C. A. de Possas, C. Puccia, A. Spielman, and M. E. Wilson. 1994. The emergence of new diseases. *American Scientist* 82:52–60.

Lewin, R., and R. A. Foley. 2004. *Principles of Human Evolution,* 2d ed. Malden, Mass.: Blackwell.

Lewis, D. E., Jr. 1990. Stress, migration, and blood pressure in Kiribati. *American Journal of Human Biology* 2:139–151.

Lieberman, D. E. 2008. Speculations about the selective basis for modern human craniofacial form. *Evolutionary Anthropology* 17:55–68.

Lieberman, D. E., and R. C. McCarthy. 1999. The ontogeny of cranial base angulation in humans and chimpanzees and its implications for reconstructing pharyngeal dimensions. *Journal of Human Evolution* 36:487–517.

Lieberman, P., and E. S. Crelin. 1971. On the speech of Neanderthal. *Linguistic Inquiry* 2:203–222.

Little, M. A., and P. T. Baker. 1988. Migration and adaptation. In *Biological Aspects of Human Migration,* eds. C. G. N. Mascie-Taylor and G. W. Lasker, pp. 167–215. Cambridge: Cambridge University Press.

Livi-Bacci, M. 1997. *A Concise History of World Population,* 2d ed. Oxford: Blackwell.

Livingstone, F. B. 1958. Anthropological implications of sickle cell gene distribution in West Africa. *American Anthropologist* 60:533–562.

Loehlin, J. C., G. Lindzey, and J. N. Spuhler. 1975. *Race Differences in Intelligence.* San Francisco: W. H. Freeman.

Lordkipanidze, D., T. Jashashvili, A. Vekua, M. S. Ponce de León, C. P. E. Zollikofer, G. P. Rightmire, H. Pontzer, R. Ferring, O. Oms, M. Tappen, M. Bukhsianidze, J. Agusti, R. Kahlke, G. Kiladze, B. Martinez-Navarro, A. Mouskhelishvili, M. Nioradze, and L. Rook. 2007. Postcranial evidence from early *Homo* from Dmanisi, Georgia. *Nature* 449:305–310.

Lordkipanidze, D., A. Vekua, R. Ferring, G. P. Rightmire, C. P. E. Zollikofer, M. S. Ponce de León, J. Agusti, G. Kiladze, A. Mouskhelishvili, M. Nioradze, and M. Tappen. 2006. A fourth hominin skull from Dmanisi, Georgia. *The Anatomical Record Part A* 288A:1146–1157.

Lovejoy, C. O. 1981. The origin of man. *Science* 211:341–350.

Lovejoy, C. O., B. Latimer, G. Suwa, B. Asfaw, and T. D. White. 2009. Combining prehension and propulsion: The foot of *Ardipithecus ramidus. Science* 326:72e1–72e8. DOI: 10.1126/science.1175832

Lovejoy, C. O., S. W. Simpson, T. D. White, B. Asfaw, and G. Suwa. 2009. Careful climbing in the Miocene: The forelimbs of *Ardipithecus ramidus* and humans are primitive. *Science* 326:70e1–70e8. DOI: 10.1126/science.1175827

Lovejoy, C. O., G. Suwa, S. W. Simpson, J. H. Matternes, and T. D. White. 2009. The great divides: *Ardipithecus ramidus* reveals the postcrania of our last common ancestors with African apes. *Science* 326:100–106.

Lovejoy, C. O., G. Suwa, L. Spurlock, B. Asfaw, and T. D. White. 2009. The pelvis and femur of *Ardipithecus ramidus*: The emergence of upright walking. *Science* 326:71e1–71e6. DOI: 10.1126/science.1175831

MacKinnon, K. C. 2007. Social beginnings: The tapestry of infant and adult interactions. In *Primates in Perspective,* eds. C. J. Campbell, A. Fuentes, K. C. MacKinnon, M. Panger, and S. K. Bearder, pp. 571–591. New York: Oxford University Press.

Mackintosh, N. J. 1998. *IQ and Human Intelligence.* Oxford: Oxford University Press.

Madrigal, L., and M. Meléndez-Obando. 2008. Grandmothers' longevity negatively affects daughters' fertility. *American Journal of Physical Anthropology* 136:223–229.

Malina, R. M. 1975. *Growth and Development: The First Twenty Years in Man.* Minneapolis: Burgess.

——. 1979. Secular changes in size and maturity: Causes and effects. *Monograph for the Society of Research in Child Development* 44:59–102.

Manzi, G. 2004. Human evolution at the Matuyama-Brunhes boundary. *Evolutionary Anthropology* 13:11–24.

Markham, R., and C. P. Groves. 1990. Brief communication: Weights of wild orangutans. *American Journal of Physical Anthropology* 81:1–3.

Marks, J. 1995. *Human Biodiversity: Genes, Races, and History.* New York: Aldine de Gruyter.

——. 2011. *The Alternative Introduction to Biological Anthropology.* New York: Oxford University Press.

Mayr, E. 1982. *The Growth of Biological Thought.* Cambridge, Mass.: Harvard University Press.

McBrearty, S., and A. S. Brooks. 2000. The revolution that wasn't: A new interpretation of the origin of modern human behavior. *Journal of Human Evolution* 39:453–563.

McLean C. Y., P. L. Reno, A. A. Pollen, A. I. Bassan, T. D. Capellini, C. Guenther, V. B. Indjeian, X. Lim, D. B. Menke, B. T. Schaar, A. N. Wenger, G. Bejerano, and D. M. Kingsley. 2011. Human-specific loss of regulatory DNA and the evolution of human-specific traits. *Nature* 471:216–219.

McDougall, I., F. H. Brown, and J. G. Fleagle. 2005. Stratigraphic placement and age of modern humans from Kibish, Ethiopia. *Nature* 433:733–736.

McEvedy, C. 1988. The bubonic plague. *Scientific American* 258(2):118–123.

McGrew, W. C. 1992. *Chimpanzee Material Culture.* Cambridge: Cambridge University Press.

McHenry, H. M. 1992. How big were the early hominids? *Evolutionary Anthropology* 1:15–20.

McKee, J. K., F. E. Poirier, and W. S. McGraw. 2005. *Understanding Human Evolution,* 5th ed. Upper Saddle River, N.J.: Pearson Prentice Hall.

McKenna, J. J. 1978. Biosocial functions of grooming behavior among the common Indian langur monkey (*Presbytis entellus*). *American Journal of Physical Anthropology* 48:503–510.

McKenzie, R. L., and J. M. Elwood. 1990. Intensity of solar ultraviolet radiation and its implications for skin cancer. *New Zealand Medical Journal* 103:152–154.

McNeill, W. H. 1977. *Plagues and Peoples.* New York: Doubleday.

McPherron, S. P., Z. Alemseged, C. W. Marean, J. G. Wynn, D. Reed, D. Geraads, R. Bobe, and H. A. Béarat. 2010. Evidence for stone-tool-assisted consumption of animal tissues before 3.39 million years ago at Dikika, Ethiopia. *Nature* 466:857–860.

Mellars, P. 2006. A new radiocarbon revolution and the dispersal of modern humans in Europe. *Nature* 439:931–935.

Mercader, J., M. Panger, and C. Boesch. 2002. Excavation of a chimpanzee stone tool site in the African rainforest. *Science* 296:1452–1455.

Mervis, J. 2006. Judge Jones defines science—and why intelligent design isn't. *Science* 311:34.

Mielke, J. H., L. W. Konigsberg, and J. H. Relethford. 2011. *Human Biological Variation,* 2d ed. New York: Oxford University Press.

Miller J. D., E. C. Scott, and S. Okamoto. 2006. Public acceptance of evolution. *Science* 313:765–766.

Miller, J. M. A. 2000. Cranifacial variation in *Homo habilis:* An analysis of the evidence for multiple species. *American Journal of Physical Anthropology* 112:103–128.

Milton J. 2011. Chimps give birth like humans. *Nature news,* April 19, 2011. doi:10.1038/news.2011.247.

Mittermeier, R. A., and E. J. Sterling. 1992. Conservation of primates. In *The Cambridge Encyclopedia of Human Evolution,* eds. S. Jones, R. Martin, and D. Pilbeam, pp. 33–36. Cambridge: Cambridge University Press.

Mittermeier, R. A., J. Wallis, A. B. Rylands, J. U. Ganzhorn, J. F. Oates, E. A. Williamson, E. Palacios, E. W. Heymann, M. C. M. Kierluff, L. Yongcheng, J. Supriatna, C. Roos, S. Walker, L. Cortés-Ortiz, and C. Schwitzer. 2009. Primates in peril: The world's 25 most endangered primates 2008–2010. *Primate Conservation* 2009 (24):1–57.

Molnar, S. 1998. *Human Variation: Races, Types and Ethnic Groups,* 4th ed. Englewood Cliffs, N.J.: Prentice-Hall.

——. 2006. *Human Variation: Races, Types, and Ethnic Groups,* 6th ed. Upper Saddle River, NJ: Prentice Hall.

Montagu, A., ed. 1984. *Science and Creationism.* Oxford: Oxford University Press.

Moran, E. F. 1982. *Human Adaptability: An Introduction to Ecological Anthropology.* Boulder, Colo.: Westview Press.

Morwood, M. J., P. Brown, Jatmiko, T. Sutikna, E. Wahyu Saptomo, K. E. Westaway, Rokus Awe Due, R. G. Roberts, T. Maeda, S. Wasisto, and T. Djubiantono. 2005. Further evidence for small-bodied hominins from the Late Pleistocene of Flores, Indonesia. *Nature* 437:1012–1017.

Morwood, M. J., R. P. Soejono, R. G. Roberts, T. Sutikna, C. S. M. Turney, K. E. Westaway, W. J. Rink, J.-x. Zhao, G. D. van den Bergh, Rokus Awe Due, D. R. Hobbs, M. W. Moore, M. I. Bird, and L. K. Fifield. 2004. Archaeology and age of a new hominin from Flores in eastern Indonesia. *Nature* 431:1087–1091.

Moyà-Solà, S., M. Köhler, D. M. Alba, I. Casanovas-Vilar, and J. Galindo. 2004. *Pierolapithecus catalaunicus,* a new Middle Miocene great ape from Spain. *Science* 306:1339–1344.

Mulcahy, N. J., and J. Call. 2006. Apes save tools for future use. *Science* 312:1038–1040.

Nemecek, S. 2000. Who were the first Americans? *Scientific American* 283(3):80–88.

Nishimura, T., A. Mikami, J. Suzuki, and T. Matsuzawa. 2003. Descent of the larynx in chimpanzee infants. *Proceedings of the National Academy of Sciences, USA* 100:6930–6933.

Noback, M. L., K. Harvati, and F. Spoor. 2011. Climate-related variation of the human nasal cavity. *American Journal of Physical Anthropology* 145:599–614.

Norton, H. L., R. A. Kittles, E. Parra, P. McKeigue, X. Mao, K. Cheng, V. A. Canfield, D. G. Bradley, B. McEvoy, and M. D. Shriver. 2007. Genetic evidence for the convergent evolution of light skin in Europeans and East Asians. *Molecular Biology and Evolution* 24:710–722.

Olshansky, S. J., and B. A. Carnes. 2010. Ageing and health. *The Lancet* 375:25.

Olshansky, S. J., D. J. Passaro, R. C. Hershow, J. Layden, B. A. Carnes, J. Brody, L. Hayflick, R. N. Butler, D. B. Allison, and D. S. Ludwig. 2005. A potential decline in life expectancy in the United States in the 21st century. *New England Journal of Medicine* 352:1138–1145.

Omran, A. R. 1977. Epidemiologic transition in the United States: The health factor in population change. *Population Bulletin* 32:3–42.

Ousley, S., R. Jantz, and D. Freid. 2009. Understanding race and human variation: Why forensic anthropologists are good at identifying race. *American Journal of Physical Anthropology* 139:68–76.

Parra, E. J. 2007. Human pigmentation variation: Evolution, genetic basis, and implications for public health. *Yearbook of Physical Anthropology* 50:85–105.

Parra, E. J., R. A. Kittles, G. Argyropoulos, C. L. Pfaff, K. Hiester, C. Bonilla, N. Sylvester, D. Parrish-Gause, W. T. Garvey, L. Jin, P. M. McKeigue, M. I. Kamboh, R. E. Ferrell, W. S. Pollitzer, and M. D. Shriver. 2001. Ancestral proportions and admixture dynamics in geographically defined African Americans living in South Carolina. *American Journal of Physical Anthropology* 114:18–29.

Parra, E. J., A. Marcini, J. Akey, J. Martinson, M. A. Batzer, R. Cooper, T. Forrester, D. B. Allison, R. Deka, R. E. Ferrell, and M. D. Shriver. 1998. Estimating African American admixture proportions by use of population-specific alleles. *American Journal of Human Genetics* 63:1839–1851.

Pavelka, M. S. M., and L. M. Fedigan. 1991. Menopause: A comparative life history perspective. *Yearbook of Physical Anthropology* 34:13–38.

Pearson, H. 2006. What is a gene? *Nature* 441:399–401.

Peccei, J. S. 2001. Menopause: Adaptation or epiphenomenon? *Evolutionary Anthropology* 10:43–57.

Pennington, R. L. 1996. Causes of early human population growth. *American Journal of Physical Anthropology* 99:259–274.

Pennock, R. T. 1999. *Tower of Babel: The Evidence against the New Creationism.* Cambridge, Mass.: MIT Press.

Penny, D., M. Steel, P. J. Waddell, and M. D. Hendy. 1995. Improved analyses of human mtDNA sequences support a recent African origin for *Homo sapiens. Molecular Biology and Evolution* 12:863–882.

Pianka, E. R. 1983. *Evolutionary Ecology,* 3d ed. New York: Harper and Row.

Pickering, R., P. H. G. M. Dirks, Z. Jinnah, D. J. de Ruiter, S. E. Churchill, A. I. R. Herries, J. D. Woodhead, J. C. Hellstrom, and L. R. Berger. 2011. *Australopithecus sediba* at 1.977 Ma and implications for the origins of the genus *Homo. Science* 333:1421–1423.

Pickford, M., and B. Senut. 2001. The geological and faunal context of Late Miocene hominid remains from Lukeino, Ethiopia. *Comptes Rendus de l'Académie des Sciences, Paris* 332:145–152.

Pilbeam, D. 1982. New hominoid skull material from the Miocene of Pakistan. *Nature* 295:232–234.

———. 1984. The descent of hominoids and hominids. *Scientific American* 250(3):84–96.

Pinhasi, R., T. F. G. Higham, L. V. Golovanova, and V. B. Doronichev. 2011. Revised age of late Neanderthal occupation and the end of the Middle Paleolithic in the northern Caucusus. *Proceedings of the National Academy of Sciences* 108:8611–8616.

Plomin, R., M. J. Owen, and P. McGuffin. 1994. The genetic basis of complex human behaviors. *Science* 264:1733–1739.

Ponce de León, M., and C. P. E. Zollikofer. 2001. Neanderthal cranial ontogeny and its implications for late hominid diversity. *Nature* 412:534–538.

Pope, G. G. 1989. Bamboo and human evolution. *Natural History,* October: 49–56.

Population Reference Bureau. 2011. *2011 World Population Data Sheet.* Washington, DC: Population Reference Bureau. http://www.prb.org/pdf11/2011population-data-sheet_eng.pdf

Potts, M. 1988. Birth control. In *The New Encyclopaedia Britannica,* vol. 15, pp. 113–20. Chicago: Encyclopaedia Britannica.

Potts, R. 1984. Home bases and early hominids. *American Scientist* 72:338–347.

Premack, D. 2007. Human and animal cognition: Continuity and discontinuity. *Proceedings of the National Academy of Sciences* 104:13861–13867.

Price, P. W. 1996. *Biological Evolution.* Fort Worth, Tex.: Saunders.

Pruetz, J. D., and P. Bertolani. 2007. Savanna chimpanzees, *Pan troglodytes verus,* hunt with tools. *Current Biology* 17:412–417.

Pusey, A. E., and C. Packer. 1987. Dispersal and philopatry. In *Primate Societies,* eds. B. B. Smuts, D. L. Cheney, R. M. Seyfarth, R. W. Wrangham, and T. T. Struhsaker, pp. 250–266. Chicago: University of Chicago Press.

Pusey, A., J. Williams, and J. Goodall. 1997. The influence of dominance rank on the reproductive success of female chimpanzees. *Science* 277:828–831.

Rak, Y. 1986. The Neanderthal: A new look at an old face. *Journal of Human Evolution* 15:151–164.

Rak, Y., and B. Arensberg. 1987. Kebara 2 Neanderthal pelvis: First look at a complete inlet. *American Journal of Physical Anthropology* 73:227–231.

Ramachandran, S., O. Deshpande, C. C. Roseman, N. A. Rosenberg, M. W. Feldman, and L. L. Cavalli-Sforza. 2005. Support for the relationship of genetic and geographic distance in human populations for a serial founder effect originating in Africa. *Proceedings of the National Academy of Sciences, USA* 102:15942–15947.

Rasmussen, D. T. 2007. Fossil record of the primates from the Paleocene to the Oligocene. In *Handbook of Paleoanthropology, vol. 2,* eds. W. Henke and I. Tattersall, pp. 889–920. Berlin: Springer-Verlag.

Ray, E. 1999a. Hierarchy in primate social organization. In *The Nonhuman Primates,* eds. P. Dohlinow and A. Fuentes, pp. 211–217. Mountain View, Calif.: Mayfield.

———. 1999b. Social dominance in nonhuman primates. In *The Nonhuman Primates,* eds. P. Dohlinow and A. Fuentes, pp. 206–210. Mountain View, Calif.: Mayfield.

Reich, D., R. E. Green, M. Kircher, J. Krause, N. Patterson, E. Y. Durand, B. Viola, A. W. Briggs, U. Stenzel, P. L. F. Johnson, T. Maricic, J. M. Good, T. Marques-Bonet, C. Alkan, Q. Fu, S. Mallick, H. Li, M. Meyer, E. E. Eichler, M. Stoneking, M. Richards, S. Talamo, M. V. Shunkov, A. P. Derevianko, J-J. Hublin, J. Kelso, M. Slatkin, S. Pääbo. 2010. Genetic history of an archaic hominin group from Denisova Cave in Siberia. *Nature* 468:1053–1060.

Relethford, J. H. 1992. Cross-cultural analysis of migration rates: Effects of geographic distance and population size. *American Journal of Physical Anthropology* 89:459–466.

———. 1994. Craniometric variation among human populations. *American Journal of Physical Anthropology* 95:53–62.

———. 1997. Hemispheric difference in human skin color. *American Journal of Physical Anthropology* 104:449–457.

———. 2001. *Genetics and the Search for Modern Human Origins.* New York: John Wiley.

———. 2002. Apportionment of global human genetic diversity based on craniometrics and skin color. *American Journal of Physical Anthropology* 118:393–398.

———. 2003. *Reflections of Our Past: How Human History Is Revealed in Our Genes.* Boulder, Colo.: Westview Press.

———. 2004a. Boas and beyond: Migration and craniometric variation. *American Journal of Human Biology* 16:379–386.

———. 2004b. Global patterns of isolation by distance based on genetic and morphological data. *Human Biology* 76:499–513.

———. 2008. Geostatistics and spatial analysis in biological anthropology. *American Journal of Physical Anthropology* 136:1–10.

———. 2009. Race and global patterns of phenotypic variation. *American Journal of Physical Anthropology* 139:16–22.

———. 2010. Race and the conflicts within the profession of physical anthropology during the 1950s and 1960s. In *Histories of American Physical Anthropology in the Twentieth Century,* eds. M. A. Little and K. A. R. Kennedy, pp. 207–220. Lanham, MD: Lexington Books.

———. 2012a. *Human Population Genetics.* Hoboken, NJ: Wiley-Blackwell.

———. 2012b. Understanding human cranial variation in light of modern human origins. In *Origins of Modern Humans,* eds. F. Smith and J. Ahern. Hoboken, NJ: Wiley-Blackwell (in press).

Relethford, J. H., and M. H. Crawford. 1995. Anthropometric variation and the population history of Ireland. *American Journal of Physical Anthropology* 96:25–38.

Relethford, J. H., and H. C. Harpending. 1994. Craniometric variation, genetic theory, and modern human origins. *American Journal of Physical Anthropology* 95:249–270.

Richmond, B. G., and W. L. Jungers. 2008. *Orrorin tugenensis* femoral morphology and the evolution of hominin bipedalism. *Science* 319:1662–1665.

Ridley, M. 2004. *Evolution,* 3d ed. Malden, Mass.: Blackwell.

Rightmire, G. P. 1992. *Homo erectus:* Ancestor or evolutionary side branch? *Evolutionary Anthropology* 1:43–49.

———. 1998. Human evolution in the Middle Pleistocene: The role of *Homo heidelbergensis. Evolutionary Anthropology* 6:218–227.

———. 2004. Brain size and encephalization in Early to Mid-Pleistocene *Homo. American Journal of Physical Anthropology* 124:109–123.

Rilling, J. K. 2006. Human and nonhuman primate brains: Are they allometrically scaled versions of the same design? *Evolutionary Anthropology* 15:65–77.

Robbins, M. M. 2007. Gorillas: Diversity in ecology and behavior. In *Primates in Perspective,* eds. C. J. Campbell, A. Fuentes, K. C. MacKinnon, M. Panger, and S. K. Bearder, pp. 305–321. New York: Oxford University Press.

Roberts, D. F. 1968. Genetic effects of population size reduction. *Nature* 220:1084–1088.

———. 1978. *Climate and Human Variability,* 2d ed. Menlo Park, Calif.: Benjamin Cummings.

Robins, A. H. 1991. *Biological Perspectives on Human Pigmentation.* Cambridge: Cambridge University Press.

Rodman, P. S., and H. M. McHenry. 1980. Bioenergetics and the origin of human bipedalism. *American Journal of Physical Anthropology* 52:103–106.

Rosenberg, K. R., and W. R. Trevathan. 2001. The evolution of human birth. *Scientific American* 285(5):72–77.

Rosenberg, N. A., J. K. Pritchard, J. L. Weber, H. M. Cann, K. K. Kidd, L. A. Zhivotovsky, and M. W. Feldman. 2002. Genetic structure of human populations. *Science* 298:2381–2385.

Rowell, T. E. 1966. Forest-living baboons in Uganda. *Journal of Zoology, London* 149:344–364.

Roychoudhury, A. K., and M. Nei. 1988. *Human Polymorphic Genes: World Distribution.* Oxford: Oxford University Press.

Ruff, C. B. 1994. Morphological adaptations to climate in modern and fossil hominids. *Yearbook of Physical Anthropology* 37:65–107.

Ruff, C. B., E. Trinkaus, and T. W. Holliday. 1997. Body mass and encephalization in Pleistocene *Homo. Nature* 387:173–176.

Ruff, C., and A. Walker. 1993. Body size and body shape. In *The Nariokotome Homo erectus Skeleton,* eds. A. Walker and R. Leakey, pp. 234–265. Cambridge: Harvard University Press.

Sabeti, P. C., S. F. Schaffner, B. Fry, J. Lohmueller, P. Varilly, O. Shamovsky, A. Palma, T. S. Mikkelsen, D. Altschuler, and E. S. Lander. 2006. Positive natural selection in the human lineage. *Science* 312:1614–1620.

Sachs, J., and P. Malaney. 2002. The economic and social burden of malaria. *Nature* 415:680–685.

Sagan, C. 1977. *The Dragons of Eden: Speculations on the Evolution of Human Intelligence.* New York: Ballantine Books.

Sauer, N. J. 1992. Forensic anthropology and the concept of race: If races don't exist, why are forensic anthropologists so good at identifying them? *Social Science and Medicine* 34:107–111.

Savage-Rumbaugh, S., and R. Lewin. 1994. *Kanzi: The Ape at the Brink of the Human Mind.* New York: John Wiley.

Sawyer, G. J., and B. Maley. 2005. Neanderthal reconstructed. *The Anatomical Record (Part B: New Anatomist)* 283B:23–31.

Scammon, R. E. 1930. The measurement of the body in childhood. In *The Measurement of Man,* eds. J. A. Harris, C. M. Jackson, D. G. Paterson, and R. E. Scammon, pp. 171–215. Minneapolis: University of Minnesota Press.

Schepartz, L. A. 1993. Language and modern human origins. *Yearbook of Physical Anthropology* 36:91–126.

Schick, K. D., and N. Toth. 1993. *Making Silent Stones Speak: Human Evolution and the Dawn of Technology.* New York: Simon and Schuster.

Schmitz, R. W., D. Serre, G. Bonani, S. Feine, F. Hillgrubber, H. Krainitzki, S. Pääbo, and F. H. Smith. 2002. The Neandertal type site revisited: Interdisciplinary investigations of skeletal remains from the Neander Valley, Germany. *Proceedings of the National Academy of Sciences, USA* 99:13342–13347.

Schoenemann, P. T. 2006. Evolution of the size and functional areas of the human brain. *Annual Review of Anthropology* 35:379–406.

Schoenemann, P. T., T. F. Budinger, V. M. Sarich, and W. S. Y. Wang. 2000. Brain size does not predict general cognitive ability within families. *Proceedings of the National Academy of Sciences, USA* 97:4932–4937.

Schoeninger, M. J. 1995. Stable isotope studies in human evolution. *Evolutionary Anthropology* 4:83–98.

Schmitz, R. W., D. Serre, G. Bonani, S. Feine, F. Hillgrubber, H. Krainitzki, S. Pääbo, and F. H. Smith. 2002. The Neandertal type site revisited: Interdisciplinary investigations of skeletal remains from the Neander Valley, Germany. *Proceedings of the National Academy of Sciences, USA* 99:13342–13347.

Schopf, J. W. 1999. *Cradle of Life: The Discovery of Earth's Earliest Fossils.* Princeton, N.J.: Princeton University Press.

Schurr, T. G. 2000. Mitochondrial DNA and the peopling of the New World. *American Scientist* 88:246–253.

Schwarcz, H. P. 2000. Fission-track dating. In *Encyclopedia of Human Evolution and Prehistory,* 2d ed., eds. E. Delson, I. Tattersall, J. A. Van Couvering, and A. S. Brooks, pp. 270–271. London: Routledge.

Schwartz, J. H. 2007. *Skeleton Keys: An Introduction to Human Skeletal Morphology, Development, and Analysis,* 2d ed. New York: Oxford University Press.

Scott, E. C. 2004. *Evolution vs. Creationism: An Introduction.* Westport, Conn.: Greenwood Press.

Sellen, D. W. 2001. Relationships between fertility, mortality, and subsistence: Results of recent phylogenetic analyses. In *Humanity from African Naissance to Coming Millennia,* eds. P. V. Tobias, M. A. Raath, J. Moggi-Cecchi, and G. A. Doyle, pp. 51–64. Firenze, Italy: Firenze University Press.

Senut, B., M. Pickford, D. Gommery, P. Mein, K. Cheboi, and Y. Coppens. 2001. First hominid from the Miocene (Lukeino formation, Kenya). *Comptes Rendus de l'Académie des Sciences, Paris* 332:137–144.

Shea, B. T., and A. M. Gomez. 1988. Tooth scaling and evolutionary dwarfism: An investigation of allometry in human pygmies. *American Journal of Physical Anthropology* 77:117–132.

Sheehan, P. M., D. E. Fastovsky, R. G. Hoffman, C. B. Berghaus, and D. L. Gabriel. 1991. Sudden extinction of the dinosaurs: Latest Cretaceous, Upper Great Plains, U.S.A. *Science* 254:835–839.

Shen G., Gao X., Gao B., and D. E. Granger. 2009. Age of Zhoukoudian Homo erectus determined with ^{26}Al/^{10}Be burial dating. *Nature* 458:198–200.

Shipman, P. 2001. *The Man Who Found the Missing Link: Eugène Dubois and His Lifelong Quest to Prove Darwin Right.* New York: Simon & Schuster.

Shipman, P. 2010. The cutting edge. *American Scientist* 98:462–465.

Shipman, P., and P. Storm. 2002. Missing links: Eugène Dubois and the origins of paleoanthropology. *Evolutionary Anthropology* 11:108–116.

Simpson, S. W., J. Quade, N. E. Levin, R. Butler, G. Dupont-Nivet, M. Everett, and S. Semaw. 2008. A female *Homo erectus* pelvis from Gona, Ethiopia. *Science* 322:1089–1091.

Smith, F. H. 2002. Migrations, radiations and continuity: Patterns in the evolution of Middle and Late Pleistocene humans. In *The Primate Fossil Record,* ed. W. C. Hartwig, pp. 437–456. Cambridge: Cambridge University Press.

Smith, F. H., E. Trinkaus, P. B. Pettitt, I. Karavanić, and M. Paunović. 1999. Direct radiocarbon dates for Vindija G_1 and Velika Pećina Late Pleistocene hominid remains. *Proceedings of the National Academy of Sciences, USA* 96:12281–12286.

Smith, F. H., I. Janković, and I. Karavanić. 2005. The assimilation model, modern human origins in Europe, and the extinction of Neandertals. *Quaternary International* 137:7–19.

Sparks, C. S., and R. L. Jantz. 2002. A reassessment of human cranial plasticity: Boas revisited. *Proceedings of the National Academy of Sciences, USA* 99:14636–14639.

———. 2003. Changing times, changing faces: Franz Boas's immigrant study in modern perspective. *American Anthropologist* 105:333–337.

Sponheimer, M., B. H. Passey, D. J. de Ruiter, D. Guatelli-Steinberg, T. E. Cerling, and J. A. Lee-Thorp. 2006. Isotopic evidence for dietary variability in the early hominin *Paranthropus robustus. Science* 314:980–982.

Spoor, F., M. G. Leakey, P. N. Gathogo, F. H. Brown, S. C. Antón, I. McDougall, C. Kiarie, and F. K. Manthi. 2007. Implications of new early *Homo* fossils from Ileret, east of Lake Turkana, Kenya. *Nature* 448:688–691.

Stanford, C. B. 2006. Arboreal bipedalism in wild chimpanzees: Implications for the evolution of hominid posture and locomotion. *American Journal of Physical Anthropology* 129:225–231.

Steadman, D. W. 2009. *Hard Evidence: Case Studies in Forensic Anthropology,* 2d ed. Upper Saddle River, N.J.: Prentice-Hall.

Stedman, H. H., B. W. Kozyak, A. Nelson, D. M. Thesler, L. T. Su, D. W. Low, C. R. Bridges, J. B. Shrager, N. Minugh-Purvis, and M. A. Mitchell. 2004. Myosin gene mutation correlates with anatomical changes in the human lineage. *Nature* 428:415–418.

Steiper, M. E., and N. M. Young. 2006. Primate molecular divergence dates. *Molecular Phylogenetics and Evolution* 41:384–394.

Stern, J. T., Jr., and R. L. Susman. 1983. The locomotor anatomy of *Australopithecus afarensis. American Journal of Physical Anthropology* 60:279–317.

Storz, J. F. 2010. Genes for high altitudes. *Science* 329:40–41.

Strachan, T., and A. P. Read. 1996. *Human Molecular Genetics.* New York: John Wiley.

Strickberger, M. W. 2000. *Evolution,* 3d ed. Sudbury, Mass.: Jones and Bartlett.

Strier, K.B. 2011. *Primate Behavioral Ecology,* 4th ed. Upper Saddle River, NJ: Prentice-Hall.

Stringer, C. B. and P. Andrews. 2005. *The Complete World of Human Evolution.* New York: Thames and Hudson.

Stringer, C., and C. Gamble. 1993. *In Search of the Neanderthals: Solving the Puzzle of Human Origins.* New York: Thames and Hudson.

Stringer, C., and R. McKie. 1996. *African Exodus: The Origins of Modern Humanity.* New York: Henry Holt.

Stringer, C. B., E. Trinkaus, M. B. Roberts, S. A. Parfitt, and R. I. Macphail. 1998. The Middle Pleistocene human tibia from Boxgrove. *Journal of Human Evolution* 34:509–547.

Strum, S. C., and W. Mitchell. 1987. Baboon models and muddles. In *The Evolution of Human Behavior: Primate Models,* ed. W. G. Kinzey, pp. 87–104. Albany: State University of New York Press.

Surbeck M., and G. Hohmann. 2008. Primate hunting by bonobos at LuiKotale, Salonga National Park. *Current Biology* 18:R906–R907.

Sussman, R. W. 1991. Primate origins and the evolution of angiosperms. *American Journal of Primatology* 23:209–223.

Suwa, G., B. Asfaw, Y. Beyene, T. D. White, S. Katoh, S. Nagaoka, H. Nakaya, K. Uzawa, P. Renne, and G. WoldeGabriel. 1997. The first skull of *Australopithecus boisei. Nature* 389:489–492.

Suwa, G., B. Asfaw, R. T. Kono, D. Kubo, C. O. Lovejoy, and T. D. White. 2009. The *Ardipithecus ramidus* skull and its implications for hominid origins. *Science* 326:68e1–68e7. DOI: 10.1126/science.1175825

Suwa, G., R. T. Kono, S. W. Simpson, B. Asfaw, C. O. Lovejoy, and T. D. White. 2009. Paleobiological implications of the *Ardipithecus ramidus* dentition. *Science* 326:94–99.

Swedlund, A. C., and G. J. Armelagos. 1976. *Demographic Anthropology.* Dubuque, Iowa: Wm. C. Brown.

Swisher, C. C., G. H. Curtis, T. Jacob, A. G. Getty, A. Suprijo, and Widiasmoro. 1994. Age of the earliest known hominids in Java, Indonesia. *Science* 263:1118–1121.

Takahata, N., Lee, S.-H., and Y. Satta. 2001. Testing multiregionality of modern human origins. *Molecular Biology and Evolution* 18:172–183.

Tamm, E., T. Kivisild, M. Reidla, M. Metspalu, D. G. Smith, C. J. Mulligan, C. M. Bravi, O. Rickards, C. Martinez-Labarga, E. K. Khusnutdinova, S. F. Federova, M. V. Golubenko, V. A. Stepanov, M. A. Gubina, S. I. Zhadanov, L. P. Ossipova, L. Damba, M.I . Voevoda, J. E. Dipierri, R. Villems, and R. S. Malhi. 2007. Beringian standstill and spread of Native American founders. *PLoS One* 2(9):e289. doi: 10.1371/journal.pone.0000829.

Tattersall, I. 1997. Out of Africa again . . . and again? *Scientific American* 276(4):60–67.

Tchernov, E., O. Rieppel, H. Zaher, M. J. Polcyn, and L. L. Jacobs. 2000. A fossil snake with limbs. *Science* 287:2010–2012.

Templeton, A. R. 2005. Haplotype trees and modern human origins. *Yearbook of Physical Anthropology* 48:33–59.

Thieme, H. 2000. Lower Palaeolithic hunting weapons from Schöningen, Germany—the oldest spears in the world. *Acta Anthropologica Sinica* 19, supplement, 140–147. Reprinted in *The Human Evolution Source Book,* 2d ed., eds. R. L. Ciochon and J. G. Fleagle, pp. 440–445. Upper Saddle River, N.J.: Pearson Prentice Hall.

Thomas, M.G., T. Parfitt, D. A. Weiss, K. Skorecki, J. F. Wilson, M. le Roux, N. Bradman, and D. B. Goldstein. 2000. Y chromosomes travelling south: The Cohen modal haplotypes and the origins of the Lemba—the "Black Jews of Southern Africa." *American Journal of Human Genetics* 66:674–686.

Thorne, A., R. Grün, G. Mortimer, N. A. Spooner, J. J. Simpson, M. McCulloch, L. Taylor, and D. Curnoe. 1999. Australia's oldest human remains: Age of the Lake Mungo 3 skeleton. *Journal of Human Evolution* 36:591–612.

Thorpe, S. K. S., R. L. Holder, and R. H. Crompton. 2007. Origin of human bipedalism as an adaptation for locomotion on flexible branches. *Science* 316:1328–1331.

Tishkoff, S.A., and M.K. Gonder. 2007. Human origins within and out of Africa. In: *Anthropological Genetics: Theory, Methods and Applications,* ed. M.H. Crawford, pp. 337–379. Cambridge: Cambridge University Press.

Tishkoff, S. A., F. A. Reed, A. Ranciaro, B. F. Voight, C. C. Babbitt, J. S. Silverman, K. Powell, H. M. Mortensen, J. B. Hirbo, M. Osman, M. Ibrahim, S. A. Omar, G. Lema, T. B. Nyambo, J. Ghori, S. Bumpstead, J. K. Pritchard, G. A. Wray, and P. Deloukas. 2007. Convergent adaptation of human lactase persistence in Africa and Europe. *Nature Genetics* 39:31–40.

Tobias, P. V. 1971. *The Brain in Hominid Evolution.* New York: Columbia University Press.

Trinkaus, E. 1981. Neanderthal limb proportions and cold adaptation. In *Aspects of Human Evolution,* ed. C. B. Stringer, pp. 187–224. London: Taylor and Francis.

——. 2006. Modern human versus Neandertal evolutionary distinctiveness. *Current Anthropology* 47:597–620.

———. 2007. European early modern humans and the fate of the Neandertals. *Proceedings of the National Academy of Sciences* 104:7367–7372.

Trinkaus, E., and P. Shipman. 1992. *The Neandertals: Changing the Image of Mankind.* New York: Knopf.

Trinkaus, E., and J. Zilhão. 2002. Phylogenetic implications. In *Portrait of the Artist as a Child: The Gravettian Human Skeleton from the Abrigo do Lagar Velho and Its Archaeological Context,* eds. E. Trinkaus and J. Zilhão, pp. 497–518. Lisbon: Instituto Português de Arqueologia.

Trotter, M., and G.C. Gleser. 1952. Estimation of stature from long bones of American whites and Negroes. *American Journal of Physical Anthropology* 10:463–514.

Trotter, M., and G.C. Gleser. 1958. A re-evaluation of estimation based on measurements of stature taken during life and of long bones after death. *American Journal of Physical Anthropology* 16:79–123.

Ungar, P. S., F. E Grine, and M. F. Teaford. 2008. Dental microwear and diet of the Plio-Pleistocene hominin *Paranthropus boisei. PLoS ONE* 3(4):e2044. doi:10.1371/journal.pone.0002044.

UNICEF. 2005. *The State of the World's Children 2006.* New York: UNICEF.

van Schaik, C. P., M. Ancrenaz, G. Borgen, B. Galdikas, C. D. Knott, I. Singleton, A. Suzuki, S. S. Utami, and M. Merrill. 2003. Orangutan cultures and the evolution of material culture. *Science* 299:102–105.

van Schaik, C. P., and A. Paul. 1996. Male care in primates: Does it ever reflect paternity? *Evolutionary Anthropology* 5:152–156.

Vaughan, W. E., and A. J. Fitzpatrick. 1978. *Irish Historical Statistics: Population, 1821–1971.* Dublin: Royal Irish Academy.

Vekua, A., D. Lordkipanidze, G. P. Rightmire, J. Agusti, R. Ferring, G. Maisuradze, A. Mouskhelishvili, M. Nioradze, M. Ponce de Leon, M. Tappen, M. Tvalchrelidze, and C. Zollikofer. 2002. A new skull of early *Homo* from Dmanisi, Georgia. *Science* 297:85–89.

Vigilant, L., M. Stoneking, H. Harpending, K. Hawkes, and A. C. Wilson. 1991. African populations and the evolution of human mitochondrial DNA. *Science* 253:1503–1507.

Voight, B. F., S. Kudaravalli, X. Wen, and J. K. Pritchard. 2006. A map of recent positive selection in the human genome. *PLoS Biology* 4(3):e72.

von Hunnius, T. E., C. A. Roberts, A. Boylston, and S. R. Saunders. 2006. Histological identification of syphilis in pre-Columbian England. *American Journal of Physical Anthropology* 129:559–566.

Walker, A., and P. Shipman. 2005. *The Ape in the Tree: An Intellectual and Natural History of* Proconsul. Cambridge, Mass.: Belknap Press.

Walker, A., and M. Teaford. 1989. The hunt for *Proconsul. Scientific American* 260(1):76–82.

Walker, J.D., and J.W. Geissman, compilers. 2009. Geological Time Scale: Geological Society of America. http://www .geosociety.org/science/timescale/timescl.pdf.

Walker, P.L., R. R. Bathurst, R. Richman, T. Gjerdrum, and V. A. Andrushko. 2009. The causes of porotic hyperostosis and cribra orbitalia: A reappraisal of the iron-deficiency-anemia hypothesis. *American Journal of Physical Anthropology* 139:109–125.

Ward, C., M. Leakey, and A. Walker. 1999. The new hominid species *Australopithecus anamensis. Evolutionary Anthropology* 7:197–205.

———. 2001. Morphology of *Australopithecus anamensis* from Kanapoi and Allia Bay, Kenya. *Journal of Human Evolution* 41:255–368.

Ward, C.V., W. H. Kimbel, and D. C. Johanson. 2011. Complete fourth metatarsal and arches in the foot of *Australopithecus afarensis. Science* 331:750–753.

Ward, C. V., A. Walker, and M. F. Teaford. 1991. *Proconsul* did not have a tail. *Journal of Human Evolution* 21:215–220.

Waters, M.R., S. L. Forman, T. A. Jennings, L. C. Nordt, S. G. Driese, J. M. Feinberg, J. L. Keene, J. Halligan, A. Lindquist, J. Pierson, C. T. Hallmark, M. B. Collins, and J. E. Wiederhold. 2011. The Buttermilk Creek Complex and the origins of Clovis at the Debra L. Friedkin site, Texas. *Science* 331: 1599–1603.

Weaver, T. D., C. C. Roseman, and C. S. Stringer. 2007. Were neandertal and modern human cranial differences produced by natural selection or genetic drift? *Journal of Human Evolution* 53:135–145.

Weeks, J. R. 2005. *Population: An Introduction to Concepts and Issues,* 9th ed. Belmont, Calif.: Wadsworth.

Weiner J. 1994. *The Beak of the Finch.* New York: Vintage Books.

Weiner, S., Q. Xu, P. Goldberg, J. Liu, and O. Bar-Yosef. 1998. Evidence for the use of fire at Zhoukoudian, China. *Science* 281:251–253.

Weiss, K. M. 1984. On the number of members of the genus *Homo* who have ever lived, and some evolutionary implications. *Human Biology* 56:637–649.

Weitz, C. A., R. M. Garruto, C.-T. Chin, J.-C. Liu, R.-L. Liu, and X. He. 2000. Morphological growth of Han boys and girls born and raised near sea level and at high altitude in western China. *American Journal of Human Biology* 12:665–681.

Wheeler, P. E. 1991. The thermoregulatory advantage of hominid bipedalism in open equatorial environments: The contribution of increased convective heat loss and cutaneous evaporative cooling. *Journal of Human Evolution* 21:107–115.

White, F. 1996. *Pan paniscus* 1973 to 1996: Twenty-three years of field research. *Evolutionary Anthropology* 5:11–17.

White, R., and J. M. Lalouel. 1988. Chromosome mapping with DNA markers. *Scientific American* 258:40–48.

White, T. D. 2003. Early hominids—Diversity or distortion? *Science* 299:1994–1997.

White, T.D., A. Asfaw, Y. Beyene, Y. Haile-Selassie, C.O. Lovejoy, G. Suwa, and G. WoldeGabriel. 2009. *Ardipithecus ramidus* and the paleobiology of early hominids. Science 326:75–86.

White, T. D., B. Asfaw, D. DeGusta, H. Gilbert, G. D. Richards, G. Suwa, and F. C. Howell. 2003. Pleistocene *Homo sapiens* from Middle Awash, Ethiopia. *Nature* 423:742–747.

White, T.D., M. T. Black, and P. A. Folkens. 2012. *Human Osteology,* 3d edition. Amsterdam: Elsevier.

White, T. D., G. Suwa, and B. Asfaw. 1994. *Australopithecus ramidus,* a new species of early hominid from Aramis, Ethiopia. *Nature* 371:306–312.

White, T. D., G. Suwa, and B. Asfaw. 1995. Corrigendum: *Australopithecus ramidus,* a new species of early hominid from Aramis, Ethiopia. *Nature* 375:88.

White, T. D., G. WoldeGabriel, B. Asfaw, S. Ambrose, Y. Beyene, R. L. Bernor, J.-R. Boisserie, B. Currie, H. Gilbert, Y. Haile-Selassie, W. K. Hart, L. J. Hlusko, F. C. Howell, R. T. Kono, T. Lehmann, A. Louchart, C. O. Lovejoy, P. R. Renne, H. Saegusa, E. S. Vrba, H. Wesselman, and G. Suwa. 2006. Asa Issie, Aramis and the origin of *Australopithecus. Nature* 440:883–889.

Whiten, A., J. Goodall, W. C. McGrew, T. Nishida, V. Reynolds, Y. Sugiyama, C. E. G. Tutin, R. W. Wrangham, and C. Boesch. 1999. Culture in chimpanzees. *Nature* 399:682–685.

Whitten, P. L. 1987. Infants and adult males. In *Primate Societies,* eds. B. B. Smuts, D. L. Cheney, R. M. Seyfarth, R. W. Wrangham, and T. T. Struhsaker, pp. 343–357. Chicago: University of Chicago Press.

Williams-Blangero, S., and J. Blangero. 1992. Quantitative genetic analysis of skin reflectance: A multivariate approach. *Human Biology* 64:35–49.

Wilmouth, J. R. 2011. Increase of human longevity: Past, present, and future. *Japanese Journal of Population* 9:155–161.

Wolde-Gabriel, G., Y. Haile-Selassie, P. R. Renne, W. K. Hart, S. H. Ambrose, B. Asfaw, G. Heiken, and T. White. 2001. Geology and palaeontology of the Late Miocene Middle Awash valley, Afar rift, Ethiopia. *Nature* 412:175–178.

Wolfe, N. D., C. P. Dunavan, and J. Diamond. 2007. Origins of major human infectious diseases. *Nature* 447:279–283.

Wolpoff, M. H. 1999. *Paleoanthropology,* 2d ed. Boston: McGraw-Hill.

Wolpoff, M. H., and R. Caspari. 1997. *Race and Human Evolution.* New York: Simon and Schuster.

Wolpoff, M. H., J. Hawks, D. W. Frayer, and K. Hunley. 2001. Modern human ancestry at the peripheries: A test of the replacement theory. *Science* 291:293–297.

Wolpoff, M. H., A. G. Thorne, F. H. Smith, D. W. Frayer, and G. G. Pope. 1994. Multiregional evolution: A world-wide source for modern human populations. In *Origins of Anatomically Modern Humans,* eds. M. H. Nitecki and D. V. Nitecki, pp. 175–200. New York: Plenum Press.

Wood, B. 1996. Origin and evolution of the genus *Homo.* In *Contemporary Issues in Human Evolution,* eds. W. E. Meikle, F. C. Howell, and N. G. Jablonski, pp. 105–114. San Francisco: California Academy of Sciences.

Wood, B., and M. Collard. 1999. The changing face of the genus *Homo. Evolutionary Anthropology* 8:195–207.

Wood, B., and B. G. Richmond. 2000. Human evolution: Taxonomy and paleobiology. *Journal of Anatomy* 196:19–60.

Wood, J. W. 1994. *Dynamics of Human Reproduction: Biology, Biometry, Demography.* New York: Aldine de Gruyter.

Woodham-Smith, C. 1962. *The Great Hunger: Ireland 1845–1849.* New York: Harper and Row.

World Health Organization. 2004. *The World Health Report 2004: Changing History.* Geneva: World Health Organization.

Wrangham, R. W. 1987a. Evolution of social structure. In *Primate Societies,* eds. B. B. Smuts, D. L. Cheney, R. M. Seyfarth, R. W. Wrangham, and T. T. Struhsaker, pp. 282–296. Chicago: University of Chicago Press.

———. 1987b. The significance of African apes for reconstructing human social evolution. In *The Evolution of Human Behavior: Primate Models,* ed. W. G. Kinzey, pp. 51–71. Albany: State University of New York Press.

Wright, P. C. 1992. Primate ecology, rainforest conservation, and economic development: Building a national park in Madagascar. *Evolutionary Anthropology* 1:25–33.

———. 1999. Lemur traits and Madagascar ecology: Coping with an island environment. *Yearbook of Physical Anthropology* 42:31–72.

Wu, X., R. L. Holloway, L. A. Schepartz, and S. Xing. 2011. A new brain endocast of *Homo erectus* from Hull Cave, Nanjing, China. *American Journal of Physical Anthropology* 145:452–460.

Xu, J., K. D. Kochanek, S. L. Murphy, and B. Tejada-Vera. 2010. Deaths: final data for 2007. *National Vital Statistics Reports,* vol. 58, no. 19. Hyattsville, MD: National Center for Health Statistics.

Yellen, J. E., A. S. Brooks, E. Cornelissen, M. J. Mahlman, and K. Stewart. 1995. A Middle Stone Age worked bone industry from Katanda, Upper Semliki Valley, Zaire. *Science* 268:553–556.

Zegura, S. L., T. M. Karafet, L. A. Zhivotovsky, and M. H. Hammer. 2004. High-resolution SNPs and microsatellite haplotypes point to a single, recent entry of Native American Y chromosomes into the Americas. *Molecular Biology and Evolution* 21:164–175.

Zipfel, B., J. M. DeSilva, R. S. Kidd, K. J. Carlson, S. E. Churchill, and L. R. Berger. 2011. The foot and ankle of *Australopithecus sediba. Science* 333:1417–1420.

Zischler, H. 2007. Molecular evidence on primate origins and evolution. In *Handbook of Paleoanthropology,* vol. 2, eds. W. Henke and I. Tattersall, pp. 861–888. Berlin: Springer-Verlag.

Zollikofer, C. P. E., M. S. Ponce de León, D. E. Lieberman, F. Guy, D. Pilbeam, A. Likius, N. T. Mackaye, P. Vignaud, and M. Brunet. 2005. Virtual cranial reconstruction of *Sahelanthropus tchadensis. Nature* 434:755–759.

PHOTO CREDITS

Introduction Figure 1: National Geographic/RF/Getty Images; fig 2: © Image State/Punchstock. **Chapter 1** Page 10: Courtesy of the National Library of Medicine; 1.1: K. Cannon-Bonventre, Anthro-Photo; 1.2: Library of Congress Prints and Photographs Division, LC-USZ62-52389; 1.3: Courtesy of the National Library of Medicine; 1.6: © The McGraw-Hill Companies, Inc./Barry Barker, photographer; 1.7: © Michael Willmer Forbes Tweedie/Photo Researchers, Inc.; 1.8: © Alan Morgan; 1.9: Kim Steele/Photodisc/Getty Images; 1.10: Nancy Nehring/Photodisc/Getty Images; 1.11: Albert J. Copley/Getty Images; 1.12: © AP Photos. **Chapter 2** Page 32: Adam Gault/OJO Images/Getty Images; fig 2.1: © Will & Deni McIntyre/Photo Researchers, Inc.; 2.7: © The National Human Genome Research Institute; 2.16: © Stockbyte/Veer. **Chapter 3** Page 60: Brand X Pictures/Getty Images; 3.1: Ingram Publishing. **Chapter 4** Page 84: © Jose Luis Pelaez Inc./Image Source/Getty Images; 4.1a: Ingram Publishing; 4.1b: Ingram Publishing/SuperStock; 4.1c: © Steve Taylor/Alamy 4.5a: PhotoLink/Getty Images; 4.5b: Purestock/Getty Images; 4.5c: Ingram Publishing/SuperStock; 4.5d: Ingram Publishing; 4.5e: Ingram Publishing 4.6: © The McGraw-Hill Companies, Inc.; 4.7: © Brand X Pictures/PunchStock; 4.8: Thinkstock/JupiterImages; 4.10a: © The McGraw-Hill Companies, Inc.; 4.10b: Purestock/Getty Images; 4.11: Peter Nicholson/Alamy. **Chapter 5** Page 108: © Brand X Pictures; 5.1: © Corel Corporation; 5.2: Royalty Free/Corbis; 5.3: Ingram Publishing; 5.5(left): McGraw-Hill Higher Education/Richard Weiss, photographer; 5.5(right): Ingram Publishing/SuperStock; 5.6: © Comstock/PunchStock; 5.7: Dynamic Graphics Group/IT Stock Free/Alamy; 5.10: PhotoLink/Getty Images; 5.11: © PhotoLink/Getty Images; 5.12: © Zoological Society of San Diego; 5.13: © MedioImages/SuperStock; 5.14: ©Purestock/PunchStock; p 5.15: © Creatas/PunchStock; 5.18: Brand X Pictures/PunchStock; 5.19a: © medioImages/SuperStock; 5.19b: © Creatas/PunchStock; 5.19c: © Brand X Pictures/PunchStock;

5.19d: © Getty Images; 5.19e: Image 100/Corbis. **Chapter 6** Page 138: © Creatas/PunchStock; 6.1: © Digital Vision; 6.2: © Harlow Primate Laboratory, University of Wisconsin, Madison, WI; 6.3: Ingram Publishing; 6.4: © Digital Vision/PunchStock; 6.6: Getty Images/Digital Vision; 6.7: © Imagestate Media (John Foxx)/Imagestate; 6.8: Corel Corporation; 6.9: © Brand X Pictures/PunchStock; 6.10: © Brand X Pictures/PunchStock; 6.11: © Comstock/PunchStock; 6.12: © Digital Vision; 6.13: © Purestock/PunchStock; 6.14: © Imagestate Media (John Foxx)/Imagestate; 6.15: © Creatas/PunchStock; 6.16: © Digital Vision; 6.17: © Brand X Pictures; 6.18: Photodisc/Getty Images; 6.19: Brand X Pictures/PunchStock; 6.20: Purestock/Getty Images. **Chapter 7** Page166: Purestock/Getty Images; 7.9: © McGraw-Hill Companies, Inc.; 7.10: © LifeART/Fotosearch; 7.14: © Jane Goodall/National Geographic Society Image Collection; 7.15: © Creatas/PunchStock; 7.16: Huntstock/Getty Images; 7.17: © H.S. Terrace/Animals Animals. **Chapter 8** Page192: © AP Photos; 8.1: © Dr. Parvinder Sethi; 8.5: Courtesy of The Laboratory of Tree-Ring Research, The University of Arizona; 8.8a: CL/LLC/Corbis; 8.8b: © Digital Vision/Getty Images; 8.9a: © The McGraw-Hill Companies, Inc.; 8.9b: © Douglas Pulsipher/Alamy. **Chapter 9** Page 214: Courtesy of Dr. Milford H. Wolpoff, The University of Michigan, Ann Arbor; 9.1: Heinrich van den Berg/Getty Images; 9.4: Courtesy of Doug M. Boyer; 9.6: © David Brill; 9.10: Courtesy of Dr. Milford H. Wolpoff, The University of Michigan, Ann Arbor; 9.12: Courtesy of Dr. Ian Tattersall, American Museum of Natural History; 9.13: © David Begun; 9.14: Copyright © 2004, The American Association for the Advancement of Science. **Chapter 10** Page 234: © John Reader/Photo Researchers, Inc.; 10.2: © Brand X Pictures/PunchStock; 10.5: Dr. Susannah Thorpe; 10.7: © 2002 Mission Paleoanthropolgique Franco-Tchadiuenne (MPFT) and Nature Publishing Group; 10.8: © Reuters/Corbis; 10.9: © Tim White/David Brill; 10.10: © 2009 Jay Matternes; 10.11: Carol V. Ward; 10.12: © Kenneth Garrett/National Geographic Image Collection; p 10.13: © John Reader/

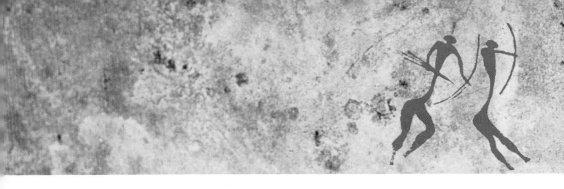

INDEX

Note: **BOLD** page numbers indicate definitions. Page numbers followed by *f* or *t* indicate figures or tables. Page numbers preceded by A1 or A2 indicate text in Appendices 1 and 2.